KEEPING THE BRITISH END UP

VOTE FOR *Timothy Lea*

...TH *Edward* ☐
...HORPE *Jeremy* ☐
...WILSON *Harold* ☐
...TIMOTHY **LEA** ☒

I LOVE TIMOTHY LEA

VOTE FOR TIMOTHY LEA

KEEPING THE BRITISH END UP

SIMON SHERIDAN

Reynolds & Hearn Ltd
London

Front cover images: (clockwise from top left) Mary Millington from the *Queen of the Blues* poster (1979); Suzy Mandel from the British *Pussy Talk* poster (1975); Sue Longhurst from the *Keep It Up Downstairs* poster (1976) and Robin Askwith from the *Let's Get Laid!* poster (1977).

Back cover images: A naughty nurse from the *What's Up Nurse?* poster (1977); Gay Soper in *The Ups and Down of a Handyman* (1975) and Lindy Benson, Anthony Kenyon, Christopher Chittell and Lyn Worral in *Erotic Inferno* (1975).

Frontispiece: The birth of a legend. Sheila White, Robin Askwith and Linda Hayden in a February 1974 publicity still for *Confessions of a Window Cleaner*.

What is pornography to one man is the laughter of genius to another.
D H Lawrence (1929)

First published in 2001 by
Reynolds & Hearn Ltd
61a Priory Road
Kew Gardens
Richmond
Surrey TW9 3DH

© Simon Sheridan 2001

All rights reserved. No part of this publication may be reproduced, in any form or by any means, without permission from the publisher.

A CIP catalogue record for this book is available from the British Library.

ISBN 1 903111 21 8

Designed by Paul Chamberlain.

Printed and bound by Biddles Ltd, Guildford, Surrey.

CONTENTS

ACKNOWLEDGEMENTS   6

AUTHOR'S NOTE   6

FOREWORD BY SUE LONGHURST   7

COMINGS...   8
    How and why the British love their sauce

DOINGS   30
    25 years of naughty British movies from 1958 to 1983

...GOINGS   196
    British sex goes down the pan

KNOBS AND KNOCKERS   210
    The biggest boys and girls in British sex film history

BIBLIOGRAPHY   235

INDEX   235

ACKNOWLEDGEMENTS

Many thanks to the following people whose invaluable memories about the British sex film era made this book possible. In alphabetical order: Linzi Drew, Peter Fairbrass, Tudor Gates, Bob Godfrey, Richard Gordon, Josie Harrison Marks, Mark Jones, Queen Kong, Stanley Long, Sue Longhurst, David McGillivray, Alan G Rainer, Kenneth Rowles, Jean Selfe, Ray Selfe, Alan Selwyn, Greg Smith, Graham Stark, David Sullivan, Norman J Warren and Omar Williams.

I am also indebted to the following who assisted me in my times of need. In alphabetical order: Darrell Buxton, Kevin Davies, Debbie and Phil Davis, Dougie Fergusson, David Hanks, Joanne Hazell, Marcus Hearn, Tim Hopewell at Granada Television, Sue Hayworth, Andrew Leavold at www.trashvideo.com.au, Howard Maxford, Marc Morris, Bernard Mullett, Richard Reynolds, Jonathan Rigby, Adrian Rigelsford, Robert Ross, Albert Tilley, Robert Vickers, Chris Voisey, Gavin Whittaker and James Willis.

My appreciation also goes to Steve Chibnall, who generously donated some particularly rare photographs.

Thanks again to my parents Pamela and Michael and all my friends, including Philip, Jonny, Katie, Alex, Heidi, Michaela, Linda and the *Burnt Toast* crew (Sally, Rachel and Hilary).

But this book is for Mark Powell for all his unflagging support and the never-ending lengths of his patience!

Until next time… ✻

AUTHOR'S NOTE

British sex films have long held a fascination for me. As a child I recall seeing newspaper advertisements for X-rated films starring Diana Dors and Willie Rushton. I knew an 'X' film was something naughty, something rude where people usually walked around nude, but I was only familiar with Dors and Rushton from *Celebrity Squares*. Did these same cuddly, funny people I laughed at on a Saturday night also lead a double life cavorting naked at the cinema? Thankfully we never really saw the great British character actors without their clothes. The undressing was left to lesser mortals like Mary Millington, Fiona Richmond and Robin Askwith, whose names I also became accustomed to. I sometimes saw photographs of them at movie premières, but I hadn't a clue who they were. All I knew was that they had sex for a living.

I was too young to see the delights of *Confessions of a Window Cleaner* at my local Odeon, but through video a decade later I caught up with the trouser-dropping antics and crude *double entendres*. And what did I think? Well, I was transfixed, but I was also perplexed. Had these sort of films really been the staple diet of filmgoers in the sixties and seventies? And the further I dug the more I realised that Robin Askwith's bum was just the tip of the iceberg, so to speak. There were well over a hundred movies I'd previously never heard of with camp titles like *Naked – As Nature Intended*, *Keep It Up Downstairs* and *Can I Come Too?*

Over the years I've probably watched an unhealthily large amount of British sex films. Some blur into each other. I honestly used to think that *I'm Not Feeling Myself Tonight!* was the worst of the genre. I now realise how wrong I was. There are far, far worse ways to spend 90 minutes of your life. Of course, there are the good (*The Wife Swappers*), the bad (*The Amorous Milkman*) and the downright ugly (*Hellcats – Mud Wrestling*), but all are intriguing in their own way. Every film has an interesting tale to tell about the era in which it was made and nobody will ever be able to deny these films' massive popularity. What British movie could run for four years in the West End or have punters queuing twice round the block today? It's all too easy to sneer at these movies, but they're part of our heritage and as sex film director Stanley Long now admits with a wry smile, 'Even the intelligentsia watch my movies now!'

To those who tirelessly took their kit off for the enjoyment of the cinemagoing public I salute you! ✻

FOREWORD

Right: Sue Longhurst in a striking 1973 portrait by Beverley Goodway.

I can honestly say that my relatively few years in the worlds of TV and cinema were the craziest and most enjoyable time of my life.

It all began in 1969 when I auditioned as a 'model who could dance' for a Hammer horror movie called *Lust for a Vampire* (although at the time it had the gentler title *To Love a Vampire*). About nine of us young girls were finally chosen and we found ourselves at Elstree Studios being choreographed in a Greek dancing sequence wearing nothing but skimpy G-strings under a few bits of well-placed chiffon! We also had to do another scene set in a girls' dormitory. Somebody asked whether I and another girl would mind taking our tops off. I've never minded tasteful nudity, and I had already posed naked for cosmetic and bath product ads, so I agreed. It was extra money and I made my first topless appearance on film!

It was a while before I made another film and, although I stunt-doubled for Susan George in *Straw Dogs* and Diana Rigg on TV, I wasn't offered my first big film role until late 1972. My model agency put me forward to audition for a comedy called *Secrets of a Door to Door Salesman*. The producer was looking for 'pretty girls who looked sexy ... and could act a bit'. I got the job somehow and I distinctly remember my debut striptease sequence. I was dressed in a stern nurse's uniform, hair tightly back under the white hat and with horn-rimmed spectacles. But soon off came the glasses, the hat, the pins from my hair bun, letting loose a cascade of golden curls, followed by my uniform, suspenders and stockings all the way to the final removal, and toss over the shoulder, of the minuscule G-string. I received a huge round of applause from the crew and suddenly realised how easy it had been and how much I'd enjoyed it.

From this point I made plenty more films like *Keep It Up Jack!*, *What the Swedish Butler Saw* in Scandinavia and *Come Play with Me* with Mary Millington. I knew they were all rather saucy and risqué and in my social circle (and family group) I generally found it difficult to discuss my new career. When *Secrets of a Door to Door Salesman* was released in 1973 my mother and grandmother stumbled across my name on the film poster outside the Bognor Picturedrome. They had no idea what it was going to be about and bought tickets for the matinée. However, once inside, they thought some of the male audience members were 'a bit strange'. They left at the end of the film looking rather white and I felt embarrassed for them both. I kept quiet about my movie career most of the time because people in my private life rather considered British films to be either Shakespeare or porn – nothing in between, although my films tended to lean towards the latter.

Whilst I was appearing as Ann Aston's replacement on TV game show *The Golden Shot* with Charlie Williams, I was offered a role in perhaps the most memorable movie of my career, *Confessions of a Window Cleaner*. My saucy scene, disappearing under the detergent bubbles in my suburban kitchen with Robin Askwith has become a favourite for a lot of people. Compared to the realistic love-making between Julie Christie and Donald Sutherland in *Don't Look Now*, which made my toes curl (even when I watched it on my own!), my movies were all pretty innocuous, lightweight stuff. There was no explicit sex in the British versions, no violence or cynicism, just plenty of naughty situations and innuendo (for added 'groan value'). In fact if anyone took the time to watch my sex scenes in slow motion it would be blatantly obvious that the positions I was in would have made intercourse physically impossible, however athletic or supple I was!

I was totally unaware during the 1970s that my films were part of something called the 'sex comedy era', but I naïvely thought my career would develop into bigger and better things. I had slowed down by the end of the decade and then suddenly my entire career came to a halt when a major operation on my middle ear left me with a bad palsy and a disfigurement of my face.

It was only years later that I was made aware that I'd been part of something special. Today I find it highly amusing that my films are being written about, but I always had tremendous fun making them and I have endless happy memories. I sincerely hope you enjoy reading about this fascinating period of British cinematic history. ✻

Sue Longhurst
Sussex, August 2001

KEEPING THE BRITISH END UP

Left: Cardew Robinson is out to impress Suzy Mandel, Mary Millington and Pat Astley in *Come Play With Me* (1977).

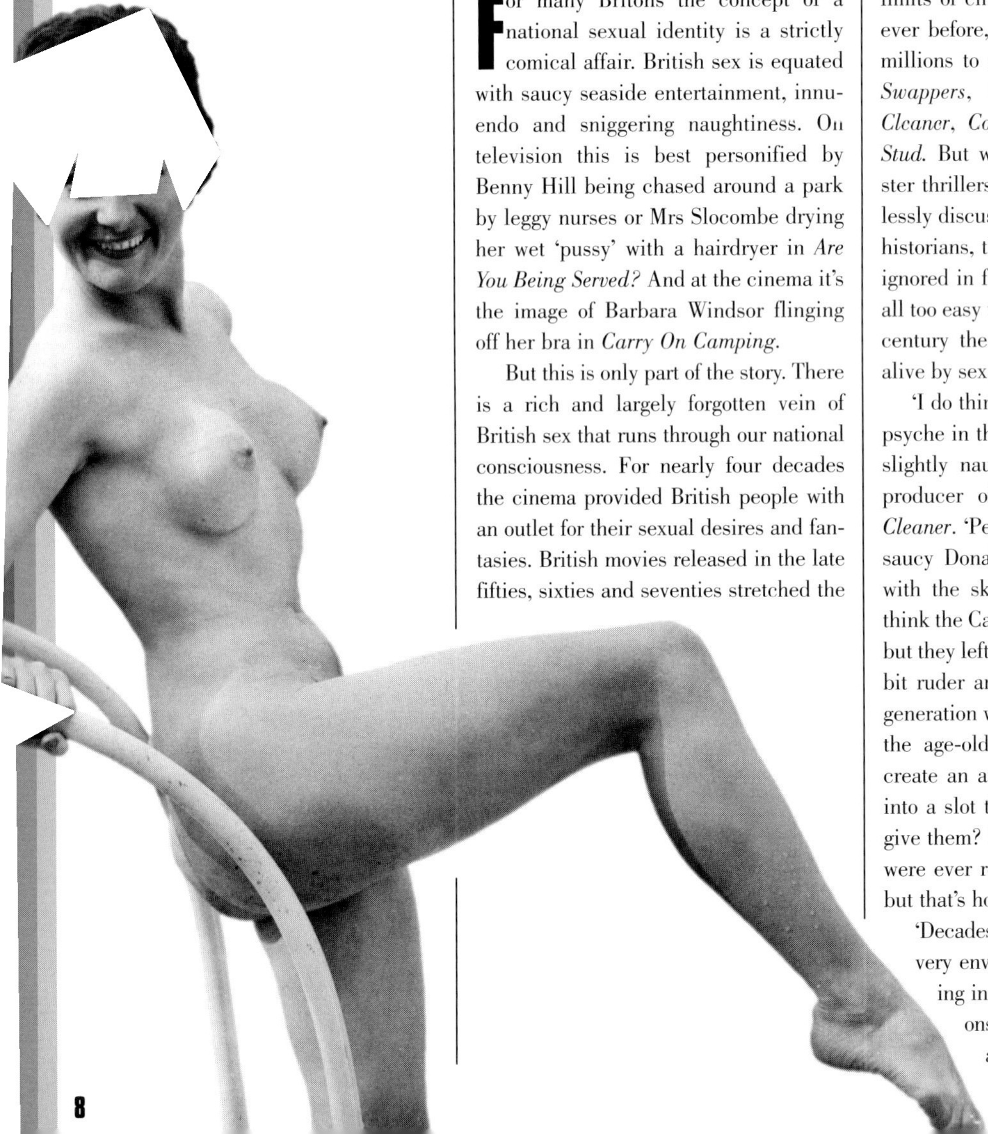

Below: Naked and unashamed in *The Nudist Story* (1960).

COMINGS... ◆◆◆

HOW AND WHY THE BRITISH LOVE THEIR SAUCE

For many Britons the concept of a national sexual identity is a strictly comical affair. British sex is equated with saucy seaside entertainment, innuendo and sniggering naughtiness. On television this is best personified by Benny Hill being chased around a park by leggy nurses or Mrs Slocombe drying her wet 'pussy' with a hairdryer in *Are You Being Served?* And at the cinema it's the image of Barbara Windsor flinging off her bra in *Carry On Camping*.

But this is only part of the story. There is a rich and largely forgotten vein of British sex that runs through our national consciousness. For nearly four decades the cinema provided British people with an outlet for their sexual desires and fantasies. British movies released in the late fifties, sixties and seventies stretched the limits of cinema censorship further than ever before, and people flocked in their millions to see the delights of *The Wife Swappers*, *Confessions of a Window Cleaner*, *Come Play with Me* and *The Stud*. But whereas horror movies, gangster thrillers and the Carry Ons are endlessly discussed by academics and media historians, the humble British sex film is ignored in favour of 'worthier' topics. It's all too easy to forget that for a quarter of a century the UK film industry was kept alive by sex, nudity and *double entendres*.

'I do think it's always been part of our psyche in the UK that we like something slightly naughty,' says Greg Smith, the producer of *Confessions of a Window Cleaner*. 'People have always loved those saucy Donald McGill seaside postcards with the skinny man and busty lady. I think the Carry Ons were wonderful films, but they left the gate open for something a bit ruder and a lot of filmmakers of my generation went that one step beyond. It's the age-old question. Do these movies create an audience or do they just drop into a slot that an audience is willing to give them? I don't think British sex films were ever really sexy. They were risqué, but that's how British people like it.'

'Decades ago English people used to be very envious of the sort of films showing in France or Scandinavia,' reckons Stanley Long, the producer and director of several home-

COMINGS...

Below: The best of British sauce – Kenneth Williams, Sandra Caron, Elizabeth Knight, Anna Karen and Barbara Windsor in *Carry On Camping* (1969).

grown sex films. 'I remember as a young man in the 1950s travelling to the other side of London just to see a film which purported to show a nipple. These so-called Continental films always looked so attractive and British movies just couldn't compete. Until the 1960s there had been such a suppression of all things sexual. I think it was a hangover from the Victorian era and this country suffered from terrible inhibitions. I think it's a national trait that we aren't very good at being erotic. The Italians pinch bums, the French have mistresses and we're not very good at either!'

HEALTH AND EFFICIENCY

The roots of the British sex film go back to 1954 and the release of an innocuous little nudist film called *The Garden of Eden*. An American production, the movie purported to extol the healthy lifestyle of naturism and was even endorsed by the US Sunbathing Association. The sight of exposed breasts and bums appalled the British Board of Film Censors, who immediately refused the film a certificate on the grounds that it was unsuitable for a UK audience. Undeterred, the movie's British distributor, Nat Miller, submitted the film to the London County Council, whose members scrutinised it closely (probably several times) and declared there was absolutely nothing obscene about it at all. In defiance of the official film censors they passed the film, rapidly followed by 180 of the 230 local authori-

Right: She's got VD. Margaret Rose Kiel in *That Kind of Girl* (1961).

ties around the UK. Within months, *The Garden of Eden* was playing to packed houses throughout the country. Cinema audiences were in raptures. Simply put, film fans had never seen nudity in such quantity ever before. The only nakedness tolerated till then was that of black people in anthropological documentaries; white women's breasts had been an unknown quantity. *The Garden of Eden* changed all that. Reluctantly, the BBFC backed down and awarded the movie a certificate.

The huge financial success of *The Garden of Eden* encouraged Wardour Street, the heart of London's film community, to turn its attention to the potentially lucrative genre of naturist films. The man who started the ball rolling, Nat Miller, decided to make his own nudie movie, *Nudist Paradise*. Shot in 1958 and released the following year, the film was the celluloid breakthrough that led to 25 glorious years of British cinematic sex. Miller, who had worked behind the scenes in TV and film for over 30 years, wasn't interested in promoting the free, unfettered life of naturism. All he wanted was to get boobs on film and bums on seats.

John Trevelyan, an ex-teacher and educational administrator, was secretary to the Board of Censors from 1958 to 1971. Responsible for steering British cinema through its most turbulent era, Trevelyan sought to impose his own ideology of 'quality and integrity', regardless of subject matter. He was well aware that naturist films were pure exploitation, but forced them to keep up the pretence of advocating a clothes-free lifestyle.

'Nudism should be shown as relevant, genuine and sincere, engaged in by people who obviously believe in it without ulterior motive,' he said. There were two further provisos. Genitals always had to remain covered up, usually with a towel draped over the offending area or by a skimpy G-string. In addition, the setting for the bare bodies had to be an officially recognised nudist camp or resort.

Nudist Paradise, like many that followed, was partly filmed at Britain's most famous naturist reserve, Spielplatz, in St Albans, Hertfordshire. Spielplatz (meaning playground) was founded in 1929 by former electrician and confirmed nudist Charles 'Mac' Macaskie. Scotsman Macaskie became the founding father of British naturism and his camp, with dozens of chalets and a 60ft long swimming pool situated in 12 acres of ancient forest, became the preferred setting for several homegrown naturist movies. Macaskie was an authority figure whose presence gave a movie an air of respectability, although the nudie film directors weren't keen to have their cameras lingering too long over the 73-year-old naturist himself. They just wanted to cut to the chase and show the naked actresses they had hired cavorting carefree and unclothed.

Since the British climate is not always conducive to showing bronzed naked bodies, a handful of early movies transported their British casts to the Isle of Levant, off the coast of the south of France, where there has been a nudist camp since the 1930s. One director who favoured sunnier climes was Edward Craven Walker, a

naturist since World War II and the only nudist filmmaker whose intentions were entirely honourable. Using the pseudonym Michael Keatering, he produced three movies between 1959 and 1963. The first, *Travelling Light*, ran for eight months at the Cinephone Cinema in Oxford Street from March 1960 and then had an even more successful run in the provinces. Craven Walker's movies made a star of Elizabeth Elcoate Gilbert, a popular *Health & Efficiency* pin-up who became known as 'Britain's Best-Known Nudist' for a while. But how many people were actually converted to naturism after seeing Elizabeth in the all-together, and how many just went to see her knockers, is debatable.

The plots of the early British naturist movies were basic to say the least. They all followed a virtually unchanging pattern. A young man or woman is secretly a nudist but is hiding the truth from his or her friends and family. Overcoming prejudice, the protagonist manages to persuade those who think nudity is disgusting to go with the flow and see the error of their anti-nudist ways. In 1961's *Nudes of the World*, the locals make their feelings clear about a nearby nudist camp by tearing down the tents and marching onto the site waving anti-nudist placards. However, they soon come to their senses and realise nudists are human too. In the most famous nudist film of them all, *Naked – As Nature Intended* (1961), a group of young lovelies accidentally stumble across a nudist beach and any preconceived ideas about taking their clothes off in public are thrown to the wall. Pamela Green, an ex-dancer and Britain's foremost nude model of the late 1950s and early 1960s, can't be converted quick enough. 'To be *ashamed* of one's body is surely more wrong and unnatural,' says the movie's voice-over. 'There's nothing shocking about enjoying the feeling of complete physical freedom that nudity brings. Their fine bronzed skins and their healthy complexions, and their obvious sincerity, show Pam how mistaken she's been to think that only peculiar people become nudists!'

The somewhat limiting narratives continually played on the virtues of men and women working in harmony with Mother Nature: fresh air, eating fruit, the sunshine, stroking donkeys and kissing babies. Frustrated viewers desperate to see bare breasts had to sit through dull travelogues, shots of leafy lanes, geese, haystacks, cattle, lots of laughing and waving and pointing at nothing in particular. Once the clothes were off the audiences got their reward: beautiful young women with clipped BBC accents tossing beachballs, trampolining, playing badminton (no shuttlecocks, naturally), scuba-diving, canoeing... In fact any activity which encouraged their breasts to wobble a bit more vigorously.

Apart from Edward Craven Walker, none of the nudist filmmakers' healthy intentions ever rang true. Frustrated by the confines of nudist camps and sandy beaches, directors tried to push the censor's limits. George Harrison Marks, Britain's most celebrated glamour photographer of the 1950s and director of *Naked – As Nature Intended*, shot footage of his star, Pamela Green, showering and towelling herself off *in her own home*. Trevelyan refused to pass the scene on the grounds that nudity could only be shown in a 'recognised setting'. Other directors, who thought they had hoodwinked the censor into believing they had made a genuine naturist movie, filled their productions with sexually suggestive scenes and *double entendres*. In *Nudes of the World*, topless Hungarian actress Jutka Gotz sings a song to her jolly friends around the campfire. The lyrics leave little doubt that she is not as innocent as she pretends to be. 'Slide your trombone, play upon your fiddle, blow the clarinet, ooh la la,' she warbles. Despite their obvious hidden agenda, nudist films were usually never rated higher than an 'A' certificate, which required children under the age of 16 to be accompanied by a responsible adult.

The cheeky credentials of the nudist filmmakers become even more suspect when you examine the sort of naughty productions they later graduated to. Whereas Craven Walker retired from movies when the naturist films began to lose their lustre, other directors, producers, editors and cinematographers, such as Stanley Long, Donovan Winter, Douglas Hill, Arnold Louis Miller and Jim Connock, all moved seamlessly into more up-front sex comedies as censorship gradually relaxed in the late 1960s. In several instances, people like George Harrison Marks and Russell Gay were even tempted into the world of hardcore pornography.

SPEED OF CHANGE

Within the space of a few years the novelty of naturist pictures began to be overtaken by a new breed of British movies, those which ignored bouncing boobs in favour of a more realistic approach to sexual relationships. The new wave of films like *Saturday Night and Sunday Morning* (1960), *A Taste of Honey* (1961) and *A Kind of Loving* (1962) shocked audiences with their portrayals of sex before marriage, swearing and so-called 'kitchen sink' realism. *The Knack ... and how to get it* (1965), *Alfie* (1966) and *Here We Go*

Round the Mulberry Bush (1967) went even further by showing the British male at his predatory worst. While these movies showed British society in a hitherto-unseen light, they weren't titillating enough to compete with the sight of bare bodies. Straightforward, cheaply made exploitation films did find themselves a limited market, wallowing in stripping, prostitution rackets and the general low-life of Soho, London's notorious red light district. The titles of B-grade movies like *The Flesh is Weak* (1957), *The Shakedown* (1959), *The Rough and the Smooth* (1959), and *Strip Tease Murder* (1961) promised exhilarating naughtiness, but delivered little more than a few cheap thrills that left the British censor singularly unmoved.

A handful of low-budget 'X'-rated movies (only to be exhibited to patrons aged 16 or over) highlighted the ills of modern society, the kind of thing that had the public scurrying back to their Sunday tabloids. Teenage pregnancies, juvenile delinquency and blackmail all had their place in the fleapits of the day, but each film had a moralistic sermon to remind audiences that it was all wrong. Two of the most famous were produced by Robert Hartford-Davis. *That Kind of Girl* (1961) dealt with venereal disease, whereas *The Yellow Teddybears* (1963) examined underage sex at a girls' grammar school. In the latter, the girls declare the loss of their virginity by wearing teddybear badges on their lapels, much to the horror of their teacher. 'Sex can be as clean or as dirty as people make it,' she says. 'As part of love it can be the most wonderful thing you'll ever know. But to trade it in for kicks and a teddybear! Why, that's like taking a Picasso and using it for a firescreen!'

'They knew these pictures weren't going to be huge artistic successes, but they would make a lot of money,' said filmmaker Ray Selfe. 'Exploitation filmmakers aimed their movies squarely at the right market to turn a profit. Many of these film's directors were regarded as the 'boys on the other sides of the tracks' and were not really accepted by the British movie community. People coming from working class backgrounds would never have been given the opportunity to make movies in the 1940s or 1950s, because we would have been excluded from the system. In those days, if you were a producer or director or a cinematographer you ate in the posh studio restaurant, while everybody else ate in the canteen. It was just like the civil service and there was a division. The filmmakers were all from the upper or middle classes who drove Rolls-Royces. But this stopped with the birth of British sex films. It provided more opportunities for everybody and it was quite a levelling thing. Whereas before the director would only have talked to his actors, now everybody was involved and it was more of a group effort. Suddenly equipment became cheaper, film-stock became faster and more and more ordinary people got involved in the cinema.'

The Cinematograph Act of 1927 stipulated that 25 per cent of features (and 30 per cent of supporting programme-fillers) shown at British cinemas had to be of UK origin, made with British money. It was an attempt to stop Hollywood dominating the market and a way of nurturing our own industry. Filmmakers were actively encouraged to produce British movies by the late lamented Eady Fund. A levy of ten per cent of all foreign films shown in the UK went into an invisible pot which was then redistributed to British directors and producers to stimulate homegrown films. And if your film cost less than £100,000 then you'd be entitled to double the money. 'Double Eady was the absolute jackpot!' says film historian and screenwriter David McGillivray. 'It was money for nothing. You just couldn't lose by making a cheap British film.'

With nudist films losing their hold on the box-office, filmmakers were putting pressure on the BBFC to relax the rulings on sex and nudity in films. Society had never known such speed of change as it did in the 1960s. People were faced with an explosion of choice in relationships and moral behaviour. The introduction of the contraceptive pill, changes in the law regarding divorce, abortion and homosexuality, and the rise of the Women's Liberation movement meant that the British censor could no longer sit back and ban films just because he didn't think they were suitable for public consumption. The increase in affordable package tour holidays to the Continent meant far more Britons were getting an eyeful of what our European cousins could see at the cinema – sex and nudity, and lots of it. Under increasing pressure from filmmakers and the general public, the Board came together in the summer of 1964 for a full and frank debate about the future of film censorship. It was decided that nudity no longer had to be confined to nudist camps. This proved to be a godsend to producers, who at long last could get nudity off the badminton court and into the strip clubs.

GODLESSNESS AND CRUDITY

In 1961 Stanley Long, the man behind several highly successful nudist films, had produced *West End Jungle*, a documentary exposé of prostitution in London. It was banned outright by the BBFC (it has never been awarded a certificate) and its salacious content was even discussed in the House of Lords. With the change in the censor's rulings, and inspired by the Italian movie *Mondo cane* (1961), Long was able to go full steam ahead with *London in the Raw* (1964) and *Primitive London* (1965). Both films provided glimpses of home-grown weirdness, nudity and lasciviousness never seen before on British screens.

Even when especially 'naughty' films like *The Naked World of Harrison Marks* (1965) were refused a certificate by the BBFC, their distributors persevered and submitted them directly to local authorities. Stuffy old councillors carefully examined the movies and invariably passed them uncut, much to the fury of the BBFC. A cinema poster with the phrase 'X certificate (London only)' was greeted with excitement by moviegoers who eagerly expected to see 'the real thing' at last. To their credit, the censors were desperately trying to walk the knife-edge of the much-maligned and badly worded 1959 Obscene Publications Act. The Act declares that the possession and production of obscene material for monetary gain is a criminal offence. But the word 'obscene' is indefinable. In British law it translates as anything which is liable to 'deprave and corrupt'. But just how corrupting watching a bit of jiggery pokery or a pair of bare knockers really is, is open to debate.

The most significant relaxation in censorship in the UK can be traced to the release of one film. *Hugs & Kisses* (aka *Puss Och Kram*), made in Sweden in 1966, was a subtitled sex picture about the power struggle within a middle class *ménage à trois*. Released in London in April 1968, the film proudly contained the very first female full-frontal seen in British cinemas. Scandinavian actress Agneta Ekmanner had the privilege of her pubic hair being seen by millions of startled moviegoers. 'In a way we deliberately made an issue of that to see what the general public, or some of the public, thought,' admitted John Trevelyan in 1968. 'It transpired that many thought pubic hair perfectly innocent and said so. We're letting the brake off slowly, because that's what people seem to want. Whether something is right or wrong is an entirely different matter. We are a barometer, not a guardian, of public morality.'

The proverbial brake continued to be gradually loosened with a succession of

Right: The première of Norman J Warren's *Her Private Hell* at London's Cameo Royal, January 1968.

films designed to create the maximum of publicity with the minimum of sex, but any sex was better than no sex. The Swedish-made *I Am Curious – Yellow* (1967), an arty, 'meaningful' porno film, finally got a UK release two years later, but only after 11 minutes of shagging had been removed. Even in its butchered state it created great excitement. Agneta Ekmanner's groundbreaking bush was quickly followed by Alan Bates and Oliver Reed exposing their tackle in the nude wrestling scene from *Women in Love* (1969). Producer David Grant provided a less cluttered view in his cinematic 'sex manual' *Love Variations* (1969), released in 1970. Germany's *W.R. – Mysteries of the Organism* (1971) went further by showing frequent bouts of love-making, slipped in between documentary footage and dramatised scenes revolving around political and sexual commentator Wilhelm Reich, although this was not to British tastes.

What *was* to British tastes was any sort of film which purported to show the sordid truth about what was really happening behind the net curtains of suburbia. With the new phenomena of wife-swapping and free love gripping the tabloids during the late 1960s, producer Stanley Long saw the perfect opportunity to make a movie dramatising various swapping case studies. Filmed in 1969 and called, naturally, *The Wife Swappers*, Long was worried how he would get the picture past the beady eyes of John Trevelyan. To better its chances the film had to adopt a 'disapproving' tone, downplaying the antics of its bed-hopping actors. In between licentious scenes of shagging, a puritanical (but fake) psychiatrist pops up to condemn sex outside marriage. It was a case of 'Look at this, but isn't it awful?' In the same way that Charles Macaskie gave the nudist movies a bit of prestige and justified their existence, so the role of disapproving 'doctor' or 'psychiatrist' cropped up in several British sex movies.

'When I made *The Wife Swappers* I took it to Trevelyan and I was honest about it,' admits Long. 'It was a pretty contentious subject and I had to present it like a cautionary tale. I would have loved to have condoned wife-swapping, but the censor just wouldn't allow me to do that. Instead I got an actor to pretend to be a Harley Street psychiatrist and give it a bit of intellectual stuff. I actually had a lot of trouble getting a certificate for it. Trevelyan refused at first because he said it pushed the boundaries of censorship too far. He waited a few months and finally relented.

However, not everyone was happy with Trevelyan's decisions reflecting the shift in public morality. Mary Whitehouse, a self-appointed crusader against permissiveness, had been campaigning zealously against 'permissiveness, sexual explicitness, Godlessness and crudities' since 1964 when she set up her Clean Up TV campaign, later the National Viewers and Listeners Association. A humble housewife and ex-school teacher from Shropshire, Whitehouse was supported by an army of Women's Institute members, Christians and big names like Lord Longford, Cliff Richard and Malcolm Muggeridge. She was also a co-founder of the Festival of Light movement which converged on Trafalgar Square in the summer of 1971. Thirty-nine coachloads of supporters from all over the UK came to sing 'Jerusalem' and decry the 'squalid abyss of erotomania'. Despite Whitehouse's favourite phrase being 'in all fairness', she was not a fair-minded or level-headed individual. She loved nothing more than whipping up her supporters into a frothing frenzy.

Whitehouse was lampooned by the media and when she appeared in public was often pelted with eggs, soot and flour bombs. Porn publisher David Sullivan even took a cheeky swipe at her by christening one of his dirty magazines after her. The anti-porn campaigner, dressed in her floral frock and floppy hat, became an easy target for the sex industry. 'Mary Whitehouse was an omnipresent figure in the news every day of the week, so she had an influence on all our lives in the industry and was easy for us to spoof,' says David McGillivray. Whitehouse appears in a variety of guises in several sex films, usually driven wild with unleashed desire or rendered speechless by a torrent of filth. In *The Love Pill* (1971) she is Mary Tighthouse, in *I'm Not Feeling Myself Tonight!* (1975) she crops up as Mary Watchtower, and in *Hardcore* (1977) she's Norma Blackhurst.

In *Every Home Should Have One* (1970), Jim Clark's clever satire on sex in advertising, the fictional Reverend Mellish presides over the England Clean England Strong Campaign, encouraging his followers to stay up late to watch prurient television films and compile their findings. 'That's 15 bloodys and five bastards,' notes his nervy secretary as the hypocritical committee tut-tuts through the films, secretly enjoying every moment. 'It's time that sex was put back where it belongs,' argues Colonel Belper, 'in the bedrooms of prostitutes and decently married couples!'

However hard Whitehouse and her supporters tried to halt the gradual acceptance of sex on TV and at the cinema, the growth of permissiveness in society and entertainment continued unabated. 'We grabbed a window of opportunity from the major film studios who had no idea what sort of film to make anymore,' says Stanley Long. 'The public were searching to find films which were much more explicit. Censorship was relaxing and audiences wanted more. Trevelyan once said to me, "You know, I don't believe in censorship. I want to relax it, but the law is the law. I really don't see myself as a guardian of public morals." He was largely responsible for pushing back barriers, but he knew it had to be a very slow process. It was a gradual thing, but he was under a lot of pressure from distributors and constantly baited by filmmakers.'

SEX AS A WEAPON

Norman J Warren's *Her Private Hell*, shot in London in 1967, is widely regarded as Britain's first proper 'sex' film. The story follows a young Italian girl who comes to London and is hoodwinked into posing naked for risqué European magazines. By today's standards the movie is extremely tame, but it caused a sensation when it was released at London's Cameo Royal cinema on the Charing Cross Road at the beginning of 1968. 'The producers were always pressing for more nudity,' remembers Warren, 'but if you look at it today it's incredibly innocent really. Even so, they sold the film as the 'first sex film made in Britain'. At the time most sex movies were French or Scandinavian, but the publicity for ours was amazing. It cost about £18,000 and was shot over two weeks, yet it was taking £5000 a week at one cinema alone and it ran in London for 24 months. People *so* wanted the opportunity to see sex in those days.'

For many rookie filmmakers, sex movies were considered the first rung on the ladder to greater, more 'respectable' successes. This didn't always happen, of course. 'I remember thinking that sex films would be a stepping stone to bigger things,' recalled Ray Selfe, the producer of 1970's *Sweet and Sexy*. 'Unfortunately, most directors just carried the baggage with them and were pigeonholed as pornographers for the rest of their careers. There were very few directors who *actually* went on to bigger and better things.'

One director who did break free was Martin Campbell, but only after a long hard struggle. The son of a New Zealand sheep farmer, Campbell came to England to become a camera operator in the late 1960s and wound up as the director of *The Sex Thief* (1973) and *Eskimo Nell* (1974), two of the most slickly made independent

Right: Seventies glamour icon Fiona Richmond loses her clothes again, much to Robin Askwith's alarm, in *Let's Get Laid!* (1977).

sex films of the decade. 'I wanted to nurture new talent,' says *Sex Thief* producer Tudor Gates. 'Martin originally came to me asking to write a script and he became my assistant and he was excellent. I couldn't wait to give him the chance to direct.' Campbell made his reputation with the classic BBC drama *Edge of Darkness* (1986), and has more recently directed big-budget blockbusters like *GoldenEye* (1995) and *The Mark of Zorro* (1998). However, Campbell is the exception rather than the rule. 'Some of the filmmakers were nothing more than talentless ragamuffins who honestly couldn't make anything else,' recalls David McGillivray. 'While others had higher aspirations.'

New directors relished the chance to helm a British film, however low-budget, because the industry was in a depressed state and there were fewer opportunities to make a lasting impression. 'A lot of people think it was easier to make a film in the sixties and seventies than it is today, but it was still pretty difficult,' says Norman J Warren. 'However, there were more avenues to go down in those days. There were more people prepared to stump up money for independent films to screen in independent cinemas. Just so long as you made a half-decent film it was possible to get it on screens around the country, but it was a smaller operation than it had been just after the war.'

The decline in domestic film production was most marked from the late 1950s onwards. With the industry going into the doldrums, fewer and fewer British movies were being made. In 1958, the year of the first *Carry On* movie, some 134 home-grown movies were produced, but by 1965 that figure had fallen to 96. The best example of how filmmaking had drastically dropped off is the mighty Rank Organisation. In 1949 they had a hand in 41 features. Twenty years later that figure had been reduced to just seven. In 1975 they made just two movies, and one of those was the play-it-safe *Carry on Behind*. Likewise, Hammer had enjoyed a steady stream of horror hits throughout the 1950s and 1960s, and were even awarded the Queen's Award to Industry in 1968. In the seventies, however, they began to feel the pinch. Once a force to be reckoned with worldwide, at their peak Hammer were regularly producing six or seven features a year. In 1975 they released just one, *Man About the House*, a familiar TV spin-off. Ironically, the only things that could get the public behind Hammer again in the 1970s were bare-breasted lesbian vampires and Reg Varney at the wheel of his double-decker in three *On the Buses* movies.

'It was mayhem in the late sixties and early seventies,' recalls Stanley Long. 'Distributors were short of new films and people just weren't bothering to go to the cinema like they had been. The big movie companies had no idea what to put out to make any money and the distributors just grabbed any gimmick to get people back so they could make a few bob. I remember there was this terrible, awful, unwatchable movie doing the rounds in the early seventies called *Double Agent 73*, starring a woman called Chesty Morgan who had a 73" bust. It was just a gimmick and people were brought in by the publicity, but I can remember speaking to a cinema owner in the West End who told me people were walking out after ten minutes because it was the pits. It was difficult to provide the audiences with something they really wanted to see.'

The reasons for the marked downturn in cinema attendance were manifold. The lack of big Hollywood blockbusters, a change in popular tastes, and the dowdy image of the cinemas themselves all played their part. But the main reason for the decline in cinemagoing was the huge popularity of television. In 1950 there were 4583 cinema screens operating in Britain. By 1970 this had plummeted to just 1529, a figure which remained more or less stable throughout the remainder of the decade. The 1946 record of 1500 million cinema admissions was now just an unrepeatable fantasy. Across the country, cinemas were starved of new films and the punters to watch them. Forced to close, many were converted into a venue for Britain's other national pastime of the era: bingo. It was a sad state of affairs which was reflected in movies of the time. In 1975's *I'm Not Feeling Myself Tonight!* the hero (Barry Andrews) is debating where to take a girl on a quiet, romantic date. 'What you need is to take her somewhere really secluded, somewhere nobody else goes,' says his friend. 'How about our local cinema?' suggests Andrews.

Filmmakers were left with one option: to offer the public something they couldn't find on television. They fought back with the only available weapon left to them. Sex.

'You had to be a very lucky independent filmmaker to make money out of any genre of movie, other than sex films,' says David McGillivray. 'Everybody wanted to make a sex film because they just couldn't fail. People just couldn't get enough. Venturing into anything else was very risky, but making sex films was easy money.'

TITS AND TITTERS

Until the 1970s, the vast majority of British sex films had concentrated on delivering fleshy pleasures with a straight face. Only a handful of titillating movies could be classed as out-and-out comedies, including the likes of *School for Sex* (1968) and *Zeta One* (1969), but, of these, few were actually successful in dragging out the belly laughs. For the most part British sex was still imbued with a sense of seriousness, fear and trepidation. However, this was all to change, and radically so.

In 1970 a major overhaul of the BBFC ratings system introduced a new 'AA' category, restricting admission to those aged 14 or over and increasing the minimum age for admission to an 'X' film from 16 to 18. With this change filmmakers were able to push the barriers of sex and naughtiness even further. And with the box-office success of films like *Percy* (1971), *Au Pair Girls* (1972) and *Secrets of a Door to Door Salesman* (1973), comedy suddenly became the deciding factor in British sex movies. 'Most British sex films had to be comedies because our movies just couldn't compete with glossy Continental films starring people like Sylvia Kristel,' observed Ray Selfe. 'Their movies had principals who could act *and* strip off. Our industry didn't have that. We figured that with a comedy the audience might not notice that the actors weren't very good. Of course, the other worry was that the audience might not laugh either. And they frequently didn't.'

And with the arrival of *Confessions of a Window Cleaner* in 1974, there was no turning back. The era of the stupefying, phenomenal, magnificent British sex comedy was upon us. The Confessions films and the legions like them combined all the successful elements of TV situation comedies (knockabout plots, gross sexual stereotypes, *double entendres*, familiar suburban settings, crusty old character actors and pretty girls) with a gigantic dollop of nudity and simulated sex. The mix was irresistible to the general public, whose seemingly insatiable appetite for titters and tits knew no bounds. But why is the love of sex and comedy such a uniformly British trait? 'The British have such an inhibition about sex,' claimed sex superstar Fiona Richmond in 1984. 'They don't like to appear interested in it so you have to lace it with humour. That way they can say that's what they really came to see, and that's what they're really entertained by.'

'Comedy is able to get away with a bit more,' thinks Confessions producer Greg Smith. 'Comedy makes the goalposts wider and, I'm not sure why, but sex and nudity are the funniest subjects anyway. All I wanted to do was make people laugh and, although the Confessions films pushed nude scenes a little bit further, I didn't want to push things just for the sake of it. I think the censor was in a state of shock after seeing *Window Cleaner*, but it was based on a very successful book and we just wanted to put all the same funny situations into the film. If it made us laugh and was sexy, we wanted to put it on the screen.'

As the British sex film became an institution during the 1970s, so the filmmakers stuck to tried and tested formulas. In the era of mirrored headboards, hot pants, crushed velvet trousers and ruffled shirts, the oversexed professional layabout became king. This was never better illustrated than in the Confessions series. Based on the bestselling paperbacks written by Christopher Wood under

KEEPING THE BRITISH END UP

Right: Mary Millington, Britain's queen of sex, shares a bed with Alan Lake in *Confessions from the David Galaxy Affair* (1979).

the pseudonym Timothy Lea, the films ran from 1974 to 1977 and followed the south London sexcapades of a long-haired klutz played by Robin Askwith. He started off his career as a trainee window cleaner, progressing through pub-rock performer, driving instructor and holiday camp host, with women throwing themselves at him left, right and centre. The stories were repetitive, episodic narratives in which Askwith was given the perfect opportunity to come into contact with as many pretty birds as possible. This safe, cosy style also applied to many of the Confessions imitators, whose working class heroes had ample chance to go on shagging sprees with women they met on their nine to five jobs, whether they were milkmen, plumbers, doctors, taxi drivers, private eyes, handymen or door to door salesmen.

The female characters also stuck to stereotypical gender roles. Middle-aged swingers, dizzy hippies, naughty 'schoolgirls' (always aged 18 or above), nurses in black stockings and suspenders, randy au pairs and Soho strippers were rife, but top of the pile was the archetypal frustrated suburban housewife, opening her front door invitingly and usually wearing nothing more than a negligée and a broad smile. The absence of their husbands, invariably much older pipe-smoking bores – who are either at work, on business conferences or playing a round of golf – provide the lusty wives with a golden opportunity to pounce on the visiting tradesman who's come to wash the windows/read the meter/check the drains etc.

'I must apologise for being in my dressing gown,' says scantily clad Olivia Munday to the male home help in *Can You Keep It Up for a Week?* (1974), 'but my husband is away on a golfing weekend and I'm afraid I overslept.' That's just a typical example, and one that naturally ends in some extramarital hanky panky, but within a year or two regular sex film audiences could see this sort of encounter coming a mile off. The working class heroes may have been king, but the seventies were really the decade when the humble housewife took absolute control. In *Adventures of a Private Eye* (1977), director Stanley Long actually spoofs this sex film perennial. Hilary Pritchard plays a sex-starved housewife leaning lustily over her garden gate and making eyes at hapless Christopher Neil. 'I'm Sally. I'm a housewife,' she says breathily, fingering the front of her blouse. 'It's rather boring, really, being a housewife.'

GORGEOUS BIRDS

The sex comedy heyday created a whole new hierarchy of British movie stars better known for their looks than their acting abilities. The curvy starlets who dominated British cinema during the 1970s had been unheard of before and just as quickly became unheard of afterwards. However, their names and faces could make or break a sex movie and to their devoted audience they were recognisable stars, guaranteed to pull in the crowds. These new screen idols were plundered from Page Three of the *Sun*, top-shelf pornographic magazines, advertising hoardings, West End striptease clubs and, not surprisingly, Thames Television's *The Benny Hill Show*, a programme which traded on its reputation for glamorous females. Leading ladies with limited acting ability, but a talent for looking good, stripping off and shagging on the big screen, included Suzy Mandel, Pat Astley, Anna Bergman (daughter of legendary Swedish film director Ingmar), Felicity Devonshire, Heather Deeley and, most prolific of all, Nicola Austine, whose career lasted over a decade.

While these women could be relied upon to deliver the sexy goods and get their names and bodies splashed across the tabloids, none of them achieved superstardom to the same degree as Britain's foremost seventies' sex goddesses, Fiona Richmond and Mary Millington. First up was Fiona, a sleek, statuesque, deeply tanned brunette from Norfolk who bypassed a career as an air stewardess in favour of becoming a *Playboy* bunny and later a nude performer in millionaire Paul Raymond's saucy stage show *Pyjama Tops*. Never out of the tabloids for long, Fiona also carved a career for herself writing a naughty column in Raymond's girlie magazine, *Men Only*. She had her first big movie role in the sex-horror blockbuster *Exposé* in 1975, which touted her as the 'the most seductive woman in Britain'.

By 1977, however, Fiona was being usurped by a new girl on the block. Mary Millington was everything the formidable Fiona wasn't. She was a short, blonde, innocent-looking bisexual; to look at, she was the archetypal girl next door. While Fiona's sexy persona was all an act, Mary lived the salacious life for real, appearing in hardcore films for John Lindsay and prostituting herself as a high-class hooker. Publisher David Sullivan installed her as the nominal 'editor' of his magazines and promoted her as his star pin-up before launching her in a stream of cheesy, box-office-busting movies. Mary's breakthrough film, *Come Play with Me*, and Fiona's latest, *Hardcore*, were released on the same day at the same cinema, the newly refurbished Classic Moulin on Soho's Great Windmill Street. Despite *Hardcore* showing on a bigger screen with a larger seating capacity, *Come Play with Me* trounced it at the box-office, netting nearly three times as much. From this moment on the unthreatening Mary overshadowed her more elegant and intimidating rival.

Neither woman ever really broke free from their sex cinema shackles and, although Fiona carried on with nude entertainments on stage before retiring gracefully, Mary never even made it that far. Addicted to cocaine and suffering from severe depression during her later years, and constantly harassed by the authorities for her anti-censorship stance, she overdosed on pills and alcohol at her Surrey mansion in August 1979. Nobody has ever come near to reaching her heights of sex superstardom since.

Female nudity was the single most vital ingredient of the seventies brand of sex comedy. If audiences just wanted a laugh they could stay at home and watch *Steptoe and Son*. If they wanted a saucier laugh they'd go and see the latest Carry On movie. But if they wanted laughs, nudity *and* sexual situations the only option was paying to see an 'X'-rated British movie at the local Odeon. 'We always made it very clear to agents not to send us any girls who weren't willing to do nudity,' says Greg Smith. 'This was so there could be no misunderstandings. And it was fair to the actresses; when they came on set they had to know exactly what was required of them. You'll never believe it, but after the first Confessions movie we had literally sackloads of mail from women who wanted to go nude in the next film. Proper actresses too.'

'I got some very good actresses in my films,' agrees Stanley Long. 'People who wouldn't have normally stripped off took their clothes off for me. If it was a funny situation, they were happy to do it in the context of the movie. I mean, Angela Scoular was a great comedy actress who had already made a name for herself and she didn't mind going nude for my films. In her scene in *Adventures of a Taxi Driver* she had to be naked because she was in the bath and it was incredibly funny. Nudity always had to be done for a reason. I never wanted to do sex just for the sake of it. There had to be a bit of credibility to a scene. All comedy, really, arises out of circumstance and error.'

Like Angela Scoular, there was a select band of established actresses who were prepared to partially or totally undress for sex films. Ex-Carry On and Ealing star Liz Fraser shocked audiences with her saucy performance in *Confessions of a Driving Instructor* and 1950s starlet Joan Collins went the whole hog several times during the late seventies. A number of actresses who dared to go bare were, at the time, complete unknowns. Lissom young ladies Joanna Lumley, Jill Gascoine, Lynda Bellingham, Kate O'Mara, Pamela Stephenson, Gabrielle Drake, Vicki Michelle, Koo Stark and Diane Keen all stripped off to varying degrees before hitting the big time on television some five or ten years later. Most interesting of all, character actress Carmen Silvera, who became a household name as Madame Edith in TV sitcom *'Allo 'Allo* during the 1980s, played a topless lesbian in 1971's *Clinic Xclusive* when she was already well into her forties. At the other end of the scale, singing star Elaine Paige made an appearance in 1978's *Adventures of a Plumber's Mate* – fully clothed throughout – but still tried to get the film's release stopped a few months later when she hit the big time in *Evita*.

Left: Before she was famous – Joanna Lumley with Diane Hart in Games That Lovers Play *(1970).*

'There were so few pictures being made in those days,' says Tudor Gates. 'People wanted to work and actors and actresses were prepared to take their clothes off in order to be in a film. I remember Diane Keen auditioning for us in the nude for *The Sex Thief*. You wanted your performers to look as good as possible but if you took them on face value you might later find out they had scars or something. Performers had to be prepared to have simulated sex too. I always remember Michael Armstrong, the writer of *The Sex Thief*, had a favourite question to ask the auditioning actresses. He'd say, "You do understand there will be simulated sex, not *actual penetration*." He loved to linger over the words, but it was all in good fun.'

The most prominent sex film distributors of the seventies – companies like Miracle, New Realm, Eagle, Oppidan and, busiest of all, Tigon – generally saw no virtue in movies unless there was wall-to-wall female nudity and as much sexual content as possible. Distributors operated primarily to make money and get punters into the cinemas. Artistic considerations didn't come into it. 'I remember sitting in a preview theatre, showing one of my films to a distributor,' says Stanley Long. 'At the end of the film he turned to me and said, "Yes, it's a great movie, but there aren't many tits in it." I couldn't believe it. I asked him how many more tits did he want: ten, twenty? I was being facetious, but it honestly got to the level where they were counting nipples. Distributors had no constructive or creative criticisms to make. It was all about nude girls and nothing else. I saw no benefit in just showing tits and arses in favour of a decent plot.'

HOUSEWIVES' FAVOURITES

It would be wrong to imagine, just because female nudity was the distributors' main concern, that naked men didn't put in an appearance. Unlike many 'X'-rated American movies of the period, the male actors who made their living from taking off their shirts and slacks in Britain were often quite presentable. Naturally, the predominantly heterosexual male sex film fans couldn't have given a monkeys about what the blokes on the screen looked like, but several directors did make the effort to cast half-decent actors. Long overlooked, let's hear it for the boys whose inclusion in the raunchy recipe was just as important. Housewives' favourite Robin Askwith became the bearer (or barer) of the most famous arse in British sex movies in his role of sexual Goliath, Timothy Lea. Askwith, who arrived at the Confessions series via Lindsay Anderson, Pier Paolo Pasolini and *Carry On Girls*, made the role of a cheeky, trouser-dropping jack-the-lad his trademark and was a remarkably good physical comedian with near-perfect comic timing.

Few male sex film performers got the mix of chuckles and pathos as dead on as Askwith did. Others followed in his wake, like baby-faced Barry Evans from LWT's *Doctor in the House* series, lanky musician Christopher Neil, ex-*Crossroads* star Barry Stokes, hardcore performer Anthony Kenyon and Shakespearean actor Mark Jones. All tried hard, but all remained in the long shadow cast by Askwith. Others, like David Pugh (*The Love Pill*), Christopher Matthews (*Come Back Peter*) and Brendan Price (*The Amorous Milkman*), had faces only a mother could love. A handful of male leads were able to juggle genuine sexiness with acting ability: Leigh Lawson, Oliver Tobias, Roger Lloyd Pack.

Most handsome of all was a former physique model, and Junior Mr Britain contestant, called John Hamill. John liked nothing more than stripping off and doing the odd full-frontal, which is more than many of his contemporaries were prepared to do. In any case, the censor always found the penis problematic and actors did more bum-flashing than anything else. In the early 1980s, the tabloids took great delight in outing *Blue Peter* presenter Peter Duncan, who had appeared in Stanley

Right: Robin Askwith tinkles the ivories while Helli Louise watches. *Confessions of a Pop Performer* (1975).

Long's prostitution comedy *On the Game* (1973) as Henry III's foppish gay lover and two years later bared all in forgotten horror movie, *The Lifetaker*.

Another important ingredient was provided by a varied supporting cast of jokers and jitterers who brought with them audiences which might not have ordinarily attended a sex film. Big-name comedy stars and character actors were installed in 'X'-rated features with astonishing regularity during the seventies. Sex film producers were well aware that their participation in a boobs-and-bums epic could make or break a film. For a fair proportion of movie fans, especially those in the provinces who didn't have salacious Soho on their doorsteps, it was a far less intimidating prospect to see a Mary Millington film when family entertainers like Bob Todd or Windsor Davies were also appearing. The distributors knew this and gave the big-name guest stars prominent billing on the posters.

For several years famous actors (many of whom, it has to be said, were well past their peak) had accepted roles in horror and sexploitation movies, both in the UK and on the Continent. Dennis Price first went lowbrow with sapphic suckers in *Vampyros Lesbos* (1970), quickly followed by Hugh Griffith in several Italian sex comedies. Dear David Niven was reduced to starring in dismal rubbish like *The Statue* (1970), a comedy about penile dimensions, and a leaden Dracula spoof called *Vampira* (1974). In saucy Restoration romp *Joseph Andrews* (1976), the 65-year-old Michael Hordern was even persuaded to do a full-frontal nude shot.

It was unsurprising, then, that famous names from the worlds of classic film comedy and TV sitcom were asked to make cameo appearances in sex films. Only a decade earlier they would have considered such films beneath them, but for the likes of comedy legends Irene Handl, John Le Mesurier, Harry H Corbett, Diana Dors, Rita Webb and Graham Stark the sex films of the seventies sustained their careers when acting jobs were thin on the ground. It also got them an extra movie on their CVs, which was always a benefit. 'There weren't many movies being made in the 1970s, so just as long as you paid the stars their standard rates they would be happy to do the films,' says Greg Smith. 'When we made *Window Cleaner*, there was just us and a Robert Powell movie in production. Just two movies and we'd just come out of the Three Day Week, so making any kind of movie was a minor miracle. Actors wanted to work.'

The Confessions films were known to be good payers, but for some lower budget productions stars were often paid cash-in-hand for their participation and were therefore prepared to take a reduction in their pay packets. Diana Dors accepted £500 for her supporting role in *Adventures of a Taxi Driver* in 1975, on condition she was paid at the end of the week in used notes in a brown envelope, so she could sneak it past the tax man. And cockney actress Queenie Watts got an insulting £75 for her appearance in 1979's *Confessions from the David Galaxy Affair*. But it was easy money; their scenes were usually polished off in a day or two. The extra kudos these cash-in-hand cameos gave to a sex film was priceless, however.

Mercifully, the (often pretty elderly) guest stars were usually kept away from the sex sequences. There were exceptions, however. Seeing Charles Hawtrey and James Robertson Justice administering kinky tortures to a naked girl in sci-fi romp *Zeta One* (1969) is a sight for sore eyes, as are the following… John Le Mesurier having a brief grope of his topless secretary's boobs in *Au Pair Girls* (1972)… Bob Todd totally naked and spanking his equally nude (but much more nubile) wife in *The Ups and Downs of a Handyman* (1975)… Tommy Godfrey posing for publicity shots with a naked Mary Millington for *Come Play with Me* (1977), then claiming in the

KEEPING THE BRITISH END UP

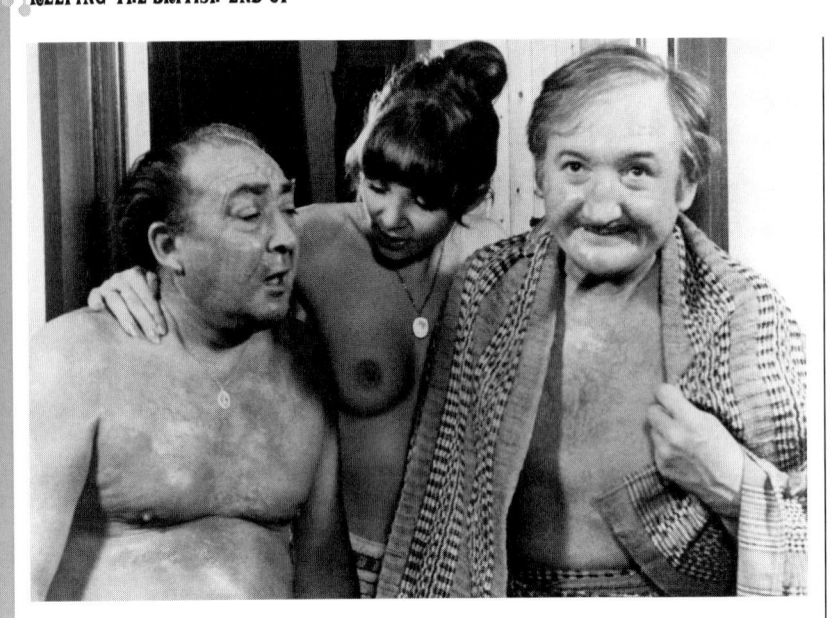

press that 'I wouldn't want to be implicated in anything like that as I sometimes appear in children's TV programmes'... Arthur Askey pinching nurses' bums in *Rosie Dixon – Night Nurse* (1978)... Not to mention Jack Douglas ogling half-dressed patients in *What's Up Nurse?* (1977) and Charlie Chester getting an eyeful in *Can I Come Too?* (1979).

And sex films didn't just attract big-name *stars*. On the other side of the camera, directors and producers were queuing up to 'go blue' after seeing that this was where the big profits lay. Val Guest, a veteran of over 70 films, took charge of *Au Pair Girls* and *Confessions of a Window Cleaner*. Ralph Thomas and Betty E Box, the duo behind the Dirk Bogarde-Leslie Phillips *Doctor* movies, entered the fornicating fray with penis-transplant comedies *Percy* (1971) and *Percy's Progress* (1974). Wolf Rilla, who had brought cinema audiences *Village of the Damned* in 1960, sidestepped into sex with *Secrets of a Door to Door Salesman* (1973), replacing the young Jonathan Demme, who was sacked part way through the project. Demme went on to direct *The Silence of the Lambs* in 1990 and won an Oscar for his trouble. Rilla opened a wine shop.

The mix of talents prepared to dabble in British sex films was bizarrely varied.

Jack Arnold had directed fantasy classics like *It Came from Outer Space* and *Creature from the Black Lagoon* but in 1974 found himself in Britain to shoot *Sex Play*. Massimo Dallamano, the cinematographer on Sergio Leone's *A Fistful of Dollars*, took English money to film *Blue Belle* (1975), starring Felicity Devonshire. Henry Herbert, 17th Earl of Pembroke, broke the family mould by directing Koo Stark in 1977 sex-fest *Emily*. But easily the most intriguing producer-writer behind seventies' sauce was a mysterious individual known as Elton Hawke. Hawke started life as the equally elusive Anthony Solomans in 1971's *Virgin Witch*, but both names concealed one of the oddest movie collaborations ever. Fearful for their reputations, wrestling commentator and ex-disc jockey Kent Walton and soap queen extraordinaire Hazel (*Crossroads*) Adair teamed up under the Hawke moniker to produce *Clinic Xclusive* (1971) and *Can You Keep it Up for a Week?* (1974), before coming clean in 1975.

1975 proved to be the most 'reproductive' year for British sex films, with an incredible 16 titles in production. The huge box-office returns of *Confessions of a Window Cleaner* in 1974 had provided a massive shot in the arm for sex film producers. By the mid-1970s sex was more commonplace than any other genre of British movie-making. A change of chief censor at the BBFC in 1975 – from Stephen Murphy, who only held the position for four years, to the more liberal New Yorker, James Ferman – meant that films could get away with even greater explicitness. But unlike most European countries, which had been producing big-budget hardcore for years, Britain remained resolutely softcore, with MPs, Christian organisations and Mary Whitehouse campaigning feverishly to stem the 'tide of filth' from abroad. Because of this, no country embraced softcore as wholeheartedly as the UK. A self-inflicted malaise, softcore sex was the only serious option for the majority of British sex film producers. They had to toe the line or face prosecution.

It became a matter of ingenuity as to how best to represent sexual intercourse without showing anything too rude. All manner of cheeky metaphors were adopted to take the place of explicit sex and arousal. These included provocatively placed sausages and bananas, trains going into tunnels, spinning clockwork toys, cannons firing, hoses spurting, inflating rubber appliances, toothpaste getting squeezed out of tubes, squirting syringes and champagne corks popping. Not to mention adjustable table lamps erecting themselves whenever a fit dolly bird walked past. Invariably, sex sequences would be intercut with this kind of imagery while the bouncing-about of the naked participants was shot at predictable, Benny Hill-style high speed. Oral sex posed more of a prob-

Left: Good clean fun. Tommy Godfrey, Suzy Mandel and Ronald Fraser in *Come Play With Me* (1977).

lem. Fellatio and cunnilingus were always filmed with the active partner licking as far away from the genitals as possible, usually six inches above the pubic area. Belly buttons never had such a good time as they did in the seventies.

THE MAN IN THE MAC

Sex film distributors pandered to the oft-mentioned, and now legendary, 'man in the mac' or 'dirty raincoat brigade', the perceived audience for British filth. Supposedly, these were middle-aged, slightly rumpled men in soiled clothing who spent their evenings manipulating themselves in dingy sex cinemas. 'I do remember them,' recalls seventies actress Sue Longhurst. 'I was once at a showing of *Come Play with Me* at a cinema in London and I looked round the auditorium and I saw quite a lot of very peculiar-looking men. I didn't really want to know what they were doing, so I didn't look too hard.'

This image of the 'man in the mac' became a much-ridiculed stereotype and, although men were indeed the predominant audience for pictures like *On the Game* (1973) and *Penelope Pulls it Off!* (1975), the filmmakers were keen to get as many people to see their humble offerings as possible, male or female. *The Wife Swappers* was probably the first to attract mixed audiences because of its marital subject matter, but the Confessions series also appealed as much to women as to men. Towards the end of the decade, as sex movies began to lose their gimmicky appeal, distributors blatantly marketed their films directly at couples. The poster for 1979's *Confessions from the David Galaxy Affair* bore the tag-line, 'Mary Millington meets Superstud in a sensationally funny film for both sexes!' Yet, just to cover all bases, the very same film was touted in top-shelf men's magazines as 'Two hours of non-stop porno!' In this particular case, neither claim was true.

'I think cinema audiences were far more gullible in the 1970s,' says Stanley Long. 'They were searching for very erotic films or hard pornography, but they didn't find it down at their local cinema. It was as simple as that. The dirty raincoat brigade really did exist. There were hordes of men who went to strip clubs in the West End and then straight to the cinema looking for nudity and explicit sex, but they just couldn't find any. I'm sure they were extremely disappointed. But movies are a funny thing. You pay your hard-earned money to see a sexy movie, but if you don't like it you can't get your money back. It's quite perverse really.'

The situation was very different in the US. Gerard Damiano's epoch-making *Deep Throat* (1972) had signalled the arrival of 'porn chic'. A grainy, cheaply made sex movie (costing around $25,000), *Deep Throat* told the story of a young woman who inadvertently discovers that her clitoris is located in the back of her throat. The film proved there was a mass audience for explicit porn and pushed back the barriers of what was deemed acceptable on the screen; it also reputedly grossed $100 million worldwide and continues to make money decades later. It heralded the birth of the billion dollar adult film industry in the US, and hundreds of other highly successful porn movies followed, like *The Devil in Miss Jones* (1972), *Behind the Green Door* (1973) and *The Opening of Misty Beethoven* (1976). Even early hardcore gay movies like *Sudden Rawhide* (1972) found their way into selected movie theatres. Over on this side of the pond, there seemed absolutely no chance that hardcore pornographic movies were ever going to go mainstream. In the meantime, a few bare bristols in *Adventures of a Taxi Driver* would have to suffice.

Of course, hardcore pornographic films *were* produced in Britain but in the most secretive of circumstances and definitely not for widespread cinema exhibition. Stag films, as they became known, had been produced in London since World War II, often exploiting the talents of Soho prostitutes and their clients. Directors like Mike Freeman, Charlie Brown, Ivor Cooke and Evan Phillips (the latter reputed to be the first Briton to make a million from pornography) all made their names in hardcore, and regularly saw the inside of prison cells for their trouble.

Nearly 20 years before videotape revolutionised the sex industry in the early 1980s, hardcore sex films, made for home consumption, were sold in small cardboard boxes containing Super Eight loops: 8mm film suitable for threading through a home projector. The original films were invariably shot on 16mm but after duplication were reduced to the smaller format for ease of use. In this way, devotees could start building up explicit film collections with titles like *Tom Cats*,

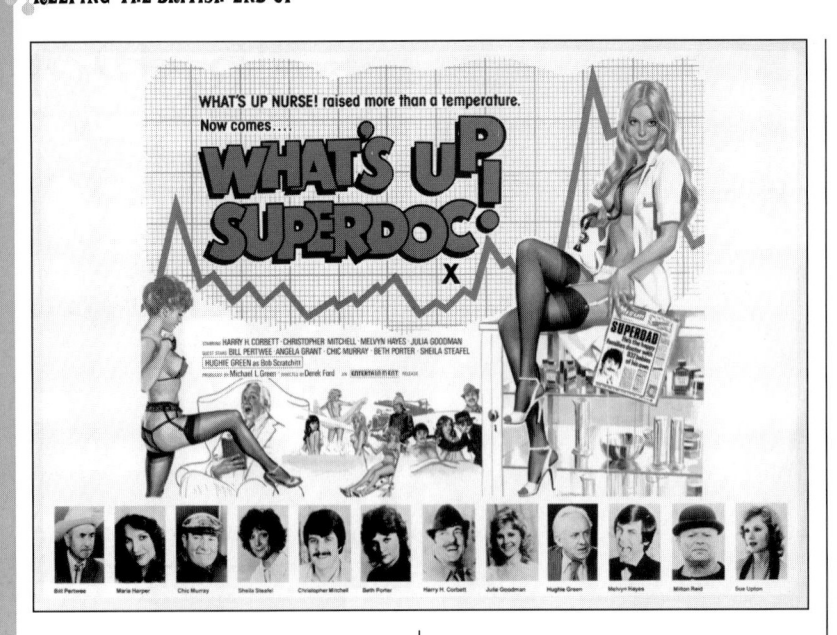

Hot Pants and *No Holes Barred*.

For those unable to accommodate home movie equipment, or to sneak it past their wives and girlfriends, the proliferation of privately owned cinema clubs provided an alternative outlet. Small, dingy clubs like the Exxon in north London, the Albatross to the east, and Swedish Paradise and Cin Cinema in Soho itself proudly offered 'continuous programmes of pornographic sound films for those who like it hot from 10.00 am to 11.00 pm', with coffee lounges provided for those needing to rest their wrists. The private cinema clubs operated under the same circumstances as small theatre clubs; there was a legal loophole stating that if you owned private premises which were only available to people who paid membership, then you could show whatever you liked and not be prosecuted. 'What nobody remembers now is that movies like *Deep Throat* had been shown around the UK in cinema clubs for over a decade,' says David McGillivray. 'By the 1970s Soho was full of cinemas showing hardcore films.'

Supposedly the most luxurious and popular cinema club in London during the mid-1970s was the Taboo in Great Newport Street, just off Leicester Square. The owner, John Lindsay, openly stressed his business was 'genuinely blue' and as a result was banned from advertising in 'family' newspapers like the *Evening Standard*, although the very same tabloids took delight in regularly exposing his business activities. Scots-born Lindsay, an ex-newspaper photographer who was once an official snapper at a Buckingham Palace ball, is usually cited as the man who brought hardcore pornography out of the back streets. Charged twice with 'conspiring to publish obscene films for monetary gain' during the 1970s, Lindsay was acquitted on both occasions. Dubbed the 'Devil's Ambassador to England' by Mary Whitehouse, Lindsay preferred a simpler description. 'Ma business is pussy' he liked to say in his heavy Glaswegian drawl.

'ADDED EXTRAS'

Whereas comedy became the preferred bedmate for sex at the British cinema, this wasn't necessarily the case on the Continent. Lighthearted romps like *Bedroom Mazurka* (1970) and *Danish Dentist on the Job* (1971), starring the Scandinavian Robin Askwith, Ole Søltoft, were massively successful both in the UK and Europe. But the most celebrated European sex films of the 1970s were fragile, arty, ethereal, inconsequential sex dramas dubbed 'coffee table porn' in the press. The first of note was Bernardo Bertolucci's notorious (and really rather boring) 1972 film, *Last Tango in Paris*, swiftly followed in 1974 by Just Jaeckin's *Emmanuelle*, a French-made movie that totally blew the world of pornography apart. The film may have lacked energy, depth, proper characterisation and a decent plot, but it captured the imagination of audiences across the Western world, who had not seen sex so beautifully or tenderly photographed before.

During the mid-1970s the French seemed to have a monopoly on this sort of featherbrained stuff. Alongside a slew of official and unofficial *Emmanuelle* sequels, there was also *Story of O* (1975), *Laure* (1975) and *Bilitis* (1976). All as fey and flighty as each other, the films were massively successful around the globe, with the makers of *Emmanuelle* claiming their film had been seen by over 100 million cinema patrons worldwide in its first 18 months. In London alone it ran for 126 consecutive weeks at the Prince Charles Cinema in Leicester Square.

British filmmakers had long been aware that foreign audiences were used to sterner stuff than indigenous ones. Since the 1950s it was not uncommon for home-grown movies to be shot with additional scenes, or stronger versions of existing scenes, for foreign markets. British horror pictures added extra gore and nudity for countries like Germany and Japan. Even light comedies, dramas and musicals were sometimes filmed with extra skin to pep up the proceedings. *Serious Charge* and *Expresso Bongo*, both early Cliff Richard films from 1959, were rumoured to have

Left: Famous names queued up to star in sex films such as What's Up Superdoc? *(1978).*

been shot with topless girls replacing the bikini-clad variety found in the British release. This also happened in the Soho-set thrillers *Beat Girl* and *Too Hot to Handle* (both 1959) and a whole slew of low-budget B-movies whose only means of recouping their costs was by filming raunchier inserts for overseas sales.

Just as Peter Cushing, the gentleman of horror, could butcher a prostitute far more graphically in the export version of Robert Hartford-Davis' *Corruption* (1967), so could Britain's foremost film comedian, Norman Wisdom, have an affair with a carefree hippy girl (Sally Geeson) in his 1969 film *What's Good for the Goose* and see her topless in the Continental version. No wonder the publicity blurb posed the question: 'What is Norman doing now that he's never done before?' In the same way, early British sex movies like *School for Sex* (1968) and *The Nine Ages of Nakedness* (1969) had significantly more flesh on view in their overseas cuts. Directors were renowned for shooting bra-on and bra-off shots of exactly the same sequences.

In the 1970s, Britain couldn't possibly compete with the huge scale of hardcore being produced in America and on the Continent, but our plucky filmmakers still gave it their best shot. Rumours circulated throughout the decade that large numbers of British sex films were being shot with 'added extras'. After hours and behind closed doors, directors were shooting hardcore pornography on a scale that has never been fully acknowledged. The 'Japanese version', as it was known by the film industry, became legendary.

'British sex films just weren't good enough to be shown on the regular cinema circuits in the USA or on the Continent in their original form,' reckoned Ray Selfe. 'The only market open to them was the hardcore porn circuit which was absolutely huge abroad, especially since *Deep Throat* had been such a hit. However, our films were far too tame for that market so British directors had to shoot extra material to get any form of overseas sales. We had these British movies starring nobody anyone had ever heard of, with very little production value and no chance of selling them abroad to distributors. They had no virtue except as pornography, so you had to shoot hardcore sequences, but very discreetly.' David McGillivray concurs. 'I remember they were always shooting two versions of these films for mysterious foreign markets. It was endemic. I became very aware of it and it happened on two or three of the movies I was involved in. These versions definitely did exist and producers were shooting hardcore porn all over the place. I'd never have found out about it if I hadn't been in the cutting-room and seen it going on.'

On a few occasions stronger material was tacked on by the distributor after filming had been completed. Norman J Warren's 1968 hit *Loving Feeling* was released overseas as *She Loved with Her Boots On* with added hardcore which the director only found out about many years later. *The Sex Thief* (1973) had lingering penetration shots slotted in for its American version, *Her Family Jewels*, on its New York début in January 1976. Despite being heralded in the American movie press as

'Britain's first hardcore porno film', the film's producer, Tudor Gates, had absolutely no idea that his movie had been tampered with. 'Somebody told me about the hardcore version when they came back from the States,' he recalls. 'The real actors hadn't participated in the extra scenes, but they'd just edited in some new footage. That's actually quite a clever thing to do, you know. I became aware of a completely separate sub-industry that would only shoot pornographic inserts for other people's films. It was quite extraordinary.'

'I'm not sure if that was always really so,' counters McGillivray. 'My own experience is that the companies themselves made the hardcore versions. A lot of directors claimed they had no idea it was going on, but I'd take that with a pinch of salt if I were you. It was all top secret and done at a time when presumably everybody involved could have been arrested, so you had to be very careful who you told. If you were involved in movies you couldn't help but know what was going on. It was a wonderful period of so many secrets and lies and that's why filmmakers enjoyed it so much.'

Quite regularly, hardcore inserts were smuggled out of the country to be developed at laboratories in more 'enlightened' countries like Sweden or Holland. If a filmmaker could persuade a British company to develop the footage it was invariably done in the early hours of the morning. 'You had to do a deal with the laboratories to process the footage in the middle of the night and nobody would watch the rushes. People were fearful of being rumbled by the police,' explained Ray Selfe.

KEEPING THE BRITISH END UP

Left: Barry Evans makes his excuses and leaves in Adventures of a Taxi Driver *(1975).*

'There were a number of cases where British films in their hardcore versions were taken to the Cannes Film Festival, but if the film was brought back into the country Customs & Excise seized it and it was destroyed. You had to be so careful.'

HARDCORE HONCHOS

Two main exponents of hardcore versions of mainstream British sex comedies were Derek Ford and David Grant. Both had seen the indigenous film industry from all angles and both had a fascination for living life on the edge. Ford, who had experienced huge success with softcore movies like *The Wife Swappers*, first took the plunge into hardcore in 1972 with *Commuter Husbands*. The film was such a hit overseas that he was encouraged to carry on with the clandestine practice for the next three years with the help of his wife, and co-producer, Valerie. Preferring to shoot the hardcore scenes in the safety of his own Essex home, his undercover methods first came to the attention of his cast on the set of 1973's *Keep It Up Jack!* 'I realised they were filming a hardcore version and several of us knew there were certain days when it was 'porn only' and nothing else,' recalls Sue Longhurst, who played the film's female lead. 'After the cast had gone home for the day Derek Ford was filming all sorts of stuff. I heard that everybody in the film crew was involved in the hardcore and other people just stood around and watched.'

Alan Selwyn, the scriptwriter of *Keep It Up Jack!*, also remembers a confusing situation during filming. 'Two young girls suddenly appeared on the location at the end of Friday's shooting and I turned to Derek Ford and said "Who the hell are they? You've finished shooting today, haven't you?" He told me they were there for a crowd scene. I believed him, but the following week everybody was talking about hardcore scenes Ford had shot over the weekend using these girls. I think Derek did it more for a hobby than anything else.'

Directors like Ford hired models from specialist agencies supplying sex performers who knew exactly what they were required to do. Although acting anonymously, many were recognisable from the 16mm home movies directed by John Lindsay. A few of these performers could be curiously temperamental. 'There were these girls on set quite prepared to have real sex for Derek Ford, but when a stills photographer came near to snap them doing it they complained,' laughs *Keep It Up Jack!* star Mark Jones. 'I just couldn't understand it. They didn't mind having it off for moving pictures, but they strongly objected to any photos being taken while they did it. I was always hearing about the bloody Japanese version, but I kept out of the way for the professionals to get on with that!'

Colleagues recall that Ford got an immense thrill from filming stronger scenes and gradually became kinkier and kinkier. His 1975 film *Sex Express* ran as support to a Swedish film when it opened at the Moulin Cinema in Soho and earned itself some positive reviews, due mostly to a mesmerising central performance by 1970s starlet Heather Deeley. A minor release running for just 50 minutes in the UK, in America it was heralded as a 'Porno masterpiece for all the family – the Manson family, that is.' Opening in New York in March 1976 under the title *Diversions*, the film was virtually unrecognisable. Running for 87 minutes, it encompasses the full gamut of weird sexual tastes and even sickening Nazi imagery. It is, without doubt, the most savage and disturbing British sex film ever made. Some foreign critics, jaded by years of hardcore, claimed that *Diversions* didn't go far enough. 'The film is a good example of the kind of dreary foreign-made pick-ups currently exploiting the sexploitation market in the US,' said American trade paper *Variety*. There's no pleasing some people.

'Hardcore was prevalent in those days,' says Sue Longhurst. 'It happened on virtu-

Right: Not quite hardcore – Sue Longhurst, Mark Jones and Maggi Burton in *Keep It Up Jack!* **(1973).**

ally all my films. You just knew it was going on all the time, behind closed doors. I really didn't much care for that side of it, but at the same time that's how they made money and it was up to them what they wanted to do. Luckily I never stayed around to see it, although I was asked if I'd participate and refused. It made me feel slightly queasy if they cut the films to make it look like I was doing it. But then these versions were shown abroad and I'd never have known anyway, would I?'

Longhurst appeared in a couple of sex films for distributor-turned-producer David Grant. He never went as far as Ford but still relished the opportunity to sell hardcore versions of his movies at the Cannes Film Festival each year. Movies like *Girls Come First* (1975) and *The Office Party* (1976) were exhibited to foreign distributors in their full pornographic glory. In their British versions Grant's movies ran for less than an hour, but were boosted to a full 90 minutes with added sex shot only after the professional actors had gone home. 'On a few of David Grant's films what you would do is cut to a close-up of genitalia belonging to a model, but still use the real actress' face in the next shot,' recalled Grant's one-time business partner Ray Selfe. 'So who's to say which is which? Everything merges into one. It was like using a body double.'

The most celebrated instance of a British film shot in a hardcore version was *Come Play with Me* (1977), produced by David Sullivan and directed by veteran George Harrison Marks. Sullivan, who at the time was the second biggest publisher of pornographic magazines in the country, promoted the film in his publications with the promise that it would be 'the British *Deep Throat*' and the first homegrown film to show actual sexual intercourse in British cinemas. Even before shooting was finished, tabloid newspapers were awash with salacious stories about what was really going on behind the shutters of the film's location, the Weston Manor Hotel near Oxford. On Sunday 13 November 1976, the *News of the World* ran the headline '*We Didn't Know it was a Blue Movie, say Stars*'. Sullivan had arranged a cleverly orchestrated leak, breaking the story that four additional hardcore sequences, three heterosexual, one lesbian, had been shot and were to be inserted into the film's narrative at the post-production stage.

The movie's 'respectable' stars were apparently outraged, an Equity representative turned up on location to investigate (and was unceremoniously told to 'Fuck off!' by the director), and cinemagoers across the land were straining at the leash. Ironically, the hardcore version of *Come Play with Me* vanished without trace. Allegedly only screened once, the unexpurgated cut never sold anywhere and has been missing ever since. Not that it did any harm to the film's box-office success in Blighty.

COUNTING THE PROFITS

The practice of filming stronger material in British films all but died out with *Emmanuelle in Soho* in 1981 and the dawn of unregulated home videos which showed just about anything you wanted to see in extreme close-up in the privacy of your own home. However, in one very rare instance the 'overseas version' was actually even more prudish than the English cut. To a few select countries the sight of Robin Askwith's bare bum was beyond the pale and had to be covered up at all costs. 'When we started filming *Confessions of a Window Cleaner*,' says Greg Smith, 'somebody from Columbia Pictures came up to us and said that there had been an incred-

KEEPING THE BRITISH END UP

Left: Linda Hayden, Robin Askwith and Greg Smith take a break from *Confessions of a Window Cleaner* (1974).

ible amount of interest from distributors in other countries. My immediate reaction was "Great", but then they started telling us you couldn't show pubic hair in South Africa and in another country you couldn't show this or that in a public cinema. We had a bit of a problem since there was quite a lot of nudity in the film.'

Columbia Pictures were keen to see *Window Cleaner* go global and increased the film's budget to accommodate foreign tastes. Crazy as it may sound, the budget provided for extra underwear for the actors to put on during the sex scenes. 'They worked out this new budget and we decided to re-shoot several scenes with the girls in knickers,' laughs Smith. 'I think for Spain we had to do a version with bras on as well. It really was a fucking nonsense and sometimes the scenes were re-cut so Robin Askwith and his female companion ended up with more clothes on than when they started. Columbia were happy to pay for the extra versions and thank goodness really, because the overseas sales were amazing. But it cost an extra £10,000 to do it. Basically £10,000 for extra knickers!'

Added underwear or not, *Confessions of a Window Cleaner* was immensely successful wherever it played. It was the highest grossing British movie of 1974, as well as being one of the biggest overseas exports of the year, with healthy sales in all the commonwealth countries like South Africa, New Zealand and Australia. But the appeal of the film was never in doubt as far as Greg Smith was concerned. 'Robin and his co-star Linda Hayden and I would go on tours for three or four weeks publicising the first Confessions film, all over the country,' he recalls. 'We did radio shows, TV, photocalls, press interviews, visited factories, even boatyards, because I strongly believed that getting to the people was very important. We had a super time. The reviews would be bad, but the figures for cinema attendances were astronomical. It became easy to knock the Confessions, but I saw people up and down the country rocking with laughter in the cinemas and it was a wonderful feeling.'

It's important not to underestimate the colossal success of British sex films. Compared with today's homegrown movies the 'X'-rated treats of the past often took up virtual residence in some London cinemas, with the punters coming back again and again just to satisfy their need to see flesh. Unbelievable as it may sound, such were the low budgets of the movies that it wasn't difficult to cover production costs within a matter of months, sometimes even weeks.

Early naturist picture *Naked – As Nature Intended* ran for 18 months in London. *Secrets of Sex* (1969) played for six months continuously at the Jacey Cinema in Piccadilly Circus, comfortably recouping its entire budget in that time. It was subsequently reissued periodically in the UK for the next ten years. Stanley Long's *The Wife Swappers* also ran for six months at one cinema in the capital. Having cost just £12,000 it went on to make nearly half a million within the space of a year. 'The film critic Peter Noble stopped me in Wardour Street and said to me that my film had the greatest title since *Gone With the Wind*,' says Long cheerfully. 'He was absolutely right because that film was box-office gold. The title alone pulled people in and other distributors were kicking themselves for not getting there first.'

'By today's standards sex movies were made with tiny amounts of money and the craziest schedules you would ever believe,' said Ray Selfe. 'You just couldn't do it today, but an entire film could be shot in less than a week and for absolute peanuts. You'd work all hours to get them finished, but you'd be very unlucky indeed if they didn't make a profit because the market for sex was so big in the sixties and seventies. I think that's why the majors started getting involved.'

By the early 1970s the financial allure of sex films had indeed attracted the attention of the major studios. Columbia Pictures bankrolled the Confessions series and EMI had a hand in the two *Percy* movies and in several others, including *Spanish Fly* (1975) and *Keep It Up Downstairs* (1976). However, the independent film companies could always make things cheaper and turn in more impressive profits. Careful not to overspend, most sex

Right: A rude awakening for Harrison Marks in *Come Play With Me* (1977). Left to right – Pat Astley, Suzy Mandel, Mireille Alonville and Mary Millington.

films were shot entirely on location, usually in the heart of Soho, which provided the perfect tacky backdrop for sexual shenanigans. Occasionally film crews ventured a little further afield to London's surrounding counties of Essex, Surrey and Kent, but only in the rarest of circumstances did filming take place in more exotic locales. *A Promise of Bed* (1969) was blessed with a little French woodland (although you'd never guess), *The Four Dimensions of Greta* (1972) took a short trip to Germany and 1973's *Commuter Husbands* enjoyed a bit of Holland, but these were definitely the exception rather than the rule.

Unanimously slated by the popular press, British sex films nevertheless continued to pull unbelievably large crowds as the 1970s wore on. Stanley Long's Confessions-style comedy *Adventures of a Taxi Driver*, shot in 1975, became the eighth most popular film in London the following year. Made for £130,000 it took nearly £48,000 in its opening week in Birmingham alone. At the ABC cinema in the city's New Street, queues snaked round the block three times over as people waited to see the film on its opening night. Eventually sold to over 50 countries and dubbed into French, Italian, Dutch and German, it grossed millions. 1978's *The Stud*, starring Joan Collins – which amusingly had extra disco footage added for American audiences rather than hardcore sex – took an incredible £550,000 in its first fortnight on release, plus an extra £640,000 in sales of the accompanying soundtrack album.

Even lesser-known movies like *I'm Not Feeling Myself Tonight!* (1976) could enjoy runs of four months in selected Soho cinemas and Derek Ford's unremarkable 1973 sex comedy *Keep It Up Jack!*, which cost just £41,000 to produce, made £3 million worldwide, helped by a 12-month run in France. 'You'd have to have been an imbecile not to make money from sex films in those days,' believes *I'm Not Feeling Myself Tonight!* scriptwriter David McGillivray. 'You shot it, released it and started counting the profits immediately. It was so easy.'

The success of these films was dwarfed by the 1977 release *Come Play with Me*, the longest-running and most profitable British movie of all time. Released at the Classic Moulin in Great Windmill Street in April 1977, the film ran daily for 201 weeks, only closing in March 1981. Opening in the cinema's tiny 134-seat auditorium, it was able to take nearly £6500 in its first week and enter the London Top Ten chart at number nine. Even three years later it was still making £1500 each week. *Come Play with Me*'s record-breaking run at this one London cinema made in excess of half a million pounds. Countrywide it took another four million.

NAFF JOKES AND BARE BUMS

The heady days when a single low-budget British movie ran for four months, let alone four years, have long gone. Film fans of a tender age can't conceive of a time when the great British public popped down to the local Odeon to be entertained and titillated by a creaky, independently made movie starring a few old sitcom stars mucking about, occasionally interrupted by scenes of naked girls and shagging. It seems a world away from the well-polished, family-orientated, multi-million pound cinema industry of today. But for the best part of 25 years British cinemas thrived on a diet of naff jokes, bare bums and bouncing breasts and the public was willing to pay again and again for the privilege of seeing them.

The great British sex film has never stood up and taken the applause for helping our indigenous film industry get through some particularly difficult times. But the images of Robin Askwith peeping through a window at a naked woman getting out of a bath, Mary Millington dressed as a nurse in black stockings and suspenders and Joan Collins squeezed into a corset with a chauffeur's cap perched on her head are just as indelible a part of our cinematic heritage as Celia Johnson and Trevor Howard embracing on a railway platform in *Brief Encounter* or Michael Caine walking menacingly along a beach in *Get Carter*. British sex films are routinely accused of being cheap, nasty and unerotic. Plenty are. But they're ours and we should be justly proud of them. ✻

KEEPING THE BRITISH END UP

Left: Robin Askwith flashes his flares in *Confessions of a Window Cleaner* (1974).

Below: Sunbathing in the studio – a publicity shot from *Nudist Paradise* (1958).

DOINGS

25 YEARS OF NAUGHTY BRITISH MOVIES FROM 1958 TO 1983

Note: The years attached to films correspond to their copyright dates, not necessarily their year of production or release. Within each copyright year, however, the films are listed in chronological order according to their eventual release dates.

1958

NUDIST PARADISE
aka *Nature's Paradise*

Great Britain / 1958 / 72 mins / cert 'A'

'For the first time a British club with British nudists is depicted on the wide screen in the full glory of Eastmancolor. Make no mistake about it, this is a major landmark in the history of British nudism!' Thus read the publicity for Britain's début nudie movie which, as it turned out, was not merely a landmark for naturists but a groundbreaking moment for British cinema. Without *Nudist Paradise* there would probably be no Robin Askwith dropping his Y-fronts, no Fiona Richmond whipping off her sparkly brassière and certainly no Mary Millington adorning cinema frontages across the length and breadth of Britain dressed as a nurse in black stockings. Proudly heralded as the first ever British movie without a stitch – filmed in 'glorious Nudiscope' – it was welcomed by excited British nudists, but more eagerly gobbled up by a male cinemagoing public anxious to see some naked British *flesh*.

'What we need,' wrote a pro-nudist in the film's publicity material, 'is a carefully edited film which will show as much as can be shown without embarrassing sensitive members of the audience. A film which will be entertainment as well as propaganda and which will be screened at ordinary cinemas up and down the country.' The movie did indeed play extensively around the UK and easily recouped its budget of £15,000 within weeks. In Australia it ran on and off for nearly ten years, and in the United States, under the title *Nature's Paradise*, it was seen as something of a British novelty. The movie's American distributors promised free admission to anyone turning up at the cinema completely naked.

The story, told in flashback, centres on Mike Malone (Carl Conway), an art student hopelessly in love with a young secretary named Joan, played by 'Britain's Exciting New Star', Anita Love. Finding it difficult to approach her, Mike plans a 'chance meeting' at the local dance, but Joan isn't having any of it. You see, Joan has a guilty secret which takes up all her time at the weekend. She likes to go starkers at a nudist camp! She confides in her office colleague Patricia (Katy Cashfield) and persuades her to visit the camp with her. They have a terrific time and the swimming pool, badminton court and trampoline are all seen at exhaustive length. Not to mention the

KEEPING THE BRITISH END UP

The FIRST BRITISH NUDIST FEATURE!

ORB PRESENTS ANITA LOVE

NUDIST 'A' PARADISE

EASTMAN COLOUR in GLORIOUS NUDISCOPE

KATY CASHFIELD · CARL CONWAY
DENNIS CARNELL

WORLD CINEPHON THURSDAY,
TRAC CINEPHONE Thurs. FEBRUAR

repetitive games of beachball-throwing. Mike, meanwhile, feels left out and secretly follows the girls. Purchasing a day-pass from the cute camp receptionist, he can't fail to miss the legend written in huge letters on the wall: 'Visitors must undress completely'. Joan goes mad when she sees that Mike has tailed her, but his firmly set quiff, big smile and flabby arse soon win her over. It doesn't take long for them to get engaged and, some months later, married. They're elected to represent their club at the Naturist World Congress to be held at Woburn Abbey and, when we join them there, we see that healthy living really does pay off since they are the proud parents of a tiny baby.

Nudist Paradise was filmed on location at Britain's most famous naturist club, Spielplatz in St Albans, Hertfordshire, with full blessing from its elderly owners, Charles and Dorothy Macaskie, who make cameo appearances, as do their daughters Iseult and Cosette, who even take part in the film's rather dodgy 'Miss Venus' competition. Spielplatz was to be the preferred location for several nudist epics over the years, with the Macaskies apparently unaware that their camp was being plundered for the delight of men in dirty raincoats.

Even the cast was hoodwinked. 'I think the thing that made it all seem so easy was the fact that we were all filming the nude sequences in a genuine naturist club,' commented Katy Cashfield, who was chosen for the part of Pat after being spotted by the film's producers stripping at London's Irving Theatre Club. She added: 'For me the most nerve-wracking moments were the screen test.' You don't have to doubt that for one moment. The lengthy, lingering scenes of undressing, copious bedroom sequences and several awkward *double entendres* expose the film's hidden agenda all too clearly.

Nudist Paradise was fairly well-received by the naturist community, not because it was especially good but mainly because it was Britain's first proper attempt at showing nudists doing what came naturally. London's *Naturist Magazine* wrote in 1959: 'No doubt the first glimpse of the top half of the moving, breathing naked woman will come as something of a shock to some people, but within minutes they will be accepting this as perfectly normal.' They were forced to concede, however, that the acting was 'of only average competence.'

The film was much joked about and spoofed for years. In 1968's *Carry On Camping*, Sid James and Joan Sims go to see it at their local fleapit. Over real clips from the film (intercut, however, with close-ups of a topless Carry On dolly), the couple discuss its artistic merits. 'You told me this film was all about camping,' complains a sour-faced Sims. 'Well, it is,' says James. 'Those are tents, aren't they?' To which Sims retorts: 'That's not what *you're* looking at!'

1959

TRAVELLING LIGHT

Great Britain / 1959 / 52 mins / cert 'A'

Edward Craven Walker, veteran naturist and regular visitor to Spielplatz, had dreamt of making a propaganda film to encourage more people to take off their clothes since the mid-1950s. With a steady influx of foreign-made nudist movies being exhibited in Britain, Walker took the plunge and directed his debut movie in 1959. Originally intended for screening at clubs, societies and Women's Institute meetings, *Travelling Light* rapidly transferred to public cinemas, much to the delight of its director. However, it didn't really attract the sort of crowd he had envisaged.

'This is the world we live in,' comments Craven Walker over scenes of coughing car exhausts, trundling commuter trains and pneumatic drills. 'Labouring under constant pressure, our nerves are strained to the utmost. Many people nowadays are beginning to find that they can only keep pace with modern life by spending more of their leisure hours in natural surroundings. But those who call themselves naturists go further!'

Ex-*Health & Efficiency* model Elizabeth is a pretty daring individual. Taking her faithful Alsatian dog 'Tough' with her, she likes nothing more than sneaking off to the sand dunes at Studland Bay to sunbathe in the all-together. Her friends wonder how on earth she gets such a fabulous, deep, all-over tan. However, Elizabeth's sordid secret is soon exposed. 'One warm summer day my dog and I were dozing blissfully in the sun when suddenly there were people all around me. I was shocked. I'd been discovered!' she says. Clutching her towel to her chest she looks terribly embarrassed, but is amazed when the three intruders start getting their kit off too. One of them comes up to her and introduces herself as a naturist. 'Naturists!' says Elizabeth indignantly. 'What in Heaven's name does she mean?'

With a little gentle persuasion these nudists encourage Elizabeth to join them on a trip to a famous nudist colony at Villata in Corsica. Leaving all her inhibitions (and her dog) in staid old England, Elizabeth has a whale of a time abroad, engaging in plenty of health-giving activities including volleyball, swimming and dancing. She also meets Yannick, 'the well-known nudist' from France, who displays her unique 'underwater ballet', without the impediment of a bathing costume, to the strains of 'The Song of India'. Yannick's nubile contortions bring a slight whiff of eroticism to the proceedings and, indeed, the censor asked for her sequence to be trimmed. Her scene culminated in an underwater kiss with a young man but was disallowed since it brought the film into 'disrepute'. Otherwise, Craven Walker concentrates on the beautiful scenic opportunities his sunny setting gives him, both on land and sea (the underwater sequences were filmed with a waterproof camera and an aqua-lung). At film's end Elizabeth has to return to 'civilisation', fully clothed, but refreshed all over and now with a perfect understanding of what 'naturism' means.

CAST: Elizabeth (*herself*), Yannick (*herself*)
CREDITS: *Director/Producer* Michael Keatering [aka Edward Craven Walker], *Underwater Photography* Michael Keatering, *Screenplay* Victor Hewitt. An E C WALKER Production. Distributed by GALA. Opened March 1960.

NUDIST MEMORIES

Great Britain / 1959 / 27 mins / cert 'A'

Director Arnold Louis Miller and cinematographer Stanley Long's first film together deliberately sets out to catch hold of the successful shirt tails of 1958's *Nudist Paradise*. Miller, a shrewd businessman, had first teamed up with Long in the mid-1950s to market and distribute 8mm glamour films showing women strip-

CAST: Anita Love (*Joan Stanton*), Carl Conway (*Mike Malone*), Katy Cashfield (*Pat Beatty*), Dennis Carnell (*Jimmy Ross*), Celia Hewitt (*interviewer*), Emma Young (*receptionist*), Walter Randall (*camp warden*)
CREDITS: *Director* Charles Saunders, *Producers* Nat Miller and Frank Bevis, *Editor* Helen Wiggins, *Photography* Henry Hall, *Screenplay* Leslie Bell and Denise Kaye, *Music* Horace Shepherd
An ORB INTERNATIONAL Production. Distributed by ORB. Opened February 1959.

KEEPING THE BRITISH END UP

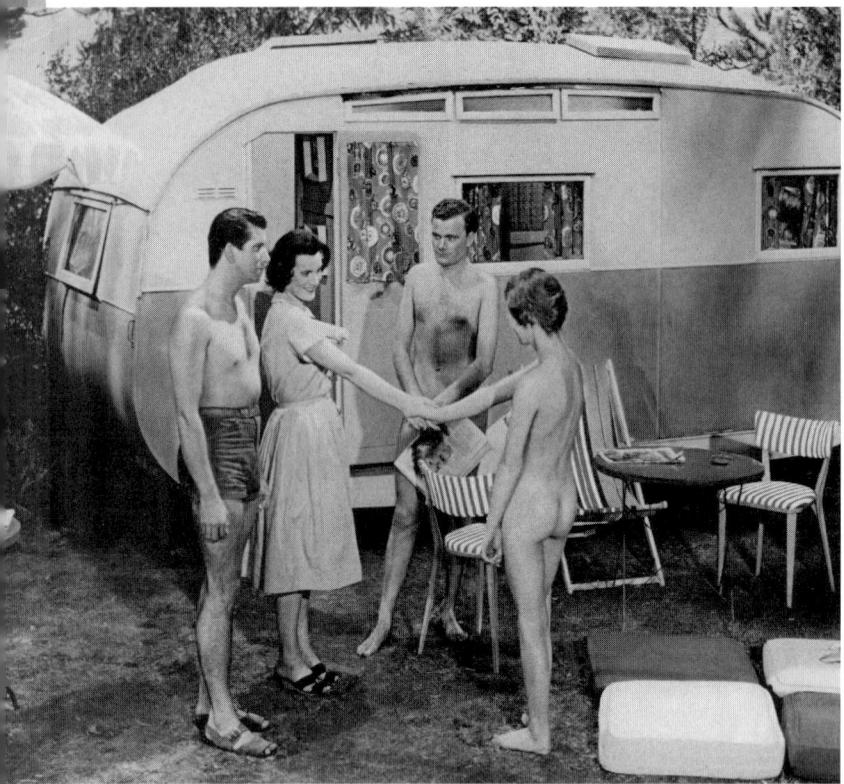

Left: Carry On Caravanning – nudist style! *The Nudist Story* (1960).

1960

THE NUDIST STORY
aka *For Members Only* aka *Pussycat Paradise*

Great Britain / 1960 / 90 mins / cert 'A'

Prim and proper Jane Robinson (Shelley Martin) is upset when her grandfather dies, but soon cheers up when she discovers that she's the main beneficiary of his will. What Jane doesn't know is that naughty grandpops was also a pioneer nudist and she has inherited the Avonmore Nudist Camp! Well, prancing about starkers just isn't Jane's bag and, feeling ashamed, she decides to close down the camp. At the last moment she is persuaded otherwise by dashing Bob Sutton (Brian Cobby), who is the camp's director and loves nothing more than letting the fresh air get into all his nooks and crannies. Jane is even encouraged to become a nudist herself, but one of the camp girls is jealous of all the attention Bob is giving the new owner. Conniving Gloria (Jacqueline d'Orsay) is French so, naturally, must be a trouble-maker. She tricks naïve Jane into believing that Bob is promiscuous and all he wants is to see her with her knickers off! Thankfully, kindly Aunt Meg (straight from the pages of Enid Blyton) intervenes, putting matters straight, and Gloria gets a jolly good telling-off.

Another film inspired by *Nudist Paradise*, this one was the work of expa-

ping. Their company, Stag Films, churned out in excess of 100 films, but the men had their sights set on bigger projects, namely a big screen movie. Shot in 'complete ignorance' over one week at Spielplatz and costing under £1000 to make, the resulting film, *Nudist Memories*, went on to run for over a year in the West End. But if anything its plot is even more simplistic than the movie it took its inspiration from.

One hot summer's day three sweet girls meet in a Soho coffee bar. It transpires that one of the girls is a nudist who frequents a nudist camp just outside London. She explains that there is no healthier way to enjoy the sunshine and invites her curious friends to join her on a day trip there. Without hesitation her mates happily accept her offer. Once at the camp the girls join in all the fun – swimming, badminton, table tennis and sunbathing – and by the day's end are extremely reluctant to return to the hustle and bustle of London. However, they promise themselves they'll be back very soon.

The most interesting thing about the film is the actress in the lead role, Anna Karen. Miss Karen, an ex-stripper from London's Panama Club, had few qualms about getting naked for her first cinema film, but a decade later was rather less glamorous in her brilliant portrayal of slovenly, bespectacled, lank-haired housewife Olive in the enduringly popular sitcom *On the Buses* (1969-73). The role, described as 'a big lump who likes her food', made her a comedy legend and she re-created the character in the brief reprise of *The Rag Trade* (1977-8). She has more recently appeared in *EastEnders* and surreal sketch show *Revolver* (2001).

CAST: Anna Karen (*Anne*), Mitzi Mayo (*Mitzi*), Carol Lynne (*Carol*), Laura Mason (*Laura*)
CREDITS: *Director/Producer* Arnold Louis Miller, *Commentary* Jill Gascoine, *Photography* Stanley Long, *Music* Neville Taylor
A SEARCHLIGHT Production. Distributed by NEW REALM. Opened March 1961.

Right: Remembering to keep their legs crossed at all times. The nudists of Michael Winner's *Some Like It Cool* (1961).

triate American brothers Harry and Eddie Danziger, who grew extremely rich on the proceeds of the Z-grade second features and TV shows churned out at their New Elstree Studios. Happy to leap on any available bandwagon, with *The Nudist Story* they provided one significant pointer to future developments in homegrown smut: they cast the first 'proper' actor (Anthony Oliver) ever to venture into British sexploitation.

CAST: Shelley Martin (*Jane Robinson*), Brian Cobby (*Bob Sutton*), Anthony Oliver (*Blake*), Natalie Lynn (*Aunt Meg*), Jacqueline d'Orsay (*Gloria*), Joy Hinton (*Carol*), Paul Hendrick (*Tim*)
CREDITS: *Director* Ramsey Herrington, *Producer* John P Wyler, *Photography* Jimmy Wilson, *Screenplay* Norman Armstrong, *Music* Tony Crombie
A DANZIGER Production in association with THE BRITISH SUNBATHING ASSOCIATION. Distributed by EROS. Opened May 1960.

1961

SOME LIKE IT COOL

Great Britain / 1961 / 61 mins / cert 'A'

Few people know that director Michael Winner started his career in the early 1960s churning out black-and-white B-movies for exploitation producer E J Fancey. His début movie, *Shoot to Kill* (1960), co-starred a young John M East, who later featured heavily in skinflicks made in the late seventies and early eighties. Now better remembered for films like *The Nightcomers* (1971) and *Death Wish* (1974), Winner tentatively dabbled in nudie cinema a decade earlier with *Some Like It Cool*, which Stanley Long has since claimed was inspired by the success of his own *Nudist Memories*. It's a simple-minded movie running barely an hour, sticking safely to the naturist movie formula and spreading on thick the pro-nudity propaganda.

There's nothing Jill (Julie Wilson) likes more than sunbathing in the nude on a quiet stretch of secluded beach, but after being rudely disturbed by a group of holidaymakers she is persuaded to join them at a local sun club. Sadly, her jealous fiancé Roger (Mark Rowland) disapproves, presumably worried that she might start comparing the size of his genitals with the other campers'. Nevertheless, Jill is still desperate to see what she's missing and, when she and Roger marry, she tricks him into going to the naturist club on their honeymoon. Miraculously, Roger is converted, as are Jill's parents, who are normally very prudish and haven't seen each other naked since 1932. The club goes from strength to strength and even buys up the adjacent field to expand its operation. The previous landowner, the blustering, red-faced, anti-nudist Colonel Willoughby-Muir (played in predictable style by Douglas Muir) is furious at what is going on, but is soon made to see the error of his ways.

Amateurish to say the least and with the sort of plot that could be written on the back on a matchbox, Winner's movie is not the camp, nudie classic that it could have been. In July 1961 the *Monthly Film Bulletin* described it as 'the sort of nudist goings-on that wouldn't bring a blush to a church outing.'

CAST: Julie Wilson (*Jill*), Mark Rowland (*Roger*), Wendy Smith (*Joy*), Brian Jackson (*Mike Hall*), Thalia Vickers (*Jill Clark*), Douglas Muir (*Colonel Willoughby-Muir*)
CREDITS: *Director* Michael Winner, *Producer* Adrienne Fancey, *Editor* Peter Austin-Hunt, *Photography* Alex Sheridan, *Screenplay* Michael Winner, *Music* Jackie Brown and Cyril Payne
An S-F FILMS Production. Released by S-F FILMS. Opened May 1961.

NAKED – AS NATURE INTENDED

aka *As Nature Intended* aka *Cornish Holiday*

Great Britain / 1961 / 65 mins / cert 'A'

If anybody was going to make a truly smashing-looking nudist film it was going to be Britain's most famous glamour photographer, George Harrison Marks. Convincing chief censor John Trevelyan that his début feature-length movie was really an impassioned plea for more people to take up the healthy life of naturism, he determined to squeeze as many breasts as possible into the film's running time and pronounced that it would be 'the nudest film of all'. And with Britain's most famous nude model, Pamela Green, in the lead role he could do no wrong.

Marks realised that he would have to play by the censor's rules to a certain extent. While he recognised that the sort of people who were going to see a Harrison Marks movie were after only one thing (two things, strictly speaking), the main bulk of the movie is taken up with a silly west of England travelogue. In fact, the working title for the picture was the less-than-titillating *Cornish Holiday*. Pamela Green later admitted the film had no script. Marks just made it up as he went along. Any poor bugger anxious to see some boobs has a long wait until all the girls start stripping off, so kindhearted Marks does give the audience a tiny taste of what's to come at the very beginning. In the incredibly drawn-out opening sequence, Pamela Green walks to camera across the beautiful sands of a Cornish beach, awkwardly holding a towel in front of her fanny.

Back to the drudgery of city life, where we are introduced to Petrina, a meek secretary who desperately needs a holiday. Her best friend is Jackie, a shoe shop assistant. Together with their more glamorous friend Pamela, the three young girls have planned a relaxing holiday in Cornwall. Pamela is a 'woman of the world' and a dancer at the Windmill Theatre, so goodness only knows what mischief they might get up to. 'How did these three different types become confirmed nudists?' asks the serious voice-over. 'We can follow them and see.' Climbing into Petrina's massive American Buick (and how can she afford *that* on a secretary's wage?), the girls set off on their journey into the naked unknown. In a secondary story, two wigglybummed, knock-kneed, busty blondes, Bridgit and Angela, are also hiking their way on holiday. The intimation, although innocently done, is that they are slightly 'more than just mates'.

After much cavorting around, pointing, waving, laughing and stopping to look at babies, the two groups' paths finally cross at the historic seaside town of Clovelly. 'The quay was built in the 16th century by George Carey, which made Clovelly the only safe harbour between Appledore and Boscastle,' we are told. Yawn! Harrison Marks must have raided every tourist information office en route for pamphlets to crib from.

Eventually, after diverting escapades at the Minack Open-Air Theatre at Porthcurno and the seat of King Arthur at Tintagel, all the girls reach the beach. And, much more importantly for the man in the mac, he knows he's finally going to see some breasts. In fact, we learn the nudity was not premeditated, but is all an accident. 'Pam, who always seems to like wandering off alone, unknowingly trespasses onto private property,' says the commentary. 'Trewyn beach is a beach owned by the local nudist society!' There she spies Bridgit and Angela in the buff playing with an inflatable beachball. Imagine her shock! However, the other girls are all smiles. The lure of the sun, sea and sand is overwhelming and suddenly everybody is completely stripped. Off come the swimming costumes and the boobs start wobbling. It's almost like the girls have never seen the seaside before,

Left: George Harrison Marks practises his art on a Cornish beach.

since they all run around like drug-addled headless chickens, playing a game of 'catch' and splashing around wildly in rock pools.

But it doesn't stop there. They all visit Spielplatz naturist club and are introduced to its owners, Charles and Dorothy Macaskie, plus several more hardened nudists, including one hot young man with muscles in places most other men haven't got places. Pamela Green sticks out like a sore thumb among the saggier, real-life nudists, but everybody gets on like a beachball on fire. Game of nude ping pong, anyone?

It has to be said that Harrison Marks does a marvellous job of photographing both the sunny countryside and the naked girls. The settings look beautiful and the director has a touching faith in the British climate. While the movie probably wasn't the 'nudest' of them all, Marks was asked, nevertheless, to remove two sequences from the film by Trevelyan. One was of Bridgit and Angela lounging on their bed, planning their holiday route in baby doll nightie and a bath towel respectively. The second was of Pamela Green showering after her dance class. Neither put nudity in their 'proper' context. Nakedness on beaches and in holiday camps was fine; stripping off indoors in suburbia was a big no-no. From a modern-day perspective, *Naked – As Nature Intended* is more interesting seen as just a travelogue with a bit of nudity tacked on at the end. However, in 1961, the historical details of Clovelly could not take precedence over swinging knockers.

CAST: Pamela Green (*Pamela*), Jackie Salt (*Jackie*), Petrina Forsyth (*Petrina*), Bridget Leonard (*Bridget*), Angela Jones (*Angela*), Stuart Samuels (*clerk/pianist/waiter/fisherman/boatman*), Guy Kingsley Poynter (*narrator*), George Harrison Marks (*himself*)
CREDITS: *Director/Producer* George Harrison Marks, *Screenplay* George Harrison Marks and Gerald Holgate
A MARKTEN COMPASS Production. Distributed by COMPTON. Opened November 1961.

NUDES OF THE WORLD
aka *Nudes of All Nations*

Great Britain / 1961 / 65 mins / cert 'A'

Hilariously old-fashioned nudist romp about Carol (Vivienne Raimon), the English entrant in an international beauty contest held on Brighton beach. When she wins the £1000 prize and a sports car, her fellow contestants accuse her of cheating by improving her chances with a fake tan. 'Zumbody ought to say zumthing,' moans the hysterical Miss France. 'Zis should not be allowed!' However, Carol explains that her healthy all-over bronzing is because she regularly bares all at nudist resorts. When the other young ladies hear this they go wild with enthusiasm and persuade her to organise a naturist holiday. Finding all the local sun clubs fully booked for the summer, they lease the grounds of a lavish stately home. While the owner, Lord Greystone (Geoffrey Denton), is away they turn the estate into a top-notch nudist camp.

The locals in the village go hopping mad and the 'not-in-my-backyard' contingent campaign for the parade of boobs and bums to be stopped immediately. Waving a placard proclaiming 'Nudist Get Out!', the protests are led by beastly, sour-faced postmistress, Mrs Haines. 'You're shameless hussies,' she screams. 'Displaying your naked bodies like depraved creatures!' Thankfully, the lusty Lord returns home just in time (revealing that he's secretly a nudist too, of course) and reassures the old bat by presenting her with the proceeds from the nudist fête, to send her wheelchair-bound daughter to America for a life-saving operation.

As well as having a great title, *Nudes of the World* is a great-looking movie, lovingly photographed in glowing colours and culminating in a terrific firework display. The film's story reads like a half-undressed version of a mid-1950s Norman Wisdom picture, but the dim-witted acting and naff story didn't put off the huge crowds who went to see it. Redhead Vivienne Raimon is a particularly dire actress, but the huge quantity of breasts and inflatable rubber rings take your mind off the dodgy central performances. 'The acting is stilted and the plot wouldn't convince a five-year-old,' wrote the *Daily Cinema* in November 1961, 'but as there aren't likely to be too many five-year-olds in the queues the film is bound to attract, who cares?'

The most fascinating element of the film is an innocuous voice-over from Valerie Singleton, who accepted the job just months before she became a presen-

KEEPING THE BRITISH END UP

Right: An exotic location for Donovan Winter's *World Without Shame* (1961).

ter on the BBC's children's programme, *Blue Peter*. Cinematographer Stanley Long recalls her well, but for all the wrong reasons. 'Valerie Singleton denied being the voice in that film,' he says. 'I just couldn't understand that. She only did a bloody voice-over for God's sake, but afterwards she wanted nothing to do with me. She didn't appear in the film naked and she did nothing to be ashamed of, but she vehemently denied having done it. I just don't know why!'

CAST: Valerie Singleton (*narrator*), Vivienne Raimon (*Carol Wilson, Miss England*), Antony Dell (*Ronald Wilson*), Colin Goddard (*Peter Graham*), Joyce Gregg (*Mrs Haines*), Douglas Cameron (*Sergeant Roberts*), Monique Ammon (*Monique, Miss France*), Sue Chang (*Sue, Miss Hong Kong*), Elaine Desmond (*Miss USA*), Jutka Goz (*Miss Hungary*), Geoffrey Denton (*Lord Greystone*)
CREDITS: *Director/Screenplay* Arnold Louis Miller, *Producer* Harry Green, *Editor* S Marks, *Photography* Stanley Long, *Music* Keith Papworth, *Song 'Oo La La' written by* Nat Mills A MIRACLE-SEARCHLIGHT Production. Distributed by MIRACLE. Opened November 1961.

SUNSWEPT

Great Britain / 1961 / 69 mins / cert 'A'

'They were naturists. They were carefree. They were... sunswept!' read the film's poster. What it failed to mention was that they were also a bit on the nutty side.

Committed naturist Elizabeth (last seen in *Travelling Light*) goes to the local sun club to meet up with her lovely friend Karen. She is introduced to a clean-living couple who have recently got married and are about to have their wedding breakfast at the club before setting off to the south of France for their idyllic, clothes-free honeymoon. The newlyweds arrive at the Rhône Valley, visit the famous naturist society at La Conche and bump into Elizabeth, who is also on holiday. She just so happens to be off to join her lissom long-haired friend Yannick on the famous stark-naked Isle of Levant (*sans* clothes since 1931). The travelogue, shot in stunning Eastmancolor by Edward Craven Walker, continues via a beautiful white schooner to the Corsican sun camp of Villata and then onto the official nudist beach on the Yugoslav island of Rab. Yannick, billed as 'the fabulous aqua star!', performs a 'dance' underwater. Karen goes nude water-skiing and the rest of the friends are happy just smiling, paddling and posing round a totem pole with huge grins on their faces. For the more cultured among the party there are midnight Tchaikovsky piano recitals! One of the better 1960s' nudies, the *Daily Cinema* wrote in January 1962 that *Sunswept* was 'a fig-leaf opus beautifully photographed ... delightful and bracing entertainment!'

Craven Walker was keen to state that his film was not to be confused with movies just cashing in on the 'craze' of nudism and without artistic merit. 'This is not another gimmick film,' he said at the time. 'It is a true representation of modern nudism.' As proof of its authenticity *Sunswept* was awarded the first ever Certificate of Approval by the British Federation of Sun Clubs. The fact that the movie clearly stated it was filmed 'by naturists and featuring genuine naturists only' made not one jot of difference to the punters in Soho. Breasts were breasts, stamped 'official' or not.

CAST: Liza Raine (*narrator*), Elizabeth (*herself*), Yannick (*herself*), Karen (*herself*), Lita (*herself*), Ingrid (*herself*)
CREDITS: *Director/Producer* Michael Keatering [aka Edward Craven Walker], *Editor* Peter Austen-Hunt, *Underwater Photography* Michael Keatering, *Screenplay* Antony Craven A MICHAEL KEATERING Production. Distributed by GALA. Opened January 1962.

WORLD WITHOUT SHAME

Great Britain / 1961 / 71 mins / cert 'A'

A long-lost nudie directed by sexploitation director Donovan Winter, who would later cause a splash with his 'X'-rated titillators *Come Back Peter* (1969) and *Escort Girls* (1974). It's the story of a young advertising executive who has a terrific win on the football pools and decides to leave the dirt and grime of London for a naturist holiday with his wife. Using the money to buy a deserted Mediterranean island (that was some pools win!), they embark on a new life free of the restrictions of the modern world. They are joined by thee other couples (surely it can only be a matter of time before a bit of wife-swapping is on the cards?), including a musician, a writer and an artist. Their happy community thrives on grape-eating, splashing about in rock pools and nude dancing and they eventually refuse to return home to 'civilisation'.

Winter's script is at least slightly more politically and ecologically minded than many contemporary nudies. The plot hinges on the youngsters' rejection of the establishment, commercialism and the threat of nuclear war. *World Without Shame* was produced by Mistral, a company run by soon-to-be top glamour photographer and pornographer Russell Gay. Gay dominated top shelves with his magazines in the late 1960s and early 1970s and directed dozens of both hard and softcore movies on 16mm, one of which, a lesbian fantasy from 1974 called *Response*, starred a young Mary Millington.

CAST: Yvonne Martell (*Yvonne*), Laura Beaumont (*Laura*), Diana Valeri (*Diana*), Laurel Grey (*Laurie*), Larry Bowen (*Larry*), Paul Christian (*Paul*), Jean Robert (*Jean*), Michael Troy (*Mike*) **CREDITS:** *Director/Screenplay* Donovan Winter, *Producers* Donovan Winter and Russell Gay, *Editor* Norman Cole, *Photography* Alex Sheridan, *Music* Ike Isaacs, *Song:* 'Come What May': lyrics by Donovan Winter A MISTRAL Production. Distributed by GALA. Opened May 1962

1962

TAKE YOUR CLOTHES OFF AND LIVE!

Great Britain / 1962 / 64 mins / cert 'A'

After the record-breaking successes of their two earlier nudist movies, Stanley Long and Arnold Louis Miller returned to the sun camps for their third and last naturist romp. The film's title is inspired in its simplicity, but the true sexual connotations were not too wholesome. 'The intimation was that it was *Take Your Clothes Off and Have Sex!* That was basically the thinking behind it,' admits Long.

Costing £14,000, the budget for *Clothes Off* was twice as much as its predecessor, partly because the producers decided to film in the south of France. Nine international beauties travel from England to the Continent, four by plane, three in a vintage car and two hitch-hiking. The different modes of transport are an obvious advantage since it pads out the running time when the narrative switches between them. They all arrive safely in Cannes and eventually meet up with their jolly bronzed hosts, John (Gino Nennan) and Tony (Ian Michael), who invite them on a nudist holiday. The boys must think all their Christmases have come at once since the nine lovelies are soon happily peeling off and taking part in various 'activities'. These include visiting a millionaire's lavish villa, going on a cruise for buried treasure and enjoying fun and frolics on the stunning beaches of the Riviera. They end up sunning themselves on the ever-popular Isle of Levant, but the movie's highlight is watching the girls doing the Twist, although they wear bikinis for this because seeing their breasts swing round at high

Right: Future Carry On favourite Margaret Nolan (left) leads the nudists in *It's a Bare, Bare World* (1963).

speed would be a little *too* indecent.

CAST: Jenny Lane (*Lee*), Maureen Haydon (*June*), Susan Irwick-Clark (*Carol*), Terri Lee (*Ingrid*), Margaret Collins (*Mandy*), Angie Lowe (*Patricia*), Hedy Borland (*Heidi*), Ku-Chich (*Esme*), Ulla Thoren (*Barbara*), Ian Michael (*Tony*), Gino Nennan (*John*), Anna Sellers (*Marie*)
CREDITS: *Director/Screenplay* Arnold Louis Miller, *Producers* Arnold Louis Miller and Stanley Long, *Photography* Stanley Long, *Music* Tony Kind
A SEARCHLIGHT-MIRACLE Production. Distributed by MIRACLE. Opened February 1963.

1963

EVES ON SKIS

Great Britain / 1963 / 63 mins / cert 'A'

Director and ardent naturist Edward Craven Walker returned to nudie films one last time with a highly creative twist; instead of naked girls frolicking on the beach he had them doing it in the snow!

A bored, blonde-haired teenage girl spends an unsatisfactory evening in a stuffy, smokey dancehall in north London. Preferring to daydream rather than boogie (the pop music is blatant padding), she fantasises about the next day when she'll be happy and naked in the crisp clean air of the Austrian Alps. There she'll join all her naked jolly friends for a frosty naturist holiday, hanging their panties on the branches of pine trees. We've seen all this a hundred times before but at least Craven Walker attempts to tweak the formula by having his naturists leaving the beachballs at home and concentrating on the healthy pursuits of skiing, throwing snowballs, making igloos and, most bizarrely of all, building snow rabbits. 'You know I've never been able to understand all this mixed-up talk about naturists or nudism or whatever it's called,' says the girl. 'I just can't see why I shouldn't be openly proud of the body I was given. Instead of having to hide it furtively all the time!'

Despite the fact that the chilly chums debate where to go for their next nudist holiday, this was Craven Walker's last foray into filmmaking. *Eves on Skis* was not a success and the director later admitted he shouldn't have made it. 'It was unnecessary because had I not shot *Eves on Skis* and *Sunswept* I would have been far better off,' he said in 1995. 'If I'd just gone ahead and exploited the one film [*Travelling Light*], which was the breakthrough worldwide, I would probably have made hundreds of thousands more. But in fact I didn't do that. I tried to make a better film and by so doing I lost the initiative and everyone else jumped on the bandwagon.'

CAST: Edward Craven Walker (*narrator*), Elizabeth (*herself*), Karen (*herself*), Karl (*himself*), Jill (*herself*), Herbert (*himself*)
CREDITS: *Director/Producer* Michael Keatering [aka Edward Craven Walker], *Photography* John Mantell, *Music* Tony Rocco

A MICHAEL KEATERING Production. Distributed by GALA. Opened September 1963.

IT'S A BARE, BARE WORLD!

Great Britain / 1963 / 33 mins / cert 'A'

Plagiarising its title from the 1963 American comedy *It's a Mad, Mad, Mad, Mad World!*, this bouncy little British nudie is as pleasing to the eye and undemanding to the brain as its predecessors. Naughty tricksters Vicki and Vera take their innocent friend Carol on a sightseeing tour of the glories of Windsor and its historic castle. However, this is just a sneaky ploy to get her to visit a nearby nudist club to which they both belong. Reluctant to end her fascinating history lesson, Carol cautiously agrees to a tour around the camp, but is allowed to keep her clothes on since she is a nudey débutante. What she sees totally blows her mind. It's like nothing she has ever experienced before! The happy campers indulge in all the nudist pleasantries: lounging about, waving at nothing in particular, laughing and giggling, endlessly splashing around in water and having a game of tug o' war. Understandably embarrassed by her clothes (they *are* awful, after all), Carol strips off, picks up a beachball and enters into the thick of it.

The storyline is as idiotic as ever, following the pattern of *Naked – As Nature Intended* in that there's a lot of picturesque scenery and perfunctory padding to sit through before the frustrated cinemagoer actually gets to see any bristols. And what bristols they are, since they belong to top-heavy ex-Harrison Marks model Vicki Kennedy. Vicki became one of the most popular nude models in Britain during the early sixties and made several saucy 8mm films for 'home use' like *One Track Mind*. Her fantastic 41-24-36 figure, innocent blue eyes and pouting lips got her noticed by several casting directors, particularly at the Cannes Film Festival where she posed provocatively on the beach.

Using her real name Margaret Nolan, she earned herself small roles in the Beatles' *A Hard Day's Night* and the James Bond picture *Goldfinger* (both 1964). She would have made an excellent leading lady in British sex comedies during the seventies had she not been snapped up by producer Peter Rogers, who featured her in a tiny role in *Carry On Cowboy* (1965) prior to building up her parts (in a manner of speaking) in *Carry On Henry* (1970) and *Carry On Dick* (1974). She also starred in the 1973 film version of *No Sex Please – We're British*.

CAST: Vicki Kennedy [Margaret Nolan] (*Vicki*), Vera Novak (*Vera*), Carol Haynes (*Carol*), Denise Martin (*Denise*), Angela Jones (*Angela*), Leslie Bainbridge (*Leslie*)
CREDITS: *Director* W Lang, *Producer* Adrienne Fancey, *Photography* Douglas Hill, *Editor* Edna Dangerfield, *Commentary written by* Monica Scott, *Music* Cy Payne
An ANTLER FILM Production. Distributed by S F FILMS. Opened March 1964.

THE RELUCTANT NUDIST
aka *Sandy, the Reluctant Nature Girl*

Great Britain / 1963 / 47 mins / cert 'A'

Sandy (played by pert brunette Annette Brand) is an awfully nice young lady of 18 who is enjoying a pure and wholesome romance with her hunky boyfriend David (Jeremy Howes). One day Sandy rings David and innocently invites him to her house for tea. In passing she asks him what he's wearing (as you do) and he replies 'a pair of shorts', but he's lying. He is as *totally nude* as the day he was born. And that is David's problem. He is a confirmed nudist who loves getting his bits out whenever he can, whether it be in the privacy of his home or the relaxed atmosphere of the Spielplatz naturist club in Hertfordshire. David confides his problem to his mate Allan, who couldn't give a toss and is more preoccupied with David winning the upcoming naked swimming competition. After all, he is the big white hope of the nudist camp.

Poor Sandy is totally in the dark about David's 'double life' and on the following Saturday invites him to a party. However, her fella has to tell a bare-faced lie. David has to take part in the swimming contest but instead tells her he's visiting his old grandma for tea and crumpets. He'd rather visit an old wrinkly than spend time with his girlfriend? Sandy nearly blows a gasket and, being the paranoid little madam she is, immediately hires a private detective to follow his every move, convinced that he's knocking off another bird. The detective (John Atkinson) follows David, but is convinced he knows him from somewhere. You'll never believe it, but the detective is a nudist too and recognises a little something about David from Spielplatz! Later that week, David and Sandy go on a camping trip and David's girly chum Brigitte tries to smooth things over between them. But Sandy, suspicious as ever, climbs into the boot of David's car, intent on catching him out. After a short ride she crawls out and discovers, to her utter horror, that she's in a nudist camp, surrounded by *naked flesh*. She's so shocked that she falls backwards into the camp pool.

KEEPING THE BRITISH END UP

After drying off, she cools down and goes on a tour of the camp, but everybody's happy, smiling faces and endless waving doesn't impress her much. Subconsciously, though, she's hooked. Outwardly furious, Sandy flees the camp in the middle of the night. Back home in chintzy suburbia she has a vivid dream about being naked and free. Waking up the following day, it suddenly dawns on Sandy that she too needs to be naked and, freeing herself of her silly inhibitions, she drives back to the naturist camp and drops her drawers!

The Reluctant Nudist was not a huge success since it sat on a distributor's shelf for the best part of three years before getting a belated release in the spring of 1966, by which time nudie movies were deemed terribly passé. It is a predictable time-filler with coy nudity, feeble dialogue and the sort of basic characterisation more akin to an episode of the *Teletubbies*. It did marginally better in America, where it was released as *Sandy, the Reluctant Nature Girl*.

CAST: Annette Brand (*Sandy*), Jeremy Howes (*David*), Vivienne Taylor (*Bridgitte*), Peter Benison (*Allan*), John Atkinson (*detective*), Mary Chapman (*Mrs Schofield*), Constance Fletcher (*Mrs Henderson*), Bertha Russell (*Mrs Dearlove*)
CREDITS: *Director* Stanley Pelc, *Producer* S M C Mitchell, *Photography* Terry Maher, *Screenplay* Michael Deeley, *Music* Dick Laurie
An AVON Production. Distributed by GALA. Opened March 1966.

1964

LONDON IN THE RAW

Great Britain / 1964 / 76 mins / cert 'X'

After the bitter disappointment of their 'prostitution exposé' *West End Jungle* being refused a certificate in 1961 for being 'obscene', Stanley Long and Arnold Louis Miller decided that their next non-nudist project would be something along the lines of a portmanteau mondo movie. Inspired by the huge international success of the emetic, Italian-made *Mondo cane* (1961), which wallowed in the unsavoury and violent side of human nature, their film would lay bare the sleazy, secretive and sordid side of London town itself, or as the posters announced, *'The world's greatest city laid bare. Thrill to its gay excitements, its bright lights, but be shocked by the sin in its shadows!'*

American actor David Gell, previously a presenter on TV pop show *Ready Steady Go*, narrates the film's peculiar scenes of oddities, debauchery, addiction and sex during a 24-hour period in the capital. The movie begins with a dejected teenage girl visiting a West End lingerie shop to buy some sexy frilly garments. We also see some Soho prostitutes at work, waving from an open window to get attention (a man hands over £3 for a 'full service'), belly dancers performing for the bowler hat brigade, gamblers using a betting shop (only recently legalised in the UK) and taking their chances on the roulette wheel in a casino. We are warned of the dire consequences for those unfortunates who risk everything on the spin of the chequered wheel. Addicts who have lost all their money at the casino are reduced to drinking bottles of methylated spirits in Piccadilly Circus.

However, the most shocking sequence in the movie shows a hair transplant with blood seeping from the patient's head all over the surgeon's gloves. It is utterly repulsive. Any punter with a stomach strong enough to bare such gruesome scenes is rewarded with a brief dollop of titillation: showgirls dancing in feathers in variety entertainments and, seediest of all, lithe young women posing nude for life-modelling classes behind a tattered curtain in a sweaty Soho basement. It's extremely doubtful whether the flesh and naughtiness were really worth the wait, however. Most balding cinemagoers will have left the auditorium with only one thought on their minds: stick with the wig.

CAST: David Gell (*narrator*)
CREDITS: *Directors* Arnold Louis Miller and Norman Cohen, *Producer* Michael Klinger, *Executive Producer* Tony Tenser, *Editor*

Stephen Cross, *Photography* Stanley Long, *Researcher* Robert Geddes, *Screenplay* Arnold Louis Miller
A SEARCHLIGHT-TROUBADOUR Production. Distributed by COMPTON CAMEO. Opened July 1964.

1965

PRIMITIVE LONDON

Great Britain / 1965 / 76 mins / cert 'X'

Primitive London manages to squeeze considerably more weirdness into its running time than its more reticent predecessor, *London in the Raw*. We see Afro hair being straightened, an operation to remove a 'fungal growth' from the gill of a living goldfish, a cheap reconstruction of Jack the Ripper's crimes, a group of hugely fat, hairy men getting a massage at a Turkish bath, some all-in wrestling with Mick McManus and, nastiest of all, a battery hen slaughterhouse in which the birds are killed, plucked and packaged in a process lasting no less than 15 minutes.

Once again, the reward for sitting through all this voyeuristic craziness is SEX. On the face of it, it seems like even the 'director' wants to see some boobs. 'Where's the shots of the girls in the topless swimsuits?' interrupts a fake American voice. 'We got any girls in this picture? Cut to the girls!' Responding to this complaint, we see the 'synthetic eroticism' of budding striptease artistes auditioning to a tuneless piano accompaniment (as if played by Les Dawson), in order to secure a place in a dingy strip club. At the Casino de Paris in the heart of the West End, girls bare their bums on stage and twirl their nipple tassels while, further downmarket, a woman is having her breasts decorated at a seedy backstreet tattooist. 'More and more young girls are going to tattooists and presenting a puzzle for psychiatry,' comments the quaintly old fashioned voice-over (David Gell again).

Long and Miller can also lay claim to the dubious distinction of bringing the new phenomenon of wife-swapping to the screen for the very first time, a phenomenon Long would return to in 1969. At an obviously faked swingers' party, a group of drunken revellers play facile games (cold teaspoon down the front of the trousers, anyone?) before chucking their car keys into a giant balloon glass and swapping partners. Unfortunately, just when the audience is getting hot and bothered at the sight of wobbling female flesh and a bit of shagging, we cut to a man having his corn removed in close-up, by far the most distasteful image in the film. If anything is going to cool the ardour then that certainly will.

KEEPING THE BRITISH END UP

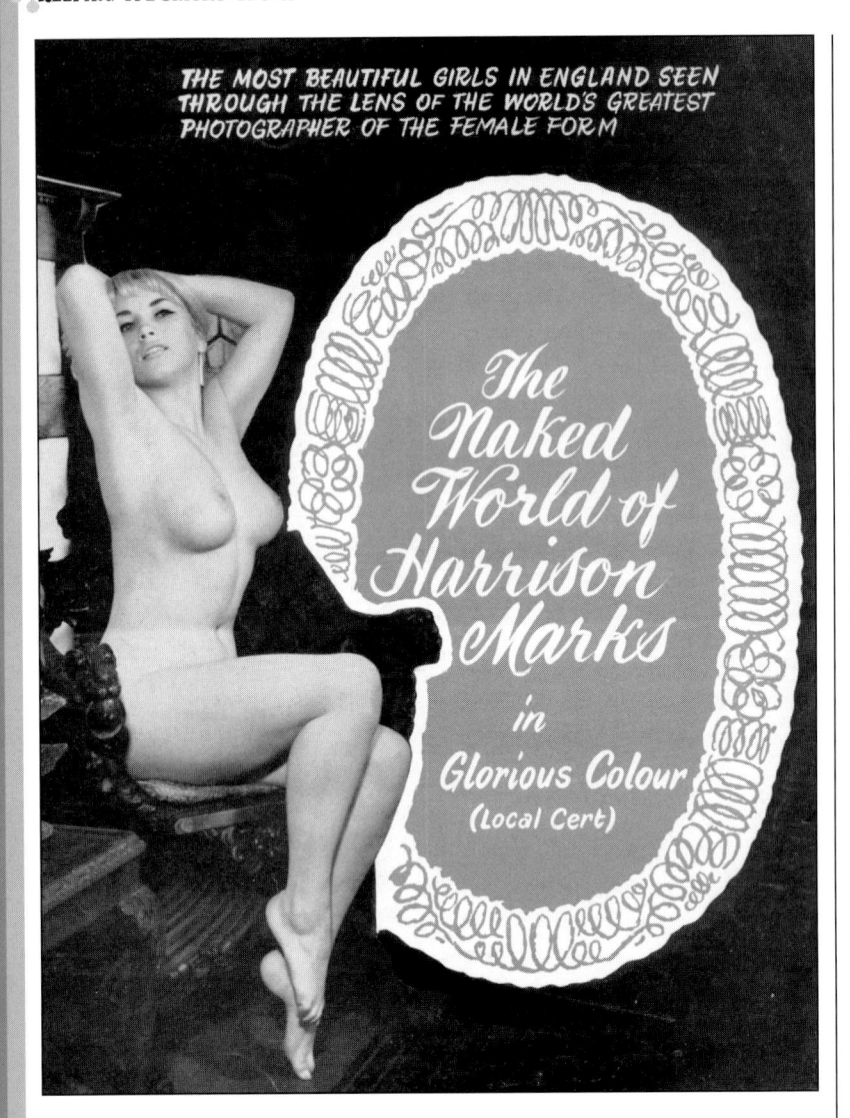

THE MOST BEAUTIFUL GIRLS IN ENGLAND SEEN THROUGH THE LENS OF THE WORLD'S GREATEST PHOTOGRAPHER OF THE FEMALE FORM

The Naked World of Harrison Marks in Glorious Colour (Local Cert)

THE NAKED WORLD OF HARRISON MARKS

Great Britain / 1965 / 84 mins / cert 'A' (London only)

George Harrison Marks enjoyed the huge financial rewards of *Naked – As Nature Intended* for several years before deciding to have another crack at the silver screen. And this time around he was brave enough to escape the confines of the nudist camp. There are no redeeming features on show in *The Naked World of Harrison Marks*, no healthy or wholesome excuses for big-breasted girls parading across the cinema screen. Yes, that's right. Harrison Marks just wanted to film tits. Not surprisingly, the BBFC saw absolutely no benefit in the movie. The women were naked just for the hell of it, for God's sake! What possible reason could the British public have for wanting to see this pornographic rubbish?

Undeterred, Marks submitted his film to London County Council and various other local authorities around Britain. It was unanimously passed and, much to the fury of the BBFC, played to packed houses around the country with an independently awarded 'A' certificate. The movie, billed as 'Luscious, delicious – it will send you delirious!', is a pretty dull affair in which Marks displays the many facets of his organisation. In pseudo-documentary style we see him designing a garish set against which his lovelies can pose, photographing a nude sitting, working on 8mm movies and even judging a beauty contest where he's on the look-out for fresh blood! Velvet-voiced Valentine Dyall (whom Marks later used in *Come Play with Me*) provides some of the commentary, explaining that 'Harrison Marks is a dreamer and the city of London is the centre of all his dreams.'

Interspersed between the nude sequences are even more nude sequences, but this time intended as 'hilarious' vignettes with Marks in various comedy disguises: naughty Toulouse-Lautrec, an Al Capone character and a blasé man-about-town fighting off gorgeous birds. The film was Britain's last fully fledged nudie and, despite Marks' modesty ('The most beautiful girls in England seen through the lens of the world's greatest

CAST: David Gell (*narrator*), McDonald Hobley (*himself*), Ray Martine (*himself*), Billy J Kramer (*himself*), Diana Noble (*herself*), Vicki Grey (*herself*), Bobby Chandler (*himself*), John Lee (*himself*), Barry Cryer [uncredited] (*Roger*), Mick McManus [uncredited] (*wrestler*)

CREDITS: *Director/Screenplay* Arnold Louis Miller, *Producers* Michael Klinger and Stanley Long, *Editor* Stephen Cross, *Photography* Stanley Long, *Music* Basil Kirchin and Johnny Coleman
A SEARCHLIGHT-TROUBADOUR Production. Distributed by COMPTON CAMEO. Opened April 1965.

44

Right: Pauline Collins (second from right) shakes a tail-feather in *Secrets of a Windmill Girl* (1966).

photographer of the female form!' screamed the film's blurb), it's all a bit dispiriting. Marks was no great filmmaker (an understatement if ever there was one), but at least the film offers a few glimpses of classic fifties' beauties like June Palmer and Pamela Green.

CAST: Valentine Dyall (*narrator*), Beryl Gilchrist (*narrator*), George Harrison Marks (*himself*), Pamela Green (*herself*), June Palmer (*herself*), Annette Johnson (*herself*), Christine Williams (*herself*), Jutka Goz (*herself*), with Stuart Samuels and Jerry Lorden
CREDITS: *Director/Producer* George Harrison Marks, *Editor* Jim Connock, *Screenplay* George Harrison Marks, Terry Maher and William Templeton, *Music* John Hawksworth A HARRISON MARKS Production. Distributed by GALA. Opened March 1966.

1966

SECRETS OF A WINDMILL GIRL
aka *Secrets*

Great Britain / 1966 / 84 mins / cert 'X'

Stanley Long and Arnold Louis Miller's final film together was originally intended to be a straightforward record of the last nude revue staged at Soho's legendary Windmill Theatre, the only theatrical venue which had steadfastly refused to close during the Blitz. But the producers 'fleshed out' the documentary with a fictitious tale about the sordid life and death of a Windmill dancing girl. Somewhere amid the tiny bikinis, big back-combed hair, fishnets and sequins sits a sparse story about flighty best friends Pat Lord (25-year-old Pauline Collins) and big-boned Linda Grey (April Wilding). Dreaming of becoming stars of the Windmill stage, they audition for nimble-footed choreographer Peter Gordeno. Though both are as stiff as a board, they manage somehow to scrape through and within 24 hours are squeezing into their sparkly corsets.

However, selfish Pat lets her paste jewellery and skimpy gold lamé knickers go to her head. Convinced she is going to become a big star, darling, she starts hanging around elderly West End producers with twirly moustaches. In the vain hope of hitting the big time, she frequents kinky masked parties and orgies as well as fraternising with butch, cross-dressing lesbians. Much to her friend's horror, Pat spirals down through seedy strip clubs and stag parties. 'She was hardly recognisable as the lively young girl who loved living,' recalls the melodramatic Linda. 'She was a burnt-out husk verging on a mental breakdown!' Naturally, Pat gets her come-uppance when she is reduced to stripping in East End pubs and smoking marijuana, eventually dying in a horrific car crash with one of her lousy pick-ups.

Linda helps the police with their enquiries, but often goes off at a tangent, rambling on, in minuscule detail, about her fellow performers. Hairdressing appointments, taxi rides to the theatre and costume fittings are all very interesting I'm sure, but will they really help with the investigation of her friend's untimely death? And she can't stop the bitching either. 'Eileen's entrances had been a bit off in the Spanish number,' she tells the glazed-over Inspector Thomas. 'Oh yes, she nearly missed one cue in the fan dance. That could have caused a sensation!'

The bulk of this quaint little movie shows the backstage primping and preening of the dancers and endless shots of them going up and down stairs and tottering down corridors in high heels and feather boas. On stage they display their colourful acrobatics, climaxing in the naughty fan dance where the barest glimpse of nipple or bum cheek is revealed behind a fluttering ostrich feather. As a historical record of the theatre it is certainly a valuable piece of filmmaking. The dancers are all genuine Windmill Girls (tellingly, we never see Pauline or April perform on stage) and

Right: Terry Skelton and Lucia Mondunio in *Her Private Hell* (1967).

other members of theatre staff also make cameos, like elderly doorman Ben. *Secrets of a Windmill Girl* is ostensibly a coy nudist film, relocated from the safety of the seaside to the seedy heart of sweaty night-time London.

CAST: Pauline Collins (*Patricia Lord*), April Wilding (*Linda Grey*), Derek Bond (*Inspector Thomas*), Martin Jarvis (*Mike*), Renée Houston (*Molly*), Harry Fowler (*Harry*), Howard Marion Crawford (*Richard Curtis*), Peter Gordeno (*Peter*), Peter Swanwick (*Len Martin*), Pat Petterson (*Pat*), Jill Millard (*Jill*), Linda Page (*Lynn*), Dana Gillespie (*singer*), Maurice Lane (*Maurice*), Leon Cortez (*agent*), Boys and Girls of the Windmill Theatre (*themselves*), Aimi MacDonald [uncredited] (*dancer*) Derek Martin [uncredited] (*man in pub*)
CREDITS: *Director/Screenplay* Arnold Louis Miller, *Producers* Arnold Louis Miller and Stanley Long, *Editor* John Beaton, *Photography* Stanley Long, *Music* Malcolm Lockyer, *Theme song* 'The Windmill Girls' *performed by* Valerie Mitchell
A SEARCHLIGHT Production. Distributed by COMPTON. Opened May 1966.

1967

I LIKE BIRDS
aka *For Men Only*

Great Britain / 1967 / 43 mins / cert 'A'

For many, director Pete Walker is the cinematic giant behind cult seventies' horror movies like *The Flesh and Blood Show* (1972) and *House of Whipcord* (1973). However, all greatness has to begin somewhere and so we look at his début movie *I Like Birds* from the dark days of 1967. Like its follow-up, *School for Sex*, the title is considerably better than the actual movie. 'I deliberately rub people up the wrong way,' the director told the *Sun* in 1975. 'I want them to come into the cinema and be shocked.' Sadly, nobody is in any danger of getting rubbed up in any direction in *I Like Birds* and the most shocking thing is the terrible acting.

Young Freddie Horne (David Kernan) leaves his job at a top women's fashion magazine because his toffee-nosed fiancée is jealous and wants him to find a more 'respectable' job. Freddie travels to sedate East Grinstead and meets Miles Fanthorpe (the anodyne Derek Aylward), founder of the Puritan Magazine Group which only publishes bland, clean-living publications. On the face of it, Fanthorpe is committed to campaigning against the decline in moral attitudes and gives lectures about the horrors of permissiveness to the local Women's Institute. However, the Puritan Group's innocuous-looking periodicals are just a front for a pornographic magazine called 'For Men Only'. And what's more, Fanthorpe's luxurious country house is home to a harem of scantily clad, cerebrally challenged dollies.

The women in Walker's film do very little but look lovely, which is just as well because when they do deliver a line of dialogue it's like a rehearsal for the school play. There's only the skimpiest amount of titillation on view. The pretty 'birds' of the title are always shot from the waist up or safely from the rear and the fellas keep their pants on at all times. The rudest thing about the entire film is that there's a character called Gussett. The film's British running time was just 43 minutes. A further quarter-hour of more risqué footage, including a bit of sleazy bondage and extra nudity, was later inserted for the American market and released under the title *For Men Only*.

CAST: David Kernan (*Freddie Horne*), Andrea Allen (*Rosalie*), Derek Aylward (*Miles Fanthorpe*), Tom Gill (*Father*), Mai Bacon (*Mother*), Glyn Worsnip (*Rudolph*), Neville Whiting (*Claude*), Joan Ingram (*Esther*), John Cazabon (*Mr Gussett*), Apple Brook (*receptionist*), Gladys Dawson (*Mrs Whitely*), Monika Dietrich (*Janet*), Jill Field (*Gunella*), Donna Reading, Valerie Stanton and April Dawson (*girls*)
CREDITS: *Director/Producer/Screenplay* Pete Walker, *Editor* Peter Austen Hunt, *Photography* Gerry Lewis, *Music* Harry South
A PETE WALKER-BORDER Production. Distributed by BORDER FILMS. Opened October 1967.

HER PRIVATE HELL

Great Britain / 1967 / 84 mins / cert 'X'

Although relatively unknown today, *Her Private Hell* quietly takes its place as Britain's first official 'sex' film; the first one passed by a more relaxed censor and the first to show men and women in bed *having sex just because they want to*. It was also director Norman J Warren's feature-length cinematic début. At the time Warren's fantasy short *Fragment* was being shown in a cinema in south Kensington by businessman Richard Schulman. He and distributor Bachoo Sen had decided to make some sex movies together to exhibit at their own chain of movie theatres, but they desperately needed a director. Warren got the job even before a script had been written. Budgeted at £18,000, the film was shot over two weeks, filming solidly every day from 10.00 am until midnight.

Compared with previous sexually suggestive British films like *Secrets of a Windmill Girl*, *Her Private Hell* goes in for the kill immediately with a montage of naked bodies over which the opening titles are displayed. Once past the wonderfully tawdry title, the sex scenes are pretty tame by today's standards, but you can clearly see what all the fuss was about in 1967: soft-focus glimpses of breasts, beds bouncing, gropings and girls stripping off at free-loving parties. The innocent soul who is plunged into this world of licentiousness is Italian actress Lucia Mondunio, in her first English part, playing wannabe *Vogue* model Marisa. Coming to England to find an agent, she is lured by a fashion photography firm, but their flowery dresses and kinky boots are just a cover. The business is ruthlessly run by an evil mastermind with a pointy beard who is more interested in getting his models to take their knickers off and pose for dirty magazines.

'I felt very sorry for Lucia,' says Warren.

'She was out of place really. Bachoo Sen, the producer, had seen an old picture of her somewhere when she was just 19 or something and now she was nearly 30. When she arrived from Italy, she wasn't really the Swinging London dolly bird we needed. She was a lovely lady but didn't look in the slightest bit innocent. She was very aware that she wasn't Twiggy and she'd put these terrible stretch things on the sides of her face to pull the skin taut under her wig. She'd also put this sparkle stuff in her eyes and she got sores on her face. It was awful.'

Marisa is persuaded to pose for some 'artistic' shots but, to her horror, they end up in a European skin magazine called *Strip* and she is blackmailed with the negatives. It's pretty cruel, sleazy stuff, but stylishly handled by the director, who allows his heroine to be terrorised but refuses to let the baddies get away with their deceitful exploitation. The mix of mini-skirts, manipulation, money and mascara makes this a milestone movie, but Warren never doubted its success. 'It was going to be a huge hit whatever happened because it had the two right ingredients, sex and nudity,' he says. 'It almost couldn't fail. The last thing the audience were doing was looking at the camera angles or the way it was photographed!'

CAST: Lucia Mondunio (*Marisa*), Terry Skelton (*Bernie*), Pearl Catlin (*Margaret*), Daniel Oliver (*Matt*), Jeanette Wild (*Paula*), Mary Land (*Sally*), Robert Crewdson (*Neville*)
CREDITS: *Director* Norman J Warren, *Producer* Bachoo Sen, *Photography* Peter Jessop, *Screenplay* Glynn Christian, *Music* Patrick John Scott
A PICCADILLY PICTURES Production. Distributed by RICHARD SCHULMAN ENTERTAINMENTS. Opened January 1968.

1968

LOVE IN OUR TIME

Great Britain / 1968 / 87 mins / cert 'X'

'Couples prepared to re-enact their happy or unhappy relationships in a documentary film called Love in Our Time *are invited to send their photographs to Elkan Allan.*' So read an advertisement placed in the *Times*, *Evening Standard* and *New Statesman*. Here was a new concept in British filth: instead of paying actors, get real people to have sex on film. Well, that's what the producers of *Love in Our Time* wanted you to

KEEPING THE BRITISH END UP

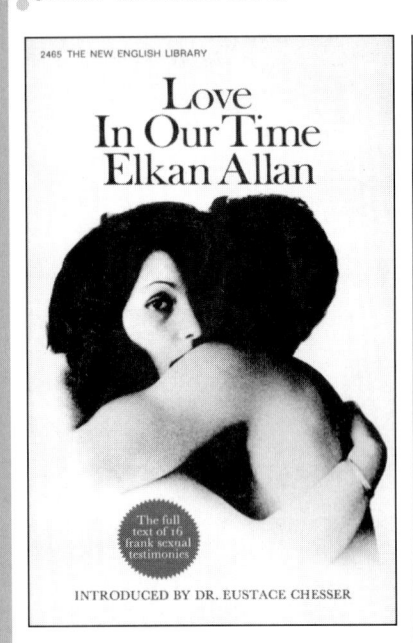

believe. Tellingly, the advert also appeared in the *Stage*, a theatrical newspaper read by every wannabe-luvvie in London.

Elkan Allan, the perpetrator of this elaborate scam, was a trained journalist and TV producer whose greatest claim to fame was as executive producer on pop show *Ready Steady Go* and as writer of several episodes of the camp American adventure series *Batman*, starring Adam West. Apparently inspired to 'examine the British public's most intimate sexual relations and the modern-day permissive society,' Allan wisely hooked up with sex-ploitation's most notorious producer and distributor, Tony Tenser. Allan must have heard the cash tills ringing in his ears.

Allan claimed, depending what publicity material you read, to have received anywhere between 500 and 1000-plus applications from randy suburban couples desperate to shed their clothes and perform for the delectation of millions of raincoated cinemagoers. 'One could judge from their photographs and their letters whether they were on principle suitable for the film,' Allan wrote in 1968. 'Many had eliminated themselves by not being real couples; one of them had gone away, or they lived too far out of London for it to be practicable. Others were illiterate.' Despite interviewing couples ranging from '18 to 70 years of age', it comes as no surprise that the couples he chose were nubile young things straight out of acting school, most notably Ann Michelle, later to star in half-a-dozen more sex films. Allan's choice of titillating subject matter is hilariously predictable: wife-swapping parties, youthful permissiveness, extra-marital affairs, the older man/younger girl scenario and 'schoolgirls'. Allan applauded his inexperienced actors for having 'exhibited themselves under a barrage of lights and in front of a dozen or so technicians and ultimately in front of millions of people.'

'We didn't make this film for sensational purposes; we didn't make it for people to giggle at sex, or to give them a thrill watching other people having sexual intercourse,' he added. Of course not. The film was greeted with howls of derision from the critics, who accused Allan of dishonesty and fancying himself as some sort of English Dr Kinsey. Needless to say, *Love in Our Time* was heavily promoted with a tie-in paperback from New English Library, featuring a further eight case histories not included in the film because they were considered 'immoral, perverted or simply obscene'. Complete with a po-faced introduction from Dr Eustace Chesser, the book flew off the shelves of W H Smith.

CAST: Elkan Allan (*narrator*) *with* Katie Allan, Ann Michelle, Declan Cuffe, Joanne Harding, Gino Melvazzi, Ann Rutter, Bill Cummings, Ian Anderson and Eddie Stacey (*as the participants*)
CREDITS: *Director/Screenplay* Elkan Allan, *Producer* Tony Tenser, *Editor* Howard Lanning, *Photography* William Brayne, *Music* Reginald Tilsley
A TIGON Production. Distributed by TIGON. Opened December 1968.

THE WINDOW CLEANER

Great Britain / 1968 / 35 mins / cert 'X'

A short sex film, this was the first effort by director Malcolm Leigh, who went on to make *Games That Lovers Play* in 1970. Donald Sumpter plays David, a window cleaner whose speciality is rubbing the panes on skyscrapers. His domineering and possessive mother (the wonderful Ann Lancaster) deliberately attempts to undermine his confidence and his nerve snaps. Reduced to swabbing bungalows, David dreams of getting his old job back and has one more crack at it. But, trying to overcome his fear of heights, he loses his nerve again halfway up a tower-block and is hauled through an open window by a sexy young girl called Sharon (Edina Ronay), who listens to his story then gives him a bit of how's yer father. With his confidence restored and extra suds in his pail, David realises he no longer has to be scared of tall buildings.

It could be said that sex films were not really Leigh's bag. He preferred documentaries. The following year he wrote and directed the feature-length *Legend of the Witches* about the historical origins of witchcraft from pagan times onwards. Containing lots of moody shots of crashing waves and swirling smoke, this seri-

48

Left: Elkan Allan's *Love In Our Time* flew off the shelves.

ous attempt also contained lots of dancing naked bodies and got an 'X' certificate for its trouble. Highly regarded, and something of a lost classic, it has remained unseen for over 30 years.

CAST: Donald Sumpter (*David*), Edina Ronay (*Sharon*), Ann Lancaster (*Mother*), Jenny Hill (*secretary*), Peggy Aitchison (*landlady*), Fred Griffiths (*foreman*), Robert Hamilton (*workman*)
CREDITS: *Director/Screenplay* Malcolm Leigh, *Producer* Negus-Fancey, *Editor* Judith Smith, *Photography* Richard Bailey, *Music* De Wolfe
A BORDER FILMS Production. Distributed by BORDER. Opened February 1969.

SCHOOL FOR SEX
aka *School for Love*

Great Britain / 1968 / 80 mins / cert 'X'

Make no bones about it, *School for Sex* is not a very good film. It's primitively shot, ponderously slow, woodenly acted and arduously unfunny. However, it does have one of the best titles ever in British cinema history, and that is primarily what sold it. 'That was a great title,' said Walker, quoted in an interview in *Films and Filming* in 1974. 'It had all sorts of connotations: blue knickers, 14-year-old girls. I mean, you could just see them reaching for their raincoats.' However, any grubby voyeurs expecting to see St Trinian's schoolgirls having underage sex will have been sadly disappointed.

Old smoothie Derek Aylward plays Giles Wingate, a bounder in classic Leslie Phillips mode, who has been taken to the cleaners one too many times by his gold-digging wives. Nine wives to be exact, including a glamorous B-movie actress (Nicola Austine), who runs off with a 'homosexual actor', and Swedish masseuse Ingeborg (Jackie Berdet), who pummels and thumps him into submission. Tired of the ruthless, scheming women he always seems to meet, Giles seeks revenge by setting up a 'school for sex' at his country house. Realising men's one Achilles heel is crumpet, he trains a motley group of bad girls – persistent shoplifters and fraudsters straight out of Holloway – to swindle fortunes out of sad old gits. Needless to say, the girls are all glamourpusses who use their womanly wiles in the crudest ways imaginable. Aylward's bikini-clad students (among them a very young Françoise Pascal) agree to sign over a third of all their future earnings to their mentor and within weeks they have fleeced thousands of pounds from elderly millionaires and rich Arab sheikhs.

School for Sex was one of Walker's most financially successful movies and it enjoyed massive popularity abroad. 'We sold it to every country in the world except Spain,' he claimed. Lucky old Spain. In America it was a huge hit, taking £2.5 million, and running for two years in New York alone. In France it enjoyed 72,000 cinema admissions in its opening week. It was like the *Come Play with Me* of the sixties but without the fun or campery. According to some, *School for Sex* can be read as a satire on British films of the period, complete with a subtext about the commercialisation of women, but I'll be buggered if I can see it. This is just terminally tedious viewing.

CAST: Derek Aylward (*Giles Wingate*), Rose Alba (*Duchess of Burwash*), Robert Andrews (*Sgt Braithewaite*), Victor Wise (*Horace Clapp*), Hugh Latimer (*Berridge*), Nosher Powell (*Hector*), Françoise Pascal (*Sally Regan*), Amber Dean Smith (*Beth Villiers*), Cathy Howard (*Sue Randall*), Sylvia Barlow (*Judy Arkwright*), Sandra Gleeson (*Jenny*), Maria Frost (*Polly*), Cindy Neal (*Marianne*), Jackie Berdet (*Ingeborg*), Gilly Grant (*stripper*), Nicola Austine (*Tania*), Robert Dorning (*official*), Julie May (*Ethel*), Wilfred Babbage (*the Judge*)
CREDITS: *Director/Producer/Screenplay* Pete Walker, *Music* Harry South, *Editor* John Black, *Photography* Reg Phillips
A PETE WALKER Film Production. Distributed by MIRACLE. Opened April 1969.

THE BEST HOUSE IN LONDON

Great Britain / 1968 / 96 mins / cert 'X'

A sumptuously staged big-budget Victorian sex comedy with a superb cast, excellent costumes, lavish sets and even a giant multi-coloured airship and a model of the Eiffel Tower thrown in for good measure. With its vivid Eastmancolor glare and big, jazzy production values, Philip Saville's film can be likened to a pornographic version of *Those Magnificent Men in their Flying Machines*.

Josephine Pacefoot (Joanna Pettet), the militant leader of the League of Social Purity, campaigns tirelessly to rehabilitate

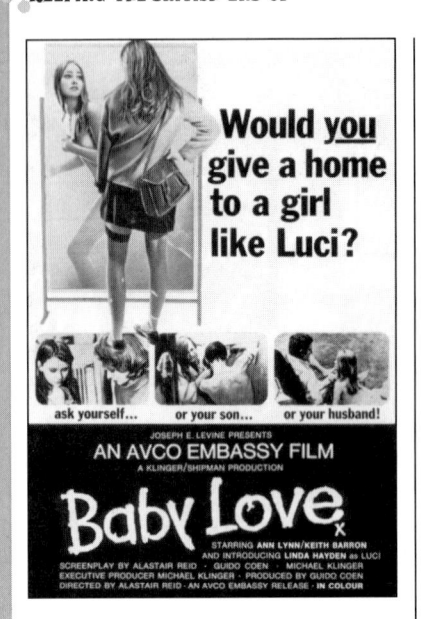

London's prostitutes. Marching her ruined girls around the capital's streets dressed in virginal white and waving placards, she attempts to get whoring outlawed, but the government is reluctant to support her. 'They fulfil functions to which a gentleman would otherwise be obliged to subject his wife,' argues one minister. Refusing an outright ban, the Home Secretary (John Bird) suggests getting the hookers off the pavements and into state-sponsored brothels along the same lines as the 'French system'. They vote for a dry-run with one experimental house of ill-repute – the opulent Libertine Club in the heart of Belgravia. Disguised as a convent school, the brothel, presided over by Gallic tart-with-a-heart Babette (Dany Robin), offers something for every sexual peccadillo: mud wrestling, orgies, whippings and young virgins.

But despite appealing to the eminent, prominent and wealthy, the new house of juicy fruit is fast running out of young ladies willing to rent out their front parlours, and naughty David Hemmings is forced to raid the Social Purity Alliance for fresh faces. Hemmings, who had made such a profound impression in Michelangelo Antonioni's 1966 movie *Blow Up*, plays dual roles in *Best House* as the kindly publicity agent Benjamin Oakes and the beastly blackguard Walter Leybourne, who delights in deflowering virgins and keeps a locket of their pubic hair in his snuff box as a memento. Supporting Hemmings, in a wide variety of billed and unbilled cameos, is a veritable Who's Who of British showbiz: Warren Mitchell, John Cleese, William Rushton, Tessie O'Shea, Queenie Watts, Margaret Nolan, Thorley Walters and even erudite newspaper columnist and Liberal MP Clement Freud.

Denis Norden's excellent script is jam-packed full of witticisms, quips and wicked one-liners and takes numerous clever swipes at leading Victorians (both real and imagined) including Prince Albert, Charles Darwin, Dr Livingstone and Sherlock Holmes, the crudest of which is a junior Emmeline Pankhurst singing her Sunday school song, 'I Love My Pussy'. Also included is a familiar little scene in which the late George Sanders and his chum John Cleese attempt to take their tiffin at the dinner table while being shelled and shot at by Indian bandits in a virtual remake of the famous dinner party sequence from *Carry On ... Up the Khyber*, which is either pure coincidence (since both movies were shot the same year) or unadulterated plagiarism. The best gag is given to moral reformer Joanna Pettet, who is astounded to learn of Hemmings' illegitimacy. 'Oh,' she exclaims, 'I've never met a bastard socially!'

CAST: David Hemmings (*Walter Leybourne/Benjamin Oakes*), Joanna Pettet (*Josephine Pacefoot*), George Sanders (*Sir Francis Leybourne*), Dany Robin (*Babette*), Warren Mitchell (*Pandolfo*), John Bird (*Home Secretary*), William Rushton (*Sylvester Wall*), Bill Fraser (*Inspector MacPherson*), Joe Lynch (*policeman*), Maurice Denham (*editor*), Wolfe Morris (*Chinese Trade Attaché*), Martita Hunt (*headmistress*), Marie Rogers (*Phoebe*), Carol Friday (*Flora Tozer*), John Cleese (*Jones*), Tessie O'Shea (*singer*), Arthur Howard (*Mr Fortnum*), Clement Freud (*Mr Mason*), Peter Jeffrey (*Sherlock Holmes*), Suzanne Hunt (*Elizabeth Barrett*), Avril Angers (*Mrs Tozer*), Betty Marsden (*Felicity*), Uncredited: Tommy Godfrey (*news vendor*), Margaret Nolan (*busty prostitute*), Milton Reid (*henchman*), Penny Spencer (*Evelyn*), Marianne Stone (*machinist*), Larry Taylor (*toff*), Thorley Walters (*Dr Watson*), Queenie Watts (*old crone*), Veronica Carlson (*blonde*).

CREDITS: *Director* Philip Saville, *Producers* Philip Breen and Kurt Unger, *Editor* Peter Tanner, *Photography* Alex Thomson, *Screenplay* Denis Norden, *Music* Mischa Spoliansky
A BRIDGE FILMS Production. Distributed by MGM. Opened June 1969.

BABY LOVE

Great Britain / 1968 / 93 mins / cert 'X'

Based on Tina Chad Christian's hugely controversial 1968 novel, *Baby Love* stars 15-year-old Linda Hayden, in her movie début, as Luci, a traumatised and malevolent 'little teaser' thrust into a world she despises. Diana Dors, in a mucky yet highly effective little cameo, plays Luci's sluttish mother, who slashes her wrists in the bath after being diagnosed with terminal cancer. Luci is entrusted to the care of her mother's ex-boyfriend, Dr Robert Quayle (Keith Barron), and his highly strung middle class family in fashionable Bayswater. Luci is overwhelmed by the splendour of their house, coming as she does from abject poverty in Merseyside. Haunted by nightmares and disturbing hallucinations of her promiscuous mother, she embarks on a twisted strategy of terrifying violence and sexual manipulation. Motivated by greed, grief, resentment and a hatred of the privileged classes, Luci does her utmost to become the focus of attention for all the family members and sets about destroying them, one by one.

As she exploits her burgeoning sexuality and complete lack of bodily inhibitions, Luci provocatively strips off at the most inappropriate moments. Quayle initially fights his feelings of attraction towards her so she turns her attentions to his hormonally charged teenage son (Derek Lamden). In a dangerous and seductive game Luci tantalises him, then rejects his clumsy advances, resulting in a frenzied attack. Quayle's wife Amy (played faultlessly by Ann Lynn, an actress sadly untroubled by the cinema much thereafter) also finds herself increasingly attracted to her orphaned guest. 'Don't you want to play with your little dolly?' Luci asks provocatively, allowing Amy to teeter on the verge of temptation before planting a passionate kiss on her lips.

Baby Love delights in gradually dissecting the prim middle class family, exposing its innermost desires and allowing it to disintegrate with terrifying ease. The tight, unfussy direction from Alastair Reid coupled with acres of stunning photography, stark close-ups, slick, sexy camera angles and judicious editing from John Glen (later to direct five James Bond movies) make this film a winner. Hayden excels as the smirking teenage temptress, stirring up electrifying tension whenever she appears on screen. One minute sucking on her thumb or turning on the waterworks and the next erupting into a lethal sexual demon, Hayden undoubtedly spawned one of the most frightening creations of sixties' cinema.

CAST: Linda Hayden (*Luci*), Ann Lynn (*Amy Quayle*), Keith Barron (*Dr Robert Quayle*), Derek Lamden (*Nick Quayle*), Diana Dors (*Liz*), Dick Emery (*Harry Pearson*), Sheila Steafel (*Tessa Pearson*), Sally Stephens (*Margo Pearson*), Patience Collier (*Mrs Carmichael*), Timothy Carlton (*Jeremy*), Christopher Witty (*Jonathan*), Vernon Dobtcheff (*lecher in cinema*), Michael Lewis (*first boy*), Julian Barnes (*second boy*), Patsy Snell (*girl at disco*), Marianne Stone (*shop manageress*), Terence Brady (*man in shop*), Katch 22 (*themselves*), Danique [uncredited] (*woman in cinema*)
CREDITS: *Director* Alastair Reid, *Producer* Guido Coen, *Executive Producer* Michael Klinger, *Editor* John Glen, *Photography* Desmond Dickinson, *Screenplay* Alastair Reid, Guido Coen and Michael Klinger, *based on the novel by* Tina Chad Christian, *Music* Max Harris
An AVTON FILM Production. Distributed by AVCO EMBASSY. Opened September 1969.

LOVING FEELING

Great Britain / 1968 / 82 mins / cert 'X'

1967's *Her Private Hell* had been such a massive hit that director Norman J Warren was approached to do a follow-up immediately, with the bonus of colour and an increased budget of £30,000. 'They wanted another film straight away and I was extremely pleased,' recalls Warren. 'It was going to be in colour this time so I insisted that it be filmed in Cinemascope, my favourite format, and as a consequence the film has got some polish to it. If you watch *Her Private Hell* and *Loving Feeling* back to back you'll see an amazing change. It all moved up a notch but, naturally, it had a lot more sex and nudity in it too. That was imperative!'

The story, set against the hip sixties'

KEEPING THE BRITISH END UP

Right: Which is which? Christopher Matthews tries to distinguish Mary from Madeleine Collinson in *Come Back Peter* (1969).

music scene, follows failed actor Stevee Day (Simon Brent), who turns his hand to radio disc-jockeying and finds himself the toast of London. Overrun by horny female fans, he just can't keep his seven inch single in his jockey shorts for long. Breaking records with a string of shapely, opportunistic fans, he leaves his beautiful wife (Georgina Ward) and takes up with a glamorous mistress (Paula Patterson), but that's only the beginning of his tangled, bed-hopping sexcapades. 'I wrote the original story,' recalls Warren. 'I'd been listening to the Righteous Brothers' song 'You've Lost that Loving Feeling' and started getting an idea for a film. In those days DJs were superstars and it was actors who struggled to make a living. I knew people at the pirate radio station Radio Caroline and I thought what about an actor who becomes a famous DJ and gets lots of groupies? The power of the record companies was huge in those days and it was commonplace to have DJs getting back-handers just to play records on air, so that's where the inspiration came from.'

Rather unusually for a British sex film documenting the promiscuity of its male lead, *Loving Feeling* shows a man who has everything but ultimately loses it all. As the advertising tag-line put it, Stevee 'got played so much, he wore out'. Despite having copious amounts of sex, at the end of the film he has lost his home and job, while his wife has rejected a reconciliation and his girlfriend has taken up with her former boss. A life of casual sexual encounters has not brought Stevee long-term happiness, nor even the kind of fulfilment that, a decade later, would come naturally to hordes of window cleaners, milkmen, door-to-door salesmen and the like.

One of the hero's inconsequential conquests is French model-turned-actress Françoise Pascal, playing a Continental knee-trembler who is seduced and stripped by Stevee. She has famously claimed that the production team had to get her blind drunk before she was willing to disrobe. 'I certainly don't remember her needing 30 brandies or her having a problem taking her clothes off,' observes Warren. 'If anything, the problem with Françoise was trying to keep her clothes *on*. It's absolutely ludicrous if you think about it. A young girl and 30 brandies? If *I* had that many I'd be out for several days!'

CAST: Simon Brent (*Stevee Daly*), Georgina Ward (*Suzanne Daly*), Paula Patterson (*Carol Taylor*), John Railton (*Scott Fisher*), Françoise Pascal (*French model*), Heather Kydd (*Christine Johnson*), Peter Dixon (*Philip Peterson*), Carol Cunningham (*Jane Butler*), Robert Hewison (*radio producer*), Richard Bartlett (*sound mixer*), Allen John (*restaurant manager*), Paul Endesby (*old man on beach*), Sonya Benjamin (*belly dancer*), Barry Stephens (*chauffeur*), John Aston (*Jane's boyfriend*)
CREDITS: *Director* Norman J Warren, *Producer* Bachoo Sen *Editor* Tristram Cones, *Photography* Peter Jessop, *Screenplay* Robert Hewison and Bachoo Sen *adapted for the screen by* Norman J Warren, *Music* Patrick John Scott, *Theme song 'Love is Now' performed by* Jacky A PICCADILLY PICTURES Production. Distributed by RICHARD SCHULMAN ENTERTAINMENTS. Opened January 1971.

1969

COME BACK PETER
aka *Some Like it Sexy*

Great Britain / 1969 / 65 mins / cert 'X'

Intended to be a dirtier version of Michael Caine's sexploits in *Alfie*, Donovan Winter's *Come Back Peter* actually does nothing more than remind the audience of Caine's immaculate central performance and *Alfie*'s sharply observed screenplay. This film has neither.

Christopher Matthews, scrawny and pasty-faced, plays a totally charmless professional ladies' man. Spending most of his time avoiding a collision in his E-type Jaguar since he can't keep his eyes on the road, he cruises for mini-skirted kewpie dolls down Chelsea way. The women can't resist his manly odour or fit body; 'I do a bit of weight-lifting,' he says unconvincingly at one point. First one out of the stalls is Lisa, a foreign au pair who talks through her teeth and wobbles her head from side to side like a *Thunderbirds* puppet. After some perfunctory chit-chat and an alcoholic beverage ('It is good, yes?' she coos), they have a partially clothed shower and then test out his bed springs. This is just the first of several tedious sexual encounters which include a *Vogue* model, a middle-aged socialite, a blues singer, a psychedelic hippy and a Salvation Army officer (a very early role for Nicola Paget). He gets the full treatment from a cross-section of British female stereotypes... But wait a minute, where's the frustrated housewife whose husband is off playing golf?

For each of Matthews' encounters he changes his outfit to match the personality of the girl he's about to shag, but his outrageous sixties clothes do little to alleviate the repetitive and episodic nature of his tacky love life. One particular ensemble (oversized crushed velvet pants, ruffled silk shirt, etc) would seem more at home in a two-ring circus than the trendy hideouts of Swinging London. More worryingly, every time he has sex, director Winter shows us a 'symbolic' shot of a butcher hacking a huge side of beef. Is he saying something about the disposable nature of sex or the way men perceive women? You decide.

A welcome twist comes at the end when it is revealed that Matthews is not the funky young legover-merchant we are led to believe. He's really just a butcher's delivery boy on the Fulham Road (hence the earlier meat shots) and he drives a tatty white van. As sex fantasy gives way to grim reality the colour rapidly drains from the film, leaving Matthews in an uneventful black-and-white world.

Come Back Peter's most eyebrow-raising sequence didn't appear in the film's initial release prints in 1969, only being inserted some 18 months later. After the international release of the film, Winter found that several countries had complained that his movie wasn't sexy enough. They demanded more breasts. Responding to this criticism, he sought a couple of models to use in an additional scene that could be slotted in without disruption to the narrative. As well as this, he spiced up a couple of the other sex scenes with body doubles. If you watch carefully, on several occasions Matthews' peachy bum is substituted for a big hairy arse, unquestionably the worst yet seen in British cinemas.

In the new version, our hero visits the basement flat of one of his conquests, the Maltese beauty Mary Collinson. Because Collinsons always come in twos, her twin sister Madeleine also turns up, nibbling on a banana. For some inexplicable reason the sisters start some bitchy dialogue and fight for Matthews' attention. Inevitably he takes them both to bed for a sisterly *ménage à trois*, but the girls ignore him and end up snogging and feeling up *each other*. Now this is where things start to blur a bit. Just to remind viewers, these actresses are *real-life twins*. Yech! But a bit of incest didn't harm the film one bit and *Come Back Peter* was re-edited to include the new sequence, coming out as *Some Like it Sexy* in November 1976.

CAST: Christopher Matthews (*Peter*), Erika Bergmann (*Lisa*), Penny Riley (*Sue*), Yolanda Turner (*Mrs Beaufort-Smith*), Madeline Smith (*Miss Beaufort-Smith*), Valerie St Helen (*Cleo*), Annabel Leventon (*Creampuff*), Nicola Paget (*Jenny*), Mary and Madeleine Collinson (*twins*)

CREDITS: Director/Producer/Screenplay/Editor Donovan Winter, Theme song 'Come Back Peter' performed by Gloria Stewart, Photography Gus Coma
A DONWIN Production. Distributed by VARIETY. Opened August 1969.

THE NINE AGES OF NAKEDNESS

Great Britain / 1969 / 95 mins / cert 'X'

Poor old George Harrison Marks. 'Wherever I go there are girls,' he laments, 'and beautiful girls, which makes it even harder. I can't get away from them!' Dreaming about big bouncing bazongas 24 hours a day, he decides to seek professional help in London's Harley

KEEPING THE BRITISH END UP

Street. However, the psychiatrist just can't understand Marks' predicament; after all, as the UK's foremost glamour photographer, isn't he in a position envied by millions of British men? Well, obviously not because Marks soon makes himself comfortable on the long leather couch and confesses all. Recalling his randy ancestors one by one, it becomes obvious that being tormented by nubile young ladies is a hereditary disease!

Setting the scene for his sexual portmanteau, Marks rewrites the history books with a selection of kinky by-gone tableaux, playing all the principal roles himself. In ancient Greece he is 'Harrison Hubergritz' the Jewish sculptor, before morphing into the wise Chinese mandarin 'Ha-Ri-Son', Greek philosopher 'Professor Marc' and 17th century portrait painter 'Sir Harrison Chandelier', who ends up in the stocks being pelted with rotten tomatoes as punishment for his debauched canvases. The period sets, although obviously plywood, are effective enough and the movie benefits from vivid Eastmancolor and lovely costumes, in particular, the sketch set in a Chinese lotus garden.

However, the most elaborate sequence is the first, set in the grunting Stone Age. Huge hairy cavemen go out hunting for big-busted prehistoric women who show considerably more flesh than Raquel Welch ever did in *One Million Years B.C.* Back in the caves Marks lifts some visual gags straight out of *The Flintstones*. There's a wind-up stone record player, a granite TV and Monique Devereaux flicks through a slate copy of *Vogue Spring Collections*. As primitive stonemason 'Harry Stone Marks', the director has mammoth fun. But it's in the Victorian pastiche that Marks is most at home. Playing music hall entrepreneur 'The Great Marko', he publicises his nude 'living statues' on the East End stage. Marks sports the same horrendous wig, powdered face and buck teeth that he would wear with even greater effect in *Come Play with Me* eight years later. So attached was Marks to this particular disguise that he had the hairpiece placed on a polystyrene head in his sitting room right up to the time of his death in 1997.

The film was initially christened *The Seven Ages of Nakedness* ('John Gielgud was playing at the Globe in a one-man show called *The Seven Ages of Man*,' Marks recalled), but halfway through filming the director realised he didn't have enough footage to make the movie run for the requisite 90 minutes. Running back to his typewriter, he hurriedly added two extra sequences, one devoted to creepy scientist 'Professor Frankenstein Marks' and the other to romantic poet 'Byron Marks'. Filling the film with familiar faces, Marks rounded up many of his old mates for cameos: Stuart Samuels from *Naked – As Nature Intended*, cockney charwoman Rita Webb, buck-toothed Cardew Robinson and comedian Max Wall in his trademark black tights. Marks' wife Toni and baby daughter Josie also make surprise contributions to the movie.

Also in the cast is Harrison Marks regular and ex-champion bodybuilder Howard Nelson, who indulges in a four-poster bed race with blonde serving wench Sue Bond and inadvertently loses his 17th century wig in the process. Bond was smitten with Nelson's impressive muscles and went after him like a dose of salts off-screen. The naughty director egged her on, knowing that Nelson (nicknamed 'Vanderhorn') would never satisfy the young actress. And he was right. Once alone together, the vain Nelson refused to make love, preferring to show off his physique and pose for her all evening. Bond made her excuses and left.

In the final tableau Marks ponders the future by imagining a space-age world where naked Amazonian women are the dominant sex. Men are redundant, except for one lone male who is kept purely for reproductive purposes and who is made to stand behind a giant mirror with his penis stuck through a hole, awaiting a 'customer'. Such is their success at eliminating men that the futuristic females

54

Right: Amorous aliens (with underwear painted on by command of the censor) in *The Nine Ages of Nakedness* (1969).

entertain a delegation of silver-skinned (and, of course, topless) Jupiterians.

Surprisingly for a late sixties movie, there is enough nudity and sex on screen to keep the average BBFC examiner busy for an entire month. Marks boasted that *Nine Ages* had 'approximately' 112 girls in the all-together and the preponderance of boobs and bums is startling. However, chief censor John Trevelyan disallowed the frivolous lesbian scenes, simulated fellatio, full-frontal nudity from the men and close-ups of male genitalia which all grace the export version. The film is nothing more than a string of naughty Harrison Marks 8mm films glued together with the tiniest dribble of Bostik. The idea behind the movie is all well and good, but *The Nine Ages of Nakedness* does go on a bit. After the tenth or eleventh pair of breasts, the endless parade of nakedness doesn't inspire much of a positive reaction. Perhaps even Harrison Marks guessed as much. 'I'm not boring you with all this, am I?' he asks at one point. Unfortunately the answer would have to be: 'Well, actually, you are a bit.'

CAST: George Harrison Marks (*himself and his ancestors*), Toni Harrison Marks (*psychiatrist*), David London (*psychiatrist's voice*), Bruno Elrington (*chief caveman*), June Palmer (*cavegirl*), Julian Orchard (*Pharaoh*), Max Bacon (*Egyptian*), Suzan Long (*Lotus*), Max Wall (*Roundhead*), Sue Bond (*buxom wench*), Howard Nelson (*Sir Rupert*), Rita Webb (*Brunhylda*), Cardew Robinson (*Judge*), Stuart Samuels (*Harry*), Terry Duggan (*policeman*), Monique Devereaux (*space leader*), Charles Gray (*narrator*), Josie Harrison Marks [uncredited] (*baby*)

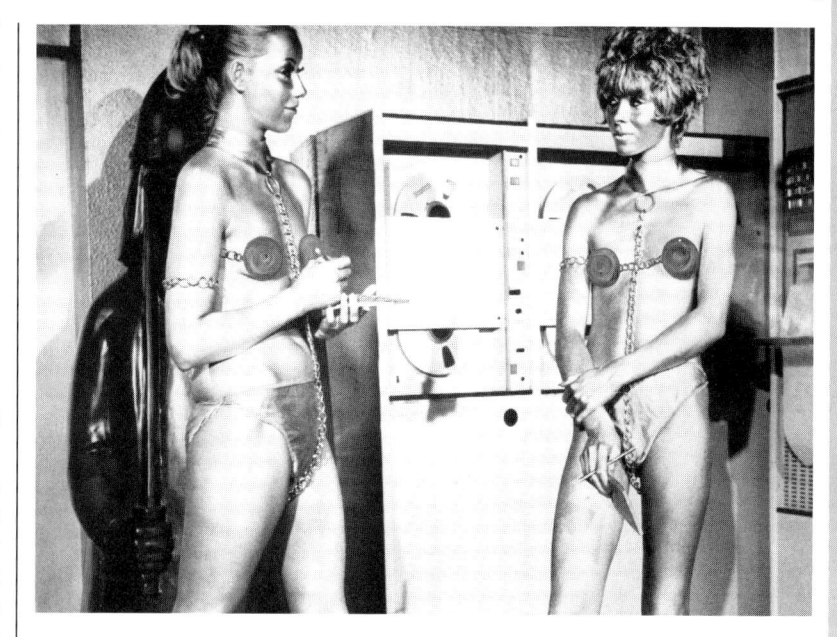

CREDITS: Director/Producer/Screenplay George Harrison Marks, *Editor* Peter Mayhew, *Photography* Terry Maher, *Music* Peter Jeffries A TOKEN FILMS Production. Distributed by ORB. Opened September 1969.

A PROMISE OF BED
aka *This, That and the Other!*

Great Britain / 1969 / 83 mins / cert 'X'

A Promise of Bed is Derek Ford's début British film and the first directed entirely on his own, but unfortunately it shows. A supposedly lighthearted look at the misadventures of three implausibly desolate characters, the movie is subtitled *A Trilogy of Comedy*, which should set alarm bells ringing immediately. There's barely a single titter on view for the entire 83 minutes, let alone an opportunity to crack a smile. To be fair it's certainly not the worst film project linked to Ford. (You only have to look at the pinnacle of awfulness which is *Don't Open 'Til Christmas* from 1984 to see just how bad things could get.) 'It was a very cheap movie and I put up all the money for it myself – £8,500,' says the film's producer, Stanley Long. 'We made it as *This That and the Other!*, but the distributors changed the name and it didn't do terribly well. It's not a film I'm especially proud of because it's quite amateurish.'

These three 'amateurish' stories can be roughly classified as a farce, a black comedy (we're talking pitch-black here) and a surreal fantasy. Starting off with the farce, we meet Italian sexpot Vanda Hudson as a struggling film actress called Susan Stress, although Doris Desperate would be more apt, such is her anxiety at never being offered any decent movie roles. The Romanesque beauty is interviewed for an upcoming movie by a brash American director, but, unable to make up his mind about her, he consults with his young son. Little Wilbur thinks vampish Vanda is too old for 'teenage appeal' and, on overhearing this, Vanda is determined to seduce the young lad and win the part. Naturally, she doesn't actually see Wilbur's face and ends up coming on to a hapless photographer (played by a very young Dennis Waterman) in error. After posing for him bedecked in chains, a feather boa, some fishnets and a black rubber outfit, she gives him a good seeing-to only to discover, to her horror, that the real Wilbur is a four-foot *Joe 90* lookalike with an over-

Left: *A Promise of Bed* (1969) was released on video as *This, That and the Other*.

sized head. It sounds funny but it's not.

The second tale is probably the best of the three, but only by a short length. George Makepeace (Victor Spinetti) is a manic depressive who likes nothing more than sitting at home listening to tape recordings of car smashes. Despairing of his empty life, he attempts to gas himself in front of the fire one evening but is disturbed in his suicide bid by a telephone call from a young woman who wrongly assumes he is a mutual friend holding a party that night. Sweet little Barbara (Vanessa Howard) duly turns up, bottle in hand, along with a crowd of hedonistic mates who trash George's flat. Even Valerie Leon, in a huge curly wig, misbehaves herself. Ironically, the theme of the party turns out to be suicides, but all ends happily when Barbara puts on George's pyjamas and invites herself to stay with him, thus ending his run of misery. The poignancy of this little vignette does manage to lift the mood for a while and is quite unusual for a British sex comedy.

The final part is the weirdest. Satirist John Bird, in a role he's probably forgotten, plays a lonely taxi driver with a passion for the beautiful birds he sees in 'X'-rated movies at his local fleapit. One late shift he picks up Scandinavian totty Yutte Stensgaard and fantasises that she lusts after him. Unfortunately, his cab has a crash and sexy Yutte runs off into the woods, hotly pursued by Bird, keen to get his 25 bob fare. Eventually he stumbles across a huge house, half-buried underground, with a gigantic sliding glass wall. Inside are a bevy of luscious lovelies cavorting topless in a swimming pool, with Yutte lying naked on the floor covered in bananas while another girl does an erotic dance with her body covered in handprints. It all turns out to be a figment of Bird's overactive mind because he suffered a bump on the head during the collision.

Unbelievably, considering the tiny budget, this final story was filmed on location just outside Paris at the house of a rich chemist (who had registered fluoride toothpaste in Europe, no less). 'We took all the actors and the entire crew over to France to film those scenes,' recalls Long. 'It was quite an achievement for a low-budget movie, but I never did it again!'

CAST: Victor Spinetti (*George*), Dennis Waterman (*photographer*), John Bird (*taxi driver*), Vanessa Howard (*Barbara*), Vanda Hudson (*Susan Stress*), Gordon Stearne (*movie producer*), Alexandra Bastedo (*Angie*), Christopher Mitchell (*Carl*), Larry Taylor (*policeman*), Robin Courbet (*Jimmy*), Michael Durant (*young playboy*), Sue Cole (*Jo*), Peter Kinsley (*Wilbur*), Roy Branningan (*Jeffrey*), Valerie Leon (*girl in bath*), Yutte Stensgard (*girl in taxi*), Cleo Goldstein (*'hands' girl*), Angela Grant (*girl with flowers*), Sheila Ruskin (*snake girl*), Siobhan Taylor, Bill Jarvis and Gregory Reid (*partygoers*)

CREDITS: *Director* Derek Ford, *Producer/Photography* Stanley Long, *Editor* Glyn Byles, *Screenplay* Donald and Derek Ford, *Music* Kongos, Demetriou and Russell, *Theme song* 'A Promise of Bed' performed by Scrugg A DORAK FILMS Production. Distributed by MIRACLE. Opened December 1969.

LOVE IS A SPLENDID ILLUSION

Great Britain / 1969 / 72 mins / cert 'X'

The third sex movie collaboration from producer-distributors Richard Schulman and Bachoo Sen following *Her Private Hell* and *Loving Feeling*, but with a change of director. This movie gave Tom Clegg his first break into films, although he later carved out a more successful career in TV, helming episodes of *Space: 1999*, *The Sweeney*, *Bergerac* and *Sharpe*.

Actor Simon Brent returns from *Loving Feeling* in the lead role of Christian Dubarry, an interior decorator holidaying in Italy with his wife Amanda. But by the seaside Brent can't help himself to the bevy of Continental girls quick enough, and beds blondes, brunettes, hotel guests and high-class hookers with Continental gaiety. His wife finds out about his indiscretions but forgives him (she has to really, since she's been carrying on behind his back too) and they get back together. Sen's sex drama is a phenomenal bonk-fest, cut by the censor by a whopping 14 minutes and denied a cinema release for over a year. In supporting roles it features future sex starlets Maxine Casson, Gay Soper, Fiona Curzon and überbabe Anna Matisse.

CAST: Simon Brent (*Christian Dubarry*), Lisa Collings (*Amanda Dubarry*), Andrée Flamand (*Michele Howard*), Peter Hughes (*Maurice Howard*), Mark Kingston (*Bernard Collins*), Fiona Curzon (*Liz*), Maxine Casson (*Debbie*), Anna Matisse (*Sophie*), Carl Ferber (*Jason*), Nancy Nevinson (*Amanda's mother*), Gay Soper (*blonde girl in bed*) Margo Mayne (*Mrs Allen*), Howard Bell (*bailiff*), Chris Clark (*architect*)
CREDITS: *Director* Tom Clegg, *Producer* Bachoo Sen, *Editor* Glenn Hyde, *Photography* Jack Atcheler, *Screenplay* David Baker and Bachoo Sen, *Music* Wilfred Burns, *Theme song 'Love is a Splendid Illusion'* performed by Lisa Collings
A PICCADILLY PICTURES Production. Distributed by RICHARD SCHULMAN ENTERTAINMENTS. Opened January 1970.

SECRETS OF SEX

aka *Multiplication* aka *Eros Exploding* aka *Bizarre* aka *Tales of the Bizarre*

Great Britain / 1969 / 82 mins / cert 'X'

In America *Secrets of Sex* was released, unrated, as *Bizarre*, a title which more accurately describes one of the most insane, perversely original pieces of crazy British movie-making ever to grace the screen. The film was directed, produced and co-written by Antony Balch, a legendary Wardour Street distributor who took several years to get the project off the ground, originally calling his multi-layered script *Multiplication*. He budgeted it at £15,000 with a running time of 65 minutes and offered it to equally legendary film producer Richard Gordon. Gordon loved the idea and six months later, after extensive script revisions from a team of writers, it finally emerged as a much longer film. Eventually costing £32,000 and running for nearly 90 minutes, the movie was shot over a period of 14 weeks. It was definitely worth the wait.

The movie is structured in portmanteau style, taking its lead from a rather oddball opening sequence. A thousand years ago, a wise and elegant Arabian judge (mutely played by *Her Private Hell*'s executive producer, Richard Schulman) is led to believe that his wife has hidden her forbidden lover in a gigantic oak chest. Pondering what action to take, he eventually orders his manservants to bury the box in a deep pit while he chucks the key off a cliff into the ocean. From this rather unconventional introduction we zoom forward to the present day, well 1969 to be precise, and meet a crusty old mummy, voiced by that indomitable boomer Valentine Dyall, who, it seems, was the poor chap doomed to a claustrophobic death all those centuries before. Lamenting his awful demise, the bandaged spirit offers snapshots of the modern-day 'battle of the sexes' and cordially invites the audience to revisit some below-the-belt tactics on the sexual battlefield. 'Who could have predicted,' he solemnly intones, 'the extremities to which mankind, and more particularly, womankind, would go on in the pursuit of, shall we say, sat-is-faction?'

From there on the movie doesn't always make an awful lot of sense, but then it doesn't really have to because the visuals are more often diverting enough. The young bronzed bodies of well-proportioned men and buxom women tumble in slow motion in a haystack as Dyall chants 'Imagine you were making love to this girl. Imagine you were making love to this boy' over and over again. A bevy of topless popsies get pelted with rotten vegetables, accompanied by boos, whereas the macho, posturing males, stripped to their waists and brandishing machine guns, are rewarded with healthy cheers. The pay-off is this: the two genders meet to the strains of 'When the Saints Go Marching In' and the action disintegrates into an orgiastic free-for-all set to fireworks.

The mummified paramour recounts several dramatised stories, including some tinged with rather more terror than titillation. A sadistic female photographer, assigned to take snaps for a book on medieval tortures (there must be a market, one supposes) suspends her weedy male model over the dreaded 'Spanish Horse' – a four-legged contraption with a razor-sharp blade for a saddle – and leaves him to dangle while she takes a leisurely lunch with her creepy assistant. When she returns, the poor chap has been sliced in half. In a more laughable tale, a fruity old financier (played by the wonderfully named Kenneth Benda) fancies his chances with a young woman half his age and gets her pregnant, only to discover that she has a hereditary defective gene and the baby is born hideously misshapen.

Right: Esme Johns and Donald Sumpter get to grips in *Groupie Girl* (1969).

After these sub-Hammer horrors we get down to some honest-to-goodness sexiness, with a topless safe-cracking British secret agent and a kinky young American who tries, but fails, to persuade the hooker he's hired for the night (Sue Bond) to make love in front of his huge pet lizard (with a microphone incongruously in shot). He's evidently more into lizard-swapping than wife-swapping. Funniest of all is a sequence with a lonesome husband (Mike Britton) who apprehends a female cat-burglar (Cathy Howard) in his house one evening. 'Christ. It's a bird!' he shrieks after unmasking her. Of course, the young madam suggests they have sex, but not before insisting on showering with her knickers still on. Dry, and back on the bed, the couple make love (still with knickers on), accompanied by the clipped tones of a BBC Radio 3 announcer enthusing about the 'old world English garden' and with a telephone cable entwined between their legs. The frantic operator's voice pleads with the subscriber to 'please replace the handset!' Finally, an old dear in a greenhouse tells her lordly butler, at unbelievable length, that all her blooms contain the souls of her former lovers

Secrets of Sex spoofs the horror genre, as well as comic strip fantasies, James Bond, silent movies, Buster Keaton slapstick and European sex pictures but chief censor John Trevelyan was not impressed with the amount of nudity (full-frontal, both male and female) the movie had on show, plus a scene with two men embracing in bed. He ordered nine minutes to be shorn off before it could be released domestically. It was shown in its original form at the 1970 Cannes Film Festival where Balch was applauded for his tongue-in-cheek approach to British filmmaking.

Balch died young in 1980, but his legacy continues. So long after his death *Secrets of Sex* is still venerated as a groundbreaking British movie. Undeniably, it is an astounding piece of work – thought-provoking and quite delightful to look at – but, while many critics talk of the movie in reverential tones, it goes without saying that it doesn't actually work. Much of it is, dare I say it, pretty tedious and overall the production has not aged terribly gracefully. The film's ideology was a little too sophisticated for the burgeoning British porn audience, but at the time of its release big screen boobs were harder to come by than they are today and as a result the movie ran solidly in London for six months. It's highly unlikely that this cerebral film could have been made even five years later, when sex comedy mania was at its unsophisticated peak. However, the irreverent *Secrets of Sex* is definitely worth another 21st century peek. Curious certainly, an oddity absolutely, it is unlike any homegrown movie before or since.

CAST: Valentine Dyall (*narrator*), Richard Schulman (*Judge*), Janet Spearman (*Judge's wife*), Dorothy Grumbar (*photographer*), Anthony Rowlands (*model*), Norma Eden (*photographer's assistant*), George Herbert (*steward*), Kenneth Benda (*Sacha Seremona*), Yvonne Quenet (*Mary-Clare*), Cathy Howard (*cat burglar*), Mike Britton (*Burglary Victim*), Maria Frost (*Lindy Leigh*), Peter Carlisle (*Colonel X*), Steve Preston (*Philpott*), Graham Burrows (*military attaché*), Mike Patten and Ray George (*Flicker Flashback men*), Karrie Lambert and Joyce Leigh Crossley (*Flicker Flashback women*), Nicola Austine (*Flicker Flashback girl*), Elliot Stein (*strange man*), Sue Bond (*hooker*), Laurelle Streeter (*woman in greenhouse*), Bob E Raymond (*butler*). **CREDITS:** *Director/Producer* Antony Balch, *Executive Producer* Richard Gordon, *Editor* John Ruston, *Photography* David MacDonald, *Screenplay* Martin Locke, John Eliot, Maureen Owen, Elliot Stein and Antony Balch, *Music* De Wolfe A NOTEWORTHY FILMS Production. Distributed by ANTONY BALCH. Opened February 1970.

GROUPIE GIRL
aka *I Am a Groupie*

Great Britain / 1969 / 87 mins / cert 'X'

Cliff Richard's *The Young Ones* was certainly never like this! Well-scrubbed teenagers singing, laughing, frolicking and waiting until they're married before having sex is a world away from Derek Ford and Stanley Long's absorbing exposé of grubby, listless youths fighting over who can get into a hippy rocker's Y-fronts first. Pruriently pandering to the contemporary tabloid image of hippies as irresponsible, amoral, drug-taking wasters, *Groupie Girl* presents the nation's youth of 1969 in the sleaziest way possible. It's a generation gap extravaganza where the squalid life of the youngsters infuriates their spluttering elders. 'You're all the same,' spits the voice of authority here. 'You long-haired layabouts!'

Filmed in 'cautionary tale' style, *Groupie Girl*'s thoughtful and perversely satisfying story follows bored suburbanite Sally, played convincingly by ex-stripper Esme Johns, who sadly never appeared in a movie again. 'I don't know what happened to her,' admits Long. 'We just pulled her out of a strip club and made her an actress. She tried extremely hard and I thought she wasn't bad at all considering.' Sally, rebelling against her conservative upbringing, has secretly been attending rock concerts and is so taken with the various bands' huge flares, facial hair and body odour that she makes the decision to become a professional groupie and promptly stows away in the back of a roadie's transit van. Ending up in London, she lives and sleeps with a succession of hirsute rockers, all of whom show her the utmost disrespect. To the musicians, girls are good for only two things: blow jobs and making breakfast.

The movie gives a beautifully blurred snapshot of hippiedom in all its compulsive nastiness. Lank hair, marijuana, partner-swapping, topless go-go girls and some genuinely good musical numbers (the title song in particular is a stormer) perfectly evoke the period, when bitter rivalries between groupie chicks spilled over into bra-bursting catfights and bitter disillusionment. The movie's accuracy is never in question since it was co-written by Suzanne Mercer, who had been a groupie herself and was at the time hooked up with the drummer from real-life rock band Juicy Lucy. Costing just £16,000 and filmed entirely on location, the film is packed with incident and thrills. 'It was extremely evocative of the period and was very much of its time,' says Long. 'I'm very proud of the way it looks because the Americans kept asking me what studio we'd shot it at. They just couldn't believe we'd done it all on location. They ended up buying it for £50,000 for distribution in the US, so we made a huge profit.'

In one especially memorable scene Sally's languid boyfriend Steve (dimple-chinned Donald Sumpter looking like a dead ringer for Marc Bolan), the lead singer with 'Orange Butterfly', gets thoroughly bored with her possessiveness and makes the decision to give her to another group, the permanently stoned 'Sweaty Betty'. Travelling at speed along a motorway in their transit van, the band pass Sally out of the window into the rival rockers' vehicle, Sally screaming in terror all the while. It's an awe-inspiring sequence, frighteningly realistic. 'It was actually filmed at Hendon airfield,' says Long. 'It was quite an ambitious effect for the budget we were working with and we did briefly use a dummy at one point, but you can't tell. It became the talking point of the entire film and encouraged a lot of people to go and see it.' *Groupie Girl* is seriously mind-expanding stuff and one of Stanley Long's grooviest moments. If you want to take a heavy trip and blow your mind, just hop on board, baby!

CAST: Esme Johns (*Sally*), Billy Boyle (*Wes*), Donald Sumpter (*Steve*), Richard Shaw (*Morrie*), Neil Hallett (*Detective Sergeant*), Bobby Parr, Bill Jarvis, Simon Probert and Emmett Henessy (*Orange Butterfly*), Tom Docherty, Simon King, Trevor Adams and Ken Hutchinson (*Sweaty Betty*), Paul Bacon (*party host*), Sue Carstairs, Ruth Harrison and Archie Wilson (*party guests*), Cherokee (*groupie at hotel*), Maureen Flanagan (*thieving groupie*), Gennie Nevinson (*Moira*), Eliza Terry (*Mooncake Girl*), Jimmie Edwardes (*Bob*), James Beck (*Bob's manager*), Lynton Guest, Paul Woloff and Paul Pride (*Bob's group*), Lynda Priest (*dancer*), Walter Swash (*hotel porter*), Mary and Madeleine Collinson [uncredited] (twin groupies)

CREDITS: *Director* Derek Ford, *Producer* Stanley

KEEPING THE BRITISH END UP

Long, Editing NCS, *Photography* Stanley Long, *Screenplay* Derek Ford and Suzanne Mercer, *Music* John Fiddy, *Theme song* 'Groupie Girl' performed by Opal Butterfly A SALON Production. Distributed by EAGLE. Opened June 1970.

MONIQUE

Great Britain / 1969 / 87 mins / cert 'X'

Thirty-something suburbanites Bill (David Sumner) and Jean Patterson (Joan Alcorn) live in the typical nuclear family bubble with their two young children, but their once-happy existence is gradually crumbling. Dissatisfied with life and tired of being at home all day, Jean wants to return to her secretarial job. 'I'm bored doing nothing,' she wails, and suggests to her husband that they hire an au pair to help with the household chores and bringing up the kids. Bill can hardly contain his delight since it might offer him new amorous opportunities. Their marital sex life is stagnant. Feeling emasculated, Bill is constantly exasperated by his wife's frigidity.

French au pair Monique (Sibylla Kay), a saucy, raven-haired minx in mini-skirt and kinky boots, duly arrives, but with unforeseen consequences for all concerned. Jean immediately returns to her job, encouraged by her new home help: 'Every woman should have something else,' Monique purrs, 'apart from just looking after her home and children.' But that 'something else' is not what she expected. Identifying Monique as a flirtatious maelstrom in their midst, Jean warns Bill to keep their employee at arm's length, but her reckless, thrill-seeking husband starts a passionate affair with Monique regardless. However, the bisexual Gallic goer wants a little more 'ooh la la'. Monique and Jean become inseparable friends, giggling and joking like teenagers, and Monique steals a few intimate caresses from her female boss wherever possible.

One morning Bill comes home unexpectedly and walks in on his wife in a nude clinch with Monique. Monique soothes the couple's worries and the situation develops into a convenient *ménage à trois* after a highly charged candlelit dinner. The groundbreaking three-way bedroom romp that follows was heavily cut by John Trevelyan, but thankfully the wonderful post-coital scene is left intact. In one of the most satisfying moments in British sex film history, the three participants sit up in bed after making love. Puffing on cigarettes and sipping wine, they nonchalantly discuss the artistic merits of an abstract painting hanging on the wall opposite. It's a delightful coda to a heart-stopping build-up.

Backed by Tony Tenser, former actor John Bown wrote and directed this marvellously stimulating and sophisticated movie and cast his wife Sibylla Kay in the title role. Largely concentrating on only three characters (no easy feat), *Monique* never once loses the audience's attention. Manipulating the theme of a disruptive sexual intruder so malevolently portrayed in 1968's *Baby Love*, Bown brilliantly succeeds in building an atmosphere of heightened sexual tension. When Monique first attempts to kiss her female employer the fear of excitement is electric and the lesbian love scenes blow the better-known *The Killing of Sister George*, made a year earlier, out of the water. The stark suburban setting is sexier than a hospital, stately home or health farm (the backdrops of so many later homegrown sex films) and the domestic scenes are beautifully naturalistic, balanced perfectly with the joyous, spontaneous performances of the children innocently playing.

Funkily directed, with snappy editing and a superb piano-led musical score, *Monique* earned great critical praise on its summer 1970 release and played to packed houses both in the UK and USA, although, incredibly, Bown never directed

Left: Not those baubles! David Sumner helps Sibylla Kay decorate the Christmas tree in *Monique* (1969).

again. He returned to acting and in 1971 he and Kay played an ill-fated husband and wife in Hammer's *Vampire Circus*.

CAST: Sibylla Kay (*Monique*), Joan Alcorn (*Jean*), David Sumner (*Bill*), Jacob Fritz-Jones (*Edward*), Nicola Bown (*Susan*), Davilia O'Connor (*Harriet*), Carol Hawkins (*blonde girl*), Howard Rawlinson (*Richard*)
CREDITS: *Director* John Bown, *Producer* Michael Style, *Executive Producer* Tony Tenser, *Editor* Richard Sidwell, *Photography* Moray Grant, *Music* Jacques Loussier A TIGON BRITISH Production. Distributed by TIGON. Opened June 1970.

THE WIFE SWAPPERS
aka *The Swappers*

Great Britain / 1969 / 86 mins / cert 'X'

The very first sex mega-blockbuster caused a sensation not only in the tabloid press, both in the UK and US, but attracted as many women as men to the cinema for an anthology of 'real life stories' which touched both sexes: the mythical, mysterious cult of the 'wife-swappers'. Although by the late 1960s the practice was only recognised as a minority social happening confined to the affluent professional middle classes, the Long-Ford partnership decided to bring the whole sordid business to a wider audience; to warn innocent working class cinemagoers of the perilous path to fornication. And quite right too. 'I was reading the *News of the World* one day,' says producer Stanley Long, 'and a story about wife-swapping just leapt off the page. I knew immediately that it could be a massive hit if I turned it into a movie.'

Master of ceremonies David Gell lends his mid-Atlantic tones to another exposé of the pink underbelly of British society. The script definitely pulls no punches this time round, equating promiscuity with the most extreme of 20th century addictions. 'It is a feature of most couples established in the so-called 'swinging set' that they will constantly seek to involve others,' Gell solemnly warns, 'a feature they share with drug addicts and alcoholics.' The subject having been 'ripped from the headlines', it provides director Derek Ford with an excellent excuse to take to the pavements of Trafalgar Square to ask the ever-willing general public what they make of all these extramarital shenanigans. 'We have it in Sweden,' remarks an excitable Scandinavian tourist. 'I don't have time to swap,' comments one cohabiting hippy. 'It's a drag, man.'

Through dramatised sequences, the movie makes less-than-tentative enquiries into the innermost workings of the wife-swapper, warning against the risks inherent in extra-marital sex yet at the same time dwelling on as much lurid detail as possible. In the bizarre opening scene a woman, naked save for a rubber mac, allows herself to be kidnapped on Westminster Bridge, driven to the countryside and chucked in a lake, on the orders of her 'master', a creep who rings her up regularly to ask, 'Marion, are you alone?' while presumably manipulating himself. In another torrid tale, a narcissistic control freak encourages his furious wife to indulge in a spot of lesbian licking for the entertainment of his mates.

The funniest story involves desperate Paul (James Donnelly) and his apprehensive wife Ellen (Valerie St John), whose sex life has waned over the past seven years. Together they embark on an evening of licentiousness which is not necessarily to Ellen's liking. Without having the grace to tell her what he's got planned, Paul invites a couple of friends round for a bout of four-way bonking. 'My first impressions of them were very hazy,' recalls Ellen when she meets the other participants. In fact, they're simply unforgettable. Jean is a peroxide blonde strumpet with an intermittently dubbed voice, and Leonard (played by Carry On supporting actor Larry Taylor) is the most irredeemably unattractive middle-aged Lothario ever to inhabit a British sex movie. Looking like a dirty gap-toothed gypsy in a cravat, he doesn't immediately win Ellen over, but when he displays his prowess at tapping ice-cubes out of the freezer tray she suddenly finds him 'quite charming'. Leonard's surreptitious grope of her arse probably won him a new fan too. Of course, she ends up in the sack with him. 'Larry never forgave me for putting him in that movie,' chuckles Long.

The individual stories are interspersed with the musings of an 'eminent London psychiatrist'. He must be for real because he's sitting behind a leather-topped desk in an oak-panelled office. Undoubtedly Harley Street. The thing is, he's not very convincing. Never have acting and reading from a script been more apparent. He

KEEPING THE BRiTiSH END UP

EAGLE FILMS present
The Wife Swappers

takes off his glasses, he puts them back on again, he casts his eyes downwards, he pauses. This really is a serious business. The 'expert' concludes that 'artificially induced lust is not an adequate substitute for real love', which is a blessed relief for all concerned, especially the audience who have just sat through an hour and a half of shagging. Now they can rest easy in the knowledge that predatory male 'swingers' can be instantly identified by their white turtlenecks and penchant for wearing sunglasses indoors.

The Wife Swappers is just as enjoyable today as it was in 1970, but now for completely different reasons. What was once viewed as titillating is now very, very funny indeed. Aside from the overblown interruptions of the phoney psychiatrist, which probably bored the damp pants off the audience over 30 years ago, the film has aged disgracefully, and all to its credit. A wonderfully camp piece of British movie-making, it is every bit as important a part of the sixties as Alfie or Up the Junction, only a hell of a lot more fun. A totally essential British sex movie and a huge hoot. As one flat-capped Londoner comments about the wife-swapping craze: 'Well, I'd like to swap my wife for a new motor!'

CAST: David Gell (narrator), Fiona Fraser (Marion), James Donnelly (Paul), Valerie St John (Ellen), Larry Taylor (Leonard), Joan Haywood (Jean), Denys Hawthorne (Cliff), Bunty Garland (Sheila), Sandra Satchwith (Carol), Andrew Lodge, Anna Bentick and Janette Richer (voices)
CREDITS: Director Derek Ford, Producer Stanley Long, Photography Mike Francis, Screenplay Derek Ford and Stanley Long, Music Michael Eaton and John Fiddy, Theme song 'Borrowed Love' performed by Jay Dee A SALON Production. Distributed by EAGLE. Opened July 1970.

LOVE VARIATIONS

Great Britain / 1969 / 80 mins / cert 'X' (London only)

The first sex education epic of its kind made in the UK but resolutely retaining all the elements which make it quintessentially safe for a British audience: no stiffies, no

DOINGS

Left: James Donelley, Joan Haywood, Larry Taylor and Valerie St John getting down to it in Stanley Long's *The Wife Swappers* (1969).

close-ups, no oral sex and, most important of all, intercourse *only* while wearing underpants. Based on David Grant's controversial illustrated sex guide published in 1968, *Love Variations* was dubbed an 'experiment in communication and education' and a film 'made to teach', but its true intentions had little to do with helping the public to better themselves in bed. It was made to titillate, but in order to get it past the censor Grant reluctantly dressed his film in the correct brain-numbing attire; in other words, a boring, clinical, characterless overcoat of the brightest Persil white.

The man in the mac was hoodwinked into seeing *Love Variations* for one purpose only. To see what he had been denied for so long: men and women bonking without the interruption of a plot. If only it was so easy. An unnamed 'family doctor' is shown in his consulting room whispering to an unsmiling pair of nodding automata. Suddenly realising the camera is on him, the doctor dives into a long and excessively dull speech about menstruation, ovulation and reproduction. Some 15 bum-numbing minutes later we still haven't seen any shagging. On come the models, helpfully identified as male and female for those unaccustomed to this sort of thing. Steven is 'five feet and nine inches' (he wishes) and works as a mechanic for a 'very well-known rally team'. Carol is 22, a housewife and looks like she needs a good night's sleep. Perhaps she's been up all night rehearsing. There's a brief shot of full-frontal nudity but, while most people take their clothes off to have sex, Steve and Carol put theirs back on (well, the obligatory knickers at least).

Sexual positions are demonstrated on a variety of white tables, rotating blocks and barrels against a stark background. All are shown in complete stillness (apart from the incessant snogging) and there is definitely no jigging about. Any inexperienced teenage boy watching this would think sex was as easy as lying in his Y-fronts on top of his girlfriend and remaining absolutely motionless. Two minutes later he'd be satisfied and she'd be pregnant. Simple! As the positions get ever more elaborate, Steven and Carol perform the very tricky lotus position, where each partner is required to stand on only one leg. They wobble and lose their footing before toppling backwards. Grant was thrilled with the scene and even more so when Soho audiences giggled their approval. 'I've discovered humour!' he told his friend Bob Godfrey excitedly. 'When the couple are doing the lotus position they fall over. It gets a fantastic laugh.' To which Godfrey replied, 'Of course they would. They're bored gutless by then!'

The film's final scene is set in a Wardour Street viewing theatre where some 'specially invited guests' (in other words, Joe Public) are asked to comment on what they've just seen. Waking up from her enforced slumber, one middle-aged lady states that the film would be of 'great interest' to her teenage daughter, but doubts whether it would show her anything she hadn't already seen. 'My children were brought up on a farm so they were fortunate,' she says, straight-faced. 'They were brought up taking sex as a matter of course.'

Amazingly refused a certificate by the British censor, *Love Variations* only got a release after London County Council passed it for selected exhibition in West End cinemas, but it still caused outrage and consternation in the tabloid press. The following year Arnold Louis Miller produced a mini-sex education film entitled *Growing Up – A New Approach to Sex Education* for showing in schools, which went a whole lot further. Banned by education authorities around Britain and denounced by Mary Whitehouse, the film showed unsimulated masturbation and intercourse, but created most consternation when one of the young actors peeled back his foreskin in close-up, with – shock, horror – dirty fingernails!

CAST: Carol Jones (*woman*), Derek Tracey (*man*) and a '*Family Doctor*'
CREDITS: *Director* Terry Gould [aka David Grant], *Producer* David Grant, *Editor* Jack Knight, *Photography* Geoffrey Glover, *Script (based on his book)* David Grant
An OPPIDAN Production. Distributed by OPPIDAN. Opened August 1970.

ZETA ONE
aka *The Love Factor*

Great Britain / 1969 / 82 mins / cert 'X'

Flaming space meteorites! A sexy sci-fi caper starring a bevy of naked alien astronauts *and* Charlie Hawtrey? Actually, scrub the word 'sexy'. The first of only

KEEPING THE BRITISH END UP

three attempts to mix British sex comedy with an episode of *Star Trek* (the others are *The Sexplorer* and *Outer Touch*), *Zeta One* is partially based on a comic strip that appeared in short-lived fantasy magazine *Zeta* in the late 1960s. Adapted for the big screen by writer-director Michael Cort, the story is told in flashback by British secret agent James Word (played with the minimum amount of effort by Robin Hawdon), whose prime objectives are shagging blonde girls in his funky plastic apartment and smoking in bed. Apart from that he does absolutely nothing.

His boss, 'W', apparently despatches his nubile secretary, Yutte Stensgaard, to visit Hawdon at home for an intimate chat. He immediately wants to slip her a few classified inches. She, however, just wants to hear him recount his latest top secret mission. They agree to compromise by playing strip poker first, a laboriously sluggish game, the build-up to which lasts some 15 brain-numbing minutes. Anyway, when he finally tells his tale it seems quite exciting.

Zeta (Dawn Addams) is the leader of a giant colony of extraterrestrial superwomen from the planet Angvia (Vagina, geddit?) who abduct earthwomen, brainwash them and transport them back to their world through a time machine. Why they do this is not entirely clear. The only benefit seems to be that the women get to wear long black wigs, suede mini-dresses and white, thigh-length, patent leather boots. As the Angvians continue their spree of kidnapping, using Valerie Leon as their chief abductor, the aliens' activities come to the attention of gruff 'public enemy number one' Major Bourdon and his simpering, effeminate 'henchman' (I use that term very loosely), Swyne.

Played by James Robertson Justice and Charles Hawtrey respectively, this has got to be the low point of both men's careers. How these two got involved in this idiotic tomfoolery is anybody's guess, because both had regular pay cheques coming in from the Doctor films and the Carry Ons respectively. In particular, it's pretty obvious that Justice *so* doesn't want to be in this film. Thinking primarily of the brown envelope stuffed with used twenties he'll get at the end of the shoot, his eyes continually flicker off-set to read his lines off idiot boards. These baffling star turns culminate in the bizarre, and not entirely welcome, spectacle of Justice and Hawtrey torturing a topless Carol Hawkins (an Angvian girl they have kidnapped) on a medieval rack.

A bunch of topless Angvians, naked bar skimpy knickers and the icing from Midget Gems stuck on their nipples, invade Justice's secret hideaway *en masse* and do battle with his calamitous band of tweed-capped gamekeepers. Suddenly all is well in the mysterious world of large-breasted space ladies and even secret agent Hawdon gets abducted by Yutte (an alien in disguise, you see) and made to inseminate all the Angvian women in a prolonged bout of fifth dimensional sperm donation.

Zeta One is camp, colourful space junk enlivened only by Martin Gascoigne's innovative set design – big plastic shapes, shimmering foil walls and flashing multi-coloured chequer-board lights – and a sequence or two filmed through a Lava Lamp. If it weren't for the topless lovelies you would definitely think this was filmed for the entertainment of children. The endless rushing-about and cheap special effects are basic in the extreme. Any more comparisons with *Doctor Who* would be churlish, but needless to say *Zeta One* will *really* have you hiding behind the sofa.

CAST: Robin Hawdon (*James Word*), Yutte Stensgaard (*Ann Olsen*), James Robertson Justice (*Major Bourdon*), Charles Hawtrey (*Swyne*), Dawn Addams (*Zeta*), Lionel Murton (*W*), Anna Gael (*Clotho*), Valerie Leon (*Atropos*), Brigitte Skay (*Lachesis*), Carol Hawkins (*Zara*), Wendy Lingham (*Edwina Strain*), Rita Webb (*clippie*), Walter Sparrow (*stage manager*), Steve Kirby (*secret agent*), Paul Baker (*Bourdon's man*), Yolanda del Mar (*snake stripper*), Angela Grant, Nita Lorraine and Vikki Richards (*Angvians*)

CREDITS: *Director* Michael Cort, *Producer* George Maynard, *Executive Producer* Tony Tenser, *Editors* Jack Knight and Dennis Lanning, *Photography* Jack Atchelor,

Right: Disaffected youth in Lindsay Shonteff's *Permissive* (1970).

Screenplay Michael Cort and Alastair MacKenzie
A TIGON BRITISH Production. Distributed by TIGON. Opened February 1971.

1970

PERMISSIVE
aka *Suzy Superscrew*

Great Britain / 1970 / 86 mins / cert 'X'

Mining the same polluted vein as *Groupie Girl* the year before, Lindsay Shonteff's *Permissive* – filmed under the gloriously bad title *Suzy Superscrew* – succeeds in being one of the dirtiest, nastiest and most squalid sex films of the seventies. Naïve, duffle-coated mouse Suzy (Maggie Stride) arrives in London to search out her old school chum Fiona (Gay Singleton), who enjoys a hedonistic life as head groupie with hippy rock group, Forever More (a turgid mix of all the worst elements of Jethro Tull combined with Slade). A genuine band signed to RCA Victor, Forever More don't seem to have any problem being portrayed in an unflattering light as drug and sex-crazed animals who look like overgrown, hair-infested gnomes. And their music's crap too.

Fiona initiates her friend into the life of groupiedom and shows her how to compete for the band member with the biggest, thickest... mane of lank hair! She takes to the life of fat spliffs, greasy layabouts and waking up each day as dazed and confused as a pigeon in Trafalgar Square, but her days as an anaemic hippy end in tragedy.

Canadian director Shonteff proved beyond doubt that he could effectively portray lurid scenes in his 1969 horror movie *Night after Night after Night*, but here he attempts something more depressingly realistic, undoubtedly helped by the cheap and grainy look of the whole picture. The bleak, meaningless life of a groupie is conveyed unpalatably, yet never heavy-handedly, and Suzy's pointless existence is effectively chronicled from her beginnings as a quiet provincial girl, who has to have the expression 'pulling' explained to her, to the end result: a competitive, hard-faced, paisley-patterned bitch. (When she finally 'steals' Forever More's hirsute lead singer from under Carol's nose, she leaves her friend to die in a bath of blood after a suicide attempt.) The film's condescending stereotypes of hippies are actually spot-on and three decades later seem more funny than tragic. Laughs aside, this is a film for lovers of nicotine-stained fingers, rusty Ford Transit vans, close-ups of white pimply flesh and shagging in toilets. And it's actually rather good.

CAST: Maggie Stride (*Suzy*), Gay Singleton (*Fiona*), Gilbert Wynne (*Jimi*), Alan Gorrie (*Lee*), Robert Daubigny (*Pogo*), Stuart Francis (*Kip*), Debbie Bowen (*Lucy*), Nicola Austine (*Coral*), Forever More (*themselves*), Mary and Madeleine Collinson, Maria Frost, Suze Randall and Cathy Howard (*groupies*)
CREDITS: *Director* Lindsay Shonteff, *Producer* Jack Shulton, *Editor* Ronald Pope, *Photography* John Taylor, *Screenplay* Jeremy Craig Dryden, *Music* Forever More, Titus Groan and Comus
A SHONTEFF FILMS Production. Distributed by TIGON. Opened October 1970.

COOL IT CAROL
aka *Oh Carol!* aka *The Dirtiest Girl I Ever Met*

Great Britain / 1970 / 101 mins / cert 'X'

'The story is true, but actual names and places are fictitious', says this movie's opening caption. And in this rare instance the claim was accurate. The story of two naïve kids, who come up from the country to a life of vice in the big smoke, came directly from a contemporary news report in the *News of the World* about a young country girl and her boyfriend who accidentally got deeply involved in prostitution and porn in London.

In Murray Smith's sleek screenplay,

KEEPING THE BRITISH END UP

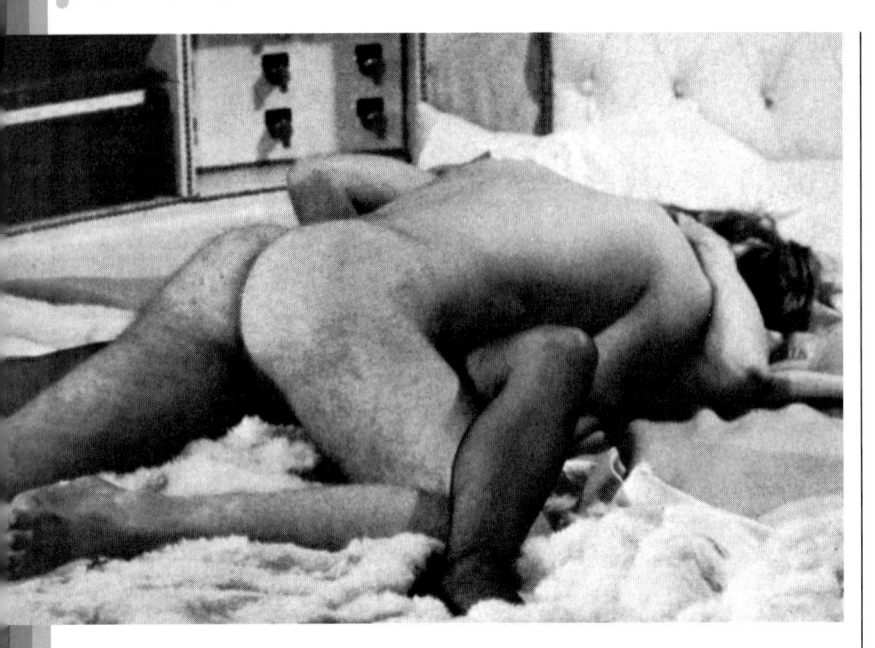

immature butcher's boy Joe Sickles (Robin Askwith doing his posh voice) tries to impress petrol pump attendant Carol (Janet Lynn) by claiming he is moving to London to become a big-shot car dealer. She calls his bluff and decides to go with him, in the hope that she'll get talent-spotted as a fashion model. Carol is more worldly wise than her long-haired companion and she makes love to him on the train. But on their arrival in London, they both have plenty to learn. 'Hey, Joe. D'you see all the black men?' Carol says excitedly the minute they step foot outside Paddington station. The young provincials are overwhelmed by the city's crowds and traffic, not to mention people's abruptness. Even hailing a taxi is an art form to be mastered.

Joe fails to find work in the luxury car showrooms of the West End, but Carol has more luck at a modelling agency, stunning the male proprietor by stripping off to her bra and panties in reception. However, cocky Joe, showing off in a gambling den, loses the little cash they have on the roulette wheel. Destitute and penniless, the pair think of other ways to earn money. Egged on innocently by Joe, Carol turns to prostitution. 'It's only a fuck,' she says. 'I can't believe people pay good money for it.' Carol awkwardly accosts men in Regent Street and eventually accepts a ride from a sinister middle-aged ponce (Kenneth Hendel), who gives her £5 for sex. Back at the creep's Battersea apartment, Joe has to wait in the next room making the tea. In a wonderfully uncomfortable sequence, Askwith grimaces while the grunts and groans from next door are intercut with the kettle boiling.

Carol uses her body dispassionately and continues to sell herself, even to old age pensioners in camel coats who queue up for cheap thrills. Later, at the Valbonne nightclub in Kingly Street, the youngsters catch the eye of Philip Stanton (Peter Elliot), a cadaverous pimp who ropes them into appearing in a blue movie in a squalid flat for £60 each. They perform innocently under the glare of the lights and camera, offering cinema audiences their first glimpse of Askwith's soon-to-be famous bum. Beside the bed the eerie 'Mr Big' of the operation, an elderly man in bowler hat and cravat, trembles with excitement.

Carol is soon in great demand for her services as a model and high-class call girl, and the money starts rolling in. The couple get their own Mayfair mansion and staff, but lavish parties and even socialising with DJ Pete Murray don't bring them true happiness. In the cold light of day, when the champagne has gone flat, they realise this is not the life for them. After catching the train home to Shropshire, they return to their old jobs and anonymity. In reality, the teenagers returned to their village but blabbed about what had happened to them. The boy was subsequently sentenced to two years in borstal for living off his girlfriend's immoral earnings, which director Pete Walker thought was a travesty of justice.

While Robin Askwith went on to become a legend in far more comical British sex films, little is known about his talented co-star. Childlike 21-year-old Janet Lynn was a stage school graduate and cabaret dancer who, remarkably, only made one other film – Sidney Hayers' *Assault*, a police drama produced by Carry On supremo Peter Rogers, also filmed in 1970. Displaying just the right amount of naïveté and girl-next-door prettiness, Lynn was applauded for her performance but the press could not understand how she had got mixed up in such a 'dirty' picture. The *Daily Mail* asked, rather loftily, 'What's a nice girl like Janet Lynn doing in a nasty film like *Cool It Carol*?'

Cool it Carol was the first British movie to truthfully show the mucky world of the four Ps: permissiveness, prostitution, pimping and pornography. But Pete Walker doesn't try to glamourise his subjects. It's his best sex film and it's frankly difficult to believe that it was made by the same man who shot the abysmal *School for Sex* only two years previously. *Cool it*

Left: *Cool It Carol* gave Britons their first lingering look at Robin Askwith's arse (1970).

Carol is relentlessly seedy, downbeat and realistic, but never exploitative, and it still packs an almighty punch today.

Unsurprisingly, the popular press of 1970 rounded on the movie, branding it immoral and filth of the lowest order. Not one reviewer actually believed the story was based on truth; one even had the temerity to believe that the movie would actively encourage petrol pump girls to flock to the big cities to seek careers in prostitution! The *Evening News* went so far as to call it 'a thoroughly nasty bit of pornography', but the film's notoriety did little to harm its box-office business: quite the opposite. The film was a smash. It was also massively popular in America, where, under the outrageously inaccurate title *The Dirtiest Girl I Ever Met*, it grossed over $2 million.

CAST: Janet Lynn (*Carol Thatcher*), Robin Askwith (*Joe Sickles*), Jess Conrad (*Jonathan*), Peter Elliot (*Philip Stanton*), Stubby Kaye (*Rod Strangeways*), Pearl Hackney (*Mrs Thatcher*), Martin Wyldeck (*Mr Thatcher*), Derek Aylward (*Tommy Sanders*), Kenneth Hendel (*pimp*), Harry Baird (*Benny Gray*), Chris Sandford (*David Thing*), Pete Murray (*himself*), Eric Barker (*signalman*), Uncredited: Nicola Austine (*stripper*), Alec Bregonzi (*Barry*), Walter Sparrow (*cameraman*), Valerie St John (*Deirdre*).

CREDITS: *Director/Producer* Pete Walker, *Photography* Peter Jessop, *Editor* Tristram Cones, *Screenplay* Murray Smith, *Music* Cyril Ornadel.
A PETE WALKER Production. Distributed by MIRACLE. Opened November 1970.

GAMES THAT LOVERS PLAY
aka *Lady Chatterley versus Fanny Hill*

Great Britain / 1970 / 91 mins / cert 'X'

Long long ago – before Joanna Lumley was officially named the woman most Britons would like to have as a next-door neighbour, before she became a household name in *The New Avengers*, *Sapphire and Steel* and *Absolutely Fabulous* – she bared all in this historical sex romp. Aged 24 and with only three bit parts behind her, Joanna was more than prepared to strip off for writer-director Malcolm Leigh. Set in the Roaring Twenties (or the Whoreing Twenties if you prefer), the film cast Lumley as prostitute Fanny Hill, the most in-demand hooker in upmarket Belgravia. Fanny's boss is also her mother, Mrs Hill (Diane Hart), who challenges rival madame, Lady Evelyn (Nan Munro), to a competition. Pitting Fanny against Lady Evelyn's top pop-tart Constance (Penny Brahms), the grand old ladies wager £1000 on who has the dirtiest dollymop. The challenge is made all the more difficult as the girls are set a virtually impossible task. They must seduce the unseducable.

Constance gets an ageing, virginal Roman Catholic bishop (John Gatrell), with whom she plays footsie under a table before unfrocking him in the orangery at the bottom of Lady Evelyn's garden. Fanny, meanwhile, gets an even shorter straw and is assigned an outrageously gay transvestite played by Jeremy Lloyd, her future husband in real life and the co-creator of *Are You Being Served?* Naturally they swap dresses, compare ostrich feathers and paste jewellery and end up in bed. (Why are gay men so easily turned straight in British sex comedies?) 'My Fanny is obviously the best!' declares Mrs Hill, but the copulation competition ends in a flat draw, with both girls successfully achieving the impossible.

Reluctant to leave matters unresolved, the old dames take a name at random out of the London telephone directory and instruct their top strumpets to get to him first, by any means possible. The lucky recipient of their amorous attentions is gentlemanly wine merchant Mr Lothran, played with relish by dear old Richard Wattis. Fanny attempts to get into his long-johns by requesting that he lay down some wine in her cellar, although her mind is on another sort of laying. Meanwhile, Constance rents an apartment over the hall from Mr L and tries to lure him over the shagpile. Neither succeeds. Lothran inexplicably rejects their fleshy charms right at the last moment, screaming: 'Not alone! Not alone!'

Unexpectedly manoeuvring the two rival girls together for a dinner date, he finally comes clean. 'I hate doing things alone,' he explains cryptically. 'It's only when I'm alone together with people that I can really be myself!' Ah, clear as crystal. The randy old goat can only get it up for threesomes. Brandishing a cat 'o nine tails, Wattis takes both the naked ladies

Left: Richard Wattis gets over-excited with Joanna Lumley and Penny Brahms on the pressbook for *Games That Lovers Play* (1970).

to the four-poster and dances the blanket hornpipe with them. However, the scene is filmed with some dignity, befitting a character actor of Wattis' standing. He does it fully clothed.

Malcolm Leigh does a smart job in helming his first feature-length sex comedy, prudently edited, lavishly decorated and with some jolly song-and-dance numbers performed by the 1920s trad band, the New Temperance Seven. Art director Bill Hutchinson has a whale of a time with the fantastic sets, creating an exuberant arena for Jeremy Lloyd's drag queen ball (complete with real female impersonators culled from the West End) and a simply stunning multi-mirrored corridor with a black-and-white tiled floor in Fanny's house of ill-fame.

However, *Games that Lovers Play* is a movie that has remained a skeleton in the closet for Lumley. In an interview two decades later she described it as a 'foul, unerotic film', but sleeping dogs never lie for long. In 1981 naughty clips from it resurfaced in an *Electric Blue* video and feature film, and Lumley has allegedly vetoed its showing on BBC Television, due to a special relationship with the corporation. On British TV it's only ever been shown on cable channels and it's been unavailable on video for many years. In May 1994 it made a belated appearance as an 'exclusive' front page story in the *News of the World*. The report claimed that bootleg videotapes of the 'seedy' film were being 'snapped up for £50 at car boot sales across the country' like it was a nationwide epidemic! Some poor bugger in Birmingham was hoodwinked into parting with cash for a copy. 'I was told it was pretty heavy stuff,' he told the newspaper, 'but you can hardly see the naughty bits. When I took it back to the guy who had sold it to me, he had already pissed off.'

CAST: Joanna Lumley (*Fanny Hill*), Penny Brahms (*Constance Chatterley*), Richard Wattis (*Mr Lothran*), Jeremy Lloyd (*Jonathan Chatterley*), Diane Hart (*Mrs Hill*), Nan Munro (*Lady Evelyn Chatterley*), John Gatrell (*the Bishop*), Charles Cullum (*Charles*), Graham Armitage (*Mr Adams*), George Belbin (*Major Thumper*), Harold Bennett (*old photographer*), Sydney Arnold (*butler*), Frank Draycott (*gardener*), Leda Felice (*Gillian*), Simon Joseph (*Simon*), June Palmer (*girl in steam room*), Michael Lee Parker (*Police Sergeant*), George McGrath (*Colonel Middleton*), Roy Stewart (*Mr Ngwanda*), The New Temperance Seven (*band*)

CREDITS: *Director* Malcolm Leigh, *Producer* Judith Smith, *Executive Producer* Negus-Fancey, *Editor* Peter Austen Hunt, *Photography* Ken Higgins, *Screenplay* Malcolm Leigh, *Music* David Lindup A BORDER Production. Distributed by BORDER. Opened December 1970.

LOVE AND MARRIAGE

aka *Sex, Love and Marriage*

Great Britain / 1970 / 81 mins / cert 'X'

More spurious 'sex education' from David Grant, based on his second best-selling sex manual. 1969's hit film version of his *Love Variations* book had the models enjoying sexual intercourse through their underpants. This sequel offers more of the same but with a greater emphasis on the emotional side of relationships and the importance of the holy union. Reluctantly, Grant knew he'd have to go that extra length if the British censor was going to pass a further 'lesson in lovemaking'. Not surprisingly, the title put many sex-starved punters off. Love and marriage were the last things they were looking for, it was sex or nothing. The movie was released in July 1971 but, sensing disquiet among the flesh-pots of Soho, Grant had the title amended to *Sex, Love and Marriage* by October.

Attempting to vary the clinical formula favoured by the BBFC, Grant enlisted the help of saucy animator Bob Godfrey to include some near-the-knuckle cartoon inserts, and increased the quota of half-naked participants in the 'demonstration' sequences. Some of his energetic models were couples in real life, which caused some critical appraisal of their 'performances'. 'I remember going to see that film in a viewing theatre in Wardour Street,' chuckles Godfrey. 'Two of the models were sitting in the row in front of me and having such a row.

"You're not very good in that position, are you?" the woman was saying to her boyfriend. She was really telling him off. Then, to make matters worse, the projectionist suddenly turned the film off halfway through. Grant shouted "What's up?" and the projectionist replied "It's the nature of the material!" He was gay, apparently, and objected to it!'

Anyone thinking our sex education movies were bad only had to look at the excruciating foreign imports. The late 1960s saw a slew of dubbed sex education films from the Continent. In the German-made *Technique of Physical Love* (1968), jointed wooden dummies acted out the sexual positions, while the Swedish *Language of Love* (1969), directed by Torgny Wickman, had eminent Danish sexologists Inge and Sten Hegeler brandishing dildos. Wickman persevered with his 'happy sex' message for over a decade with a string of sequels. But *More About the Language of Love* (1970), released in the UK in 1974, went beyond the pale with a dramatised sequence on 'the use of bidets'.

CAST: David Jackson (*narrator*) *with models* Carol Jones, James Peterson, Stephanie Stevenson, Richard Stevenson, Barbara Christie, Jean Watson and Tony Clarke
CREDITS: *Director* Terry Gould (David Grant), *Producer* David Grant, *Editor* Jack Knight, *Photography* John Millcocks, *Animation* Bob Godfrey, *Script (based on his book)* David Grant
An OPPIDAN Production. Distributed by TIGON. Opened July 1971.

SWEET AND SEXY

aka *Foursome*

Great Britain / 1970 / 58 mins / cert 'X'

Cameraman, director, editor and actor Ray Selfe had made hundreds of commercials and documentaries and in 1969 decided to branch out into feature films. 'It was a co-operative sex film, whereby none of the people involved would get paid, not even the actors, in order to save money,' he explained. 'Miracle Film distributors liked the idea straight away and accepted it. I knew that if it could make a sizeable profit we'd be OK.' The directing duties were handed to the inexperienced Anthony Sloman, whom Selfe had taught cinematography when he was a teenager.

Sweet and Sexy's meandering story concerns rough and ready Northerner Ted (Robert Case) trying to track down his sister, Joan, in London to inform her that their mother is seriously ill. Unconcerned about leaving his mother alone in a critical condition, he sets off by train to find her. Phoning her or sending a letter would be too simple. ('It's a pretty puerile script, but there you go,' commented Selfe ruefully.) Once in London he discovers that she's gone missing and, following her trail, he is 'forced' into having sex with a selection of hot, sex-starved women, including Rose Alba as a frustrated landlady and cute Cathy Howard as an S & M freak who lives in a house decorated with tinfoil. He ends up popping his cork with a

KEEPING THE BRITISH END UP

CLASSIC MOULIN
(formerly CAMEO) PICCADILLY CIRCUS, Great Windmill St 437 1653

SWEET AND SEXY X AND **The Lustful Vicar** X

Progs. Daily 11.35, 12.40, 3.10, 5.45, 8.15.
Sunday 2.15, 3.15, 5.45, 8.20.
Late Cinema Friday and Saturday 11.00 p.m.

good-time girl in a dingy flat, but only after making love does he realise… yes, you guessed it… that he's just slept with his own sister! What a mistake to make. Actually, it's only his half-sister, so that's all right then.

At the start of the project Selfe had little idea how badly the filming was going to go. 'My mother had died a week before filming was due to start and I was working 20-hour days during the shoot just to get it finished,' he remembered. 'I was the producer, camera operator and director of photography and I even loaded up all the equipment at the end of the day. It was back-breaking work.' All the locations were the cast and crews' own houses and flats. Shot, amazingly, for a paltry £8000, the film managed to come in on budget. However, much to Selfe's horror, the sound quality was so bad that the entire film had to be re-dubbed. And worse was to come.

As Selfe explained, 'Anthony Sloman had shot an awful lot of sex scenes against my advice and, because I was the movie's producer, I said perhaps it shouldn't be quite as strong as it was. I mean not strong by today's standards, but then it was pretty hot.' It came as no surprise when John Trevelyan saw the first cut of *Sweet and Sexy* and declared that it had not one single redeeming feature. 'I knew he was going to complain,' recalled Selfe. 'It wasn't a social comment movie or a protest picture or anything. It was just an out-and-out titillation film and Trevelyan said we'll have to cut this or that, but Sloman wouldn't budge an inch and Trevelyan got very upset.'

The censor originally demanded nearly 45 minutes of cuts to be made, almost unheard-of in a British film. This was reduced to 21 minutes, with Selfe eventually abiding by the decision. 'I don't blame him,' he said. 'Some of the sex scenes were pretty boring. One part was just a guy humping with a camera moving round his bum, but it showed no detail of anything in particular. The plot was worth only 20 minutes of anyone's time anyway.' Because of Sloman's arguments with Trevelyan, the film, running at just 58 minutes, took nearly two years to reach the screen. It finally opened in March 1972 at the Cameo Moulin in Great Windmill Street. To add insult to injury, it played alongside a Swedish sex shocker called *The Lustful Vicar*, cheekily billed as 'a tale of a rising young man of the cloth'.

CAST: Robert Case (*Ted*), Quinn O'Hara (*Sarah*), Susanne Rogers (*Julie*), Rose Alba (*landlady*), Jason Twelvetrees (*Bert*), Max Burns (*Tony*), Cathy Howard (*Olivia*), Raymond Cross (*Dennis*), Prudence Paige (*Janet/Joan*), Susie Reilly (*Amelia*), Harriet Allen (*Louise*), Tessa Lewis (*stripper*).
CREDITS: Director Anthony Sloman, Producer Ray Selfe, Editor Martin Amstell, Photography Howard Edward [aka Ray Selfe], Screenplay Anthony Sloman and Andrew Best [aka David Korr], Music Jeremy Paul. A LIONGRADE Production. Distributed by MIRACLE. Opened March 1972.

HENRY NINE TILL FIVE

Great Britain / 1970 / 6 mins / cert 'X'

In bleak, grim, rainy suburbia, a short, fat, balding, egg-headed man travels to work on the tube train. Identical to all his fellow commuters, Henry wears a bowler hat, tiny spectacles and reads the newspaper. Every day is exactly the same, but don't be fooled by Henry's appearance. Underneath he's a raging tiger. In his bare city office he spends the day endlessly stamping bits of paper, but his unfulfilled daylight hours are fuelled by extravagant fantasies. 'I don't like my job very much,' he moans. 'But I have discovered a way of defeating boredom and all its vicissitudes. I think about sex.'

Bob Godfrey's groundbreaking cartoon had originally been commissioned by another animation company who recoiled in horror when they say the final script. '"This is utter filth. We can't do this," was their reaction,' says Godfrey, 'but they offered it to me and I absolutely loved it. Up until then sex was either shown as very romantic or very serious, but I decided to go for a big laugh.' Godfrey himself voiced the monotone, lethargic Henry. 'I wanted his voice to be a boring drone like he was talking about a broom, not sex,' he explains. 'It's funnier with a flat voice when he tries to get his tongue around those French phrases. Anyway, with me doing the voice we saved a lot of money. Our first choice, Michael Bentine, was too expensive!'

Henry's varied, and often bizarre, sex-

70

Right: George Best and Penny Brahms take a break from filming a fantasy sequence with Hywel Bennett in *Percy* (1971).

ual fetishes are painstakingly illustrated, whether it be partaking in Roman orgies, flashing in the park or being whipped by a statuesque Amazonian woman in fishnet stockings. The latter fantasy is usually saved 'for afternoon tea-breaks'. He even shocks the plump tea-lady by indulging in a little transvestism, wearing a huge decorated bonnet in the office. If Henry's imagination flags he can always find inspiration elsewhere. 'I keep the complete works of the Marquis de Sade in plain wrappers, secreted amongst my egg and tomato sandwiches,' he explains.

The pay-off is that when Henry returns home to his grey suburban terrace his wife turns out to be a breathless nymphomaniac who is absolutely crazy about him. 'You look ravishing tonight,' she purrs. 'Take me, Henry, take me!' But poor Henry has exhausted himself with his nine-to-five fantasies and has no energy left to make love. 'Not tonight, beloved,' he mutters guiltily. 'I've had such a hard day at the office.' Voiced by glamour girl Marilyn 'Knockers' Rickard, Henry's wife, the epitome of sexual desirability, is heard but not seen. 'We were going to draw this sexy woman,' recalls Godfrey, 'and I mean she had to be absolutely "Phwoarr", but as the weeks went by we decided just to have a disembodied voice, which was much better because you had to imagine her.'

Henry Nine Till Five became the first British cartoon to get an 'X' certificate, but what did John Trevelyan make of it? He bumped into Godfrey one day in Soho Square and told him: 'It's a great film Bob. I saw it twice, but I had to give it an 'X'. It's pretty rude, but short of swinging male genitalia we can show almost anything nowadays!'

CAST: Bob Godfrey (voice) (*Henry*), Marilyn Rickard (voice) (*wife*)
CREDITS: *Director/Producer* Bob Godfrey, *Editor* Tony Fish, *Photography* Bev Roberts, *Screenplay* Stan Hayward
A BOB GODFREY Production. Distributed by BRITISH LION. Opened May 1973.

1971

PERCY

Great Britain / 1971 / 103 mins / cert 'X'

Based on Raymond Hitchcock's perky 1969 novel of the same name, *Percy* tells the cock-and-ball story of an antique dealer, Edwin Anthony (Hywel Bennett), who

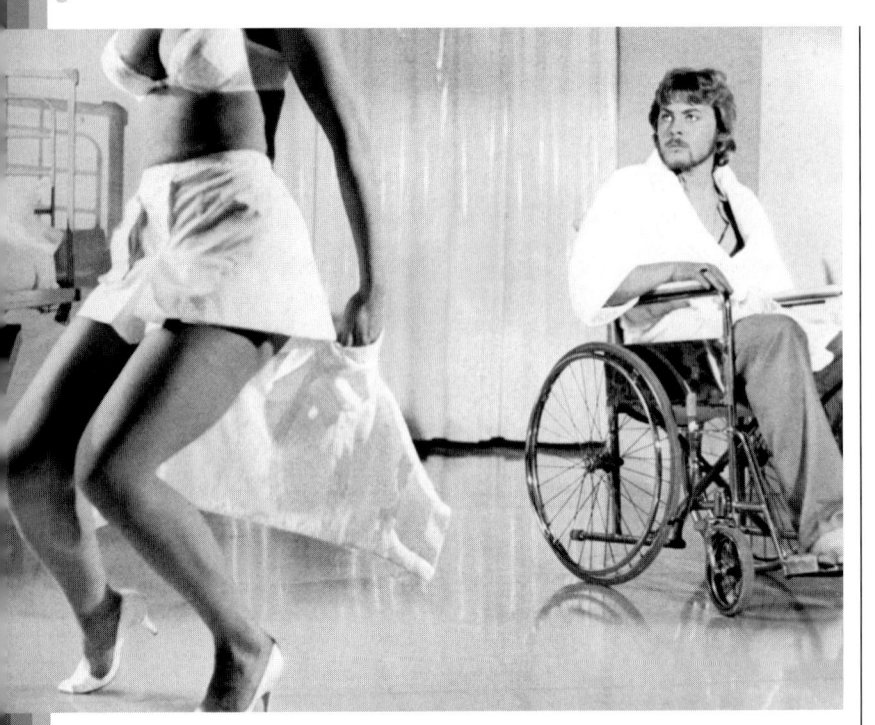

Left: The swingingest transplant ever – Hywel Bennett in *Percy* (1971).

is separated from his favourite part following a tragic accident involving a cut-glass chandelier. As a result, he becomes the recipient of the world's most sensational transplant in medical history: he gets a brand-new cock! Denholm Elliott is the pioneering surgeon who performs the operation and loves the resulting publicity, but refuses to tell his patient where his new pecker came from. Bennett soon starts to resent his new todger (nicknamed 'Percy' by those around him), as he is ridiculed wherever he goes. After the sensational story gets on the front page of the *Sun* ('The Swingingest Transplant Ever!'), his penis becomes the main topic of conversation in pubs across the land.

The worldwide media are soon on Edwin's tail and as a consequence he sets out to trace the organ's original owner. When the surgeon's kindly assistant Sister Flanagan (Pauline Delany) gets him a list of all the male patients who died on the day of his operation, he is able to track down the ex-lovers of several different deceased men, and is gradually able to eliminate them. One had an identifiable penile birthmark, one was a black man, another a homosexual burnt to a crisp in a car crash and one a circumcised Jew. He eventually discovers the unwitting donor had been a philandering sex maniac. The cad's melancholy widow Moira (Cyd Hayman) tells him: 'You're a very lucky man. You've inherited the equivalent of a vintage Rolls-Royce.'

Why he makes the pointless search for the dick's original owner is baffling, and a further hunt for the philanderer's ex-mistresses (including European totty Elke Sommer and Britt Ekland) takes the singularly unfunny idea one bulge too far and the trouser-snake gags eventually lose their impetus. The best scene occurs at the start of the film when the surgeon appears on a BBCTV chat show and refuses to temper his 'medical' language. The movie makes reproving digs at the double standards of British television as the BBC producer frantically attempts to bleep out the 'offending' words, 'penis' and 'vagina'.

The famous filmmaking double-act of director Ralph Thomas (brother of Carry On director Gerald) and producer Betty E Box (wife of Carry On producer Peter Rogers), so beloved of movie fans because of their long-running Doctor series (1954-1970), wandered into the realms of the 'X' certificate for the first time with *Percy*, their 31st film together. The movie's nudity, 'come' jokes, four-letter words and endless knob gags initially shocked many in the British film establishment. When Anglo-EMI originally announced production of the film in 1970 they were criticised in the press for going downmarket, and pressure groups like Mary Whitehouse's National Viewers and Listeners Association were said to be 'appalled' at such a 'poor taste' movie. The public condemnations were excellent publicity for the film, which built on its pre-release notoriety with an extensive advertising campaign asking 'How big is Percy?' Despite the bad-mouthing *Percy* did not stiff at the box-office and became one of Box's biggest cinematic successes, even getting the green light from the director of the National Society for Transplant Surgery, who issued a distinctly odd press release saying: 'I am delighted by your new film *Percy* in the firm belief that humour is the only weapon required to beat a path to the hearts of those delightful idiots – the British public.'

CAST: Hywel Bennett (*Edwin Anthony*), Denholm Elliott (*Emmanuel Whitbread*), Elke Sommer (*Helga*), Britt Ekland (*Dorothy*), Cyd Hayman (*Moira Warrington*), Janet Key (*Hazel Anthony*), Tracey Crisp (*Miss Elder*), Antonia Ellis (*Rita La Rousse*), Patrick Mower (*James Vale*), Pauline Delany (*Sister Flanagan*), Adrienne Posta (*Maggie Hyde*), Julia Foster

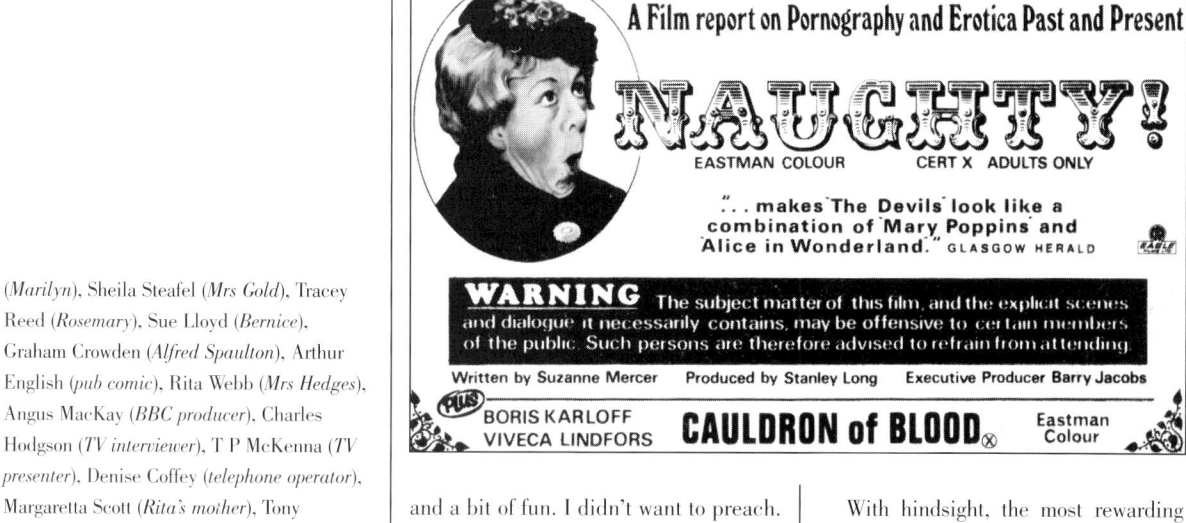

(*Marilyn*), Sheila Steafel (*Mrs Gold*), Tracey Reed (*Rosemary*), Sue Lloyd (*Bernice*), Graham Crowden (*Alfred Spaulton*), Arthur English (*pub comic*), Rita Webb (*Mrs Hedges*), Angus MacKay (*BBC producer*), Charles Hodgson (*TV interviewer*), T P McKenna (*TV presenter*), Denise Coffey (*telephone operator*), Margaretta Scott (*Rita's mother*), Tony Haygarth (*Purdey*), Ronnie Brody (*reporter*), George Best [uncredited] (*himself*), Penny Brahms [uncredited] (*football fan*)

CREDITS: *Director* Ralph Thomas, *Producer* Betty E Box, *Editor* Roy Watts, *Photography* Ernest Steward, *Screenplay* Hugh Leonard *based on the novel by* Raymond Hitchcock, *Music* Ray Davies and The Kinks An ANGLO-EMI-WELBECK Production. Distributed by MGM-EMI. Opened February 1971.

NAUGHTY!

Great Britain / 1971 / 83 mins / cert 'X'

Stanley Long's semi-documentary report on pornography and erotica is a jolly hotch-potch of the real, the historical and the imagined which he hoped would provide a basis for a better understanding of sex as a commodity. '*Naughty!* was saying why do some people think they can be the guardians of public morality, while others are denied what they want to see?' says Long. 'I just wanted to say that pornography has been with us forever and the demand is still there. I was having a go at the Mary Whitehouses of the world, but I wanted to make the film with a bit of integrity and a bit of fun. I didn't want to preach. I wanted to entertain and I think I did it quite well.'

Long starts the movie off with a bit of old-school comedy stereotyping. Gloomy middle-aged Horace (played by C Lethbridge-Baker) has been starved of sex for three months by his nagging wife. Seeking fulfilment, he trundles around Soho gawping at lurid cinema posters and sex-shop windows. All the while his wife's screeching voice reverberates around his head. 'I'm tired. I've got a headache. Can't you just go to sleep like other people?'

From present-day permissiveness, Long delves back into the murky past. He obviously has most fun with the historical re-enactments, particularly of the staunch Victorian variety, where he relishes the opportunity to expose the hypocrisy of 19th century society. In his fictional Victorian family, pious Papa (Lee Donald) is a scowling Bible-bashing patriarch who abhors bad language and insists on having all the legs of his furniture covered up. Yet after dark he reads pornographic novels, entertains his mistress and sleeps with child prostitutes. Meanwhile, Mama (Brenda Peters) gives her daughter some sound advice for her wedding night: 'When it happens, hold tight and remember that it happened to the Queen'.

With hindsight, the most rewarding element of *Naughty!* is the contemporary (pre-*Deep Throat*) footage of hardcore pornography and the attitudes surrounding it. Shooting at the 1970 International Wet Dream Festival in Amsterdam, Long shows groups of blitzed-out hippies watching flickering cinema images of, as one person describes it, 'people fucking, being sucked, women with dogs…' One critic predicts that it is only a matter of time before we get to see the same thing legally in the UK. (He couldn't have got it more wrong.) Plus, we also get some rather pithy observations from Al Goldstein, the New York editor of *Screw* magazine, who claims that 'Porn is basically dull.'

Back in London, Long secures his biggest coup by documenting, for the very first time, the making of a British hardcore sex film with infamous pornographer, John Lindsay. The voice-over announces we will see a 'genuine, unstaged account of a modern blue movie'. The three participants (two female, one male) acting in Lindsay's ten-minute epic *Sex After School* look thoroughly miserable rather than enthusiastic, although the director is totally fired up. 'It's got to be sexy,' says Lindsay. 'The competition is fierce nowadays and they're churning them out in

Right: Eva Whishaw lusts after future *Emmerdale* star Richard Thorp in *Suburban Wives* (1971).

Denmark and we in London want to do the best and really turn quality out. I want 100 per cent action. I want everything. Sucking, licking, fucking, screwing. You name it. I want it and I want it good!'

Long had heard about Lindsay's reputation and was keen to use him in *Naughty!* in order to bring his documentary completely up to date. 'He was actually my stills photographer on *The Wife Swappers* in 1969,' Long points out, 'but at the time I had no idea he was so heavily involved in hardcore stuff. He was a likeable rogue with the right idea but totally the wrong approach. He pushed it way too far and as a result got his collar felt.'

CAST: C Lethbridge-Baker (*Horace*), Lee Donald (*Victorian Papa*), Brenda Peters (*Victorian Mama*), Nina Francis (*daughter*), Shane Raggett (*son*), Lois Penson (*maiden aunt*), Debbie Fairbridge (*youngest daughter*), Rosalie Westwater (*lady in museum*), Arthur Skinner (*Doctor*), Jane Cardew (*Papa's mistress*), Bill Ward (*street hawker*), Declan Mulholland (*policeman*), Hamish Roughead (*gent*), Jim O'Connor (*Henry Spencer Ashbee*), Derek Glynne-Percy (*John Hotten*), Olive MacFarland (*Mary Wilson*), David Grey (*Henry Hayler*), Vivienne Carmichael (*Mrs Hayler*), Yvonne Paul (*prostitute*), Heather Chasen (*madame*), *Uncredited as themselves:* Al Goldstein, Germaine Greer, John Lindsay, Lucienne Camille
CREDITS: *Director/Producer/Photography* Stanley Long, *Editor* NCS, *Screenplay* Stanley Long and Suzanne Mercer
A SALON Production. Distributed by EAGLE. Opened October 1971.

NOT TONIGHT DARLING!

Great Britain / 1971 / 85 mins / cert 'X'

You'd have thought that rookie movie director Anthony Sloman would have learnt his lesson after his previous sex movie, *Sweet and Sexy*, had been severely criticised by the censor for having too much explicit sex in it and as a result got torn to ribbons. For his follow-up, *Not Tonight Darling!*, Sloman fell into the honey trap again with a rampant orgy, frenzied coupling, pseudo-lesbian massage, men running naked through a muddy field and more group-groping than a British audience could ever hope to take in one sitting. Taking umbrage with Sloman a second time, the censor shaved a whole five minutes off this one, a tale of a bored suburban housewife who has tired of her unresponsive husband and yearns to find sexual excitement outside marriage.

Luan Peters (an ex-Paul Raymond protégée whose alleged 42" bust had been known to make grown men weep) is the neighbourhood nympho seeking nine-to-five thrills. But the object of her desire, Australian door-to-door salesman Vincent Ball, wants more than just a daytime diversion on her divan; he wants to make her into a porn star. Luan's dull solicitor husband is downing the whiskies and ogling the girls in a seedy Soho watering hole one night when he is horrified to see his wife frolicking naked on a projector screen. It seems that his wife's secret lover has blackmailed her into taking part in an orgy and the whole event was committed to celluloid in a home-made skin flick.

Filmed as *Sex in the Suburbs* (why nobody had ever thought of that title before is a mystery), the movie had its name changed by its catchpenny distributors, presumably to cash in on the long-running Ray Cooney farce *Not Now Darling!*, which had been playing to packed houses in the West End. The film also features a performance by late-1960s one-hit wonders Thunderclap Newman, who scored a Number One in 1969 with *Something in the Air*.

CAST: Luan Peters (*Karen Williams*), Jason Twelvetrees (*John Williams*), Vincent Ball (*Alex*), Nicki Howarth (*Joan*), James Hayter (*Mr Finlay*), Bill Shine (*Captain Harrison*), Sean Barry (*Eddie*), Lance Barrett (*Gary Williams*), Amber Harrison (*Suzanne*), Mike O'Malley (*Ben the Click*), Carol Catkin (*Jill*), Jenny D'Arcey (*Celeste*), David Vorhaus (*George*), Patti Walby (*Anna*), Jay Lee (*Bill*), The Tiffany Sisters (*strippers*), June Palmer, Nicola Austine and Samantha Bond (*girls at health club*), Thunderclap Newman (*themselves*)
CREDITS: *Director* Anthony Sloman, *Producer* John M Taylor, *Executive Producer* Negus-Fancey, *Editor* Ean Wood, *Photography* Harry Waxman, *Screenplay* Ean Wood
A MINTDENE Production. Distributed by BORDER. Opened December 1971.

SUBURBAN WIVES

Great Britain / 1971 / 87 mins / cert 'X'

Seven salacious stories from the fevered

mind of director Derek Ford, filmed in a similar pseudo-documentary style, but with much less success, as *The Wife Swappers*, which he made two years earlier. There's some swapping going on here too, but the main thrust of Ford's movie is an 'examination' of the new social phenomenon of 'nine-to-five widows' twiddling their thumbs while their husbands are in the City with pretty secretaries sitting on their laps. The film is presented by glum-looking Eva Whishaw as an investigative journalist assigned the task of exposing sex in the suburbs. 'They are not wild teenagers, nor are they the jaded, wealthy jet-set,' explains Whishaw. 'They are middle class, affluent, professional people. They have good homes, colour television sets, two cars, help in the house and foreign holidays. Most have families, but all are bored. They are nothing extraordinary. They are the suburban wives.'

The individual tales are told mainly from a female perspective, which was unusual in sex films up to then, but the raunchy re-enactments are, not surprisingly, purely shag-by-numbers stuff aimed at the predominantly male Soho brigade. Despite the shots of neat, soulless post-war housing estates, the bored housewives are portrayed as a pretty unsympathetic bunch: manipulative, vengeful, secretive women in love with their own reflections and determined to have some sexual fun at their partners' expense. They begin idle affairs to give themselves a hobby, turn to prostitution for excitement and sleep with the au pair in order to punish the cheating husband and give themselves a lesbian thrill.

It's pretty low-wattage stuff all round, too convoluted and rather too wordy to be authentically sexy. In fact, the best sequence has no shagging or nudity in it at all. The marvellously feline Heather Chasen plays a wife suspicious that her randy husband is having an affair with his bitchy, busty PA (Gabrielle Drake) and visits his office unexpectedly to stir up trouble. Swapping unpleasantries with the secretary, she goes into hubby's office and asks for a shoulder rub after her tiring day of shopping. Her exaggerated grunts and groans infuriate Drake, who imagines her lover is having it off with his own wife over the leather top and consequently breaks off the affair. Simply told and timed to perfection, it's better than any amount of kinkiness Ford could think up.

CAST: Eva Whishaw (*Sarah*), Nicola Austine (*Fox*), Tony Barton (*Hound*), Maggie Wright (*Irene Marriott*), Peter May (*John Marriott*), Barry Linehan (*Bill*), Claire Gordon (*Sheila*), James Donnelly (*client*), Heather Chasen (*Kathy Lambert*), Denys Hawthorne (*George Lambert*), Gabrielle Drake (*secretary*), Yocki Rhodes (*Yocki*), Jane Cardew (*Corale*), Robin Culver (*photographer*), Pauline Peart (*Mavis*), Richard Thorp (*Sarah's husband*), Brian Miller (*husband's friend*), Sidonie Bond (*Jill*), Timothy Parks (*Leonard*), Mia Martin (*Helene*) **CREDITS:** *Director/Screenplay* Derek Ford, *Producer* Morton M Lewis, *Editor* Terry Keefe, *Photography* Bill Holland and Roy Poynter, *Music* Terry Warr A BLACKWATER Production. Distributed by BUTCHERS. Opened December 1971.

VIRGIN WITCH

aka *Virgin Witches* aka *Lesbian Twins*

Great Britain / 1971 / 89 mins / cert 'X'

A supernatural sex shocker with real-life sisters Vicki and Ann Michelle as a couple of dollies descending into Hell via Surrey. Based on the spellbinding novel by Klaus Vogel, the sisters leave behind dreary village life and head for the big bad smoke in search of fame and fortune. Ann signs up with Sybil Waite's fashion agency in Chelsea but, unluckily for her, Sybil (played by Michael Caine's fearsome first wife, Patricia Haines) is a butch lesbian more interested in seeing a young girl's

KEEPING THE BRITISH END UP

Left: James Chase ensures that Vicki Michelle is no longer a *Virgin Witch* (1971).

knockers than getting her into *Harpers and Queen*. Having her latest recruit strip off and taking her breast measurements, Sybil is reduced to a quivering, twitching mess of sapphic hormones.

The Michelle girls are persuaded to go with Sybil to her friend's Tudor mansion, Wychwold, for a photographic assignment, but obviously neither girl has been to the flicks to see a Christopher Lee film recently. Ann gets to work on a shoot for a 'cider advertisement', but as she peels off the clothes and has her wicked way with the photographer it becomes more Humpy Jack than Scrumpy Jack. Meanwhile, Vicki stumbles across the Dark Arts, but is comforted by the owner of the house, Gerald Amberley (Neil Hallett), a foxy, lip-licking scoundrel and high priest of a secret coven. Hallett is his devilish best here in a part he was born to play, a 'world authority' on witchcraft but with a passion for naïve young popsies who lay themselves bare for a poke with his ceremonial dagger.

As the Sabbat arrives, the girls are initiated into the world of black magic and wanton witchery. Hallett has his wicked way with Ann on the altar, while the rest of the kinky coven strip off and dance orgasmically around them (crazy old housekeeper included) in a nude variation on the Twist. Thereafter Sybil takes a lesbian liking to her new Satanic signing, but Ann conspires to eliminate her, culminating in a blood-curdling, and naturally rather nude, climax.

Ex-stunt arranger Ray Austin – who had previously worked on TV's *The Avengers* and *The Saint* – directs his first film with enthusiasm, gleefully gobbling up every last horror cliché. The sounds of the creepy church organ, owls hooting, flickering black candles, creaking doors and scenes draped in seductive red lighting are all well-thumbed pages straight out of the Gothic recipe book, but here he executes them in a pulse-racing new fashion, making the film a damn sight more spooky and sexy than most of Hammer's early seventies efforts. The Michelle sisters strip off with gusto at every available juncture and Haines, also seen ripely nude, is creepy *par excellence* as the pervy priestess. The ungodly mix of witchcraft and nudity did not amuse the BBFC, however, who refused *Virgin Witch* an 'X' certificate. It was only screened in London after the local authorities decided that naked Devil worship was just what the people of Kensington and Chelsea were crying out for.

CAST: Ann Michelle (*Christine*), Vicki Michelle (*Betty*), Patricia Haines (*Sybil Waite*), Neil Hallett (*Gerald Amberley*), James Chase (*Peter*), Keith Buckley (*Johnny*), Paula Wright (*Mrs Wendell*), Christopher Strain (*milkman*), Esme Smythe (*horse rider*), Peter Halliday (*club manager*), Garth Watkins (*Colonel*), Prudence Drage and Maria Coyne (*coven members*)

CREDITS: *Director* Ray Austin, *Producer* Ralph Solomans [aka Kent Walton and Hazel Adair], *Editor* Philip Barnikel, *Photography* Gerald Moss, *Screenplay (based on his novel)* Klaus Vogel, *Music* Ted Dicks, *Song* 'You Go Your Way' *written by* Hazel Adair and Ted Dicks, *Performed by* Helen Downing
A UNIVISTA Production. Distributed by TIGON. Opened January 1972.

THE LOVE PILL

Great Britain / 1971 / 82 mins / cert 'X'

Against a backdrop of eerie music and blistering sunshine, the women of an idyllic country village, young and old alike, are being turned into sex maniacs. What's more, no child has been born in the community for six whole years. Curiouser and curiouser. At first glance this looks like a kinky case straight out of *The Avengers*' casebook. What would John Steed make of all this? An alien invasion? A plot to take over the world? A megalomaniac on the loose? Back in the unreal world of sex comedy the actual cause for this unusual phenomenon is far more predictable. It's all down to balls. Sugar balls to be pre-

Right: David Pugh finds himself irresistible to both sexes after popping *The Love Pill* (1971).

cise, being sold at the village shop. Old Fred Crudleigh, the shop proprietor, has formulated a minty sweet which not only converts the most frigid of women into raving nymphomaniacs, but also acts as the most effective contraceptive known to man, after just one suck! What a concept for the randy male. Unlimited sex with any woman, but without the nasty aftertaste of pregnancy. It's the perfect fantasy. But who could have thought of such a dastardly plot? Well, none other than John Lindsay, pornographer extraordinaire and the director of hundreds of hardcore 16mm quickies, now turning his hand to softer centres on the big screen.

Poor old Fred gets killed in a tragic shooting accident and his sugar-coated business is inherited by his gormless, socially inadequate son, Arnold (played by Welsh actor David Pugh). Looking like the bastard son of Cardew Robinson and Olive from *On the Buses*, Pugh wins the prize, in a tough field, for the most desperately unattractive male sex comedy lead of the 1970s. When his character manages to woo the pretty girl, it gives hope to twitching, squinting, pigeon-chested, chinless wonders everywhere. Perhaps it's just his money they're after, since Arnold hitches up with slimy wideboy Libido (Henry Woolf, better known to 1970s children as the host of *Words and Pictures*), who wants to market the love pills to a wider audience.

Hoping to attract women nationwide to this revolutionary discovery, he naturally chooses country bumpkin Arnold as the face of his TV campaign. The pills are an immediate success, with horny women mobbing chemists for extra supplies and pouncing on unsuspecting men in the street for instant relief. Lindsay, rather pleasurably, turns the sex formula on its head by hallucinating an alternative Soho where the overwhelming demand is for male prostitutes and big-boy strip shows. In one of the few refreshing ideas of the sex comedy era, Lindsay shows the dingy fleshpots of the West End packed to capacity with women in dirty raincoats baying for tumescent todgers and hairy bum-cheeks.

CAST: Toni Sinclair (*Sylvia*), Melinda Churcher (*Linda*), Henry Woolf (*Libido*), David Pugh (*Arnold*), Kenneth Waller (*Professor Edwards*), John Stratton (*newsreader*), Maureen Flanagan (*country blonde*), Jacqueline Andrews (*Lady Feellitt*), Tilly Tremaine (*Mary Tighthouse*)
CREDITS: *Director* Kenneth Turner, *Producers* John Lindsay and Laurence Barnett, *Editors* David Lane and Mike Campbell, *Photography* John Mackey, *Screenplay* John Lindsay and Laurence Barnett, *Music* Paris Rutherford
A MAYFAIR Production. Distributed by TARGET INTERNATIONAL. Opened February 1972.

SHE'LL FOLLOW YOU ANYWHERE

Great Britain / 1971 / 96 mins / cert 'X'

'The final question in our survey on sex in Britain today was answered by 8345 adult males and 6320 females. To the question "What do you do immediately following the sex act?", two per cent said they did it again. Four per cent said they had something to eat or drink. Five per cent said they lit a cigarette and seven per cent said they went to sleep and 82 per cent said they got up and went home!' So says the plummy psychiatrist in *She'll Follow You Anywhere*, a sex-obsessed comedy full of gags far older than that one and following the well-trodden aphrodisiac path of *The Love Pill*.

Keith Barron and Kenneth Cope, the latter fresh from *Randall and Hopkirk (Deceased)* and sporting the very worst handlebar moustache since Salvador Dalí, play a couple of useless research chemists who stumble across an invention which could revolutionise the sexual revolution. The two chumps work for their traditionalist boss Richard Vernon at 'Parker's

KEEPING THE BRITISH END UP

Left: Kenneth Cope and the Collinson twins feeling bashful in *She'll Follow You Anywhere* (1971).

Perfumes', formulating new after-shaves. It's not much of a life until one day, quite by accident, the fellas discover that pink liquid compound BK142 does something absolutely extraordinary – it can part a pretty girl's thighs within seconds and drive her insatiable for sex.

Cope sets about testing the formula by covering himself in the scent and getting chased round Piccadilly Circus by a Bunny Girl, much to the consternation of real-life passers-by. His escapades make the front page of the *Sun* and, realising they're sitting on a sexual goldmine, the lads set up in business together in a secret laboratory which they dub their 'nookie palace'. Dousing themselves in BK142, unsuspecting lovelies get one whiff of the potion and follow the guys anywhere. The unsuspecting women are brainwashed by the aroma into thinking that they're making love to a catalogue of glamorous male stars like Mick Jagger, Hugh Hefner, Englebert Humperdinck and George Best. Naturally, Cope gets so much sex that he suffers from an inflamed penis, so swollen and unsightly that his doctor chooses to handle it with a pair of metal tongs in one of the most tasteless scenes ever to come out of British cinema.

Cope and Barron mess about like adolescent, over-ripe schoolboys in a sweet factory (until they end up snogging each other in the film's creaky denouement), but they have peerless support from fractured-voiced Hilary Pritchard and wonderful old pro Richard Vernon at his mad, barking best. When Vernon unwittingly gets a splash of the stinky stuff, his formerly frigid secretary, Miss Cawfield (Penny Brahms), falls to her knees and gives him a blowie. Her fantasy man is HRH Prince Philip, who makes his first and last appearance (via ITN news footage) in a British sex comedy.

CAST: Keith Barron (*Alan Simpson*), Kenneth Cope (*Mike Carter*), Richard Vernon (*Andrew Coombes*), Hilary Pritchard (*Diane Simpson*), Philippa Gail (*Jane Carter*), Penny Brahms (*Miss Cawfield*), Sandra Bryant (*Sue*), Mary and Madeleine Collinson (*Janet and Martha*), Anna Matisse (*Erika*), Josie Baxter (*girl on train*), Andrea Allen (*girl with dog*), Linda Cunningham (*Betty*), Valerie Stanton (*Sally*), Sheila Ruskin (*Jackie*), Me Me Lay (*Bride*), Ray Barron (*Groom*), William Job (*Psychiatrist*), Michael Darbyshire (*Doctor*), Bob Todd (*car salesman*), Joyce Windsor (*cleaner*), Ron Pember (*Corporal*), Ken Keeling (*Jackie's dad*), Hilary Mason (*Jackie's mum*), Nancy Gabrielle and Beryl Cooke (*perfume testers*), Jennifer Watts (*Bunny Girl*)
CREDITS: *Director* David C Rea, *Producer* Peter Newbrook, *Editor* Maxine Julius, *Photography* Ted Moore, *Screenplay* David C Rea and Theo Martin, *Music* Gordon Rose, *Theme song* 'She'll Follow You Anywhere' performed by Davy Clinton
A GLENDALE Production. Distributed by SCOTIA-BARBER. Opened February 1972.

EROTIC FANTASIES

Great Britain / 1971 / 44 mins / cert 'X'

After the success of the feature *Games That Lovers Play*, it was surprising to see talented director Malcolm Leigh return to a short portmanteau piece for his next production. At least *Erotic Fantasies* delivers considerably more than its clichéd title and is certainly unique, mixing heavy breathing with a semi-documentary style. A virginal young woman is placed under hypnosis by a psychiatrist who asks her to recollect the moment of her sexual awakening and describe her fantasies in detail. Neither of the participants is actually shown. We only hear the voices of debonair Patrick Allen (the distinguished voice of TV's Barrett Homes adverts) and actress Susan Engel.

The woman's memories of puberty are accompanied by some beautiful shots of fish, birds and spiders while her amorous dreams (lesbian and heterosexual) consist of huge Oriental phalluses, erotic art and Hindu sculptures set to classical music. It's strange, considering the woman has no

Right: An American advert for *Fun and Games* (1971).

knowledge of sex, that she is able to conjure up such explicitly erotic images. It is only when she finally snaps out of her trance that she can finally imagine herself having a healthy love life with a man. The film did upset several critics who considered it beyond the pale. 'I have no doubt that many people would find the film objectionable,' wrote *CinemaTV Today* in January 1972, 'if they wandered in to see it without taking heed of the title.' Leigh's next few films turned their back on sexual matters and concentrated on his favoured subject – Eastern religions, traditions and folklore – in *The Sword and the Geisha* (1971), *Pillars of Islam* (1973) and *The Manifestations of Shiva* (1980).

CAST: Patrick Allen (voice) (*psychiatrist*), Susan Engel (voice) (*patient*)
CREDITS: *Director/Screenplay* Malcolm Leigh, *Producer* Malcolm Leigh, *Editor* Peter Austen-Hunt, *Photography* Harry Waxman, Ken Withers and Dick Bailey
A LEIGH FILMS Production. Distributed by TARGET INTERNATIONAL. Opened February 1972.

FUN AND GAMES
aka *Story of a Nympho* aka *1,000 Men and a Girl* aka *1,000 Convicts and a Woman*

Great Britain / 1971 / 92 mins / cert 'X'

This lusty prison drama directed by ex-stuntman Ray (*Virgin Witch*) Austin was subtitled *A Portrait of a Nymphomaniac* in Britain, which was pretty daring for 1971. The nymphomaniac in question is played by American actress Alexandra Hay. A native of Los Angeles, Hay moved to England in 1964 and had a very successful career as a fashion model before returning Stateside and getting snapped up by Columbia Pictures. Over time she cultivated her reputation as a sexpot by appearing in a succession of naked roles, including the controversial stage play *The Beard*, which was raided by police every night after being branded indecent. Hay was arrested 12 nights on the trot before the play was closed. Compared to that, returning to Britain in 1970 to start work on a saucy sex movie was a piece of cake.

Hay plays 17-year-old Angela Thorne, a curvaceous blonde minx who arrives at Greybourne, an experimental 'open prison', to join her stern father (super-smooth Neil Hallett), the prison governor, after spending four restrictive years in a Massachusetts girls' school. She's in trouble as soon as she sets foot in England, stripping off in the back of the car that has been sent to collect her, much to the arousal of her father's friend Paul (Sandor *Crossroads* Elès). Unfortunately, Governor Thorne has spent too long locked up with big, butch, tattooed felons and is unable to give his daughter the attention she deserves. Instead, she decides to play a naughty game by strutting up and down in front of the sexually frustrated prisoners,

KEEPING THE BRITISH END UP

wiggling her arse and unzipping her jeans to taunt them. Hardened criminals have never been so hard.

The stage set, petulant Angela commences an insatiable campaign of seduction among selected inmates and guards. She obtains sadistic pleasure in prick-teasing sex offenders and delinquents, but gets herself into a whole heap of trouble when she tangles with a violent sex murderer who attacks her. Fearing for her safety and blind to any notion that his daughter is a sneaky little hussy, the governor recommends that she returns to the USA. Wounded by her father's coldness, attention-seeking Angela smokes some hash, shags a warder and a black inmate and helps a couple of prisoners escape to France. However, it all goes tits up when pater catches her at the sea port and realises what a manipulative, promiscuous little strumpet she actually is.

Often the re-titling of films for an overseas market can be a bland exercise, but very occasionally the foreign title can blow the original into orbit. When American International Pictures got their hands on this film they just couldn't hold back. One can imagine AIP's head honcho Samuel Z Arkoff thought, 'Fun and Games is too bland – how about something a little more titillating? I mean, here's a nympho being slavered over by sex-starved inmates. How about *1000 Convicts and a Woman?*' It's a killer title which, although totally inaccurate, would have probably boosted the movie's chances here in Blighty. Naturally the budget didn't stretch to a thousand extras playing prisoners, it's more like 20, but hey, what the hell!

CAST: Alexandra Hay (*Angela Thorne*), Sandor Elès (*Paul Floret*), Harry Baird (*Carl*), Neil Hallett (*Governor of Greybourne*), Robert Brown (*Ralph*), Frederick Abbott (*Forbus*), David Bauer (*Gribney*), Peter J Elliott (*Matthews*), Tracey Reed (*Linda*), Stella Tanner (*Mrs Jackson*), Ronnie Brody (*inmate*)

CREDITS: *Director* Ray Austin, *Producer* Philip Krasne, *Editor* Phil Barnikel, *Photography* Gerald Moss, *Screenplay* Oscar Brodney, *Music* Peter J Elliott, *Theme song* 'Fun and Games' performed by Mike Felix
A MOTION PICTURES INTERNATIONAL Production. Distributed by SCOTIA-BARBER. Opened February 1972.

THE YES GIRLS
aka *Take Some Girls*

Great Britain / 1971 / 86 mins / cert 'X'

Teenage blonde Maria (Sue Bond) gives an old man a heart attack just by taking off her bra and is so traumatised by the experience (and who wouldn't be?) that she flees to London. There she meets up with a wannabe actress called Angela (Sally Muggeridge), who invites Maria to share a flat with her and Caron (Felicity Oliver). Realising the magical properties of her cleavage, she offers sexual favours to the creepy landlord when the girls fall behind with the rent.

Nobody can keep their mince pies off Maria and her picturesque bosom, and when Angela auditions for a role in a 'big budget movie in the south of France' produced by down-at-heel production company 'Ritzy Films', Maria gets the lead part instead. The other two girls cadge themselves supporting roles. Unfortunately, the promised all-expenses-paid cinematic extravaganza is actually a sexploitation movie entitled *Flesh in the Fields* being shot on location at the chilly seaside resort of Broadstairs. Instead of expanding their thespian talents, the three girls are just told to run around fields with no clothes on.

Lindsay Shonteff's satire on ultra-cheap sex movies is all the more convincing because *The Yes Girls* is itself an ultra-cheap sex movie. The filmmakers within the film are a grim bunch of Wardour Street stereotypes. The cigar-chewing producer is anxiously watching the pennies, the direc-

Left: Jack May wants to make Sue Bond a star in The Yes Girls *(1971).*

tor is attempting to be artistic and the cameraman just wants to do his close-up of Maria's breasts. Shonteff doesn't have to look very far for inspiration when the girls' nudie film finally has its 'world premiere' in London and it turns out to be a depressingly tatty affair. *The Yes Girls*, by contrast, ran for nearly a year in Soho between 1972 and 1973. Sue Bond, in her first and last leading role, is both charming and ballsy as the ever-ready strumpet who gets exploited by the 'X'-mongers.

CAST: Sue Bond (*Maria*), Sally Muggeridge (*Angela*), Felicity Oliver (*Caron*) with Jack Smethurst, Ray Chiarella and Jack May
CREDITS: *Director/Screenplay* Lindsay Shonteff, *Producer* Mike Elam [aka Lindsay Shonteff], *Editor* Jackson Bodell, *Photography* John C Taylor, *Music* Alan Gorrie
A LINDSAY SHONTEFF Production. Distributed by MIRACLE. Opened March 1972.

CLINIC XCLUSIVE
aka *Clinic Exclusive* aka *With These Hands*

Great Britain / 1971 / 91 mins / cert 'X'

A rather ingenious little sex drama with a wicked twist in the tail, set against the backdrop of a busy health clinic in London. The constant comings and goings, hysterical phone calls, double-dealings and wicked stereotypes of staff and customers alike give it an exaggerated soap opera flavour. This is a fair assessment since *Clinic Xclusive* was co-written and produced by *Crossroads* co-creator Hazel Adair, in conjunction with her business partner Kent Walton, using the pseudonym 'Elton Hawke'.

The proprietor of Adair's clinic is ruthless, hard-faced bitch Julie Mason (menacingly played by Georgina Ward), who as well as running the business also offers 'special treatments' to her wealthy clients. She is just as likely to massage the aching shoulder blades of an elderly gentleman as to let him have a crafty nibble on her nips. And it's not just sex which is on the health-club menu. Raven-haired Julie also administers spankings, lashings and birchings to those who pay through the nose. And pay they do, because she's also a ruthless blackmailer who extorts thousands of pounds out of her prominent customers to keep their kinks from going public.

Unfortunately, her wealthiest client is giving her big trouble. Middle-aged Belgravia widow Elsa Farson (Carmen Silvera) is a mentally unstable lesbian who craves the touch of a younger woman. Previously, Julie had played along for the money, but as the socialite's bank account has run dry she finds herself disgusted by their gay encounters. She has to scrub herself in the shower after each sapphic sex session. Having her sexual advances continually spurned, Elsa kills herself with an overdose of sleeping pills. But Julie gets a taste of her own medicine when a mysterious stranger arrives on the scene. Looking like the man from the Milk Tray ads, Lee Maitland (Alex Davidson) woos the cold fish and takes her to the cleaners to the tune of £50,000. It transpires it was all a vengeful plan, as Elsa was his late mother and he wanted payback. Reissued as *Sex Clinic* in May 1975, Adair's film is a competently produced scandal rag, made all the more shocking by the amount of saggy male flesh revealed by the establishment's clientele and mature actress Carmen Silvera going topless a decade before her leading role in TV sitcom '*Allo 'Allo*. She probably leaves this one off her CV.

CAST: Georgina Ward (*Julie Mason*), Alex Davidson (*Lee Maitland*), Polly Adams (*Ann*), Carmen Silvera (*Elsa Farson*), Mike Lewin (*Roger Dawes*), Vincent Ball (*Bernard Wilcox*), Basil Moss (*Philip Eveleigh*), Tony Wright (*Inspector*), Geoffrey Morris (*Roderick Clyde*), Maria Coyne (*Marilyn*), April Olrich (*Paula*), Windsor Davies (*Geoffrey Carter*), Peter Halliday (*Mr Fawcett*), Nicola Austine [uncredited] (*first girl in pool*)
CREDITS: *Director* Don Chaffey, *Producer* Elton Hawke [aka Hazel Adair and Kent Walton], *Editor* Mortimer Lodge [aka John Trumper], *Photography* Brendan Stafford, *Screenplay* Elton Hawke, *Music* Ted Dicks
A PYRAMID Production. Distributed by DOVERTON. Opened July 1972.

KAMA SUTRA RIDES AGAIN

Great Britain / 1971 / 9 mins / cert 'X'

For Bob Godfrey's second naughty cartoon (which he liked to call 'sextoons'), he again visits the secret sexual world of suburbia and peeks through the curtains at middle-aged married couple Stanley and Ethel. Fans of sex manuals like *Love Variations* (which gets a plug for author David Grant), the pair put the spice back into their humdrum lives by trying every sexual position currently in print. Demonstrating sex on a bicycle, against a coconut tree, on roller skates and sliding down a banister, Stanley explains these are nothing but 'simple variations' on intercourse. More advanced lovemaking involves 'the stapler', a terrifying mechanical invention which *hammers* poor red-faced Stanley straight into his waiting wife. As in *Henry Nine Till Five*, director Godfrey is resourceful as ever when thinking up new sexual pastimes. 'We went through the 57 varieties of sexual positions,' he laughs. 'I had all the animators acting out the positions on the floor, but we were seriously running out by the end!'

The film's scriptwriter said at the time that he thought the animators' enthusiasm for their saucy subject resulted in him being immortalised on screen. 'The hero Stanley was really the writer Stan Hayward,' chuckles Godfrey. 'He really looked like that with eyes on the side of his head and eyebrows that go straight across!' The film's nicest touch, however, is having Godfrey's previous sex-mad anti-hero, Henry, obliviously sailing past as Stanley and Ethel have naked sex on an escalator on the London Underground. Considering his heightened sexual awareness, it's funny to see Henry blissfully ignorant of this bit of public fornication. In 1971 *Kama Sutra Rides Again* was Oscar-nominated as the best cartoon short, but Godfrey nearly knew nothing about it. 'I had sold a print of *Kama Sutra* to a wealthy American who wanted to give it to his son for a wedding gift,' says Godfrey. 'Suddenly it was up for an Oscar. I knew nothing about it. It was very close but Richard Williams eventually got it for his *A Christmas Carol*.' Four years later Godfrey was finally able to claim an Oscar for his 1975 film *GREAT – Isambard Kingdom Brunel*.

CAST: Bob Godfrey (voice) (*Stanley*), L J Dickens (voice) (*Ethel*)
CREDITS: *Director* Bob Godfrey, *Producer* Ron Inkpen, *Photography* Paul Whibley, *Screenplay* Stan Hayward, *Music* John Hawksworth
A BOB GODFREY Production. Distributed by EMI. Opened October 1977.

1972

THE FOUR DIMENSIONS OF GRETA
aka *The Three Dimensions of Greta*

Great Britain / 1972 / 89 mins / cert 'X'

Australian actor Tristan Rogers plays Hans Weimar, a German journalist asked to investigate the strange disappearance of spunky 18-year-old Greta Gruber (*Mayfair* covergirl Leena Skoog), who has gone missing in London after starting work as an au pair. She has not been heard of for several months and the only leads Hans has are some old letters and a couple of black-and-white photographs. He uses Greta's unfortunate disappearance as an excuse to come to London to do an exposé on the 'serious social problem' of au pairs being taken advantage of by their cruel English employers. Packing wisely for his trip, he decides only to take a small suitcase containing two cartons of peppermints, a map of London and eight condoms.

His investigations take him to Greta's ex-boss in Golders Green, the bitter Mrs Marks (Carole Allen), who sums up au pairs quite succinctly: 'They're lazy and disobedient and most of them are thieves.' Hans learns Greta often frequented a fruity topless disco in the West End and hung around with a bunch of degenerate groupies before becoming an exotic dancer at a seedy strip joint. 'They are quite naked and they move on stage!' advertises droll strip-club doorman Bill Maynard when Rogers tries to gain entrance to the establishment. Sultry stripper Original Cyn (Minah Bird in her most substantial 1970s sex film role) finally points him in the direction of Greta's football player boyfriend (Robin Askwith), who in turn claims Greta has been abducted by sadistic East End gangland boss Carl Roberts (Alan Curtis).

As Hans interviews those who knew Greta during her stay in London, each interviewee has a different slant on the personality and morality of Greta. It's a devilishly simple idea, cleverly executed, in which several individuals can perceive the same person in totally different lights.

DOINGS

The funniest of the four stories comes from tarty German groupies Jane Cardew and Felicity Devonshire, who pretend that butter wouldn't melt in their innocent mouths and recall Greta as a money-grabbing sex-mad bitch with a liking for threesomes, which is exactly what they're like themselves. To put the cherry on the cake, each of the flashback scenes was filmed in luxurious 3D, a new idea for a British movie and for director Pete Walker.

'Pete had this idea to do a movie with some sexy 3D sequences in it,' recalled the film's associate producer, Ray Selfe. 'He asked me to find some cameras to do it, but it wasn't that easy. Eventually I tracked down a couple from a movie museum which had been used in the Festival of Britain short film from 1951. We cleaned up the equipment and did some practice shots to see if everything still worked. We didn't do anything rude though, it was just Pete holding a broom handle up to the camera lens and waggling it about a bit!' Broom handles are strangely absent from the finished film. Leena Skoog instead throws her underwear at the camera, wobbles her boobs and bends over to show the audience her bum. Most crudely, and cheekily, of all she pokes a banana towards the camera and seductively eats it. The cinema poster promised 'a girl in your lap', but the banana was extra.

The Four Dimensions of Greta has been awarded cult status as Britain's very first 3D feature film, but unfortunately it is lead actor Tristan Rogers (who subsequently became a daytime soap star in America in *General Hospital* and *The Bold and the Beautiful*) who rather lets the side down. His German accent is frankly terrible. At times he actually sounds more like Arthur Askey than a Continental stud. During one scene somebody actually asks him 'Are you German?', so unconvinced are they by his faltering monotone speech. Thankfully, the whole movie is played very tongue in cheek so perhaps the crappy accents don't detract from the fun too much.

Anyway, Rogers is not the film's main draw and neither, really, is Leena Skoog. Karen Boyes (now retired from acting and married to nobility) is the undoubted star of the film as Hans' beautiful English girlfriend Sue. Boyes is a stunning-looking woman who acts and strips with equal aplomb. Certainly one of *the* faces of the seventies, her incredible cheekbones, heavily powdered complexion and soft, sexy, educated voice makes her a force to be reckoned with. Her beauty positively radiates off the screen thanks to Peter Jessop's superb cinematography. *Greta* would come even more recommended and score higher on the 1970s sex-o-meter if it wasn't for Pete Walker's carefree handling of Sue's rape. Brutally attacked off screen, but with terrified screams and yells audible, she emerges from the experience totally untraumatised and without a blonde hair out of place.

The movie was immensely popular and, even though the 3D sequences added an extra £7,000 to the budget, it was money well spent since the result enjoyed a record-breaking run in London. Walker was so pleased that he went back to the much-publicised 'pleasures of the third dimension' for his next film, the saucy horror picture *The Flesh and Blood Show*. But *Greta* will always be remembered as the original and best. '*Greta* did a bomb when it opened at the Classic Cinema on Baker Street,' remembered Ray Selfe. 'They actually had to install a new entrance just to get people in because they were queuing from nine in the morning. It was madness, but that film was so hyped-up in the press. We got so much publicity because people were so desperate to see breasts in 3D. Those were the days!'

CAST: Tristan Rogers (*Hans Weimar*), Karen Boyes (*Sue*), Leena Skoog (*Greta Gruber*), Alan Curtis (*Carl Roberts*), Robin Askwith (*Roger Maitland*), Jane Cardew (*Kirsten*), Felicity Devonshire (*Serena*), Minah Bird (*Cynthia*), Bill Maynard (*Big Danny*), Martin Wyldeck (*Herr Schickler*), Godfrey Kenton (*Herr Gruber*), Pearl Hackney (*Frau Gruber*), Elizabeth Bradley (*Frau Schickler*), Erika Raffael (*Karen*), Carole Allen (*Mrs Marks*), Marion Grimaldi (*American*), Ken Hendel (*Percy*), John Clive (*Phil the Greek*), Nick Zaran (*Johnny Maltese*), Ralph Ball (*Fred Sharprock*), Ivor Salter (*hotel porter*), Richard O'Brien (*balding hippy*), Max Mason (*policeman*), Steve Patterson and Mike Britton (*hippies*), Pete Walker (*waiter*)
CREDITS: *Director/Producer* Pete Walker, *Associate Producer* Ray Selfe, *Editor* Matt McCarthy, *Photography* Peter Jessop, *Screenplay* Murray Smith, *Music* Harry South, *Theme song* 'Greta' performed by Huckleberry Flynn
A PETE WALKER Production. Distributed by HEMDALE. Opened May 1972.

AU PAIR GIRLS

Great Britain / 1972 / 86 mins / cert 'X'

'They come from here, they come from there. No matter where they may come from they're always welcome, everywhere... au pair!' run the lyrics of this film's rousing bossa nova theme tune. Really it matters not a jot where the au pair actually originates from. Only one thing is certain. She invariably ends up with her knickers round her ankles grossly misinterpreting her English employer's instructions.

Sitting in the director's chair for *Au Pair Girls* was veteran movie-maker Val Guest. Having been writing movies since the 1930s and directing them since the 1940s, and working with just about everybody including Will Hay, David Niven, Peter Sellers, Cliff Richard and the Crazy Gang, it was considered quite a shock to see Guest masterminding a more permissive movie. Guest was an innocent when it came to sex films. 'I had never seen any films of this type before,' he told an interviewer in *Photoplay* magazine in 1972, 'and, deciding I'd make one myself, I asked John Trevelyan, the ex-film censor, to recommend a good example.' Guest went to see a couple of Danish sex comedies which had been doing big box-office in the UK, *Seventeen* and *Bedroom Mazurka*, both starring Ole Søltoft, and took his inspiration from them, although he later admitted he could do 'a lot better'.

'I was shocked when they showed me the original script for *Au Pair Girls*,' Val told *Cinema X* magazine, 'and I said I'd only do it if I could rewrite it. Even then I wondered if I should.' It's not terribly surprising that Guest balked at the first draft screenplay since it was based on a raunchy story outline by self-appointed 'King of British Sex', David Grant, who had recently raised cinemagoers' temperatures with his naughty *Love Variations*. After extensive rewrites by Guest, the movie finally went before the cameras in spring 1972. The film follows 24 chaotic hours in the lives of four sexy au pair girls who arrive in London from abroad. There's Swedish Anita (Astrid Frank), Danish Randi (Gabrielle Drake), German Christa (Nancie Wait) and Nan Lee (Me Me Lay) from China. At the Overseas Employment Agency all the young ladies are assigned their new placements and immediately get to work. But as the movie's catch-line says: 'They came to make the beds... and made everything!'

Busty Gabrielle Drake – who had just starred in Derek Ford's *Suburban Wives* and was saddled with the nickname 'Wotta Pair' on the set of this – is the most alluring of the four au pairs. Driving to her new place of work with eager young lech Richard O'Sullivan, Randi's car gets a puncture and the couple are forced into taking refuge in a barn, which, as anticipated, leads to a tumble in the hayloft and a poke with a pitchfork. The long-legged brunette provides the most enduring image in the whole movie when she has a ducking in a water trough and emerges in her clinging wet dress, nipples ahoy! RADA-trained Gabrielle (an ex-au pair herself) is a stunner, but it is German-born Astrid Frank who lassoes most of the laughs. A hyperactive chatterbox with no inhibitions and an obsession with colour TV, Astrid's squeaky-voiced innocent has little or no grasp of the English language. 'In the evening I play with myself,' she answers blithely when asked if she can occupy her spare time.

The film is a funky, swinging feast of fun, which pushed the limits of on-screen nudity at the time and shows London at its sexy, wiggling, mini-skirted best. The scenes at 'Groovers' nightclub, where the rum and cokes flow like water, and in the happening boutiques of the King's Road Chelsea, are wonderful. So it is rather regrettable that the film's director has attempted to blot the memory of *Au Pair Girls* from his mind. In all his interviews publicising *Au Pair Girls* Guest stressed, almost to the point of tedium, that his film was 'art' not pornography. Desperate to distance himself from 'dirty' movies, he repeatedly claimed that his film was good clean fun and *not* perverted. 'The outcry at the moment is about sex. Too much sex,' he told *Cinema X* in 1972. 'I think it depends entirely on how sex is presented. In *Au Pair Girls*, it's all fun, it's bubble! There is absolutely no violence or kinks. There are no lesbians, no queers and no whips. Nothing like that at all.'

Unwilling 'to pop up from the same trap twice', Guest said he'd never direct a sex comedy again. Yet two years later he helmed one of the biggest movies of his long career, *Confessions of a Window Cleaner*. Thereafter, however, he's been rather reluctant to talk about his brief dalliance with sex films, admitting that he would rather be remembered for his 'cleaner' pictures like *Ask a Policeman* or *The Day the Earth Caught Fire*.

CAST: Gabrielle Drake (*Randi Lindstrom*), Astrid Frank (*Anita Sector*), Nancie Wait (*Christa Geisler*), Me Me Lay (*Nan Lee*), Richard O'Sullivan (*Stephen Wainwright*), John Le Mesurier (*Mr Wainwright*), Johnny Briggs (*Malcolm*), Geoffrey Bayldon (*Mr Howard*), Daphne Anderson (*Mrs Howard*), Rosalie Crutchley (*Lady Tryke*), Julian Barnes (*Rupert*), Lyn Yeldham (*Carole Fairfax*), Marianne Stone (*Mrs Fairfax*), Ferdy Mayne (*Sheik El Abab*), Steve Patterson (*Ricky Strange*), John Standing (*Buster*), Harold Bennett (*Lord Tryke*), Norman Chappell (*shoe salesman*), Milton Reid (*guard*), Christine Donna (*Karen*), Joyce Heron (*Mrs Stevenson*), Trevor Bannister (*photographer*), Roger Avon (*Rathbone*)
CREDITS: *Director* Val Guest, *Producer* Guido Coen, *Editor* John Colville, *Photography* John Wilcox, *Screenplay* Val Guest and David Adnopoz *based on a story by* David Grant, *Music* Roger Webb
A KENNETH SHIPMAN Production. Distributed by LMG. Opened September 1972.

THE LOVE BOX

aka *Looking for Love* aka *The Sex Box*

Great Britain / 1972 / 89 mins / cert 'X'

'Open up your love box, please don't lock me out. I want to eat you like a plate of sauerkraut. I'm gonna open up your love box and take what you have. I'm gonna die unless I get into your love box!' say the sexually unambiguous lyrics to the theme song of 1972's *The Love Box*. If you didn't know what the film was about before, you definitely did after hearing that naughty little ditty.

The movie is about a personal column published in fictional London magazine 'This is Your Week', edited by Tris Patterson (Chris Williams), who spends more time feverishly poring over the contact ads and fantasising about what the advertisers are like than actually doing any work. 'It was an idea I'd had about people responding to personal ads,' says the movie's producer Tudor Gates. 'I wanted to call it *Looking for Love*, because I thought that was far more relevant, but the distributors wanted a sexier angle. I hoped to make an intellectual erotic movie, but of course they weren't interested. We shot it over an absolutely punishing two-week schedule doing a scene a day and we just put lots of sex in it, I suppose.'

And an unashamed sex film it certainly is, with a series of imagined (and mainly nude) happenings occurring in the hotbeds of London's suburbia. The individual stories are illustrated in a series of comedy vignettes very much in the style of Benny Hill, but going for the naked jugular in much the same way as 1969's *The Wife Swappers* did. Among other things, we have frustrated housewives (led by Jane Cardew), stuck at home eating French fancies, who decide to hire a male prostitute to liven up their coffee mornings. An ancient old man answers an advert for a busty blonde masseuse and tells her 'Some of my limbs I haven't used for years' – but she soon remedies that. A pompous, fat idiot is tricked into appearing in a blue movie and a virgin schoolboy orders a service from an older woman (Maggie Wright) but is so inexperienced he even has to have kissing explained to him.

In addition there's an orgy in a grotty flat in Kilburn involving enormous grilled sausages and some good old wife-swapping where the women dress up in pantomime costumes. Rather oddly, the film eventually careers into a drippy hippy fantasy, where any notion of lasciviousness is replaced with carefree warmth and affection. The magazine's editor is so thrilled with the way the new-style personal ads have revitalised his publication that he dreams of a sexual utopia where men and women run about naked through

KEEPING THE BRITISH END UP

flower beds, making love and receiving diplomas 'in the art of love'.

The Love Box was directed, produced and scripted by the elusive twosome Billy and Teddy White, who didn't really exist. They were nothing more than pseudonyms for American producer Wilbur Stark (father of Koo) and English playwright Tudor Gates. 'Wilbur decided on the name Billy White early on and so I went with Teddy White. It was a bit of a joke,' says Gates. 'I suppose we used different names just in case the film flopped. There was every chance that the film could come out looking awful, but thankfully it did very well at the box-office. It was a tremendous hit.'

CAST: Chris Williams (*Trish Patterson*), Maureen Flanagan (*Helen*), Alison King (*Margery Nicholls*), Simon Legree (*Rod*), Paul Aston (*Peter*), Maggie Wright (*Mrs Simpson*), Christine Bradwell (*Miss Harvey*), John Mattocks (*Tom Cat*), Lizbeth Lindeborg (*Blonde Kitten*), Minerva Smith (*Brunette Kitten*), Jane Cardew (*Fran*), Julia Breck (*Doreen*), Lita Petrou (*Hilda*), Rose Burton (*Shirley*), Anthony Bailey (*male prostitute*), Leonore Little (*stripper*), Basil Clarke (*old man*), Elaine Baillie (*masseuse*), Raymond Young (*Mr Middleton*), Jennifer Guy (*foreign student*), Ann Henning (*Gerda*), Peter Burton (*Charles Lambert*), Charlie Miller (*Harry*), Marianne Morris (*Janet*), Freddie Earle (*Bill*), Cheryl Gilham (*Sally*), Dick Hayden (*Johnny*), Emmett Hennessey (*Martin*), Trudi Blue (*Sandra*), Georgina Symonds-Rose (*Kit*), Joan Alcorn (*Kathy*), Craig Israel (*Texan*), Dave Carter (*Kathy's husband*), Minah Bird (*black girl*), Vivienne (*Chinese girl*), Kerima (*Indian girl*), Pauline Anderson (*Eskimo*), Nicola Austine, Rena Brown, Sue Bowen, Jeanette Marsden and Liz Carlson (*girls*)

CREDITS: *Directors/Producers/Screenplay* Teddy and Billy White [aka Tudor Gates and Wilbur Stark], *Editor* Rex Graves, *Photography* Grenville Middleton, *Music* Mike Vickers

A SHORT CIRCUIT Production. Distributed by EAGLE. Opened October 1972.

SEX AND THE OTHER WOMAN
aka *The Other Woman*

Great Britain / 1972 / 88 mins / cert 'X'

Stanley Long dips his hand into another takeaway party bag of sexual misdemeanours, this time with a theme of adultery or, to be more specific, the power of women to reduce men to jelly and to prove irrevocably that they are the not the weaker sex. Genial uncle, Richard Wattis, presents four dramatised case studies with his usual sardonic wit. Looking every inch the figure of authority behind his desk, Wattis delivers his lines with piquant dryness. 'Let us not forget,' he says, 'that nature has given most of the powers of attraction to women. They provide the attraction. Men are purely the iron filings.'

The 'other women' of the title are portrayed as over-the-top seductresses and manipulating money-hungry bitches, stirring up testosterone wherever they go and squeezing poor defenceless husbands into servile submission. Maggie Wright is an evil gold-digger who proudly shows off her erect nips under her sports bra and spoons out her boobs during a flight on a private jet, causing her married lover to go into temporary free-fall. Jane Cardew is the big-busted office tease who hunts out otherwise-attached men and seduces them in the stationery cupboard. And Felicity Devonshire plays a precocious schoolgirl spread-eagled on a sheepskin rug for the delectation of her best friend's middle-aged Brylcreemed father, who fancies himself as a bit of a Lothario. Performing with some vigour, the

Left: Jane Cardew and Paul Greenwood have fun in the office in *Sex and the Other Woman* (1972).

female cast go through the sex comedy motions without a care and don't bat an eyelid when stripping off. As an extremely camp photographer comments to one of his models part way through the proceedings: 'Right, tits out, fannies up, tums in. You're supposed to look glamorous, you know!'

However, the film ends on a more upbeat note for downtrodden men who are martyrs to their raging hormones. Every British sex film fan's fantasy comes true when a cheeky jack-the-lad has his conniving mistress move into the family home so his downtrodden wife can have a bit of rumpy-pumpy too. 'Take a tip from me, fellas,' he smirks. 'If you've got a problem with the other woman, try introducing her to the wife. You never know, you might have my luck!'

CAST: Richard Wattis (*presenter*), Bartlett Mullins (*Henry*), PeggyAnn Clifford (*Henry's wife*), Maggie Wright (*Liz*), Anthony Bailey (*Reggie*), Margaret Burton (*Flora*), Gordon Gale (*Arnold*), Barbara Wendy (*model*), Jane Cardew (*Lisa Biggs*), Gillian Brown (*Sue*), Anthony Howard (*MD*), Stacy Davies (*Kershaw*), Raymond Young (*Guy Parkinson*), Felicity Devonshire (*Sarah*), Louise Rush (*Louise*), Mary Barclay (*Cynthia*), Louise Pajo (*Shirley*), Max Mason (*Ted*), Barbara Meale (*Barbara*), Stella Tanner (*mother-in-law*), Paul Greenwood [uncredited] (*Chris*)

CREDITS: *Director/Producer* Stanley Long, *Photography* Michael Boultbee, *Screenplay* Adrian Reid, *Music* De Wolfe, *Songs performed by* Jacky Taylor
A SALON Production. Distributed by EAGLE. Opened December 1972.

COMMUTER HUSBANDS
aka *Sex Games*

Great Britain / 1972 / 85 mins / cert 'X'

Six more implausible stories about the battle of the sexes in a partial sequel to *Suburban Wives*. Director Derek Ford dispenses with the pseudo-documentary feel for this one in favour of a more straightforward porn portmanteau introduced by 1970s starlet Gabrielle Drake. The busty actress – an ex-player for Birmingham Repertory Company and later the boss of TV's *Crossroads* motel – had proffered a glimpse of nipple in *There's a Girl in My Soup* and *Connecting Rooms*, but remained resolutely covered up in silk blouse and mini-skirt in *Suburban Wives*, despite being heavily promoted as that film's star. In this film she reveals only marginally more curves, although she did the full monty for Val Guest in *Au Pair Girls*. Looking gorgeous with kholed eyes, beehive hairdo and clinging outfits, she presents the half-dozen reports from the Penthouse Club in London with a theme of man as 'the most dangerous animal of them all'.

However, despite her anthropological generalisations purporting to prove that the human male is a 'predatory hunter', the vignettes on display do not support the wonky theory one bit. Instead, men are presented as sad victims of circumstance and social inadequates: a genteel, failed adulterer who gets caught out by his own equally deceitful wife; a cheap, randy plumber desperate to see some breasts; a bowler-hatted fantasist with a thing for motorbikes; a pitiful middle-aged voyeur; a nervous, clumsy innocent abroad and a dispiriting square.

The blandness of the male characters is slightly off-set by lively performances from the aforementioned Drake as well as Robin Bailey, Heather Chasen and the naked loveliness of model Nicola Austine. Ford has also made a concerted effort to squeeze in more humour and visual gags. One couple are busy eating and drinking while they copulate for 18 solid hours, and the stupid plumber's filthy dungarees are admired by a dizzy hippy who proclaims 'Man, where did you get the wild gear? So soiled and worn!' Sending up sex films themselves, Claire Gordon plays porno queen Carla Berlin, the star of such classics as *The Private Lives of King Kong* and *Sex Raiders from Outer Space*. There's plenty of sex too, including some location footage filmed in the red light district of Amsterdam and an almost avant-garde orgy sequence with leathered-up bikers. Notable as the first of Ford's movies to be shot in a hardcore version for foreign markets, *Commuter Husbands* also wins the prize for the most unsexy, unappealing, turn-off title of the 1970s. Realising their folly, the distributors rapidly changed it to the more generic *Sex Games*.

CAST: Gabrielle Drake (*Carol Appleby*), Robin Bailey (*Dennis*), Jane Cardew (*Dennis' secretary*), Heather Chasen (*Dennis' wife*), Dick Hayden (*Arthur Benbow*), Claire Gordon

KEEPING THE BRITISH END UP

(Carla Berlin), Dervis Ward (Arnold), Dorothea Phillips (Arnold's wife), Brenda Peters (Lola), Mike Britton (Peter Harris), Nicola Austine (Dream Girl), Tim Parks (Raymond Hardacre), Yocki Rhodes (Trudi), Robin Culver (John Appleby), George Selway (Mr Charlesworth), John Barcroft (Mario Abrizzi), Valerie Stanton (Marion), Tara Lynn [uncredited] (second Dream Girl)
CREDITS: Director Derek Ford, Producer Morton M Lewis, Editor Roy Deverell, Photography Roy Poynter and Morton M Lewis, Screenplay Derek Ford, Music Terry Warr, Song 'Man Is a Hunter' performed by Samantha Jones
A BLACKWATER FILMS Production. Distributed by CHILTON. Opened March 1973.

LAYOUT FOR 5 MODELS

Great Britain / 1972 / 90 mins / cert 'X'

Little-known soft-porn portmanteau about the lives and loves of five pleasure-seeking poppets. Hedger Wallace plays the editor-in-chief of an erotic magazine who listens attentively to wanton tales of lust from his photographic models. Sexy Stephanie (Erica Gene) wants to be photographed *in flagrante* with her flamboyant hairdresser; Minah Bird participates in an orgy with hippy rock group 9.30 Fly; Elizabeth, a frumpy Swiss au pair girl (played by *Permissive*'s Maggie Stride), proves she's no square in bed when she sleeps with a pervy photographer and his missus; blonde Joanna (Vicki Hodge) endures having her nipples made erect for a magazine layout but dislikes posing nude, and lastly, Monique (Hilary Lebow) begins researching a saucy novel by going undercover at a strip joint. She enjoys stripping so much that she dispenses with the book and makes performing her career. *Layout for 5 Models* marked the sex film débuts of 1970s studs Alan Lake and Mark Jones.

CAST: Hedger Wallace (*magazine editor*), Tim Pearce (*art director*), Alan Lake (*Andy*), Erica Gene (*Stephanie*), Simon Kent (*Allesandro*), Minah Bird (*Maria*), Louisa Livingstone and Carol Catkin (*dancers*), Maggie Stride (*Elizabeth*), Chris Williams (*Tony*), Sally Faulkner (*Kitty*), Vicki Hodge (*Joanna*), Gil

Left: Glamorous Gabrielle Drake in *Commuter Husbands* (1972).

Barber (*Derek*), John André (*George*), Hilary Lebow (*Monique*), Mark Jones (*David*), Leo Kharibian (*Mr Quinto*), 9.30 Fly (*Pop Group*) **CREDITS:** *Director* John Gaudioz, *Producer* Sergei Seiffe, *Editor* Dick Mason, *Photography* Vernon Layton, *Screenplay* Peter Stafford and John Stewart, *Music* Hal Shaper A PLAYGIRL Production. Distributed by AMANDA. Opened November 1973.

SINDERELLA

Great Britain / 1972 / 5 mins / cert 'X'

If cinemagoers were shocked by Bob Godfrey's sexy little cartoon fantasies like *Henry Nine Till Five* then they certainly weren't going to relish David Grant's first animated free-for-all, based on an innocent children's fairy-tale about a sweet young girl and her glass slipper. Grant's twisted version was called, rather obviously, *Sinderella*.

Beautiful Sinderella stumbles across a cock-shaped magic toadstool in the forest and gives it a vigorous rub. Lo and behold her fairy godmother arrives out of thin air and speeds her off to meet Prince Charming at the grand ball. She falls in love with the Prince and they enjoy a bit of nookie, but on the stroke of midnight she is forced to flee, leaving the Prince only her skimpy brassière with which to identify her. He soon tracks down her house and Sindy's horrendously ugly sisters ungraciously try the bra on for size before the Prince is successfully reunited with her lover. The ugly sisters, feel-ing pretty pissed off that they didn't get any sex, are then raped by the Three Bears who burst into the house.

Mmm, it's not the version most of us are familiar with and the Establishment took particular umbrage. Refused a certificate by the BBFC, it was declared obscene at Bow Street Magistrates' Court and the High Court of Appeal in 1973, before Grant re-submitted it for an 'X' certificate after snipping 25 seconds of 'bear rape' and erections. Naturally, Grant was absolutely thrilled with the bad publicity. He was able to proudly exhibit the film at his cinemas as the 'first obscene cartoon made in Britain'.

Animated graphically with cut-out images more akin to Terry Gilliam's *Monty Python* inserts or kiddie's TV favourite *Captain Pugwash*, *Sinderella* was filmed entirely anonymously. The animator's name was known by most of Wardour Street, but few actually had much idea who he was. He was Marcus Parker-Rhodes, a recently graduated art student. 'He was just out of art school and I think he was probably conned into making the film,' says Bob Godfrey. 'Nobody put their names to it. It was so badly made. Badly everything. Just rubbish!'

Parker-Rhodes is reluctant to talk about the film today, which is fair enough. He has carved out a successful career for himself as the animator of schools programmes on TV as well as working for both his heroes, Terry Gilliam and Bob Godfrey. *Sinderella* is a film he would probably prefer to forget, but not half as much as its cartoon cousin, *Snow White and the Seven Perverts* [qv], which fared even less well at the hands of British law.

CREDITS: *Director* Marcus Parker-Rhodes [uncredited], *Producer* Ron Inkpen [uncredited], *Executive Producer/Screenplay* David Grant An OPPIDAN Production. Distributed by BORDER. Opened November 1973.

1973

TIFFANY JONES

Great Britain / 1973 / 90 mins / cert 'X'

Pete Walker's sex comedy follow-up to *The Four Dimensions of Greta* is a major disappointment. No-one can doubt Walker's directorial talents, but he totally loses the plot here in an excruciatingly unfunny and irksome production. Based on a popular newspaper comic strip which originally appeared in the *Daily Sketch*, Miss Tiffany Jones is a beautiful, dizzy model who continually finds herself in one dastardly predicament after another, usually involving the loss of her clothes. Real-life model-turned-actress Anouska Hempel takes the role of Tiffany, playing the winsome wide-eyed card with all her might but not engaging the audience in the least. New Zealander Hempel – now Lady Weinberg and retired from acting – is really rather pretty but completely lacks charisma or sex appeal. She also starred

89

KEEPING THE BRITISH END UP

in 1973 in Russ Meyer's *Blacksnake* (released in the UK as *Slaves*), and Meyer was so disappointed that she didn't match up to his mammary specifications that he edited footage of larger breasts into her nude scenes.

In *Tiffany Jones* Hempel doesn't meet such an ignominious fate. Instead, she gets herself mixed up with some evil Eastern Bloc-ers led by ruthless dictator President Jabal (Eric Pohlmann) and attempts to help a murdered king's son overthrow the heartless regime which has taken over his country. Along the way her top comes off rather a lot. Johnny Foreigner is always good for a laugh and a variety of English performers try their best to sound menacing and European (Liverpudlian actor Geoffrey Hughes' accent has to be heard to be believed). The only vaguely amusing bit occurs when Tiffany is kidnapped and tortured by a bunch of Marxist chefs who tie her to their kitchen table and threaten her with soup, dishcloths and spaghetti. 'You are going to tell us everything,' says their villainous ringleader. 'If you refuse we will ladle the *consommé Julien* onto those naked shoulders of yours, one spoonful at a time.'

CAST: Anouska Hempel (*Tiffany Jones*), Ray Brooks (*Guy*), Susan Sheers (*Jo*), Damien Thomas (*Salvador*), Eric Pohlmann (*President Jabal*), Richard Marner (*Vorjack*), Ivor Salter (*Karatik*), Lynda Baron (*Anna Karekin*), Martin Benson (*Petcek*), Alan Curtis (*Marocek*), John Clive (*Stefan*), Geoffrey Hughes (*George*), Bill Kerr (*Morton*), Martin Wyldeck (*Brodsky*), Nick Zaran (*Anton*), Walter Randall (*Jan*), Kim Alexander (*Harry Wheeler*), Sam Kelly (*film director*), Rose Hill and Tony Simpson (*couple in Gullivers*), Pearl Hackney (*demonstrating woman*), David Hamilton (*TV presenter*)

CREDITS: Director/Producer Pete Walker, Editor Alan Brett, Photography Peter Jessop, Screenplay Alfred Shaughnessy *based on the comic strip by* Pat Tourret and Jenny Butterworth, Music Cyril Ornadel
A PETE WALKER Production. Distributed by HEMDALE. Opened April 1973.

THE SEX VICTIMS

Great Britain / 1973 / 40 mins / cert 'X'

A long-unseen spooky ghost story-cum-sex film. A lorry driver named Jack (Ben Howard) is driving along a quiet road winding its way through a forest when he is startled by a beautiful girl (Jane Cardew, recently seen in *The Four Dimensions of Greta*), riding naked on a horse. Jack is haunted by the girl's image but is unable to find her when he returns to the spot the following day. After a dalliance with lusty stable lass Felicity Devonshire at a local riding school, which he has joined in the vain hope of tracking the mysterious girl, he eventually finds her, but only after a lengthy chase across country. They make love and the mysterious girl promises to meet up with him again, but on one condition: that he brings with him his colleague George, who until recently has always driven the forest route.

Jack and the reluctant George return to the woodlands but are ambushed by police, who insist that the girl was raped and murdered there several weeks earlier. George confesses to the murder, but innocent Jack is arrested as an accomplice, unable to convince the authorities that a ghostly apparition has tricked him. *The Sex Victims* is director Derek Robbins' first movie and he displays a deft touch in handling a daytime ghost story with all the sexual trimmings. The film is noteworthy for featuring a young Alun Armstrong in the days before he starred in popular TV shows like *Our Friends in the North* and *Oliver Twist*.

CAST: Ben Howard (*Jack Piper*), Alun Armstrong (*George*), Jane Cardew (*naked girl*), Felicity Devonshire (*stable lass*)
CREDITS: Director/Producer/Screenplay Derek Robbins, Editor Peter Austen-Hunt
A BORDER Production. Distributed by BORDER. Opened April 1973.

DOINGS

Left: High-speed sexual acrobatics from David Warbeck and Linda Coombes in Martin Campbell's The Sex Thief *(1973).*

THE SEX THIEF

aka *Her Family Jewels* aka *Handful of Diamonds*

Great Britain / 1973 / 89 mins / cert 'X'

'I'd seen a lot of British sex films and I thought they were a bit crap, frankly,' admits *Sex Thief* producer Tudor Gates. 'With this film we were attempting to make a more literal sex film with a good story. We filmed it in a fortnight and it cost the princely sum of £40,000, but we'd never have had the opportunity to make it unless it was sexy. I still wanted to make a decent film with a funny script, a story and attention to detail and I really think we achieved that.'

Thanks to a sharp, snappy script from actor-director-writer Michael Armstrong (who also stars), *The Sex Thief* is helped by some surprisingly smooth direction from Martin Campbell. Often quoted as Campbell's début, *The Sex Thief* was actually his second bite of the sex comedy cherry. 'When I co-directed *The Love Box* in 1972 Martin was my assistant and from my point of view he more or less directed my bits,' confesses Gates. 'He had an excellent talent for filmmaking. That's why I was desperate for him to do this film too.'

Dishy David Warbeck stars as a plummy-voiced paperback writer who supplements his royalties by donning a black mask and working nights as a cat burglar. However, he's also prone to leaving a pearl necklace as his calling card since all the wealthy women he robs demand sex from him. Indeed, his 'victims' are so keen for their jewellery boxes to be raided again that they deliberately feed the police false descriptions of what their assailant looks like. As the coppers (Armstrong and Terence Edmond) keep coming up against brick walls in their investigations, Armstrong turns his attention to his collection of confiscated pornography. His admiration for Danish porn films knows no bounds: 'They give minge a bit of class, don't they?'

Even starchy insurance investigator Diane Keen (years before she became the TV face of Nescafé coffee) falls under the sex thief's wicked spell. In the film's most original sequence, Warbeck seduces rich Lady Prescott while her husband is out watching the wrestling. As he beds her, their forceful lovemaking is intercut with legendary grappler Big Daddy doing his famous 'splashdown' on the canvas. The BBFC were not amused and asked for the sequence to be trimmed.

The film was released in America in January 1976 under the name *Her Family Jewels*, with added hardcore footage, mainly explicit genital close-ups, cut into the narrative to give the impression that the likes of Warbeck and Keen (though mercifully not Big Daddy) were really doing the squirt and squeeze.

CAST: David Warbeck (*Grant Henry*), Diane Keen (*Judy Marvin*), Terence Edmond (*Inspector Robert Smith*), Michael Armstrong (*Sergeant Plinth*), Christopher Neil (*Guy Hammond*), Linda Coombes (*Jezebel Lorraine*), Jenny Westbrook (*Emily Barrow*), Gerald Taylor (*Mr Barrow*), Harvey Hall (*Jacobi*), Gloria Walker (*Angie*), Eric Deacon (*Crabshaw*), Christopher Mitchell (*Ian Wensleydale*), Christopher Biggins (*Lord 'Porky' Prescott*), Susan Glanville (*Lady Florinda Prescott*), David Landor (*Guido*), Neville Barber (*auctioneer*), Val Penny (*stripper*), Veronica Doran (*traffic warden*), Dave Carter (*jeweller*), James Aubrey and David Pugh (*reporters*), Derek Martin (*strip club doorman*), Big Daddy [aka Shirley Crabtree] [uncredited] (*wrestler*)

CREDITS: *Director* Martin Campbell, *Producers* Michael Style and Teddy White [aka Tudor Gates], *Editor* Rex Graves [aka Peter Musgrave], *Photography* Grenville Middleton, *Screenplay* Edward Hyde [aka Michael Armstrong and Tudor Gates], *Music* Mike Vickers

An OCARINA-DRUMBEAT-RAINBOW Production. Distributed by LMG. Opened July 1973.

THE PORNBROKERS

Great Britain / 1973 / 86 mins / cert 'X' (London only)

The Pornbrokers was John Lindsay's response to Lord Longford's pious 1972 book *Pornography: The Longford Report*, in which he concluded that pornographers in Britain were the lowest of the low. 'Lord Longford knows nothing about pornography,' scoffed Lindsay. By the early 1970s Lindsay was the most prolific and high-profile blue filmmaker in the country, and in *The Pornbrokers* he stakes out his argument effectively enough. In the opening titles he displays photos of children in South Vietnam suffering from the effects of napalm gas, political prisoners in China facing the firing squad and a man being beheaded in the Middle East. This is the 'real' pornography, he argues.

Lindsay enjoyed goading the authorities and never once sought anonymity. In *The Pornbrokers* he lays himself bare like never before, and not always in a flattering light. The voice-over claims that 'Everything we show in this film is fact,' but there is every indication that most of it is cleverly stage-managed. Britain's king of the triple-'X' is shown in the stark white offices of his Berwick Street HQ, above his blue cinema club. A nervous, sullen 17-year-old school-leaver, Maureen O'Malley, arrives for an interview. Lindsay asks her to do a colour test and she happily poses on a red sheepskin rug, legs akimbo, while he snaps away. The test turns into a full-blown photo session and Lindsay smoothes over any worries she might have. 'Men are such suckers when it comes to pretty birdies. They take one look and their brains go bang,' he says, spreading it on thick and pretending to be ignorant about the business he has made his own.

'Naïve' Maureen nods appreciatively until Lindsay fires his exocet: magazine work is a 'bit slack' at the moment, apparently. 'Have you ever heard of a Swedish movie?' he asks. She seems a little unsure, but Lindsay perseveres. He's won seven international awards, the guys he uses are always handsome young studs and he often films in Trinidad. Maureen is immediately hooked. 'I think men are nutters, you know,' says Lindsay, turning on the charm. 'Because obviously if you want a girl why not have one for real? Why look at it on film?' he adds, quite blatantly missing the whole point of pornography. 'You know it's crazy, but anyway they do and that's what makes the money, so who am I to question it?'

The voyeuristic viewer is then taken on a journey to see Lindsay's latest epic, *Wet Dream*, being filmed in a 'luxury penthouse'. It's Maureen's first hardcore movie and she meets her co-stars, three guys and two girls. Lindsay makes much of the fact that his models are just 'ordinary' people – secretaries, students and housewives – and nobody is ever coerced into having sex on camera. After the shoot, he interviews his young actors to find out what motivates them. Irish Pauline is rebelling against her strict Catholic upbringing, bisexual Kevin hopes it will break him into the world of acting and good-looking John just enjoys the sex and the money, although he draws the line at some things. ('I wouldn't do a scene with a guy,' he explains.) As for Maureen, it's worth noting that she would later court controversy when persuaded to change her name to 'Mary Whitehouse' and pose in hundreds of explicit photo shoots, so that cheeky publisher David Sullivan could make a few cheap shots at Britain's foremost moral campaigner through his top-shelf magazines.

Lindsay next takes us around Europe. In Amsterdam we meet Joop Wilhelmus, a treacle-haired troglodyte whose porno magazine *Chick* is the best-selling adult publication in the Netherlands. Tubby Joop is portrayed as a family man, with a wife and nine-year-old daughter, although, tellingly, his involvement in child pornography is not touched upon. In Stockholm Lindsay visits Ulrich Geismar at his notorious sex club Chat Noir, where live bed shows are *de rigueur*, and then we meet Berthe Milton, who has built his empire on the most famous porn label of all, Private. Finally, in Copenhagen ('the porn capital of the world'), Lindsay interviews the legendary Lasse Braun, the world's single biggest 'X'-rated film producer who sells an incredible – by today's standards – 100,000 copies of each of his 16mm movies.

By contemporary standards *The Pornbrokers* contains some very explicit material. Aside from the 'live' footage,

Left: John Lindsay's hardcore hopefuls in *The Pornbrokers* (1973).

Lindsay also includes images taken straight from the pages of hardcore magazines: erections, ejaculation, oral sex and anal intercourse. Not surprisingly, the film was refused a certificate by the BBFC and chief censor Stephen Murphy had a major run-in with Lindsay over the movie. 'He called me a liar,' Lindsay claimed in a 1976 *Penthouse* interview. 'Murphy wouldn't believe that I could get ordinary girls to do what they did in that film. According to him it was all faked. My reply was to ask him if he had a daughter. Yes, he had, he said. I said, "Mr Murphy, it doesn't matter how you are brought up. I bet if I talked to your daughter I could make blue films with her." His reply to that was to tell me to get out of his office. He hasn't spoken to me since.'

Lindsay eventually had to apply to the Greater London Council, which awarded the film an 'X' certificate for London only. It played at two cinemas, the Royal in Charing Cross Road and the Jacey on Trafalgar Square, to exceptionally good business. *The Pornbrokers* is the sort of documentary you would now see (in abridged form) late at night on Channel 5 — and you'd barely bat an eyelid. However, because of its great age and the fact it was documenting an industry which was still illegal in Britain, the movie remains the only true document of 1970s hardcore. Fascinating stuff.

CAST: Roger Heathcot (*narrator*), John Lindsay (*British pornographer*), Lasse Braun (*Danish movie director*), Nicholas Treadwell (*art gallery owner*), John Freshwater (*editor of* Experience *magazine*), Joop Wilhelmus (*Dutch porno producer*), Ulrich Geismar (*owner of Chat Noir*), Berthe Milton (*editor of* Private), Fleyming Kornrer (*ad-man for Lasse Braun*), Maureen O'Malley [aka Mary Whitehouse] (*British model*)
CREDITS: *Director/Producers* John Lindsay and Laurence Barnett, *Editor* John Pipkin, *Photography* John Lindsay and Mike Kubicki, *Concept* John Lindsay
An ELMSIDE FILMS Production. Distributed by TARGET. Opened August 1973.

SECRETS OF A DOOR TO DOOR SALESMAN
aka *Naughty Wives*

Great Britain / 1973 / 80 mins / cert 'X'

Right, you live in a beautiful cottage in an idyllic Cornish seaside town, happily making your living as a lobster fisherman and bedding all the local crumpet, and then suddenly you come into a lot of money when your father dies. What do you do? Yes, you jack it all in and move to dirty, polluted London, where you try your hand as a door to door salesman flogging vacuum cleaners. If you can suspend your disbelief for one moment, you might just enjoy *Secrets of a Door to Door Salesman*.

Supremely accident-prone David Clyde (Brendan Price) is our fishy hero, taking up lodgings in a north London b 'n' b run by a battleaxe landlady and her brood of five nubile, sex-mad nieces. The girls fall over themselves trying to assist David in finding a new occupation by giving him a job manual entitled *101 Different Positions*, but the only position they want is a horizontal one. Before settling down to selling Hoovers, David gets himself a walk-on (or should that be hard-on?) part in a blue movie being shot by kinky Jewish director Jake Tripper (Bernard Spear), the man behind the huge international success of *Werewolf Virgins*, starring Nora Titzoff.

David's beautiful co-star is Penny (Sue Longhurst in her very first sex comedy role), dressed as a saucy nurse and harbouring very definite ideas about the acting profession. 'I will only appear in the nude if it is artistically dictated by the emotional complexities of the character I portray,' she says earnestly. 'Like when I was a teenage virgin.' David needs eight re-takes to do his stuff and then, after a welcome cuppa, is invited to do the hardcore scenes for the 'overseas' version. Exhausted, he retires immediately, but has cause to regret it when the suburban housewives on his door to door rounds initially reject his dubious charms. Eventually he finds true love with a fruity German Fraulein, Martina (Jean Harrington).

The film brims over with lots of good Carry On-style jokes, no doubt helped by the input from veteran gag-man Denis Norden (albeit using a pseudonym) and writing partner Joseph McGrath. And the good-humoured script happily sends up the sex movie industry — Tripper's porn movie is filmed behind a kosher butchers on the Edgware Road for a company called Anglo Titanic International Films (an in-joke at the expense of producer David Grant) — and provides plenty of slick one-liners, particularly for Chic

KEEPING THE BRITISH END UP

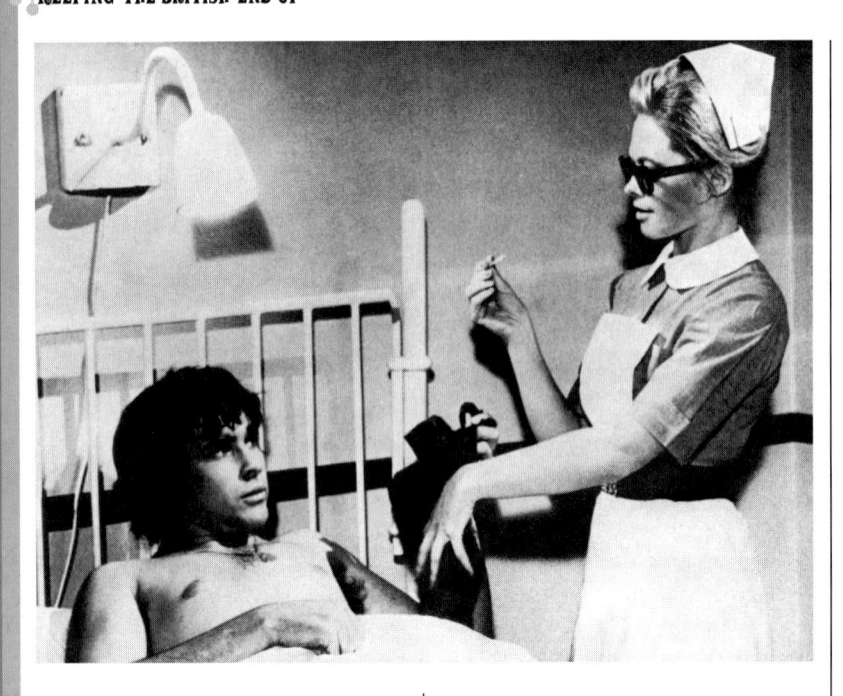

WHITE CARGO
aka *Albert's Follies*

Great Britain / 1973 / 62 mins / cert 'AA'

'*White Cargo* was all Ray Selfe's doing,' claims screenwriter David McGillivray. 'He had a script for a sex comedy for the Goodies, who were extremely big on television at the time. He got the money together but not, alas, the Goodies. They just read the script and didn't want to do it, so Ray was left with this script and needed it rewritten in a hurry so that the film could be made for somebody else. That lucky person was David Jason in his first leading movie role. Jason was very excited about doing the film, but his excitement diminished somewhat during shooting.'

Fresh from his success in the stage version of *No Sex Please – We're British*, Jason plays Albert Toddey, a scruffy no-hoper who fantasises about becoming a slick, sharp-suited government agent. McGillivray's script is a dead ringer, albeit saucier, for the sort of farce Norman Wisdom would have played in a decade earlier. ('I've always been a great fan of Norman,' admits McGillivray. 'I think he is one of the great British clowns.') In the story, Albert visits a Soho strip joint owned by devious Dudley Fox (Raymond Cross) and gets mixed up with a glamorous showgirl called Stella, played by top totty Imogen Hassall (nicknamed 'The Countess of Cleavage' in the tabloids at the time). Stella explains that strippers keep disappearing from the club and before long she goes missing too, sold into

Murray as a pervy policeman, continually accosted by peeping toms, flashers and naked girls. Referring to lusty Felicity Devonshire, he comments, 'A girl shouldn't be given a body like that until she's old enough to be trusted with it!'

There's nudity and humping by the bucketload, but on the whole the movie is more sentimental than downright sexy. That said, the fabulously sassy, up-tempo theme song stays in your head long after the film has ended (courtesy of Laurie Holloway, later the musical director on TV's *Parkinson*). The film was directed by no less than Wolf (*Village of the Damned*) Rilla, while the opening scene was handled by Jonathan (*Silence of the Lambs*) Demme, on leave from his apprenticeship with Roger Corman and booked to direct the entire movie – it would have been his first – until 'creative differences' intervened. *Secrets of a Door to Door Salesman* would also have been Mary Millington's first feature film (playing a topless traffic warden), had she not been cut from the film at the editing stage. In the final version you only catch a fleeting glimpse of the woman who later became a sex film legend.

CAST: Brendan Price (*David Clyde*), Sue Longhurst (*Penny*), Felicity Devonshire (*Susanne*), Jean Harrington (*Martina*), Chic Murray (*policeman*), Graham Stark (*Charlie Vincent*), Bernard Spear (*Jake Tripper*), Johnny Briggs (*Loman*), Jacqueline Afrique (*Rachel*), Elizabeth Romilly (*Nancy*), Jan Servais (*Jane*), Jacqueline Logan (*Mrs Donovan*), Vicky Burgoyne (*Sally Cockburn*), Noelle Finch (*Edith Simons*), Tara Lynn (*Mrs Bell*), Tony Doonan (*Mr Bell*), Jenny Westbrook (*pregnant actress*), Geraldine Hart (*Mrs Barling*), Valerie Bell (*Mrs Green*), Karen Boyes (*David's girl-friend*), Lesley Roach (*singer at disco*), David Rayner (*Bruce, the art director*), Peter Vernon (*Crossways*), Judi Stevenson (*voluptuous girl at disco*), Alan Selwyn (*man at disco*), Monika Ringwald and Rosemary Chalmers (*topless waitresses*), Mary Maxted aka Mary Millington [uncredited] (*traffic warden*)

CREDITS: *Director* Wolf Rilla, *Director of opening sequence* Jonathan Demme, *Producer* David Grant, *Associate Producer* Malcolm Fancey, *Editor* Peter Horrey, *Photography* Marc McDonald, *Screenplay* Joe McGrath and Roy Nicholas [aka Denis Norden], *Music* John Shakespeare and Derek Warne, *Theme song* 'Love Makes Two People Swing' performed by Linda Saxone

An OPPIDAN Production. Distributed by NEW REALM. Opened September 1973

Left: Brendan Price gets the full treatment from nurse Sue Longhurst in *Secrets of a Door to Door Salesman* (1973).

white slavery in an unnamed 'Arabian oil state'. Albert tracks the missing girls to the evil Mr Fox's country mansion, where they're all manacled to a basement wall, and is pursued throughout by a couple of bowler-hatted civil servants played by TV favourites Hugh Lloyd and Tim Barrett.

The movie, originally called *Albert's Follies*, was inspired by director Ray Selfe's own experiences of working in Soho during the glory days of the striptease clubs. 'It's based on a Walter Mitty-type thing,' said Selfe. 'It's about a guy who imagines he's somebody else. It's only a split second in his brain, but in that split second he becomes James Bond. I put it to producer Olive Negus and she loved it, so the idea was that all the fantasy sequences would be shot in 3D, like the stuff I'd done in *The Four Dimensions of Greta* for Pete Walker.'

'It was a baptism of fire for Ray because it was the first feature film he had directed,' remembers McGillivray. 'Changes kept being presented to him and it was very stressful.' Things did indeed change, and drastically so. The 3D was abandoned at the insistence of producer Olive Negus, who also wanted the sex toned down for a 'U' certificate. Her partner, E J Fancey, had different ideas, however. 'Suddenly they wanted an 'X' certificate,' explains Selfe, 'and I'd shot half the bloody movie already. So E J came down onto the set the next day and I did a scene with the girls being led naked out of the cellar. I shot the scene twice, once naked, once covered up, but Hugh Lloyd objected, saying he had a following in America and if they saw this film they would think he was making porn. I told him, "They're not coming out fucking, Hugh, it's just the naked body, for God's sake."'

The nude footage was never to see the light of day, because it would have made little sense stuck in the middle of a rather less raunchy film. 'E J was happy anyway,' said Ray. 'He'd seen a lot of muffs on set that day.' The film was finished at Twickenham in less than two-and-a-half weeks on a budget of £70,000, which was pretty luxurious for a British comedy of only 60-odd minutes' duration, while several of the sets were recycled from the Peter O'Toole vehicle *The Ruling Class*. *White Cargo* has some genuinely funny moments and, though no classic, offers a hint of what was to come for star David Jason, just eight years away from his creation of Del Boy in the classic sitcom *Only Fools and Horses*.

Of all British sex comedies, *White Cargo* is one of the least raunchy but also one of the most frequently seen. The film frequently turns up on British TV (on at least one occasion in a 74 minute version) at around three in the morning. 'It's baffling, isn't it?' says McGillivray. 'I had no idea it still existed until it was shown on TV. If that's still around then it means that some others I was involved with which are even worse might exist too, and that sends shudders down my spine!'

CAST: David Jason (*Albert Toddey*), Imogen Hassall (*Stella*), Hugh Lloyd (*Chumley*), Tim Barrett (*Fosdyke*), Dave Prowse (*Harry*), Raymond Cross (*Dudley Fox*), Sue Bond (*Desirée*), John Barber (*special agent*), Geraldine Hart (*housewife*), Stan Stewart (*Jim*), Roger Adamson (*carpet salesman*), Paddy McQueen (*old lady*), Nik Zaran (*strip club owner*), David McGillivray (*customer*), Kirstie Pooley, Vivienne Stokes, Deirdre Lindsay, Jacqui Hurst and Bozena (*girls*), Ruxton Hayward [uncredited] (*comedian*), Albert Moses [uncredited] (*Arab*)
CREDITS: *Director* Ray Selfe, *Producer* Negus-Fancey, *Editor* Peter Austen-Hunt, *Photography* John Barnard, *Screenplay* Ray Selfe and David McGillivray, *Music* David Lindup
A BORDER Production. Distributed by BORDER. Opened November 1973.

SNOW WHITE AND THE SEVEN PERVERTS
aka *Some Day My Prince Will Come*

Great Britain / 1973 / 11 mins / cert 'X' (London only)

The 1973 release of *Snow White and the Seven Perverts* whipped up a storm of controversy because of its juxtaposition of childhood fairy-tales with explicit sexual imagery. A far ruder, and cruder, cartoon than any of Bob Godfrey's 'X'-rated shorts, it was refused a certificate outright by the BBFC and only saw the light of day after being reluctantly passed by the Greater London Council for showing in the capital only. Opening as support film to a cut-down hardcore German sex thriller called *Climax* at the Classic Piccadilly Circus, the poster read in bold letters: 'David Grant's Controversial Permissive Cartoon

KEEPING THE BRITISH END UP

Right: The sexiest, sassiest crime-fighter of the 1970s – Linda Marlowe as *Big Zapper* (1973).

(title censored)'. Several cinemas were raided, the cartoon was confiscated by the police and a destruction order was placed on the print. In several instances copies were actually incinerated. 'It was very rude,' said filmmaker Ray Selfe, 'but it was actually a lot closer to the Brothers Grimm than the Disney version. In fact, Grant got nasty letters from Disney threatening to sue, but of course they didn't own the title.'

Why all this fuss over such a little thing? It's a vulgar but amusing cartoon in which an unnamed narrator tells the traditional story of Snow White at odds with the explicitly sexual visuals. Most of the characters are identified by the size of their phalluses or breasts; in fact, the Wicked Queen's only beef with Miss White is that her boobs are bigger than her own. The dwarfs are seedy, raincoated midgets who spend most of their time scampering around Soho flashing at passers-by. And the handsome Prince Charming doesn't awaken his love with a kiss but with a ride on his enormous knob. Filmed anonymously by Marcus Parker-Rhodes, *Snow White and the Seven Perverts* was released simultaneously with its equally mischief-making sibling *Sinderella*. However, bowing to pressure, and following a suggestion from Ray Selfe, David Grant reluctantly reissued the film under a new title: *Some Day My Prince Will Come*. Absolutely inspired!

CREDITS: *Director* Marcus Parker-Rhodes [uncredited], *Producer* Ron Inkpen [uncredited], *Executive Producer/Screenplay* David Grant An OPPIDAN Production. Distributed by BORDER. Opened November 1973.

BIG ZAPPER

aka *The Sex Life of a Female Private Eye*

Great Britain / 1973 / 90 mins / cert 'X'

In perhaps the kookiest film of Lindsay Shonteff's career, the uncompromising Linda Marlowe ('the girl with the long legs and the short fuse') stars as the sexy, sassy, white-suited private eye Harriet Zapper, who can handle a gun as well as she handles her men. Her boyfriend Rock Hard (Richard Monette) is a male nymphomaniac who continually pesters Harriet with demands for masochistic sex and regular whippings, whether it be in bed, in the back of her Mercedes sports car or up against any available wall. While he's losing weight from all the carnal exercise, all she gets is backache. 'For Christ's sake, Rock!' Marlowe moans. 'You've lost 11 pounds in two days and I'm still aching. Cut it out!'

Choosing to advertise her services in the local *Village Gazette*, Harriet is hired by the saucily named Jeremiah Horn (Jack May), a randy old soak who asks her to find his daughter, Pandora, who has mysteriously gone missing without a trace. Narrating her adventures *à la* her fictional namesake Philip ('Flagellation just wasn't my scene'), la Marlowe follows the trail to a sadistic country house criminal named Kono (played by Gary Hope as a combination of Christopher Lee and Nicholas Parsons). Hope is a seriously deranged gangland pimp with a penchant for kinky sex and is responsible for the brutal murder of young Pandora.

Taking her hostage, Kono wants Harriet for some slap and tickle – with emphasis on the slap – but when she pulls down her panties, the reason for her 'Zapper' moniker becomes all too apparent. In one of the most brilliantly bizarre moments of seventies' cinema, a flashing, dazzling, pulsing ball of electric light zaps out of her fanny and momentarily stuns her assailant. There's no real reason for this and it's never fully explained how she came to have this most unusual super power, but no matter. It's an incredibly funny scene and many viewers will have to scrape their jaws off the floor having seen it.

Thereafter, Harriet single-handedly takes on Kono and his leering henchmen in a super-silly pastiche of James Bond. Twirling her twin .357 Magnums (a Shonteff trademark), she makes mincemeat of the baddies, succeeds in bringing down a helicopter (in a very expensive, un-sex comedy special effect, it must be said) and dispenses with ten of Kono's men using a machine-gun suggestively positioned between her spread-eagled legs, before polishing off a group of Samurai warriors! Shonteff goes to town with the violent set-pieces, with shootings, stabbings, choppings, severed heads and dollops of blood and guts aplenty, and it's a movie you'll not forget in a hurry. A stunning, fast-paced kinky comic strip adventure, *Big Zapper* is an exceptional film and Marlowe absolutely takes no prisoners as the fast-talking, ball-crunching, ass-kicking Harriet. Tremendous fun and totally unmissable. Followed, less successfully, in 1974 by *Zapper's Blade of Vengeance*, which replaced the Epping Forest location with the south of France, firearms with swords and sexiness with Alan Lake.

CAST: Linda Marlowe (*Harriet Zapper*), Richard Monette (*Rock Hard*), Gary Hope (*Kono*), Sean Hewitt (*Fingers*), Michael O'Malley (*Strawberry Jim*), Jack May (*Jeremiah Horn*), Penny Irving (*Maggie*), Stuart Lock (*Septimus/Randy Horn*), Bobbi Anne (*Pandora Horn*), Parnell McGarry (*Lesbian Rose*), William Ridoutt (*Shawn Cobra*), Graham Ashley (*Mr Cortina*), Nova Llewellyn, Jo Peters, Sonia Camara and Paula Tinker (*prostitutes*), Michael Crane (*Cecil*), Kristopher Kum, Hock Chuan and Tony Hiew (*Samurai swordsmen*), William Hootkins, John Salthouse and Gaylord Burr (*Kono's henchmen*)

CREDITS: *Director/Producer* Lindsay Shonteff, *Editor* Spencer Reeve, *Photography* John Taylor, *Screenplay* Hugh Brody, *Music* Colin Pearson
A LINDSAY SHONTEFF Production. Distributed by MIRACLE. Opened December 1973.

ON THE GAME

Great Britain / 1973 / 87 mins / cert 'X'

A historical companion piece to *Naughty!*, this was Stanley Long's cheeky delve into the vaults to serve up, as the subtitle has it, *A Chronicle of Prostitution*. Leaving no stone unturned, Long even opens the film with two models in monkey suits humping in a quarry for the price of five fresh eggs, a naughty rip-off of Stanley Kubrick's *2001: A Space Odyssey* which strangely omits the big black (phallic) obelisk.

Long's whirlwind TARDIS tour through time and space takes us past Babylonian broads, Ancient Grecian flappers and Roman giglets before settling down in Long's favourite historical era – the Victorian one. The director gets well into his stride with our ancestor's favourite pastime: flagellation. Carmen Silvera (better known as Edith in TV sitcom '*Allo 'Allo*) plays the fearsome Mrs Berkeley of 28 Charlotte Street. Dressed like a black widow and more frightening than Anne Robinson in *Weakest Link* mode, she proves herself an expert in wielding the rod and demonstrating her 'adjustable whipping machine' on some poor septuagenarian, whose trembling buttocks go as red as his face. Long punctuates his quaint dramatisations with some fascinating facts that would impress any Trivial Pursuit fan. Did you know Roman prostitutes dyed their hair blue, or that the loose women of Victorian England wore face masks, or that there was a horse-drawn mobile brothel which toured the trenches during World War Two? Did you *want* to know?

There are some cute little vignettes along the way: Napoleon's waxed moustache droops after intercourse; Gladstone's favourite call-girl has his face tattooed on her arse; ex-Page Three girl Maureen Flanagan plays a prostitute who has cream buns thrown at her fanny. The hoary historical framework is an ideal canvas for swaying boobs and thrusting buttocks, but there's less sex and more jollification in *On the Game* than Long's two previous portmanteaux. However, the stirring sight of starlet Nicola Austine as Empress Messalina, naked save for a yellow wig and gold-painted nipples, is an image to be cherished!

KEEPING THE BRITISH END UP

CAST: Charles Gray (*narrator*), Pamela Manson (*brothel keeper*), Charles Hodgson (*Roman aedile*), Suzie Bowen (*young prostitute*), Nicola Austine (*Empress Messalina*), Allen Morton (*Henry III of France*), Peter Duncan (*François*), Louise Pajo (*Veronica Franca*), Allan McClelland (*doctor*), Eva (*jailed prostitute*), Val Penny (*ducked prostitute*), Francis Batson (*Napoleon*), David Brierley (*Prince of Wales*), June Palmer (*wife*), Lloyd Lamble (*Mr Gladstone*), Gloria Walker (*Jenny*), Carmen Silvera (*Mrs Berkeley*), Heather Chasen (*madame*), Maureen Flanagan (*Lil*), Mildred Mayne (*Lulu White*), Tommy Eytle (*pianist*), John McLloy (*Mr Lusty*), Lucienne Camille (*sex therapist*)

CREDITS: *Director* Stanley Long, *Producers* Stanley Long and Barry Jacobs, *Editor* Patrick Foster, *Photography* Mike Boultbee, *Screenplay* Suzanne Mercer, *Music* De Wolfe. A SALON Production. Distributed by EAGLE. Opened January 1974.

KEEP IT UP JACK!

Great Britain / 1973 / 87 mins / cert 'X'

Put simply, *Keep It Up Jack!* is director Derek Ford's attempt to restage *Charley's Aunt* in a knocking shop. End-of-pier variety act Jack James (Mark Jones) is summoned to a London law firm where he learns that his old Aunt Letitia has died in a car crash. If that wasn't shock enough, he also finds that she has left him a substantial Edwardian house in Ascot. Unfortunately the house happens to be a working brothel and his dear-departed relative was actually a legendary madame specialising in whippings. All her hookers have flown the coop apart from one occupant, the beautiful Virginia (Sue Longhurst), who is desperate to re-start the business. Jack is instantly attracted to Virginia and, in an attempt to persuade her to stay, decides to pose as his aunt. Why is never properly explained, but presumably men in frocks are always good for a giggle.

Raiding auntie's wardrobe and making good use of her wigs and make-up, Jack makes a convincing replacement and keeps up the pretence for much of the movie, even resorting to tucking his penis between his legs. Virginia, it transpires, has lesbian leanings, fancies 'auntie' and is desperate to have a bit of girl-on-girl action. In an astoundingly eye-popping joke, she climbs into bed with the dragged-up Jack and makes a grope for 'her' crotch. She assumes his erection is a strap-on dildo. 'It's such a real one. Isn't it good?' she squeals with delight.

Several new girls are hired to get the business up and running again, including rubber dominatrix Jenny Westbrook, ex-*Penthouse* pet Maggi Burton, baby doll Linda Regan and busty black model Veronica Pieters, who was the daughter of the British Guyanan Ambassador to London and terribly posh. (After the film was completed she married an English lord and retired.) Naturally, Jack hasn't got a clue how to run a house of ill-repute and when the invaluable little black book goes missing he is forced to pose as the *clients*. Sadly, the comedy struggles fruitlessly for laughs when Jack resorts to dressing up in silly costumes. These, rather bizarrely, take the form of a Japanese businessman, an Arab Sheikh, a brash Texan and a Spanish bullfighter.

The action rushes around in farcical fashion with numerous cases of mistaken

DOINGS

Left: Sue Longhurst and Mark Jones swap style tips in *Keep It Up Jack!* (1973).

identity, Jack zipping through one quick change to the next, doors flying open and slamming closed, and the male lead spending considerably longer in the nude than any of his curvaceous co-stars. *Keep It Up Jack!* was shot with hardcore inserts on location at Derek Ford's Essex house (which had previously stood in as a country retreat in *Suburban Wives* and as a luxury hotel in *Commuter Husbands*). The film's thespians were a little surprised to see all manner of fornication going on behind the scenes. Sue Longhurst was even asked to participate, but declined. In her startling opening sequence she is seen blissfully pleasuring herself on a water bed covered in pink satin sheets. 'I had quite a fight with them over that scene,' Sue recalls. 'I don't know quite how raunchy they wanted me to be, but I was supposed to be thoroughly enjoying myself on my own. But there's no way I was doing any stronger stuff. I have a stop button if you like and that was as much as they were going to get!'

CAST: Mark Jones (*Jack James*), Sue Longhurst (*Virginia*), Maggi Burton (*Fleur*), Linda Regan (*Gloria*), Jenny Westbrook (*Caroline*), Paul Whitson-Jones (*Mr Fairbrother*), Frank Thornton (*Mr Clarke*), Queenie Watts (*charlady*), Veronica Pieters (*Francine*), Yvette Vanson (*Sylvie*), Steve Viedor (*Muscles*), Jack Le White (*stagehand*), Juliet Groves (*Lily*), Marian Brown (*Marian*), Jan Foster (*Jan*), Gideon Kolb, Anthony Kenyon and Bob Raymond (*clients*), Derek Martin [uncredited] (*client with swing*)

CREDITS: *Director* Derek Ford, *Producer* Michael L Green, *Editor* Patrick Foster, *Photography* Geoff Glover, *Screenplay* Derek Ford and Alan Selwyn, *Music* Terry Warr A BLACKWATER FILMS Production. Distributed by VARIETY. Opened March 1974.

MISTRESS PAMELA

Great Britain / 1973 / 91 mins / cert 'X'

The redoubtable Ann Michelle stars in this bawdy tale of strumpets, trollops and saucy sluts, set in 1740 and based upon the classic by Samuel Richardson, celebrated as the 'first dramatic novel written in the English language' (or, in other words, the very first one-handed read). Hard-faced Michelle plays Pamela Andrews, a comely country lass, daughter of a ditch-digger, who is taken into domestic service at the kinky Bedfordshire household of lusty Lord Devenish (Julian Barnes). He provides her with food, lodgings and wages of one guinea per year, and if she's lucky, one and a half days' off every 12 months. However, naïve Pamela is warned by her father of the perils of menfolk. She takes on board what he has said, but her determination to keep her virginity is assailed by the lecherous footman, the lesbian housekeeper and, most of all, the dastardly Devenish.

His loins stirred by her innocent beauty, Devenish sets about bedding the wench by any means necessary. Try as he might to get her frilly drawers down or get a peek at her cleavage, the Lord is thwarted at every turn. Eventually he kidnaps her, taking her to his second country pile in Lincolnshire, and during the night attempts to mount her. He fails again and she only submits to his persistent passions when he promises to marry her and declare his undying love.

Mistress Pamela tries hard to amuse, but its skinny story and repetitive, drawn-out scenarios frustrate more than titillate. Even the sex scenes offer little except apathy. During a couple of bonking bouts a message flashes up on screen proclaiming 'Pray be patient! We are being censored!', but the joke is a huge turn-off. A couple of cunning cameos – from Fred Emney as a decrepit doctor prescribing a 'hot toddy' for every ailment, and obsequious Ken Parry, as oily as ever, as the corrupt country parson – raise the odd laugh, but the film generally lacks a light touch and Ann Michelle looks resolutely miserable throughout. Produced by cousins Michael Glass and Julian Sacher, both of them heirs to High Street giants Marks and Spencer, *Mistress Pamela* was intended as the first of five sex films they would finance. It never happened.

CAST: Ann Michelle (*Pamela Andrews*), Julian Barnes (*Lord Robert Devenish*), Dudley Foster (*Jonathan*), Anna Quayle (*Mrs Jelks*), Anthony Sharp (*Longman*), Rosemarie Dunham (*Mistress Blimper*), Derek Fowlds (*Sir Percy*), Jessie Evans (*Widow Parr*), Ken Parry (*Parson*), Fred Emney (*Dr Livesey*), Fredric Abbott (*John Andrews*), Marianne

KEEPING THE BRITISH END UP

Stone (*Katie*), Barbara Hickmont (*Beattie*), Betty Turner (*Sarah*), Terry Plummer (*Giles*)

CREDITS: *Director/Producer* Jim O'Connolly, *Executive Producers* Michael Glass and Julian Sacher, *Editor* Fergus McDonell, *Photography* Arthur Ibbetson, *Screenplay* Jim O'Connolly based on the novel *Pamela, or Virtue Rewarded* by Samuel Richardson, *Music* David Whitaker A MERLOT FILMS Production. Distributed by MGM-EMI. Opened March 1974.

SEX FARM

Great Britain / 1973 / 84 mins / cert 'X' (London only)

Covering much the same torpid terrain as 1971's *Clinic Xclusive*, Arnold Louis Miller's hedonistic health farm creates the perfect setting for those wishing to play away from home. Cheryl (Hilary Lebow) and Diane (Amber Kammer) are two neglected wives who, frustrated by their husbands' sexual inadequacies, visit a high-class health and leisure establishment for a relaxing weekend. However, it's not crunchy lettuce salads, whirlpool baths and bracing physical jerks they're after. They have their minds set on some extramarital jiggery-pokery.

The farm's managing director Dr Schroeder (Gordon Whiting) advocates abstinence from all alcoholic beverages, fatty foods and sex, but secretly indulges himself with every bit of skirt passing his office. The girls soon cotton on to the truth behind the farm's healthy façade and joyfully throw themselves in for the 'full treatment', taking advantage of the masseur's hands, the cook's ladle and the gym instructor's chest expander. And if that wasn't enough excitement for an off-peak break they have it away with all the other guests too in a climactic, drunken orgy. Refused a certificate by the BBFC for 'excessive sexual content'.

CAST: Hilary Lebow (*Cheryl Hope*), Amber Kammer (*Diane Waitman*), Kim Alexander (*Tom Hope*), Tristan Rogers (*Robert Waitman*), Gordon Whiting (*Dr Schroeder*), Claire Gordon (*receptionist*), Max Mason (*Frank Collins*), Ray Edwards (*Charles Truelove*), Elsie Winsor (*Miss Lowndes*), Tommy Wright (*Wilson*), Barry Rhode (*gym instructor*), Steve Patterson (*masseur*), Sui Lin (*masseuse*), Susan Glanville (*typist*), Patrick Tull (*dietician*)

CREDITS: *Director* Arnold Louis Miller, *Producers* Arnold Louis Miller and Sheila Miller, *Editor* Howard Lansing, *Photography* Tony Leggo, *Screenplay* Alan Pas, *Music* De Wolfe A GLOBAL-QUEENSWAY Production. Distributed by MONARCH. Opened March 1974.

SOFT BEDS, HARD BATTLES

aka *Undercover Hero*

Great Britain / 1973 / 107 mins / cert 'X'

Pity poor Roy Boulting. Beset with problems from the outset, Boulting is on record as saying that this movie was the 'unhappiest experience in my whole career.' Oddly it was his star, whom he had worked with many times before, who created the problems – Peter Sellers, no less.

The legend 'A Boulting Brothers Production' was synonymous with high-quality satire around the world. After many comic triumphs, in 1970 twins John and Roy had produced *There's a Girl in My Soup*, a silly romantic comedy with Sellers as a middle-aged Don Juan temporarily tamed by a funky 19-year-old popsie played by Goldie Hawn. Laced with a few naughty tit-bits and a couple of glimpses of boob, the film was a big hit. Three years later Roy, deciding to go it alone, approached Sellers for a far saucier movie. Smarting from a long line of flops, Sellers was keen to be associated with the Boulting name again and *Soft Beds, Hard Battles* was the nearest he ever got to an out-and-out sex come-

Left: Ann Michelle rejects Ken Parry's dubious advances in Mistress Pamela *(1973).*

dy. Sellers agreed to star but halfway into pre-production refused to sign on the dotted line. After much negotiation, Boulting got him to change his mind and filming finally started, but not before the script, co-written by Leo *Peeping Tom* Marks, had been re-jigged numerous times at Sellers' insistence.

Set during World War Two, the story centres on a vast high-class brothel, decked in red velvet, gold tassels and crystal chandeliers, in the heart of Paris. Madame Grenier (Lila Kedrova) oversees her girls, all of them tantalisingly kitted out in frilly negligées, stockings and suspenders, garters and feather boas and puffing away on Gauloises. Pandering to the perverted needs of the nasty Nazis, the whorehouse is a front for the French Resistance and Madame Grenier sets about training her young ladies to kill their high-ranking German clients, turning the establishment into a knocking-off shop rather than a knocking shop.

Sellers plays six roles (à la Alec Guinness in *Kind Hearts and Coronets*) and also narrates. His Adolf Hitler is uncannily realistic, but he's best as the doddering old General Latour with a penchant for ladies a quarter his age. Sellers wears such heavy prosthetics that when Jenny Hanley nibbles his ear one worries that it might come off in her mouth, and as Japanese Prince Kyoto he is simply unrecognisable. Occasionally Sellers' French accent drifts off into *Pink Panther* territory and at times the idea of idiotic Nazis and saucy French girls is reminiscent of TV's *'Allo 'Allo*. In fact, Sellers' portrayal of the limping, leather-coated Gestapo chief undoubtedly provided the inspiration for the comedy series' Herr Flick. Coincidentally, *'Allo 'Allo*'s Richard Marner crops up, uncredited, as (what else?) a Nazi.

Boulting's temperamental star was absent for much of the schedule, the shooting coinciding with his latest infatuation, this time for American star Liza Minnelli, 20 years his junior. Sellers would flounce off early from Shepperton in order to see Minnelli at the London Palladium, causing major disruption for the production crew. In several instances a double had to be used. With a wrecked shooting schedule and an unpredictable star, the cost of the film spiralled out of control. The finished film was rumoured to have cost in excess of a million pounds, nearly bankrupting Boulting.

Despite a solid script, big-budget sets, excellent costumes and some amusing performances from Lila Kedrova and Curt Jürgens in particular, laughs are a bit thin on the ground. Obviously the strain of working with Sellers in a studio under seige from reporters took its toll on Boulting and the production as a whole. However, the film does contain a few honest-to-goodness chuckles. At one point the hookers surreptitiously spike the Nazis' drinks with pills designed to give *elephants* life-threatening flatulence, let alone humans. Seeing the Hun belching and farting their way into oblivion is hilarious. The girls eventually succeed in sabotaging the Nazis' plans and freeing Paris. The French President awards them all with medals (dropping Rula Lenska's down her cleavage) and the famous whorehouse gets national monument status. A wall plaque is placed by the entrance: 'In this house the foundations of freedom were well and truly laid.' Sadly, *Soft Beds* was the last cinema film Boulting made and is the only picture he is ashamed of. And what's more, after all that trouble and strife, Sellers and Minelli never married. Their tempestuous affair lasted exactly one month.

CAST: Peter Sellers (*General Latour/Major Robinson/Herr Schroeder/Adolf Hitler/Prince Kyoto/French President/narrator*), Lila Kedrova (*Madame Grenier*), Curt Jürgens (*General von Grotjahn*), Beatrice Romand (*Marie-Claude*), Jenny Hanley (*Michelle*), Françoise Pascal (*Madeleine*), Gabriella Licudi (*Simone*), Rula Lenska (*Louise*), Daphne Lawson (*Claudine*), Carolle Rousseau (*Hélène*), Hylette Adolphe (*Tom-Tom*), Rex Stallings (*Alan Cassidy*), Timothy West (*chaplain*), Vernon Dobtcheff (*padre*), Thorley Walters (*Erhardt*), Patricia Burke (*Mother Superior*), Phillip Madoc (*Weber*), Windsor Davies (*Monsieur Bisse*), Tony Simpson (*Felix*), David Toguri (*Prince Kyoto's aide*), Michael Sheard (*military governor*), Gertan Klauber, Stanley Lebor and Barry Gordon (*Gestapo agents*), Helli Louise [uncredited] (*prostitute*), Richard Marner [uncredited] (*Nazi gaoler*)
CREDITS: *Director/Producer* Roy Boulting, *Editor* Martin Charles, *Photography* Gil Taylor, *Screenplay* Leo Marks and Roy Boulting, *Music* Neil Rhoden
A CHARTER FILMS Production. Distributed by FOX-RANK. Opened March 1974.

1974

ESCORT GIRLS
aka *All Lovers are Strangers*

Great Britain / 1974 / 95 mins / cert 'X'

Donovan Winter's previous 'X'-rated film, *Come Back Peter*, displayed an exuberant, carefree, fantastical approach to sex, yet *Escort Girls* shows the downside. Written as *All Lovers are Strangers* – a far more accurate title, since the escorts in the film are both female and male – the script wallows in several tales of rejection, disappointment and loneliness. Using Christmas as a background, Winter provides not only an original setting for a British sex film but also the single most important time of year when people yearn for the company of others. The opening shots of sparkling Christmas windows in Regent Street department stores are alternated with down-and-outs sleeping rough and the tawdry displays in sex shops with raincoated men shuffling past.

Quite a serious and realistic sex movie, Winter's persuasive direction and grainy camerawork almost give the film a fly-on-the-wall quality, with only the occasional bit of wobbly acting giving the game away. Among Winter's desperate vignettes of the single life in London, a wealthy middle-aged woman seeks companionship with a much younger stud, but he balks at the thought of sex with her and does a runner. An aggressive American businessman tries to rape his pretty escort but is blackmailed in an elaborate sting involving a waiting photographer. And two randy Scotsmen on the look-out for 'wee lassies' to fill their Christmas stockings find it near-hopeless picking up English girls and so hire two lovelies for the evening. Trying to impress them with champagne, they demand 'their money's worth' but get a clout round their heads for their trouble.

Two of the stories, however, end happily. Veronica Doran plays an ugly but rich socialite (despite a continuity error to the contrary, in which she is seen working in a pet shop in the film's opening sequence), who needs to impress her dreadful friends at a Christmas Eve soirée. Hiring a big black man called Lester for the night, she introduces him to her racist friends. A 'White Christmas' toast goes down like overcooked plum pudding and Lester does his best to keep his head while all around him are losing theirs. Winter has some interesting things to say about early seventies racial stereotypes, with the jealous men imagining their guest as a Zulu warrior while the twittering women fantasise him as Muhammad Ali or Johnny Mathis. Back home, Doran challenges her suitor to prove he's 'as good as they say you are' and the couple make love and find contentment with each other.

The stand-out sequence features David Dixon (later to find cult fame with the lead role in *The Hitch-hiker's Guide to the Galaxy* a decade later) as a lonely Welshman who works as a humble clerk in a London firm of accountants. Seeking companionship, he goes to an escort agency and is introduced to the delightful Susan (Maria O'Brien) for the princely sum of £12. Dixon is splendid as the naïve, unsophisticated virgin and when Susan takes him back to her flat to make love the scene hits all the right notes. In a believable and touching sex scene, he finally loses his virginity and finds the confidence which has always eluded him. Endearing as this story is, and as distressing as some of the others are, this is far and away Winter's best film.

CAST: David Dixon (*Hugh Lloyd*), Maria O'Brien (*Susan*), Veronica Doran (*Vicky*), Ken Gajadhur (*Lester*), Marika Mann (*Emma Gouldman*), Gil Barber (*Wayne*), Helen Christie (*Mary Hockstadler*), Richard Wren (*Barry*), David Brierly (*James*), James Hunter (*Ian*), Teresa Van Ross (*black dancer*), Brian Jackson (*Harvey Matelow*), Barbara Wise (*Sheila*), Max Mason (*photographer*), Karen Boyes (*blonde*)
CREDITS: *Director/Producer/Editor/Screenplay* Donovan Winter, *Photography* Gus Coma and Austin Parkinson
A DONWIN Production. Distributed by VARIETY. Opened May 1974.

THE HOT GIRLS

Great Britain / 1974 / 40 mins / cert 'X'

Watching *The Hot Girls* is an uncomfortable experience, not just for the audience but for the poor harrassed scriptwriter who penned the original story, David McGillivray. 'Oh God, this is agony. Do we really have to talk about that film?'

McGillivray says with a groan. 'I wrote the script for that, but it was thrown out. I ought to be able to look back and laugh because it was so ludicrous, but that film caused me so much grief. I was a young man with ambitions and it all went horribly wrong. As far as I can remember New Realm had just £8000 to make a film and I had to write a script in two days, which I thought was pretty damn decent of me actually, because that was fast even by my standards. And then the producer Laurie Barnett said to me "We can't use this script." All because they needed to shoot the following week!'

Incredibly, the film was just made up as they went along with very little or no expertise from those involved. 'Laurie Barnett was a boom-swinger with ambitions to be a film producer,' says McGillivray. 'He was a bit of a jack-the-lad really. And in those days it was possible for anyone to become a film producer. He was a great talker and was able to get money out of distributors like New Realm. That's the only reason they got the film made.'

As it turned out, *The Hot Girls* does indeed look improvised, with dialogue and plot careering directionlessly all over the place. 'They were working with Roger Corman's method of thinking up a vague idea and just shooting it the next week, no matter what,' remembers McGillivray. 'It didn't seem that unusual during the early seventies.' Co-produced (and rewritten) by hardcore supremo John Lindsay, the film was envisaged as a follow-up to his earlier documentary on the flourishing porn industry. In *The Hot Girls* he attempts to blow the lid off the world of nude modelling, but this time around the 'documentary' is pure fabrication. The Rag Dolls Agency provides the fictional framework in which many of Lindsay's veteran porno performers show and tell. Lindy Benson poses as Dracula's victim for a book cover. Janet Adler gets sprayed with beer over a bar counter for an advertising promotion and Andee Cromarty, Stephanie Marrian and Ava Cadell wear a selection of cutaway panties and rubberwear while posing for cameramen more interested in their crotches than their smiles. Despite his shoddy treatment at the hands of the movie's producers, McGillivray does make a cameo appearance as himself, interviewing Danish porn star Helli Louise on the set of her latest hardcore movie, *Lust to Kill*.

In Britain *The Hot Girls* ran for barely 40 minutes, with extra hardcore scenes filmed for the overseas market, but even in its 'cleaner' version it is still enough to give McGillivray the willies. 'That film is a real skeleton in my closet and the thing I hate the most,' he winces. 'In my experience everything gets unearthed sooner or later and now we're talking about it somebody is bound to dig it up!'

CAST: Timothy Blackstone (*photographer*), Lindy Benson (*Linda*), Eva Chatt [aka Ava Cadell] (*Eva*), Helli Louise (*Helli*), Janet Marsden (*Jan*), Stephanie Marrian (*Stephanie*), Linda Rimington (*Linda*), Pamela Foster (*Pam*), Patsy Allen (*Patsy*), David McGillivray (*interviewer*), Lyn Worrell (*Lyn*), Ray Selfe (*photographer*), Andee Cromarty (*Andee*), Fiona Kendall (*Fiona*), Jan Adair (*Jan*), Janet Adler (*Janet*), Zoe (*Zoe*)
CREDITS: *Directors/Producers/Screenplay* John Lindsay and Laurence Barnett, *Editor* Bob Nadkarni, *Photography* Ray Selfe, Bill Patterson and Roy Brewington, *Music* De Wolfe A BASKFORM Production. Distributed by NEW REALM. Opened May 1974.

THE OVER-AMOROUS ARTIST
aka *Just One More Time*

Great Britain / 1974 / 46 mins / cert 'X'

This naughty bit of mid-seventies David Grant-produced twaddle provides dishy ex-Junior Mr Britain, John Hamill, with his first lead in a sex film. A favourite of David Grant (who probably fancied him), Hamill plays Alan Street, a philandering jack-the-lad with an artistic bent, an undemanding role which he would return to twice more. Taking his kit off became something of an obsession for Hamill, who admitted at the time that he was a 'born flasher'.

Finding it impossible to juggle his office job with his paint-splashing hobby, Alan takes the brave decision to switch stereotypical gender roles with his glamorous wife Sue (Sue Longhurst). She becomes the main breadwinner but Alan hasn't anticipated the amorous attentions of a lusty army of female admirers who pester him for sex all day long. His artistic neighbour Carole (Claire Russell) invites him to take a peek at her 'etchings' and gets more than she bargained for.

KEEPING THE BRITISH END UP

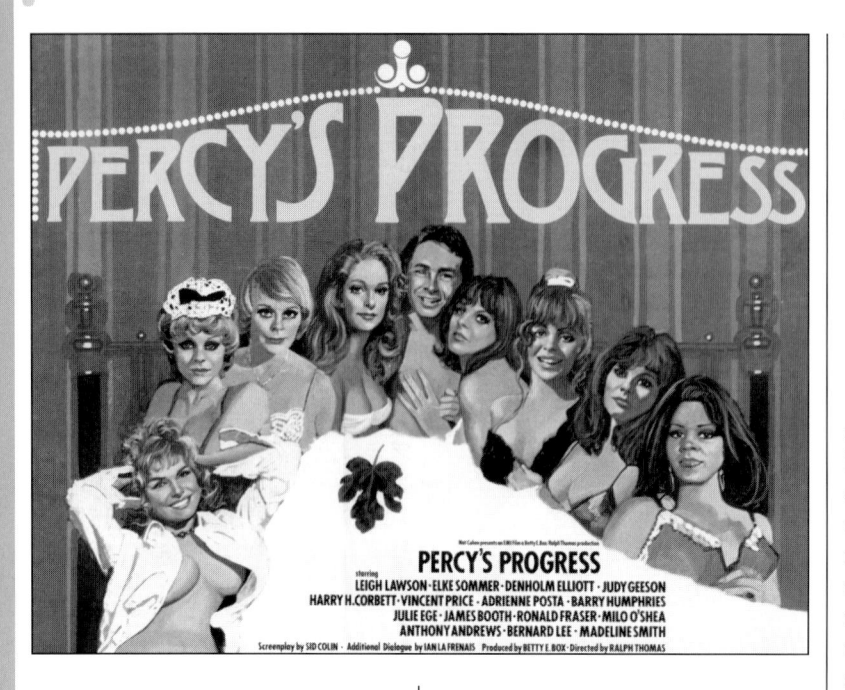

Right: Leigh Lawson tries to retain his trousers in Percy's Progress *(1974).*

Hyperactive Bev (Hilary Pritchard) from the flat next door shows off her sexy lingerie, and mother and daughter double-act Geraldine Hart and Felicity Devonshire both jump at the chance to get their hands on his stiff-bristled brush.

At the end of three days on the job, Alan's easel is starting to droop and he is completely unable to satisfy the bedtime demands of his wife when she returns home from the office. Attempting to save his skin, Alan attributes his flaccid performance to excessive housework and Sue takes pity on him. Her solution is to hire a pretty young au pair to help Alan with the scrubbing, but he is petrified of their new employee. What if she seduces him too? Envisaging further demands on his overworked physique, Alan collapses into a knackered heap. Also filmed in a hardcore version and reissued under a new title (and a rather bad one too), *Just One More Time*, in March 1975.

CREDITS: John Hamill (*Alan*), Sue Longhurst (*Sue*), Claire Russell (*Carole*), Marianne Morris (*Anne*), Geraldine Hart (*Fran*), Felicity Devonshire (*Barbara*), Hilary Pritchard (*Bev*), Jan Adair (*Sandra*), Bob Todd (*postman*), John Bluthal (*salesman*), Fred Griffith (*window cleaner*), Debbie Monroe (*au pair*), Bobby Sparrow (*dancer*). **CREDITS:** *Director* Maurice Hamblin, *Producer* David Grant, *Associate Producer* Malcolm Fancey, *Editor* Ian Duncan, *Photography* Geoffrey Glover, *Screenplay* Peter Horrey, *Music* John Shakespeare and Derek Warne An OPPIDAN Production. Distributed by NEW REALM. Opened May 1974.

PERCY'S PROGRESS

aka *It's Not the Size That Counts!*

Great Britain / 1974 / 101 mins / cert 'X'

If 1971's *Percy*, a silly romp about the world's first penis transplant, was a prime example of sex comedy credibility-testing, then the sequel, in which our hero has the only fully functioning pecker in the entire world, stretches the dick jokes to breaking point. For producer Betty E Box and director Ralph Thomas it's a return to more fertile ground after their last big screen venture, the contraceptive 'comedy' *It's a 2' 6" Above the Ground World*, released in 1972. A chronically humourless comedy about a young Catholic bra and girdle manufacturer (Hywel Bennett) re-claiming his marital rights after getting his reluctant wife pregnant six times in eight years, the film is basically 90 minutes of rowing and coy sexual jokes. The resulting flop encouraged Box to look to stiffer stuff. Hywel Bennett declined a further opportunity to make penis jokes and the title role was handed over to handsome, athletic 28-year-old newcomer Leigh Lawson (soon to be Twiggy's husband) in his first British film. 'We were looking for someone who could make sex funny, not sleazy and erotic,' said Thomas.

Well, *Percy's Progress* certainly isn't erotic, relying more on sniggering innuendo than sexual thrills. *Carry On Dick* would have been a better title had it not already been bagged by Box's husband Peter Rogers. The first *Percy* film made no reference to the size of the transplanted todger; all Bennett could say was that he thought it was 'ugly'. Now a virtue is made of its size and the virility of its owner. It's nine inches long, or nine and a half 'depending on humidity'.

At the end of the first film, our hero Edwin Anthony was happily living with his new wife, Moira. Three years later Edwin, now prudently referred to as just 'Percy', seems to have adopted the philandering characteristics of his schlong's previous owner. Tracked down to the south of France where he's been hiding the sausage with lissom Elke Sommer, he is brought back to Britain to face his wife's wrath in the divorce court, accused of a dozen or more counts of adultery. The high-profile case takes its toll and a morose Percy takes to the high seas for a

104

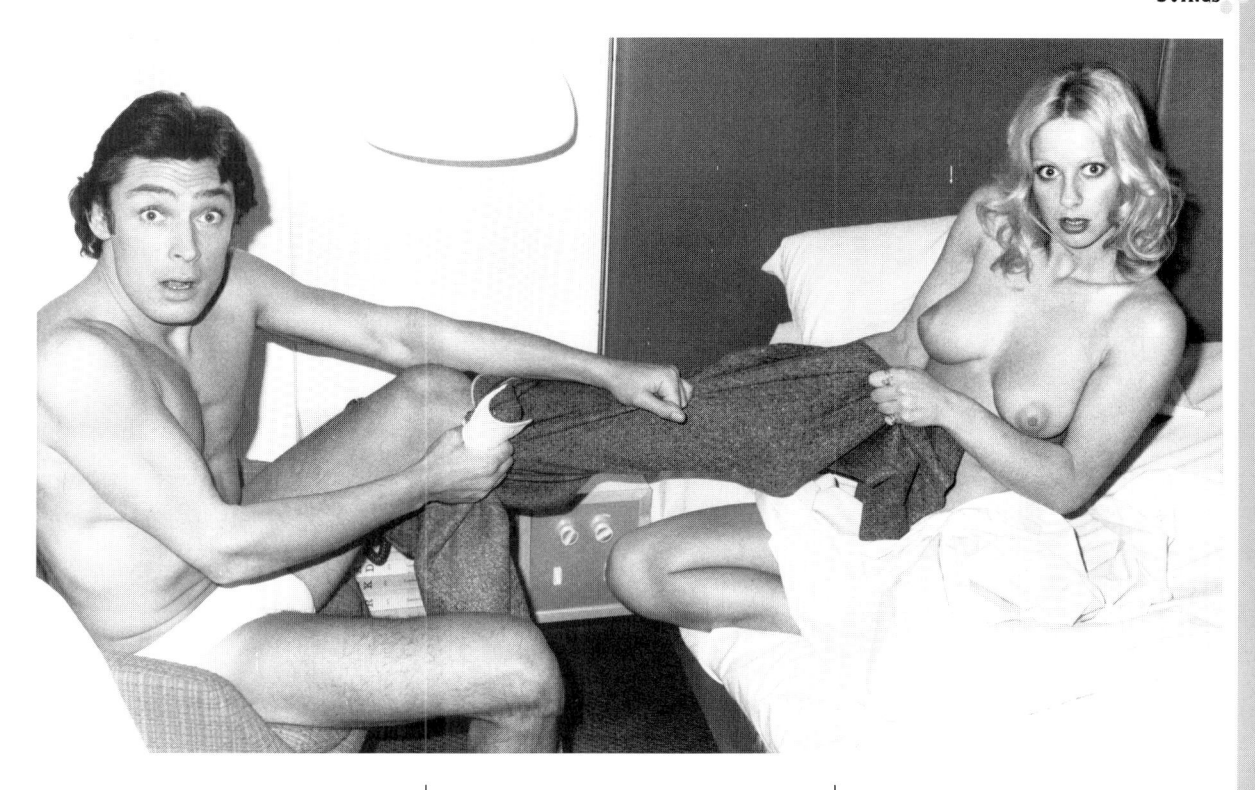

life of forced solitude and celibacy.

But adrift for 12 months without nookie and only drinking bottles of Bollinger 69, Percy's raging hard-on soon needs a thoroughly good work-out. Unbeknown to him, an American B-52 transporter plane, containing canisters of poison PX123, has crashed into the Pacific Ocean, polluting the domestic water supply of every country in the world. Apart from killing all the fish, the poison has the unpleasant side-effect of making every man on the planet impotent. Because Percy hasn't had a drop of water all year, he has the world's only working stiffy. When he finally returns home the British government decides to commandeer his purple-helmeted avenger for the sake of the human race. The United Nations order each of the world's countries to select a woman to have sex with him in a 'Miss Conception' contest. Presented with the choicest birds in the world, Percy has to do his duty for England, again and again, before going into post-coital collapse.

Box assembles an impressive cast of guest stars including Denholm Elliott, returning from the first movie but now as director of the Whitbread Institute for Sexual Inadequacy, plus Adrienne Posta and Elke Sommer. The new faces are Harry H Corbett (doing a close approximation of PM Harold Wilson), bunny-loving zoologist Barry Humphries (also appearing as Dame Edna Everage), Vincent Price no less, James Booth, Madeline Smith, Julie Ege, Minah Bird and *Playboy* Playmate of the Month for April 1974, Marlene Morrow. All go through the motions effectively enough, although the best line is reserved for Ronnie Fraser: 'The *crème de la crème* of the Earth's crumpet is competing for the privilege of your nine bleedin' inches,' he says, chastising our Percy. 'In my day, lad, it was twelve!'

CAST: Leigh Lawson (*Percy Edward Anthony*), Elke Sommer (*Clarissa*), Denholm Elliott (*Sir Emmanuel Whitbread*), Judy Geeson (*Dr Faithweather*), Harry H Corbett (*Prime Minister*), Vincent Price (*Mammonian*), Adrienne Posta (*Iris*), Julie Ege (*Miss Hanson*), Barry Humphries (*Dr Anderson/Dame Edna*), James Booth (*Jeffcott*), Milo O'Shea (*Dr Klein*), Ronald Fraser (*Bleeker*), Anthony Andrews (*Catchpole*), Bernard Lee (*Barraclough*), Madeline Smith (*Miss Bristol*), Alan Lake (*Derry Hogan*), Jenny Hanley (*Miss Teenage Lust*), Diane Langton (*Maureen Sugden*), George Coulouris (*Professor Godowski*), Carol Hawkins (*Maggie*), Marika Rivera (*Madame Lopez*), Penny Irving (*Chiquita*), Judy Matheson (*Maria*), Gertan Klauber (*Pablo*), T P McKenna (*London news editor*), Norman Chappell (*valet*), Olga Anthony (*Whitbread's PA*), Minah Bird (*Miss America*), Marlene Morrow (*Miss Australia*), Ludmilla Nova (*Miss France*), Karen David (*Miss Israel*), June Bolton (*Miss Thailand*), *Uncredited:* Jeannie Collings (*Miss Margate*), Marianne Morris (*Miss Buxton*), Monika Ringwald (*Miss Hove*), Ina Skriver (*Miss Ulla Bergström*), Marianne Stone (*reporter*)

CREDITS: Director Ralph Thomas, Producer Betty E Box, Editor Roy Watts, Photography Tony Imi, Screenplay Sid Colin, Music Tony Macauley, Theme Song 'God Knows I Miss You' performed by Carl Wayne
A BETTY E BOX-RALPH THOMAS Production. Distributed by EMI. Opened July 1974.

KEEPING THE BRITISH END UP

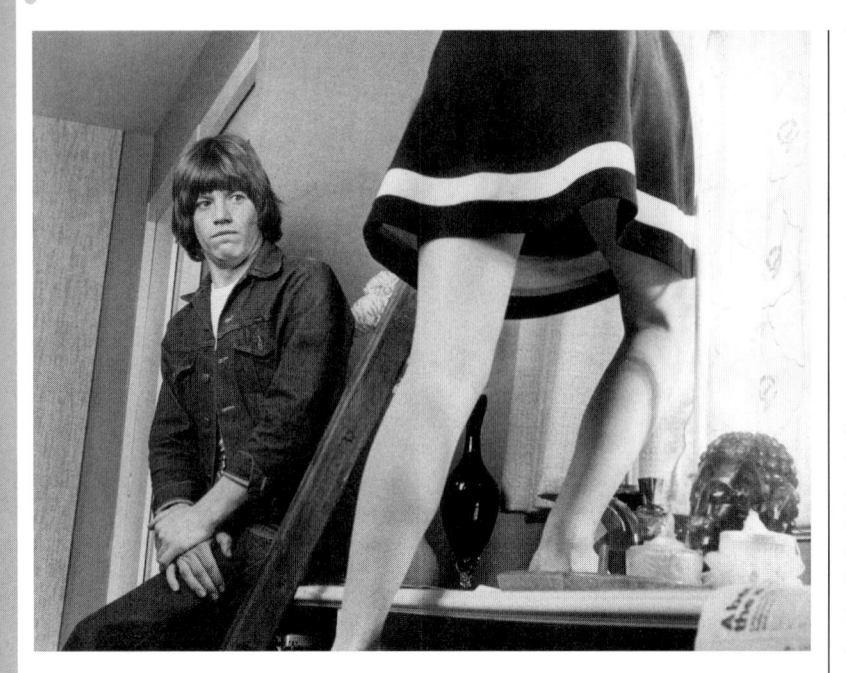

Left: Robin Askwith gets an eyeful of Anita Graham in *Confessions of a Window Cleaner* (1974).

Right: A defining moment in British sex comedy as Robin Askwith and Sue Longhurst romp amid the bubbles in *Confessions of a Window Cleaner* (1974). The underpants stayed on.

CONFESSIONS OF A WINDOW CLEANER

Great Britain / 1974 / 86 mins / cert 'X'

For up-and-coming 31-year-old film producer Greg Smith, a seemingly insignificant train journey in 1971 was to change his life and create a new style of filmmaking that would revolutionise British cinema. 'I was going to a business meeting by train and while standing at Paddington I realised that I'd left my briefcase at home with all the paperwork which I had intended to do on the journey. So I thought I'd have to get something to read,' says Smith. 'I bought a newspaper and then this paperback book called *Confessions of a Window Cleaner* caught my eye. I thought "What a great title!" So I paid for it and read it on the train. I chortled all the way there and thought to myself this is very funny stuff. When I got off at the other end I had already decided that I wanted to make it into a wonderful movie.'

As soon as Smith stepped off the train at Folkestone he rang the book's publishers, Sphere, and tracked down the author, Timothy Lea. In reality Mr Lea was a clever marketing gimmick. He didn't exist. *Confessions of a Window Cleaner*'s real author was Christopher Wood, a Cambridge law graduate and ex-advertising executive who was later to pen a further 18 novels in the series. 'The books were massive at that time,' recalls Smith. 'They were selling in their millions and Chris Wood just couldn't write them quick enough. I met him and we got on really well so I bought the film rights to the first book, with an option to buy the sequels if a first film was successful.'

It actually took nearly two and half years to finally get the project off the ground. All the big distributors turned it down until Columbia Pictures finally came on board in 1974, but only after they'd been offered the proposition for a third time. At the time Columbia were investing in several British films and their president, David Begelman, told Smith that if they could make the film for no more than £150,000 – peanuts to a big American company like Columbia – and on a five-week schedule then they had a deal on their hands. 'They were keen to make British movies in order to get some Eady money and I honestly think that *Window Cleaner* just slipped through their net,' reckons Smith. 'It was like, "For God's sake make this film, just so long as it comes in on budget and is funny." I think it was all down to timing and good luck.' Columbia were even happier to finance the project when veteran director Val Guest climbed aboard. 'It was a real coup to get Val to direct the movie,' adds Smith. 'He'd just done another sexy comedy called *Au Pair Girls* at Twickenham Studios and he was a real old pro. I was thrilled.'

With all the paperwork signed the significant matter of finding a leading actor to play the 'autobiographical' role of Timothy Lea – a naïve, virginal window cleaner finding his way through the sexual jungle of Clapham, south London – became a priority. Auditions were held in December 1973 at Val Guest's plush St John's Wood home, but finding the right actor was not easy. Smith remembers that 'Dennis Waterman, Richard Beckinsale, Richard O'Sullivan [and, according to his own account, Nicky Henson] all turned it down. As I recall, Dennis Waterman refused even to see us.'

Eventually a young 23-year-old, blond-haired actor named Robin Askwith (who had previously appeared, and bared his arse, in two low-brow sex films for Pete Walker) took his turn in Guest's lounge. Askwith had been recommended to Greg Smith by his then-girlfriend, the actress Lynda Bellingham, whom he had acted with on television. By coincidence, Askwith had recently appeared as a cheeky window cleaner in a TV commercial for KitKat. Within the space of a few days Askwith was offered the part and a bonking legend was born. Exuding naïve gullibility, Askwith plays the role of self-conscious, good-looking boy-next-door with spirited vigour. And, as in the original Christopher Wood novels, Timmy narrates the story in voice-over. 'We took an early decision, even if it was going to be compared to *Alfie*, that Timmy should be telling his own story to the audience,' says Smith. 'It was the right device for the movie.'

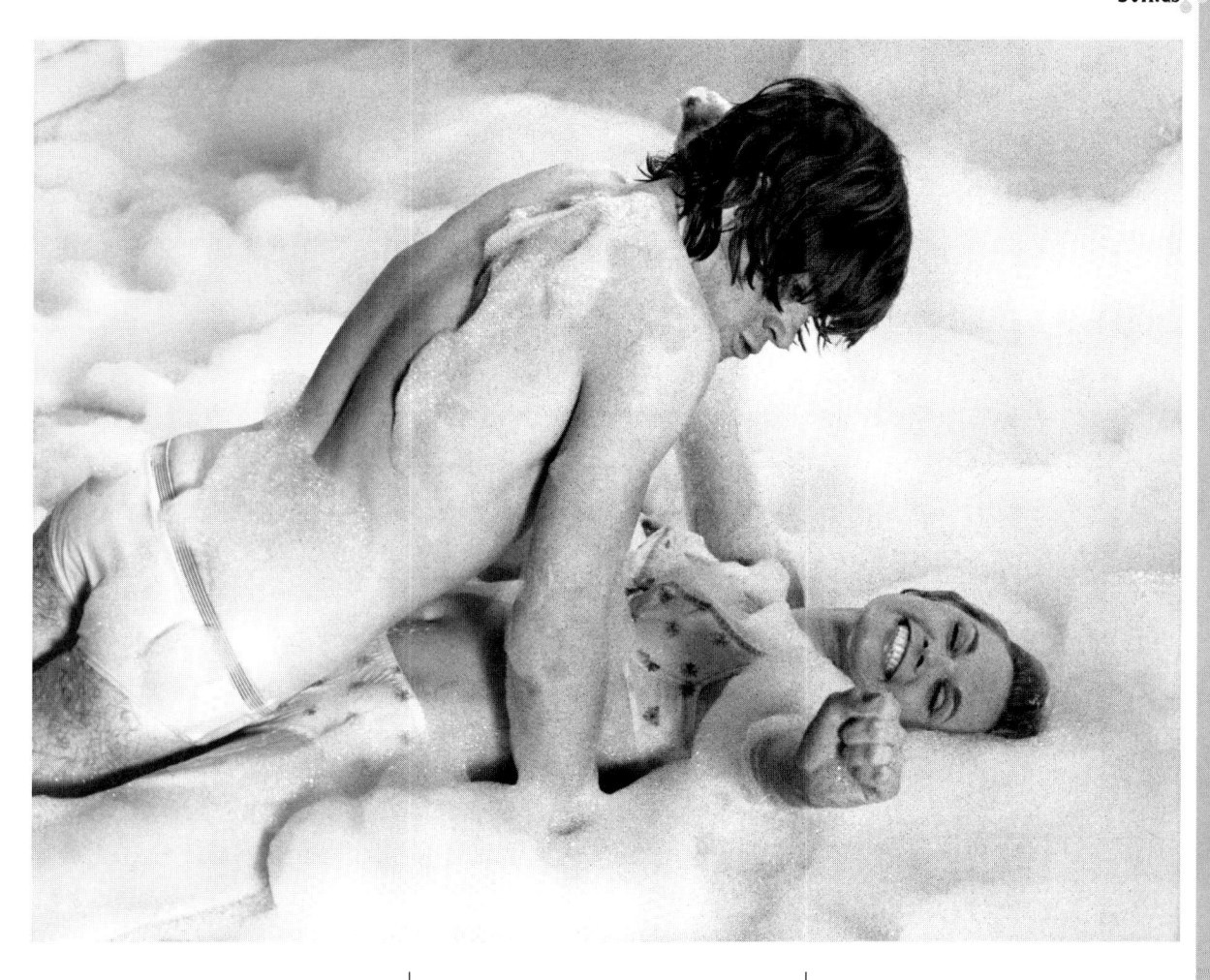

Bill Maynard was cast as Timmy's kleptomaniac, cloth-capped father, his peace-keeping wife was Dandy Nichols and their daughter, the ever-suspicious Rosie, was Sheila White. The role of her errant cheating husband, Sidney Noggett, was taken by Liverpudlian actor, Anthony Booth. 'Bill Maynard had committed to the film from day one. He loved the script,' says Smith. 'Tony Booth and Dandy came on board because my business partner Norman Cohen and I had done the film of *Till Death Us Do Part*, and John Le Mesurier signed up because of the *Dad's Army* picture we'd worked with him on.' Le Mesurier was just one of the comedy legends who graced *Window Cleaner* with invaluable special guest appearances; alongside him were Joan Hickson, Richard Wattis (in his last film) and ex-Hammer star Melissa Stribling. The film set an immediate trend by mixing the raunch with dollops of funny business from big-name character actors, often direct from the world of TV situation comedy. It was a route that all slapstick sex films would follow from 1974 onwards.

Womanising Sidney Noggett (Booth) runs his own window cleaning business (motto: 'We rub it better for you!'), but spends most of his time shagging the clients. Cocksure Sid desperately wants to educate virginal Timmy in the ways of the world, but is tiring of his brother-in-law's failure to lose his cherry. Setting Timmy up with local stripper Lilly Lamour – 'the biggest sensation since natural gas' – he hopes to finally fill the gap in the lad's sexual education. Backstage at the strip joint, Lilly (played by newcomer Christine Donna) happily agrees to show him the ropes, but the experience isn't exactly earth-shattering. Poor Timmy accidentally fucks her suspender belt! Thankfully, after a false start, he has better luck with other women on his window cleaning round and eventually loses his virginity in *the* single most talked-about sequence in 1970s sex comedies.

Jacqueline Brown (Sue Longhurst), a well-known nymphomaniac housewife,

KEEPING THE BRITISH END UP

Left: *Confessions of a Window Cleaner* (1974) – producer Greg Smith, director Val Guest, starlet Katya Wyeth and associate producer Norman Cohen.

invites Timmy round to soap up her windows. Attempting to fill his bucket in her sink, Timmy accidentally knocks over his bottle of industrial detergent, slips and is spread-eagled on the linoleum, powerless to defend himself from his lust-driven client. Water cascading out of the sink mixes with the detergent and creates football-sized bubbles covering the entire room, in which the two randy participants enjoy a squeaky-clean sex romp. On his exit, the exhilarated Timmy stands proudly on the doorstep to the sound of a chorus of 'Hallelujah'. 'Jacqui had certainly taught me how to come clean!' he quips.

'That single scene was definitely the defining moment of *Confessions of a Window Cleaner*,' believes Greg Smith. 'It became the single moment when that type of film just clicked. We built a set of the kitchen with a three-feet-tall sealed wall all around it and we just pumped in the detergent,' he adds. 'I kept the bubbles in and stopped Robin from getting out!' It proved to be an unforgettable experience for the two young actors, totally naked in a huge paddling pool full of bubbles. 'Val Guest was a terribly big director and some of us were worried how he'd be around nudity,' says Sue Longhurst. 'On my first day on set, myself and Robin stripped off and I felt slightly odd being naked in front of Val. Anyway we just had to get on with it and Robin and I started to do the sex scene on the floor covered in bubbles and they had these firemen with pressure hoses firing foam all over us. It was quite hilarious.'

Funny as it may look today, the scene was not without its perils. Askwith has since claimed that, with the scene taking two days to film, the corrosive nature of the foam badly burnt his bollocks. Uncomfortable from the experience for some days afterwards, Askwith says he developed an itchy rash, but his producer was not keen to get involved in a discussion regarding his star's red-raw gonads. 'I never saw them and nor did I ask to take a look!' Smith laughs.

Long ignored by highbrow cinema critics, *Window Cleaner* contains some quite poignant and heartfelt moments focusing on how the inexperienced Timmy learns to cope with the opposite sex, unravelling the complicated rules of courtship and sexual etiquette. Actress Linda Hayden plays Timmy's love interest Elizabeth Radlett, and the scene in which he debates whether to put his hand on her knee or around her shoulders at the cinema is both touching and funny. It is a scene many young men could actually relate to. Greg Smith agrees. 'It's a rites of passage film in essence,' he says, 'about a young man finding his way through the minefield of relationships. Plus, I think there's a lot of blokes out there who would like to be accosted by as many beautiful women as Timmy Lea and get away with it! Putting it simply, sex and relationships *are* funny.'

With the laughs coming thick and fast, some wickedly corny one-liners and Askwith's superb clowning, the tone is set for undoubtedly the best sex comedy series of the 1970s. *Confessions of a Window Cleaner* broke box-office records in the UK and was the highest-grossing British movie of 1974, as well as cleaning up in Europe and several commonwealth countries like South Africa, New Zealand and Australia. Despite this, back home it was extremely difficult to find a single critic who had a kind word to say about the movie. But, says Greg Smith, 'I just didn't care because the film made me laugh. Christopher Wood's script made me laugh, Robin made me laugh, Bill Maynard made me laugh. So by the time we got to the reviews I didn't care one bit. It came out towards the end of 1974 and was in profit by March 1975. The petty criticisms were cushioned hugely by the

Right: Jeremy Bulloch is sandwiched between Jenny Cox and Venicia Day in *Can You Keep It Up For a Week?* (1974).

numbers of people going to see the movie. There were still queues of people going to see that film in its tenth or eleventh week. People love to laugh and laughter is such a cure-all for almost anything.'

CAST: Robin Askwith (*Timothy Lea*), Anthony Booth (*Sidney Noggett*), Linda Hayden (*Elizabeth Radlett*), Bill Maynard (*Mr Lea*), Dandy Nichols (*Mrs Lea*), Sheila White (*Rosie Noggett*), John Le Mesurier (*Inspector Radlett*), Joan Hickson (*Mrs Radlett*), Katya Wyeth (*Carole*), Richard Wattis (*Carole's father*), Sue Longhurst (*Jacqui*), Melissa Stribling (*Mrs Villiers*), Anita Graham (*Ingrid*), Christine Donna (*Lilly Lamour*), Olivia Munday (*Brenda*), Judy Matheson (*Elvie*), Elaine Baillie (*Ronnie*), Jenny Westbrook (*girl in street*), Carole Augustine (*sunlamp girl*), Sam Kydd and Brian Hall (*removal men*), Marianne Stone (*woman in cinema*), Jeannie Collings, Monika Ringwald, Joanna Peters, Claire Russell (*Baby Dolls*), Porjai Nicholas (*second stripper*), Derek Lord (*policeman*), Christopher Owen (*Vicar*), Peter Dennis (*waiter*), Andee Cromarty (*window dresser*), David Rose (*store manager*), Eva Chatt [aka Ava Cadell], Petula Noble, Glenda Allen, Zoe Hendry (*naked college girls*)
CREDITS: *Director* Val Guest, *Producer* Greg Smith, *Executive Producer* Michael Klinger, *Associate Producer* Norman Cohen, *Editor* Bill Lenny, *Photography* Norman Warwick, *Screenplay* Christopher Wood and Val Guest, *Based on the novel by* Timothy Lea, *Music* Sam Sklai, *Theme song* 'This Is Your Life Timmy Lea' *performed by* Sue Cheyenne A SWIFTDOWN-COLUMBIA Production. Distributed by COLUMBIA-WARNER. Opened August 1974.

CAN YOU KEEP IT UP FOR A WEEK?

Great Britain / 1974 / 94 mins / cert 'X'

Only in a British sex comedy could you get a plot like this. Annette (Jill Damas), a prim young madam with big knockers, promises to marry her accident-prone boyfriend Gil (Jeremy Bulloch), on the condition that he keeps his hands off other women and holds down a proper job for seven days. If he breaks the bargain then he has to march up to Buckingham Palace stark naked. The trouble is, Bulloch, very much playing the Robin Askwith card here, just can't keep a job for five minutes and is continually getting into sexual misunderstandings with luscious females.

While trying to make a go of it at the local garage, he assists a frumpy female mechanic. 'What's that?' she asks him as he brushes past. 'I've got an adjustable spanner in my pocket,' he innocently replies. It's a fabulous sex film occupation, affording him plenty of gags about tools, stiffness, big equipment and 'filling it up', but Gil gets the sack for accidentally soaping up a topless dolly in the car wash and sticking a nozzle up some poor woman's arse. Seeking solace in the At Your Service employment agency, he meets the boss – a philandering old smoothie in a polo neck, Gerry Grimwood (Neil Hallett) – who promptly despatches his latest employee into the big bad world with a mop, bucket and vacuum cleaner.

Mrs Bristol (Sue Longhurst) is a consultant psychiatrist who just can't wait to put a new dent on her leather couch. Longhurst, who has never been so sexually predatory in a role, succeeds in turning their lovemaking into an impromptu foursome with a massive tangle of arms and legs. Busty Olivia Munday plays a bored housewife who 'inadvertently' gets her big toe stuck in her bath and seeks lubrication, and Valerie Leon is a butch whip-cracking lesbian with a liking for PVC body-suits and S & M. The most interesting client is a frilly gay photographer played by Richard O'Sullivan, whose agent presumably got him this job while he was 'resting' between series of hit Thames TV sitcom, *Man About the House*. Camping it up something rotten, he asks for somebody to dust his stone busts. 'I want someone to touch up my marbles with a feather duster,' he squeals. Klutzy Gil isn't doing very well but redeems himself at the agency's tenth anniversary party (shot on location at the Holiday Inn at Heathrow Airport), which is not much more than an excuse for zoom shots of jiggling boobs, naked bouncing on space hoppers and men in drag.

When Annette finally forgives him for his numerous indiscretions the couple get married. However, pulling a cliché right out of the sex comedy tombola, her new husband is too exhausted to make love because all the shagging-about wearing Marigolds has sapped his energy. Bulloch, who flits around gormlessly in a script salvaged out of Confessions screenwriter Christopher Wood's dustbin, was not asked to repeat his performance in another trousers-down romp. Now better known for keeping all his clothes on, having his face covered up and not uttering a single line of dialogue, Bulloch found greater fame as alien bounty hunter Boba Fett in the *Star Wars* films *The Empire Strikes Back* (1980) and *Return of the Jedi* (1983).

CAST: Jeremy Bulloch (*Gil*), Jill Damas (*Annette*), Neil Hallett (*Gerry Grimwood*), Sue Longhurst (*Mrs Bristol*), Richard O'Sullivan (*Mr Rose*), Jenny Cox (*Dr Livingstone*), Valerie Leon (*Miss Hampton*), Olivia Munday (*Mrs Hobson*), Mark Singleton (*Mr Hobson*), Joy Harrington (*Gloria Grimwood*), Venicia Day (*Sue Anne Stanley*), Sally Lahee (*Madam Chairman*), Sally Harrison (*car wash customer*), Frances Burnett (*driver*), Lyn Ross (*garage secretary*), Valerie Phillips (*mechanic*), Jules Walters (*John Thomas Smallpiece*), Nick McArdle (*drunkard*), Catherine Howe (*singer*), Wendy Wax (*Baby Doll*), Sarah Frampton (*Pamela*), Stephanie Marrian (*Lesley*), Maria Coyne (*receptionist*), Lindsay Marsh (*Gigi*)

CREDITS: Director Jim Atkinson, Producer Elton Hawke [aka Hazel Adair and Kent Walton], Editor Dave Docker, Photography Ricky Briggs, Screenplay Robin Gough, Music Harry South, Theme song 'Keep It For Me' written by Hazel Adair and Ted Dicks, Performed by Catherine Howe
A PYRAMID Production. Distributed by TARGET. Opened October 1974.

SEX PLAY
aka *The Bunny Caper* aka *The Games Girls Play*

Great Britain / 1974 / 90 mins / cert 'X'

Quite what persuaded American science fiction maestro Jack Arnold to come to England in 1974 to make a softcore porn movie is baffling. The veteran of *It Came from Outer Space* (1953), *Creature from the Black Lagoon* (1954) and *The Incredible Shrinking Man* (1957), as well as innocent TV series like *Gilligan's Island*, can only have been tempted by a suitcase of cash and the promise of quivering English flesh, although he did insist on bringing over with him an all-American beauty for the leading role.

Christina Hart, who plays *Sex Play*'s teenage temptress, was a popular face and body in primetime TV series like *Streets of San Francisco*, *Happy Days* and *Charlie's Angels*. She also made several 'scream queen' B-movies during the seventies, but waited to come to the UK before agreeing to take everything off. Perhaps she thought nobody would ever find out. Arnold, meanwhile, seems as much at home with naked girls as he does with oddities from outer space. His skill as a director saves *Sex Play* from being another run-of-the-mill sexploitation movie with a dot-to-dot plot – in which schoolgirls hold a sex competition where the winner must provide photographic proof.

Blue-eyed blonde Bunny O'Hara (Hart) is a rampant 16-year-old with a taste for older men in Washington's highest positions (or any position, come to think of it). She has become an embarrassment to her government official father and he accepts the job of US ambassador to London in the hope that the famous English reserve will subdue his daughter's unbridled sex drive. No such luck. Whisked away to her quaint Victorian finishing school, Bunny meets

DOINGS

Left: Gilligan's Island was never like this – a scene from Jack Arnold's Sex Play (1974).

her roommates (over-age vamps Jill Damas, Drina Pavlovic and Jane Anthony) and sets about instructing them in the ways of seduction.

Initially making them strip off and parade nude for the horrified headmistress, Bunny then sets them a humping challenge. Each girl draws a straw to see who can sleep with one of four VIPs currently making headlines in the tabloids: a visiting Chinese ping-pong champion, a Russian diplomat, the American foreign minister and HRH Prince Charles. They have varying success in their tasks (succulent Miss Damas gets steamed up with the entire Chinese ping-pong team in the pool), but the only bedroom target not to make an appearance is Britain's then-most eligible Royal bachelor. Charles was not forthcoming in a cameo role and the nearest the filmmakers got to him was a sentry box outside Windsor Castle.

CAST: Christina Hart (*Bunny O'Hara*), Gordon Sterne (*O'Hara*), Jane Athony (*Jackie*), Jill Damas (*Christine*), Drina Pavlovic (*Salina*), Erin Geraghty (*Ducky*), Ed Bishop (*Secretary Beard*), Murray Kash (*Dr Wolfgang Meyer*), Carolyn Whitaker (*Agnes*), Sarah Brackett (*Harriet*), Eunice Black (*Miss Grimm*), Myvanwy Jenn (*Judith*), Irena Peters (*Melinda*), Steve Plytas (*Krashneff*), David Beale (*Lord Teakwood*), Eric Young (*Wang Lo*), Rex Wei (*Chen Ling*)

CREDITS: *Director* Jack Arnold, *Producer* Peer J Oppenheimer, *Editor* Don Deacon, *Photography* Alan Hume, *Screenplay* Peer J Oppenheimer and Jameson Brewer, *Music* John Cameron

AN ELITE SYNDICATE Production. Distributed by ATLANTIC. Opened December 1974.

Eskimo Nell

aka *The Sexy Saga of Naughty Nell and Big Dick* aka *The Ballad of Eskimo Nell*

Great Britain / 1974 / 82 mins / cert 'X'

'If you're looking back at the sex comedy era then *Eskimo Nell* is the one that says it all,' says Stanley Long unequivocally. 'It was my way of having some fun at the expense of the industry, arising out of frustration at the way distributors were treating sex films in Britain. They were pushing for more explicitness all the time. They thought, quite wrongly, that the more tits and arses you had in a film the more successful it would be. That's bullshit.'

Long has described *Eskimo Nell* as his 'ultimate statement' on sex in the British cinema. While it's not a raunchy sex film *per se*, it is a vividly colourful and funny portrait of the British exploitation cinema of the mid-1970s. Nattily directed by *The Sex Thief*'s Martin Campbell and full of extremely funny jokes, it's a plucky British classic. The droll screenplay by Michael Armstrong takes wicked pot shots at the industry and his targets are all vaguely disguised members of the Wardour Street community. Armstrong also plays young, idealistic film school graduate Dennis. Desperate to direct his first film, he gets chucked out of every major film company in Soho (United Artists, Columbia-Warner etc) before spotting a sign for 'BUM Productions' in a dingy Soho doorway. Benny U Murdoch (Roy Kinnear), the breast-obsessed head of the company, offers Dennis the opportunity to direct a film version of the saucy Victorian poem 'Eskimo Nell'. Dennis has lofty ideas about how to make the movie, but Benny just wants naked girls.

Four potential backers come forward, but all have very different ideas about how the film should look – and all want their protégés to take the starring role. What follows is based entirely on Armstrong's experiences of trying to keep all of the people happy some of the time just to get a film made. Millionaire Ambrose Cream (Richard Caldicot) wants a Kung Fu musical version of *Eskimo Nell* starring his karate-chopping girlfriend (Prudence Drage). Old queen Vernon Peabody (Jeremy Hawke) sees the project as a cross-dressing gay Western with 'young boys having their bottoms spanked'. Lady Longhorn (Rosalind Knight), chairwoman of the Society for Moral Reform, envisages the movie as pure family entertainment with religious overtones. And sex producer Big Dick (Gordon Tanner) demands hardcore pornography. 'What I need is 90 minutes of good solid pornography, none of that simulated crap,' barks Big Dick. 'I want to see everything, so you shoot it for real. I want to see girls being whipped, plenty of flagellation, bondage, rubber appliances, leatherwear, chains, lesbianism, kinky gadgets and you can throw in a bit of bestiality at the same time.'

With Dennis' scriptwriter (Christopher

Left: Christopher Timothy is distracted by Beth Porter in *Eskimo Nell* (1974).

Timothy) tearing his hair out trying to write several very different screenplays, Benny absconds with the money, leaving his director up to his neck in trouble. With four different versions of the same film in the can, a cataclysmic cock-up occurs at the Royal charity première when the hardcore version is accidentally screened for the entertainment of Her Majesty.

Armstrong's excellent script is complemented by some standout comedy performances, particularly from Diane Langdon as the tarty and untutored Gladys Armitage, Benny's busty protégée, and priceless Beth Porter as Big Dick's sex-obsessed starlet who can do tricks with her breasts and a wine glass. Kinnear's character, forever proclaiming his virility ('No-one can call *me* a poof'), is loosely based on Tony Tenser, the sexploitation producer and owner of Tigon Film Distributors. Foul-mouthed Big Dick is really Samuel Z Arkoff, co-founder of the infamous American International Pictures. Armstrong himself plays a rough approximation of Michael Winner, while Lady Longhorn is a thinly veiled caricature of Mary Whitehouse. But did any of the real-life targets realise they were being lampooned? 'No, I don't think so,' says Stanley Long. 'We were just having a bit of fun and it was a comment on that whole period of filmmaking. Nobody came and had a go at me about it. I hope they would have been quite flattered!'

CAST: Michael Armstrong (*Dennis Morrison*), Roy Kinnear (*Benny U Murdoch*), Terence Edmond (*Clive Potter*), Christopher Timothy (*Harris Tweedle*), Diane Langton (*Gladys Armitage*), Gordon Tanner (*Big Dick*), Beth Porter (*Billie Harris*), Richard Caldicot (*Ambrose Cream*), Prudence Drage (*Millicent Bindle*), Jeremy Hawke (*Vernon Peabody*), Raynor Bourton (*Johnny*), Rosalind Knight (*Lady Longhorn*), Katy Manning (*Hermione Longhorn*), Anna Quayle (*Reverend Mother*), Jonathan Adams (*Lord Coltwind*), Christopher Biggins (*Jeremy Longhorn*), Stephen Riddle (*Simon*), Christopher Neil (*Brendan*), Sheila Bernette (*actress at casting*), Lloyd Lamble (*the Bishop*), Max Mason (*Dave*), Jenny Short (*Maggie*), Tony Sympson (*grandfather*), Beatrice Shaw (*grandmother*), David Toguri (*Kung Fu artist*), Mike Worsley (*Charlie*), Nicholas Young (*Deadeye Dick*), Lewis Barber (*Mexican Pete*), Graham Ashley (*projectionist*), Dave Carter (*laboratory man*), Connie Brodie (*the Queen*), Bill Maelor-Jones (*cinema manager*), Uncredited: Derek Martin (*floor manager*), Mary Maxted [aka Mary Millington] (*traffic warden stripper*), Charles Pemberton (*policeman*)
CREDITS: *Director* Martin Campbell, *Producer* Stanley Long, *Editor* Patrick Foster, *Photography* Peter Hannon, *Screenplay* Michael Armstrong, *Music* Simon Park, *Choreography* David Toguri
A SALON PRODUCTION Film. Distributed by EAGLE. Opened January 1975.

THE STUD
aka *The Importance of Being Randy*

Great Britain / 1974 / 81 mins / cert 'X'

Not to be confused with the identically titled sex movie from 1978 starring Joan Collins, this particular brand of stud-u-like started life as a sexy, big-budget spy spoof entitled *The Importance of Being Randy*, but was abandoned by its wealthy backers during pre-production. Director Billy White (aka Wilbur Stark), in his first solo venture since splitting with his film partner Tudor Gates, downsized the whole production, economised the title and plumped for satire over sexiness. As it turned out, *The Stud* is a piece of cheap-looking whimsy, randomly taking the piss out of James Bond, Hollywood musicals and, a decade too late, Andy Warhol and his artistic cronies.

The British security forces are concerned that somebody connected with the film studio operated by pop artist Randy Warpshot is smuggling top secret information to the Ruskies. Julian Holloway and buxom brunette Pamela Roland are MI6 undercover agents despatched to Warpshot's studio to track down the security leak, which takes the form of microdots disguised as beauty spots. Posing as models, they are forced into accepting parts in the eccentric artist's new softcore porn film, with Holloway in the lead.

A totally bizarre concoction with *Monty Python* overtones and softcore thrills, *The Stud* is an incomprehensible, amateurish mess of the highest order. Dudley Sutton does manage a close approximation of Warhol and Julian Holloway finally gets to grips with more female flesh than Barbara Windsor ever afforded him in the Carry On movies. However, the mixture of topless cat fights, music from ex-Manfred Mann guitarist Mike Vickers and contemporary satire does not work here. A humongous flop at the box-office, it never got a full release in the UK and today remains the sort of camp obscurity waiting to be rediscovered by cinephilic anoraks.

CAST: Dudley Sutton (*Randy Warpshot*), Julian Holloway (*Spencer*), Pamela Roland (*Jilly*), Jean Gilpin (*Nika*), Vicki Hodge (*Brigit*), Lindsay Kemp (*Topstar*), Cher Cameron (*Black Velvet*), Antony Scott (*Billy*), Jeremy Nicholas (*Allboy*), Bozena (*Olga*), Ken Benda (*Mr Carruthers*), Catherine Willmer (*Mrs Carruthers*)
CREDITS: *Director/Producer* Billy White [aka Wilbur Stark], *Editor* Rex Graves, *Photography* Grenville Middleton, *Screenplay* Jonathan Peeler, *Music* Mike Vickers
A GLOBEBEST Production. Distributed by MIRACLE. Opened May 1975.

THE AMOROUS MILKMAN

Great Britain / 1974 / 94 mins / cert 'X'

'Are you getting plenty? Ask your milkman!' reads the side of randy Davey Canning's trundling milkfloat. Clearly the local women don't need encouragement, since he is regularly besieged by fiery female customers demanding more than an extra pinta and a carton of clotted cream. Having his apron snatched and peaked-cap pinched by the grabbing hands of women on his patch (including Diana Dors at her terrifying best, all hair, tits and lips) becomes a regular breakfast routine.

Actor Derren Nesbitt, best remembered for playing baby-faced thugs and hit-men in films from the fifties and sixties, takes the reins of his first film as director, as well as producing, writing (he adapted his own novel) and making a Hitchcock-like cameo as a milkman. Unfortunately, placing so many important jobs in such inexperienced hands makes the film a bit of a curdled mess. Nesbitt, obviously thinking he can write comedy innuendo as well as Carry On maestro Talbot Rothwell, rather over-eggs the pudding with an overdose of painfully unfunny dialogue, delivered in utterly banal fashion. When the hero accidentally bangs into a young woman,

Right: Christopher Chittell, another future *Emmerdale* star, and Jeannie Collings in shagfest *Erotic Inferno* (1975).

bending down to feed her mewing cat, he says, 'I hope I didn't hurt your pussy.' We also have lines like, 'D'you think I could have a bit extra tomorrow?', 'Do you like the organ?' and a sex orgy at a house in 'Stilorgan Road'. In more accomplished hands these lines may have raised a titter, but they certainly don't here. Brendan Price is an absolutely hopeless male lead playing much the same prattish character he gave us in *Secrets of a Door to Door Salesman*, but with even less enthusiasm.

Nesbitt's extremely set-bound story comes across like a half-baked, second-rate Ray Cooney stage farce, continually hindered by the flabby direction. He attempts to compensate with considerable nudity and big-name cameos from the likes of Bill Fraser and Roy Kinnear. But, just when you think the film couldn't get any more annoying, Alan Lake turns up as a would-be Casanova (with his shirt open to the waist and a medallion hanging round his wringable neck) and Dors accuses Price of rape after he spurns her advances. Oddly, it is Price, not Dors, who is examined by the police doctor in a really unpleasant scene where his underpants and genitals are examined for 'residue'. Thereafter, the film briefly degenerates into a 'comedy' about sexual assault, with about as many laughs as you would expect from such a subject. As sex pictures go, this is the dregs, a thoroughly irksome experience for all involved, probably none more so than Nesbitt himself, who seems so fed up with the film he just abruptly ends it

after 90 tedious minutes.

On a slightly more positive note, Brendan Price is surrounded by an assemblage of beautiful leading ladies including Hammer Horror starlet Julie Ege, American Nancie Wait and Benny Hill girl Jenny Westbrook. Had Derren Nesbitt played his cards right he could have got the lovely Sue Longhurst too, but the role he offered was a little on the droopy side. 'I went for an audition, but what a joke!' Sue exclaims. 'Nesbitt offered me this terrible part. No acting, no words, no nothing. All he wanted me to do was groan. Just go "Uuuhh" and that was it. Well, I turned him down flat. By that stage I wanted to act, not just fake orgasms!'

CAST: Brendan Price (*Davey Canning*), Bill Fraser (*Gerald Jones*), Diana Dors (*Rita Jones*), Julie Ege (*Diana*), Donna Reading (*Janice Peters*), Nancie Wait (*Margo*), Alan Lake (*Sandy*), Megs Jenkins (*Iris Peters*), Patrick Holt (*Tom Peters*), Sam Kydd (*Wilf*), Janet Webb (*Vera*), Ray Barrett (*John*), Roy Kinnear (*Police Sergeant*), Fred Emney (*Magistrate*), Anthony Sharp (*Counsel*), Ivor Salter (*policeman*), Arnold Ridley (*cinema attendant*), *Uncredited:* Jenny Westbrook (*Joan*), Norman Chappell (*first ambulanceman*), Derren Nesbitt (*new milkman*), Marianne Morris (*Dora*), Monika Ringwald (*party girl*)
CREDITS: *Director/Producer/Screenplay* Derren Nesbitt, *Editor* Russell Lloyd, *Photography* Jim Allen, *Music* Roger Webb
A LANKA Film. Distributed by VARIETY. Opened June 1975.

CONFESSIONS OF A SEX MANIAC
aka *Design for Lust* aka *The Man Who Couldn't Get Enough*

Great Britain / 1974 / 81 mins / cert 'X'

As sexually opportunistic professions go, an architect isn't really the most terrific job in the world, but all the obvious ones were rapidly being gobbled up. The eager sex comedy audience of the 1970s had already exhausted door to door salesmen, amorous milkmen and cheeky window cleaners, all of which offered ample chance to meet half-naked women on suburban doorsteps, don't forget. But a man who designs tower blocks for a living? What's so interesting about that? Well, you'd be surprised!

Egghead master-architect Sir Bernard Storm (Derek Royle) is off on a prestigious lecture tour of the USA when a new commission is suddenly dropped on his desk – a multi-million dollar marina complex in Sydney Australia. What's more, the plans need to be completed within just four weeks. Unable to deal with the lucrative new project, he hands it over to his sex-mad, long-haired layabout assistant, Henry, played by then-little-known actor, Roger Lloyd Pack. Today, people more used to Lloyd Pack playing nitwits in TV sitcoms *Only Fools and Horses* and *The Vicar of Dibley* will be surprised to see what a lithe, fit young man he was in his youth, totally naked and romping about in some pretty raunchy sex scenes. Unfortunately, this isn't the sort of performance that could ever be recycled on

Before They Were Famous.

Young Henry is undoubtedly talented, but he just can't keep his mind on his work. All he can do is dream about naked girls, but if he doesn't deliver the goods he gets the sack. He endures a fitful night's sleep, both tossed and turned (though primarily just tossed), until inspiration finally hits him: knockers! Yes, you heard right, a building that looks like a giant breast. 'But you can't have a great boob straddling the skyline!' complains his secretary Hilary (Vicki Hodge). In order to achieve his aim Henry has to find the superlative hooters on which he can model his design. After placing an advert in *Time Out*, his office is inundated with wobbling bosoms of all shapes and sizes to be examined with expert precision (in other words, a protractor and a ruler). He meets all the various sex-toy females, a neglected housewife, a wistful hippy and a young nympho, until his quest for the 'perfect pair' hits him straight in the face: the norks belonging to office dolly Hilary. Sir Bernard summarily returns and Henry's design is a roaring, if unconventional, success – a big bulbous building with a huge pink nipple on the roof.

Director Alan Birkinshaw's one-joke movie was first known as *Design for Lust* but powerful distributor Oppidan, owned by David Grant, who always had his eye on the box-office takings, dispensed with the original title and gave it a far more in-yer-face approach. *Confessions of a Window Cleaner* had already lathered up the British cinemagoing public, so Grant thought he'd 'borrow' part of the title and add an unsubtle twist of his own. Thus, the deep and meaningful *Confessions of a Sex Maniac* was born. Columbia Pictures were not impressed and slapped an injunction on the film; I mean, could the world really cope with two rival Confessions series?. It was hastily reissued in February 1976 under a third title, *The Man Who Couldn't Get Enough*. As one character comments in the movie: 'If it wasn't so predictable it would be obscene!'

CAST: Roger Lloyd Pack (*Henry Milligan*), Vicki Hodge (*Hilary*), Derek Royle (*Sir Bernard Storm*), Stephanie Marrian (*Susan*), Louise Rush (*Val*), Candy Baker (*Millie*), Ava Cadell (*last girl*), Cheryl Gilham (*housewife*), Jeanette Marsden (*hippy*), Carole Hayman (*piano girl*), John Aston (*postman*), Bobby Sparrow (*girl in pub*), Monika Ringwald, Zoe Hendry, Glenda Allen, Audrey Frank and Jo Peters (*girls*)

CREDITS: *Director/Producer* Alan Birkinshaw, *Editor* David White, *Photography* Arthur Lavis, *Screenplay* Alan Paz, *Music* John Shakespeare and Derek Warne
A ROTHERNORTH Production. Distributed by OPPIDAN. Opened July 1975.

1975

EROTIC INFERNO
aka *Adam and Nicole* aka *The Naked Key* aka *Naked and Willing*

Great Britain / 1975 / 80 mins / cert 'X'

Erotic Inferno is a bit of a British sex film rarity. This hasn't got anything to do with the acting, the direction or production values (all above average, incidentally). No, what makes this sex movie unusual is that it's genuinely full of shagging. Jon York's slim screenplay (for which he was paid £250) has more frenzied rural rutting and nudity than a whole library of Jilly Cooper bonkbusters. And the sex isn't just confined to the bedroom either. We see it in the stable block, against a wall, over a cooker, on the breakfast table, in the hall, in the barn, in the bathroom and even in the back of a Range Rover.

After the mysterious disappearance of their lecherous father at sea, devious tough guy Martin Barnard (Chris Chittell) and his ditchwater-dull younger brother Paul (Karl Lanchbury) are called

Keeping the British End Up

to his grand country estate by solicitor Eric Gold (played by Michael Sheard, later to gain infamy as Mr Bronson in children's serial *Grange Hill*). With their daddy missing presumed dead, they prepare themselves for the reading of his last will and testament, but are bemused to find the manor house locked and bolted. Under strict instructions from the solicitor, all beneficiaries must bed down in the housekeeper's cottage, currently occupied by butch estate manager Adam (Michael Watkins) and his sometime girlfriend Nicole (Jenny Westbrook). Having to wait 24 hours, the randy devils amuse themselves with a bed-hopping merry-go-round. Martin manages to keep his pecker up for his girlfriend Brenda (Jeannie Collings), winsome Nicole and lusty bisexual stable lass Gayle (Heather Deeley), who is currently shacked up with her domineering girlfriend (Mary Millington in a very early role). Adam, meanwhile, has also been greasing the weasel with Gayle, Nicole and Brenda, while Brenda has been sleeping with Paul who, in turn, is also shagging Nicole. Got that? No? You really need a spider diagram to keep up with things.

The men are universally charmless bastards and the women demure, pitiful, 'dirty little bitches' who get roughed up and forced to have sexual intercourse but secretly 'quite like it'. Experienced thespian Christopher Chittell is mesmerising (and unintentionally very funny) in the central role of randy womaniser Martin. Unable to keep his hands to himself or his dick in his pants, he can smell a woman at 10,000 feet. Chittell, a veteran of such movies as *To Sir With Love*, shows expert handling of the deep and meaningful porn dialogue. 'You little hot sex kitten,' he growls. 'This is what you want. You love it, don't you?' It comes as no surprise to learn that Chittell had previously appeared in a hardcore movie, *The Intruders* aka *Let Us Play Sex* (1974) in Sweden, directed by porn pioneer Torgny Wickman, and later starred in two more: *Country Life* and *Molly* (both 1977). Shaking off his stud image, Chittell went on to plough entirely different furrows in Yorkshire Television's hit primetime soap, *Emmerdale*.

The silly twist in the film's tale is that old Mr Barnard (Tony Kenyon) is not actually dead at all. He's been secretly holed up in the manor house with a couple of champagne-quaffing blonde nymphos watching how his offspring react to his 'passing' during their dirty weekend. *Erotic Inferno* was a return to British sex movies for producer Bachoo Sen, who had first entered the fray with Norman J Warren's *Her Private Hell* in 1967. Shot in just 22 days, the film was also director Trevor Wrenn's last movie. Wrenn had previously been a cinematographer on José Larraz' sex-horror films *Scream and Die* and *Symtoms* (both 1973) – actor Karl Lanchbury was also borrowed from the Larraz stable – and Wrenn's moody direction, effective use of lighting, great locations and sound performances (most of the cast being dubbed, notwithstanding) made *Erotic Inferno* a big hit.

The film opened at Bachoo Sen's own cinema, the Astral in Soho's Brewer Street in May 1975 but in June the following year the precious landlords of the cinema's premises sought a High Court injunction to stop the film being shown, claiming that *Erotic Inferno* was 'lewd and pornographic'. Well, of course it was! Had it taken them a year to realise that? The legal action failed and the landlords, George and Billy Walker, adopted the attitude 'If you can't beat 'em, join 'em' by later ploughing money into several dirty movies of their own. *Erotic Inferno* continued to entertain the dirty raincoats of Soho, on and off, for nearly four years. It's a tidy little movie without too much plot to get in the way of the nudity and one of the few actually tailor-made for its intended audience. Oh, and did I mention? It's full of sex.

CAST: Michael Watkins (*Adam*), Jenny Westbrook (*Nicole*), Chris Chittell (*Martin Barnard*), Karl Lanchbury (*Paul Barnard*), Jeannie Collings (*Brenda*), Heather Deeley (*Gayle*), Mary Maxted [aka Mary Millington] (*Jane*), Michael Sheard (*Eric Gold*), Brian Hawksley (*Vicar*), Anthony Kenyon (*Old Mr Barnard*), Monika Ringwald (*girl in hotel bed*), Lindy Benson (*first blonde*), Lynne Worral (*second blonde*).
CREDITS: *Director* Trevor Wrenn, *Producer* Ken Coles, *Executive Producer* Bachoo Sen, *Editor* John Rogers, *Photography* Dudley Lovell, *Screenplay* Jon York
Produced and distributed by THE ENGLISH FILM COMPANY. Opened May 1975.

GIRLS COME FIRST

Great Britain / 1975 / 45 mins / cert 'X'

Light, fluffy, sweet and just long enough to savour, *Girls Come First* is just like a bubbly chocolate bar. With the slimmest of silly story-lines bulked out by an exceedingly attractive cast and fairly raunchy sex scenes, the movie, produced by master sexploiter David Grant, is an excellent example of frugal British filmmaking, emphatically tailored to its intended audience but executed with a certain style. The sex scenes are passionate and well directed without ever being tacky and the dreamy, French-tinged romantic score from Grant's favourite composer, John Shakespeare, complements the well choreographed naked grapplings perfectly.

Former Tony Hancock stooge Bill Kerr plays a loud, cocky American who owns a top-shelf periodical called *The Swinger* but, tiring of the magazine's style, asks hunky erotic artist Alan Street to inject a bit of oomph into the pages. Alan (John Hamill, reprising his character from the previous year's *Over-Amorous Artist*) accepts the job (much to his girlfriend Sue Longhurst's consternation) and moves into Kerr's Soho swingers' club to paint the nude hostesses. Within minutes of getting his easel out Alan is beset by pretty women turned on by his muscles. Those queuing up for a feel are Heather Deeley, mini-blonde bombshell Bobby Sparrow and Hazel Glyn, in the days before she became pop sensation Hazel O'Connor. Her porn past caught up with her thanks to clips resurfacing on an *Electric Blue* video a decade later, but obviously she had some happy memories of making love to John Hamill. One of her 1981 hits was entitled 'Give Me An Inch'.

Complementing the bonking, there's the odd flash of wit – a rabbi reading a porn magazine behind a copy of the *Jewish Chronicle* – and a few chuckles to be had at the expense of Kerr's Japanese chauffeur (Burt Kwouk), who eats dogs for breakfast and treats Sue Longhurst to some of his *Pink Panther* Kung Fu moves, and loses.

Running at only 45 minutes, but shot in a hardcore version for overseas markets, it's fortunate that *Girls Come First* was ever finished. Grant's previous movie *Pink Orgasm*, made only months earlier and starring Heather Deeley and Victor Spinetti, ran out of steam part-way through shooting. Only two or three sequences were filmed and only 15 minutes of footage ended up in the can. 'With a lot of David Grant's films he just ran out of impetus,' said his business partner Ray Selfe. 'It was just a question of filming a little scene and he was happy with that. He made films to please himself. He had to be pushed to finish a film.'

Girls Come First was filmed by TV director Joseph McGrath (who disliked sex movies, but needed the work) under the exotic moniker Croisette Meubles. Grant hoped that excited cinemagoers would think this was the first sex picture to be directed by a woman. In fact, Croisette Meubles is a street name in Cannes which Grant had spotted out of the corner of his eye the last time he attended the famous film festival.

CAST: John Hamill (*Alan Street*), Bill Kerr (*Hugh Jampton*), Sue Longhurst (*Sue*), Burt Kwouk (*Sashimi*), Rikki Howard (*Sonia Drysdale*), Cheryl Gilham (*Zoe*), Hazel Glyn [aka Hazel O'Connor] (*Claire*), Bobby Sparrow (*Miss Broad*), Heather Deeley (*French maid*), David Grant [uncredited] (*pedestrian*)

CREDITS: *Director* Croisette Meubles [aka Joseph McGrath], *Producers* David Grant and Malcolm Fancey, *Editors* Paul Hennessey and Malcolm Lowry, *Photography* Robin Brown, *Screenplay* Joseph McGrath and Gordon Exelby, *Music* John Shakespeare and Derek Warne, *Theme song* 'Girls Come First' *performed by* Ross McManus
An OPPIDAN-NEW REALM Production. Distributed by NEW REALM. Opened July 1975.

CONFESSIONS OF A POP PERFORMER

Great Britain / 1975 / 91 mins / cert 'X'

'*Confessions of a Window Cleaner* had only been on release for two months when Columbia Pictures turned round to me and said they wanted a sequel,' says producer Greg Smith. 'It's weird because I never wanted to do a series of comedies really, but we had the books to work from and we went along with it. Then by the time we were already shooting the follow-up we knew that there'd be a third one too, and then very possibly a fourth one after that.'

By the end of 1974 there were already eleven Christopher Wood novels on the market, plus an unofficial rival paperback series penned by Jonathan May. After

KEEPING THE BRITISH END UP

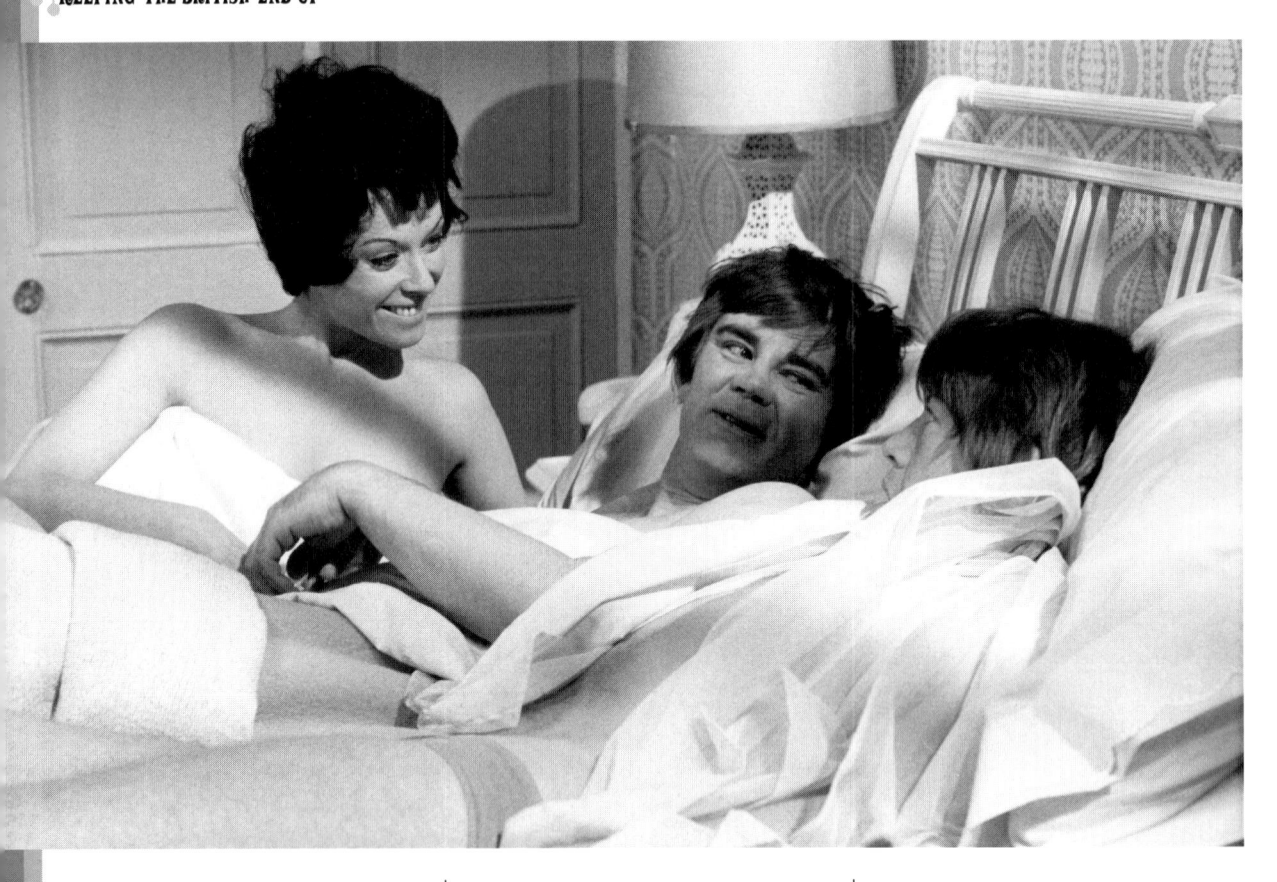

Window Cleaner the next book in the series had been *Confessions of a Driving Instructor*, but Greg Smith took the decision early on to adapt one of Wood's more recent novels, *Confessions from the Pop Scene*, which had been published in the spring of 1974. 'We changed the name to *Confessions of a Pop Performer* because we thought 'performer' was more of a double entendre,' admits Smith.

With Val Guest unwilling to do another sex comedy (his wife Yolande Donlan was not keen to see her husband go down that route again), *Window Cleaner*'s associate producer Norman Cohen was drafted in to helm the sequel. All the principal cast members were happy to reprise their roles but Dandy Nichols, who had played Mrs Lea in the first movie, was unavailable due to the movie's shooting dates conflicting with the filming of what was to be the last original series of Johnny Speight's BBC series *Till Death Us Do Part*. She was immediately replaced by a comedy character actress of considerable standing, Doris Hare, well known as Reg Varney's devoted mum in long-running ITV sitcom *On the Buses*.

Tiring of window cleaning and its attendant dangers (like Bill Pertwee and his well-sharpened javelin), Sid and Timmy set up 'Noggo Enterprises' to promote up-and-coming local pub band 'Kipper', featuring Peter Cleall (from *Please Sir!*), David Auker, Richard Warwick and Bill Maynard's real-life son, Maynard Williams (the spitting image of Liam Gallagher). Sid arranges for them to play their first big showcase gig at the local civic centre, but when the group's drummer hurts his finger Timmy takes over at short notice to perform their theme tune 'Do the Clapham'. Unfortunately, Sid's attempts at getting together a bunch of screaming teenage fans fall flat when the only rent-a-crowd he can manage are members of the Clapham Old Girl's Club. In a very amusing scene, the geriatric groupies (average age: 68), dressed in 'I Love Kipper' T-shirts, storm the stage and cause a riot.

Unlikely as it may sound, *Pop Performer*'s musical numbers, produced by Ed Welch and Mike King (from 1950s band the King Brothers), are actually pretty catchy and the movie was released with a tie-in soundtrack album on Polydor Records. In addition to incidental music for the film, the LP also included all of Kipper's 'hits' and the charming ditty 'I Need You (Like a Hole in the Head)', as performed by the band's main rivals, the outrageous Climax Sister. Played by Diane Langton and Linda Regan, the gruesome twosome are crude, lewd, sexually voracious temptresses described in the movie as 'two wonderful old pros'. Kipper's musical prowess somehow gets them onto TV talent show *Opportunity Knockers*, compèred by Peter Jones as Maxy Naus, whose close approximation of *Opportunity Knocks*' Hughie Green hits just the right note. However,

Left: Jill Gascoine entertains Tony Booth and Robin Askwith in *Confessions of a Pop Performer* (1975).

Right: Timmy Lea and his family from *Confessions of a Pop Performer*. Clockwise – Bill Maynard, Tony Booth, Sheila White, Robin Askwith and Doris Hare.

no surprises here, their television début ends in cataclysmic disaster when the band blow up the show's 'applause-o-meter'. It goes from bad to verse when the accident-prone band put in a farcical performance at the Royal Variety Show, shocking the Queen and Prince Philip.

As usual there's the familiar smattering of rattling bed posts, creaking doors and trembling drinks trolleys as Timmy takes advantage of the nubile young ladies of the record business. One young groupie mistakes him for Mick Jagger making a comeback and is determined to find out if it's really a 'rolled-up sock' down his jeans. Scandinavian Helli Louise is the well-upholstered contortionist, Eva the acrobat, who takes to limbering up backstage with a little help from our hero, while severe Maggie Wright unwittingly makes Timmy the subject of primetime entertainment through a two-way mirror at a record executive's party. For future star-spotters it's interesting to see Askwith bed down with breathless nymphomaniac Mrs Barnwell, played by 28-year-old Jill Gascoine. She's better known today for her role in ITV's detective series *The Gentle Touch* and as a bestselling authoress based in California with actor-husband Alfred Molina. Ms Gascoine strips off with great aplomb in her movie début and, in addition to shagging Askwith, has to fake embarrassing orgasms with Tony Booth, plus – horror of horrors – Benny Hill stooge, Bob Todd!

Director Cohen brings a quicker pace and more physical comedy to the second Confessions movie and fills the running time with wall-to-wall slapstick. Walking disaster area Timmy Lea's clumsy antics with foam-filled fire extinguishers, spilt beer, pots of paint and theatre trapdoors take him dangerously close to Norman Wisdom territory, only Norman was never seen on film engaging in cumbersome sexual intercourse while dressed as a pantomime horse. The crowning glory of the movie comes when dear old headscarfed cockney Rita Webb makes a bravura appearance as a furious mother looking for her groupie daughter on the Kipper 'tour bus'. Wielding a lethal-looking umbrella, she has one of the most unforgettable lines in British sex comedy: 'Have you seen my Fanny?'

CAST: Robin Askwith (*Timothy Lea*), Anthony Booth (*Sidney Noggett*), Doris Hare (*Mrs Lea*), Bill Maynard (*Mr Lea*), Sheila White (*Rosie Noggett*), Bob Todd (*Mr Barnwell*), Jill Gascoine (*Mrs Barnwell*), Peter Cleall (*Nutter Normington*), Peter Jones (*Maxy Naus*), Carol Hawkins (*Jill Brown*), Richard Warwick (*Petal*), Maynard Williams (*Eric*), Mike King (*Blow*), David Auker (*Zombie*), Diane Langton (*Ruby Climax*), Linda Regan (*Brenda Climax*), Margaret Heald (*Linda*), Andee Cromarty (*Fanny*), Rita Webb (*Fanny's mother*), Ian Lavender (*Rodney*), Bill Pertwee (*Fred*), Robert Dorning (*Augustus Brown*), Maggie Wright (*Ruth*), Suzette St Clair (*Sharon*), Irene Gorst

KEEPING THE BRITISH END UP

(*Penelope*), Anita Kay (*Sonia*), Sally Harrison (*Patsie*), Lynda Westover (*Carole*), David Hamilton (*Peter Moorcock*), Helli Louise (*Eva the acrobat*), Rula Lenska (*receptionist*), Vicki Woolf (*secretary*), Jackie Blackmore (*woman on doorstep*), Bobby Sparrow (*girl at cinema*), Dave Prowse (*man at cinema*), Emma Booth (*little girl*), Jane Hayden (*girl at crossing*), Helen Ford (*old lady with ear trumpet*)

CREDITS: *Director* Norman Cohen, *Producer* Greg Smith, *Executive Producer* Michael Klinger, *Editor* Geoffrey Foot, *Photography* Alan Hume, *Screenplay* Christopher Wood *based on the novel by* Timothy Lea, *Music* Bugatti Musker
A SWIFTDOWN-COLUMBIA Production. Distributed by COLUMBIA-WARNER. Opened September 1975.

THE SEXPLORER
aka *The Girl from Starship Venus* aka *Diary of a Space Virgin*

Great Britain / 1975 / 85 mins / cert 'X'

For some inexplicable reason *The Sexplorer* is supposed to be cult American filmmaker Quentin Tarantino's favourite British film. Quite why the director of *Pulp Fiction* is so taken with this trifling little piece of sexploitation is utterly mystifying. In Derek Ford's film a heroic alien explorer from Venus is despatched to Earth to survey mankind in all its lasciviousness. And what better place to start than the neon-illuminated heart of Soho? The spacecraft is actually a ball-bearing suspended on a piece of cotton (no expense spared), which plops into a puddle in Piccadilly Circus. As if by magic, out pops a full-sized alien, who has helpfully adopted the form of a naked German girl. Attempting to remain inconspicuous, she is instructed by her mothership to recite a line of 'Earth dialogue': 'I am a writer. I am 170 years old. My name is Mark Twain.'

The luscious extraterrestrial is played by Teutonic blonde model, Monika Ringwald, who was never any great shakes as an actress, but is absolutely perfect here, since she's not called upon to talk much and all she has to do is look moronic and walk in a bewildered state round sex shops like a wind-up robot. As a few of her ex-colleagues have suggested, that's exactly how she was all the time. On the night-time streets of Soho, Monika's nudi-

Left: Mark Jones and Monika Ringwald get ready for refuelling in The Sexplorer *(1975).*

ty makes her an obvious target, so she is kitted out with a fetching overall from a sauna to cover her modesty. Continuing her travels through the dirtiest square mile in London she is transfixed by sex toys, strip clubs and all the breast-swinging activities on offer. Although she probably looks most startled seeing John Inman's name emblazoned on the *Let's Get Laid!* poster outside the Windmill Theatre.

Men are a huge source of fascination to her. Stumbling blithely into a gents' toilet she assumes a penis ('a large probe') is probably 'some sort of refuelling equipment', while the raincoated perverts in the Focus Cinema (later the Astral) on Brewer Street are visiting a 'building of an educational nature'. Monika's nearly right and she certainly learns one lesson, by mimicking the on-screen porn action and giving seedy patron Anthony Kenyon a deft blow-job. Attempting to blend into her surroundings, she also blows something else – her cover – when a sip of alcohol inadvertently turns her green from head to toe. She later gets herself into even more trouble when another lech, Mark Jones, discovers, to his cost, that her fanny is electrically charged!

While Monika's innocent observations of London are really quite sweet, the film only gets going when she is furnished with a full set of sensory organs which give her an exaggerated sexual drive. 'I'm ready for refuelling,' she says excitedly after discovering the true meaning of sex. Alan Selwyn's theme song is also rather jovial. *'She's the girl from Starship Venus. She's arrived from outer space and she's landed on our planet just to watch the human race. She's got turned on to permissiveness and now keeps up with the pace.'* You can't get better than that! The film was also shot with hardcore inserts and additional scenes for America. Dare I say it, perhaps that's why Tarantino likes it so much.

CAST: Monika Ringwald (*the Sexplorer*), Andrew Grant (*Allan*), Mark Jones (*best man*), Alan Selwyn (*Bert*), Anthony Kenyon (*man in cinema*), David Rayner (*Lenny*), Michael Cronin (*doctor*), Dave Carter (*Inspector*), Catriona Nurse (*policewoman*), Elaine Baillie (*sauna attendant*), Prudence Drage (*Doris*), Anna Dawson (*shop manageress*), Chris Gannon (*store detective*), Beatrice Shaw (*Old Ethel*), Maria Ski (*usherette*), Ros Strang (*girl in sauna*), Tanya Ferova (*club stripper*), Albin Pahernik (*man in toilet*), Juliet Groves and Roy Scammell (*club dancers*)

CREDITS: *Director/Screenplay* Derek Ford, *Producer* Morton M Lewis, *Editor* Howard Lanning, *Photography* Roy Poynter, *Music* John Shakespeare, *Theme song* 'Girl from Starship Venus' *performed by* Don Lang, *Theme song written by* Alan Selwyn and Bruce Graham
A MEADWAY FILMS Production. Distributed by BUTCHERS. Opened October 1975.

SEX EXPRESS
aka *Diversions*

Great Britain / 1975 / 50 mins / cert 'X'

A pretty female prisoner and her two escorts, one male and one female, arrive handcuffed together at Paddington Station. Sentenced to five years' imprisonment for grievous assault, the woman is to be transferred to another prison. Entering the crowded railway carriage, Imogene (Heather Deeley) stares out of the window as suburbia whizzes past. Feeling a little drowsy she starts fantasising about some of the other passengers...

Imogene imagines making love to the hippy student (Jeffrey Morgan) sitting opposite her, in a barn strewn with apples. She next turns her attentions to a fedora-hatted stranger (Timothy Blackstone) who sits silently in the carriage reading a *Vampirella* comic book. Imogene is thrust back in time to when she was a nurse in the Vietnam war gang-raped by a group of soldiers. Exacting her revenge on men, she cruises the streets of Soho in her convertible, picking up guys and taking them back to her apartment to have sex before stabbing them to death. Blackstone is one of her unfortunate victims, but she soon meets her match in a real-life vampire. Next she fantasises about moving into an ex-call girl's flat and, when a handsome gentleman caller arrives to view the property, she poses as the hooker and sleeps with him for £100. In the last dream sequence, Imogene buys a 19th century camera and tripod from a Victorian memorabilia shop, but the ghost of the previous owner (Anthony Kenyon) and his parlour maid return for a little out-of-body slap and tickle.

The twist in the tale is that Imogene is not the prisoner at all. She is really one of the escorts. The real gaol bird is her sullen-faced companion, prisoner

Left: The biggest sex star of 1975 – Heather Deeley in *Sex Express*.

Brown (Jacky Rigby). Quite clever, but this all seems pretty straightforward stuff from sex film director Derek Ford. Although it's undeniably the most visually stimulating of his many productions, and enjoys a much more mature tone than his earlier works, standing alone it would be indistinguishable from a lot of low-budget British fare of the seventies. Of course, the film still contains a smattering of lighter touches so beloved of the British audience and enjoyed a lengthy run at the Moulin Cinema as one half of a double-bill with Torgny Wickman's melancholy Swedish drama *Anita* (1973). And Deeley got a few kind notices for her central performance.

However, don't be taken in by all the innocent bum-tickling, cute smiles and comedic flourishes. In its unexpurgated overseas version *Sex Express* is one of the most genuinely disturbing and horrific British films ever shot. This is made all the more shocking because of its great age. Hardcore versions of British sex comedies were commonplace by the mid-1970s. Back then it was an open secret in Wardour Street that some directors were dabbling with things better left alone. Even today several British sex comedy veterans will not admit publicly what they really got up to. The late Derek Ford was one of the main perpetrators of hardcore, slipping in a bit of penetration and oral sex into films like *Keep It Up Jack!*. In *Sex Express* he goes beyond the pale. Released in America in March 1976, his film was a full 27 minutes longer than its British counterpart and sported a new title: *Diversions*. Ford made no attempt to cover his tracks by adopting an overseas pseudonym for himself or any of his cast members. This was a British film for kinkier overseas tastes and he was proud of it.

Diversions follows exactly the same framework as the original. Deeley daydreams her peculiar fantasies, but instead of pretending to have intercourse she does it for real. Nothing surprising in that, except that she totally dominates every sex scene and acts the rest of the cast off the screen. But in an additional scene, never included in the UK print, Deeley is shown being forced to have sex with Nazis. With Deeley made to suck on the end of a rifle, having a knife rubbed over her body and then indulging in a bisexual threesome complete with anal penetration… no wonder Ford refused to submit this sequence to the BBFC. But this is nothing compared to Deeley's scene with Timothy Blackstone. In the unedited version (and readers of a nervous disposition please turn away now), the heroine stabs Blackstone to death, masturbates with his blood, cuts off his penis and sucks it. A deeply unpleasant scene (obviously faked, since Blackstone carried on his bonking career for some years) which even today would certainly be disallowed – let alone in 1975, when Ford could have been sent to gaol for distributing it.

Right up until his death in 1995 Ford continued to deny he had anything to do with *Diversions*, but everybody in the sex film community knew the real story. Others involved in the production still refuse to talk about it. It's a sobering thought that kinky pornography is not the sole prerogative of Continental filmmakers. It was happening here decades ago, but in the most cloak-and-dagger circumstances imaginable.

CAST: Heather Deeley (*Imogene*), Derek Martin (*escort*), Jacky Rigby (*Brown*), Jeffrey Morgan (*student*), Terry Walsh (*mercenary*), Timothy Blackstone (*victim*), James Lister (*vampire*), Tim Burr (*gentleman caller*), Tony Kenyon (*Victorian photographer*), Gilly Sykes (*parlourmaid*). **CREDITS:** Director/Screenplay Derek Ford, Producer Valerie M Ford, Production Supervisor Alan Selwyn, Editor Patrick Foster, Photography Geoffrey Glover, Music De Wolfe A BLACKWATER FILMS Production. Distributed by VARIETY. Opened November 1975.

Right: Helli Louise wants to know if Barry Stokes has the right tool for the job in *The Ups and Downs of a Handyman* (1975).

UPS AND DOWNS OF A HANDYMAN

aka *The Happy Housewives* aka *Confessions of an Odd Job Man*

Great Britain / 1975 / 84 mins / cert 'X'

Virtually overnight, the huge popularity of *Confessions of a Window Cleaner* inspired a slew of copycat films vying for a slice of the sex film pie and all following the formula of a young working class lad being besieged by hordes of randy women. *Ups and Downs of a Handyman*, released at the tail end of 1975, was no exception, as producer Kenneth Rowles readily admits. 'I liked sexy comedies. I'd seen Pete Walker's work and was also at Twickenham Studios when Val Guest was making *Au Pair Girls*, so I knew they had great potential. Because *Confessions of a Window Cleaner* had been such a successful series I wanted to go the same way, but a lot more economically.'

Just as Confessions and later Adventures were to become brand-name prefixes, so Kenneth Rowles sought a catchy title for his film. 'A writer friend of mine, who was also an actor, Derrick Slater, said he had this comedy script which was at that stage just called 'The Handyman'. I came up with the title 'Ups and Downs'. I had originally toyed with the 'Ins and Outs' but thought that was a bit much!'

Confident of the film's potential and with a competent cast of comedy names like Bob Todd and Chic Murray, plus a bevy of young actresses willing to strip off, Rowles and his cinematographer Douglas Hill actually re-mortgaged their houses in order to finance the picture. The story follows the ups and downs of sex-mad young newlyweds Bob (Barry Stokes) and Margaretta (Penny Meredith) who manage to escape the polluted, congested, noisy streets of Hammersmith to the rural idyll of the fictitious Surrey town Sodding Chipbury (not to be confused with Chipping Sodbury, of course) after being left a luxury cottage in an elderly aunt's will. Finding that job opportunities in the village are non-existent, Bob is forced into offering his 'services' as a handyman on a postcard in the newsagent's window. As the lusty local women invite him round on the pretext of sorting out their plumbing there is a plethora of 'Have you got the right tool?'-type jokes and the predictable *double entendres* are better sign-posted than the M25.

In the space of a week it seems like Bob has shagged the entire female population of Surrey, beginning with a bisexual threesome with hugely endowed Danish poppet Helli Louise and her friend Jeannie Collings in a grubby bathroom sequence straight out of a Scandinavian porn film, complete with some of the sleaziest music ever heard in a Brit sexcom. (Interestingly, this scene was deleted from a 1998 video reissue, such was its perceived naughtiness.) He also has a mother-daughter bunk-up in a hayloft, is seduced by the Squire's wife on the kitchen floor, enjoys a tumble in the back of a vintage Bentley with Sue Lloyd, as well as dalliances with ex-Carry On actresses Alexandra Dane and Valerie Leon (both of whom stay resolutely covered up). Barry Stokes, in his first lead role after a short stint on *Crossroads*, spends most of the film naked. But the real shock to the system is his atrocious wailing of the film's theme tune, and other incidental songs, especially when you consider that he had the lead role in the London stage production of *Godspell* between 1973 and 1974.

By the weekend our handyman hero is so knackered that he can't even get it up for his poor sweet wife. Confiding his troubles to local prostitute Maisie (it all goes on in this village!) – played by Stokes' soon-to-be real-life wife Gay Soper – he admits he is beginning to resent his forthright customers and is in danger of being booked by the law for obstreperous behaviour. 'Next time I catch him, I'll slap a ticket on it,' vows the local bobby.

KEEPING THE BRITISH END UP

The role of the bumbling, accident-prone policeman is played with twitching vigour by legendary Scottish comedian Chic Murray. Virtually reprising the role he played in *Secrets of a Door to Door Salesman* two years previously, Murray displays mock-outrage as he repeatedly stumbles across nudity and lasciviousness in the picturesque village, while at the same time taking great interest in the Mary Millington magazines on sale in the local newsagents, run by Robert Dorning. 'I'm just doing my duty,' he splutters. 'Protecting the citizens from moral decline.' Also on board is Benny Hill regular Bob Todd as the randy Squire with a predilection for spanking schoolgirls. Watching paunchy, middle-aged (and totally nude) Todd spanking his screen wife in a shower is a grim horror not to be repeated.

Ups and Downs of a Handyman was immensely popular at the box-office and Ken Rowles was keen to start work on a sequel immediately. *Handyman*'s UK distributors, Target, had also started handling Stanley Long's *Adventures* series and, although initially keen to do a deal on a series of *Ups and Downs* movies, the idea was eventually pushed to one side. 'It was a real shame,' says Rowles, 'but they just didn't want two rival series going up against each other and I lost a lot of money.' The proposed sequel was entitled *Ups and Downs of a Soccer Star*, co-scripted by *Handyman* director John Sealey and, incredibly, Ken Follett, husband of MP Barbara Follett and soon to be the writer of international bestsellers like *Eye of the Needle*. The sequel was still being promoted at the Cannes Film Festival as late as 1979, with up-and-coming starlet Julie Lee attached to the project. Robin Askwith had been approached to play the lead, but declined.

CAST: Barry Stokes (*Bob*), Penny Meredith (*Margaretta*), Gay Soper (*Maisie*), Chic Murray (*PC Fred Knowles*), Bob Todd (*Squire Bullsworthy*), Robert Dorning (*Arthur*), Sue Lloyd (*blonde*), Valerie Leon (*redhead*), John Blythe (*Charlie Elgin*), Alexandra Dane (*Mrs Knowles*), Helli Louise (*Arthur's daughter*), Julia Bond (*Polly Elgin*), Pauline Letts (*mother*), Harold Bennett (*Gasper*), Jeannie Collings (*Mary Wain*), Olivia Syson (*Mrs Bullsworthy*), Nita Lorraine (*Jenny Elgin*), Ava Cadell (*schoolgirl*), Jannette Carol (*barmaid*), Christopher Rowles [uncredited] (*stable lad*)

CREDITS: *Director* John Sealey, *Producer* Kenneth F Rowles, *Editors* Jim Atkinson and John Carr, *Photography* Douglas Hill, *Screenplay* Derrick Slater and John Sealey, *Music* Vic Elms, *Theme Song* 'The Ups And Downs of a Handyman' performed by Barry Stokes

A KFR Production. Distributed by TARGET INTERNATIONAL. Opened December 1975.

Left: Rascally rogues Leslie Philips and Terry-Thomas surrounded by Euro-popsies in Spanish Fly *(1975).*

SPANISH FLY

Great Britain / 1975 / 86 mins / cert 'AA'

Who could ask for more? The two greatest comedy bounders of British cinema, Terry-Thomas and Leslie Phillips, together in one movie for the very first time. Quite simply it's inspired. Why it took until 1975 to get them together is perplexing, but perhaps movie producers expected sparks to fly between the two rascally rotters. After all, the opening credits indicate this is Leslie Phillips *versus* Terry-Thomas!

Terry-Thomas is allowed to exaggerate every one of his famous mannerisms at full throttle here as gap-toothed old rogue Sir Percy de Courcy, living it up in Spain after presumably being chucked out of England for tax evasion. A beautiful sun-bleached villa, a private yacht and a swanky Rolls-Royce don't come cheap, not to mention his faithful manservant-cum-chauffeur Perkins (Graham Armitage), who is considerably smarter than him. Sir P secretly plans a wicked wheeze to restore his lost fortune by buying up 10,000 gallons of cheap red wine. By putting a fancy label on it, pretending it's French and giving it a false '64 vintage, he hopes to sell it to silly English merchants and make a fortune. When he meets up with his raffish old school chum Mike 'Spotty' Scott (Phillips), he intends to offload a few cases immediately. There's just one teensy weensy problem: the wine tastes like paint stripper, or worse. 'It's cat's piss,' one girl remarks after taking a sip. 'No, it's not cat's,' winces Phillips, 'it's dog's!'

The ingenious Perkins attempts to make the wine more palatable by mixing it with a variety of ingredients, a mixture featuring herbs and 'dead flies' proving to be the most potent. With just one taste the locals are turned into marauding sex maniacs. It seems that the innocent 'flies' are actually the greeny-gold 'Spanish Fly' beetle, famed in ancient times as an aphrodisiac! Suddenly everybody wants a bottle, with pretty young women the most profoundly affected. The aphrodisiac plot is as old as time and a dogged sex comedy stand-by, but never has it been so funny or looked so appealing. The high production values, sweet Eurovision-esque theme tune, super location work in Menorca and fabulous interplay between the two legendary leads is priceless.

Director Bob Kellett is a veteran of many big screen comedy flicks like *Up Pompeii* and *The Alf Garnett Saga*. Frisky fox Leslie Phillips plays an underwear marketing man, in the Mediterranean to take photographs of his four delicious models sporting Janet Reger's best frilly knickers, and to escape his fearsome missus (Sue Lloyd). The invigorating wine has Leslie's curvy companions clamouring for his loins... rather! He's come a long way since eyeing-up Joan Sims' rump in *Carry On Teacher*. Here he actually gets his hands on some naked girls and has his first-ever nude bed scene with luscious Sophia Loren lookalike Julie (played by mono-named German actress and ex-ballet dancer, Nadiuska). Even dirty trickster Terry-Thomas has a sniff of the action with a bare girl cavorting about on his boat. 'Absolutely splendid!' he comments with a broad smile across his face.

The passion plonk proves to be the 'greatest invention since the double bed', as Phillips puts it, and reliable retainer Perkins has to find as many Spanish Flies as possible just to keep up with the demand. He enlists the help of the local children and in a charming scene the Spanish bambinos scramble over the hillside with nets and jam jars in search of creepy crawlies. *Spanish Fly* is a cute, flirty little movie which succeeds in being much sexier than many of its more explicit contemporaries. It's worth watching just to see Terry-Thomas calling out the lifeguards when he runs out of tonic water and hearing him say 'You absolute shower!' one last time. As fruity, full-bodied sex comedies go this is a fine vintage.

CAST: Leslie Phillips (*Mike Scott*), Terry-Thomas (*Sir Percy de Courcy*), Graham Armitage (*Perkins*), Sue Lloyd (*Janet Scott*), Nadiuska (*Julie*), Frank Thornton (*Dr Johnson*), Ramiro Oliveros (*Juan*), Andrea Allan (*Bruce*), Sally Farmiloe (*Francesca*), Jaleh Haddah (*Annette*), Nina Francis (*Isabel*), Sergio Mendizabal (*Pons Prades*), Emiliano Villena (*clean Domingo*), Fernando Porcel (*dirty Domingo*), Marisa Porcel (*Maria*), José Luis Lifante (*Pedro*).
CREDITS: *Director* Bob Kellett, *Producers* Peter James and Gerald Flint-Shipman, *Editor* Al Gell, *Photography* Jack Atcheler, *Screenplay* Robert Ryerson, *Music* Ron Goodwin, *Theme song 'Fly Me' performed by* Geraldine A WINKLE-QUADRANT Production in association with IZARO FILMS. Distributed by EMI. Opened January 1976.

Left: Anna Bergman and Linda Marlowe stripping off in Hamburg for *Penelope Pulls It Off!* (1975).

PENELOPE PULLS IT OFF!
aka *Penelope*

Great Britain-Germany / 1975 / 84 mins / cert 'X'

Penelope Pulls It Off! opens with a dizzying kaleidoscope shot of spinning breasts, but this incomprehensible Anglo-German co-production rapidly loses any artistic impetus in favour of knockabout stupidity. Super-sexy Linda *Big Zapper* Marlowe is a well-healed art dealer whose grand ancestral home is about to be taken over by the bailiffs unless she comes up with the readies, and quickly. Enlisting the help of her sexually precocious teenage daughter (Anna Bergman), she persuades a derelict Welsh artist friend to forge great works by Constable and Picasso and sneakily sells them off to pay her debts. The clever fakes fool the art market for some time, but eventually the ladies have to adopt more ruthless methods of securing their fortune.

Marlowe and Bergman joyously strip off at every available juncture and look terrific, but the crude plot searches for direction. Bergman in a buttock-length St Trinian's outfit, and hair in bunches, makes an unconvincing 15-year-old; she was 26 at the time. But the lollipop-licking Lolita directs coy glances at horny English art dealer Jeremiah Jones (Nicholas Day) and before long is making passionate waves on his boat. Hardly needing much encouragement to break the law, her lover cries: 'Who cares about the age of consent?'

Filmed entirely on location in Hamburg in 1975, all the supporting actors were dubbed into English, which sometimes makes for distracting watching. The film has all the Teutonic touches British viewers had come to expect from the never-ending stream of imported sex films flooding UK cinemas in the mid-1970s. Extravagant facial hair, fat ugly Germans, drunkenness, gorging on rich food, animals getting involved in the comedy bonking and 'jokes' as thin on the ground here as in the depressing *Schulmädchen Report* series. The narrative is intermittently interrupted by a nonsensical subplot in which a temperamental artist (Benno Hummer) is harassed by his dolly bird life-studies. Tiring of bothersome females, he 'marries' his extremely well-hung black butler, Othello, and holding his lover's large penis in his hand waggles it down the phone to a bemused Marlowe. Not terribly good really, the film is best summed up by a talking parrot which squawks 'What a load of rubbish!' throughout.

CAST: Anna Bergman (*Penelope Charterley*), Linda Marlowe (*Lady Charterley*), Nicholas Day (*Jeremiah Jones*), George Murcell (*Owen Glendower*), Horst G Fleck (*Herman*), Benno Hummer (*Quentin Roberts*), Ronald Kitchen Jnr (*Andre Copin*), Judith de la Couronne (*Madame Dupont*), Ernst Mark (*Nero*), Reiner Brounecke (*Mark Anthony*), Harald Eggers (*Claudius*), Karin Janssen (*Fortunata*), Stefani Roos (*Habineas*), Marian Koos (*Diana*)

CREDITS: *Director* Pete Curran, *Producers* Elizabeth Curran and Rosemarie Walters, *Editor* Karl Brauer, *Photography* Jost von Hardenberg, *Screenplay* Jonathan Walters An ELSINORE Production. Distributed by TARGET. Opened January 1976.

Right: James Booth inspects his troops in I'm Not Feeling Myself Tonight! *(1975).*

I'M NOT FEELING MYSELF TONIGHT!
aka *The Sex Ray* aka *The Love Ray*

Great Britain / 1975 / 84 mins / cert 'X'

I'm Not Feeling Myself Tonight! was the latest in a long line of 1970s sex film storylines concerned with an aphrodisiac intended to turn women into hot-blooded nymphomaniacs. At least here the device used to get pretty women in miniskirts to have a bit of how's yer father with very ugly men is not a love potion, pill or perfume (so passé, darling!), but... high frequency soundwaves. The script, written by David McGillivray, was originally called *The Sex Ray*, based on an anonymous American porno novel which was a favourite one-handed read of producer Laurence Barnett.

Anglicised and restructured, the story runs as follows: Jon Pigeon, 'a born wanker' played by seventies heart-throb Barry Andrews, is an unfulfilled virgin who never manages to succeed with the birds he is repeatedly accosted by on the way to work (including an ultra-saucy Mary Millington). Seeking refuge in his vast collection of jazz mags, blow-up dolls and 'sex instruction' videotapes, he dreams of the day when he can finally take a turn among the cabbages with his object of desire, spunky Cheryl (Sally Faulkner). Considering his immense sexual frustration, it's a cruel twist of fate that the poor lad holds the lowly position of janitor at the Hilderbrand Institute of Sexual Research, in which naked women running through the corridors chased by white-coats and topless 'research assistants' bouncing up and down on exercise bikes are ten-a-penny. The institute's staff take a dim view of anyone not indulging in a little office hanky panky. 'What's a lovely girl like you doing in a dreadful sex institute like this?' asks doorman Chic Murray, feeling up an innocent young secretary on her first day, and ancient tea-lady Rita Webb thinks nothing of grabbing at any passing crotch on her trolley rounds.

One day in his pokey broom cupboard, Pigeon accidentally invents a 'sonic device' which he hopes will put an end to his nightly knuckle-shuffling. Aided by his little friend, Keith, a congenital idiot (played by Billy Hamon, giving a superb performance), he tries out his new invention, which emits sound waves at such a high pitch as to hit any unsuspecting woman's g-spots full-on and turn her into a sexual whirlwind. Before long the institute's slobbering director Willie Nutbrown (James Booth) wants to get his greasy hands on the pulsating audio aphrodisiac and claim it as his own, which leads to a dumb Benny Hill-style chase and some predictable hole-mongering at a garden party, with all the guests bonking in the bushes.

Some sophisticated McGillivray wit does occasionally rise above the tide of smut and his really inventive stuff stands out a mile. The fearsome Mary Watchtower (no guesses who that's supposed to be) of the Clean Up the World Campaign gets blasted with the sex ray and comes over hotter than a freshly fucked fox in a forest fire. Indulging in a drunken orgy with a vicar while watching a porn video, Watchtower comments: 'This one's so much more technical than the others. And so much more corrupting!' A running gag throughout the movie is the monotone female voice blaring out of the sex institute's tannoy system, with such droll gems as 'Doctor Smith to the ejaculation room please' and 'Coitus has commenced in room 504, please do not interruptus'. Unfortunately, director Joe McGrath misguidedly thought McGillivray's original script was a bit too clever for its own good and set about rewriting most of it himself. 'Joe didn't really think the script was very funny, so he got all his mates in to help and re-drafted bits of the script each day,' says McGillivray wearily. 'When I went to the preview I was under the seat in embarrass-

Right: Linda Hayden seduces Fiona Richmond in the controversial *Exposé* (1975).

ment, because my name was on the film but nobody in the audience was laughing. I did think my jokes were better than his.'

Apart from the flourishes of inspired sex movie piss-taking courtesy of McGillivray, the most enjoyable thing about the whole movie is its fabulous *double entendre* title which has become the writer's greatest gift to the sex film genre. 'This is a bit of a scoop,' admits McGillivray, 'but when I was writing the movie I was actually a virgin and a title like *I'm Not Feeling Myself Tonight!* could only have come from somebody who was obviously masturbating a lot. That was my idea of humour, but it has nothing whatsoever to do with the film. It's just a typical British innuendo – I'm not going to be wanking tonight, I'm going to be having real sex!'

CAST: Barry Andrews (*Jon Pigeon*), James Booth (*William Nutbrown*), Sally Faulkner (*Cheryl Bascombe*), Billy Hamon (*Keith Furey/Keith's parents*), Ben Aris (*Trampas B Hilderbrand*), Chic Murray (*Fred*), Rita Webb (*tea lady*), Ronnie Brody (*neighbour*), Freddie Earl (*cowboy*), W G Maelor-Jones (*lecturer*), Brian Murphy (*caretaker*), Marjie Lawrence (*caretaker's wife*), Graham Stark (*hotel MC*), Katya Wyeth (*Wendy*), Geraldine Hart (*Mrs Watchtower*), Gennie Nevinson (*Vera*), Juliette King (*Heidi*), Jo Peters (*Deirdre*), Jean Collins (*Miss Bagnell*), Sally Harrison (*videotape girl*), Mike Grady (*boy scout*), Robert Dorning (*man at party*), Marianne Stone (*consultant*), Bob Godfrey (*postman*), Steve Amber (*policeman*), Penny Croft (*traffic warden*), Andrea Lawrence (*Mrs Nutbrown*), Gracie Luck (*Mrs Hilderbrand*), Heather Deeley (*girl in lecture theatre*), Suzanne Bass, Bobby Sparrow and Glenda Allen (*Nutbrown's girls*), Monika Ringwald, David McGillivray, Lindy Benson, Tim Blackstone, Laurie Goode and Andee Cromarty (*party guests*), *Uncredited:* Pat Astley (*Saloon Girl*), Jeannie Collings (*Sylvia*), Mary Maxted [aka Mary Millington] (*girl in sunglasses*)

CREDITS: *Director* Joseph McGrath, *Producer* Malcolm Fancey, *Co-Producers* Laurence Barnett and John Lindsay, *Editors* Jim Atkinson and John Carr, *Photography* Ken Higgins, *Screenplay* David McGillivray, *Music* Cy Payne An ANTLER FILM Production. Distributed by NEW REALM. Opened February 1976.

IT COULD HAPPEN TO YOU

Great Britain / 1975 / 78 mins / cert 'AA'

'I did a complete mock-up of a sperm and there was a really lovely sequence showing how VD got passed around,' says director Stanley Long. You read right. In the decade before AIDS hit the headlines the main worry for promiscuous teenagers was catching a dose of syphilis or gonorrhoea and Long was contracted to make a film to warn youngsters of the dangers. It's probably the most sedate and serious-minded of all his productions. 'There was an Australian sex education film doing the rounds and it was pretty dreadful, even worse than the one I made, and I was asked to remake it for a British audience,' he says. 'The whole idea was to make a fairly serious film about venereal diseases, but have a bit of comedy in it to make it more acceptable.'

The movie was made in conjunction with Dr R D Catterall, a senior consultant at Middlesex Hospital who, in pure British sex film tradition, appears sitting behind his desk and delivering a sombre message to the general public in much the same way that the 'doctors' did in *The Wife Swappers* and *Love Variations*. Only on this occasion he's genuine and Catterall's scenes were shot at the James Pringle Clinic in London's Charlotte Street. The doctor is one of the old school, going misty-eyed about the time before 'package tours and the pill' made his job so difficult, but he doesn't advocate abstinence from sex. The spread of disease is dramatised by Eric Deacon having a bit of heave-ho with 'mature and sophisticated' Rula Lenska and contracting gonorrhoea. The disease is then spread around his social circle, including a gay couple who contract syphilis.

'It all starts with a couple snogging at a party and it goes on from there. I didn't want it to be preaching,' claims Long. 'There were some pretty horrid close-ups of infected organs, but they had to be there. It was about casual sex, but it was vital that young people learnt to communicate with each other to stop VD. It was supposed to be shown to a primarily teenage audience and I was happy that it got an 'AA' rating, but then the distributors got their hands on it.'

Didn't they just. A few months after its initial release Variety Film Distributors, who were handling the film, changed its title to the more sensational *Intimate Teenage Secrets*. As 'punishment' the film was re-certificated by an infuriated censor as an 'X'. 'Dr Catterall was a very eminent man and he had been thrilled with the movie, but he wasn't so happy to see his name on a film poster saying *Intimate Teenage Secrets*,' says Long. 'Nor was I. When it got the 'X' certificate it immediately lost its intended audience and I was totally pissed off. It wasn't made to titillate. It didn't pander to the sex comedy market really. It was completely the reverse of erotic. It was totally un-erotic.'

CAST: Eric Deacon (*Mick*), Vicky Williams (*Jenny*), Martin Skinner (*Colin*), Robert Cotton (*Dan*), Nicholas Young (*Raymond*), Peter Vaughan-Clarke (*Robbie*), Rula Lenska (*Rita*), Richard Mathews (*Mr Ramlin*), Rosalind Knight (*Mrs Ramlin*), Sue Holderness (*Christine*), Bernadette Milnes (*Mrs Peterson*), Catherine Crewe (*Miss Harris*), Freddie Earle (*Gon*), Bernard Hill (*Syph*), Jonathan Adams (*Henry VIII*), Veronica Doran (*Queen*), Christopher Biggins (*apothecary*), Dave Carter and Graham Ashley (*workmen*)

CREDITS: *Director/Producer* Stanley Long. *Editor* Jo Gannon. *Photography* Peter Sinclair. *Screenplay* Michael Armstrong. *Medical Advisor* Dr R D Catterall A NITREV-SALON Production. Distributed by VARIETY. Opened March 1976.

EXPOSÉ

aka *The House On Straw Hill* aka *Trauma*

Great Britain / 1975 / 82 mins / cert 'X'

This violent tale of blood, boobs and rubber gloves is infamous for at one time being the only British entry in the Department of Public Prosecutions' list of banned movies during the 'video nasties' furore of the early 1980s. Unavailable on video for nearly 15 years, *Exposé* has become something of a cult movie, though why it was withdrawn from sale and surrounded in controversy for so long is something of a mystery. For years the film gained the sort of notoriety more associated with the likes of *Straw Dogs* and *The Texas Chain Saw Massacre*. There's a bit of nasty business with a knife, also a rape and plenty of nudity, but *Exposé* portrays them carefully in context and the movie is one of the most brilliantly atmospheric sex films of the 1970s.

Linda Hayden displays more of the terrifying menace she first let rip in 1968's *Baby Love*. Here she's a manipulative secretary, Linda, who goes to work for Paul Martin (played by German actor Udo Kier), a best-selling author of pulp fiction who can only work in complete silence and seclusion in his rented country cottage. Under huge pressure to meet the publisher's deadline for his new book, he is tormented by nightmarish delusions and bloody hallucinations. A control freak, only able to make love to his girlfriend Suzanne (Fiona Richmond) while wearing surgical gloves, Kier feels certain that he is descending into madness, a mental state

Right: Diana Dors harangues Barry Evans in *Adventures of a Taxi Driver* (1975).

encouraged by his new employee. After the arrogant Suzanne sashays out of the house back to London on a business trip, Linda asserts her position in the household, dismissing the housekeeper and sexually taunting Paul. It transpires that Paul's last book, 'Deadly Silence', was actually written by Linda's husband Simon, who was driven to suicide when Paul tricked him out of the manuscript. And now Linda wants him to pay.

Director James Kenelm Clarke gets the very most out of his location, the quiet Essex village of Little Baddow, and the unusually high production values are a pleasant surprise, including a fantastic shot where the camera whizzes around a field of corn. The intriguing shots of fingers, guns, typewriter keys, lights flickering and doors creaking – right up to the final shot of combine harvesters threshing menacingly forward – all create an electric atmosphere of considerable agitation.

The film cracks on at a thunderous pace with shocking images flying across the screen at 100 miles per hour and the incredible sexual tension is enough to cause a cinematic migraine. Scenes of Linda masturbating on her bed, hand down the front of her knickers, and later seducing Suzanne in front of a window while she repeatedly whispers 'You look good, *really* good' bring the over-heated stew to boiling point. By the time Linda gets around to the climactic butcher-knife slaying of the stark naked Suzanne in the bathroom, blood swirling down the plughole, and Paul gets his razor-sharp cheekbones carved up even further, the film seems ready to implode.

What stops this from happening are the well-measured performances by the game cast of basically just three protagonists. Kier is sufficiently deranged-looking to be believable, and Hayden again excels in the mouth of madness. *Exposé* also gave *Men Only* editor Fiona Richmond her first sizeable cinema role and provided the movie with the hook with which to ensnare the paying public. It worked astoundingly well. The movie played continuously for six months in London's West End and begat two more Kenelm Clarke/Richmond sexploiters.

CAST: Udo Keir (*Paul Martin*), Linda Hayden (*Linda Hindstatt*), Fiona Richmond (*Suzanne*), Patsy Smart (*Mrs Aston*), Vic Armstrong (*big youth*), Karl Howman (*small youth*), Sydney Knight [uncredited] (*Smedley the gardener*)
CREDITS: *Director* James Kenelm Clarke, *Producer* Brian Smedley-Aston, *Executive Producer* Paul Raymond [uncredited], *Editor* Jim Connock, *Photography* Denis Lewiston, *Screenplay* James Kenelm Clarke, *Music* Steven Gray
A NORFOLK INTERNATIONAL Production. Distributed by TARGET. Opened March 1976.

FEELINGS
aka *Whose Child Am I?*

Great Britain / 1975 / 90 mins / cert 'X'

Barbara (Kate O'Mara from classic TV serial *The Brothers*) and Paul Martin (Paul Freeman) are a blissfully happy couple who enjoy a very healthy sex life (as the film's opening bout of belly-bumping to classical music testifies), but their life is missing one thing: a child. While they can't get enough of playing mummies and daddies, she is frustrated and he is infertile. 'Without children, it's no marriage,' Barbara wails. Visiting the local family planning clinic to see sanctimonious Dr Benson (Edward Judd), Barbara decides to attempt to get pregnant by artificial insemination and, in case you don't know what that is, the triumphantly bad dialogue makes it clear as crystal. 'You mean taking another man's sperm and injecting it into my wife to fertilise her?' asks Paul, managing somehow to keep a straight face.

Barbara fails to become pregnant, however, and is advised that she would stand a better chance of producing a child through 'normal mating'. Although the 'thought of making love without loving' appals her, she's soon dropping her knickers for blond physiotherapy student Michael (Bob Sherman), both at the clinic and also (naughty, naughty) *back at his flat*. Naturally she doesn't tell her husband what she's been getting up to and when she falls pregnant their matrimonial problems really start.

Director Gerry O'Hara (wisely using the pseudonym Lawrence Britten) throws all he's got into this inglorious mess. There's a proliferation of mid-Atlantic accents (it is never made clear whether the story is supposed to be set in Britain or Canada), some preposterous characterisations and TV star O'Mara is exploited to the max, being totally naked in virtually all her scenes. There are several frothy subplots bubbling under too. Dr Benson's jolly assistant Helen (Frances Kearney) is sleeping with an ageing, silver-haired roué (Ronan O'Casey), because the 'best wine comes in old barrels' apparently. Unfortunately, Helen's mother (Melissa Stribling) guiltily confesses that her daughter was conceived by artificial insemination too and the old guy she is sleeping with is actually her own father! Interestingly, Canadian actor O'Casey had previously found fame playing Peggy Mount's gormless son-in-law, Jeff Rogers, in the cockney sitcom *The Larkins* (1958-63). After enjoying the bed scenes in *Feelings*, O'Casey went on to produce and direct an all-out hardcore feature of his own, *The Double Exposure of Holly*, in New York in 1977. What must Peggy have thought?

The clinic quack also has trouble with a couple of lesbians (Felicity Devonshire and Diane Fletcher) who are desperate to have a child of their own. After some reluctance, and incredible ignorance – 'Without the normal male-female balance in the family the odds are that your child will also become a homosexual!' – he agrees to inseminate one of them. Plus there's a bit of drama with mixed-up sperm samples and a dope-smoking hippy (Beth Porter) getting a sample from an 'African donor'.

Feelings is top-notch camp entertainment. It has all the characteristics of a bad daytime American medical soap combined with a 1950s grindhouse B-movie and a big dollop of gratuitous 1970s nudity. The movie's ludicrous story – with implausible situations, tears, hysteria, blackmail, double-takes, sententious revelations, open mouths and wide eyes – could come straight out of an episode of *Sunset Beach* or *The Bold and the Beautiful*. In fact, Kate O'Mara, who later went on to star in top US soap *Dynasty* during the 1980s, blesses the movie with its most fantastic line of bedroom dialogue, which not even Joan Collins could have got away with: 'Every time we make love I feel more like some sort of sperm disposal machine than a woman!'

CAST: Kate O'Mara (*Barbara Martin*), Paul Freeman (*Paul Martin*), Edward Judd (*Dr Benson*), David Markham (*Professor Roland*), Bob Sherman (*Michael*), Frances Kearney (*Helen Randall*), Diane Fletcher (*Renate*), Felicity Devonshire (*Carrie*), Melissa Stribling (*Charlotte Randall*), Ronan O'Casey (*John Roberts*), Beth Porter (*Mrs Lustig*), Freda Bamford (*Barbara's mother*), Rikki Howard (*Michael's girlfriend*), Sally Faulkner (*Mrs Linden*), Jean Gilpin (*receptionist*)
CREDITS: *Director* Lawrence Britten [aka Gerry O'Hara], *Producer* Basil Appleby, *Editor* Tony Lenny, *Photography* Ken Hodges, *Screenplay* James Stevens, *Music* Pierre Dutour
A PLAYPONT Production. Distributed by MIRACLE. Opened July 1976.

ADVENTURES OF A TAXI DRIVER

Great Britain / 1975 / 89 mins / cert 'X'

At the time of its filming in 1975 Stanley Long strongly refuted any comparisons between his latest cinematic venture and Greg Smith's Confessions series. 'They are very different types of films. Mine are based on comedy truth, whereas they are basically slapstick,' he told the trade press. Today he takes a more measured view: 'Yes, *Adventures of a Taxi Driver* was partly inspired by the Confessions films, but I wanted to give mine a different emphasis that wasn't so reliant on the *double entendre*. And I honestly thought I could do it better.'

Barry Evans, a TV star from the *Doctor* sitcoms, takes the Robin Askwith-type role here as a randy London cabbie who 'gets

Right: Early 1980s video cover for *Secrets of a Super Stud* **(1975).**

more than his *fare* share'. While Evans certainly has plenty of impressive comedy credentials, he badly lacks Askwith's warmth and naïveté and as a consequence is too self-assured, conceited and smug to be a truly likeable hero. Thinking he can have absolutely any woman he likes, Evans' Joe North even sets his sights on his best mate's bird, co-star Judy Geeson. 'She fancies me, I can tell,' he thinks to himself. 'I could pull this one dead easy, no problem!' Strangely for a script written by a woman (Suzanne Mercer, the woman behind *Groupie Girl*), Joe consistently comes out on top, while the movie's females are, almost universally, whining, paranoid, weak-willed characters taken in by his cockiness and into his bed.

What the movie does offer is the alluring Anna Bergman in her début British movie and a roll-call of comedic talent in the Confessions tradition, including Diana Dors (as Evans' slovenly mother), Stephen Lewis, Ian Lavender, Henry McGee, Angela Scoular and Liz Fraser. The latter plays a mature prostitute who entertains clients in the back of Evans' cab. 'C'mon love, don't be nervous,' Fraser tells her agitated client as they drive past the poster for *Jaws* at the Odeon Leicester Square. 'I won't bite it off.'

Adventures of a Taxi Driver seemed to hit the right note with the general public and was placed 19th in the end-of-year most profitable films of 1976, an incredible achievement for a low-budget, independently distributed movie. In Britain Long carefully marketed the movie and it was released region by region throughout the country. It was also sold to a mighty 36 overseas territories including South Africa, New Zealand, Canada and Australia. Down Under alone, it was the most popular film of the year, with audience members queuing round the block to see the film at Sydney theatres.

For the film's London press showing the director arranged a performance at the Casino Cinema in Old Compton Street with a specially invited audience. 'I got all the London taxi drivers along,' recalls Long. 'We had an audience of about 300 cabbies plus all the press people. I was very conscious that if I only invited snobby critics they would just sit in stony silence so I made sure I had the right kind of audience to get some atmosphere. It was a knock-out idea because the cabbies were falling about with laughter. It's weird because all you could hear was laughter. It's actually the favourite of all my films because it was so popular and I don't think I ever topped it.'

CAST: Barry Evans (*Joe North*), Judy Geeson (*Nikki*), Adrienne Posta (*Carol Hodgkiss*), Diana Dors (*Mrs North*), Robert Lindsay (*Tom*), Liz Fraser (*Maisie*), Ian Lavender (*Ronald*), Angela Scoular (*Marion*), Henry McGee (*Inspector Rogers*), Stephen Lewis (*club doorman*), Brian Wilde (*Harold*), Anna Bergman (*Helga*), Jane Hayden (*suicidal Linda*), Stephen Riddle (*Bunny McQueen*), Prudence Drage (*Mrs De Vere Barker*), Marc Harmon (*Peter North*), Graham Ashley (*Gerry*), Dave Carter (*Bill*), Charles Pemberton (*Sergeant Jeeves*), Gloria Walker (*Dora*), Andrew Secombe, David Auker and Lee Crawford (*kidnappers*), Desmond McNamara and Mike Worsley (*robbers*), Sue Vanner (*hostage*), Beatrice Shaw (*nun*), Natasha Staiteh-Masri (*Alice*), David Brierley (*narrator*), Uncredited: Michael Armstrong (*customer*), Jack Haig (*priest*), Pete Walker (*crashed motorist*). **CREDITS:** *Director* Stanley Long, *Producers* Peter and Stanley Long, *Associate Producer* Michael Armstrong, *Editor* Jo Gannon, *Photography* Peter Sinclair, *Screenplay* Suzanne Mercer, *Music* De Wolfe, *Theme song* 'My Cruisin' Casanova' performed by Adrienne Posta. A SALON Production. Distributed by ALPHA. Opened July 1976.

SECRETS OF A SUPERSTUD
aka *It's Getting Harder All The Time!*

Great Britain / 1975 / 90 mins / cert 'X'

Custer Firkenshaw (Anthony Kenyon) is a crinkly middle-aged Casanova and erstwhile editor of *Bare Monthly* magazine who lays every model he can get into his centrefold. When the superstud's Great Uncle Charlie dies, he bequeaths the bulk of his £3 million fortune to Custer on condition that the ageing philanderer marries and provides a male heir within 12 months. If he fails, all the money will go to conniving Aunt Sophie and her greasy son Cousin Henry. If this wasn't enough to think about, Custer visits the London clinic of German potency expert Dr Halldenberger and finds that he has only a handful of 'units of sexual activity' left. Just 13 more screws then kaput! So it's a race against time to find an attractive, fertile partner without using up all his sperm reserves in the meantime. However, Firkenshaw can't resist temptation, particularly when his money-grabbing relatives are conspiring to chuck every busty beauty in London at him in order to get him despunked as quickly as possible. If he's not careful it's soon going to be Custer's last stand!

This outlandishly bad comedy was shot in a hardcore export version (entitled *It's Getting Harder All the Time!*) with Kenyon ploughing his way through most of the cast of inexperienced actresses. A few frayed remnants of explicit sex remain in the British cut. At alarmingly regular junctures humping is chucked in for the sake of it along with large dollops of kinkiness. In one scene Kenyon has his genitals covered in fruit salad, cream, mixed nuts and several carefully placed pineapple rings before one of his lovers chows down!

Secrets of a Superstud's credits claim it was produced and directed by Morton Lewis, a minor player in British films since the 1930s and a famed football fanatic. He produced *The World at Their Feet* in 1970, the 'official' record of the World Cup in Mexico, and yearned to go mainstream with family films like *Speaking of Spooks*, a 1973 comedy vehicle for TV comics Mike and Bernie Winters, but never made it. Instead he went in the opposite direction, falling headlong into sex, producing the hardcore versions of *Commuter Husbands* (1972) and *The Sexplorer* (1975). *Superstud* would have been his first attempt at feature direction, but Alan Selwyn, the film's writer and an omnipresent figure in seventies' sex cinema, claims he did most of the job. Somebody has to take the blame for the movie's threadbare production values (surprisingly filmed at Twickenham Studios), extremely crude and static direction, and editing which bears all the hallmarks of being done by a one-armed chimp. It's an unusually fractured movie playing on menopausal man's fear of impotence coupled with promiscuous fantasies. But with its Zimmer frame pace you'd find more excitement in a seaside nursing home.

CAST: Anthony Kenyon (*Custer Firkenshaw*), Mark Jones (*Peter*), Alan Selwyn (*Bernie Selby*), Margaret Burton (*Aunt Sophie*), Raymond Young (*Uncle Clifton*), David Pugh (*Cousin Henry*), Maggie Wright (*Sybil Firkenshaw*), Jenny Westbrook (*Miranda*), Bobby Sparrow (*Beryl*), Janet Adler (*Rita*), Paula Martin (*Jane*), Joanna Richards (*Susan*), Juliette Groves (*Julie*), Candida Hershman (*Nurse Lashing*), David Rayner (*Dr Lemmon*), Michael Cronin (*Dr Halldenberger*), Bill Boazman (*Toogood*), Daniella Fletcher (*Miss Effingwell*), Gabrielle Blunt (*Aunt Cissy*), Heather Deeley (*intruder*), Jaqui Rigby (*Lulu*), Jeanette Charles (*the Lady*), Ellie Reece Knight and Andee Cromarty (*fake old ladies*)

CREDITS: Directors Morton M Lewis and Alan Selwyn [uncredited], Producer Morton M Lewis, Editor Peter Pitt, Photography Roy Poynter, Screenplay Gerry Levy, Morton M. Lewis and Alan Selwyn, Music John Shakespeare and Derek Warne, Song 'It's Getting Harder All the Time' performed by Ross MacManus
A MEADWAY INTERNATIONAL Production. Distributed by BUTCHERS. Opened July 1976.

BLUE BELLE

aka *The End of Innocence* aka *Emmanuelle's Daughter* aka *Annie: The True Story of Annie Belle*

Great Britain-Italy / 1975 / 87 mins / cert 'X'

Blue Belle is an Anglo-Italian rip-off of *Emmanuelle* which manages to beat the celebrated original at its own game. In the lead role (and allegedly playing 'herself') is 17-year-old Parisian beauty Annie Belle, famous during the 1970s for her trademark, bleached platinum, boyish hair-cut. She had previously enjoyed the lead role in Emmanuelle Arsan's erotic odyssey *Laure*, produced by 20th Century-Fox, and went on to become a staple of European sex and horror flicks for the next decade. Her best film, *Blue Belle*, has been unjustly ignored in favour of its more famous French cousin starring Sylvia Kristel, but it's actually a whole lot better.

Belle (because of her tender age) plays the role of a teenage nymphette perfectly, balancing her childlike, ice-cream-licking innocence with new found Lolita-like confidence. The film exploits every cliché out of the glossy pages of *Vogue* and *National Geographic*, which made *Emmanuelle* and its sequels so successful: lots of pointless nudity, slow-motion running along beaches, superbly photographed locations (here including a Tibetan monastery) and a dash of lesbianism all set to a repetitive, breathy, Jane Birkin-like musical soundtrack.

The barely identifiable plot centres on a different sort of 'little orphan Annie' and her pervy, impotent, middle-aged guardian, Michael (who makes her call him 'Daddy'). Travelling to Hong Kong on a business trip, Michael is arrested for smuggling and young Annie is thrust into the care of a kinky couple, jet-setter Linda (English beauty Felicity Devonshire) and her slimey husband Angelo (actor-director Ciro Ippolito). Introduced to the endless rounds of cocktail parties, art galleries and the glamorous elite, she continually runs off for sex with the chic men and women she meets socially. Her insatiable need for attention annoys those who want her all to themselves. 'I really believe that two of us won't be enough for her,' complains Angelo. 'So what do you suggest?' retorts his wife. 'Set up a coalition to satisfy her?'

While the allure of the Orient was so irresistible for many great big-budget sex movies of the 1970s, *Blue Belle*'s Italian director Massimo Dallamano (in his penultimate film before his death a year later) frames his characters in a more sympathetic and engaging way against the fantastic landscapes. The director had already gained notoriety for his infamous sex fantasy *Venus In Furs* (1969), and his previous British co-production was a drugs thriller with Stephanie Beacham called *Superbitch* (1973). *Blue Belle* does have some of the tired trappings of empty European erotica, including a rape which the heroine eventually starts to enjoy; sex in the stable-block with horse harnesses tied round the lovers' buttocks; and lots of laughing about absolutely nothing whatsoever (the revelation that Annie is a virgin is met with howls of merriment). Belle's performance, however, is startlingly mature, a hundred times more erotic than Kristel's, and there's also a mesmeric cameo from shaven-headed model Ines Pellegrini as a female monk, while Felicity Devonshire displays an acting talent not yet seen in her British-based sex comedies. It's the sort of film that could never have been set on home turf because exotica and Surrey don't really mix (1977's *Emily* tried and failed). But *Blue Belle* is a welcome alternative to the stranglehold which the likes of *Confessions of a Window Cleaner* and *Come Play with Me* had on the British box-office.

CAST: Annie Belle (*Annie*), Felicity Devonshire (*Linda*), Ciro Ippolio (*Angelo*), Charles Fawcett (*Michael*), Al Cliver (*Philip*), Ines Pellegrini (*Sarah*), Maria Rohm (*Susan*), Tim Street (*Harry*), Linda Ho (*Genevieve*), Ted Thomas (*George*), Linda Slade (*Cornelia*), Chan Yiu Lan (*Chan*)

CREDITS: *Director* Massimo Dallamano, *Producer* Harry Alan Towers, *Editor* Nick Wentworth, *Photography* Franco Delli Colli, *Screenplay* Massimo Dallamano and Harry Alan Towers *based on a story by* Annie Belle A BARONGREEN-ITALIAN INTERNATIONAL Production. Distributed by MIRACLE. Opened February 1977.

1976

INTIMATE GAMES
aka *Fantasies*

Great Britain / 1976 / 90 mins / cert 'X'

A day's filming around the grand old university buildings of Oxford was definitely money well spent because it sets the scene perfectly for this sex comedy set on a college campus. Although it's an odd college where the students spend most of their work time studying sex fantasies. 'Everyone has their private, secret thoughts and amongst these secret

Left: Annie Belle and Al Cliver enjoy a snog while the mysterious Ines Pellegrini watches in *Blue Belle* (1975).

thoughts, difficult though it may be for you to visualise, everyone has their own sexual fantasies.' So says university academic Professor Gottlieb (George Baker), spouting a load of pseudo-intellectual claptrap. 'Our diet of sex has become as inviting as dry bread and water, while our need is for cakes and wine.'

Lecturing his attractive young class with the aid of vibrators and a blow-up doll (how modern!), Gottlieb sets his panting students an exhaustive project to be completed over the Christmas vacation. They must explore their own sexual fantasies as well as finding case studies outside the confines of the college buildings. Having been paired up (naturally there's an an odd number so there has to be a girl girl combination), the eager students retreat to their digs for some in-depth practical humping. Anna Bergman reveals her passion for sucking. 'It's always been a great comfort to me, sucking something,' she coos. Unfortunately for her co-student it's only thumbs she wants to pop in her mouth. Volcanic Felicity Devonshire dreams of being a 'fresh deodorised virgin' ravished by hundreds of black natives, but her real liking is just for well-hung men. Imagine her delight when she realises her fellow student Edward Kalinski, a wimp in corduroy, has been blessed with an 'enormous chopper'. She doesn't walk straight for a week. Suzy Mandel (sporting an appalling pudding bowl haircut) and cute Heather Deeley, meanwhile, are the 'reluctant lesbians' who explore their homosexuality in a dimly lit sex scene filmed in slow motion.

After they've split college the hippy students dig some crazy tales from friends and family. Queenie Watts plays the wife of pigeon fancier Hugh Lloyd, who spends most of the time in the coop at the bottom of the garden but dreams of stroking the plumage of a different type of bird. Isla Blair performs an elaborate (by sex film standards) dance number with three fellas in black tails. Doing a Hollywood-style 'walk down', she undoes their flies as she goes. To top it all, 20-stone character actress Claire Davenport rides around the stage of the Cambridge Theatre like a horse with tiny jockey Johnny Vyvyan on her back. *Intimate Games* also provides a minor showcase for sex superstar Mary Millington, in her last uncredited bit part, as a choir singer getting a hand up the back of her. It was the first and last time Mary ever appeared fully clothed and holding the top note of 'Morning Has Broken'.

The first film directed by playwright and screenwriter Tudor Gates under his own name, he acknowledges it was a step forward for him. 'The distributors wanted a name to direct it. I suggested Martin Campbell who had done a super job on *The Sex Thief*, but they wanted me,' he says. 'I did all the studio work and Martin ended up helping with the location shots.' *Intimate Games* never overstays its welcome, with Gates balancing the sex and comedy sequences perfectly and fleshing out his well-constructed – though clichéd – story with an excellent young cast who can actually deliver their lines with some conviction. For some reason, randy students have never really had a presence in British sex films, but this 'Carry On Campus' partly restores the balance and provides some honest laughs along the way. The film's high production values make it look a lot more expensive than it actually was (budget: £60,000) and Gates' laudable sense of place and first-rate use of location inject some air and space into the proceedings. (The 'college' where most of the action takes place was the home of Laurie Marsh, head of Tigon Film Distributors, in Wentworth.) A success all round, except for veteran actor George Baker, who has since disowned the film. 'I'm not surprised,' says Gates ruefully. 'He's on TV now.'

The movie was filmed at Twickenham Studios under the less-than-original working title of 'Fantasies', but just before release Tigon changed the name to *Intimate Games*, directly inspired by the upcoming Olympic Games in Montreal. The film poster even mimicked the five-ringed Olympic symbol, with the star's faces and chests bursting through the circles. The Olympic Association took the view that their logo was being brought into 'disrepute' by a lot of naked girls and threatened to sue. Somehow managing to wiggle out of it, Heather Deeley, Suzy Mandel, Anna Bergman and Felicity Devonshire were promptly despatched to Piccadilly Circus for an entire Saturday in June 1976 to collect money for the British Olympic team. By five o'clock their rattling tins were full to the brim. Wearing unfeasibly skimpy dresses,

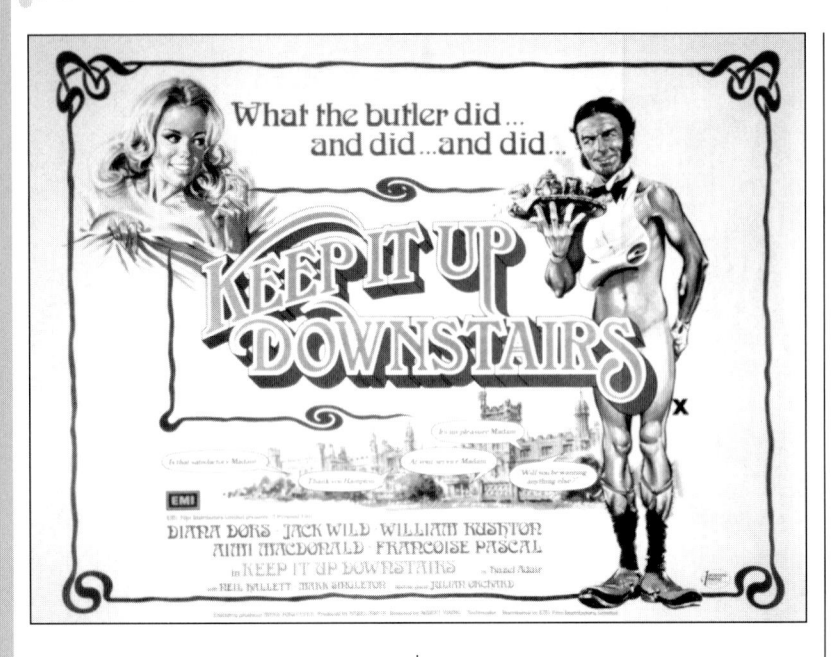

KEEP IT UP DOWNSTAIRS

aka *Can You Keep It Up Downstairs?*

Great Britain / 1976 / 90 mins / cert 'X'

After the success of 1974's *Can You Keep It Up for a Week?*, producer Hazel Adair immediately began writing a follow-up, this time a period spoof of the popular TV series *Upstairs, Downstairs*. Filmed entirely on location at beautiful Knebworth House, near Stevenage in Hertfordshire, and with an increased budget of £120,000, *Keep It Up Downstairs* is a swanky production with a superior cast, luxurious costumes and polished direction from Robert Young. Adair's script sparkles with witty word play, dirty *double entendres* and some funny, if obvious, visual gags. Notable for being the first 'X'-rated film she publicly put her name to, Adair faced a backlash from some corners of the film community who considered sex comedy the prerogative of men only. 'I don't know why it should be so strange,' she retorted during production in 1975. 'That's implying that women don't know anything about sex or don't enjoy it!'

In 1904, the fortunes of grand stately home Cockshute Towers are in disrepair. Lord Cockshute (Mark Singleton) is down to his last brass farthing and has even pawned the silver teapot. If the family can't find some money fast to pay the mounting bills then they'll be out on their arses. Thankfully there are pleasant distractions provided by the downstairs staff. Wily butler Hampton (Adair's favourite actor, Neil Hallett), who is considerably more intelligent than his blue-blooded employers, brings more than just breakfast in bed to his rampant mistress Lady Cockshute (Sue Longhurst), while cheeky French maid Françoise Pascal dallies with the Lord on the four poster. The rest of the servants can't keep their hands to themselves either and Mary Millington, Anthony Kenyon and Simon Brent all seize any lusty opportunity that comes their way. The family bank account is only restored after Cockshute's nerdy experimenter son Peregrine (ex-'Artful Dodger' Jack Wild) inadvertently invents a pliable 'rubber sheath' in the basement, which proves to be an excellent contraceptive. Longhurst, who looks scintillating and gives her best comedy performance of the decade, is more interested in getting her hands on her virginal stepson. 'I've heard sex isn't good for one,' Wild stutters. 'It isn't,' she replies, 'but it's marvellous for two!'

Keep It Up Downstairs was also filmed in a hardcore version which several of the 'straight' cast objected to. Longhurst was asked to go a 'bit further' and refused, Pascal said if they made her go nude she'd walk off the set and Wild now refuses to talk about the film because of the backstage shenanigans he was witness to. Mary Millington was more accommodat-

hanging just beyond the buttock, probably swung things in their favour, and it certainly didn't do the film's chances any harm either.

CAST: George Baker (*Professor Gottlieb*), Suzy Mandel (*Erica*), Anna Bergman (*Suzy*), Felicity Devonshire (*Cathy*), Heather Deeley (*Marion*), Maria St Clair (*Jane*), Peter Blake (*John*), Hugh Lloyd (*John's father*), Queenie Watts (*John's mother*), Ian Hendry (*Uncle Rodney*), Joyce Blair (*Beryl*), Chet Townsend (*Benny*), Edward Kalinski (*Nick*), Norman Chappell (*Principal*), Claire Davenport (*fat woman*), John Vyvyan (*jockey*), Martin Neil (*Joe*), Susan Glanville (*frustrated housewife*), Steve Amber (*housewife's lover*), Barbara Eatwell (*pigeon girl*), Forbes Collins (*Squire*), Lindy Benson (*blonde wife*), Monika Ringwald (*secretary*), Norma Lean (*maid*), Michael Clarke (*gay motorist*), Guy Standeven (*psychiatrist*), John Benson (*executive*), Peppi Borza, John Melainey and Roger Finch (*dancers*), Mary Millington [uncredited] (*girl in choir*).

CREDITS: *Director/Screenplay* Tudor Gates, *Producer* Guido Coen, *Production Supervisor* Martin Campbell, *Editor* Pat Foster, *Photography* Frank Watts, *Music* Roger Webb. A PODENHALE Production. Distributed by TIGON. Opened June 1976.

Right: Sue Longhurst lusts after Jack Wild in *Keep It Up Downstairs* (1976). Nowadays Wild refuses to talk about the movie.

ing, doubling for Pascal's bottom and indulging in a remarkably libidinous lesbian threesome with co-stars Olivia Munday and Maria Coyne. One man who saw all of it going on was casting agent Alan Selwyn, a friend of *Keep It Up Downstairs*' cinematographer Alan Pudney. 'Alan asked me to go along for the day and see it being shot and it was really funny seeing everybody rushing about. They used body doubles for the main stars, but Neil Hallett really seemed to be enjoying it. He was hilarious.'

Considering the problems that beset the production, it's a credit to the stars that *Keep It Up Downstairs* ever got finished. 'It was a chaotic movie to work on,' recalls Sue Longhurst. 'Nobody knew what was going to be shot from one day to the next. We didn't know whether we were doing an interior, an exterior, wearing day-wear or night-wear, doing a dialogue scene or a sex scene. It was chaos, but I loved doing it all the same because I love period costumes, the hair, the hats, everything. Although I was glad to get all the filming out of the way, it turned out to be a really classy film.'

CAST: Neil Hallett (*Percy Hampton*), Diana Dors (*Daisy Dureneck*), Jack Wild (*Peregrine Cockshute*), Mark Singleton (*Lord Cockshute*), Sue Longhurst (*Lady Cockshute*), John Blythe (*Francis Dureneck*), Willie Rushton (*Snotty Shuttleworth*), Françoise Pascal (*Mimi*), Olivia Munday (*Kitty Cockshute*), Seretta Wilson (*Betsy-Ann Dureneck*), Julian Orchard (*Bishop*), Aimi MacDonald (*Christabelle St Clair*), Carmen Silvera (*Lady Bottomley*), Simon Brent (*Rogers*), Anthony Kenyon (*Mellons*), Sally Harrison (*Maud*), Mary Millington (*Polly*), Joan Newall (*Mrs Burgess*), Nigel Pegram (*Count Von Schilling*), April Olrich (*Duchess*), Peter Halliday (*PC Harbottle / Old Harbottle*), Maria Coyne (*Vera*), Craig Marriott (*newsboy*). **CREDITS:** *Director* Robert Young, *Producer/Screenplay* Hazel Adair, *Executive Producer* Mark Forstater, *Editor* Mike Campbell, *Photography* Alan Pudney, *Music* Michael Nyman and Clare Moray, *Theme song* 'Always A Pleasure' performed by Neil Hallett A PYRAMID FILM COMPANY Production. Distributed by EMI. Opened July 1976.

THE OFFICE PARTY

Great Britain / 1976 / 55 mins / cert 'X'

The Office Party is a prime example of ultra-cheap, rock-bottom, shot-in-two-versions British sex film production. Filmed in April 1976 and exhibited in cinemas just three months later, the movie is a testament to how quickly producer David Grant could churn out his 'X'-rated extravaganzas. *The Office Party* is easily his cheekiest cheap shot at the 'X' film market because he didn't even have to find a location. He shot it in the offices of his own film distribution company, Oppidan, over the Easter weekend. Grant was about to move his over-filled movie operation into plush new spacious offices (complete with bar) in Coventry Street, Piccadilly, just above his Pigalle cinema. Around the same time he was in dire need of a short film to release as part of a double-bill with the American production *Linda Lovelace for President* and naturally decided to exploit his new locale. Apart from a tiny bit of outdoor location filming in Piccadilly Circus, the bulk of the film is entirely shot indoors and he has to be applauded for actually pulling the whole thing off. His offices were slightly re-dressed with potted plants and garish cinema posters (and naked girls), but basically what you see is a genuine British porn mogul's lair.

The resulting film is an ebullient little affair about an office secretary departing to get married and having her final fling during the inevitable office leaving party. The undistinguished direction and slimline

Left: Boss Alan Lake asks his secretary Pamela Grafton to take dictation in *The Office Party* (1976).

tonic of a plot (both from Grant himself) make it typical mid-1970s sex fare, but the super cast act their hearts out as a variety of tasty office stereotypes. Alan Lake (looking uncharacteristically bloated) is the boss of 'S-X Films' who arrives to work bright and breezy in order to shag his voluptuous blonde secretary. The chirpy Irish charwoman disturbs their love-making but is more concerned with reminding her employer that new loo rolls need ordering. Later the rest of the staff arrive: Judith (Caroline Funnell), the office dumpling who refuses sugar cubes in her tea because she's on a diet but scoffs scotch eggs between typing letters, Mr Palmer (Chris Gannon) the groping, sex-mad old Steptoe who scrupulously checks the company accounts, and Peter (Johnny Briggs), the office rake who lusts after all the pretty girls. Best of all is David Rayner (agony aunt Claire Rayner's real-life brother) as Francis, a simpering queen who brings his dog into work and is continually disturbed by male admirers. 'That was some silly bugger ringing me up,' he moans to his colleague. 'Asking me to go out with him tomorrow night to see some awful sex film called *The Erotic Milkman*. I ask you, what does he think I am?'

As afternoon approaches, the party for the departing Sally gets underway with the desks buckling under the weight of alcoholic drinks. José, the Spanish tea boy, arrives with a projector and blue movie, and staff gate-crash the party from adjacent offices. Peter tries to seduce toffee-nosed temp Samantha (Julia Bond) with a slow dance and soon everybody is slinking off for passion among the paper-clips.

Running at just 55 minutes, *The Office Party* was bumped up to 90 minutes with the inclusion of hardcore footage for the overseas market. In the leading female role is bubbly newcomer Teresa Wood (or, as Grant saucily billed her, 'Teresa Wood and does'), who acts competently enough when required and who strips off for the hardcore scenes with equal enthusiasm. Her bonking partner is actor-model Steve Amber, the Oppidan in-house stud and close friend of Grant. Grant was such an admirer of Amber's ever-ready, ever-stiff penis he dubbed it 'Napoleon'. Although Johnny Briggs wasn't required to act in any of the hardcore sequences, Grant did ask him to drop his strides for his love scene with starlet Julia Bond. Briggs refused and the pair had an almighty row. Vowing never to work for Grant again, Briggs contacted his agent and compromised by filming the scene in pants only.

The 'S-X Films' office walls are plastered with real Oppidan posters like *Frankenstein was a Lesbian*, *Blue Movie Party* and *Hollywood Bitch*, the sort of hardcore movies Grant was playing at his cinema clubs, but the tongue-in-cheek in-jokes don't stop there. At one point the radio is switched on and the DJ reads out a birthday dedication. 'Here's a request for Ray Selfe of Streatham,' says the DJ. 'Wishing you love and kisses on your birthday... from Norman!' Having a friendly dig at his business partner was just the director's style and Grant even makes a cameo appearance as an angry motorist in the film's early moments. His beloved Shih Tzu dogs also have a wag-on role. 'He had those dogs with him everywhere,' recalled Selfe, 'but he chose that breed just to offend people when they asked what they were.' The best self-spoofing comes during the pornographic film show. As the office staff settle down to watch the (unseen) sex action on the screen, the more naïve members of the audience pass comment. 'How could people make them?' asks frumpy Judith incredulously. 'And how can actors act in them?'

CAST: Alan Lake (*Tom Barnes*), David Rayner (*Francis*), Chris Gannon (*Palmer*), Johnny Briggs (*Peter Leigh*), Steve Amber (*Bryan*), Teresa Wood (*Sally*), David Rodigan (*José*), Pamela Grafton (*Miss Mavis Peabody*), Caroline Funnell (*Judith*), Ellie Reece-Knight (*Jackie*), Julia Bond (*Samantha Worthington*), Jeanne Starbuck (*Mrs O'Flaherty*), Jason White (*Bruce*), Vicky Hamilton-King (*Mrs Barnes*), David Grant [uncredited] (*car driver*)

Right: Lynda Bellingham and Robin Askwith in *Confessions of a Driving Instructor* (1976).

CREDITS: *Director/Producer* David Grant, *Editor* John Shirley, *Photography* Peter Jessop, *Screenplay* David Grant and Gordon Exelby, *Music* John Shakespeare and Derek Warne An OPPIDAN Production. Distributed by NEW REALM. Opened July 1976.

CONFESSIONS OF A DRIVING INSTRUCTOR

Great Britain / 1976 / 90 mins / cert 'X'

By the late 1970s British moviegoers could be forgiven for thinking 'It's August, there must be a Confessions film on!' At the climax of *Confessions of a Pop Performer* Timmy and his crafty brother-in-law Sid (Tony Booth) were reduced to busking on street corners in order to earn a dishonest crust after their brief excursion into rock 'n' roll had ended in disaster. Never ones to be easily beaten, the budding entrepreneurs now try their hand at driving instruction, but with the usual catalogue of calamities.

Taking over a dilapidated driving school – not straying too far, since it was filmed in Borehamwood High Street, only a few doors up from their window cleaning business – and re-naming it the 'Noglea School of Motoring', Timmy and Sid have the perfect opportunity to live life in the fornicating fast lane with a bulging client book of women determined to lose more than just their 'L' plates. Suzy Mandel (her voice dubbed on this occasion) is a slinky, crimson-lipped hussy who can't take her hands off Timmy's gear stick. Sally Faulkner is another unsatisfied wife, a golf widow whose husband cruelly neglects her at weekends. 'Every Sunday morning I wake up to the rattle of my husband's balls going out the front door,' she explains to Timmy before letting him play 'a round' in a sand-filled golf bunker during a driving lesson diversion. Lynda Bellingham (producer Greg Smith's wife at the time) plays a 'jolly super' upper class archery-lover who is also romanced by Timmy. When she briefly flashes her left breast while getting to know Timmy a little better, she quickly covers it up again, saying, 'Gosh, how rude!' By Confessions standards it's an insignificant contribution yet, to Bellingham's discomfort, the image was reproduced to help sell the movie, particularly on video after she had become famous as TV's Oxo gravy mum – much to the embarrassment of her youngest son.

With Sid and Rosie living over the driving school business, Timmy decides to make the break from the family home too and takes up lodgings with veteran blonde bombshell Liz Fraser as lusty landlady Mrs Chalmers. Mrs C dotes on her new guest but secretly yearns to give him more than just a signature in her rent book. In a far meatier role than her *Adventures of a Taxi Driver* part, Fraser was called upon to display more flesh in *Driving Instructor* than one would expect from such a well-known comedy actress. Greg Smith was desperate to have her on board but wasn't sure if she'd go for such a saucy part. 'I said to her, "Would you like to do one? We promise there'll be no nudity, but you'll have to do some knickers and bra stuff. Have a read of the script and if you don't like it, don't take offence." Thankfully she did like it and I think she's very sexy in the movie.'

Indeed she is. Playing the part to perfection, Liz created one of the most voluptuous comedy characters in the whole seventies' sex film era. Seeing Liz in black stockings, suspenders and corset (a potent visual later reused to even greater effect by Joan Collins in *The Bitch*), with her big boobs wobbling like jelly, is a sight that stayed with cinemagoers for quite some time after they'd left their local Odeon. If *Driving Instructor*'s brief chocolate eclair sequence, in which

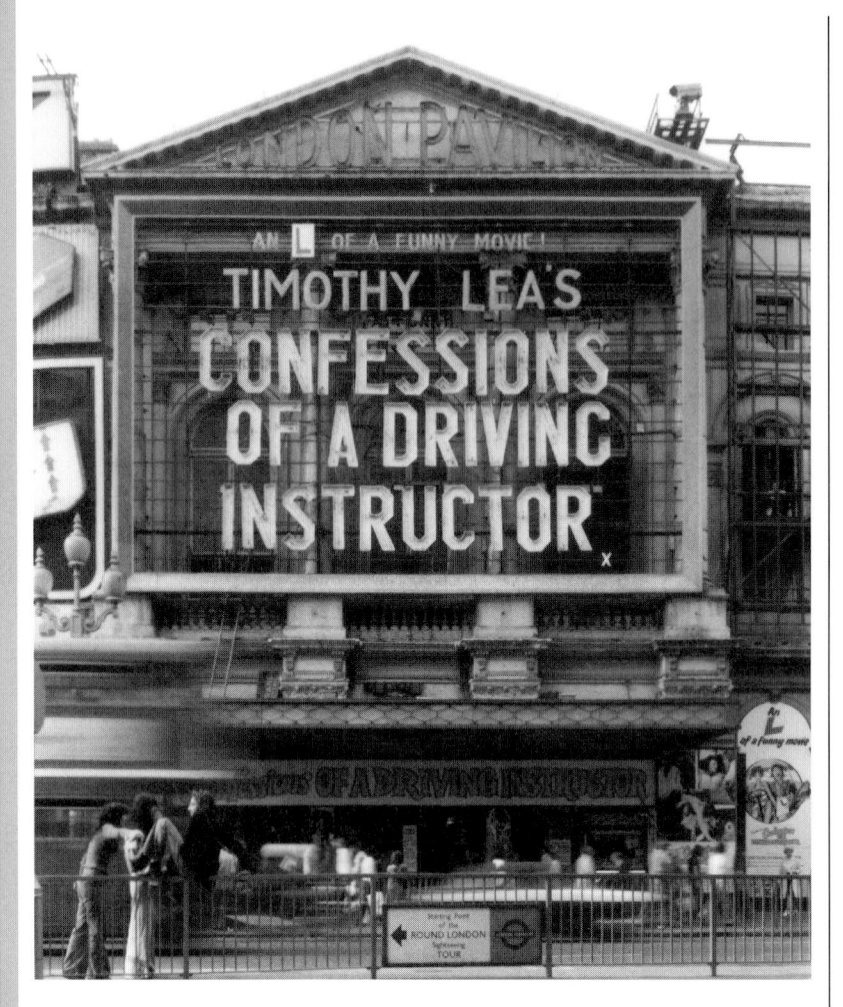

Fraser's expansive chest accidentally gets splashed with cream, raises a few male eyebrows more used to seeing her covered up in the early Carry On films, then it is even more surprising to see her shagging Timmy in a bubble-filled bath with a squeaky rubber duck.

Aside from Askwith's continuing sexcapades, Bill Maynard's performance as Timmy's uncultured, oafish, flat-capped father was rapidly becoming the funniest turn in the series, and his interplay here with clucking wife (Doris Hare) and whining, sour-faced daughter (Sheila White) is as marvellous as ever. A cleaned-up TV spin-off featuring the dysfunctional Lea family was definitely a missed opportunity, especially since the cast gelled so well. 'We all had a wonderful social life outside of work,' recalls the movie's producer, Greg Smith. 'We had a solid regular team and we'd all meet up off set to go down the pub and to parties. It was a very happy family.'

As with the previous Confessions movies, *Driving Instructor* comes up trumps with guest stars. The unforgettable Irene Handl joins the team as 'Miss Slenderparts' (one of writer Christopher Wood's most inspired character names), an elderly one-woman disaster area who's failed her driving test an incredible 43 times. Also guest-starring is booming Welshman Windsor Davies, playing against national type and doing his best Sean Connery impersonation as Lynda Bellingham's fearsome, sporran-swinging father. It's a joy to see his eyes bulging and moustache twitching in disgust as he watches Sally Faulkner (who has been concussed from a flying golf ball) on her knees at crotch level, head lolling from side to side in the film's funniest sight gag.

The third Confessions movie is a hugely enjoyable affair, considered by some fans to be the best of the bunch. Greg Smith, Norman Cohen and Christopher Wood had taken on all comers and proved themselves the best triple act in big screen British comedy. Greg Smith never wanted to go head to head with the Carry Ons but, like it or not, the Confessions were beating the more recent Carry Ons hands down. Well established as Britain's best loved 'junior Sid James', by 1976 Robin Askwith's character had become part of the cinematic fabric, and even the makers of his trademark pressed denim suits get an end credit in this one. In pure 'James Bond will return' style, *Confessions of a Driving Instructor* ends with a tentative plug for the fourth in the series. Eyeing up a billboard advertising 'Funfrall Holiday Camp' (with an illustration that looks suspiciously like actress Linda Hayden), the conniving Sid asks his naïve brother-in-law, 'How d'you fancy a trip to the seaside, Timmo?'

CAST: Robin Askwith (*Timothy Lea*), Anthony Booth (*Sidney Noggett*), Doris Hare (*Mrs Lea*), Bill Maynard (*Mr Lea*), Sheila White (*Rosie Noggett*), Windsor Davies (*Mr Truscott*), Liz Fraser (*Mrs Chalmers*), Irene Handl (*Miss Slenderparts*), George Layton (*Tony Bender*), Lynda Bellingham (*Mary Truscott*), Avril Angers (*Mrs Truscott*), Maxine Casson (*Avril Chambers*), Suzy Mandel (*Mrs Hargreaves*), Chrissy Iddon (*Lady Snodley*), Ballard

*Left: **Confessions of a Driving Instructor** opened at the London Pavilion in August 1976.*

Berkeley (*Lord Snodley*), Sally Faulkner (*Mrs Dent*), Donald Hewlett (*Chief Examiner*), Sally Adez (*female examiner*), John Junkin (*Luigi*), Geoffrey Hughes (*postman*), Damaris Hayman (*tweedy golfing lady*), Daniel Chamberlain (*Jason Noggett*), Lewis Collins (*rugby player*), Timothy Blackstone [uncredited] (*party guest*)
CREDITS: *Director* Norman Cohen, *Producer* Greg Smith, *Executive Producer* Michael Klinger, *Editor* Geoffrey Foot, *Photography* Ken Hodges, *Screenplay* Christopher Wood *based on the novel by* Timothy Lea, *Music* Ed Welch, *Theme song 'My Name is Timmy Lea' performed by* The Ronnie Bond Singers
A SWIFTDOWN Production. Distributed by COLUMBIA-WARNER. Opened August 1976.

SEXTET

Great Britain / 1976 / 56 mins / cert 'X'

Or more accurately, *Quartet*, since this obscure little programme-filler is a composite of four individual sex stories that all take place in a plush London apartment block. It was to be the last British sex film to use the well-mined anthology device that had been so popular with directors since the late 1960s. Directed and scripted by Derek Robbins, who had previously brought *The Sex Victims* to the screen in 1973, *Sextet* was heavily cut by the British censor because of the vast acres of flesh on show and virtually disowned by a furious Robbins. As a protest, his credits on the film are listed as 'Sam Spade', a sideways homage to Humphrey Bogart's character in *The Maltese Falcon*.

The four separate tales – billed 'How to cheat your way into bed!' – are dominated by a handful of limp couplings and a running theme of sexual favours for monetary gain. In the last and most amusing story, the producer of a nude Soho revue (played by Bruce Montague, later to find fame as Wendy Craig's paramour in hit BBC sitcom *Butterflies*) is auditioning new girls. One of them, Dolly, catches his eye but, rather unusually for a stripper, she has a mental block when it comes to taking her clothes off in public and refuses to disrobe for him. But back at Jonathan's apartment Dolly suddenly loses all her inhibitions, stripping her clothes off with wild abandon, pouncing on the producer and leaving him drained and exhausted by her sexual demands.

Dolly gets the job after the bedroom audition, but on her opening night is booed off stage when she again refuses to shed her threads. Suddenly she takes matters in hand and defiantly tugs off her knickers to prove she can be as liberated as the next girl, serenading the audience with a song. Interestingly, Dolly is played by ex-cabaret star Jenny Cox, who the previous year had featured as a stripper in *Carry On Behind*. *Sextet* offers Jenny a fleshier role, in every respect, and she even gets to sing the closing tune, 'Liberation Has Come!', as she pulls down her panties!

CAST: Kate Harper (*Eleanor*), Richard Cornish (*Terry*), Robin Stewart (*Bernie*), Julia Bond (*Sally*), Michael Richmond (*Edgar*), Bruce Montague (*Jonathan*), Jenny Cox (*Dolly*), Philip Bowen (*Algernon*), Peter Attard (*Des*), Caroline Grenville (*Desdemona*), Lorraine Layton (*Julie*)
CREDITS: *Director/Producer/Screenplay* Sam Spade [aka Derek Robbins], *Editor* Tony Palk, *Photography* Dudley Lovell, *Music* Bob Kerr, *Song 'Liberation Has Come' performed by* Jenny Cox
A WATCHGROVE Production. Distributed by BORDER. Opened August 1976.

UNDER THE DOCTOR
aka *The Way You Smile*

Great Britain / 1976 / 86 mins / cert 'X'

Rather unwisely, actor Barry Evans turned down the lead in the copper-bottomed *Adventures of a Private Eye* in favour of this, the début feature from former TV cameraman Gerry Poulson. 'I took him to dinner one night and offered him all sorts of incentives to do the sequel to *Adventures of a Taxi Driver*,' recalls director Stanley Long. 'He told me he didn't want to do another sex comedy, but then he got a bit hard up and was forced to take *Under the Doctor*. By that stage I'd already recast the male lead in my films and it was too late.'

In this medical concoction Evans plays eminent Harley Street psychiatrist Dr Boyd, who has an appointment book bulging with female clients desperate to offload their sexual problems in his consulting room. Unfortunately Evans' baby-face looks prove irresistible to all his patients and their problems rapidly turn into fantasies with the doctor getting the

KEEPING THE BRITISH END UP

Right: Charles Erskine finds it hard to keep his eyes on the road after picking up two leggy hitch-hikers in *Take An Easy Ride* **(1976).**

plum part in each. Evans, in his role as consultant, is shown only in discreet glimpses from behind his big leather chair puffing on his cigar, but adopts a variety of other, more visible, guises in a trilogy of saucy stories.

Marion (played by ex-*Please Sir!* pupil Penny Spencer) is a sexually repressed office secretary who reads *double entendres* into all of her boss' dictation and is desperate to get his silver balls clacking on the desk. Although she claims to lack confidence, she has no qualms about strolling through Knightsbridge topless under a see-through blouse, much to the surprise of real-life shoppers. Next up is Lady Victoria Stockbridge (Hilary Pritchard), a high society débutante romancing an upper class twit (Jonathan Cecil) at his huge country house. At dinner, sitting at opposite ends of a gargantuan table, the couple have to shout at each other in order to make conversation. Finding him a terrible bore, she dreams of a more chivalrous era where men duelled with swords for the hand of their lady. Pritchard demands incredibly high standards from her suitors. 'I've never been under less than a third viscount,' she declares.

In the final story the irrepressible Liz Fraser plays Sandra, a housewife who has invented an imaginary husband as a result of being jilted at the altar some years previously. She talks about her partner as if he really exists. 'If I'm in the kitchen, for instance, bending over the oven to see if my Yorkshire puddings have risen and he comes in, the next thing I know he's got both his hands up my skirt and he's putting the meat in!' she explains straight-faced. The film provides Fraser with the most sexually upfront role of her comedy career, as she spends much of her time romping in black bra and knickers, brandishing a whip and squeezing her wobbling breasts in order to get the desired response from an uninterested Evans.

CAST: Barry Evans (*Dr Boyd/Mr Johnson/Lt Cranshaw/Colin Foster*), Liz Fraser (*Sandra*), Hilary Pritchard (*Lady Victoria Stockbridge*), Penny Spencer (*Marion Parson*), Jonathan Cecil (*Rodney Harrington-Harrington/Lord Woodbridge*), Elizabeth Counsell (*Nurse Addison*), Peter Cleall (*Wilkins*)
CREDITS: *Director* Gerry Poulson, *Producer* Ron Bareham, *Editor* Mike Kaufman, *Photography* Ray Parslow, *Screenplay* Ron Bareham, *Music* Jean Bouchety, *Theme song* 'Talk of Love' performed by Vince Hill
A THORRAWOOD production. Distributed by ALPHA. Opened November 1976.

TAKE AN EASY RIDE

Great Britain / 1976 / 44 mins / cert 'X'

Take an Easy Ride proudly takes it place as one of the most confounding, curious and kinky movies in the history of British sex films. Certainly it's one of the most jaw-droppingly memorable. Now so beloved of media students, if the film didn't exist it would have to be invented. Running under three quarters of an hour, *Take an Easy Ride* manages to squeeze in just about every salacious tit-bit of home-grown exploitation in one tasty package, and although it's not always easy to digest, the movie richly deserves the title of true 'cult classic'. Where else can you witness a blonde Swedish sexpot, dope-smoking, Soho strippers, murder, naturism, juvenile delinquency, long-haired hippies, lesbianism, a groovy disco, up the mini-skirt shots, threesomes, voyeurism and even a dash of T-Rex?

The original premise of *Take an Easy Ride* was to illustrate the dangers of the 1970s craze for hitch-hiking. The newspapers regularly detailed rapes and murders associated with accepting lifts from complete strangers and director-producer Ken Rowles decided to take his inspiration from there. As a cautionary tale with vox-pop from real members of the public mixed with dramatic reconstructions, one can't help but be reminded of Stanley Long's *The Wife Swappers*, which covered another 'ripped from the headlines' subject and portrayed it in much the same style.

Amazingly, the film was never intended as a sex picture but started life as a television short. 'It was going to be made as a TV documentary for what was then Southern Television,' says Ken Rowles. 'I was given a budget of just £10,000, but while I was still shooting it the rushes were seen by David Grant and he said to me, "Would you be interested in it playing in one of my cinemas?" He was obviously thinking how easy it would be to get some Eady money for it, so I said yes, fine!' Grant made only one condition: the film had to contain some more sex. 'As a filmmaker I don't feel like I added anything to the film that cheapened it,' says Rowles. 'I definitely didn't feel compromised adding the extra sex scenes. I was already filming a couple of scenes which were a bit stronger anyway. I just thought that having the movie at the cinema would be much better than one solitary showing on the telly.'

So Southern Television's loss was sexploitation's gain. Originally shot over two weeks in the summer of 1974 in the Kent village of Doddington and on the outskirts of Leeds Castle in Maidstone, *Take an Easy Ride* was finally released with the extra, sexier footage in March 1977. But the long wait was worth it. The film played at the Pigalle Cinema on Piccadilly Circus, adjacent to David Grant's Oppidan offices, for an incredible 48 continuous weeks. 'At its peak I reckon it was making about five grand a week,' says Rowles. 'Grant made a helluva lot of money out of that film.'

The movie follows several distinct stories. Teenage tearaways Mary and Anne bop the night away at a club (fronted by the most annoying DJ since Keith Chegwin) and learn that their favourite band are playing at the upcoming Ashford Pop Festival. The footage of hippies walking around naked and playing 'Greensleeves' on guitars was actually from the ITN archive of the Isle of Wight pop festival from 1970; it's a dead giveaway since landlocked Ashford doesn't have a beach! The two girls take a chance and hitch a ride in an open-topped Triumph from a dodgy individual in flat cap and black gloves, who has a secret stash of hardcore porn in his glove compartment. 'So you like these pop things?' he asks in his sleazy West Country drawl. 'Plenty of boys there. I bet you like that!' His passengers, feeling distinctly uncomfortable, are then driven down a leafy lane and shown some of his girlie magazines. 'Do you like it?' he asks, but the girls, disgusted, ask to get out of the car. He pulls over and knifes one girl, chucking her in the river, and sexually assaults the other. The sequence is nasty and sledgehammers the message home. The girls wind up in casualty, not the festival, and 'Mr Black Gloves' goes on to pick up other unsuspecting women. Even today the identity of the movie's villain is a closely guarded secret, since he was only filmed from behind. 'We don't talk about that! It's a joke,' Rowles says with a chuckle. 'It's for you to guess. We're still trying to find out if he's alive!'

Another couple of delinquent girls (Gennie Nevinson and Stella Coley) prove that it can be the passing motorist who suffers, not the hitcher. High on drugs and seeking 'a whole new scene, a completely different trip,' the bad girls nick a knife, rob a café of its takings and steal a ride on the A20. The meek, unsuspecting driver gets relieved of his wallet and then stabbed in the belly, resulting in a lot of tomato ketchup seeping everywhere.

The undoubted star of the movie is unbilled Danish actress Ina Skriver, who plays the vivacious but naïve 'Scandinavian bird' Suzanne. Accosted coming out of a grocery store, she is called upon to give her views on hitch-hiking. 'Oh yes, I used to hitch,' she says, 'but it's not a pretty story!' A beautiful, statuesque woman, Skriver has long been the movie's main focus of interest. 'I don't know who she was,' says Rowles. 'We just got her from an agency, but how long she was in Britain for I just don't know. She disappeared afterwards.' In fact, it wasn't Skriver's only British film. She had already appeared uncredited in *Percy's Progress* and in 1976 enjoyed a lesbian romp with Koo Stark in *Emily*. A soldier's girlfriend who is in England to visit him at his army base, Suzanne prefers to thumb lifts, happily getting into a Rolls-Royce driven by a suspiciously over-friendly husband, Alan (Alan Bone, by trade a stage manager and great friend of Sid James), and his wife Margaret (minor porn actress Tara Lynn).

Alas, the 'respectable' couple have

no intention of getting their nubile passenger to the army base on time. Instead they stop en route at a hotel and get her thoroughly pissed. 'I'll hire a room,' Alan suggests helpfully. Poor innocent Suzanne decides to take a bath but is shocked when Margaret walks in, naked and unannounced, and starts feeling her up. Tubby Alan shows up, taking snaps with his camera and whipping off his briefs in order to join them on the bed for a sweaty threeway tumble. 'After a drink and everything I wasn't able to put up much of a fight,' laments Suzanne, which is the understatement of the year. And it all ends in tears because she gets dumped by her beloved squaddie after getting pregnant form the experience.

As with *The Wife Swappers*, the film doesn't boast any major-league names, being largely populated by complete unknowns or minor supporting players like Tony Doonan and Tara Lynn. Gennie Nevinson went on to much bigger things after she emigrated to Australia and Helen Bernat, who plays the tragic Anne, is now a bit-part player on BBC soap *EastEnders*. However, had Ken Rowles known then what he knows now, his film may have boasted a performance from the biggest sex star of the 1970s. 'We were doing some casting in Wardour Street for *Take an Easy Ride*,' says Rowles, 'and Mary Millington came to see us for a part. Of course she was just Mary Maxted then because it was 1974. So we had a chat and I thought she was lovely, but she wasn't an actress and I had my doubts about her suitability.

Before she left she said to me, "Don't you want to see me nude?" I replied that we didn't need to because at that stage we just wanted to see what she looked and sounded like. But Mary wasn't having any of that. She was wearing this dress, buttoned up the front, and she just pulled the buttons open and let it drop to the floor so she was completely naked. Then she grabbed my hand and placed it on her bare bum. "Just as smooth as a baby's skin, isn't it?" she said. It was quite a surprise really!'

One day Rowles met an audience member coming out of *Take an Easy Ride*, who told him: 'I'm a teacher and I want all my pupils to see that film, because it really shows how dangerous hitch-hiking is.' Quite why a prim schoolteacher was spending an afternoon watching movies in one of London's most notorious porn cinemas is another thing. Unfortunately, while the film may have been envisaged as a well-intentioned cautionary tale, the intended audience never got to see the finished product. Very few, if any, teenage girls would have found themselves drawn to the Pigalle in Piccadilly Circus to watch an 'X'-rated film in an auditorium jammed with middle-aged men in raincoats. Even the earnest voice-over introduction from Alan Reeve-Jones seems tailor-made for an older, strictly male audience. 'At times you may wish the wife and kids were out of the way as you pass that mini-skirt thumbing a lift. The producers of this film wish to give you the opportunity to judge for yourself whether hitch-hiking should be banned. Is it a form of Russian roulette?'

Looking at the film nearly three decades later it seems unimaginable that it could ever have been shown on television, but Rowles claims that he *meant* the film to be seedy and sleazy. Believe it or not, he was attempting to burnish *Take an Easy Ride* with some *Cathy Come Home*-style realism. 'It has some of that documentary feel to it because I was trained as a documentary filmmaker and therefore I treated the film as such,' he says. 'Perhaps it was before its time. Back in the mid-seventies you just wouldn't have got away with a lot on television, but today on Channel 4 I'm sure you would.' *Take an Easy Ride* has long been a forgotten classic of seventies' filmmaking and one that deserves a wider audience. Even Ken Rowles has jokingly expressed an interest in making a sequel in which 'Mr Black Gloves' gets released from prison after ten years, but at the same time he recognises its limitations. 'It's a load of rubbish,' he says with a smile, 'but I can still be proud of making a load of rubbish, can't I?'

CAST: Margaret Heald (*Mary Ford*), Helen Bernat (*Anne Davis*), Derrick Slater (*Mr Ford*), Jeanne Field (*Mrs Ford*), Sam Avent (*Police Inspector*), Gennie Nevinson (*Pam*), Stella Coley (*Ruth*), Charles Erskine (*Jock the lorry driver*), Terry Francis (*murdered car driver*), Fred Hogarth (*second lorry driver*), Pauleen Bate (*first hitch-hiker*), Christianne (*second hitch-hiker*), Tony Doonan (*hospital doctor*), Ron Patric (*Mr Davis*), Sue Allen Carstairs (*Mrs Davis*), *Uncredited:* Alan Bone

(*Alan*), Tara Lynn (*Margaret*), Alan Reeve-Jones (*voice-over*), Christopher Rowles (*drug pusher*), Ina Skriver (*Suzanne*)
CREDITS: *Director/Producer/Editor* Kenneth F Rowles, *Photography* Douglas Hill, *Screenplay* Derrick Slater, *Music* De Wolfe A MIDAS-KFR Production in association with ACTION PLUS. Distributed by CHILDS ASSOCIATES. Opened March 1977.

1977

UNDER THE BED!
aka The Wedding Party

Great Britain / 1977 / 53 mins / cert 'X'

Under the Bed! was originally envisaged as a direct continuation of the sexcapades of the horny pen-pushers seen in *The Office Party*. In that film, young secretary Sally (played by spirited brunette newcomer Teresa Wood) enjoys one last fling with office stud Bryan before her upcoming nuptials. The movie was a big success for director David Grant, who managed to sell the hardcore version to over a dozen countries in the Palais des Festival building at the 1976 Cannes Film Festival and also secured the finance (a reputed £100,000) to shoot a sequel, to be filmed that summer. 'The sequel was supposed to have been called *The Wedding Party* and the idea was that this and *The Office Party* could be run together,' said producer Ray Selfe. 'In the end it was called *Under the Bed!* because David couldn't get all the same actors back, so the two films never got released together.'

In a strange way the movie does hold together as a sequel of sorts. The action centres on a wedding reception held at Sally's stuffy parents' beautiful riverside home, filmed entirely on location beside the Thames at Wraysbury in Berkshire. Poor Sally has got hitched to a famous photographer, Timothy 'Ever-ready' Harton, but balks at the thought of having to make love to him (square, balding, prudish) on her wedding night. She retreats to her bedroom to take off her ivory finery but is shocked to find her old flame Alan (John Hamill) hiding under the bed. Slightly drunk, he cajoles Sally into having a farewell fuck for old time's sake, which she accepts without too much soul-searching. Their mattress manoeuvres make for the best scene in the movie.

Thereafter the sexual activity comes thick and fast for everybody. The unlikeliest wedding guests pair up for sex in various rooms, including stuttering office virgin Penny (Jayne Lester), who finally loses her cherry to a friend of the bride's. 'I want to make love to you until you beg me to stop,' her suitor says. 'Well, I'm b-b-begging you now,' she stammers – and as a result miraculously loses her speech impediment. The caterer (Michael Cronin, later to become the sports master in children's TV series *Grange Hill*) has difficulty coping with the lecherous guests. And you just know there's going to be trouble when hardcore actress Lisa Taylor arrives as the caterer's flirtatious younger sister, Maria-Teresa. Dressed and plaited like Heidi, she momentarily leaves the finger food to abscond over the fence for a bonk on a boat with Sally's athletic neighbour, Terry. In quite a raunchy scene, Maria is on top when Terry comes a little too rapidly. 'Maria's not-a-finished yet!' complains the Italian sexpot, demanding they make love again, this time uncomfortably hanging from a tree.

Though hardly a classic – the majority of the jokes fall agonisingly flat – the standard of acting from the sex performers is especially good. In particular, Teresa Wood and Lisa Taylor manage to be both sexy and comedically convincing, putting a great deal of 'oomph' into the predictable proceedings. Ultimately though, the abridged UK version of *Under the Bed!* is neither one thing nor the other. The hardcore footage, provided by leading lady Wood and rent-a-stud Timothy Blackstone among others, would seem to have been the only saleable thing this little movie had going for it. But a lack of substance was a failing David Grant's movies had suffered from before. 'He didn't obey the rules of filmmaking,' reckoned Ray Selfe. 'I know I'm old-fashioned, but you need to base a film around a three-act play. You need protagonists, a problem and a resolution. David's films didn't do that. You'd get to the end of the movie and you'd say, "What was all that about then?"'

CAST: Teresa Wood (*Sally*), John Hamill (*Alan*), Jayne Lester (*Penny*), Lisa Taylor (*Maria-Teresa*), Caroline Funnell (*Judith*),

KEEPING THE BRITISH END UP

Pamela Grafton (*Miss Mavis Peabody*), Michael Cronin (*caterer*), Carol Reyment (*mother*), Jon Prince (*father*), Bill Boazman (*Uncle Bertie*), Brian Godfrey (*Timothy*), Alix Krista (*Auntie Bessie*), Peter Jolley (*Arthur*), Adrienne Conway (*Françoise*), Pam Green (*Mrs Harton*), Frank Coda (*Mr Harton*), David Rodigan (*José*), Adrian Ropes (*Frank*), Timothy Blackstone (*guest in velvet suit*), Roy Scammell (*milkman*)
CREDITS: *Director* David Grant, *Producer* Ray Selfe, *Editor* Bill Lenny, *Photography* Peter Jessop, *Screenplay* David Grant and Gordon Exelby, *Music* Derek Warne and John Shakespeare, *Theme Song* 'Wedding Party' *performed by* Ross MacManus
An OPPIDAN-NEW REALM Production. Distributed by NEW REALM. Opened January 1977.

EMILY
aka *The Awakening of Emily*

Great Britain / 1977 / 86 mins / cert 'X'

Watching this film's opening scene of a beautiful old steam train chugging through the verdant English countryside, with the innocent face of a young girl gazing out of a carriage window accompanied by the tinkling music of composer Rod McKuen, you might be forgiven for thinking that it's a sequel to Lionel Jeffries' *The Railway Children*. Well, you'd be wrong. *Emily* was seriously intended to be Britain's answer to 1974 French sexfest *Emmanuelle* and, although it wasn't even a fraction as financially successful, the similarities between the two films are blatant. Both movies are about the sexual awakening of a young girl who enjoys erotic experiences with men and women alike and both are ultimately just as windy and meaningless as the other. However, while *Emmanuelle* became the Bollinger of seventies' porn, *Emily* is strictly 7Up. This *is* England after all and erotica doesn't come easy. Having said that, Koo Stark (future girlfriend of Prince Andrew) has considerably more innocent warmth than Sylvia Kristel as the impressionable young woman floating down a stream of sexual discovery.

In the autumn of 1928, 17-year-old Emily Foster (Koo) returns to her home in England after a year at a Continental

Left: Before she met Prince Andrew. Koo Stark in *Emily* **(1977).**

finishing school. During her absence she has become aware of her sexuality and is eager to get cracking. Her mother (Sarah Brackett) could teach her a few lessons, since she is secretly a prostitute who pays for the upkeep of her lavish house by serving up a bit of split mutton to her houseguests for cash in hand. Her best customer is lecherous old aristocrat Richard Walker, played by Victor Spinetti, who flashes his bare arse once too often. On her first night back on home turf, Emily's mother organises a dinner party in which she meets zesty American schoolteacher James Wise (Richard Oakfield). She immediately fancies him rotten and accepts a flight in his bi-plane. Emily pays absolutely no attention to the view above the clouds, preferring to enjoy the feel of the vibrating joystick between her legs – clenching the joystick so hard she nearly causes the aircraft to plummet out of the sky.

Everybody wants to get their hands on sweet little Emily whether it be randy Richard, her young suitor James, or her middle-aged neighbour Rupert (Constantin de Goguel) and his bisexual Swedish wife Augustine (Ina Skriver). The infamous lesbian shower scene, which got Koo into such trouble with the Royal Family a decade later, is a purely decorous affair. A bit of steam, some tentative nipple-licking and no explicit below-the-waist shots hardly makes for gasket-blowing erotica, but without it the *Sun* could never have revelled in the inspired headline, 'Koo Starkers!'

Emily was Old Etonian director Henry Herbert's second feature. His first had been a children's adventure picture called *Malachi's Cove* in 1973, starring Donald Pleasence, which was far more in keeping with titled nobility. You see, Herbert also happens to be the 17th Earl of Pembroke, the 14th Earl of Montgomery and 6th Baron Herbert of Lea. Now there's a porn pedigree. *Emily* is a big, airy, empty film which is more tedious than sexy. Despite fancying himself as the Anglo-Saxon Just Jaeckin, Herbert seems reticent to direct erotic sex scenes, a failing one could put down to a public school upbringing were it not for the fact that other British sexmongers were generally just as clueless. And while everything is very easy on the eye it's also incredibly dull. As somebody once said, nothing really happens and what does happen isn't very interesting.

CAST: Koo Stark (*Emily Foster*), Sarah Brackett (*Margaret Foster*), Victor Spinetti (*Richard Walker*), Jane Hayden (*Rachel*), Constantin de Goguel (*Rupert Wain*), Ina Skriver (*Augustine Wain*), Richard Oldfield (*James Wise*), David Auker (*Billy*), Jeremy Child (*Gerald*), Jeannie Collings (*Rosalind*), Jack Haig (*taxi driver*), Pamela Cundell (*Mrs Prince*)

CREDITS: *Director* Henry Herbert, *Producer* Christopher Neame, *Editor* Keith Palmer, *Photography* Jack Hildyard, *Screenplay* Anthony Morris, *Music* Rod McKuen, *Song* 'Secret Emily' performed by Ken Barrie An EMILY Production. Distributed by BRENT WALKER. Opened February 1977.

STAND UP VIRGIN SOLDIERS

Great Britain / 1977 / 90 mins / cert 'AA'

Stand Up Virgin Soldiers was an enjoyable digression for actor Robin Askwith, director Norman Cohen and producer Greg Smith, nicely sandwiched between *Confessions of a Driving Instructor* and *Confessions from a Holiday Camp*. A follow-up to the 1968 Columbia Pictures film *The Virgin Soldiers*, directed by John Dexter, it is again based on a bestselling novel by Leslie Thomas. Unlike the original, the sequel's screenplay was entrusted to Thomas himself and the result is a much funnier and sexier film. Hywel Bennett was brilliant as Private Brigg in the first movie, but Robin Askwith stepped in for the follow-up. Unfortunately, when Columbia announced their intention to make the new film in the trade press, critics denounced the casting, claiming the film would be nothing more than 'Confessions of a Virgin Soldier'. 'There was nothing that we considered Confessions-esque about that film,' insists Greg Smith. 'I was worried about some of the sex scenes, but they were in Leslie Thomas' original book so we had to include them. It could be argued that the characters of Timmy Lea and Private Brigg are similar. One is patently fictional, while the other is largely autobiographical. However, I thought there was nobody better for the leading role than Robin and he took a lot of fans with him to that picture.'

Set in Malaya in 1950 during the Communist bandit war, soldiers Brigg (Askwith) and Jacobs (George Layton) –

'a fine pair of privates' – and their fellow recruits are all set to return to dear old Blighty when PM Clement Attlee regretfully informs them that they will have to serve a further six months in the rain-drenched tropics, much to the delight of masochistic Sergeant Wellbeloved (Edward Woodward). The sweaty recruits drown their sorrows at the Golden Grape bar, nicknamed the 'Golden Grope' since it's the favourite haunt of the local Singapore prostitutes. Top attraction is the fearsome 20-stone Eurasian hooker Elephant Ethel (Miriam Margolyes), who can be bought for as little as ten dollars and a few crushed ribs. A more desirable dish is the beautiful Juicy Lucy (returning from the first film, but now portrayed by Fiesta Mai Ling), who offers a 'good fluck'. While Brigg seeks solace with Lucy, Jacobs reluctantly beds Ethel, whose passionate maulings literally bring the house down.

Thankfully the two lads meet a couple of pretty nurses, sprightly Pamela Stephenson and her posh mate Lynda Bellingham, the latter in her second film role for husband Greg Smith. The actresses bring much-needed glamour (and bare breasts) to the movie, but audiences will gain just as much pleasure from seeing gentle John Le Mesurier as a golf-obsessed soft-touch Colonel and Irene Handl as a dotty old colonial lady taking tea and cakes in the tropical heat. Warren Mitchell is unrecognisable as Welsh soldier Morris Morris and displays another side to his talents – a full-frontal nude scene.

Not surprisingly, when *Stand Up Virgin Soldiers* opened critics refused to look beyond the film's obvious Confessions pedigree. Robin Askwith has never looked better or acted more convincingly; even his innocent love scene with virginal Pamela Stephenson is played for tenderness rather than laughs and is more romantic than anything seen under the Timothy Lea guise. 'Columbia Pictures were very keen for Robin to star in it,' explains Greg Smith, 'and he surprised quite a few people with his performance. I think he was exceptionally good.' Of course, there *are* a couple of Confessions-type touches (apparently added at Columbia's insistence), like a patient running amok in his wheelchair, Briggs' clumsiness and bad manners at a high-ranking dinner party and a well-bandaged Jacobs tumbling backwards down a flight of steps, but the film also portrays the harsh realities of war unflinchingly. The vivid battle scenes, though obviously not on the scale of *We Dive at Dawn*, are handled magnificently by Norman Cohen. Also, the poignancy of grown men crying because they want to go home and Briggs' realisation that he's killed somebody bring a legitimate lump to one's throat.

Left: Fiesta Mai Ling, Robin Askwith, George Layton and Pamela Stephenson promoting *Stand Up Virgin Soldiers* in October 1976.

CAST: Robin Askwith (*Brigg*), Nigel Davenport (*Sgt Driscoll*), George Layton (*Jacobs*), John Le Mesurier (*Colonel Bromley Pickering*), Warren Mitchell (*Morris Morris*), Robin Nedwell (*Lt Grainger*), Edward Woodward (*Sgt Wellbeloved*), Irene Handl (*Mrs Philimore*), Pamela Stephenson (*Berenice*), Lynda Bellingham (*Valerie*), Fiesta Mai Ling (*Juicy Lucy*), Miriam Margolyes (*Elephant Ethel*), David Auker (*Lantry*), Robert Booth (*Field*), Peter Bourke (*Villiers*), Leo Dolan (*Tasker*), Brian Godfrey (*Foster*), Paul Rattee (*Browning*), Patrick Newell (*MO Billings*), Monica Grey (*Mrs Billings*), Rosamund Greenwood (*Miss Plant*), Pearl Hackney (*Miss Burns*), John Clive (*man in wheelchair*), Dino Shafeek (*Indian watchman*), Anna Dawson and Brenda Kempner (*glams*), Albert Moses (*Indian shopkeeper*)
CREDITS: *Director* Norman Cohen, *Producer* Greg Smith, *Editors* Geoffrey Foot and Bryan Tilling, *Photography* Ken Hodges, *Screenplay (based on his novel)* Leslie Thomas, *Music* Ed Welch
A GREG SMITH-MAIDENHEAD Film Production. Distributed by WARNER BROS. Opened March 1977.

HARDCORE
aka *Fiona* aka *Frankly Fiona*

Great Britain / 1977 / 82 mins / cert 'X'

Before you get excited, *Hardcore* it ain't. It's just a soft-focus, fictionalised, cinematic 'autobiography' of 1970s sex superstar Fiona Richmond, partly based on her 1976 book *Fiona* and claiming to be the 'frankly sensational adventures of a liberated lady'. Die-hard Richmond fans won't find it that sensational really, but it's still a sex comedy deluxe, head and shoulders above the competition.

Fiona plays herself (who else could do the role justice?) through eight chapters of her lascivious life story. Arriving in the south of France, Fiona meets the enigmatic Anthony Steel in his luxurious white-washed villa. Although unknown to each other, Fiona recounts her life to him, some of it slightly true but most of it utter rubbish. She does admit to being a vicar's daughter in Norfolk, but seeing her playing a 15-year-old with hair in bunches is faintly ridiculous. Dramatising all the myths and legends of her history, Fiona gets through school by having it away with the chemistry master, joins the mile-high club when she becomes an air hostess and auditions for a theatrical agent played by Ronald Fraser and cheekily named Marty Kenelm-Smedley in tribute to the film's director and producer. Marty (who surely is far too common to be an accurate caricature of Paul Raymond) is a difficult man to impress, but after Fiona strips for him in his office and floors him with a left hook, she is signed to a year's contract, wages: £200 per week plus luncheon vouchers.

Soon Fiona's name is splashed across the West End and she makes her dramatic stage début at the Windmill Theatre in a show full of whips, giant steaming phalluses and shagging. Her big début climaxes with her timidly exposing a large silver star stuck to her fanny. Everybody gasps and a star is born. The well-tanned Fiona looks fabulous throughout and is a good sport at playing herself, tongue firmly planted in cheek. She's sexy, passionate and raunchy, even during her obviously faked and uncomfortable lesbian sex scene with a fellow air stewardess. Director James Kenelm Clarke again shows he's the classiest sex film director around; even when the story sags, his thoughtful direction does not. Getting the most out of the fabulously hot, record-breaking summer of 1976 (plus beautiful locations in France and Norfolk coupled with Mike Molloy's soft, sunny photography), Clarke succeeds in making an unusually expensive-looking Brit sex flick.

The film's financier Paul Raymond makes sure that his various businesses get discreetly plugged, notably his Revuebar, the Windmill and Whitehall theatres and his magazine *Men Only*. Getting so damn famous, Fiona arrives at the real *Men Only* offices at Millbank Tower and gets a job 'road-testing' working class men around the UK. 'I need direct experiences with lusty sons of toil,' she exclaims before humping sex actor John Hamill on a bed of root vegetables. Fiona's so-called reality constantly smudges into film fantasy, but *Hardcore* offers every naked variety of the Fiona Richmond legend and stands as a lasting testament to her immense popularity.

CAST: Fiona Richmond (*Fiona*), Anthony Steel (*Robert Charlton*), Donald Sumpter (*Mark*), Arthur Howard (*Vicar*), Murray Brown

KEEPING THE BRITISH END UP

COME PLAY WITH ME

Great Britain / 1977 / 94 mins / cert 'X'

The most famous of all British sex films started life as a script bashed out on George Harrison Marks' ancient typewriter in the early seventies. Marks had tried to flog his idea for years to no avail. By 1976 he had endured two trials at the Old Bailey for sending obscene materials through the post, had seen his business empire go into receivership and was now an alcoholic. Britain's most famous glamour photographer was reduced to selling a few colour transparencies of naked girls to publisher David Sullivan on a month-to-month contract. But unknown to Marks, Sullivan had recently been harbouring a dream to move into feature film production. One afternoon while he and Marks sat chatting about the state of British cinema, Marks happened to mention that he had written a 'very funny story' about randy nurses at a health farm. Sullivan was hooked immediately. Five weeks later *Come Play with Me* was being shot on location in Oxfordshire and at Bushey Studios in Hertfordshire. Sullivan hadn't even read the script.

Sullivan knew a lot about selling magazines. He knew nothing about making movies, but no matter. He has since admitted he never really cared what the finished film looked like; he simply stumped up the £120,000 budget and only bothered to visit the set twice. Sullivan was certain that, with the power of his huge stable of girlie magazines, he could make *Come Play with Me* a mas-

(*Charles*), Patricia Bourdrel (*Madeleine*), Ronald Fraser (*Marty*), Victor Spinetti (*Duncan*), Graham Stark (*Inspector Flaubert*), Graham Crowden (*Lord Yardarm*), Harry H Corbett (*Art*), Roland Curram (*Edward Emmett*), Michael Feast (*photographer*), John Clive (*Willi*), Percy Herbert (*Hubert*), John Hamill (*Daniel*), Linda Regan (*secretary*), Neil Cunningham (*Mr Foster*), Adam West (*Oliver*), Joan Benham (*Norma Blackhurst*), Howard Southern (*TV director*), Heather Deeley (*Jill*), Eddie O'Dea (*Buddy*), Jeremy Child (*Tenniel*), David Cole (*youth*), Stephen Calcutt (*Karl*), Norman Bacon (*Manfred*), Kevin Sheehan (*ticket collector*), Helli Louise [uncredited] (*third Men Only girl*)

CREDITS: Director/Music James Kenelm Clarke, *Producer* Brian Smedley-Aston, *Executive Producer* Paul Raymond [uncredited], *Editor* Jim Connock, *Photography* Mike Molloy *Screenplay* James Kenelm Clarke and Michael Robson

A NORFOLK INTERNATIONAL Production. Distributed by TARGET. Opened April 1977.

Left: Fiona Richmond's school days? Not quite. Hardcore *(1977).*

sive success. And he wasn't wrong.

The only conditions imposed on Marks were that (a) Sullivan's star pin-up and then-girlfriend, Mary Millington, had to be the 'star' of the film and (b) there had to be lots of nudity. Marks nodded in agreement but had wholly different ideas. Writing, directing and starring in the movie, Marks let the whole thing go to his head and the finished product is bizarre to say the least. 'I'm not sure that George Harrison Marks actually knew he was making a sex film,' said *Come Play With Me*'s associate producer Willy Roe in 1998. 'He really wanted to make something that was just more of a comedy. The script was probably written to be a different sort of film, a more expensive production.'

The story focuses on two elderly forgers, Clapworthy (Harrison Marks himself) and his Jewish companion Kelly (Alfie Bass), who are responsible for a million faked £20 notes currently in circulation. On the run from their East End boss (Ronald Fraser), they scarper with the printing plates and hop over the border to Scotland. The two old boys find refuge at Bovington Manor, a health farm run by Lady Bovington (Irene Handl). Unfortunately, poor Lady B faces financial ruin because she just can't attract enough paying guests. When her dreadful choreographer nephew, Rodney (Jerry Lorden), turns up unexpectedly with his troupe of dancers, they hit on a saucy idea to restore their fortunes. Rodney's professional ballet dancers, curiously attired in kinky boots, stockings, corsets and see-through blouses, calmly agree to become prostitutes to attract new clients and convert Bovington Manor into the biggest knocking shop in Britain. The girls, including Mary Millington, Suzy Mandel, Anna Bergman, Nicola Austine and Pat Astley, happily don nurses' outfits and are photographed for some sexy press ads. Within weeks the manor is full to capacity with ugly old men seeking the 'full treatment'.

A subplot featuring an outrageously camp government agent (Ken Parry), assigned by the deputy PM (Henry McGee) to discover the source of the forged bank notes, fits in there somewhere but it's difficult to say quite how. *Come Play with Me* is a bit of a mess all round but endearing nevertheless. It's not sexy in the slightest and if the few scraps of nudity were removed it could safely be screened on a Sunday afternoon on BBC1. In a vain attempt to make the film work, Marks tries to cover all bases. There are attempts at slapstick comedy, a bit of stripping, a really freaky song-and-dance sequence which comes out of nowhere, some antediluvian music hall banter, 'contemporary' pop music and a Benny Hill-style chase. However, Marks' total inability to direct with a firm hand leaves his cast to basically do their own thing. Parry clearly hasn't learnt his lines, Irene Handl makes hers up, Bob Todd (as the vicar) looks suspiciously drunk, Henry McGee looks straight into camera in desperation and the pregnant pauses from Jerry Lorden (surely the worst actor on Equity's books) are blissfully awful. Some of the scenes look totally improvised, including American actor Thick Wilson getting a talcum powder rubdown from German porn star Sonia and Isabella Rye having an utterly nonsensical conversation with her masseur.

When Sullivan saw the finished film he realised what he'd let himself in for. He didn't care about the film's varying quality, but he was concerned that it just wasn't rude enough to get an 'X' rating. 'I saw a rough cut of *Come Play with Me* and I was pretty shocked,' admits Sullivan. 'There really was no nudity in it for the first 45 minutes and not enough of Mary. And the distributors weren't exactly very happy either. It would never have got a release the way it looked then. I had to get George back and he shot some new stuff and we added it in.'

Marks was extremely reluctant to film any new footage, especially since Willy Roe had chucked out 40 pages of the screenplay during the early stages of production. Eventually he agreed, but the extra sequences (including an uncredited stripper putting her stockings and suspenders on, naked bodies romping about in a plunge pool at Sullivan's Croydon sauna club and Mary Millington giving Howard Nelson some 'colonic irrigation') stand out like swollen thumbs. Four hardcore scenes were also shot – three heterosexual, one lesbian (the latter featuring Mary Millington and Penny Chisholm) – but they seemed to disappear almost as soon as they were filmed. Only scraps of them remain in the finished British cut, and Sullivan and Marks both refused to take the blame for their inclusion in the shooting schedule.

Come Play with Me opened to universally scathing reviews at the newly refurbished Classic Moulin in Great Windmill Street on 28 April 1977. Sullivan had signed a contract with the cinema stating that, so long as his film's weekly takings did not fall below a 'break figure' of £1000, they were obliged to keep running it. Determined to keep the film showing for as long as possible, Sullivan embarked on the most dishonest cinema marketing campaign in history. Through his stable of publications the millionaire publisher continually promoted Mary Millington as the star of *Come Play with Me*, despite the fact that she appears only fleetingly. The hardcore footage was also hyped to boiling point. Readers were promised that Sullivan's début film would be the very first to feature 'real sex' passed by the BBFC. 'We must warn filmgoers that *Come Play with Me* contains scenes of a highly explicit nature which may prove too shocking for some,'

claimed one of his editorials. For months Sullivan's magazines contained photo-spreads of models indulging in penetrative sex, claiming they were stills taken from the film. Pictures of Mary in open-legged poses purported to have been taken on set and even Marks was roped in to do a bit of publicity. Describing it as the 'funniest, sexiest film ever made in Britain', the director even claimed it featured 'nearly 50 great girls and they all strip off!'

The unrepentant hype paid off. In London *Come Play with Me* ran solidly for four years. Impressed by the film's longevity, the *Guardian* dubbed it *Mousetrap at the Moulin*. Around the country it played on over 1000 separate screens. Britain's longest running movie ever confounded critics and filmmakers alike; even the film's own editor, Peter Mayhew, claimed that it 'set back the industry ten years'. Many fellow sex comedy veterans blamed

Sullivan for the beginning of the end of the industry. He still faces their wrath today. '*Come Play with Me* is a dreadful effort,' says Stanley Long. 'I'm not being bitchy because we're past all that, but there was no thought behind it. It annoys me especially when that film is lumped in with mine.' Whatever the criticisms, rightly or wrongly *Come Play with Me* has entered cinema history. Its title is as synonymous with British sex now as it was in 1977.

CAST: George Harrison Marks (*Cornelius Clapworthy*), Alfie Bass (*Maurice Kelly*), Irene Handl (*Lady Bovington*), Ronald Fraser (*Slasher*), Tommy Godfrey (*Norman Blitt*), Ken Parry (*Podsnap*), Cardew Robinson (*McIvor*), Bob Todd (*Vicar*), Sue Longhurst (*Christina*), Jerry Lorden (*Rodney*), Henry McGee (*Deputy Prime Minister*), Rita Webb (*Madame Rita*), Queenie Watts (*café owner*), Talfryn Thomas (*Nosegay*), Norman Vaughan (*seaside per-

Left: Mary Millington, Harrison Marks, Suzy Mandel, Mireille Alonville, Alfie Bass, Nicola Austine and Pat Astley relaxing in *Come Play With Me* (1977).

former), Derek Aylward (*Sir Geoffrey*), Valentine Dyall (*Minister for Finance*), Michael Balfour (*Nosher*), Milton Reid (*bouncer*), Howard Nelson (*Mr Benjamin*), Thick Wilson (*Mr Wilson*), Suzy Mandel (*Rena*), Mary Millington (*Sue*), Pat Astley (*Nanette*), Suzette St Claire (*Tina*), Anna Bergman (*Josie*), Mireille Alonville (*Michelle*), Nicola Austine (*Toni*), Penny Chisholm (*Tess*), Marta Gillot (*Petrina*), Sonia (*Mandy*), Suzette Sangalo Bond (*Patsy 'The Amazon'*), Lisa Taylor (*Sir Geoffrey's lover*), Isabella Rye (*Denise Wilson*), Toni Harrison Marks (*Miss Dingle*), John Denny (*Capital Radio DJ*), Josie Harrison Marks (*Trixie the brownie*), Billy Maxim (*welk seller*), Deirdre Costello (*blonde stripper*), Tara Lynn [uncredited] (*auditioning stripper*), Suzie Sylvie [uncredited] (*bikini girl*)

CREDITS: *Director/Producer/Screenplay* George Harrison Marks, *Executive Producer* David Sullivan, *Associate Producer* Willy Roe, *Editor* Peter Mayhew, *Photography* Terry Maher, *Choreography* Mireille Alonville, *Music* Peter Jeffries, *Theme song 'Come Play with Me' performed by* Coming Shortly
A ROLDVALE Film. Distributed by TIGON. Opened April 1977.

WHAT'S UP NURSE?

Great Britain / 1977 / 84 mins / cert 'X'

Robert Todd (Nicholas Field) is a naïve, cack-handed young doctor who takes up his first appointment at a crummy little hospital at so-called Banham on Sea (the movie was actually filmed entirely on location in Southend). He doesn't make a terribly good impression when, on his first day, he is wheeled in on a stretcher 'intimately stuck' to the daughter of the blustering consultant (John Le Mesurier). The beautiful Felicity Devonshire plays the girl in question, Olivia, whose vaginal muscles are so convulsive she attaches herself to all her partners. After this inauspicious start, Todd finally settles into his new job, getting to grips with a bizarre assortment of luckless patients.

Field, who bears an uncanny resemblance, both physically and vocally, to Hugh Grant, makes for a pretty bland hero (he retired from acting in 1978 to become an interior designer), but the supporting actors are impressive. Le Mesurier wanders through in a daze, but Kate (*Love Thy Neighbour*) Williams makes a fun alternative to Hattie Jacques as Matron and Graham Stark enjoyably overplays know-it-all porter Carthew. Stark was also the film's associate producer but was unhappy with the finished product. 'I cherish my reputation and I'm happy to say that I've made some pretty classy films in my time, but *What's Up Nurse?* wasn't one of them,' he recalls. 'I went into the film in good faith, but frankly I was appalled. Constantly trying to make it funny was difficult and I spent all of my time trying to get rid of the vulgarity in it, but I couldn't just walk out of my contract. I was very disappointed by it.'

It was thanks to the well-connected Stark that director Derek Ford was able to assemble such a superior cast. Also involved are Andrew Sachs (*Fawlty Towers*) as another Spanish waiter, Anna Karen (*On the Buses*), Le Mesurier's *Dad's Army* co-stars Bill Pertwee and Frank Williams, the much-missed Barbara Mitchell (*Please Sir!*) as a flirtatious neighbour spouting double *entendres* nineteen-to-the-dozen and music hall star Chic Murray in a throwaway cameo. Most interesting are the twin appearances of Carry On regulars Peter Butterworth and Jack Douglas as a couple of coppers; with no Carry On in production in 1977 they were reduced to appearing in this drivel.

With all that talent it comes as no surprise that the script is barrel-scrapingly dreadful and the starry players are shamefully wasted. The movie's only decent gag is lifted straight off a famous seaside postcard. A patient clutching his burning crotch is followed from a cubicle by a dippy young nurse (Julia Bond) holding a pan of steaming water. 'You stupid girl,' reprimands Matron. 'I told you to prick his boil!' If Ford, who also wrote the torpid screenplay, had invested as much time in writing a half-decent story as he did on bringing together his cast then the movie would have been a winner. As it is, the childish, hackneyed one-liners fight for space with some of the crudest, most tasteless sequences seen in any 1970s sex comedy. In *Carry On Nurse* Wilfrid Hyde White had a daffodil famously placed between his buttocks. Nearly 20 years later Ford goes one better by having patient Ronnie Brody with a jam jar wedged up his rectum. The fact that real-life medical students are reportedly faced with this kind of thing on a daily basis doesn't make the sequence any more palatable.

KEEPING THE BRITISH END UP

Worst of all, Ken Parry, as a mincing, sour-faced old queen worried about his boyfriend's acute constipation, takes the prize for playing the grossest gay stereotype ever. Prescribed with pessaries after five weeks without a bowel movement, Parry is furious that there's been no change in his lover's condition. 'He said they tasted horrible,' he screams. 'For all the good that it did him, he might as well have just stuck 'em up his arse!' Convinced he is actually pregnant, his limp-wristed partner endures an enema, only to wake up with an escaped chimpanzee (don't ask!) in his bed, which he claims as his child. It's a nasty scene, written with utter contempt.

CAST: Nicholas Field (*Dr Robert Todd*), Felicity Devonshire (*Olivia Ogden*), John Le Mesurier (*Dr Ogden*), Graham Stark (*Carthew*), Kate Williams (*Matron*), Cardew Robinson (*ticket collector*), Barbara Mitchell (*neighbour*), Angela Grant (*Helen Arkwright*), Peter Butterworth (*Police Sergeant*), Jack Douglas (*Constable*), Julia Bond (*nurse*), Elizabeth Day (*2nd nurse*), Ronnie Brody ('*Jam Jar Man*'), Sheila Bernette (*Mrs Garrett*), Chic Murray (*pet shop owner*), Bill Pertwee (*Flash Harry*), Frank Williams (*Vicar*), Keith Smith (*Mr Newberry*), Andrew Sachs (*Guido*), Kate Harper (*club girl*), Ken Parry and Peter Greene (*gay couple*), Anna Karen (*knitter*), Terry Duggan (*old salt*), Zoe Hendry (*topless patient*), Michael Cronin (*workman*), Albert Moses (*first Asian*), Monika Ringwald (*party guest*), Lisa Taylor (*head nudist*), Serena Lyn (*fire eater*). **CREDITS:** *Director* Derek Ford, *Producer* Michael L Green, *Associate Producer* Graham Stark, *Editor* Richard Marden, *Photography* Les Young, *Music* Roger Webb, *Theme song* 'The Love Bug' performed by Tony Burrows A BLACKWATER FILM Production. Distributed by VARIETY. Opened May 1977.

ADVENTURES OF A PRIVATE EYE
aka *Adventures of a Private Dick*

Great Britain / 1977 / 96 mins / cert 'X'

With Barry Evans reluctant to sign on the dotted line for another saucy *Adventures* comedy, director Stanley Long was forced to look elsewhere for a replacement. 'We had all sorts of names lined up,' admits Long. 'People like Robin Nedwell and Richard Beckinsale, but nobody wanted to do it. That's how we got Christopher Neil, because he was relatively unknown.' Neil, a musician by trade and the songwriting partner of pop star Paul Nicholas, actually succeeds in giving a far more agreeable central performance than Evans ever did. Neil's innocent glances to camera and double-takes blow Evans' out of the water. Plus Michael Armstrong's gag-laden script gives Neil more manoeuvrability to get the most out of his naturalistic performance. And with a change in actor came a shift in character name – from Joe North to Bob West. In the third film, he'd mutate into Sid South.

The original idea for a second *Adventures* comedy was *Adventures of a Roving Reporter* before it eventually morphed into *Adventures of a Private Dick*, then *Private Eye*. Neil plays boneheaded assistant to studly, hard-nosed private detective Judd Blake (Jon Pertwee). When Judd goes on holiday to Beirut, he leaves his second-in-command, and his big magnifying glass, in sole charge. Bob's first case arrives in the shape of big-name guest star Suzy Kendall (playing it straight), who is being threatened by an unknown blackmailer, demanding thousands of pounds in return for some photographic negatives of herself in sexually compromising positions. The trail takes Bob to the creepy ancestral home of Kendall's crazy family, Grimsdyke Manor, presided over by a huge stuffed vulture. We're seriously into *Addams Family* territory here with a kooky bunch of eccentric relatives, all of whom are under suspicion. There's twitching hypochondriac Violet (Liz Fraser), insane, eyeball-rolling, alcoholic Sydney (Harry H Corbett), and the psychic Medea (Anna Quayle), who dabbles in witchcraft. They're all crude caricatures but lovable ones nonetheless.

In addition to the Grimsdyke clan, Long assembles his greatest ever cast of comedy stalwarts who greedily gobble up Armstrong's bubbly dialogue. Irene Handl is the delightfully dotty Miss Friggin, Fred Emney plays a bewildered, short-sighted Lord who mistakes Bob for a female prostitute, and Hilary Pritchard is a whip-cracking, porn-loving, suburban nympho who tries to entice Bob into bed. ('How about a bit of *Last Tango in Paris*? I've got loads of butter in the fridge. I would have suggested *Deep Throat*, but I tried it with the window cleaner last week and I nearly choked myself!') There's also Adrienne Posta doing a remarkable impersonation of Liza Minnelli in a neatly staged song-and-dance sequence filmed at London's Burlesque strip club.

Private Eye is the most consistently entertaining of the *Adventures* trilogy with abundant fun and games. It had the biggest budget of the three movies, best script and most enjoyable performances. Strange, then, that it was the least successful at the box-office. 'I don't know why really,' says Long. 'We spent a lot of time on that one to get it right and it cost an extra ten grand, but it wasn't quite as popular as *Taxi Driver*. The strange thing is that we reduced the budget for the next one, *Adventures of a Plumber's Mate*, and it was a much bigger hit. You just can't predict it.'

CAST: Christopher Neil (*Bob West*), Suzy Kendall (*Laura Sutton*), Harry H Corbett (*Sydney*), Liz Fraser (*Violet*), Diana Dors (*Mrs Horne*), William Rushton (*Wilfred*), Irene Handl (*Miss Friggin*), Anna Quayle (*Medea*), Fred Emney (*Sir Basil*), Jon Pertwee (*Judd Blake*), Ian Lavender (*Derek*), Veronica Doran (*Maud Gubbidge*), Adrienne Posta (*Lisa Maroni*), Julian Orchard (*police cyclist*), Linda Regan (*Clarissa*), Hilary Pritchard (*Sally*), Jonathan Adams (*Inspector Hogg*), Angela Scoular (*Jane Hogg*), Jonathan Caldicott (*Craddock*), Robin Stewart (*Scott*), Nicholas Young (*Legs Luigi*), Graham Ashley (*Mr Prentiss*), Nicola Austine (*Mrs Prentiss*), Peter Greene (*policeman*), Derek Martin (*desk sergeant*), Milton Reid and Jon Robinson (*bodyguards*), Linda Cunningham (*Zelda*), Teresa Wood (*Millie*), Maria (*Miss Walker*), Shaw Taylor (*himself*), Hot Toddy (*chorus girls*)
CREDITS: *Director* Stanley Long, *Producers* Peter and Stanley Long, *Editor* Jo Gannon, *Photography* Peter Sinclair, *Screenplay* Michael Armstrong, *Music* De Wolfe, *Theme song 'Private Eye' performed by* Christopher Neil
A SALON Production distributed by ALPHA. Opened July 1977.

DEAR MARGERY BOOBS

Great Britain / 1977 / 5 mins / cert 'X'

Another tiny 'X'-rated production off Bob Godfrey's 'sextoons' conveyor belt, *Dear Margery Boobs* is a spoof on Marge Proops' *Daily Mirror* agony column, though Godfrey claims it was originally inspired by screenwriter Stan Hayward's frantic correspondence with the Inland Revenue. Once again, the hero is a small middle-aged suburbanite who writes a series of saucy letters (all signed 'Worried Streatham') to an agony aunt, detailing his odd sexual practices. Margery Boobs is unruffled by his erotic tales of sex with an electrified rubber doll, but when she reads of his desire to be pelted with

Right: Julia Bond, Robin Askwith and Caroline Ellis grin and bare it out of season in Confessions from a Holiday Camp *(1977).*

cream eclairs while swinging from a trapeze she can contain her lust no longer and proposes marriage.

Godfrey indicated at the time it would be his last sexual cartoon (it wasn't) and certainly the finance for the five-minute project was not as forthcoming this time round. *Kama Sutra Rides Again* had been made with financial assistance from the legendary Boulting Brothers, but Godfrey had to go downmarket for *Margery Boobs* and knocked on the grimy door of infamous porn producer David Grant. 'You had to be a bit desperate to go to him for money,' laughs Godfrey. 'I mean he wasn't the sort of person you'd want round for dinner!'

CAST: Imogen Claire (*voice*) (*Margery Boobs*), Bob Godfrey (*voice*) ('*Worried Streatham*')
CREDITS: *Director* Bob Godfrey, *Producer* David Grant, *Editor* Tony Fish, *Photography* Julian Holdaway, *Screenplay* Stan Hayward, *Music* Jonathan Hodge
An OPPIDAN Production. Distributed by OPPIDAN. Opened August 1977.

THE KISS

Great Britain / 1977 / 18 mins / cert 'X'

Blonde bombshell Felicity Devonshire (in her final film) and boyfriend Barry Cranwell enjoy a sexy picnic in the country. They make love tenderly before going for an idyllic walk, but are shocked to stumble across the hooded form of the Grim Reaper. Perplexed rather than terrified, they follow the hideous apparition and are finally deposited, still fearless, on an open hillside. They enjoy a lingering kiss whereupon it transpires they are actually sitting in a car which crashes into a tree and explodes into flames, killing them both.

This peculiar 18-minute short was co-scripted by photographer Kevin Pither and David Grant, the latter uncharacteristically drifting into the avant-garde. Pither originally worked as a cameraman on Ray Selfe's numerous documentaries during the 1960s. The following decade he had become chief projectionist at Selfe and Grant's cinemas, but had a hankering to direct his own pictures. He kept nagging Grant and *The Kiss* was the curious result. During shooting, however, Pither realised his screenplay was not all it appeared to be, and the news was brought to him by his old boss, Ray Selfe. 'I said to him, "I don't know how to tell you this, but you've stolen the plot from another movie." It was basically a sexier variation on *Incident at Owl Creek*.'

An Oscar-winning French short made in 1964, directed by Robert Enrico and based on the famous Ambrose Bierce story, *Owl Creek* told of a condemned Civil War soldier who fantasises an exhilarating break for freedom before, to the audience's astonishment, the hangman's rope breaks his neck. 'We ran *The Kiss* as a support movie at the Pigalle,' recalled Selfe, who also edited the film. 'It never ran anywhere else because there was no market for that sort of film. I don't think anybody liked it at all. The audience would complain. They wanted something sexy, not arty!'

CAST: Felicity Devonshire (*woman*), Barry Cranwell (*man*), Digby Runsey (*Grim Reaper*)
CREDITS: *Director/Photography* Kevin Pither, *Producers/Screenplay* David Grant and Kevin Pither, *Editor* Ray Selfe, *Music* Kieran White
An OPPIDAN-INTERGALACTIC COSMIC FILM Production. Distributed by OPPIDAN. Opened August 1977.

CONFESSIONS FROM A HOLIDAY CAMP

Great Britain / 1977 / 88 mins / cert 'X'

The final Confessions outing takes our heroes away from the cosy setting of south London and drops them slap bang in the middle of a hedonistic holiday camp in a chilly March, providing them with plenty of 'crumpet opportunities'. Like a dirtier version of *Carry On Camping* (which, incidentally, was also filmed at the height of winter), *Confessions from a Holiday Camp* prickles all over with copious goose-bumps and erect nipples. This holiday getaway proves that the British don't mind sunbathing in a force ten gale.

'Costing £220,000, it was the most expensive Confessions we'd made and for this film we even had a 'foreign location', so to speak,' laughs producer Greg Smith. 'The movies were so huge by 1977 that it wasn't difficult to get decent locations.' In fact, the 'exotic' setting for the movie was a less-than-glamorous holiday park on Hayling Island, Hampshire which they only got because it was out of season. 'We filmed in February and March of that year so several of the girls got slightly blue, so to speak,' adds Smith. 'I think the most-heard expression during filming was "It's fucking cold".' Because of the extensive location work away from Elstree Studios, *Holiday Camp* enjoyed the luxury of a six (rather than five) week shooting schedule.

Timmy (Robin Askwith) and Sidney (Tony Booth) are working at Funrall Holiday Camp as green-coated holiday hosts. 'Only Sid could have come up with the brilliant idea of re-opening a holiday camp in March,' says Timmy. 'It was so cold the Russians were trying to send political prisoners there!' When stern ex-prison governor Willie Whitemonk (John Junkin) takes over the business he demands an end to the sexy shenanigans that have been going on. In an effort to appease the ferocious camp comandant, the likely lads decide to organise a beauty contest and have no shortage of ready, willing and able applicants. The vacationing vamps – including Nichola Blackman (dubbed by Miriam Margolyes), Caroline Ellis and the beautiful Penny Meredith – promise Timmy sexual favours if he fixes it for them to win. But does our hero accept bonking bribery? Of course he does!

Timmy also goes the extra length with the campsite radio annoucer (Kim Hardy) and inadvertently creates his own version of *Je t'aime ... moi non plus* as their orgasmic groans are broadcast over the tannoy system. However, Timmy soon realises he has bitten off more than he can screw when Whitemonk's nymphomaniac wife, Antonia (the delectable Liz Fraser, back for second helpings after *Driving Instructor*), demands a bit of bump 'n' grind on the local ghost train. Also back in the cosy Confessions camp is Linda Hayden, after a two-film break, as a saucy French 'ow you say? 'oliday 'ost' named Brigitte. But her Gallic accent is nearly as bad as her German one in David Niven's *Vampira* a few years earlier. Deadpan comic Colin Crompton (Bernard Manning's co-host from TV's *Wheeltappers and Shunters Social Club*) rounds out the cast in his one and only movie role. But, as usual, the most chucklesome scenes are reserved for the Lea family, immortalised by Doris Hare, Bill Maynard and Sheila White.

Holiday Camp has fewer belly laughs than usual and the gags are more whiskery than ever. Askwith gurns and grimaces through the usual cavalcade of calamities – usually involving regular drenchings in the camp pool – but some of the jokes are overly familiar or just variations on what has gone before. Timmy's romp with Brigitte in a shed full of bulging inflatables, for example, recalls similar outings in foam (*Window Cleaner*) and a pile of 7" singles (*Pop Performer*). And today the movie looks more dated than its predecessors thanks to some egregiously racist and homophobic quips. Lance Percival brings new meaning to the expression 'holiday camp' as the mincing entertainments officer, though he predictably turns straight by the end after snogging Brigitte under a table, while Nichola Blackman as the slinky Blackbird endures tired old jokes about her skin colour every time she appears on screen.

The film closes, less than triumphantly, with the classic comedy standby of a pie fight and Timmy laments his continuing failure to hold down a decent job. 'We've got to find something more suited to our talents,' he reflects. 'Brain surgery maybe, or plumbing perhaps. I've been a bit worried about my plumbing lately...' It is the series' most obvious signpost to the next misadventure, the draft script of which was called *Confessions of a Plumber's Mate*. But, as Greg Smith explains, 'Takings were slightly down on *Holiday Camp*. Not drastically, but a little less than normal. I had a tingling down my spine that told me we couldn't carry on forever.' Smith's mind was made up for him when Columbia Pictures' president David Begelman, who had always been very supportive of the company's British output, left the company under a very dark cloud in February 1978. His successor wasn't keen to finance any more low-budget UK productions and, as a result, poor old Timmy Lea was never seen again.

CAST: Robin Askwith (*Timothy Lea*), Anthony Booth (*Sidney Noggett*), Doris Hare (*Mrs Lea*), Bill Maynard (*Mr Lea*), Sheila White (*Rosie Noggett*), Linda Hayden (*Brigitte*), Lance Percival (*Lionel*), Liz Fraser (*Antonia Whitemonk*), John Junkin (*Mr Whitemonk*), Sue Upton (*Rene*), Caroline Ellis (*Gladys*), Penny Meredith (*married woman*), Nichola Blackman ('*Blackbird*'), Julia Bond (*bikini girl with grapes*), Nicholas Owen (*Kevin*), Mike Savage (*Kevin's father*), Janet Edis (*Kevin's mother*), David Auker (*Alberto Smarmi*), Marianne Stone (*waitress*), Deborah Brayshaw (*go-cart Girl*), Carrie Jones (*Timmy's bikini girl*), Kim Hardy (*announcer*) Margo Field (*Mrs Dimwiddy*), Lauri Lupino Lane (*mayor*), Leonard Woodrow (*chaplain*), Jake Cooper (*Jason Noggett*)

CREDITS: *Director* Norman Cohen, *Producer* Greg Smith, *Executive Producer* Michael Klinger, *Editor* Geoffrey Foot, *Photography* Ken Hodges, *Screenplay* Christopher Wood *based on the novel by* Timothy Lea, *Music* Ed Welch, *Theme song* 'Give Me England' *performed by* The Wurzels
A SWIFTDOWN-COLUMBIA PICTURES Production. Distributed by COLUMBIA-WARNER. Opened August 1977.

A LUSTFUL LADY

Great Britain / 1977 / 35 mins / cert 'X'

A peculiar, little-seen 35-minute programme filler, filmed on location in the Seychelles with an unappealing inflatable doll in the title role. Tubby Aubrey Morris plays an unfortunate passenger who has fallen overboard from a luxury cruise liner. Stranded on an exotic island, his only company is a sex doll, voiced by Marcella Markham. He falls in love with his artificial girlfriend, hijacks a small boat and escapes to civilisation intending to spend the rest of his life with her. However, once settled at a luxury hotel the doll turns into a flesh and blood woman who refuses to give herself up to him unless they get married first.

CAST: Aubrey Morris (*shipwrecked man*), Marcella Markham (voice) (*inflatable doll*), Julian Holloway (voice) (*shipwrecked man*), John M East [uncredited] (*sailor*)

CREDITS: *Director/Photography* Hal E Woode, *Producer* Jay Sinclair, *Editor*

Left: Caroline Ellis, Colin Crompton and Lance Percival get the beauty contest under way in *Confessions from a Holiday Camp* (1977).

Wulfert Bodo Rintz, *Screenplay* Hal E Woode and Jay Sinclair, *Music* John Leach and George Fenton
A BORDER-DEWMOSS Production. Distributed by WATCHGROVE. Opened November 1977.

CRUEL PASSION
aka *Marquis de Sade's Justine*

Great Britain / 1977 / 97 mins / cert 'X'

Arthouse meets grindhouse in this supposedly highbrow adaptation of the Marquis de Sade's notoriously depraved novel *Justine*. Set in 1785, the film chronicles the trials and tragic tribulations of two teenage sisters, Justine and Juliette. Justine is a frigid, introspective young innocent while her slightly older sister is a sexually voracious, sinful, shag-happy raver. Residing in a convent full of fornicating lesbian nuns, a kinky pastor and a corrupt money-grasping Mother Superior, the sisters couldn't have got off to a less wholesome start. Expelled from the nunnery after Justine refuses to let the Mother Superior have a grope under her habit, the girls set out into the big bad world. 'There is a simple rule of nature,' Juliette tells her younger sibling, 'that the wicked will flourish and the good must flounder.' And boy, does Justine flounder.

With Koo (*Emily*) Stark as the sweet Justine and Lydia Lisle as Juliette, the movie's casting director has made little or no effort to get actresses who look anything like the 16 and 17-year-olds they are supposed to be. If anything, Ms Lisle looks like she's pushing 30. The sisters flee to London where Juliette's friend Pauline (Ann Michelle) has made a terrific living for herself in an upmarket whorehouse. When they finally arrive at the lavish Mayfair brothel, overseen by a fruity French tart called Madame Lorande, the girls are checked to see if their cherries are intact. Juliette is set to work immediately and takes to her new profession like a cat-o-nine-tails to a trembling buttock.

Poor Justine isn't terribly impressed watching her sister give a blow-job to the brothel's resident coke-snorting fop and hastily flees back to the countryside. But, of course, being a goody-two-shoes is her downfall. The randy old pastor tries to rape her then falls to his death from the roof, she gets kidnapped by a bunch of lecherous ale-swigging graverobbers who just happen to be plundering her parents' plot, and she suffers horrific nightmares of being placed on a flaming crucifix surrounded by pasty-faced spectres. Anything that can go wrong does go wrong, ridiculously so. Even when an innocent coachdriver gets shot through the head by the villains, his bloody corpse falls, where else, right on top of wretched Justine.

The whole thing is reminiscent of the famous 1914 silent serial *The Perils of Pauline*, in which the luckless Pearl White lurched from one calamity to another. There's even cliffhanger 'da-da-da...' music (probably nicked from *Dick Barton*) to warn the viewer when there's a dramatic bit coming up. The principle underpinning the whole piece is 'Why be good, when you can be really bad?' Naughty Juliette lives the life of Reilly as a hooker but being sweet and virtuous doesn't get Justine anywhere, and in the movie's incredibly downbeat denouement she gets raped by the man who hours earlier saved her from the graverobbers, is savaged by a couple of Dobermanns, raped twice more, and then thrown half-dead into a freezing lake. If *Cruel Passion* weren't so thoroughly dismal and depressing it could actually be quite funny. The finished film was not to everybody's taste and failed to set the box-office alight. For Koo it was her last chance to break into the celebrity A-list. Instead, she set her sights on something bigger, HRH Prince Andrew. But that's another story.

CAST: Koo Stark (*Justine Jerome*), Lydia Lisle (*Juliette Jerome*), Martin Potter (*Lord Carlisle*), Hope Jackman (*Mrs Bonny*), Katherine Kath (*Madame Laronde*), Maggie Peterson (*Mother Superior*), Ann Michelle (*Pauline*), Barry McGinn (*George*), Louis Ife (*Pastor John*), Jason White (*Pearce*), Malou Cartwright (*Sister Clare*), David Masterman (*Archer*), Ian McKay (*Brough*), Alan Rebbeck (*Lord Claverton*), Jeannie Collings, Jennifer Guy and Barbara Eatwell (*prostitutes*), Glory Annen (*nun/prostitute*).
CREDITS: *Director/Producer* Christopher Boger, *Editor* Peter Delfgou, *Photography* Roger Deakins, *Screenplay* Ian Cullen based on writings of the Marquis de Sade, *Music* Richard Wagner
A CEE EUROPA Production. Distributed by TARGET. Opened April 1978.

LET'S GET LAID!
aka *The Love Trap*

Great Britain / 1977 / 96 mins / cert 'X'

Loosely based (and I mean *loosely*) on Paul Raymond's long-running Windmill stage farce, *Let's Get Laid!* is a momentous moment in British sex film history, bringing together two of the genre's biggest stars, Fiona Richmond and Robin Askwith. Sadly, it's not the frenzied shag-fest that the producers would have you believe. 'Now, Britain's sexy superstars get it together!' announced the poster. Get it together? They barely even get it apart.

Set in London in 1947, Askwith plays completely against Timothy Lea type in his role of a softly spoken Northerner called Gordon Edistone Kitchener Laid. Demobbed from the army, he is given the key to a luxury Mayfair apartment owned by his rich cousin. Hearing groaning from across the hall, he finds a dying secret service agent in a flat owned by crappy B-movie actress Maxine Lupercal (Fiona Richmond). Asking him to dispose of the body, Maxine draws the naïve Lancastrian into a confused plot that's less espionage thrills than sexpionage frills. Laid has inadvertently pocketed the dead man's cigarette lighter, a potentially dangerous device code-named PJ46, and soon the police, the secret service and an evil international crook with a gravity-defying coiffeur (Anthony Steel) are all after him. Lucky police inspector Graham Stark gets the chance to utter the line everybody has been waiting to hear: 'Let's get laid!'

Wary that the man in the mac might be finding all this plot a bit too much to cope with, director James Kenelm Clarke allows Fiona to show off one of the best bodies in British porn at regular intervals, courtesy of several arbitrarily inserted Technicolor fantasy scenes. They're all much the kind of thing we've come to expect from her – romping on a giant bed, tarting it up as a saucy French maid and playing a Nazi Miss Whiplash. For lovers of stocking tops, sock suspenders, feather boas and ATS uniforms these sequences are a dream come true. For anyone else they just get in the way. The whole thing is reminiscent of an old black-and-white George Formby caper with added nudity.

Let's Get Laid! is a somewhat muted sex movie; even poor Robin Askwith doesn't get to shag as many birds as he was used to in the Confessions series. The one person who seems to be having fun is minor-league sex actress Lisa Taylor, who, in the film's running gag, is seen shagging a variety of men (sometimes two at a time) whenever Askwith rings her up. The film is significant from a historical point of view, however, as a fond farewell to one of the great British sex sirens of the 1970s. This was Fiona Richmond's final big fling in 'X'-rated cinema. The ending of her relationship with Paul Raymond meant she was left out of his next film, *Erotica* (1980), and instead took to the road with her increasingly awful stage shows.

CAST: Fiona Richmond (*Maxine Lupercal*), Robin Askwith (*Gordon Laid/Jimsy Deveroo*), Anthony Steel (*Moncrieff Dovecraft*), Graham Stark (*Inspector Nugent*), Linda Hayden (*Gloria*), Roland Curram (*Rupert Dorchester*), Tony Haygarth (*Sgt Costello*), John Clive (*Piers Horrabin*), Charles Pemberton (*Constable Barclay Baxter*), Lisa Taylor (*Eleanor Midwinter*), Anna Chen (*Hyacinth*), Richard Manuel (*Fenton Umfreville*), Patrick Holt (*Commissioner*), Peter Cartwright (*film director*), David Millicent (*Sgt Sterne*), Clare Russell (*Marti*), Shaun Curry (*Greenleaf*), Fanny Carby (*woman in phone booth*), James Marcus (*Quentin Rusper*), Murray Salem and Ted Burnett (*heavies*), Tony Hughes (*Goddard Ronaldshay*), Jayne Lester (*Ruby the tart*), Donna Scarf (*ATS girl*), Frank Ellis (*mortician*), Uncredited: Pat Astley (*ATS girl*), Timothy Blackstone (*Eleanor's lover*), Vicki Scott (*girl at poolside*)

CREDITS: Director/Music James Kenelm Clarke, Producer Brian Smedley-Aston, Executive Producer Paul Raymond [uncredit-

Left: Robin Askwith sweeps Fiona Richmond off her feet in *Let's Get Laid!* (1977).

ed], *Editor* Jim Connock, *Photography* Philip Meheux, *Screenplay* Michael Robson *based on the play by* Sam Cree
A NORFOLK INTERNATIONAL Production. Distributed by TARGET. Opened May 1978.

1978

ROSIE DIXON – NIGHT NURSE

Great Britain / 1978 / 88 mins / cert 'X'

When production of *Confessions of a Plumber's Mate* was cancelled, *Rosie Dixon* unknowingly marked Columbia Pictures' last foray into British sex comedy. Filmed in the autumn of 1977, the picture was again based on a novel by Christopher Wood – *Confessions of a Night Nurse*, published in 1974. As a literary cousin to Timothy Lea, Wood followed the character of naïve suburban teenager Rosie over nine books between 1974 and 1977, casting her as escort, baby sitter, riding mistress, bar maid and so on.

When Columbia announced its intention to mine another rich vein of paperback pokery, not everybody was convinced that a sex comedy series with a female lead was going to be successful, none more so than Confessions supremo Greg Smith. 'I didn't really want to get involved because I wasn't sure it was wise to have two rival Confessions-type series running at the same time, but I took the role of executive producer on it just to keep an eye on things,' he explains. 'I did insist that they didn't use the Confessions prefix though, because I figured that if the film flopped it would taint my series.'

Adopting the title *Rosie Dixon – Night Nurse*, the film was produced by experienced filmmakers Davina Belling and Clive Parsons, who spent over a year auditioning young hopefuls to take the leading role. 'I've seen a lot of 18-year-old scrubbers in the last 18 months,' Belling told *Screen International* in August 1977. 'But when we found Debbie Ash we knew she was right!' For pretty blonde-haired Ash the role was gold-dust and the trade papers talked of her becoming 'the next big thing'. Sadly it wasn't to be. Her fame was eventually eclipsed by her sister Leslie, who incidentally takes a small supporting role, with uncharacteristic brown hair, in *Rosie Dixon*.

Inspired by primetime medical soap opera 'Doctor Kilmore', starry-eyed 18-year-old virgin Rosie Dixon (Ash) decides to become a nurse and enrols at nearby St Adelaide's Hospital. The harsh realities of life on the wards is somewhat different from television, however, since the nurses are dominated by a tough, unfeeling Scottish Matron (Beryl Reid, wonderful as usual). Sharing a room in the nurses' home with an upper class nympho called Penny Green (Caroline Argyle), Rosie becomes the focus of sexual attention for a gaggle of lecherous student doctors whose main priority is shagging rather than treating patients. The guest stars (both in and out of bed) are of the usual Columbia calibre. Many faces are re-used from previous Confessions episodes, notably Liz Fraser as a dizzy housewife obsessed with winning newspaper competitions and John Le Mesurier as head surgeon Sir Archibald, more interested in the 3.30 at Newmarket than whipping out an appendix. The biggest shock is seeing veteran comic Arthur Askey as a dirty old man whizzing about in his motorised wheelchair pinching nurses' arses.

The film's director Justin Cartwright, an old university chum of Christopher Wood, attempted to distance himself from the Confessions movies, but by attempting to alter the tried-and-tested formula, and instead make a dirtier version of *Doctor in the House*, he shot himself in the crotch. 'It is smut for all the family,' he joked at the time. 'But we're deliberately not being grubby, we're going for a glossier look instead.' Cartwright was an ex-commercials director and helming a full-scale 90-minute movie was a totally new experience for him. Nobody can deny the film looks great. It's certainly as glossy as Cartwright intended, but with none of the cheerful effervescence of the Confessions series. Soft-focus prettiness sits awkwardly with comedy capers with a skeleton, humping in hospital laundry baskets and patients mistakenly drinking urine samples. Even some of the corny jokes are well below the quality threshold we've come to expect from Christopher Wood. 'Are you intimidated?' asks the ferocious Matron. 'I don't think so, but I've had a flu jab!' Rosie replies. In the title role, Debbie Ash tries hard but lacks the clumsy phys-

161

Right: Caught on camera – Oliver Tobias and Joan Collins in *The Stud* (1978).

icality of Robin Askwith. Playing Rosie virtually straight, she just doesn't have the personality to pull it off.

Rosie Dixon's funniest moment probably happened off screen. When the movie was nearing completion, Belling and Parsons innocently invited the parents of cast members Peter Mantle and Caroline Argyle onto the set. What the Reverend W E Mantle and Judge Major Michael Argyle thought of their offspring appearing in a softcore porn film was never reported. We can but guess. Major Argyle was a circuit judge for 18 years who vigorously spoke out against permissiveness and pornography and famously presided over the 1971 *Oz* magazine obscenity trial, handing out severe prison sentences to the editors. 'I will not tolerate filth!' he famously pronounced.

CAST: Debbie Ash (*Rosie Dixon*), Caroline Argyle (*Penny Green*), Beryl Reid (*Matron*), John Le Mesurier (*Sir Archibald MacGregor*), Arthur Askey (*Mr Arkwright*), Liz Fraser (*Mrs Dixon*), John Junkin (*Mr Dixon*), Lance Percival (*Jake Fletcher*), Bob Todd (*Mr Buchanan*), Leslie Ash (*Natalie Dixon*), David Timson (*Geoffrey Ramsbottom*), Jeremy Sinden (*Dr Robert Fishlock*), Peter Mantle (*Dr Tom Richmond*), Ian Sharp (*Dr Seamus MacSweeney*), Christopher Ellison (*Dr Adam Quint*), John Clive (*Grieves*), Glenna Forster-Jones (*Staff Nurse Smythe*), Patricia Hodge (*Sister Belter*), Harry Towb (*Mr Phillips*), Joan Benham (*Sister Tutor*), Claire Davenport (*Mrs Buchanan*), Sara Pugsley (*Night Sister*), Peter Bull (*august visitor*), Pat Astley, Teresa Wood, Margaret Heald, Fiona Douglas

Stewart and Sue Lambarth (*nurses*)
CREDITS: *Director* Justin Cartwright, *Producers* Davina Belling and Clive Parsons, *Executive Producer* Greg Smith, *Editor* Geoffrey Foot, *Photography* Alex Thomson, *Screenplay* Christopher Wood and Justin Cartwright *based on the novel by* Rosie Dixon, *Music* Ed Welch, *Theme song 'Rosie' performed by* Greengage A COLUMBIA PICTURES Production. Distributed by COLUMBIA-WARNER. Opened February 1978.

THE STUD

Great Britain / 1978 / 91 mins / cert 'X'

Jackie Collins' most famous bonkbusting novel, published in 1969, had originally been set to go before the cameras the following year. In fact, it wasn't until 1977 (by which time the book had sold over one million copies) that the film finally went into pre-production, and only after virtually every studio, both in the UK and US, had turned it down. Jackie's elder sister Joan had loved the story of a manipulative, sexually liberated older woman having lashings of sex with a handsome young club owner and apparently told Jackie modestly, 'I must play the part. I would be fabulous!' Desperate to see the book come to life on the big screen, Joan persuaded her third husband, businessman Ron Kass, to put up the dough. He'd never dabbled in filmmaking before but it wasn't a risk he'd ever regret.

With Joan self-cast as man-eating bitch Fontaine Khaled, the search was on for an actor to play the title role. In October 1977 the movie's distributors placed advertisements in the trade press, launching the hunt for 'the greatest STUD of all time!' The only requirements were that the actor had to be British, over six feet tall and between 27 and 30. Adam Faith, George Best and even Tom Jones were all mentioned, but finally muscular, cleft-chinned newcomer Oliver Tobias was chosen. Legend has it that Jackie Collins took one look at him and had him signed up on the spot.

Jackie reshaped her original novel into a more contemporary screenplay, with all the seventies' *Saturday Night Fever* disco trimmings but still concentrating on the central premise of the selfish upper class ball-breaker taking advantage of all and sundry. Joan is fantastic as the filthy-rich, pouting, posturing bitch with an insatiable lust for young men. Unhappily married to her middle-aged businessman husband (played with restraint by Walter Gotell), she seeks thrills and spills on the dancefloor of her West End nightclub, Hobo, managed by the handsome and promiscuous Tony Blake (Tobias). Joan's dialogue is chock-full of bitchy one-liners, Fontaine Khaled being easily identifiable as the blueprint for Alexis Carrington Colby in the American primetime soap *Dynasty*, in which Joan starred for eight years.

Managing to get Tony back to her elegant apartment in Eaton Square, Fontaine seduces him in the elevator. Viewing him as nothing more than a 'working class bum in Gucci shoes', she is happy to belittle Tony. Much is made elsewhere of Tony's supposed virility and sexual prowess. He invites a never-ending stream of pretty young ladies to test his mattress. None leave disappointed. He's beautiful and well-hung and he knows it. 'It's not often I get to eat that much,' remarks one of his female conquests the morning after an extended humping session. Impeccably dressed and with more pairs of shoes than Imelda Marcos, the lantern-jawed Tony poses in front of his mirror and murmurs, 'You handsome bastard.' Several contemporary critics accused Tobias of being emotionless in his role, but in fact his moody performance is extremely believable. If anything, he underplays the part, injecting some much-needed vulnerability into Tony Blake.

As Tony gets drawn further into Fontaine's web of sex, drugs and decadence, he's flown to Paris and encouraged to take part in an outrageous orgy in a private swimming pool. Tony takes an immediate shine to a couple of decorative party popsies (Pat Astley and Suzie Sylvie), but it's Fontaine's waspish best mate Vanessa (Sue Lloyd) who has really set her sights on him. After she ensnares him into a bit of water-logged rumpy-pumpy, her bisexual husband (Mark Burns) attempts to give Tony a sneaky blow-job, but instead Tony blows his top and hurriedly departs for London. Weary of everybody wanting a piece of him (well, one piece in particular), Tony suddenly realises he is being devoured by the very lifestyle he's so addicted to.

On release, *The Stud* traded shamelessly on its very considerable sexual imagery. Joan's nudity caused a sensation in newspapers and magazines across the world, although she had shown a bit of flesh already in 1975's *Alfie Darling*. Nevertheless, a famous British actress, over 40, baring everything was something of an unknown quantity and the media couldn't get enough of her. Male audiences certainly loved the 'new look' Joan and by the end of 1978 she had been voted the sexiest woman in the world. Lately her career had been going down the pan in various low-budget clinkers like *Empire of the Ants*, shot in the swamps of the Florida Everglades, but *The Stud* gave her the shot in the arm she desperately needed. The film's spin-off merchandise reached fever-pitch, meanwhile, with the launch of a brand-new aftershave ('a distinctive masculine fragrance with the sexual powers attributed to musk and ginseng'), tackily called 'Monsieur Le Stud' and available from the fragrance counters at Boots and Debenhams!

KEEPING THE BRITISH END UP

While the movie was just what the doctor ordered for its fading female star, Oliver Tobias didn't fare so well. In Britain his career petered out, but he continued to make pictures on the Continent, although no role became as iconic as that of sex machine Tony Blake. *The Stud* is unquestionably one of the most exhilarating British movies of the late 1970s and blissfully evocative of its decadent, groove-fuelled era. The terrific, pulsating, pumping disco soundtrack adds great atmosphere to the story. It's truly invigorating to watch sex starlet Minah Bird wiggling her tush to Hot Chocolate's *Every One's a Winner* amid a sea of lip-gloss, satin pants, crimped hair and sparkly boob tubes – and that's just the fellas!

CAST: Joan Collins (*Fontaine Khaled*), Oliver Tobias (*Tony Blake*), Sue Lloyd (*Vanessa Grant*), Mark Burns (*Leonard Grant*), Doug Fisher (*Sammy Marks*), Walter Gotell (*Benjamin Khaled*), Tony Allyn (*Hal*), Emma Jacobs (*Alexandra*), Peter Lukas (*Ian Thane*), Natalie Ogle (*Maddy*), Constantin de Goguel (*Lord Newton*), Sarah Lawson (*Anne Khaled*), Guy Ward (*Peter*), Peter Dennis (*Flowers*), Peter Bourke (*Gordon*), Tania Rogers (*Janine*), Felicity Buirski (*Deborah*), Jeremy Child (*Rupert Scott*), Minah Bird (*Molly*), Sharon Fussey (*Denise*), Chris Jagger (*Terry*), Hal Dyer (*Maxine*), Margot Thomas (*Mamie*), Hilda Fenemore (*Tony's mum*), Bernard Stone (*Tony's dad*), John Conteh (*himself*), Billy Walker (*himself*), Legs and Co (*dancers*), Uncredited: Pat Astley and Suzie Sylvie (*girls in shower*), 'Gypsy' Dave Cooper (*naked man*), Suzanne Danielle (*disco dancer*), Howard Nelson (*Sandro*), The Real Thing (*themselves*), Lady 'Bunny' Rothermere (*herself*), Vicki Scott (*clubber*), Milo Sperber (*Kamara*)

CREDITS: *Director* Quentin Masters, *Producer* Ron S Kass, *Editor* David Campling, *Photography* Peter Hannan, *Screenplay* (based on her novel) Jackie Collins, *Choreography* Flick Colby, *Music* Biddu and John Cameron, *Theme song 'The Stud'* performed by The Biddu Orchestra

A STUD Production. Distributed by BRENT WALKER. Opened April 1978.

ADVENTURES OF A PLUMBER'S MATE

Great Britain / 1978 / 84 mins / cert 'X'

On the face of it, it seems like more than just coincidence that, within months of Robin Askwith's *Confessions of a Plumber's Mate* being cancelled in pre-production, Stanley Long waded in with a plumbing extravaganza of his own, but coincidence it was. *Adventures of a Roving Reporter* had been mooted as the title of the third *Adventures* comedy, but Long played safe and decided to concentrate on the lowbrow laughs afforded by a multitude of plumbing, waterworks and toilet bowl gags. And lead actor Christopher Neil was back again to stem the flow.

Neil, whose compass-hopping character is now called Sid South, lives in a squalid north London flat struggling to make ends meet and working as a plumber for sanitary engineer B A Crapper. As Crapper, poor Stephen Lewis is stuck firmly, as ever, in *On the Buses* mode; he's got Blakey's trademark Hitler moustache and looks, as usual, like he's swallowed an ashtray. On his rounds, Sid visits frustrated, bondage-loving housewife Prudence Drage to replace her toilet seat. Unbeknown to her, she's been literally sitting on a fortune; it's made of solid gold, melted down by her violent gangland boyfriend. After a bit of mild handcuffed hanky panky with Drage, our hero takes the old loo seat and flogs it to a junk shop for a couple of quid. Naturally, the villains soon come looking for him and he gets involved in a lot of largely humourless business trying to get it back. Three quarters of the way through, this plot is largely discarded in favour of traditional blue-tinged escapades with naked popsies Lindy Benson, Teresa Wood and Suzy Mandel. The stand-out scene is Sid's encounter with giant-sized character actress Claire Davenport as a topless

164

Left: Christopher Neil comes to clear a blockage for John Wyman and Lindy Benson in *Adventures of a Plumber's Mate* (1978).

masseuse, her huge boobs dangling frighteningly close to Long's camera lens.

The big-name comedy guest stars seem a little thin on the ground here. William Rushton and Anna Quayle make valuable contributions but, amazingly, the top-billed character actor is '17-stone punch drunk ignoramus' (his own description) Arthur Mullard as a bookmaker's heavy. 68-year-old Mullard, with his battered face, huge weight and big polyester trousers pulled right up to his nipples, makes for an unconvincing bully boy and is about as frightening as your grandad.

The biggest surprise is seeing soon-to-be West End star Elaine Page as Sid's love interest, with an astounding *Charlie's Angels* flick and a friendly sympathetic ear. Interestingly, Paige's insignificant contribution to the movie nearly ended in court. 'She had quite an innocuous part really,' says Long. 'She isn't naked, she doesn't swear, she's not in any compromising positions. She doesn't do anything but be the nice little girlfriend. Just after she made the film she became a big hit in Andrew Lloyd Webber's *Evita* and she attempted to stop *Plumber's Mate* being released. Her lawyer got involved and I had to promise not to use her name on the paid advertising. She was a nice girl, but I couldn't understand her as soon as she became a star.'

The general tone of *Adventures of a Plumber's Mate* is much more serious and downbeat than its predecessors. There are violent villains, people 'roughed up' and put in hospital, an old lady getting 'shit scared' and a cat getting squashed under a mattress. Most disconcerting of all, Prudence Drage's character is called a 'silly bitch', slapped round the face and has her hair pulled over a banister by her vicious gangland husband. This scene is like something out of *The Sweeney* and totally out of place. The series ends ungraciously with Stephen Lewis leaping about in agony after having a mechanical drain cleaner stuck up his arse. It really was the final word in toilet humour. As with the Confessions series there were plans to make one more – *Plumber's Mate* had actually been considerably more successful than its predecessor – but Long decided to quit while he was ahead. 'I felt like I'd run out of gags and I wasn't prepared to repeat myself. It's always a struggle to find new funny situations. I did have a script for a fourth movie, *Adventures of an Electrician*,' says Long with a twinkle in his eye, 'but I thought it was absolutely shocking!'

CAST: Christopher Neil (*Sid South*), Stephen Lewis (*Crapper*), Elaine Paige (*Daisy*), Arthur Mullard (*Blackie*), William Rushton (*Dodger*), Nina West (*Sally*), Prudence Drage (*Janice*), Anna Quayle (*Loretta Proudfoot*), Peter Cleall (*Carson*), Claire Davenport (*Belinda*), Richard Caldicot (*Wallings*), Christopher Biggins (*Robin*), Stephen Riddle (*Willie*), Jonathan Adams (*rent collector*), Leon Greene (*Biggs*), Neville Barber (*Charteris*), Suzy Mandel, Linda Hartley, Tessa Skola and Vicki Scott (*tennis girls*), Lindy Benson (*Maisie*), John Wyman (*Maisie's husband*), Christine Donna (*Anna*), Teresa Wood (*plunger girl*), Derek Martin (*motorcycle dealer*), Pat Astley [uncredited] (*party guest*)

CREDITS: *Director/Producer* Stanley Long, *Editor* Jo Gannon, *Photography* Peter Sinclair, *Screenplay* Stephen D Frances and Aubrey Cash, *Music* Christopher Neil, *Theme song* 'I'm Flying' performed by Christopher Neil A SALON Production. Distributed by ALPHA. Opened June 1978.

THE PLAYBIRDS
aka *The Playbird Murders* aka *Secrets of a Playgirl* aka *The Blue Girl*

Great Britain / 1978 / 94 mins / cert 'X'

Barely six months after *Come Play with Me* opened to record box-office figures in London, producer David Sullivan announced the next starring vehicle for his girlfriend, 1970s sexbomb Mary Millington. Sullivan promised that *The Blue Girl*, as it was initially known, was going to blast its mighty predecessor to smithereens; it would be the 'hottest film ever to be screened in Britain'. And Sullivan was taking no chances. He rejected George Harrison Marks' offer to direct another film for him and instead asked *Come Play with Me*'s associate producer Willy Roe, who had had no previous experience of directing, to helm the new movie.

Roe's brief was to make a much sexier film than *Come Play with Me* with a raunchier, more up-to-date storyline, a pared-down budget, a leaner shooting schedule, lots more naked girls and a pivotal part for Mary. Against all odds, Roe by and large succeeded. The film's title was changed to *The Playbirds* on Mary's

KEEPING THE BRITISH END UP

suggestion and Sullivan agreed that the new movie could be an excellent 90-minute marketing gimmick for his stable of publications, notably his flagship top-shelf magazine *Playbirds*. In the finished film actor Alan Lake plays Harry Dougan, a flared-trousered, wide-lapelled, race-horse-owning, millionaire publishing magnate who auditions models for his girlie magazines by getting them to strip for him in his office. If he likes them they make the centrefold and, as a bonus, get to see his bedroom ceiling. Now where have we heard that one before? 'Yes, Lake is playing me,' Sullivan reluctantly admitted in 1997, 'but only vaguely.'

Lake's character is a bit of a kinky old devil, getting his models to pose nude for a series of supernatural-themed photoshoots. However, the subject matter is attracting the attention of a deranged stalker who is systematically murdering each centrefold one by one. Poor Pat Astley gets choked in her kitchen and sugary Suzy Mandel soon goes the same way. The killer, nicknamed 'The Chopper' in the tabloids, confounds Scotland Yard's dippiest detectives Holbourne (Glynn Edwards) and Morgan (future *That's Life* presenter Gavin Campbell), until pretty WPC Lucy Sheridan (Mary) agrees to go undercover as a glamour girl. In real life Mary relished the chance to play a Metropolitan police officer, many of whom had tangled with her when her sex shop was regularly raided. Dressing Britain's foremost 4' 11" hardcore porn actress in a police uniform was Sullivan's idea of a joke.

Roe gives Mary plenty of colourful opportunities to get her kit off as over-enthusiastic Lucy begins taking her responsibilities a bit too far. Getting a feel for her new 'career', she starts working as a prostitute in a London sauna, has a lesbian fling, shags the slippery Dougan and makes it onto the front cover of *Playbirds* magazine, never once blowing her cover, or her cool. But who is the murderer? The smart money's on Dougan himself, but there's also a religious zealot, a hideous photographer and a pervy MP who rants about 'pornography being the heroin of the soul' on TV chat shows but likes nothing better than going home at the end of the day and pulling his pudding over a John Lindsay film. The laughable 'shock' ending is a terrible cop-out and still disappoints even after repeated viewings. The crazy Bible-basher (Dudley Sutton) is arrested and charged with the murders, but when Mary returns to her flat she is brutally slain in her bathtub. The real identity of 'The Chopper'? The Bible-basher's hitherto unsuspected twin brother!

With its overall style reminiscent of a 1950s black-and-white B movie, *The Playbirds* bears uncanny similarities to Terry Bishop's 1959 quota quickie *Cover Girl Killer* as well as Lindsay Shonteff's 1969 thriller *Night after Night after Night*, both featuring puritanical psychopaths

Left: Mary Millington ironically cast as WPC Sheridan in *The Playbirds* (1978).

killing young lovelies. Wherever the inspiration came from, *The Playbirds* is still unbeatable as a piece of British sexploitation. It's the film where Mary finally stood up and was counted. Although the naff ending hits a bum note, the tempting mix of nudity, excitement, car chases, overblown theme tune and blatant self-publicity makes it an irreplaceable masterpiece of seventies smut and an invaluable record of Soho in all its tackiness.

CAST: Mary Millington (*WPC Lucy Sheridan*), Alan Lake (*Harry Dougan*), Glynn Edwards (*Chief Supt Jack Holbourne*), Gavin Campbell (*Insp Harry Morgan*), Suzy Mandel (*Lena Cunningham*), Windsor Davies (*Assistant Police Commissioner*), Kenny Lynch (*Police Doctor*), Derren Nesbitt (*Jeremy Roe*), Dudley Sutton (*Hern*), Ballard Berkeley (*trainer*), Alec Mango (*George Ransome MP*), Pat Astley (*Doreen Hamilton*), Sandra Dorne (*Dougan's secretary*), Penny Spencer (*Sgt Andrews*), Michael Gradwell (*Terry Day*), John M East (*radio interviewer*), Anthony Kenyon (*Dolby*), Ron Flanagan (*Detective Wilson*), Suzie Sylvie (*WPC Taylor*), Uncredited: Derek Aylward (*older massage man*), Gloria Brittain (*crucifix model*), Debra (*Foxy*), Howard Nelson (*caped man*), Suzette Sangalo Bond (*poolside party girl*), Tony Scannell (*man at depot*).

CREDITS: *Director/Producer* Willy Roe, *Executive Producer* David Sullivan, *Editor* Jim Connock, *Photography* Douglas Hill, *Screenplay* Bud Tobin and Robin O'Connor [aka George Evans and Willy Roe], *Music* David Whitaker, *Theme song 'Playbirds' performed by* John Worth A ROLDVALE Film. Distributed by TIGON. Opened July 1978.

YOU'RE DRIVING ME CRAZY!

Great Britain / 1978 / 53 mins / cert 'X'

In early 1978 prolific producer David Grant was approached by two naïve scriptwriters who had written a script humorously entitled *The Au Pair Wore Spurs*. Grant liked their idea but, as always, was reluctant to pay them for it. Instead, Grant just ripped the cover sheet off their treatment and thought up a new title, passing it off as his own. The first the writers heard of it was when they happened upon the film playing in a West End cinema. Grant reluctantly took them to one side and paid them off. 'He was the typical con-man, pushing things to the limit every time,' said Ray Selfe. 'But he'd only ever get caught out once every 25 or so times.' Whoever takes responsibility for it, the storyline for *You're Driving Me Crazy!* could be written on the back of a postage stamp since it involves nothing more than a collection of hurriedly put-together sex scenes and birds stripping off. What makes the finished movie slightly more interesting is the setting. It was filmed on Magna Carta Island on the River Thames near Runnymede where the famous charter was signed in 1215.

Michael Watkins (the male lead in 1975's *Erotic Inferno*) stars as Tom, a naughty photographer temporarily unable to drive after a serious car crash. He advertises for an au pair-cum-chauffeur and is all set to hire a sexy German lass when his possessive girlfriend Jacqui (Lisa Taylor) vetoes the idea. She insists he hire young buck Aron, played by Steve Amber with a yucky American accent, instead. Aron wastes no time in shagging Tom's luscious models and banging the tasty next-door neighbour (Pat Astley), while Tom has his hands full with Anthea (Suzy Mandel in her final British film). The interminable bed-hopping finally ends happily with a cosy foursome involving Tom, Aron, Jacqui and Aron's ex-girlfriend Mary Lou (Pauline Abner). Running 53 minutes in the UK, the movie was also filmed in a hardcore export version.

You're Driving Me Crazy! was David Grant's last movie before he concentrated his efforts exclusively on film distribution and the burgeoning video market. It also marked his last collaboration with long-time business partner Ray Selfe. Their Oppidan film partnership had served them well and by 1978 they had a turnover of £500,000 and a staff of 45. However, when their offices in Coventry Street were bought up for redevelopment, and subsequently turned into the Trocadero complex, Selfe decided to throw in his hat. He realised that the boom years of British sex cinema were at an end. Grant moved to new offices in Berkeley Square and when Selfe finally walked out Grant cried like a baby. From then on it was all downhill.

CAST: Michael Watkins (*Tom*), Steve Amber (*Aron*), Pat Astley (*Monica*), Suzy Mandel (*Anthea*), Lisa Taylor (*Jacqui*), Nikki Kelly (*Bente*), Pauline Abner (*Mary Lou*), Suzie Alexander (*Petra*), Alan Selwyn (*Monica's husband*), David Grant (*Tom's assistant*), Ray Selfe (*publican*)

KEEPING THE BRITISH END UP

CREDITS: *Director* David Grant, *Producer* Malcolm Fancey, *Editor* John Pipkin, *Photography* Peter Jessop, *Screenplay* David Grant and Norman Arch, *Music* John Shakespeare, *Theme song 'You're Driving Me Crazy!'* performed by Nick Curtis
An OPPIDAN Production. Distributed by NEW REALM. Opened July 1978.

WHAT'S UP SUPERDOC?
aka *What's Up Number 2*

Great Britain / 1978 / 93 mins / cert 'X'

So what have we learnt so far about what really gets the seventies' woman going? Is it an aphrodisiac contraceptive (*The Love Pill*), a whiff of perfume (*She'll Follow You Anywhere*), a sip of fruity wine (*Spanish Fly*) or a tingle from a sex ray (*I'm Not Feeling Myself Tonight!*)? No, no, no! What the average housewife wants is a great big dollop of British spunk! Yes, it had to happen. In 1978 director Derek Ford inflicted his masterstroke on British cinema: a comedy about masturbation and semen!

A slap and tickle 'sequel' to Ford's earlier *What's Up Nurse?*, the story follows the latest adventures of Dr Robert Todd, now played by *It Ain't Half Hot Mum*'s fresh-faced recruit Christopher Mitchell. The dirty doc is back in London after his failed excursion to Southend-on-Sea and now has his own practice in Bayswater. Not that he needs much practice since his eager female patients can't wait for a tug on his stethoscope. Quite why this is the case is bemusing since Mitchell is the saggiest, flabbiest, chubbiest mummy's boy ever to become the leading man in a sex comedy. Throughout the film he struggles to hold his stomach in during his nude scenes and, as a lover, he has all the charm of an off-duty tax advisor.

Todd is visited by glam doctor Annabel Leith (Julia Goodman) from the Artificial Insemination Donation Service (AIDS for short: these are the innocent days of 1978 remember), who reminds him that when he was a medical student back in the sixties he donated a considerable amount of sperm to the national reserves. Now it can be revealed that Todd has fathered an incredible 837 babies, all of them boys. His spunk is, quite simply, the most exceptional in Britain. The remarkable story makes the front page of the *Daily Mirror* and suddenly every woman in the country is clamouring for his cum. Besieged by frantic housewives, Todd is chased down the street by women waving empty test tubes, desperate for some of his baby gravy.

Todd's infamy eventually gets him invited onto an LWT chat show presented by *Opportunity Knocks* host Hughie Green. The family favourite tries to skirt around words like 'sperm' and 'masturbate' during the interview, but finally blows his top. 'How could you put me on TV with a man who wanks for a living?' he screams at his producer. The 'superdoc' is forced to go into hiding, protected by stiff ex-military man Harry H Corbett, who insists on putting him through regular physical jerks (like he needs any more of *them*). And everything goes tits up when Todd is abducted by a Texan billionaire (Bill Pertwee) who values oyster juice more highly than oil.

Writer-director Ford struggles to find enough *double entendres* to fill 90 minutes (several ideas are brazenly pinched from *Percy* and *Percy's Progress*),

168

Left: Christopher Mitchell gets more than his fair share in *What's Up Superdoc?* (1978). Left to right: Anna Bergman, Alison Begg, Mary Millington, Maria Harper, Vicki Scott and Nicola Austine.

although he should be congratulated for filling his movie with more references to having one off the wrist than had been heard in the entire back catalogue of British sex comedies up to that point. (Even the classic Sam & Dave number, 'Hold On I'm Coming', is given a seventies makeover as the theme tune.) Despite the dream team of naked talent on offer (Mary Millington, Anna Bergman, Nicola Austine, Vicki Scott, Lisa Taylor and Dick Emery's girlfriend Fay Hillier), the only good-looking nude scene in the film has nothing at all to do with the director. In a blatant bit of padding, Todd visits the Raymond Revuebar in the heart of Soho to watch real-life 'speciality act', the Blue Angels. The two blondes, naked bar for diamante g-strings and chokers, go through a beautifully synchronised routine which sits uneasily among the pervading silliness elsewhere. The tender erotica of this scene, staged by Paul Raymond's French choreographer Gerard Simi, provides one of the only truly trouser-tightening moments in all British sex films. It's surprising that Ford left the scene in since it puts the rest of his work to shame.

Once again Ford fails to get the most out of his motley bunch of old comedy troupers. Harry H Corbett is irritating rather than funny, Hughie Green gives a tasteless performance and both Bill Pertwee and Melvyn Hayes adopt accents that vary wildly from scene to scene. Only Sheila Steafel and Marianne Stone contribute appetising cameos as a couple of skittish doctors fascinated by Todd's genitals. *What's Up Superdoc?* is marginally better than Ford's first medicom but if the sex scenes were cut the movie would be indistinguishable from a Children's Film Foundation production. But perhaps even kids are too sophisticated for this stuff.

CAST: Christopher Mitchell (*Dr Robert Todd*), Julia Goodman (*Dr Annabel Leith*), Harry H Corbett (*Sgt Major Goodwin*), Bill Pertwee (*Woodie*), Chic Murray (*Bernie*), Angela Grant (*Kim*), Hughie Green (*Bob Scratchitt*), Melvyn Hayes (*Pietro*), Ronnie Brody (*The Boss*), Beth Porter (*Melanie*), Sheila Steafel (*Dr Pitt*), Marianne Stone (*Dr Maconachie*), Maria Harper (*Julie*), Milton Reid (*Louie*), Sue Upton (*Marlene*), Nora Llewellyn (*Monika*), Lisa Taylor (*wife*), Ronald Alexander (*husband*), Julie Kirk (*Dr Todd's receptionist*), Fay Hillier (*Raymond Revuebar stripper*), Jack Silk (*PC Robinson*), Geoffrey Leigh (*Hermann*), Mary Millington (*girl with champagne*), Anna Bergman (*first maid*), Nicola Austine (*second maid*), Vicki Scott (*stripper in house*), Alison Begg (*girl up tree*), Peter Greene (*man in audience*), Norman Lawrence (*solicitor*), Jackie Moran (*make-up girl*), Ian Ford (*boy in park*), The Blue Angels (*speciality act*)
CREDITS: *Director/Screenplay* Derek Ford, *Producer* Michael L Green, *Editor* David Campling, *Photography* Geffrey Glover, *Music* Frank Barber and Paul Fishman, *Theme Song* 'Hold On I'm Coming' written by Isaac Hayes and David Porter, *performed by* Fingers A BLACKWATER FILMS Production. Distributed by ENTERTAINMENT. Released September 1978.

CARRY ON EMMANNUELLE
aka *Emmanuelle in London*

Great Britain / 1978 / 88 mins / cert 'AA'

Now it could be argued that all the Carry On films are basically sex comedies, but as there's just not the space to discuss the whole lot here, it's this one which deserves a little adult attention. The *pièce de résistance* of the Carry Ons is the moment where Kenneth Williams finally strayed into Robin Askwith territory and grasped the sexual nettle with both hands. Or was it?

Producer Peter Rogers and director Gerald Thomas had been curious to work out what made their rivals' so-called 'adult' sex comedies so popular and in September 1976 went to see *Confessions of a Driving Instructor*. Seeing a naked Robin Askwith scampering around in the all-together with ex-Carry On star Liz Fraser, the filmmakers were convinced that the next fully fledged Carry On should aim for an 'X' certificate. The Carry Ons had been getting gradually ruder ever since *Carry On Girls* (1973). That film's reliance on busty cat fights, an end of the pier beauty contest and saucier language – topped off with ex-Harrison Marks glamour girl Margaret Nolan squeezed into a silver bikini astride a donkey – very nearly got the series its first 'AA' rating. And with 1976's WWII barrack-room comedy *Carry On England* the series finally did get an 'AA'. An unmitigated disaster by Carry On standards, the film often lasted no more than a week in

169

Left: The scene we thought we'd never see — Suzanne Danielle beds Kenneth Williams in *Carry On Emmannuelle* (1978).

provincial cinemas and was hurriedly re-edited in order to get an 'A'.

Licking his wounds, Rogers made the strange decision to go ahead with an even naughtier Carry On, determined as he was to get a slice of the Confessions cake. As early as May 1977, *Carry On Again Nurse* had been announced as the 30th in the series and had been widely reported in the trade press as strictly 'X'-certificate material. Unfortunately the Rank Organisation backed out and Rogers was forced to seek private backing and new distribution from Hemdale. While Hemdale were keen to take over the Carry Ons, they were not so enamoured with *Again Nurse*. They preferred *Carry On Emmannuelle*, a spoof on Sylvia Kristel's mega-hit *Emmanuelle* written by a young Australian TV writer called Lance Peters, with the spelling adjusted to avoid copyright infringement. There was just one small problem. The investors wanted it sexy, but they didn't want it *too* sexy.

Lance Peters' original script contained scenes of masturbation, oral sex, lesbianism and a pornographic magazine shoot. Rogers claimed that he completely rewrote the screenplay several times in order to tone down the sexual content. 'I want to be left out of this piece because I don't like any of it,' Kenneth Williams grumbled in March 1978. 'It isn't a question of what can be cut, or what scenes can be modified or rewritten. The very essence of it is offensive.' Realising the movie was a dead duck without Kenny's involvement, Rogers had the script re-tweaked again. Kenny still didn't like it, but finally signed on the dotted line in exchange for a pay rise.

The pivotal role of Emmannuelle was given to leggy newcomer Suzanne Danielle, whose largest movie role to date was as an uncredited mascara-caked disco dancer in *The Stud*. The film was clearly not going to be the usual ensemble piece, but Carry On regulars Kenneth Williams, Joan Sims, Kenneth Connor, Peter Butterworth and Jack Douglas did have something to get excited about. After 20 years of thwarted amorous adventures, the old Carry On cast were finally promised their nirvana. They were going to have sex.

Filming started on 10 April and immediately rumours were rife that the once sacred Carry Ons were going porno-graphic. When Barbara Windsor turned down a featured role on 19 April, the very next day a national newspaper ran the headline *'Barbara Windsor says Carry On without me'* above a report alleging that she stormed out of the studio and branded the film 'one long nude scene'. The truth was that Ms Windsor had never even stepped on set but several of the film's backers were moved to write to Kenneth Williams, much to his dismay, demanding assurances that the film would not be a 'dirty picture'.

The plot (and there's not much of it, which is one similarity to the Sylvia Kristel original) centres on the lissom wife of the French Ambassador to London, Emile Prevert (Kenneth Williams). The Embassy staff, housekeeper Mrs Dangle (Sims), chauffeur Leyland (Connor), elderly boot-boy Richmond (Butterworth) and butler Lyons (Douglas), are fascinated by their employers' unfulfilled sex life and it becomes their main topic of below-stairs conversation. Rebuffed by her weight-lifting-fixated husband, the nymphomaniac Emmannuelle seeks her pleasures elsewhere, seducing all her husband's high-ranking friends, leaving her 'calling card', a pair of her panties, wherever she goes. To top it off, she takes on Harry 'Mr Super Muscle' Hernia, a TV bodybuilder whom Emile idolises (played by ex-porn star and veteran of *Come Play with Me*, Howard Nelson).

Lance Peters' script suffers from attempting to be a sex-free parody of the

Right: The first *Carry On Emmannuelle* home video appeared on the short-lived Betamax format.

"A hilarious sex comedy in the true 'CARRY ON' tradition"

CARRY ON Emmannuelle

STARRING:

KENNETH WILLIAMS

★

JOAN SIMS

★

PETER BUTTERWORTH

★

KENNETH CONNOR

★

JACK DOUGLAS

★

BERYL REID

AND

SUZANNE DANIELLE AS EMMANNUELLE

world's most commercially successful sex movie, rather like shooting *Carry On Cowboy* without Stetsons or *Carry On Screaming!* without monsters. Seeing old-timers like Kenneth Connor prancing around in his underpants, Joan Sims rubbing dirty laundry over her breasts and Kenneth Williams flashing his bum over and over again is neither funny, attractive or sexy. As one critic put it, sitting through the film was like watching 'elderly relatives disgracing themselves at a party'. Indeed, it's nothing short of grotesque to see poor old Connor, as the leering, lecherous chauffeur, taking Emmannuelle for a sightseeing tour of London and telling her that 'I'm driving you now, you know, in a Daimler Pervertible. The hood doesn't go down but the chauffeur does!'

The reason this sauciest ever Carry On was awarded an 'AA' rating has more to do with what you *hear*. Though it's the last original Carry On, it's notable for a multitude of firsts: the series' first blow job (just out of shot), first 'I'm coming' joke, first ever utterance of 'shit', an armed kidnap, a suicide bid, plus references to incest, pornography, spanking and voyeurism. And after years of Charlie Hawtrey campery and 'I feel queer' jokes from Williams, the series gets its first genuinely (though grossly stereotyped) gay characters. But it's the pseudo-sex scenes which really have audiences squirming in their seats. Danielle offers a few discreet glimpses of breast and bum and appears totally naked in a steamed-up shower (from behind), which comes as quite a shock since Barbara Windsor herself had been showing considerably more over the past decade. One can't help thinking how much better Windsor would have been in the lead role, marvellously miscast as a Continental sexual predator. Danielle cuts a striking figure and certainly looks the part, but she plays it completely straight. A 4'11" giggly blonde would have made a far superior parody.

As a satire on British sexual mores, it says a lot that a sexy 'French' bird has to set foot in the cosy world of Carry On to teach the old-timers how to finally get their legs over. Sadly, the comedy of frustration is gone and the characters are far too knowing about the art of seduction. Sex isn't even called 'it' anymore. It's called, well, *sex*. And the possibility of promiscuity being as funny as frustration is killed stone dead by far too many laugh-free sequences, coupled with very feeble jokes, an unnaturally slow pace

171

Right: Carroll Baker and Anthony Franciosa as the angst-ridden protagonists of Robert Young's *The World is Full of Married Men* (1979).

and way too much extraneous dialogue. Director Gerald Thomas, who usually had such a good understanding of the mechanics of comedy, lets scenes which should have been nipped in the bud after the first gag peter out aimlessly into stony-faced silence; Emmannuelle's on-air seduction of smarmy TV presenter Henry McGee is a case in point.

With the Carry On audience non-existent by 1978 and even the sex film market hanging on by a thread, *Carry On Emmannuelle* suffered the humiliating fate of being the biggest commercial flop of the entire series. Gaining only a limited release outside London, it was ignominiously put out as one half of a double-bill with a five-year-old American thriller, *Speedtrap*, starring Tyne Daly. And the stigma surrounding *Carry On Emmannuelle* has remained. Its patchy theatrical release and relative invisibility on video during the 1980s made the myth that it was a 'dirty' movie all the stronger. Terrestrial TV, normally more than happy to plump up the schedules with classic Carry On capers, seemed reluctant to broadcast the film and it was only slipped into the late night schedules in May 1998, a full 20 years after it was made. Barbara Windsor didn't see the film on its original release but caught the TV showing. As she told the *Sunday Telegraph Magazine* in March 1999, 'It was so awful it made me cry.'

CAST: Kenneth Williams (*Emile Prevert*), Kenneth Connor (*Leyland*), Joan Sims (*Mrs Dangle*), Jack Douglas (*Lyons*), Peter Butterworth (*Richmond*), Suzanne Danielle (*Emmannuelle Prevert*), Beryl Reid (*Mrs Valentine*), Larry Dann (*Theodore Valentine*), Henry McGee (*Harold Hump*), Albert Moses (*Doctor*), Tricia Newby (*nurse*), Howard Nelson (*Harry Hernia*), Victor Maddern (*man in launderette*), Dino Shafeek (*immigration officer*), Robert Dorning (*Prime Minister*), Michael Nightingale (*Police Commissioner*), Bruce Boa (*US Ambassador*), Steve Plytas (*Arabian Minister*), Llewellyn Rees (*Lord Chief Justice*), Jack Lynn (*Admiral of the Fleet*), Eric Barker (*ancient General*), Joan Benham (*dinner party guest*), Claire Davenport (*fat woman in pub*), Norman Mitchell (*drunken husband*), John Carlin (*French priest*), Gertan Klauber (*German soldier*), Suzanna East (*Colette*), Louise Burton (*girl at zoo*), James Fagan (*Concorde steward*), Malcolm Johns (*sentry*), Guy Ward (*gay flirt*), Philip Clifton (*injured footballer*), Nick White (*sent-off player*), John Hallett (*substitute player*), Bruce Wyllie (*football referee*), Corbett Woodall (*ITN newscaster*), Tim Brinton (*BBC newscaster*), Bill Hutchinson (*first reporter*), Neville Ware (*second reporter*), Jane Norman (*third reporter*), Stanley McGeogh (*journalist*), Deborah Brayshaw (*French blonde*), Marianne Maskell (*hospital nurse*)

CREDITS: *Director* Gerald Thomas, *Producer* Peter Rogers, *Editor* Peter Boita, *Photography* Alan Hume, *Screenplay* Lance Peters, *Music* Eric Rogers, *Theme Song* 'Love Crazy' *performed by* Masterplan, *composed by* Kenny Lynch
A CLEVES INVESTMENTS-PETER ROGERS Production. Distributed by HEMDALE. Opened November 1978.

1979

CAN I COME TOO?

Great Britain / 1979 / 43 mins / cert 'X'

Director Ray Selfe's last seventies' sex comedy took him back to his roots and his first love, the cavernous suburban cinema. Filmed entirely on location at the Ritzy Cinema in Brixton (here renamed the Savoy as a tribute to the cinema in Croydon where Selfe had worked as a youngster), *Can I Come Too?* attempts to reflect upon the sorry state of British film exhibition by the late 1970s. The cinema here, starved of blockbusters, is forced to play B-movie sexploiters like *King Kong Meets Emmanuelle* to a half-empty auditorium of slow-clapping pensioners and teenagers only there for a quiet grope. Selfe's amusing film gently takes the mickey out of the sex film business, while happily contributing to it at the same time, and could be comfortably screened alongside the equally tongue-in-cheek satire *Eskimo Nell*, made five years earlier.

Can I Come Too?'s cinema plays host to the première of fictional low-budget sex film *Love in the Undergrowth*, starring air-headed former waitress Gloria Overtones (played enthusiastically by Suzie Sylvie). Unfortunately, the event is pretty low-key all round. Terry the projectionist (Graham White) has his hands full shagging one of the randy usherettes, Sue Longhurst and Mark Jones (in the final sex film for both of them) spend more time snogging than selling tickets, and it remains to be seen who will actually turn up for the gala showing. 'Is the Queen coming?' asks the aristocratic Lady Wickhampton (Jean Selfe). 'I doubt it,' replies Gloria. 'Maybe a few hairdressers though!'

Judiciously scripted by producer Alan Selwyn (who also appears as Sam Seagull, producer of the successful *Sore Throat*), the film was shot at break-neck speed. 'There was a new movie doing the rounds and the distributors suddenly needed a second feature to go with it,' recalls Selwyn. 'On Thursday they gave me the idea for the story and told me they wanted a script by Monday because that's when filming started! It was madness, but I managed to write it in just three days. Then I rang a couple of my mates up that weekend and persuaded them to star in it. On the Monday we went in front of the cameras and filmed it in less than a week.'

The movie is notable for turns from old comedy troupers Charlie Chester (as the cinema manager) and the indomitable cockney loudmouth Rita Webb (as the elderly usherette). Chester, who was often cited as Max Miller's main rival, was rather under-used by British cinema but shines here in all his dilapidated glory. Although Chester desperately tries to keep his eyes off the naked girls cavorting on his premises, in real life the comedian adored a bit of naughtiness, having written dozens of semi-pornographic novels under the pseudonym Carl Noone. His novels concentrated on his favourite subjects: nymphomania, masochism and whippings. In *Can I Come Too?* Chester has the temerity to accuse Webb of lowering the tone of the proceedings. 'You *are* a little uncouth, you know!' he reprimands her. 'Well, I like that!' she replies. 'Bleedin' cheek! I've got just as much couth as you 'ave!' Rollicking good fun all round.

CAST: Charlie Chester (*Mr Royal*), Rita Webb (*Laverne*), Tony Wright (*George Skinner*), Chic Murray (*Manny McTavish*), Mark Jones (*Freddy Lawrence*), Sue Longhurst (*Vera Ball*), Jean Selfe (*Lady Wickhampton*), Susie Sylvie (*Gloria Overtones*), Clive Wouters (*Roddy Wickhampton*), Lindy Benson (*Maxine*), Maria Harper (*Sylvie Denby*), Lou Raynes (*Manny Glowpick*), Graham White (*Terry*), Julia Rushford (*Georgina*), David McGillivray and Raymond Cross (*critics*), Ray Selfe (*man in restaurant*), John Pipkin (*drinks deliveryman*), Alan Selwyn (*Sam Seagull*), Howard Selfe (*boy*), Vicki Scott [uncredited] (*girl in opening titles*)

CREDITS: *Director* Ray Selfe, *Producer/Screenplay* Alan Selwyn, *Editor* John Pipkin, *Photography* Alan Pudney, *Music* John Shakespeare and Derek Warne, *Theme song 'Can I Come Too?'* *performed by* Ross MacManus

An OVAL REGION Production. Distributed by New Realm. Opened March 1979.

THE WORLD IS FULL OF MARRIED MEN

Great Britain / 1979 / 106 mins / cert 'X'

After the huge success of *The Stud*, Jackie Collins' movie producer husband Oscar Lerman turned his attentions to his wife's début novel *The World is Full of Married Men*, first published in 1968. Oddly, it was the sequel, *The World is Full of Divorced Women*, which was first earmarked for big screen treatment in November 1975 by Warner Bros. Wanting to keep a tighter reign on her new project (mindful of Gerry O'Hara's tinkering with the plot of the upcoming *The Bitch*), Jackie took it upon herself to write the movie's screenplay herself.

The movie very nearly stalled in the planning stages. Jackie had been good friends with snapper Terence Donovan, dubbed the Orson Welles of photography.

KEEPING THE BRITISH END UP

Right: Willy Roe directs Alan Lake and Mary Millington in *Confessions from the David Galaxy Affair* (1979).

His only movie, *Yellow Dog* (1973), was an incoherent, camp, 'X'-rated Oriental espionage thriller starring Robert Hardy. And it proved to be a dog at the box-office too. Jackie hadn't seen the film, but was keen to get Donovan on board to direct *Married Men*. Knowing Donovan's only previous excursion into filmmaking wasn't really up to scratch, Jackie's co-producers Adrienne and Malcolm Fancey advised her to watch *Yellow Dog* first. After a private screening Jackie was allegedly pretty pale-faced. Skilled director Robert *Keep it Up Downstairs* Young was chosen instead. And, following the lead provided by *The Stud*, the new film's soundtrack was packed to bursting with the likes of Tavares, the Three Degrees, Gladys Knight and a gutsy title song by Bonnie Tyler.

The two leading roles, unhappily married David and Linda Cooper, were taken by Americans actors Anthony Franciosa and Carroll Baker, the latter once infamous for her role in fifties shocker, *Baby Doll*. Womanising David takes up with an irresponsible, publicity-seeking 21-year-old strumpet called Claudia Parker, who has lofty aspirations of becoming a top model and actress. Claudia is played by American newcomer Sherrie Lee Cronin, whose acting is even flatter than her chest. She wasn't first choice for the part; *Carry On Emmannuelle* actress Suzanne Danielle originally took the role but was released from her contract a couple of weeks into filming due to 'disagreements' with the producers. All her scenes had to be re-shot.

Linda, weary of her husband's errant ways, reluctantly falls for the big lapels and tousled locks of sappy singer Gem Gemini, played with complete indifference by Paul Nicholas. Despite being heralded as 'Britain's top rock star', Gemini gets himself the classy gig of singing the jingle to a TV soap commercial in which Claudia sits in a giant clamshell full of bubbles. It's the equivalent of Robbie Williams doing a promotion for Bloo Loo.

Coming as it did at the tail end of the British sex film era, the movie finds space for several veteran sex sirens. Babycham beauties Pat Astley and Nicola Austine play a couple of giggling blondes engaged by David to schmooze one of his kinky clients in a nightclub. Looking adorable in flowing white gowns and peroxide hair, the two lovelies charge around the dancefloor before getting paid to partake in a threesome. (Incidentally, at the film's close, both beauties dance in silhouette under the end credits.) David, meanwhile, is rendered impotent after all the hullabaloo surrounding his marriage break-up and the sluttish behaviour of new love Claudia. The 'last of the great shafters' (as Gareth Hunt's character dubs him) can't even get it up for a succession of frisky female escorts played by Suzie Sylvie, Lindy Benson, Stephanie Marrian and Penny Kendall.

The script lurches from one outrageous soap opera set-piece to another with numerous hysterical public confrontations in restaurants, bedrooms and driveways. The softcore manipulations and plastic situations, not to mention various dangling loose ends, have all the hallmarks of an American mini-series, a genre Jackie Collins was later to move into during the 1980s. The crude dialogue is classic Collins. 'If it was up to you I'd be laying on the bed with my legs in the air, waiting for Father Christmas to come through the damn door!' Claudia screams at David at one point. As a cousin of the far more profitable *The Stud* and *The Bitch*, *The World is Full of Married Men* fails to deliver the same quality of devilish decadence, and Joan Collins is sorely missed.

CAST: Anthony Franciosa (*David Cooper*), Carroll Baker (*Linda Cooper*), Gareth Hunt (*Jay Grossman*), Georgina Hale (*Lori Grossman*), Anthony Steel (*Conrad Lee*), Sherrie Lee Cronin (*Claudia Parker*), Paul Nicholas (*Gem Gemini*), Jean Gilpin (*Miss Field*), John Nolan (*Joe*), Moira Downie (*Gerda*), Alison Elliott (*Sharon*), Eva Louise ('*Mercedes Benz*'), Roy Scammell (*Jeff Spencer*), Nicola Austine (*Alice*), Pat Astley (*Wendy*), Joanne Ridley (*Joanie*), Emma Ridley (*Lucy*), Suzie Sylvie, Stephanie Marrianne, Penny Kendall, Lindy Benson, Christine Donna and Vida (*girls in hotel*), Helli Louise, Nova Llewellyn and Adele Neatour (*Gem's backing singers*), Jeannie Starbuck (*cleaning lady*), Maxine Cunliffe (*Jay's girlfriend*), Corbett Woodall (*TV announcer*), Hot Gossip (*dancers*)
CREDITS: *Director* Robert Young, *Producers* Malcolm Fancey and Oscar Lerman, *Screenplay (based on her novel)* Jackie Collins, *Music* Frank Musker and Dominic Bugatti, *Theme song 'The World Is Full of Married Men' performed by* Bonnie Tyler and Mick Jackson
A MARRIED MEN Production. Distributed by NEW REALM. Opened May 1979.

CONFESSIONS FROM THE DAVID GALAXY AFFAIR

aka *Star Sex*

Great Britain / 1979 / 96 mins / cert 'X'

David Sullivan's follow-up to *The Playbirds* has all the hallmarks of being a cut-and-shunt job. Unable to make up its mind whether it's a Confessions-style comedy, a thrilling drama or an erotic odyssey, it succeeds only in being total garbage. Sullivan's biggest blunder was not ensuring that Britain's most famous pin-up, Mary Millington, was the movie's main focus. Stupidly, she is cast aside in a throwaway subplot completely incidental to the rest of the wretched narrative. It was a crazy mistake for Sullivan and director Willy Roe to make. It was Mary, and *only* Mary, the fans wanted to see. Not Diana Dors, not Bernie Winters, not a handful of numbingly awful Page Three girls and certainly not Alan Lake. It made no odds that Mary clearly wasn't the best actress in the world. The paying audience didn't care.

Unfortunately, *Confessions from the David Galaxy Affair* is all Lake's film. In the most uncontrolled, self-indulgent and downright annoying performance of his career, he plays a promiscuous astrologer being fitted up by the police for his part in a Securicor robbery five years previously, in which a man was killed. That's the dramatic bit. With the threat of gaol preying on his mind, Galaxy still has time to sleep with the entire female cast (except, tellingly, his real-life wife Diana Dors). Medallion sparkling and eyes bulging wildly, Lake seems to be acting in a completely different film, if not planet, to everyone else. At regular intervals he breaks into a series of excruciating and seemingly unrehearsed impressions (John Wayne, Humphrey Bogart, Bruce Forsyth, a Pakistani, a Jamaican etc). This culminates in an embarrassingly unwatchable impersonation of a mincing homosexual which should definitely have been left on the cutting-room floor.

The only times when *David Galaxy* drags itself out of the shit are when the shapely Rosemary England appears as 'Miss Beauty Bust' and Mary Millington makes her all-too-brief cameo. Mary plays Millicent Cumming, a high society heiress who, despite having entertained 1,756 men, has never experienced an orgasm. Mary's sweet tongue-in-cheek innocence shines through her dialogue, as does her unflagging enthusiasm. She is set up on a blind date with Galaxy in the hope that the 'super-stud' will finally cure her problem.

Intoxicated by Campari and soda and a prawn cocktail, Millicent finally reaches sexual nirvana in a startlingly explicit, multi-positioned sex scene played out against Galaxy's mirrored headboard.

The film was a bitter disappointment for Mary Millington fans who expected more and deserved much better. It is a cataclysmic waste of opportunity, time, talent and money. Compared to the alluring delights of Come Play with Me and The Playbirds the film was a resounding box-office flop. And Sullivan wonders why!

CAST: Alan Lake (*David Galaxy*), Glynn Edwards (*Chief Inspector Evans*), Anthony Booth (*Steve*), Diana Dors (*Jennie Stride*), Mary Millington (*Millicent Cumming*), John Moulder-Brown (*Sgt Johnson*), Bernie Winters (*Mr Pringle*), Kenny Lynch (*Joe*), Rosemary England (*Sandra*), Sally Faulkner (*Amanda*), Queenie Watts (*David Galaxy's mother*), Milton Reid (*Eddie*), Cindy Truman (*Anne the traffic warden*), Maria Parry (*Susan Carter MP*), Ballard Berkeley (*Judge*), Alec Mango (*Cllr Pembleton*), Barbara Eatwell (*Kate, first lesbian*), Vicki Scott (*Charlotte, second lesbian*), Faith Daykin (*Julia Shorthouse*), Penny Kendall (*Angela Kripp*), Pamela Healy (*Gina Kirby*), Valerie Minifie (*Sylvia*), Jeanette Caron (*Edie*), Tina Kirsch (*Jill the nurse*), John M East (*Willie*), Luigi Deanjioy (*Luigi*), George Lewis (*George*), Steve Kane (*Steve*), Diana Hicks (*Steve's girlfriend*), Lindy Benson (*Evelyn*), Claire Nicholson (*Janet*), Lou Soames (*girl in bar*), John Roach (*warder*)
CREDITS: *Director/Producer* Willy Roe, *Executive Producer* David Sullivan, *Editor* Jim Connock, *Photography* Douglas Hill, *Screenplay* Joe Ireland [aka George Evans] *based on the novel by* George Evans, *Music* David Whitaker, *Theme song 'His Name Is Galaxy' performed by* Diana Dors
A ROLDVALE Film. Distributed by TIGON. Opened June 1979.

QUEEN OF THE BLUES
aka *Queen of Spades*

Great Britain / 1979 / 62 mins / cert 'X'

Mary Millington, in her last film (released just weeks before her suicide), plays the star attraction at a flashy West End strip joint ('licensed to sell booze and boobs at exorbitant prices') owned by shady brothers John M East and Allen Warren. Certainly separated at birth, East must have been brought up by giraffes and Warren by a family of munchkins since they are the most unlikely siblings you've ever seen. Unfortunately East also doubles as the club comic, dressing up in flashy Max Miller togs and raiding his ancient joke book. 'I'm a very refined gentleman,' he says. 'I even serve breast of chicken in a bra.' All is going sparklingly, but the club is being done over each night by a couple of braindead heavies (Felix Bowness and Milton Reid) running a protection racket for a local thug, while the strippers are also being menaced by a backstage ghost.

Director Willy Roe, whose efforts seem to get worse with every succeeding film, yet again ignores the cardinal rule of sexploitation cinema, by shamefully denying the audience their right to see what they paid their admission for: plenty of female nudity, and in particular the film's big draw Mary Millington. The minimalist plotline serves as an excuse for a series of stripteases, but Roe insists on filming the majority of the girls in static longshot, thereby reducing any perceived notion of titillation. Instead, Roe prefers to give us shot after shot of ugly men – smug-faced Bowness leering and sneering at the girls and Reid sticking a Vicks Synex up his hooter.

It gets even more frustrating when Mary takes to the stage to do her striptease. Radiating glamour in a voluminous cape and feather boa, she prances around the stage only to be cut off mid-flow as the film slices straight into another scene. All momentum and

Left: Mary Millington takes to the stage at The Burlesque in *Queen of the Blues* (1979).

excitement goes to the wall. The film was made in less than two weeks and rushed into cinemas to recoup some of the losses of David Sullivan's previous film *Confessions from the David Galaxy Affair* (only released the previous month!), and it shows.

Jim Connock's editing seems to have been done with a lawnmower and the continuity is abysmal. There is absolutely no concept of timescale since the strip club punters remain glued to their seats night after night, wearing the same clothes and laughing hysterically at East's terrible gags. Characters disappear for no reason, East seems to be a quick-change artist, actress Nicola Austine strips on stage while at the same time sitting in the audience clapping herself, and various strippers walk off stage when they haven't even been on it. Mary Millington is given a brief scene backstage where she actually gets to act and does quite well bitching at the other strippers, but the rest of the film is a gigantic mess and a disheartening end to Mary's sex comedy career.

CAST: Mary Millington (*Mary, Queen of the Blues*), John M East (*Mike Carter*), Allan Warren (*Tony Carter*), Ballard Berkeley (*Uncle Fred*), Lynn Dean (*Lucille*), Rosemary England (*Jill*), Felix Bowness (*Eddie*), Milton Reid (*'Brother' Richard*), Robert Russell (*Rex Roscoe*), Valerie Minifie (*Enid*), Harry Littlewood (*Derek*), Geraldine Hooper (*receptionist*), Cindy Truman (*Mirabelle*), Pat Astley (*Rosetta*), Nicola Austine (*Teresa*), Faith Daykin (*Charmaine*), Lydia Lloyd (*June*), Rosalind Watts (*Jane*), Fiona Sanderson (*Valerie*), Steve Kane (*Alfredo*), Tony Allef [uncredited] (*moustachioed Arab patron*), John Roach [uncredited] (*patron*).

CREDITS: Director/Producer Willy Roe, Executive Producer David Sullivan, Editor Jim Connock, Photography Douglas Hill, Screenplay Joe Ireland, Music David Whitaker A ROLDVALE Film. Distributed by TIGON. Opened July 1979.

OUTER TOUCH
aka *Spaced Out*

Great Britain / 1979 / 78 mins / cert 'X'

Hot on the heels of *Star Wars*, *Close Encounters of the Third Kind* and *Battlestar Galactica*, director Norman J Warren also entered the space race, albeit with a slightly saucier approach. 1979's *Outer Touch* marked his first foray into sex films for over a decade, having won popular acclaim for his horror movies *Satan's Slave* (1976), *Prey* (1977) and *Terror* (1978). 'I've always adored horror,' says Warren. 'That's the genre I like, but that didn't mean I was going to exclude any other type of film. When I was offered *Outer Touch* I really thought it was going back to the days of *Her Private Hell* and *Loving Feeling* and I wasn't entirely sure that there was still a market for that kind of film. But I did it anyway.' Curiously, Warren didn't look to the current slew of sci-fi blockbusters for inspiration but instead to British B-movie *Fire Maidens from Outer Space* (1956), about the all-female inhabitants of the thirteenth moon of Jupiter. It was once dubbed the 'worst movie ever made'.

In Warren's film a malfunctioning spacecraft lands on Clapham Common and four Londoners are taken prisoner by the female crew so they can assess the physical and mental capabilities of Earthlings. Having never seen men before, the inquisitive trio of insatiable extraterrestrials (Kate Ferguson, Ava Cadell and Glory Annen) are quick to notice the 'extra limb' sported by three of their subjects. Cadell, playing an intergalactic grease-monkey, is transfixed by myopic, masturbation-mad Willy (Tony Maiden, looking uncannily like a junior Robin Askwith). Startled by his semi-erect penis she is suspicious of his true intentions. 'What's that?' she asks. 'Have you got a weapon down there? Space rats! It's changing shape!' As the spacewomen experiment on each of the earth males (and discover the joys of sex), Willy is found to be one of the 'most advanced bodies in the universe' and they want to keep him as their pet.

It must be said that *Outer Touch* looks like it was shot with hand-me-downs from *Doctor Who*. Old Cyberman suits and silver-sprayed sets are much in evidence but the abundance of tin-foil, creaky plastic, DFS off-cuts and odds and ends from a TV repair shop make it all the more ludicrous, although they sit awkwardly with the excellent special effects and spacecraft exteriors craftily culled from Gerry Anderson's *Space: 1999* TV series. The film did far better in America than the UK, where it was released by Miramax in re-edited form under the title *Spaced Out*. As well as a new musical soundtrack, the voice of the ship's talking Wurlitzer was re-dubbed by wisecracking cult comedian, Bob Saget, who brought a lot of new fans to the movie. 'I much prefer the American version to be honest,' admits Warren. 'It's much funnier, but you can't take *Outer Touch* seriously for one minute anyway. It makes me cringe in a way, but I think that's a plus for it. It's fun to look at and it's now a very popular film in America to watch on video with a few beers. I think that's its level now. It's dreadful in a nice kind of way.'

CAST: Barry Stokes (*Oliver*), Tony Maiden (*Willy*), Glory Annen (*Cosia*), Ava Cadell (*Partha*), Kate Ferguson (*Skipper*), Michael Rowlatt (*Cliff*), Lynne Ross (*Prudence*), Bill Mitchell (*voice of Wurlitzer, UK*), Bob Saget (*voice of Wurlitzer, USA*)
CREDITS: *Director* Norman J Warren, *Producer* David Speechley, *Editor* Jim Elderton, *Photography* John Metcalfe, *Screenplay* Andrew Payne, *Theme song (UK) 'Outer Touch' performed by* Emil Zoghby, *Theme song (USA) 'Spaced Out' performed by* The Chance
A THREE-SIX-TWO Film Production. Distributed by MIRACLE.
Opened August 1979.

THE BITCH

Great Britain / 1979 / 88 mins / cert 'X'

A little over a year after Jackie Collins' *The Stud* had hit cinema screens with such an almighty bang came the super-sexy sequel *The Bitch*, based on her latest novel and continuing the sexploits of hedonistic anti-heroine Fontaine Khaled (Joan Collins). Fontaine got her comeuppance in the last instalment when her weary billionaire husband divorced her after finding a naughty videotape of her shagging Tony Blake in a lift. Now, 12 months on, she's feeling the pinch. The separation has cost her dearly and she can no longer keep up with her extravagant lifestyle of Cartier jewellery and Bruce Oldfield dresses. Her nightspot, Hobo, is losing money and her clientele are enjoying wilder nights out at a new gay club round the corner. But fruity Fontaine isn't about to take this lying down. 'What do you want me to do?' she protests to her business advisor. 'Stay at home at night watching the box in a

Left: Ava Cadell and Tony Maiden in *Outer Touch* **(1979).**

Marks and Sparks dressing gown?'

To make matters worse, Fontaine gets mixed up with an unappealing Italian jewel thief, Nico Cantafora, played by disappointing Oliver Tobias replacement Michael Coby, whose veneer is as smooth as a Parker Knoll coffee table and just as wooden. She meets him on a flight from New York, where Fontaine has been dancing the night away at Studio 54. Cheekily, the in-flight movie just happens to be *The Stud*, in a scene where Tony dines with Fontaine's stepdaughter. 'I can't make up my mind whether it's funnier with the sound or without,' says a bemused Nico. 'It's not meant to be funny!' chastises Fontaine.

From here on we are served up with a crappy Mob plot involving a stolen diamond ring planted in Fontaine's fur coat, a bit of racehorse fixing and some bloody awful Mafia villains with dark glasses and extended sideburns, controlled by raddled Ian Hendry as the delightfully named underworld boss, Thrush Feather. It's definitely more decadent than *The Stud*, with location work in New York, aerial photography and a dozen or so racehorses, but the whole package is much less sleazy and, as a consequence, much less fun. Even Joan has lost some of her bitchy bite, as Fontaine implausibly falls in love with her greasy Mediterranean suitor.

The less engrossing story means there's more reliance on the disco element. Sadly, this time round the movin' and a-groovin' is pure padding, although it's fabulous to see Joan on the dancefloor shaking her booty to the Gibson Brothers. Also enjoying a boogie is Cherry Gillespie from Pan's People and 'British John Travolta' Grant Santino, the UK's real-life reigning disco dancing champion of 1978. There are enjoyable turns from returning supporting actors like the underrated Doug Fisher, Mark Burns, Chris Jagger and the wickedly saucy Sue Lloyd. And there's still a fair amount of fornication on offer. Fontaine has a couple of ribald romps with Nico (whose modesty is always covered by a well-placed sheet or raised thigh) and, in an attempt to recreate the famous waterlogged orgy of the earlier movie, there's an underwater grope-a-thon in a private pool with Nico taking advantage of 'X'-rated starlet Vicki Scott.

The Bitch's most noteworthy sex scene comes early on when Fontaine, feeling slightly randy, seduces her chauffeur Ricky (played with just enough cockiness by Peter Wright). The image of Joan half dressed, with a chauffeur's cap jauntily placed on one side of her head, became the movie's defining moment and later adorned the poster, tie-in novel and accompanying soundtrack album. It was not, however, to the star's liking. 'I absolutely despise that photograph,' she told *Photoplay* in November 1979. 'It's cheap. I wear that outfit for about 30 seconds … but this is what they have chosen to sell the movie on. I think they could have done it with more class and style. I'm not going to pose for any more pictures like that.'

By the film's finale Fontaine has lost her disco to gangster Thrush Feather and looks utterly desolate and abandoned, which inevitably led to speculation in the press that there would be a third instalment of Jackie Collins' most infamous literary creation. The idea was mooted by distributors Brent Walker, who had once again cleaned up at the box-office with *The Bitch*, but Joan was reluctant to step back into the role of London's very own Lucretia Borgia. And more to the point, Jackie had no intention of pulling another Fontaine story out of the bag, especially since the novel of *The Bitch* had a more upbeat ending. Joan admitted that she had been approached to don the black corset one last time, but had balked at the idea. 'I'm sure they'd be quite happy to make something called *The Further Adventures of Fontaine* but I don't want it any more,' she said just after the movie's release. 'I want to get Fontaine out of my system. After all, what more can she do? *Fontaine Meets the Huggetts*? No way!'

CAST: Joan Collins (*Fontaine Khaled*), Michael Coby (*Nico Cantafora*), Ian Hendry (*Thrush Feather*), Sue Lloyd (*Vanessa Grant*), Mark Burns (*Leonard Grant*), Kenneth Haigh (*Arnold Rimstead*), Doug Fisher (*Sammy Marks*), Carolyn Seymour (*Polly Logan*), Pamela Salem (*Lynn*), John Ratzenberger (*Hal Leonard*), Steve Plytas (*Louis Almond*), Sharon Fussey (*Denise*), Peter Wright (*Ricky*), George Sweeney (*Sandy Roots*), Chris Jagger (*Terry Langham*), Maurice Thorogood (*Paul*), Bill Mitchell (*Bernie*), Alibe Parsons (*Bernice*), Mela White (*Mrs Walters*), Maurice

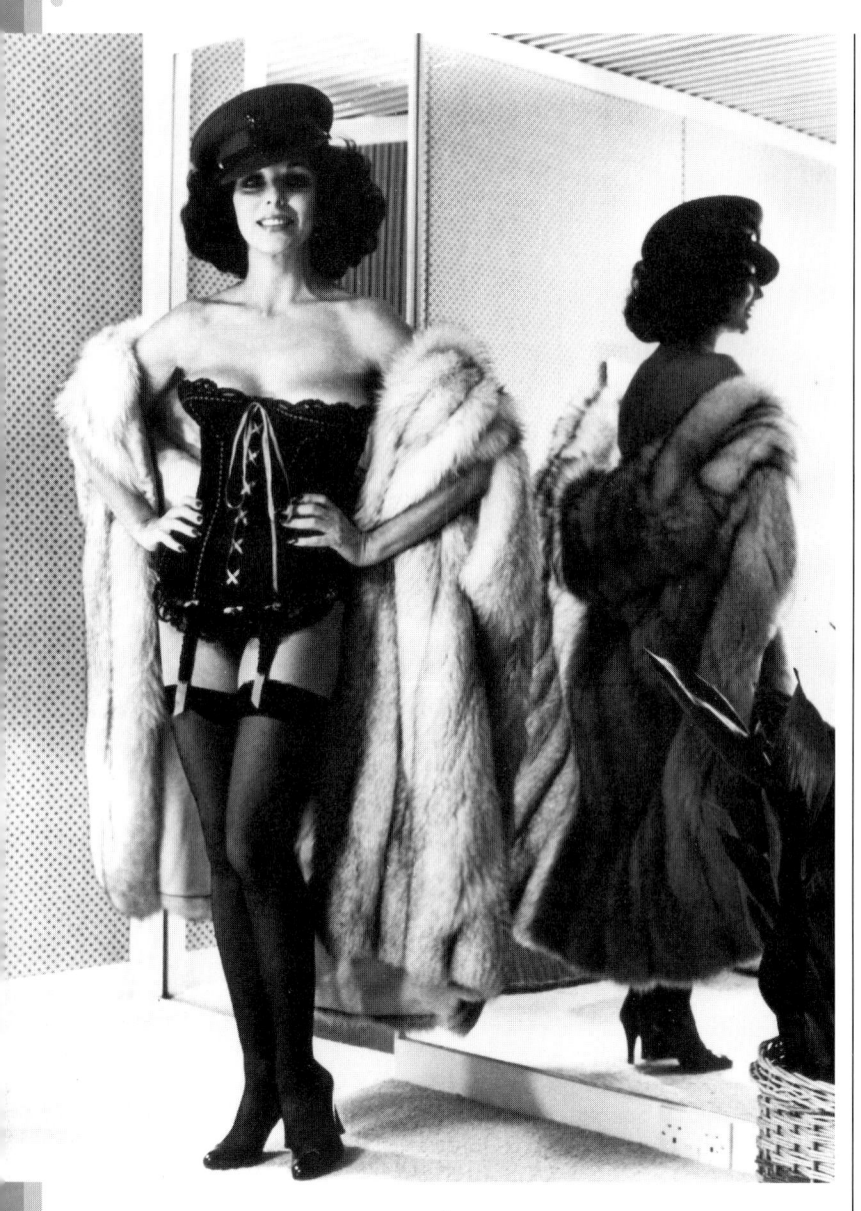

GIRLS AND BOYS TOGETHER

Great Britain / 1979 / 57 mins / cert 'X'

...or boys who like girls to be boys. This is a real curiosity and quite unlike anything you would expect to come out of the David Sullivan stable. *Boys and Girls Together* is directed by Ralph Lawrence Marsden, an Australian who had previously directed, produced and written *Sabbat of the Black Cat* (1973), an Edgar Allan Poe-inspired movie about a man terrorised by a spooky pussy. Working in England, he concentrated on wholly different pussies for this weird piece of sexploitation. Running under an hour, it was only ever intended to be a supporting feature (it played alongside Boney M's *Disco Fever* and *Mary Millington's True Blue Confessions* in 1980), but it seems unlikely that this little film would complement either disco dancing or cod-documentary since it exists in an indescribable world of its own. Produced by Willy Roe, who had taken control of Mary Millington's more traditionally structured sex blockbusters like *The Playbirds*, it is remarkable that Sullivan's Roldvale company, always with its eye on the box-office, ever gave him financial backing for this oddity.

Boys and Girls Together is a clumsy, crude piece of filmmaking but a completely fascinating one. Quirky camera angles, hand-held judderings and depressing close-ups (of pants being washed in a sink) give it the feel of a student film, while at other times the subject matter is strictly slapstick. It's also filmed in silence, with only a couple of lines of crudely dubbed dialogue breaking the monotonous musical soundtrack, performed by somebody called Clift Ritchard. The ultra-basic screenplay follows the lonely lives of six multi-racial, multi-sexual boys and girls in a sprawling Hampstead guesthouse. With very little interaction between the 20-something individuals, they spend most of their time furtively

O'Connell (*John-Jo*), Anthony Heaton (*Luke*), Tim Carlton (*Jamie*), Jill Medford (*Sharon*), Graham Simpson (*Mario*), Grant Santino (*disco dancer*), Cherry Gillespie (*disco girl*), Vicki Scott [uncredited] (*pool girl*)
CREDITS: *Director* Gerry O'Hara, *Producer* John Quested, *Screenplay* Gerry O'Hara *based on the novel by* Jackie Collins, *Music* Biddu and Don Black, *Theme song* 'The Bitch' *performed by* Olympic Runners A SPRITEBOWL-BITCH Production. Distributed by BRENT WALKER. Opened September 1979.

Left: Kinky chauffeuse Joan Collins in *The Bitch* (1979).

looking at each other on the stairwell then going back to their rooms for some masturbation.

And there is *a lot* of masturbation in this movie. Indian Lily buys a poster of rock star Roger Daltrey, pins it to the wall, finds a carrot, then sucks and wanks with it while fantasising about him. Next door, Singaporean Jat gets excited reading *Gay News* and imagining his ex-boyfriend playing tennis. All the housemates are yearning for some physical contact but initially make no headway at all. Don from the USA gets cheated out of a tenner by a Soho prostitute and German Ilsa has been cruelly jilted, while West Indian Leroy (when he's not doing nude press-ups over a full-length mirror) is fretting about being dumped by his girlfriend. Rather strangely, the sombre tone is occasionally lightened with totally bizarre 'comedy' sequences which make *Boys and Girls Together* feel like a porno version of Eric Sykes' *The Plank*. Born-again Christian Jenny is taking a bath when she slips on the soap and skewers herself on the handle of the loo brush with a shocking 'boing!' sound. She enjoys the sensation so much she stays sitting on it.

In the end all the couples come together (as the film's title implies), but in unexpected combinations. Gay Jat seduces 'straight' Leroy, Ilsa and Jenny have a lesbian affair and Don beds Jenny after foreplay involving a spilt cup of tea. The gay sequences are notable because British porn films up to then had never actually shown two men making love (comedic or otherwise). Although the kissing, caressing and fucking are brief – the film was trimmed of two minutes' sex by the censor – they're groundbreaking by British standards. Predictably, the three couples (two homosexual, one heterosexual) meet up on Hampstead Heath and split up again into strictly boy-girl pairings for some more sexual experimentation, culminating in a bisexual free-for-all with all six housemates hugging and kissing in the summer sunshine. Their raised hands and hippy-dippy swaying have all the hallmarks of Tudor Gates' *The Love Box*, made nearly a decade earlier.

Ultimately the film is trying to say something about loneliness and the awakening of slumbering sexuality. But what the raincoats in Soho, more used to models in nurses' outfits being chased by Bob Todd, thought of it all is anybody's guess.

CAST: Roger Furse (*Don, USA*), Cherry Patel (*Lily, India*), Helen Fitzgerald (*Ilsa, Germany*), Christine Maskelle (*Jenny, UK*), Paul Ong (*Jat, Singapore*), Anthony Thomas (*Leroy, West Indies*)
CREDITS: *Director/Screenplay* Ralph Lawrence Marsden, *Producer* Willy Roe, *Editor* Wulfert Bodo Rintz, *Photography* Stewart Neale, *Musical Director* Sean Ore, *Theme song* 'Boys And Girls Together' performed by Nuefrunt, *Composed by* Clift Ritchard [sic]
A ROLDVALE Production. Distributed by JAY JAY. Opened February 1980.

DREAM DOLL

Great Britain-Yugoslavia / 1979 / 13 mins / cert 'X'

Bob Godfrey's last animated sex cartoon of the decade is a cheeky spoof on the 1955 French short *The Red Balloon*, only here the innocent little Gallic boy enchanted by a lively balloon is replaced by a downtrodden Parisian with an inflatable sex doll. 'When I first saw the script for *Dream Doll* I thought it was so sordid,' recalls producer Bob Godfrey. 'This guy's basically not getting any so he goes to a sex shop and buys a rubber woman. I thought, "We can't have this. It's just too sleazy." So we made it romantic, with a sad and lonely hero who finds companionship.'

The doll in Godfrey's film (co-financed by Yugoslavia's Zagreb Films) doesn't take it lying down and becomes the dominant partner, making her male owner a sexual plaything. But when the doll is abducted in a public park by three thugs the little man defends her honour, despite getting beaten up. At the end, all the inflatable sex dolls in the capital come to his aid and carry him into the sky. 'It's a charming ending,' says Godfrey. 'He goes to Heaven and everybody's all rubber up there!'

CREDITS: *Directors* Bob Godfrey and Zlatko Grgic, *Producer* Bob Godfrey, *Animators* Zlatko Grgic and Turido Paus, *Screenplay* Stephen Penn, *Music* John Hyde
A BOB GODFREY Production in association with ZAGREB Films. Distributed by 20th CENTURY-FOX. Opened November 1980.

KEEPING THE BRITISH END UP

Right: Suzie Sylvie has a blast from Martin Burrows in *Sex with the Stars* (1980).

1980

THE GREAT BRITISH STRIPTEASE

aka *An Unbelievably Dirty Night Out with Bernard Manning* aka *The Great British Striptease Festival*

Great Britain / 1980 / 54 mins / cert 'X'

This was infamous blue comedian Bernard Manning's first and thankfully last excursion into the world of cinema. It's allegedly a straightforward documentary recording of the 1979 British Striptease Festival, apparently 'a great British event' in which the best stripper of the evening wins a cool £500. Shot direct onto videotape and then blown up to 35mm for cinema exhibition, the very dated video effects (straight out of *Top of the Pops*) make the whole farrago appear even grubbier. The movie was filmed on location at the Blackpool Tower Ballroom in front of a capacity audience of both men and women who had the final vote on who won and who lost.

According to Manning, there's not a professional stripper in sight. But any 'X'-rated film buff worth his salt will immediately identify a smattering of seasoned sex film actresses from the past decade of Stanley Long, Derek Ford and David Sullivan productions. These include Nina West, Vicki Scott, Gloria Brittain, Lisa Taylor, Cheryl (Cherry) Gilham and Camille Lorelei. (The latter was a veteran of a dozen or more hardcore John Lindsay shorts and identifies herself as a 'beauty consultant', which is one way of putting it, I suppose.) The women come on in pairs to do their stripteases, usually involving a little quasi-lesbian stocking-peeling, groping or kissing, and are dressed in a variety of well-worn costumes: schoolgirl, French maid, belly dancer. Vicki Scott catches her sparkly bra-top in her hair while removing it and is forced to continue the rest of her performance with her underwear hanging from her barnet. It's all so hideously British.

The thoroughly indecorous Manning punctuates the action with a stream of appallingly racist gags which tickle the audience no end. His assistant for the night is comedy actress Su Pollard – embarrassingly, the movie opened just weeks after her first sitcom hit, *Hi De Hi*, had débuted on BBC1 – who scampers around the stage picking up discarded knickers and feather boas, but not saying very much since the producers have wisely not given her a microphone. With a strained smile she tries to interact with her co-host, who tells the assembled throng: 'You'd have to be a leper to sleep with this one, believe you me!' Most frightening of all, Manning and Pollard get to sing 'The Lady is a Tramp' during the interval, which is guaranteed to induce a cerebral haemorrhage.

The entire event is obviously stage-managed from beginning to end. Comedy writer-performer John Junkin is credited as 'story consultant', which seems a little surprising as this is supposedly an honest recording of the event. Considering that the audience laugh loudest at the painfully unfunny racist jokes it comes as quite a surprise to see black model Lucienne Camille (one-time glamour girl from the TV version of *Up Pompeii!*) win the competition and bag the £500 prize. To celebrate, Manning attempts a little striptease himself, but the film ends before the voluminous trousers come off. Saints preserve us.

CAST: Bernard Manning (*compère*), Su Pollard (*his assistant*) with Lucienne Camille, Diane Foster, Cheryl Gilham, Lisa Taylor, Julia Rushford, Nina West, Gloria Brittain, Vicki Scott, Veronica Plunkett, Jane Lucas, Rosalind Edwards, Christine Shaw, Shirley Knight, Bobby Buckley and Lorraine Lorelei (*as themselves*)
CREDITS: *Director* Doug Smith, *Producer* Tim Stone and Kent Walwin, *Editors* Philip Stone and Robert Hartwell, *Music* the Jack Dorsey Orchestra, *Script* Bernard Manning, *Story Format* John Junkin
An AMARANTH Production. Distributed by TARGET. Opened March 1980.

SEX WITH THE STARS

aka *Confessions of the Naughty Nymphos*

Great Britain / 1980 / 92 mins / cert 'X'

In the second star-gazing sex comedy in less than a year (the other was the appalling *Confessions from the David Galaxy Affair*), roly-poly American actor Thick Wilson plays a brash, obnoxious, cigar-sucking media mogul who, after enormous success with his last magazine (*John Thomas Weekly*, no less), buys up a quaint English periodical called *Happy Homes*. Giving it an 'instant sex makeover', he re-launches the title as, ho-hum, *Horny Homes*. Only one of the original features is retained, the magazine's astrological forecast: 'Clara looks at the stars'. Old Clara is actually dead and her monthly prediction page has been inherited by her diffident, drippy nephew Peter Bates (Master Bates to you and me). The new owner is obsessed with Bates' column (if you'll pardon the pun) and demands a complete overhaul. He wants first-hand accounts of the sexual characteristics of each star sign, and he wants them now. But the nervous, stuttering Bates is not only a slow worker, he's also a 29-year-old virgin.

You can see where this is going, can't you? It's a dumb story, reminiscent of a dozen sex comedy plots we've seen before, only on this occasion it's spread even thinner than Marmite. The script was actually written a decade before by writer-director Tudor Gates, around the same time as his *The Love Box*, which had a similar magazine-based story. Hawked around for ten years, it finally got picked up in 1979 by 27-year-old Syrian director Anwar Kawadri, who wanted to cut his teeth on a big-budget British movie. Needless to say, the big budget never came, nor did the big-name stars or flashy locations. But with limited resources he eventually got the job done for £70,000. When the film was completed, however, Kawadri was unable to find a distributor willing to exhibit it. Gates had originally written the script using his Teddy White pseudonym, and only after he reluctantly agreed to put his real name to the film did Tigon sign a deal to distribute it.

The film was modestly successful at the box-office, though its only saving grace is a wonderfully ethereal score by Pierre Bachelet, who also wrote the music for the original *Emmanuelle*. Despite the hero's shortcomings, Bates manages to bed a luscious lady of each star sign without any trouble whatsoever and thus saves his pimply skin. His starry-eyed conquests include late-1970s sexpots Suzie Sylvie, Faith Daykin and Rosemary England (using the name Poula Grifith Jada), who all helped to attract the crowds. However, it is veteran porn actress Nicola Austine, incredibly in her 20th film in only ten years, who steals the show in a slow-motion fantasy featuring strobe lighting and a squirting water bed. Her acting hasn't improved much in ten years, granted, but she is sexier than ever and gives the most elegant and sensuous performance of her extensive career.

CAST: Martin Burrows (*Peter Bates*), Thick Wilson (*Mr Terson*), Janie Love (*Susie, Sagittarius*), Suzie Sylvie (*Shirley, Gemini*), Terri Mitchell (*Brenda, Aquarius*), Simone St Laurent (*Mrs Simmons, Taurus*), Nicola Austine (*Mrs Doyle, Libra*), Carrie Allen (*Scorpio*), Poula Grifith Jada [aka Rosemary England] (*Leo*), Faith Daykin (*Cancer*), Clair Bastin (*Virgo*), Loretta Smith (*Pisces*), Caroline Grenville (*Capricorn*), Suzannah Willis (*Mrs Terson, Aries*), Danique (*Peter's landlady*), Daniella Gonella

and Max Roman (*interviewees*)
CREDITS: *Director* Anwar Kawadri, *Producers* Panos Nicolaou and Anwar Kawadri, *Editor* Ray Millichope, *Photography* Peter Jessop, *Screenplay* Tudor Gates, *Music* Pierre Bachelet, *Theme song 'Sex with the Stars' performed by* Neil Lancaster
A JEZSHAW Production. Distributed by TIGON. Opened July 1980.

MARY MILLINGTON'S TRUE BLUE CONFESSIONS
(INCORPORATING MARY MILLINGTON 1946-1979 PROLOGUE)
aka *The Naked Truth*

Great Britain / 1980 / 6 mins and 39 mins / cert 'X'

Immediately after Mary Millington's suicide on 19 August 1979, her producer and manager David Sullivan announced that he would not make another movie for 'at least 12 months as a mark of respect'. But, even in death, Mary was too valuable a commodity to ignore. Numerous 'tribute' magazines appeared on news-stands, recordings of her voice, both faked and real, were sold at sex shops and, most significantly of all, a new movie went into production in the spring of 1980. Sullivan has claimed he was 'bullied' into making the film by Mary's 'friend', publicist and sometime co-star, John M East.

Mercifully, clips of the deceased star weren't woven into a new narrative, as with both Bruce Lee and Peter Sellers. Instead, *Mary Millington's True Blue Confessions* was envisaged as a biography-cum-tribute. Costing just £24,000, the results are variable, gruesome, but undeniably compelling. East, who wrote the screenplay and narrates the film, prefers to sensationalise his friend rather than eulogise. Instead of untangling her legend, he piles on even more innuendo: her alleged promiscuity, her bisexuality and her reputation as a 'harlot' and a 'notorious woman'. 'She achieved her effects with extraordinary ease and grace,' he announces over nude clips of her from *The Playbirds*. 'A lush, ripe girl. Mary, whose beautiful, passionate body opened the door to dreams.'

Rather cynically, the film's six-minute prologue acts as nothing more than an elongated trailer for her films still in release, with no mention, naturally, of her non-Sullivan productions. From there, the movie opts for a morbid trawl through the places rather than events of her life. East's galloping, tabloid-style commentary describes Soho as 'the spiritual home of pornography in all its forms. To the liberated an oasis of naughtiness. To the puritans a boil on the buttocks of London!' But everything smacks of pure fakery. There are unsexy re-creations of one of Mary's so-called uninhibited parties, partly shot in her own home in Walton-on-the-Hill and partly in Sullivan's luxury apartment in Woodford Green. The awkward lesbian gropings, unsatisfactory threesomes and colourful bath scenes are watched by model Faith Daykin (playing a young Mary), and a sex scene filmed in the cubicle of a ladies' clothing boutique is lifted directly from the pages of Mary's ghost-written autobiography. 'Her dogs still pine for their mistress,' drools East. But her real Alsatians had already been disposed of and the ones pictured had been hired for the day.

The film will long be remembered for its excessively bad taste, like nothing seen before or since in British cinema. East made a calculated decision to film in the bedroom where Mary had died only months before. Rumpling her bed sheets and lying her negligée on the covers, he then spilled pills across them. Most ghoulish of all was his decision to leave the telephone handset off the hook. Considering that Mary's last phone call was a cry for help to East himself and was brushed off

Left: Mary Millington's photo session from *The Playbirds* appeared in re-edited form in the posthumous *True Blue Confessions* (1980).

by him, this seems the most brutal and alarming image of all. East even has a quivering female voice reading abridged passages from Mary's suicide note to David Sullivan and uses model Marie Harper to pose as Mary's body lying in a coffin. The shocking sequence was filmed at a real undertakers in Palmers Green. But it could have been far worse: certain associates of Mary had photos of her body laid out on the mortuary slab and it had been debated whether they, too, should be included in *True Blue Confessions*.

Does any of this really matter? Would Mary really have minded? It's doubtful, since nobody exploited Mary as much as Mary did herself. But this quasi-documentary still leaves a nasty taste in the mouth. Mary herself comes out of it exceedingly well, however, as a kindhearted innocent, an animal lover and a loyal friend. And, for all its grotesquerie, *True Blue Confessions* was a huge hit, running for over six months at the Cinecenta on Piccadilly Circus and setting a new house record in its opening week. As Marilyn Monroe and James Dean had demonstrated, exploitation does not stop at the grave.

CAST: John M East (*narrator*), Faith Daykin (*young Mary*), Geraldine Hooper (*boutique owner*), Mike Gallagher and Louise London (*party guests*), John Roach and Gavin Clare (*men in cinema*), Marie Harper (*Mary in coffin*) with contributions from John Lindsay, David Sullivan, Tom Hayes, Kathy Green and Rex Peters
CREDITS: *Directors* Nick Galtress and John M East, *Producer* David C Kenten, *Executive Producer* David Sullivan, *Editor* Roy Deverell, *Photography* John Shann and Richard Crafter, *Music* De Wolfe and David Whitaker, *Costume* She and Me, *Lingerie* Silver Rose, *Original Millington Footage* Taboo Films, *Concept and Script* John M East A ROLDVALE Film. Distributed by JAY JAY. Opened October 1980.

PAUL RAYMOND'S EROTICA
aka *Erotica*

Great Britain / 1980 / 86 mins / cert 'X'

After standing in the shadows for his three Fiona Richmond pictures during the seventies, *Men Only* publisher Paul Raymond stepped into the light in 1980. Not only does he grace this film's title, he also 'acts' for the first time, but only in a role he has stage-managed for years – himself. Wisely realising, however, that the average punter wasn't going to pay to see *him*, Raymond imported a much more ravishing star: French hardcore porn actress Brigitte Lahaie, cast as a journalist and photographer for *Paris aujourd'hui* magazine, over in England for an 'in-depth' investigative report.

Determined to find out if the British really *are* sexy, Brigitte wastes little time in having it away with everybody she sets eyes on, both male and female. She is instantly bewitched by Raymond's real-life girlfriend, and inadequate Fiona Richmond replacement, Diana Cochran, a toothy 21-year-old blonde in a flying suit. The rest of her adventures could loosely be described as 'erotic vignettes' or 'utter boredom', depending on your point of view. Brigitte has a lesbian foursome, a boogie at a nude nightclub called Starkers, and a romp in a stable block at Knebworth House where one poor sod acts as a coffee table while the other three participants balance perilously on top.

Even less appealing, she visits Smithfield meat market and seduces a blood-soaked delivery man, having sex with him in the back of a refrigerated lorry among the pig carcasses. How romantic! From a censorship point of view the most eye-opening scene occurs when the saucy French filly visits a crowded nude sauna underneath the Windmill Theatre. The solitary male patron has a wonderful time as his penis is massaged in close-up and he gets an undeniable erection, albeit flat against his belly. Raymond must have slipped the censor quite a bung to get that through.

Tellingly, little is revealed about the most interesting performer in the film, Paul Raymond himself. He is painstakingly portrayed as a pin-striped, tough-talking businessman with an autocratic control over every aspect of his empire. Ready to record the great man's thoughts on her tape-recorder, Brigitte gives him a lacklustre probing and the answers are dispiritingly scripted. Somehow managing to cram in even more nakedness, we're also entertained with some really dated sequences of performers literally throwing themselves around the Revuebar stage. It's like a porno version of the Russian acrobats seen every

Saturday on *The Paul Daniels Magic Show*. But the jerking muffs, open-legged shots and lesbian gropings go a lot further than anything seen before and must have had David Sullivan hanging his head in shame.

This is just complete nonsense. And it goes on... and on... and on. After an hour and a half you'll be begging for mercy. Only at the end do the producers really come clean about their true cinematic intentions. '*You have seen the show,*' flash the end credits, '*now see the show live at the Raymond Revuebar.*' Allegedly costing £1,500,000, *Paul Raymond's Erotica* became the most expensive, long-winded cinema advert ever and the public stayed away in droves. The *Daily Express* reported that you couldn't hear the soundtrack of the film because of the cinema seats snapping noisily up as the audience rushed for the exits.

CAST: Brigitte Lahaie (*Brigitte*), Diana Cochran (*Diana*), Paul Raymond (*himself*), the Raymond Revuebar Girls (*themselves*), Faith Daykin and Vicki Scott [uncredited] (*models*), Gerard Simi [uncredited] (*himself*), Carl Snitcher [uncredited] (*himself*)
CREDITS: *Director/Screenplay* Brian Smedley-Aston, *Producer* James Kenelm Clarke, *Executive Producer* Paul Raymond, *Editor* Jim Connock, *Photography* Alan Hall, *Music* Steven Gray
A PAUL RAYMOND Film in association with NORFOLK INTERNATIONAL Productions. Distributed by BRENT WALKER.
Opened September 1981.

1981

ELECTRIC BLUE – THE MOVIE

Great Britain / 1981 / 96 mins / cert 'X'

It seems odd that the *Electric Blue* video series, which marked the beginning of the end for British sex at the cinema, should attempt a big screen spin-off in 1981. The *Electric Blue* brand, which offered a top-shelf magazine-type format but with moving flesh, had been launched in 1979 by photographer Adam Cole. Several volumes were released each year with big-name glamour girls used to front the videos. Cole himself directed the movie version, with US hardcore legend Marilyn Chambers providing the naughty linking material. Chambers had previously worked in Britain, incidentally, in the US-financed *Insatiable* (1980), co-starring legendary cocksman John C Holmes and veteran British music hall star Joan Turner.

As Mistress of Ceremonies, Chambers seems happy enough to smile and strip off while presenting all the features that made Cole's videos so successful: repetitive nude disco dancing, faked lesbian jiggery pokery, discreet masturbation, suburban wives and depressingly unerotic fantasies, all mixed up with 'candid clips' (read: recycled rubbish) culled from other people's movies. Brigitte Lahaie makes an appearance as does *Hustler* centrefold Desirée Cousteau, while cheeky *Emmanuelle in Soho* actress Angela Quick (aka Mandy Miller) keeps the British end up by having a wank for the camera.

The 1980 video release *Electric Blue 002* had featured clips from *Games That Lovers Play*, showing Joanna Lumley naked with fully clothed character actress Diane Hart. Furious that her artistry was being defiled, Hart sued *Electric Blue* and won considerable damages. Wanting to re-use the footage for the movie version, Cole trod more carefully and edited Hart out of the picture. More interesting are clips of pneumatic blonde bombshell Jayne Mansfield in a frothy bathtime sequence from her 1963 B-movie *Promises! Promises!*. Also on display is 'a unique piece of film' of, allegedly, a pre-Hollywood Marilyn Monroe, shot sometime in 1946. She's quite obviously not the genuine article and several years later was revealed to be post-war glamour pin-up and stag film performer Arline Hunter.

In 1974 another British-made compilation movie, *Ain't Misbehavin'*, had cleverly re-edited clips of colourless old American stag films set to the music of George Gershwin and Fats Waller. But in the *Electric Blue* concoction the Mansfield and 'Monroe' footage sits uncomfortably among the 1980s crudity of awkward, tottering housewives attempting to look sexy in high heels and Ann Summers underwear. Most of the film looks all the more grubby because it's been blown up from the original video. *Film Review* put it beautifully when it described the film as 'a sort of deluxe wanker's digest'.

CAST: Marilyn Chambers (*compère*), 'Marilyn Monroe' [ie, Arline Hunter] (*herself*), Desirée Cousteau (*herself*), Brigitte Lahaie (*herself*), Britt Ekland (*herself*), Joanna Lumley (*herself*), Mandy Miller [aka Angie Quick] (*herself*), Jayne Mansfield (*herself*)
CREDITS: *Director* Adam Cole, *Producer* Adam Cole, *Executive Producers* Tony Power and Roger Cook
A SCRIP GLOW Production. Distributed by TIGON. Opened January 1982.

EMMANUELLE IN SOHO

Great Britain / 1981 / 65 mins / cert 'X'

Carry On supremo Peter Rogers may have been worried about the spelling of his particular 'Emmannuelle' in 1978, but producer David Sullivan had no such qualms about stepping on copyright toes for his last full-scale feature film, *Emmanuelle in Soho*. The movie, originally entitled *Funeral in Soho*, had been announced as a vehicle for Mary Millington as early as 1978, with a script written by director Willy Roe and Mary's close friend David Weldon. Purporting to be a thriller about London's gangster underworld, the film endured several extensive rewrites before landing up with Mary's acting coach, and sometime co-star, John M East. By the summer of 1979 the script was called *Emmanuelle in Soho* and, just two weeks before Mary's death, Sullivan had placed an advertisement in the trade press proclaiming that the movie would be 'Mary Millington's New Blockbuster for 1980'.

His star's suicide meant the entire project was put on ice for nearly two years, but in the spring of 1981 the movie finally went into pre-production. Sullivan had begun promoting his then-girlfriend, the strikingly beautiful half-Chinese, Yorkshire-born model Julie Lee, as his new discovery and wanted her to play the lead part of the insatiable Emmanuelle. Unfortunately nobody had bothered to find out if Julie could act. During rehearsals the poor girl could barely get a line out. Reluctantly, Sullivan had to reduce Julie's part to a supporting role and elevated another of his magazine models, Angela Quick, to prime position. Cynically cashing in on the alliteration of Mary's name, Angela was rechristened Mandy Miller, a pseudonym also designed to trick the audience into thinking it was child actress Mandy Miller who had appeared in several movies during the 1950s, now all grown up and presumably having a healthy sex life.

Lee plays Kate Benson, an unsatisfied wife whose spindle-shanked husband Paul (Keith Fraser) is a jobbing nude photographer who never earns enough cash to support their apparently lavish Bayswater-with-Mercedes lifestyle. Thankfully, they have a lodger, Emmanuelle, who surely can't be adding much to the household coffers since she hasn't got a job. (Angela Quick acts cheerfully enough, but Julie Lee *looks* the part much more. When one imagines Emmanuelle, however you spell it, one thinks of an exotic beauty, not a perky young scrubber from Islington. But there you go.) Out of desperation, Emmanuelle decides on a porn career, choosing the classy showbiz name Peggy the Pushover. Kate, meanwhile, pursues her dream of a stage career and successfully auditions for a part in a nude revue entitled *Hang About Sebastian*. The show consists of little more than a dozen naked women 'dancing' around in see-through mackintoshes to disco music, while looking thoroughly bored and trying not to bump into each other. 'I distinctly remember,' says Linzi Drew, 'spending all day dancing in these transparent coats in some dilapidated theatre in south London; Streatham or Tooting it was. It was funny because nobody knew what they were doing or how to dance.'

This now-infamous 'mackintosh' scene is just one of the laughably unerotic low-points the movie has to offer. A woeful lesbian sequence at the beginning features Angela Quick and Mary Millington's real-life ex-girlfriend, Kathy Green. Kathy, sporting a fetching purple bruise on her back, manages to writhe around on top of her co-star and feign cunnilingus without actually touching her; no mean feat. 'Look as though you're dying for a length,' urges snap-happy Paul. 'Come on, girls, this isn't the real thing, you know!' Never was a truer word spoken. And in another scene, a barrel-shaped, four-foot-nothing 'exotic dancer' (Suzanne Richens) auditions for the stage show with the most dismally unprofessional striptease ever shown on screen.

Screenwriter John M East wrote himself a plum part as lecherous Jewish porn agent Bill Anderson, but acquits himself

Right: Do not adjust your dress — Nicholas Clay and Sylvia Kristel in Just Jaeckin's *Lady Chatterley's Lover* (1981).

as charmlessly as ever, with hackneyed jokes recycled (again) from the Max Miller joke book. Anderson has been selling Paul's porn pics to various European magazines on the quiet and, when Paul finds out, he blackmails Anderson at an unintentionally hysterical house party at his Bayswater mews. All the upwardly nubile guests strip off except the men, who defiantly keep their pants on. A couple of soggy lesbians make out in a whirlpool full of dirty water and a fat man, who has some difficulty in getting his trousers undone, enjoys a threesome with Kathy Green and another young lady who hides in bed with the sheet over her head. 'These bits were filmed in a luxury apartment in Green Street in Mayfair,' says Linzi Drew, who donned an outrageous Zandra Rhodes wig for the scene. 'There were half a dozen houses in Green Street that were owned by Arabs. But for some reason, when they went away for their religious festivals, film directors would take over the flats and start shooting porn films. It happened quite regularly.'

As in *Come Play with Me*, Sullivan made the decision to produce *Emmanuelle in Soho* in a hardcore version too. His company, Roldvale, hired none other than Ray Selfe to shoot the extra footage. 'The film originally only ran for about 65 minutes,' said Ray, 'but I shot another half hour. There's a party scene and we cut away to completely different people going into separate rooms.' It was Ray's one and only foray into hardcore, a mode he wasn't totally *au fait* with. 'I honestly didn't know any actresses who would do hardcore and I didn't have a set,' he said. 'No studio would allow me to film it on their premises and I wasn't keen on getting a reputation as a porn director. So Roldvale got me two girls and a fella and we shot it in a student's dormitory flat in Hendon. One of the girls wore clown's make-up to disguise herself.' However, Ray had an unexpected surprise when he arrived on location. 'I thought it was just going to be me, my lighting assistant and the actors. But at 8.30 am Roldvale's accountant turned up, along with a couple of others plus Julie Lee and her mother! They all sat on chairs on one side of the room and stayed all day to watch.'

Ironically, Sullivan got into trouble over the hardcore footage, but not the *real* hardcore footage. Long renowned for advertising his films as being far stronger than they actually were, *Emmanuelle in Soho* had been promoted in *Whitehouse* and *Playbirds* with a series of explicit stills purporting to be taken from the movie. However, these were faked photographs featuring a bearded man and a blonde girl. The BBFC, fed up with Sullivan attempting to hoodwink the British cinemagoing public, decided once and for all to take him to task. After the film had been certificated for adults only, BBFC boss James Ferman threatened to withdraw its 'X' certificate.

Sullivan was livid and responded by taking the unprecedented step of paying for a full-page advertisement (which must have cost a bob or two) in *Screen International* in May 1981. He argued that, whenever hardcore pictures were printed in his magazines, it was clearly stated that they were from the oft-mentioned 'overseas version' only. Crazily, Sullivan even got into a spot of bother with Westminster Trading Standards, who claimed the film was not pornographic enough. Oh please! Only after some tough negotiating did the film get a full, and very profitable, release.

The full American version of *Emmanuelle in Soho* is worth tracking down since the first six minutes contain a documentary about London's most famous 'naughty square mile'. Easily the most salacious and lurid portrait of Soho ever committed to film, the documentary acts as a kind of debauched travel brochure for American tourists. The uncredited voice-over artiste sounds like a perverted, salivating schoolmaster and relishes every word of his sleazy commentary, chewing over every last succulent morsel of 'flesh peddling', 'strange devices' and 'well-oiled bodies'. David Sullivan is to be heartily congratulated for falsely selling Soho to the Americans as some depraved Disneyland. What a shame, then, that by 1981 Westminster City Council had already begun a thoroughgoing Soho purge.

It is difficult to convey just how grotesquely bad *Emmanuelle in Soho* really is. The three young leads all look like they're reading off idiot boards and the late Julie Lee, in particular, can barely string a sentence together. Her monotone voice and flat Northern vowels redefine the word leaden. Obviously the public didn't object to the shocking acting and flaccid sex scenes, since it was one of David Sullivan's most successful movies. The film had its UK première in Lee's home town of Sheffield on Saturday 4 July 1981, with Ms Lee in attendance and a heaving press presence. In London it opened at the Eros in Piccadilly, taking over £35,000 over ten weeks and then running for a further 25 consecutive weeks at the Moulin until March 1982.

Many of Sullivan's contemporaries cite him as being the man who brought British sex films into disrepute. In the case of *Emmanuelle in Soho*, however, that was surely the whole point.

CAST: Mandy Miller [aka Angie Quick] (*Emmanuelle*), Julie Lee (*Kate Benson*), John M East (*Bill Anderson*), Keith Fraser (*Paul Benson*), Gavin Clare (*Adie Cole*), Tim Blackstone (*Derek*), Geraldine Hooper (*Jill*), Anita Desmarais (*Sheila Burnette*), Georges Waser (*Tom Poluski*), Erika Lea (*Judy*), Kathy Green (*Sammy*), Suzanne Richens (*Suzie*), John Roach (*Albert*), Linzi Drew (*guest with pink hair*), Vicki Scott, Louise London, Natalie Newport, Marie Harper, Samantha Devonshire, Carla Lawrence, Ruth Chapman, Kalla Ryan (*showgirls*)
CREDITS: Directors David Hughes and Ray Selfe [uncredited], *Producer* John M East, *Executive Producer* David Sullivan, *Photography* Don Lord, *Screenplay* Brian Daly and John M East, *Music* Barry Kirsch, *Choreography* Anita Desmarais
A ROLDVALE Film. Distributed by TIGON. Opened July 1981.

LADY CHATTERLEY'S LOVER

Great Britain-France / 1981 / 103 mins / cert 'X'

By the dawn of the 1980s the Confessions series was just a bleary-eyed memory for the big-wig executives at Columbia Pictures. They realised, however, that 'where there's muck there's brass' and didn't think twice about distributing a film version of the sauciest story of the 20th century. Written in 1928, D H Lawrence's *Lady Chatterley's Lover* had only been available, unexpurgated, in Britain since Penguin Books' famous 1960 obscenity trial at the Old Bailey.

No filmmakers had come forward with an express wish to turn the book into a movie, however. A lowbrow American production, *Young Lady Chatterley*, had been made in 1976; starring Harlee McBride and Ann Michelle, it focused on Lady C's promiscuous young niece and enjoyed some success. But it wasn't until 1981 that somebody had the bright idea to make an English language version filmed on home turf. The director and star were not obvious choices to bring England's most infamous sexual heroine to life. Louche French director Just Jaeckin had previously worked with Dutch actress Sylvia Kristel on *Emmanuelle* in 1974 and had shocked audiences even further with his naughty spank-a-thon *Story of O* the following year. Mercifully, *Lady Chatterley's Lover* is far tamer stuff and is all the better for it.

You can say what you like about Jaeckin's work, but he does know how to make a film look good. His attention to period detail in *Lady Chatterley's Lover* is unsurpassed and his photography of the mist-cloaked, dew-drenched countryside is often beautiful. The only drawback is that Jaeckin's well-crafted imagery can never be as overtly sexy as Lawrence's original text, with its fruity language and sexually explicit situations. So Jaeckin does have a slight tendency to come over a little 'Mills and Boon' every so often. The 31-year-old Kristel, meanwhile, looks pretty bored throughout, although her natural body has filled out into more English-friendly curves since her *Emmanuelle* days. Despite filming her part in English, her voice was distractingly dubbed into quasi-Joanna Lumley for the movie's British and American release.

Lady Constance (Kristel) is a lively, vivacious young bride whose sex life is shattered when her husband is paralysed from the waist down after experiencing a bomb blast in World War One. Lord Clifford Chatterley (Shane Briant) rejects his wife's amorous advances, preferring to play endless games of cards, chess and snooker and zip around the grounds in a bizarre motorised bathchair. The Lord's indomitable Aunt Eva (Elizabeth Spriggs)

189

KEEPING THE BRITISH END UP

The delirious sex scenes in *Lady Chatterley's Lover* are lovingly photographed; both romantic and passionate, they're quite unlike anything previously seen in homegrown softcore. Mellors tenderly laying flower petals on his lover's naked body is a world away from the usual comedic shagging offered up as entertainment in the UK, and yet the film was hardly the runaway success Columbia had predicted. Was the film's more believable approach to erotica what the British public really wanted? It would appear not. The only other homegrown narrative sex film made that year, David Sullivan's *Emmanuelle in Soho*, trades instead on an awkward, unreal, sniggering approach to sex. Whereas one film delights in the art of love-making, the other merely drools over 'having it off'. You can guess which one made the most money.

CAST: Sylvia Kristel (*Constance Chatterley*), Nicholas Clay (*Oliver Mellors*), Shane Briant (*Lord Clifford Chatterley*), Ann Mitchell (*Mrs Bolton*), Elizabeth Spriggs (*Lady Eva*), Pascale Ridault (*Hilda*), John Tynan (*Roberts*), Michael Huston (*footman*), Fran Hunter (*maid*), Ryan Michael and Mark Colleano (*gigolos*)
CREDITS: Director Just Jaeckin, Producers Chris Pearce and André Djaoui, Editor Eunice Mountjoy, Photography Robert Fraisse, Screenplay Christopher Wicking and Just Jaeckin based on the novel by D H Lawrence, Music Stanley Myers and Richard Harvey A LONDON CANNON Production in association with PRODUCTEURS ASSOCIÉS (Paris). Distributed by COLUMBIA-EMI-WARNER. Opened December 1981.

seems preoccupied with Constance not getting her daily oats and, planting seeds of doubt in Constance's head, she covertly encourages her to experiment with other men. It does the trick because Constance immediately starts fantasising about big white stallions and sturdy oak trees.

The bitter Lord Chatterley surprisingly gives Constance his blessing and, no sooner said than done, enter Mellors (Nicholas Clay), the rough and ready gamekeeper.

The very next day Constance goes to Mellors' cottage to check on her husband's pheasants, only to find the brash Yorkshireman washing himself stark naked at his front door. Unlike British directors, Jaeckin isn't shy of the naked male form. Clay's posterior puts Robin Askwith's hairy arse to shame and, after two decades of homegrown sex films, it's significant that it finally took a French director to eroticise an Englishman's body.

MARY MILLINGTON'S WORLD STRIPTEASE EXTRAVAGANZA
aka *Miss International Striptease*

Great Britain / 1981 / 46 mins / cert 'X'

Directly inspired by Bernard Manning's *Great British Striptease* movie released the year before, John M East set his sights even lower, producing a virtual remake, shot on film at the Burlesque Club in Mayfair and purporting to be a 'tribute' to Britain's first lady of sex. In Manning's film the strippers competed for a brown envelope stuffed with 500 quid. Not to be outdone, the strippers here are fighting over 'a £1000 prize, a holiday in Jamaica and an exclusive film contract'. It's all complete bollocks of course. In order to justify this tasteless farrago, East falsely describes Mary as 'the great stripper' and, as if to demonstrate his point, gets all dewy-eyed and shows a re-edited clip of Mary disrobing in *Queen of the Blues*. From this sickening starting point Mary is hastily forgotten and it's on with the show. After all, why spend thousands of pounds making a film with a story? Just cut to the chase, dispense with the narrative and get the tits out.

Executive producer David Sullivan had originally approached blue comic Jimmy Jones to compère the film but he had asked for too much money. Sullivan took the cheaper option and hired Jewish family comedian Bernie Winters. Definitely an unknown quantity when it came to blue material, Winters fails miserably to be funny, instead taking a few cheap shots at the expense of racial minorities and grinning like an idiot throughout. At first glance he has the punters in convulsions, yet most of the laughter is jarringly dubbed. The audience reaction shots are also pretty stale, since they too have been cheekily culled from *Queen of the Blues*.

Winters inaccurately introduces '16 beautiful girls from all over the world'. Well, firstly there are 17 girls and Winters knows damn well they've been roped in from various London boroughs. Without a trace of irony we are informed that Middlesex-born glamour girl Gloria Brittain hails 'from Spain' and Sheffield's own *Emmanuelle in Soho* actress, Julie Lee, is rather predictably 'from Hong Kong'. Julie, wisely not given the luxury of dialogue after her unfortunate performance in her début movie, has to make do with twirling a pink parasol while the impatient audience serenades her with a chorus of 'Get 'em off!' At least Angie Quick (aka Mandy Miller) has the dignity to tell Winters she's from the exotic locale of Islington.

The bulk of the film presents some of the clumsiest, most uncoordinated stripping routines you've ever seen, which isn't surprising since the girls are all models or actresses rather than professional dancers. Director Roy Deverell's camera lingers relentlessly on faceless shots of bobbling boobs, gyrating crotches and jiggling, cellulite-dimpled arses. The terminally bored Katrina ('from New Zealand' apparently) provides the absolute low point by merely swinging her considerable breasts from side to side in a virtually trance-like state. Blonde Brighton-based model, Kathy Green, seems to get the audience vote. She's banking on winning since she apparently gave the chief judge a blow-job earlier. We're then treated to an incongruous sex scene, spliced in from *Emmanuelle in Soho*, of Green indulging in some tatty humping with a fat hairy bloke and her female friend, all set to music. 'I even got my friend to screw him and she fucked him good and proper!' she says in a menacing voice-over.

Giving the judge a meat whistle must have paid off since Kathy wins the competition, although, as anticipated, the £1000 prize and holiday in Jamaica are not forthcoming. However, in real life, the film contract came true for Kathy, sort of. She carried on taking her knickers off in a series of plotless video potboilers for David Sullivan, but it was more Wood Green than Hollywood. As in the Bernard Manning film, compère Winters strips off at the climax, forcibly 'assisted' by the girls. He looks very uncomfortable as they violently yank at the front of his strides. 'We're making this up as we go along, you know,' he comments. We would never have guessed.

CAST: John M East (*Master of Ceremonies*), Bernie Winters (*compère*) *with the Roldvale Striptease Girls:* Kathy Green (Brighton), Julie Lee (Hong Kong), Angie Quick [aka Mandy Miller] (Islington), Gloria Brittain (Spain), Maxine (Botswana), Chantel (Australia), Katrina (New Zealand), Vicky (Turkey), Vicky 2 (Sweden), Samantha (USA), Joy (Wales), Rita (France), Christina (Holland), Helena (Greece), Carol (New Zealand), Marie (Sweden), Shereen (South Africa) and John Roach (*Mr Hare*), Christine (*drag act*)
CREDITS: *Director* Roy Deverell, *Producer*

KEEPING THE BRITISH END UP

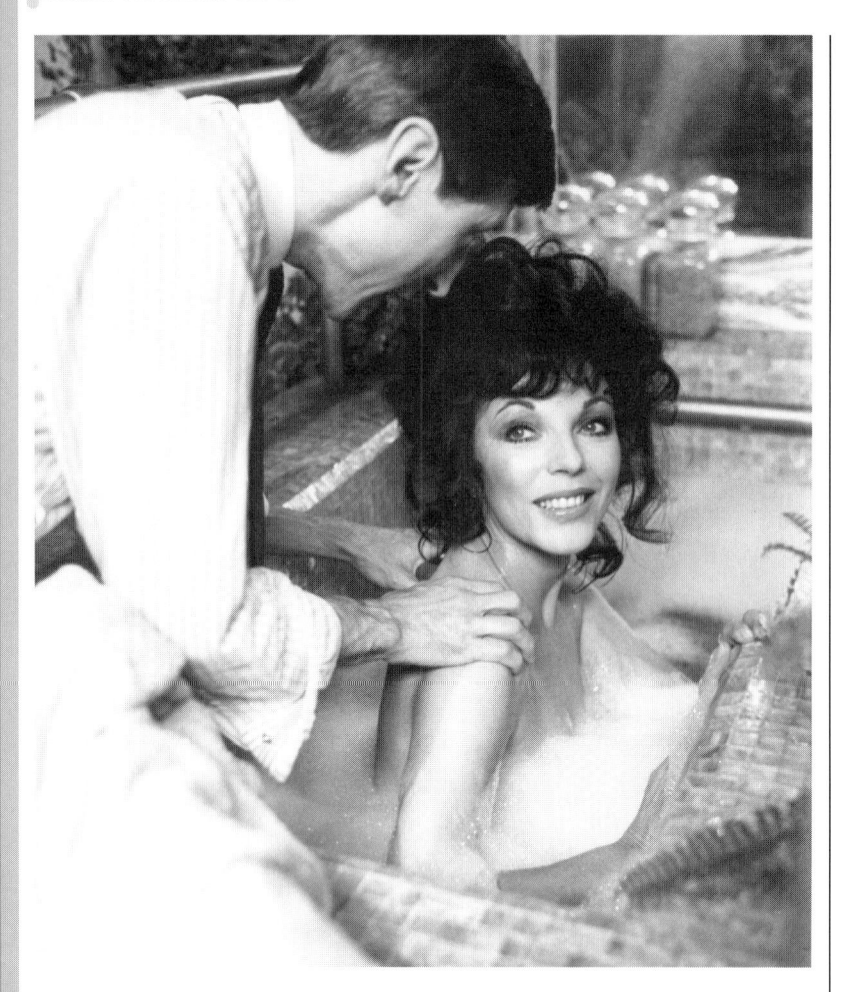

John M East, *Executive Producer* David Sullivan, *Editor* Roy Deverell, *Photography* Julian Doyle, *Music* De Wolfe and Barry Kirsch, *Devised by* David Sullivan
A ROLDVALE Film. Distributed by TIGON. Opened March 1982.

1982

NUTCRACKER
aka *Nutcracker Suite*

Great Britain / 1982 / 97 mins / cert 'X'

Despite Joan Collins' worry that after *The Stud* and *The Bitch* she would always be typecast in nymphomaniacal mode, she did dip her toe one last time into the tepid waters of sinful cinema. For *Nutcracker* she was paid $50,000. 'It was by sheer luck they got her,' recalls filmmaker Tudor Gates. 'Just after she made the movie she got signed up by Aaron Spelling for *Dynasty*.' By 1984 she was on that amount of money per episode. With hindsight, Joan may have wished that she'd held out a little longer for her big break as *Nutcracker* vies with 1976's *Empire of the Ants* as Ms Collins' most criminal movie ever.

A silly, soapy melodrama with a ridiculous plot and even more ridiculous acting, the script has all the hallmarks of having been written by a dizzy 12-year-old in her creative writing class. In fact, it was based on a story by a portly middle-aged Greek, Max Roman. Actor-writer Roman had appeared briefly in director Anwar Kawadri's last movie, *Sex with the Stars*, and during the late 1970s had had a hand in several hardcore movies shot in Greece. Attempting to emulate the successful ingredients of *The Stud*, Roman created a story which he hoped would do for ballet what Jackie Collins had done for disco. No such luck.

Finola Hughes plays a young Russian ballerina who, while on tour in Scotland, sneaks out of her cruddy theatre and runs away to London with the intention of defecting to the West. She seeks refuge at Joan's Carrère International Ballet Company in Covent Garden, which has all the appearance of a very high-class hairdressing salon with Leslie Ash on reception. The flustered Russians try to cover up the scandal by claiming their star has hurt her ankle in rehearsals and is unable to perform. Meanwhile, bland tabloid reporter Mike McCann (Paul Nicholas) is poking his lens around Joan's premises, hoping to sniff out an exclusive.

Overall, *Nutcracker* is a trashy, cheap-looking production with lousy dialogue ('I must dance, for that I would forsake everything!') and comic-book Cold War Russians with cod accents and names like Boris, Gargarin and Popov. There's even a Madame Olga in the mix, played by Jo Warne (later to become the first Peggy Mitchell in *EastEnders*) with exaggerated facial expressions that are pure pantomime. The strangely old-fashioned plot makes few concessions to believability and is peppered with gratuitous shots of the young ballerinas scrub-

Left: Joan Collins receives a soaping from Murray Melvin in *Nutcracker* (1982).

bing up in the shower.

Since la Collins was hoping to exorcise the spirit of Fontaine Khaled, she is more discreet in her nudity this time round, leaving the stripping to another mature British actress whose career had recently been on the skids, the ill-at-ease Carol White. The film's climax involves an outrageous fancy dress ball and a crappily choreographed 'modern interpretation' of *The Nutcracker*; among the dancers is future *Generation Game* hostess Rosemarie Ford, dressed as Wonder Woman. The party soon degenerates into abandoned sexual revelry, with sex film legends Anna Bergman and Nicola Austine making cameo appearances as a couple of naked lesbians snogging in an armchair.

Disappointingly, Joan lends very little oomph to her role as Madame Carrère. Even seeing her in stern schoolma'am mode, dressed in lycra and leg-warmers while giving her ballet pupils what for, is just not exciting enough. Mercifully for her, *Nutcracker* sank with barely a ripple and Joan was soon ensconced in the world of primetime American soap. The public was given one last glimpse of the celebrated Collins bosom, however, when she posed nude for the Christmas 1983 edition of *Playboy* in the States. It became the bestselling issue ever.

CAST: Joan Collins (*Laura Carrère*), Carol White (*Margaux Lasalle*), Paul Nicholas (*Mike McCann*), Finola Hughes (*Nadia Gargarin*), William Franklyn (*Sir Arthur Cartwright*), Leslie Ash (*Sharon*), Murray Melvin (*Leopold*), Vernon Dobtcheff (*Markovich*), Geraldine Gardner (*Markova*), Cherry Gillespie (*Mireille*), Jane Wellman (*Grace*), Ed Bishop (*Sam Dozier*), Jo Warne (*Madame Olga*), Martin Burrows (*Tom*), Morgan Sheppard (*George Peacock*), Fran Fullenwider (*Vi*), Anna Bergman (*Tashi*), Nicola Austine (*Sylvie*), Olivier Pierre (*Alex Lasalle*), Steve Kelly (*Boris*), Jimmy Mac (*stage doorman*), Rosemarie Ford (*dancer*)

CREDITS: *Director* Anwar Kawadri, *Producer* Panos Nicolaou, *Screenplay* Raymond Christodoulou *based on a story by* Max and Yvonne Roman, *Music* Simon Park, *Theme song 'Time to Love You' performed by* Paul Nicholas A JEZSHAW FILM Production. Distributed by RANK. Opened October 1982.

1983

FANNY HILL

Great Britain / 1983 / 92 mins / cert 'X'

Following the same bawdy tradition as Restoration comedies like *Lock Up Your Daughters!* (1969), *The Bawdy Adventures of Tom Jones* (1975), *Joseph Andrews* (1976) and *The Wicked Lady* (1982), the movie version of *Fanny Hill* – based on the notorious 1748 one-handed novel by John Cleland – is a great deal ruder than any of its predecessors and demonstrates clearly how the boundaries of censorship had been pushed to the limit by the early 1980s. There's sex by the ton here, with camera angles and direction more reminiscent of hardcore pornography than the usual tepid British rompage.

Lisa Raines plays the titular heroine, a destitute orphan who travels 200 miles to find her fortune in London. Looking for work, she is taken in by blowzy old madame, Mrs Brown (Paddy O'Neil), who recognises her potential and employs her to 'look after the linen', a sexual euphemism if ever there was one. Anxious to get Fanny to work, the Madame organises some 'on-the-job training' in an unexpurgated girl-on-girl scene with Maria Harper's head hooker Phoebe (an absolutely startling scene in its explicitness). She later has a secretive peep at what her other girls get up to behind closed doors in an outstanding montage of doggie-style humping, threesomes, energetic banging, groaning, panting and bouncing involving three of the most captivating porn princesses of the era – Vicki Scott, Suzie Sylvie and Angela Quick.

Eventually Mrs Brown is forced to relinquish her 'ownership' of her fresh new Fanny and the young girl is passed into the capable hands of another madame (played by Shelley Winters, no less) at an upmarket house of ill-fame in Covent Garden. There she is expected to participate in even more depravity. In another eye-popping montage, we're treated to an abundance of boobs, hairy bushes, naked men, bum-biting, shagging, spanking and blow-jobs, and although the practice of filming hardcore inserts in British sex films had ceased in

KEEPING THE BRITISH END UP

Right: Tantalising sleeve design for the straight-to-video sequel to *Hellcats – Mud Wrestling*.

1981 with *Emmanuelle in Soho*, if ever there was an instance where the cameras should have carried on rolling well into the night, this is it.

Director Gerry O'Hara goes a hell of a lot further in his depiction of sex than he ever did in *Feelings* or *The Bitch* and it's doubtful that his distinguished cast of big names had any idea of how explicit the final movie would be. (For its American release, however, all the sex was removed so it could get a mainstream airing.) Oliver Reed contributes an undistinguished cameo as a camp lawyer and veteran American actress Shelley Winters seems lost among the fornication. Most shocking of all, catatonic old Wilfrid Hyde White, in his last big screen movie, can barely walk, let alone deliver his lines. His dialogue appears suspiciously ad-libbed and his bedroom roll with Fanny is pretty unsavoury stuff, although it's doubtful he'd had this much fun since having a daffodil stuck up his arse in *Carry On Nurse* in 1959.

CAST: Lisa Raines (*Fanny Hill*), Shelley Winters (*Mrs Cole*), Oliver Reed (*Mr Widdlecombe*), Wilfrid Hyde White (*Mr Barville*), Paddy O'Neil (*Mrs Brown*), Jonathan York [aka Barry Stokes] (*Charles*), Maria Harper (*Phoebe*), Lorraine Doyle (*Martha the maid*), Liz Smith (*Mrs Jones*), Alfred Marks (*Lecher*), Angie Quick (*Harriet*), Suzie Sylvie (*Jane*), Vicki Scott (*Polly*), Tracy Dixon (*Emily*), Janet Henfrey (*lady in Intelligence Office*), Harry Fowler and Gordon Pollings (*beggars*), Howard Goorney (*Mr Croft*), Fanny Carby (*old wench*), Philip Herbert [uncredited] (*tubby client*)

CREDITS: *Director* Gerry O'Hara, *Producer* Harry Benn [aka Harry Alan Towers], *Editor* Peter Boyle, *Photography* Tony Spratling, *Screenplay* Stephen Chesley *based on the novel by* John Cleland, *Music* Paul Hoffert A FANNY HILL FILM Production. Distributed by BRENT WALKER. Opened April 1983.

HELLCATS – MUD WRESTLING
aka *The Hellcat Mud Wrestlers*

Great Britain / 1983 / 45 mins / cert 'X'

So what began with an innocent game of volleyball in a sunswept nudist camp in Hertfordshire ended in a disused Croydon nightclub in three feet of mud. 1983's *Hellcats – Mud Wrestling* spelt the end of the British sexploitation era. And what an egregious end it was.

David Sullivan had tried his hand at narrative comedy, documentary and striptease but now he attempted to embrace the world of *cinéma verité*. His latest venture was to bring the crazy world of American circus sideshows to Britain and along with it a most unlikely star, Miss Queen Kong. Californian Queenie (6'5" and weighing in at 20 stone) was the leader of a troupe of female grapplers touring the States. Sullivan first saw her mountainous act in Las Vegas in 1981 and immediately asked her to come to Britain to make a film. 'I remember David Sullivan as a very eccentric, randy man,' recalls Queenie. 'He really loved American girls and pursued them during the making of this movie. He also had an eye for talent and called me his 'star'. David believed in my talent and the possibilities of mud wrestling taking off in London.' It never did take off and Sullivan couldn't care less anyway. He just wanted to make an ultra-low-budget B-movie showcasing Queenie's considerable talents.

The resulting film was shot on location in just one day in a Croydon night spot, since female wrestling was illegal in London at the time. Sullivan co-directed the movie and is proud to have created one of the tackiest productions of his undistinguished career. The centrepiece of the film is a child's paddling pool full of mud in which Queenie and her American cohorts take on Sullivan's pitifully under-rehearsed homegrown wrestling team. 'The British girls were all very nice,' Queenie recalls, 'but were no competition for us experienced American girls.'

That's an understatement. The 'European Champion' (a-hem), Miss Deathwish, looks more like a House of Fraser beautician than a bone-crusher. 'Hungry' Helen Hammer has the appearance of a suburban hairdresser who couldn't even manage a pork pie let alone a leg-lock, and popular porno model and sex film actress Vicki Scott (a more petite and unthreatening woman you could never hope to find) is falsely heralded as the 'Scottish Welterweight Champion'. This is nothing but a silly, staged sham, and the sheepish audience seem bemused by the whole thing, as well as hiding behind their pints of beer whenever Miss Kong comes within ten feet of them.

The wrestling bouts are a mud-spattering, ear-pulling, cheek-smacking, head-splitting feast and the British girls take an absolute thrashing. Queen Kong makes a bravura appearance, knockers falling out of her bikini and giving the cameras a lovely close-up of her big muddy arse. Titillation is never far from the mind of the film's presenter, the unavoidable John M East, who continually goads the contestants, finding out when they last had sex and interviewing them while they're partially nude. At the end of Vicki Scott's interview, in which she looks like she wants to burst out laughing, the camera pans down to her crotch for an inconsequential shot of her pubic hair. Of course, this was all good clean fun for the film's brightest star. 'I loved every minute and felt very lucky to have been chosen to visit London as David Sullivan's guest,' says Queenie. 'I stayed at his mansion and it was gorgeous, and his cook and butler were really sweet to me. He even took me and my sister mud wrestlers to Stringfellows and we were treated like celebrities.' When the film eventually opened at London's Eros Cinema in 1983 she was flown back to Britain to do some publicity on radio and TV. She even went on a much-reported tour of the Scottish Highlands.

Such was the success of this cheap little movie that Sullivan rushed a sequel into production. *Foxy Female Boxers* (1983) transported Queenie from the paddling pool to the boxing ring and is notable for being even more amateurish than its predecessor. Sullivan, who sat in the director's chair a second time, once again filmed his performers from behind and allowed interviewer John M East to make things up as he went along. Featuring all-female boxing for the first time in Britain, East desperately tries to hype things up. 'Foul her. Kick her in the bum!' he suggests to one contender. Old hands like Vicki Scott are used to his banter but the American lady boxers are totally bemused by his constant stream of sexual innuendo and suggestive remarks.

The film would have been Britain's very last sexploitation movie had it not been rejected by the British censor. During the second boxing bout, model Zena Whitehouse (Sullivan's then-girlfriend and new face of *Whitehouse* magazine) takes on her American counterpart, Terrible Terri. The two ladies are topless and really slug it out in the ring, despite having been reminded of the rules ('no knock-knock on the knock-knockers'). It's the dubious highlight of the movie ('Their fists are flying. Their boobs are bouncing,' screams the slavering commentator), but the BBFC took exception to the juxtaposition of violence and titillation. They ordered the sequence to be removed, but Sullivan refused. As a consequence the film went straight to video in an abridged version and was later re-edited with *Hellcats* into a feature-length production, *Queen Kong – The Amazonian Woman*.

So it came to pass that *Hellcats – Mud Wrestling* was the very last British film to pander directly to the faithful dirty mac brigade. The exhausted censor finally groaned a sigh of relief at no longer having to evaluate such low-budget shockers for cinema exhibition ever again. 'That was the most appalling film I've ever had the misfortune to sit through in my life,' chief examiner James Ferman told East. 'You have brought the British film industry to the lowest depths of depravity.' What a way to go.

CAST: John M East (*interviewer*), Sandy Wolshin (*compère*), Queen Kong [aka Deanna Booher] (*herself*), Shelly Selina Savage (*herself*), Helen Hammer (*herself*), Rose Rock (*herself*), Vicki Scott (*herself*), Miss Deathwish (*herself*), John Roach (*referee*), Big Harry (*British coach*), Hal 'The Animal' Stone (*American coach*), Jock McPhearson (*promoter*)

CREDITS: *Directors* Alan Hall and David Sullivan, *Producer* John M East, *Executive Producer* David Sullivan, *Music* De Wolfe and Barry Kirsch, *Devised by* David Sullivan and John M East
A ROLDVALE Production. Distributed by TIGON. Opened May 1983.

...GOINGS

BRITISH SEX GOES DOWN THE PAN

So, as far as big screen British bonking went, that was about it. Or was it?

Well, the 1980s certainly couldn't have got off to a worse start for the trusty homegrown pornographer. In 1982, the new Conservative government scrapped the quota which had ensured that all cinemas screened a minimum percentage of British movies, and the Eady Fund went the same way soon after. Legend has it that a government minister walked into a Soho cinema one day and suddenly realised just what sort of British movies public money was being used to make. 'Many government ministers honestly thought that the Eady money was backing quality period drama,' says David McGillivray. 'Then they realised that the whole fund was going to produce movies like *Come Play with Me*.'

For the Tories, these new measures were nothing more than a cost-cutting exercise, denying filmmakers a 'petty extravagance' they'd been enjoying for far too long. Film production continued its downward spiral during the 1980s, with only a handful of indigenous movies turning a profit at the box-office. Notable exceptions included *Chariots of Fire* (1981) and *Gandhi* (1982), but when actor Colin Welland famously announced at the 1982 Oscar ceremony that 'The British are coming,' it definitely wasn't the sort of 'coming' the denizens of Soho had been anticipating. *Deep Throat*'s prediction that hardcore sex would soon be as commonplace as violence in mainstream movies never materialised. Tinto Brass'

notorious *Caligula*, released uncut in America in 1980, showed that hardcore could be intermingled with Shakespearean actors like John Gielgud, Peter O'Toole and Helen Mirren. But the mixture wasn't exactly welcomed by cinemagoers, and even less so by the unsuspecting thespians. 'Are we in a blue movie?' Gielgud exclaimed halfway through filming.

The early eighties saw the final sad dribble of new sex films being exhibited at British cinemas, often released in double-bills with reissues of homegrown stuff from the previous decade. From a pulsating torrent of breasts, bums and skimpy knickers just five or six years earlier, the production and distribution of sex films, like everything else, had ebbed away to virtually nothing by the beginning of the new decade. From the mighty peaks of 1975, British sex film production had slumped dramatically to only nine films in 1979 and just two by 1983.

SEX-STARVED

Starved of British sex films, distributors like Tigon and Jay Jay had increasingly turned to overseas producers, retitling the movies and, if need be, dubbing them into English. As usual, these imported movies were heavily cut by the ever-watchful censor, determined to omit anything that was in the slightest bit sexy. The French-made *Secrets of a Nymphomaniac* (1980) was trimmed from 84 to 67 minutes. *Ecstasy Girls*, shot in the USA in 1979 but

released here two years later, went from 84 minutes to only 50 and, most shocking of all, *Desires Within Young Girls* (1977), starring US sex legend Georgina Spelvin, lost a whopping 44 minutes on its belated British release in 1980. Desperate distributors vainly scratching around for new sex films to screen rapidly found new avenues of exploitation, namely Italian zombies and kung fu from Hong Kong.

The prevalence of imported sex films had at least one amusing side-effect. After the rip-roaring success of our own *Confessions of a Window Cleaner* in 1974, there was a sharp increase in European films being retitled to cash in on the Confessions craze. These counterfeit Confessions were happy to masquerade as their British counterparts, aping poster design, trade publicity and, in some cheeky cases, even being re-tooled with spanking new opening credits exactly imitating the distinctive seaside-postcard title typeface. It was all part of a cynical distributors' ploy to get in as many punters as possible by any dishonest means necessary. If it meant tarting up a crappy European movie so it looked like it starred Robin Askwith, then so be it.

The sheer quantity of these phoney Confessions is pretty astounding. The following titles were all released in the UK between 1974 and 1980: *Confessions of a Nymphomaniac*, *Confessions of a Male Escort*, *Confessions of an Au Pair Girl*, *Confessions of a Bigamist*, *Confessions of* a Sexy Photographer, Confessions of a Frustrated Housewife, Confessions of a College Girl, Confessions of the Campus Virgins, Confessions of a Danish Covergirl, Confessions of a Sixth Form Girl, Further Confessions of a Sixth Form Girl, Confessions of the Sex Slaves, Confessions of a Teenage Virgin, Confessions of a Concubine. And best, and most salacious, of all: Confessions of a Naked Virgin.

As late as 1982 the saucy Spanish movie Madame Olga's Pupils was getting a cumbersome release as The Confessions of Madame Olga's Pupils. It didn't exactly trip off the tongue. And, with the name Emmanuelle proving just as popular in the phoney retitling stakes, it's not surprising that some distributors attempted to cover both bases. Witness the bowdlerised concoctions that were The Confessions of Emmanuelle and Emanuelle's Swedish Confessions. Given half a chance, the brass-necked marketing men would even mix randy oddjob men with the latest sci-fi craze, as when a 1978 West German pornfest cropped up on UK screens as Close Encounters of a Handyman.

The most famous of all British sex films, Come Play with Me, also gave rise to several bogus soundalikes, including Come with Me My Love in 1977 and Come Make Love with Me in 1979. The poster for 1979 shocker Nympho Girls, directed by West German smutmeister Walter Boos, was a rough approximation of the original Come Play with Me artwork and sported the impertinent tag-line 'Come Play with Us!' In 1980, Come Play with Me producer David Sullivan picked up Les Bourgeoises de l'amour, a Brigitte Lahaie vehicle produced and directed by Zurich-based 'Pope of Porn' Erwin C Dietrich, and put it out as an 'in name only' sequel, Come Play with Me 2. Two years later, Sullivan acquired another Dietrich/Lahaie collaboration, cumbersomely entitled Julchen und Jettchen – die verliebten Apothekerstöchter (Julie and Yvette the Chemist's Lovestruck Daughters). Sullivan lost no time in changing its title to copper-bottomed old Come Play with Me 3.

Sullivan was virtually the very last British producer to persevere with the dying genre. But after the commercial drubbing of Confessions from the David Galaxy Affair in 1979, his next five films all had significantly reduced running times and considerably pared-down budgets. Sullivan had begun to lose confidence in filmmaking, feeling that it was too risky putting up the money for a picture only for it to take a beating at the box-office. His later movies often required a year or more on release before making any significant profit, and that wasn't quick enough for him. The pot of gold that had been Come Play with Me had long run dry and Sullivan retired from the film business in 1983. 'Occasionally I think I should have carried on with the sex films,' he reflects. 'I concentrated on the 45-minute things at the end but I wish I'd stuck with the 90-minute features and carried on a bit longer. If I'd really put my mind to it they could have succeeded, because I was good with publicity. Instead of the three or four features I made, I think I should have made 30 or something. Yes, 30 films would have been nice, but there just weren't the cinemas to show them.'

Sullivan is right. The closure of cinemas continued apace, and the independent cinemas, sex films' greatest allies, were the first to go. A greater reliance on US product, coupled with the era of new-style Hollywood blockbusters ushered in by Star Wars in 1977, proved once and for all that British productions didn't have a hope in hell of attracting the crowds. And ticket sales had never been more depressing. The 1946 high of a billion-plus had collapsed by an incredible 96 per cent to just 54 million by 1984. The same year, the number of cinema screens had fallen to just 1355, down by over 50 per cent in 20 years. 'So few towns had more than one cinema by the early eighties,' Sullivan

197

Right: *Sexy Secrets of the Kissogram Girls* (1985). Exmouth was not amused.

points out. 'Cinemas were shutting everywhere and there was nowhere to get your movies shown, which was incredibly sad. The game was up. It was like banging your head against a brick wall. I mean, to be honest with you, I was in it to make money and without the cinemas there to support you there was just no point in carrying on.'

CRACKDOWN

The downward trend in cinemagoing did not pick up to any degree until 1985, when Britain's first multiplex (another US import) opened in Milton Keynes. By the end of the year a further nine multiplexes had opened in the UK, but by that time the sex film era was dead and buried. Just as the independent cinemas were disappearing, so too were the anything-goes Soho cinema clubs. On 1 November 1982 the BBFC introduced its new simplified certificates for cinema exhibition. The 'A' became a 'PG' (for Parental Guidance), the 'AA' became the '15' and the evocative 'X', so X-ploited by sex filmmakers for the past 20 years, was overturned in favour of the plain old '18'. Most contentiously of all, a new rating was slipped into the equation: the infamous 'R18'.

The most misunderstood and heavily policed certificate in cinema history, the 'R18' was awarded only to sex films to be exhibited or sold on licensed premises. The 1982 Local Government (Miscellaneous Provisions) Act put an immediate end to cinema clubs evading censorship regulations. All exhibited films now had to be certificated 'R18', which put pornographers like John Lindsay in an untenable position. Showing an explicit movie on 'private' property with 'strict' membership rules (which in effect amounted to nothing more than 'instant' membership on the door) was just not acceptable any longer.

The 1982 Act also set about restricting the opening of sex shops and the exhibition of pornographic films by ordering that all sex-related businesses must obtain licenses from local councils. With licenses costing in the region of £20,000, few could afford to stay in business. Any cinemas persevering were forced to show heavily cut sex films, since the 'R18' certificate meant an end to raunchier material being shown. The porn-loving punter had to endure inflated admission costs and was presented with movies cut to ribbons, which only a year before he'd been able to watch with little or no tampering. All sex businesses had to be licensed annually and it was solely up to local councils to decide whether to award such licenses. Trading without a license led to a hefty fine and usually a closure order within 28 days.

The porn barons of Soho fell like ninepins. Police raids on fleshpots became ever more commonplace in the early eighties and dozens of long-established businesses went bankrupt within weeks. Early in 1982, Westminster City Council heard 29 appeals against licensing enforcement, dismissing them all. Several porn filmmakers were sent to gaol for supplying 'obscene' films for monetary gain and John Lindsay went the same way for exhibiting them. Pornographers were suddenly being treated like pariahs. Suddenly pornography was almost universally reviled in Britain. It became the cause of all society's ills, to be stamped out at all costs.

Even before the Local Government Act there were signs that draconian anti-sex legislation was finding favour with the Conservative government. The 1981 Indecent Displays Act was initially introduced as a private members bill by Tory MP Tim Sainsbury, and followed a 'Nationwide Petition for Public Decency' which had been doing the rounds for nearly ten years, since its launch by supporters of the Festival of Light in 1971. The Act sought to restrict external displays of 'indecent material' on the frontages of sex shops, cinemas and theatres, namely flashing neon signs advertising 'Hardcore XXX sex!' and illuminated photographs of topless starlets.

This was a huge victory for Mary Whitehouse and her National Viewers and Listeners Association, which had long complained about the public face of sex establishments. With the new backing afforded her by the 1982 Act requiring all sex premises to hold a license, Whitehouse mobilised her provincial troops to write to their local councils objecting to any applications for a license. 'A sex shop attracts undesirable persons into the neighbourhood,' she wrote. 'Offence would be caused to all decent people who live locally. Pornography endangers marriage, leads to adultery and encourages promiscuity among teenagers.'

Hardly inundated with letters proclaiming any support for the easy availability of porn, local councils were instead bombarded with hundreds of angry

Women's Institute members demanding an end to sex shops. One such vociferating letter, in opposition to a Bristol sex shop, reasoned: 'We don't want a sex shop here because no *normal* person needs pornography.' David Sullivan, who had embarked on a massive operation to open over a hundred Private Shops throughout the British Isles between 1978 and 1981, suddenly found people protesting outside his shops and complaining to their local MPs.

Whitehouse's well-choreographed tactics usually worked. In some counties she succeeded in getting all sex premises closed down and she was particularly pleased when a Bible-reading room opened on the site of the old Private Shop in Weston Super Mare. Back in London, the traditionalist Soho Society, which had been appalled by the escalation of sex shops since the mid-1970s, pressed Westminster City Council to 'clean up' the West End. Already reeling from police raids, expensive licenses and a clampdown on window displays, the pornocrats were dealt one final blow. The 1986 General Powers Act gave Westminster Council additional legislation to regulate the number of sex establishments in the West End. With the steady gentrification of Soho, sex shops were replaced by delicatessens, cappuccino coffee bars, Italian restaurants, advertising agencies and gift shops.

The re-developments had, in fact, been a long time coming. As early as 1978 the famous Pigalle Cinema in Piccadilly Circus had closed down when developers moved in to turn the site into the new Trocadero centre. Many other sex businesses fell foul of the 'new' Soho. In 1980 it was estimated that there were 163 sex establishments in the district. Seven years later that figure had shrunk to just five sex shops, three peepshows and two specialist sex cinemas: the Astral in Brewer Street and the Moulin complex in Great Windmill Street. 'Soho was wall-to-wall neon in the 1970s,' remembers David McGillivray, 'but walking down Brewer Street a decade later it was almost unrecognisable. There was hardly anything left. Over a period of a couple of years it changed completely. It had been a neon-lit night town which I had loved, and suddenly it was all closed down.'

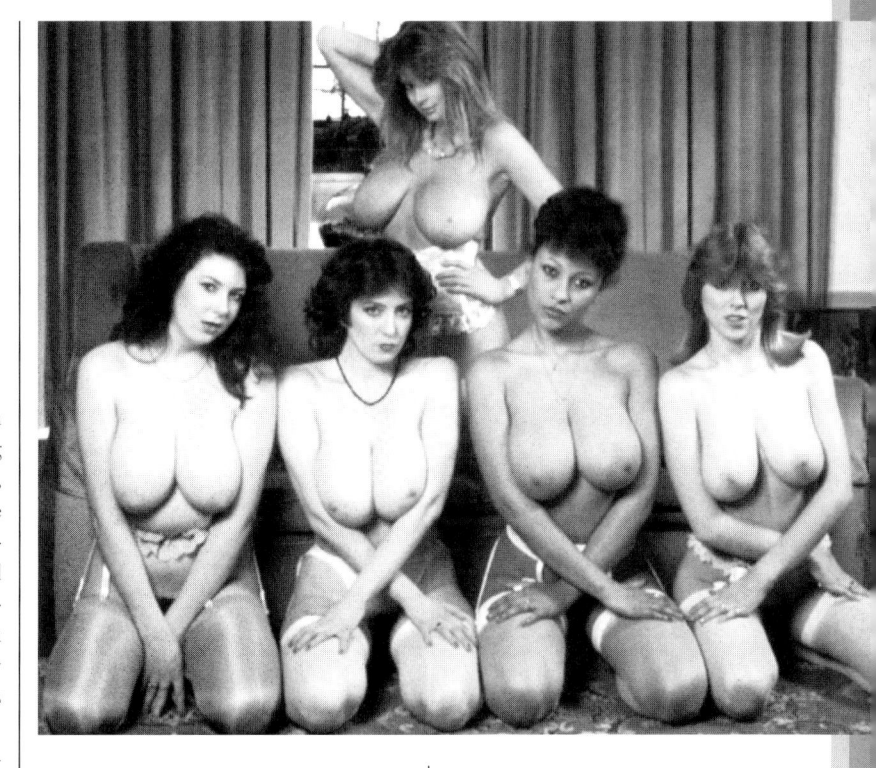

VIDEO PANIC

But without the auditoria showing jolly sex comedies, where had the loyal sex film audience been finding an outlet?

Pornography has always been quick to exploit new technologies and throughout the Western world video was seen as the saviour of the sex film. There had been excited talk of the new-fangled video recording machine since the late 1960s, but it wasn't until the following decade that the public finally got their hands on what they'd been reading about for so long. The first video machines were launched in the UK in 1978 with a campaign fronted by French saucepot and ex-porn actress, Françoise Pascal. Initially, porn had the video market cornered, with at least one quarter of all tapes sold in Britain between 1979 and 1981 being of a 'sexual nature'. Never missing a lucrative business opportunity, David Sullivan immediately jumped on the video bandwagon. Released on the Hokushin label in 1979, *Come Play with Me* was one of the first clutch of British titles to transfer to the new medium. Retailing for the extortionate price of £99, it still sold well and was rapidly followed by *The Playbirds* and *True Blue Confessions*. The Confessions, Adventures and What's Up series followed suit.

But since there was no regulatory body controlling the production and distribution of hardcore films on video, sex shops were soon saturated with heavy-duty porno titles. In America, video had transformed the porn industry, directors and producers immediately being won over by the eco-

KEEPING THE BRITISH END UP

Right: Renowned poster artist Tom Chantrell designed this photo montage for the video cover of *Queen of the Blues*.

nomic benefits of shooting films straight onto videotape. Back in Britain, pornographer Mike Freeman, who had made his fortune making hardcore loops in the 1960s (and as a consequence had spent most of the seventies in gaol), transferred to video in the eighties with ultra low-budget titles like *Flat Sharing Shaggers* (1980) and *Truth or Dare* (1981), often starring his protégée Paula Meadows. Sullivan made his own tapes too. His *Whitehouse Video Show* and *Playbirds Video Show* series trod the thin line between hard and softcore and he also released compilations of other people's hardcore movies. John Lindsay, who had been in continuous hardcore production for well over a decade, saw his chance to reissue many of his 1970s' 8mm classics on video (some featuring Ava Cadell and the young Mary Millington), as well as shooting brand-new titles direct to video.

The 1980s saw a flourishing black market in illegally imported hardcore porn tapes. The Beate Uhse sex shop organisation, based in Germany, famously boasted that Britain was easily their most profitable market. Such was the demand for hardcore porn over here that the company distributed and sold over 10,000 video cassettes of one porn title alone between 1979 and 1983. *Color Climax* and *Private* tapes from Scandinavia were openly advertised in magazines and discreetly displayed behind the counter in Soho sex shops. For the best part of five years, tens of thousands of 'uncertificated' hardcore tapes from the US and Europe were illegally imported into Great Britain, where they were duplicated, distributed and sold.

To the dedicated porn lover and experienced masturbator, the arrival of video was a dream come true. No more tiresome trips into Soho for a wank in a draughty, cramped little cinema club full of other blokes all doing the same thing. No more fiddly home projectors, no tricky focusing, no more big cumbersome screens to put up, no 8mm film spools that split or tangled in the machine, no distracting projector noise to keep mother awake upstairs. Just invest in a top-loading VCR, slip in a porno tape, turn down the sound and play away!

However, the advent of the video age brought with it unforeseen consequences and an added headache for the authorities. Films on video, whether they were *The Exorcist*, Walt Disney's *Lady and the Tramp* or John Lindsay's *Oral Connection*, were all uncertificated. Unlike cinema films, the BBFC had no formal powers to certificate movies on video. With no governing body to regulate videotapes, the spread of previously unavailable films like *Deep Throat* continued unchecked. Soon the tabloids were chock-a-block with scare stories of impressionable teenagers exposed to 'nightmarish' adult material on video. The tapes vilified in the press were not, it must be noted, sex titles, but gory horror films like *I Spit on Your Grave* (1978), *The Driller Killer* (1979) and *Zombie Flesh Eaters* (1979). These and many other tapes like them were dubbed 'video nasties'. How can it be possible, argued the police, that films banned on the big screen are now readily available for viewing in the privacy of people's homes?

As a response, the Director of Public Prosecutions issued a list of potentially damaging titles. Spurred on by the apparent inconsistency in the law, Mary Whitehouse launched her campaign against video nasties as early as August 1980. Her National Viewers and Listeners Association called for immediate legislation to control 'this unacceptable video pornography'. She described the burgeoning video industry as 'the biggest ever threat to the quality of life in Britain.' Everything went back to the creaky old Obscene Publications Act of 1959 and what was deemed 'corrupting' and what was not. As always, juries were divided. But Whitehouse continued to whip up a frenzy of panic whenever she spoke in public, never more so than during the 1983 general election when she travelled round the Home Counties in a van emblazoned with the legend 'Children at Risk'. She relished recounting the tale of an adolescent boy who had become so addicted to porn and horror videos that his parents had noted how 'dark patches under his eyes had became a permanent feature, as well as weight loss, lack of concentration and illegible handwriting.'

In an attempt to curtail the sale of obscene videos, Tory MP Graham Bright championed his proposed Video Recordings Bill throughout the 1983 election. Intended to bring videos in line with the rest of the law, the bill was vocally supported by Mary Whitehouse, Margaret Thatcher and the Archbishop of Canterbury, Dr Robert Runcie. It proved to be a major vote-winner and contributed to Thatcher's re-election. By July 1984 it was on the statute books as the Video Recording Act. The new legislation solely concerned itself with the classification of videos. Any video which failed to obtain a classification was automatically deemed illegal. Unsurprisingly, the BBFC (the 'C' now standing for 'classification' rather than 'censors') was chosen by the Home Secretary to face the mountainous task of reclassifying in excess of 10,000 tapes from September 1985 onwards. The UK now had the strictest video controls in the whole of Europe.

The early '18' certificate sex videos were cut to shreds by the censor. The sexual partners would meet, there would be 20-odd minutes of close-ups of feet and orgasmic faces, a few long shots filmed from the back, 'optical softening' (ie, manipulation of the image so as to focus on only one enlarged area – a clean one, with genitals absent) creating a grainy look in certain scenes… and then the video would end and titles, if any, would roll. 'R18' videos fared little better but *were* allowed to show real sex, masturbation and more nudity, on condition that they were edited in such a way as to provide no *evidence* that the participants were doing it for real. The films were cut so heavily they looked all the more seedy and unpleasant.

Spurred into action by Mary Whitehouse, Sir Bernard Braine, Conservative MP for Castle Point, campaigned vigorously to ban the new 'R18' videos, but failed. Had he actually taken the trouble to view one he would have realised immediately that he had very little to worry about. Few could be genuinely offended by their content and – here's the real irony – the average punter couldn't buy them anyway. 'R18's were supposed to be available only from licensed sex shop premises. But since these were on the decrease you couldn't buy the tapes in the first place. By the late 1980s, video distributors had stopped submitting their films to the BBFC because they knew the movies would never turn a profit because there was nowhere for the public to buy them.

SEX ON TAPE

There was a continuation of the softcore sex comedy genre on video. *Take an Easy Ride* director Ken Rowles briefly flirted with video when he produced *The Perils of Mandy* (1981), the story of a dim-witted schoolgirl (Gloria Brittain) who escapes her seedy headmaster to pursue a career in modelling. She dances to Shirley Bassey's version of 'Light My Fire' at Bayswater's Concordia Restaurant only to get kidnapped and tied to a railway line by the headmaster's crooked associates. The video was left unfinished by Rowles and the existing footage was rendered almost incomprehensible by slipshod and disorderly editing. It's distinguished only by its opening titles, with credits written in red lipstick on two gyrating female arses.

Veteran filmmaker George Harrison Marks took to video like a duck to water with his 'schoolgirl caning' series from 1984, revealing just how bad a director he really was. Others totally turned their back on the new medium. The original Confessions series had transferred well to video and become a mainstay of video rental shops across the UK, but when Greg Smith was offered the chance to make a new film to be shot straight onto video in 1983, he declined. 'It would have looked tacky and the backers wanted to make it in something like three weeks,' he says. 'It would have compromised everything we had done before.'

For some young directors, video provided their first opportunity to make a movie. Filmed on location in Smarden, Kent, by rock star turned porn star Lindsay Honey, *Death Shock* (1982) was billed as a cheeky crossbreed of Hammer Horror and Carry On but failed to score in either department, despite plenty of unintentionally entertaining moments. A group of six over-ripe, sex-mad twenty-somethings stumble across a rural devil worshipping cult led by a kinky lord. Honey was good-humoured enough to include a reel of out-takes at the end entitled *It Will Be Alright on the Bed*, but it's not surprising that his largely inexperienced cast created over ten minutes of bloopers from a film that runs for little more than three quarters of an hour. Linzi Drew, however, playing the raunchy, simple-minded maid, deserved better dialogue than she was given.

Director Peter Kay and his Hove-based Strand International company nearly made home-made video an art form in *Sexy Secrets of the Kissogram Girls* (1985), *Sexy Secrets of the Sex Therapists* (1987), *Miss Adventures at Mega Boob Manor* (1987) and *The Will of Ebeneezer Grimsdyke* (1989). The videos, instantly recognisable by their bon-tempi organ music, mis-spelt credits, abrupt editing, juddery zooms, large-breasted 'actresses' and improvised dialogue, served as nothing more than lengthy and repetitive nude scenes strung together by the thinnest of plots. *Kissogram Girls*, which actually runs for a full 90 minutes, was the first video of its kind to cash in on the mid-eighties craze for unfeasibly enormous British boobs and created a right old rumpus when it was filmed in staid Devon seaside town, Exmouth. The lead actress, ex-*Mayfair* centrefold Zoe Lee, undergoes extensive 'training' at a posh country house to become a naked kissogram girl. Seeing her jogging in her leotard and doing topless aerobics with her 42DDs bouncing everywhere is an experience not easily forgotten. It's delightfully, charmingly awful. Other made-for-video sex shockers of the period included *The Naughty Dreams of Miss Owen* (1987), *The Initiants* (1988: billed as 'a film of rare quality', which is an understatement) and *Unbelievable Experience* (1989).

The *Electric Blue* video series was launched in 1979 by fashion photographer Adam Cole and publisher Paul Raymond. Initially sold by mail order and promoted in Raymond's magazines, within a couple of years the series became the most recognisable porn brand name in the UK. The tapes introduced to the world the first erotic video 'magazine' format, with each tape presenting sexy vignettes of girls-next-door stripping, nude 'wives' writhing on beds and wanking to camera, silly comedy sketches and archive material of nude celebrities all linked together by a glamorous talking head. It was no surprise to see Raymond's famous consort Fiona Richmond presenting *Electric Blue 001* (1979), but rather more eyebrow-raising to find Britt Ekland doing the same in 1980 for volume three. Other stars called upon to present various volumes included Desirée Cousteau, Seka and Marilyn Chambers. Over the years the *Electric Blue* brand proved itself consistently successful, often with three or four volumes released annually. Softcore, but certainly more explicit than many of their contemporaries, the series fought off numerous challengers and copycat labels and also branched out into magazine titles. *Electric Blue* productions and their ilk concentrated on subjects that were mainly left untouched by the BBFC, like lesbianism (no erections to get in the way), endless boob-rubbing and nipple-licking, mud wrestling, shower scenes, rubber fetishism and spanking. As already noted, the videos spawned a one-off excursion into cinema with *Electric Blue – The Movie* in 1981; 'as opposed to *Electric Blue – The Building Site* presumably,' wrote one waggish critic in *Film Review*.

The popularity of 1980s softcore did not in any way subdue the market for full-on hardcore material. There was a thriving underground market of unlicensed sex shops selling uncertificated material imported from the US and mainland Europe. The police continued their crackdown but a few dissenting voices were demanding a change to the ageing and unworkable Obscene Publications Act. The dissent dated back to the late seventies, when the Arts Council of Great Britain had produced a report on pornography in the UK, suggesting that the government consider suspending the Obscene Publications Act for a trial period to see whether the UK falling in line with the rest of Europe would have an adverse effect on British society. Prompted by this, in July 1977 Labour Prime Minister Jim Callaghan commissioned a Home Office report on obscenity and film censorship. The committee was headed by eminent philosopher Professor Bernard Williams and also featured a High Court judge, a former chief constable, a journalist, a bishop and a psychiatrist.

In October 1979 the Williams committee announced its findings, claiming that there was 'no evidence' to support any harmful side effects of pornography, recommending the abolition of the Obscene Publications Act and advocating the widespread opening of sex shops selling whatever sexual material they liked. Sadly, by the time the report was published, Labour had been ousted from power and the new

Left: New Romantic nightmares in *The Initiants* (1988).

Tory Home Secretary summarily rejected its findings, claiming the report was 'curiously inconclusive'. A campaign for the repeal of the Obscene Publications Act continued, headed by actor-turned-activist David Webb, who set about exposing the idiosyncratic and purely subjective standards of the British authorities.

Mary Millington had already become almost a martyr to the cause. In her suicide note to David Sullivan, she wrote that 'The police have framed me yet again … I do so hope that porn is legal one day, they called me obscene names for being in possession of it and I can't go through any more … Please print in your magazines how much I wanted porn legalised.' But Mary's desperate plea went unheeded. The British establishment insisted that the UK was to remain steadfast and isolated in its attitude towards porn, while the BBFC, Canute-like, continued to hold back the rising tide of European 'filth'.

The demand for more explicit films continued unabated for 20 years. By the mid-1990s the Obscene Publications Squad was seizing and incinerating in excess of 100,000 tapes annually. But the Metropolitan Police were fighting a losing battle. If a sex establishment was raided in the morning, clearing out the entire stock, the shopkeeper could easily have his shelves entirely restocked by the afternoon. Where once protection rackets, pimping and dealing in illegal firearms had kept the criminal fraternity of Soho busy, the ease and profitability of video piracy proved far more appealing to them. In anonymous lock-ups and garages, rows upon rows of video duplication machines were busy making copies of hardcore tapes to be sold in Soho sex shops. The authorities had little trouble arresting the man behind the counter, sending him to court and fining him a derisory sum, but they rarely apprehended the 'Mr Bigs' of the business.

In an attempt to beat the authorities at their own game, hardcore sex shops often filled over 95 per cent of their shelf space with battered paperback novels, water-damaged tapes of *Only Fools and Horses* and ex-rental made-for-TV videos. No license is required if less than five per cent of overall stock is sex-related. The imprecisely worded Local Government (Miscellaneous Provisions) Act of 1982 defines a sex establishment only as 'a shop selling sexual articles of any significant degree'. Some sex shops filled their premises with slimming pills and vitamins, with hardcore stashed under the counter. Despite 'Private Shop' still being emblazoned over the door, they had the gall to call themselves 'Health Food Shops'.

These illegal outfits were usually based in London, yet provincial sex shops often contained a smattering of hardcore tapes and could certainly order virtually anything the customer wanted at an exorbitant price. Seventies films like *Queen of the Blues* and *Confessions of a Sex Maniac* were repackaged in startlingly explicit covers showing full-colour penetration shots (quite blatantly taken from a more contemporary European magazine) and passed off as 'hardcore Scandinavian sex comedies', all for £50 a throw. Hardcore tapes were openly advertised in top-shelf magazines (almost to saturation point within the pages of David Sullivan's *Daily Sport* newspaper), and often with hilariously straight-to-the point titles: *Lesbians in Wellies*, *Fat and Recently Divorced*, *Pakistani Women Having Sex in Unusual Places* and so on.

SEX: THE SECOND COMING

In 1991, a revitalised genre of British film-making burst, seemingly out of nowhere, onto video store shelves: the sex education tape. Throwing the authorities into disarray and setting new standards with their explicit imagery and language, the tapes showed unsimulated penetrative sex, oral sex and masturbation, marking the first time that the BBFC had passed such scenes in its 78-year history. The groundbreaker was *The Lovers' Guide* (1991), created and presented by psychosexual therapist Dr Andrew Stanway, which stirred up howls of disgust among the readers of the *Daily Mail*. The tapes did not in any way promote promiscuity, but instead stressed the need for commitment and understanding. However, the calm and collected voice-overs were sometimes at odds with the extremely explicit images. Many viewers preferred to turn down the sound and just watch the pictures *sans* commentary. The emphasis leaned heavily towards titillation and offered many video collectors their first chance to buy a 'porno movie' legally in the UK.

When high street newsagent W H Smith agreed to stock the '18' certificate title, *The Lovers' Guide* suddenly became very big news indeed. Detective Superintendent Michael Hames, head of Scotland Yard's

KEEPING THE BRITISH END UP

Left: The Lovers' Guide was a home video phenomenon in the 1990s.

Obscene Publications Squad, attacked the 'slack' censorship laws which allowed 'pornographic videos to go on sale in the high street masquerading as sex education.' The public obviously disagreed, as *The Lovers' Guide* shifted an incredible 500,000 copies in less than 12 months and was followed by a rush of copycat titles in 1992, including *Making Love*, *A Woman's Guide to Loving Sex*, *Better Sex for Lovers*, plus two sequels to the original *Lovers' Guide*. The videos harked back, of course, to an age nearly 20 years previously: the dark days of David Grant's *Love Variations*, when the only way to sneak smut in through the back door was to have sex scenes interspersed with the musings of a medical 'expert'. The 1990s pundits were slightly more animated and jolly than their predecessors, however, and included psychologists, sex therapists and marriage counsellors. Even TV hypnotherapist Paul McKenna slipped through the net somehow.

While the *Daily Mail* contingent continued to be disgusted (fuelled, no doubt, by a helpful double-page spread in the paper with accompanying stills), the videos carried on being big sellers throughout the mid-1990s. The BBFC made it clear that the films were purely for 'educational' purposes and the video producers were quick to point out that most of the participants were 'real-life married couples'. Funnily enough, several of the models went on to become bona fide porn stars in their own right, appearing in several 'under the counter' productions thereafter. Ultimately, two of the most controversial but genuinely well-intentioned sex education titles, *The Gay Man's Guide to Safer Sex* (1992) and *Getting It Right* (1993), managed to clear up several ugly misconceptions about the spread of HIV and AIDS and further pushed back the barriers of what the BBFC deemed acceptable. Despite the homosexual sex education tapes being tailored to a very specific market, *The Gay Man's Guide* sold 20,000 copies in just three months (much to the horror of Christian family groups) and immediately went to number one in the video sell-through chart.

The sex education boom also paved the way for another neglected video 'art form' to make an appearance in high street video outlets. Male striptease had been spoofed in movies like *The Love Pill* (1971) and *The Sexplorer* (1975), and documented in James Katz's *The Rise and Fall of Ivor Dickie* in 1977, but never before had it been fully exploited as an entertainment for women. The craze for naked male flesh first erupted in Britain when a heavily muscled American dance troupe, the Chippendales, arrived for a club tour in the late eighties, causing a sensation among British women more used to native beer bellies and saggy arses. Rival British striptease troupes imitated their act and within the space of a few years even the most upmarket of nightclubs were bulging at the seams with 'women only nights'.

Video cashed in on the new sensation with dozens of titles, mostly filmed on location in Essex venues awash with dry ice, hairspray and hyperventilating women. It was the release of *London Knights* in 1991 that really created a stir, however. As well as buffed buttocks and twitching pectorals, the cheeky chappies in *London Knights* offered a little (and sometimes a rather big) extra – full-frontal nudity. Well-oiled, semi-erect cocks could be seen dangled in ladies' faces, all in the name of home entertainment, although the BBFC discouraged too many lingering close-ups.

To some degree the popularity of *The Lovers' Guide* and *London Knights* paved the way for a greater sexualisation of British entertainment throughout the 1990s. The expansion of cable television created a brand-new market for pornography. In 1993 a Holland-based adult film channel, Red Hot Dutch, began beaming non-stop hardcore into Britain via a European satellite, creating media outcry and lurid headlines in every daily newspaper. Powerless to physically block the signal, the government instead made it impossible to purchase the decoder cards required to access the service. Other porn channels like Rendezvous, TV1000, FilmNet and TV Erotica tried the same trick, while softer British-based cable channels like Playboy TV, Television X and The Adult Channel provided new opportunities for sex film producers. But did it really matter where the porn was being broadcast from? With the

204

Right: Shirley Stelfox, Anthony Collin and Julie Walters in Terry Jones' *Personal Services* (1987).

massive expansion of the internet, the global communications network made terrestrial borders irrelevant. The British were gradually coming round to the idea that with the tap of a computer keyboard you could obtain whatever flavour of pornography you wanted, providing access to material which the rest of the Western world had taken for granted since the late 1960s.

In 1986 Labour MP Clare Short had put forward a proposal to outlaw topless models in newspapers like the *Sun* and the *Star*, at the same time supporting a well-publicised feminist 'Off the Shelf' campaign which demanded that even soft porn titles like *Mayfair* and *Playboy* should be removed from high street newsagents and dumped in the fast-disappearing licensed sex shops. If Ms Short could have foreseen the revolution just around the corner, she probably wouldn't have wasted her time. Later that year David Sullivan launched his newspaper the *Sunday Sport*, promising more than just breasts on page three, and in 1992 came *For Women* and *Women on Top*, the first British porn magazines to be aggressively marketed at young women. *Desire* came next, aimed squarely at couples of every sexual persuasion. Soon high street newsagents' shelves were bulging with new titles tailored to every sexual whim. Customs were even turning a blind eye to imported magazines showing erections, like *Hustler* or *Black Inches*, encouraging old British reliables like *Whitehouse* and *Playbirds* to jump on the stiffy bandwagon. *British Sex*, the first hardcore magazine to be openly published in the UK, was launched in 1998 and European imports *Private* and *Color Climax* were on public display in corner shops around the country.

On the lower shelves the new breed of 'lads mags' fought for space. *FHM*, *Loaded*, *Maxim* and *GQ* flourished on a monthly diet of scantily clad cover girls and articles on wanking and blue films. Even long-established film magazines devoted whole issues to the history of the pornographic movie. Home entertainment retailers like HMV and Virgin devoted large sections of their stores to '18' certificate sex videos and in 1997 London's Olympia Exhibition Centre played host to Britain's first Erotica trade fair, attracting as many women as men. The sex toy and bondage demonstrations were a huge hit with an enquiring British public and the queues of visitors weren't shy about being approached by television journalists anxious to know what 'Tina from Tooting' made of it all. Suddenly sex was trendy again.

THE EARTH MOVES

Sex at the cinema, while far less prevalent than it had been during the 1970s, maintained a select presence in the nation's ABCs and Odeons. Incredibly, *Come Play with Me* was still playing in selected theatres around the provinces until as late as 1985. Sex just for the sake of it was increasingly frowned upon by the politically correct British censor but, naturally, sex for art's sake was quite acceptable, as Peter Greenaway proved in his kinky movies *A Zed and Two Noughts* (1985), *The Cook, The Thief, His Wife and Her Lover* (1989) and *The Pillow Book* (1996). A few British films actually persevered with the once-potent mix of sex and comedy, albeit in a much diluted form. *Personal Services*, released in 1987, starred Julie Walters as infamous brothel-keeper Cynthia Payne and suddenly made prostitution a dinner table conversation point. The grimly funny *Rita, Sue and Bob Too* (1986) looked at threesomes on a council estate and Mel Smith's *The Tall Guy* (1989) featured one of the funniest and most energetic sex scenes yet seen on screen. (Participants: Emma Thompson and Jeff Goldblum.) *Wilt* (1989) centred on the misadventures of an inflatable doll and *Preaching to the Perverted* (1997) was a brave, but flawed, attempt to make S & M funny.

The Big Swap (1998), filmed in the sedate Somerset seaside town of Clevedon, harked back to Stanley Long's productions nearly 30 years before with its story of mass wife-swapping. Male nudity captured the public imagination in *The Full Monty*

Left: Bored Bradford teens Siobhan Finneran and Michelle Holmes in Alan Clarke's *Rita, Sue and Bob Too* (1987).

(1997), about a group of unemployed steelworkers who form a striptease troupe and find their fortune. The film created an international sensation and spawned a thousand copycat theatre revues. For a while British moviegoers became oblivious to men in the buff, with the once-taboo penis almost becoming commonplace. Scottish heart-throb Ewan McGregor famously exposed his dick in *Trainspotting* (1996) and seemingly got it out in every one of his movies thereafter. Grittier depictions of British sex were passed in *Stella Does Tricks* (1996), a disturbing story of teenage prostitution which brought back memories of Tony Garnett's bleak 1980 Birmingham docudrama *Prostitute*, and *The Acid House* (1997), with its seedy, and realistic, images of anal intercourse. Over the past two decades the BBFC has become ever-more relaxed about sex in the movies. Cut films diminished from 40 per cent of the total in 1974 to under four per cent by 1998. The boom in big screen shagging stimulated some BBFC examiners to jokingly dub themselves the 'British Board of Fuck Counters'.

In 1997, three hardcore videos were passed by the BBFC on an experimental, 'suck it and see' basis. Though cut, the tapes showed erections, penetrative sex and oral sex. One was US production *Batbabe* (1995), the others were home-grown tapes *Charlie's Private Sessions* and *Ladies Behaving Badly* (both 1997), and all three were distributed by Shropshire-based Prime Time Productions. Lacking extreme close-ups and minus any scenes of ejaculation, the videos could, if anything, be described as 'medium core'. It was really a little piece of history in the making, taking everybody by surprise.

James Ferman described the 'crazy situation' whereby he spent all his time deciding upon the acceptability of movie releases at the BBFC while his top-floor office in Soho Square overlooked the biggest porn business in Britain. Each day Ferman had to live with the ridiculous anomaly of an alternative, uncertificated film network operating on his own doorstep. He criticised the police and magistrates for a heavy-handed interpretation of the Obscene Publications Act and for persecuting members of the public who wanted stronger material. 'I think Britain is trying not to be repressive,' he told the *Times* in August 1998, 'but the public are prepared to go further than the regime within which the censors have to work and I think the police are way behind public taste.' He was accused of overstepping the mark when he started allowing more explicit 'R18' videos to be released while conveniently forgetting to inform the police. Ferman didn't see sex as a threat to British society, preferring to concentrate his efforts on violence in films. There was no evidence, he argued, that civilised societies in Holland and Germany were awash with widespread sexual depravity due to the relaxation of sexually explicit material.

In 1998, David Sullivan's Sheptonhurst video distribution company submitted a hardcore American tape, *Makin' Whoopee!*, which was awarded an 'R18' certificate with minor cuts. Pro-family campaigner John Beyer, Mary Whitehouse's limp successor as head of the NVALA, got wind of the BBFC's new attitude and publicly criticised Home Secretary Jack Straw for failing to restrain the ongoing efforts of the 'depraved pornographers who continually test the boundaries of decency.' Straw was furious at not being kept up-to-date with developments at the BBFC and ordered an immediate halt to the more explicit tapes. The following year Sheptonhurst, pleased with the *Makin' Whoopee!* result, submitted a further seven hardcore tapes, including *Nympho Nurse Nancy*, *Office Tart* and *Wet Nurses 2*, but were surprised to see all of them rejected outright. Smarting from the BBFC's decision, Sheptonhurst complained to the Video Appeals Committee (VCA), which ruled, by a majority of four to one, that the BBFC had been wrong in not granting the tapes a certificate and that the films should be made available as 'R18'. The BBFC wasn't happy at having its decision overturned and, in a tit-for-tat move, sought a judicial review from the High Court in May 2000.

The Court upheld the VCA's findings and this damning result had serious implications for the BBFC. As a result, the Board

Right: Mel Smith and Griff Rhys Jones with their inflatable co-star Angelique in 1989's saucy comedy *Wilt*.

drew up new guidelines which were published in September 2000. Aroused genitalia, masturbation, penetrative sex, oral sex, group sex and ejaculation would all be allowed in 'R18' videos, uncut, with no distinction between heterosexual and homosexual activity. Only degrading material (like child porn, coprophilia and extreme sexual violence) was exempt, and therefore illegal. It was a landmark decision that left the Home Office spluttering and took the porn fraternity by surprise. 'Now for the very first time you can see hardcore porn legally,' says a triumphant David Sullivan. 'All that stuff with the Video Appeals Committee changed the law. In fact, *we* changed the law. If you'd told me ten years ago that we'd be in this situation I'd never have believed it. Certainly not in my lifetime. In defence of the BBFC I think they've laid down a very healthy set of rules. They're right to say no to pissing and degrading stuff, but getting normal sex passed in videos is extremely good news.'

The BBFC examiners were apparently sent on an exhaustive, week-long hardcore porn course in order to brace themselves for the new era of film classification. When they returned they could barely cope with the huge backlog of hardcore tapes submitted by producers rushing to get their films classified. 'We never had a market in this country before,' says Linzi Drew, partner of sex legend Ben Dover. 'It's been a sudden change, but we're all for it. The key thing is that sex should be consensual and I think the BBFC has finally come round to accepting that nobody is forced into making porn films.'

Ben Dover, the 'Housewive's Choice' in British porn, has been making his own hardcore tapes since 1995 and has clocked up somewhere in the region of 50 titles so far. Dover, also known as Lindsay Honey, directed *Death Shock* back in 1982 and became a popular model in the pages of David Sullivan's magazines and in other people's films before taking the plunge with his own company, producing immensely popular 'camcorder classics' like *Little Smart Arses*, *Housewives' Fantasies Part 1* and *English Porno Groupies 2*. As of 2000 the British public could finally see his films uncut.

'The new ruling on porn videos has opened up the British market a lot,' says enormously endowed black British porn star Omar Williams. 'But you have to look for names you can trust, just like you look for Cruise or Schwarzenegger at the cinema. The public want good quality tapes like mine or Ben Dover's. Unfortunately you can still only buy hardcore in the 90 or so sex shops in this country. I'd like to see 300 or so.' Northampton-born, Williams has made 20 volumes of his *Amazing Omar Triumphs* series on his Big Willy label in three years. In tongue-in-cheek videos like *Big Black Shagger*, Williams plays for laughs as much as titillation, taking the role of a cheeky, ever-beaming innocent abroad, a kind of Robin Askwith for the new millennium only you get to see him have real sex. 'I loved the Confessions films,' says Williams. 'When I was a schoolboy I'd sneak round to a mate's house and watch those type of movies, Robin Askwith, Russ Meyer, all that. I've always found them funny and my videos certainly have similarities. I use that cheeky approach in my films, like being a window cleaner, an estate agent or sex toy demonstrator. Comedy makes porn films much more accessible and I've always wanted to give my videos a lot more humour than my contemporaries. The Confessions were raunchy for their time, but you see everything in mine!'

SEX ON THE TELLY

The dawn of the new millennium saw a stylish makeover of many of the sex shop premises in the heart of London, thanks in the main to the demand for the new 'R18' classification. 'Soho has managed to fight back thanks to the new ruling on videos,' reckons David McGillivray. 'We're going back to the way it was in the seventies now. You can walk down Brewer Street and it's virtually the same as it was back then, only cleaner. Britain is now experiencing the thrill of buying legal hardcore films, which everyone else in Europe has been doing for the last 20 or 30 years. It's lovely to see the expressions on people's faces; they had no idea that hardcore tapes came with covers, so used were they to seeing tenth-generation bootleg copies of porn films. Inevitably it will become a novelty, but I hope it continues for a while

KEEPING THE BRITISH END UP

Left: Early 1980s video makeover for *Erotic Inferno*.

yet because it's such a thrill.'

On average, each Soho sex shop now makes in excess of a quarter of a million pounds in profit every year. At the time of writing there are 16 licensed sex shops in Soho and a further 18 unlicensed premises, but while Westminster Council still regularly raids the illegal premises few shops are actually prosecuted. 'Juries never give a guilty verdict any more,' says one licensing officer for Westminster Council. 'We're only looking for dodgy 'Section II' material now: child porn, bestiality and violent stuff. The licensed premises are greatly improved and we don't have to bother them. They're run like proper businesses and they have to be because the owners are forking out annual licenses of £22,500 and they want to see a good profit. The public are Westminster's masters if you like and, to be honest, sex shops attract very little criticism nowadays.'

The sexualisation of Great Britain has also edged its way into the nation's sitting rooms, with more liberal TV companies prepared to dish the dirt after the nine o'clock watershed. In Desmond Morris' *The Human Animal* series, broadcast on BBC1 in 1994, a model had a camera inserted in her vagina to show how her body reacted when her male partner made love to her. To broadcast that would have been unthinkable even five years previously, yet 13 million eager viewers tuned in. Channel 4, launched in 1982, had originally paved the way to more sexually explicit material on late-night TV but in 1997 handed over the baton to the excitable Channel 5, which tended to programme sex every night of the week. Several TV series embraced porn culture and sex like never before, pushing the limits of the broadcasting regulators. Series like *British Sex* (Sky 1998), *Sex and Shopping* (C5 1999), *Pornography: The Secret History of Civilisation* (C4 1999), *European Blue Review* (C5 2000), *Vice: Inside Britain's Sex Business* (ITV 2001), as well as countless one-off documentaries, were all guaranteed to get more than just the nation's net curtains twitching. Many, though not all, focused on the sleazier or more comical side of the sex business. Viewers didn't have to search the *TVTimes* very hard to find listings of any amount of sexually orientated material.

By the 1990s there was little evidence left of the Great British sex film boom of the sixties and seventies, with only the perennially popular Confessions movies being periodically re-packaged and re-released, while more obscure titles like *Girls Come First* and *What's Up Nurse?* occasionally turned up in dog-eared boxes with sun-bleached covers. It wasn't until 1992, when David McGillivray collected his thoughts and recollections on the sex film era and put them into his book *Doing Rude Things*, that various film historians began to sit up and take notice. In the post-modern age, where everything has some sort of intrinsic value, the great British sex film was well overdue for reappraisal.

A tongue-in-cheek documentary based on McGillivray's book, also called *Doing Rude Things*, was broadcast on BBC2 in May 1995 and scored a very impressive 4.93 million viewers. The following year Channel 4 produced an informative and moving documentary called *Sex & Fame: The Mary Millington Story*, which placed our Number One sex star in her historical context and hailed her as an icon of the seventies. These documentaries elicited a sudden rash of official sex film re-releases, first on video, then on DVD. Exactly 20 years to the month after its original release, *Come Play with Me* débuted on the Medusa label in April 1997, swiftly followed by a shed-load of long-forgotten and previously unavailable movies, some of which, critics were wicked enough to comment, 'should have stayed unavailable'.

Channel 5 must be applauded for providing British viewers not only with their first terrestrial showing of the *Emmanuelle* series but also for staking their claim on never-before-screened British sex comedies, including *Adventures of a Taxi Driver*, *The Amorous Milkman*, *Hardcore* and *Rosie Dixon – Night Nurse*. Even the BBC took the plunge by screening *Keep it Up Downstairs* (1976), albeit after midnight and cautiously editing out all of the sex and most of the nudity. What seems utterly incredible is that, despite healthy video sales and frequent cable showings,

208

Right: Will we ever see their like again? Robin Askwith and Tony Booth in Confessions from a Holiday Camp (1977).

it took terrestrial TV over 20 years to realise the ratings potential of *Confessions of a Window Cleaner*, Britain's number one film of 1974. Even more startling is that *Come Play with Me* has never been screened. Regular showings of Robin Askwith's bum have proved to be amazingly popular and Channel 5 has invested in a complete catalogue of nostalgic naughtiness. Even the likes of *The Ups and Downs of a Handyman* (1975) could easily score two million viewers in a single showing, proving itself to be perfect Friday night, post-pub entertainment.

'They're always shown on a Friday night when people are probably too drunk to care what they're watching,' observes David McGillivray cynically. 'Apart from a few film historians who know the story behind the making of these movies, I don't think it's possible for anybody else to sit through them. I doubt that the audience for this sort of material has ever stopped existing, but I think people would rather be sitting at home watching hardcore videos now.' Veteran director Stanley Long agrees. 'I don't think the sex comedy era has died,' he says. 'It's still there, only it's been taken over by TV. If a television channel wants to increase its audience they put boobs on. If they could put hardcore on TV to get viewers they'd do it and at the end of the day they probably will.'

A NEW ERA?

Just as home entertainment has been revolutionised, so there have also been significant changes in the BBFC's attitude towards sex in the cinema. In 1998 the BBFC allowed Lars von Trier's *The Idiots*, featuring unsimulated group sex scenes, to be released to British cinemas, followed a year later by *Romance*, featuring Rocco Siffredi, a veteran of over 1000 hardcore videos. Despite very explicit sex scenes, the movie was released uncut after being classed 'a serious work' by examiners. The fact that it was directed by a woman, Catherine Breillat, presumably did it no harm either. *Intimacy* (2000), filmed in London by another French director, Patrice Chéreau, became the first mainstream English language movie with unsimulated sex scenes to be passed uncut in Great Britain. Even more startling was the fact that the participants were both 'names', Kerry Fox and Mark Rylance. The movie's two-hour running time included a horny half hour of erections, blow-jobs and bonking. All this despite the prevalent thinking at the BBFC that 'images of real sex will usually be brief and justified by content'.

In recent years there have been persistent rumours that there are plans to revive the most famous of all the British sex film series, the Confessions. Robin Askwith certainly seemed keen. 'I'm ready. My backside's still in pretty good shape!' he told the *Sunday Times* in 1995. But would a Confessions film for the 21st century actually work? Would it have to contain hardcore sex scenes? Any chance of a revival is refuted by producer Greg Smith. 'No, it won't happen,' he says. 'I wouldn't make another one now for a King's ransom. I love the movies and love talking about them, but in this politically correct world some people might find them verging on the objectionable. And if you made them politically correct they just wouldn't be funny.'

With the 1970s revival in full flow and famous American porno movies like *Deep Throat* and *The Devil in Miss Jones* finally getting uncut releases in Britain, along with once-problematic S & M drama *Story of O* being theatrically released here 25 years after the rest of Europe, can it be long before the uncut version of *Come Play with Me* finally sees the light of day? 'There is still a huge market for well-made sex films today,' reckons David Sullivan. 'If they were making sexy cinema movies with a good story, some funny scenes plus a bit of penetration then I think they'd be very popular, that's if only the cinema chains would show them, of course. If I could market one like that then I could make it tremendously successful.' Few would doubt the word of the most successful marketing man ever, so maybe we could be entering a new golden era of British sex films… ✲

KEEPING THE BRITISH END UP

KNOBS AND KNOCKERS

THE BIGGEST BOYS AND GIRLS IN BRITISH SEX FILM HISTORY

Left: Pamela Green was Britain's glamour superstar of the 1950s and 60s.

This is purely a personal choice, but listed here are the most influential and interesting movers and shakers in British sex film history.

Hazel ADAIR (1921-)

One of the most unlikely participants in British sex movies would have to be writer-producer and soap opera queen Hazel Adair. In 1955 she devised and wrote one of Britain's first ever daily TV serials, *Sixpenny Corner* for Associated Rediffusion, and later was co-creator (with Peter Ling) of *Compact* (1962-65) and, most famously, *Crossroads* (1964-88). In 1970 she formed Pyramid Films with fearsome *Cool For Cats* DJ and wrestling commentator Kent Walton, the partners using the joint pseudonym Elton Hawke, and produced the sexcoms *Clinic Xclusive* and *Can You Keep It Up For a Week?* After the partnership was exposed by a newspaper in 1975, the pair reverted to their real names for 1976's *Keep It Up Downstairs*. In 1979 Adair changed genres when she produced the thriller *Game For Vultures*, recycling several faces from her sex film past. There was an outcry when *Crossroads* was axed in 1988 after 4,510 episodes but, like the proverbial phoenix from the flames, the motel doors re-opened in the spring of 2001, with a burst of tabloid publicity and a £10 million revamp.

GENRE CREDITS: *Virgin Witch* (1971) (co-producer/co-composer of theme song), *Clinic Xclusive* (1971) (co-producer/co-writer), *Can You Keep It Up For a Week?* (1974) (producer/co-composer of song), *Keep It Up Downstairs* (1976) (producer/writer)

Michael ARMSTRONG (1944-)

Armstrong is a RADA-trained actor who turned to directing in 1968 with a 14-minute short, *The Image*, starring an up-and-coming David Bowie. The same year he directed and co-wrote *The Haunted House of Horror*, a grim and gruesome vehicle for Frankie Avalon of all people. In 1970 he helmed the notoriously violent *Mark of the Devil* (*Hexen bis aufs Blut gequaelt*) in Germany, which is yet to be released in the UK uncut. He contributed to his first sex film in 1973, co-writing (under an assumed name) and appearing in Tudor Gates' *The Sex Thief*, although it's his sardonic script for *Eskimo Nell* which gained him most critical praise. Armstrong worked extensively for producer-director Stanley Long and completed a saucy script for the unfilmed Sex Pistols movie, *A Star is Dead*, due to have been directed by Pete Walker. On television he has worked on series like *The Saint* and *The Professionals*. Today he is managing director of Armstrong Arts, whose national tour in 2000 of Strindberg's infamous *Miss Julie* was dubbed a 'sex shocker' by the local press and billed as 'the play they want to ban'.

GENRE CREDITS: *The Sex Thief* (1973) (actor/co-writer), *Eskimo Nell* (1974) (actor/writer), *Adventures of a Taxi Driver* (1975) (actor/associate producer), *It Could Happen to You* aka *Intimate Teenage Secrets* (1976) (writer), *Adventures of a Private Eye* (1977) (associate producer/writer), *Adventures of a Plumber's Mate* (1977) (casting)

Robin ASKWITH (1950-)

A blond mop-topped cheeky monkey, Askwith perfected his chosen role of suburban jack-the-lad in films like *The Four Dimensions of Greta* (1972), *Bless This House* (1972) and *Carry On Girls* (1973) before being offered the role he will always be associated with, Timothy Lea. The four *Confessions* films made his name worldwide and in 1975 he was voted 'most promising newcomer' by the *Evening News*. 'I'm not sure that there'll ever be another Robin Askwith,' admits *Confessions* producer Greg Smith. 'He has the ability to be rude and drop his strides and not offend anybody. That is an incredible talent!' When the series was scrapped in 1977, Askwith continued his ribald adventures on stage. *The Further Confessions of a Window Cleaner* (1978), directed by none other than Val Guest, cleaned up in theatres around the world. Further stage work followed and, a decade after Timmy Lea's first appearance, Askwith created a similar character, saucy milkman Dave Deacon, in LWT's sitcom *The Bottle Boys* (1984-1985), which at its height attracted nine million viewers a week. Askwith is still busy today in stage farces and guest appearances on television. He cropped up again at the cinema, rather unexpectedly, in Hollywood blockbuster *U-571* (2000), as a herpes-ridden merchant sailor who gets shot by the Germans. 'I'd never been offered anything like this,' he admitted at the time. 'In England, you know, I'm just a trouser-dropping imbecile!' Ironically, his character was billed as 'British Seaman'.

GENRE CREDITS: *Cool It Carol* (1970), *The Four Dimensions of Greta* (1972), *Confessions of a Window Cleaner* (1974), *Confessions of a Pop Performer* (1975), *Confessions of a Driving Instructor* (1976), *Stand Up Virgin Soldiers* (1977), *Confessions from a Holiday Camp* (1977), *Let's Get Laid!* (1977), *Doing Rude Things* (TV 1995)

Pat ASTLEY

Two sides of Pat Astley in *Queen of the Blues* (1979).

Blackpool-born Pat moved to London with her baby daughter in the early 1970s and made fleeting appearances in hardcore 16mm shorts for John Lindsay and George Harrison Marks including *Nymphomania*, *End of Term* and *Doctor Sex*. In the pages of *Whitehouse* and *Private* she was often paired with Mary Millington and the two women became good friends. In 1977 she got her big break in television (albeit uncredited and rapidly replaced by Vivienne Johnson), as Young Mr Grace's leggy nurse in the saucy sitcom *Are You Being Served?* Suddenly, her career in 'X'-rated films really started to take off. Pat is great in *The Playbirds*, despite falling foul of the murderer in the film's first five minutes, and in 1984 gained her meatiest film role as a nude model (what else?) in the unpleasant slasher flick *Don't Open Till Christmas*. Now completely retired from acting, she apparently works part-time in a shop in Lancashire.

GENRE CREDITS: *I'm Not Feeling Myself Tonight!* (1975), *Come Play with Me* (1977), *Let's Get Laid!* (1977), *Adventures of a Plumber's Mate* (1977), *Rosie Dixon – Night Nurse* (1978), *The Playbirds* (1978), *The Stud* (1978), *You're Driving Me Crazy!* (1978), *Queen of the Blues* (1979), *The World is Full of Married Men* (1979)

Nicola AUSTINE

In a 13-year film career, Nicola enlivened any film in which she appeared. In 1972's *Commuter Husbands*, for example, she steals the show as a seductive 'dream girl' scurrying naked through the English countryside. Constantly in demand throughout the 1970s, she was often credited as Nikki, Nicole or Nicky, with a variety of spellings of her surname. In addition to her sex film work she was an uncredited participant in a Roman orgy in the film of *Up Pompeii* (1970) (undoubtedly her bare boobs helped the movie get an 'AA' rating); one of Hywel Bennett's fantasy women in *It's a 2' 6" Above the Ground World* (1972) and a Playboy bunny in *Vampira* (1974). She was also a *Sun* Page Three girl and *Top of the Pops* record sleeve model. In 1976 she appeared on the paperback cover of *Confessions of a Driving Instructor*, although she didn't feature in the movie. She also made a rather self-conscious appearance, as herself, in Peter Cook and Dudley Moore's filthy documentary *Derek and Clive Get the Horn* and, bizarrely, featured as a sex-change strongman named Bruce (with dubbed butch voice) in Lindsay Shonteff's *Licensed to Love and Kill* (both 1979).

GENRE CREDITS: *Secrets of Sex* (1969), *Cool It Carol* (1970), *Permissive* (1970), *Suburban Wives* (1971), *Not Tonight Darling!* (1971), *The Love Box* (1971), *Commuter Husbands* (1972), *Clinic Xclusive* (1972), *On the Game* (1973), *Come Play with Me* (1977), *Adventures of a Private Eye* (1977), *What's Up Superdoc?* (1978), *Queen of the Blues* (1979), *The World is Full of Married Men* (1979), *Sex with the Stars* (1980), *Nutcracker* (1982)

Derek AYLWARD (1922-)

A native of Maidenhead, Aylward entered the British film industry as a child actor. His largest role came as Charles Wesley in the 1954 religious biopic *John Wesley*, funded by the Methodist Church of Britain, and other roles followed in *The Trials of Oscar Wilde* (1960) and John Schlesinger's *Darling* (1965). His rebirth as a performer in 'X'-rated productions was down to director Pete Walker, who starred Aylward in four of his early exploitation movies including *The Big Switch* (1968) and *Man of Violence* (1970). His preferred roles were amoral ex-army cads who drank dry Martinis or raffish old lechers with an eye for underage girls. After *Cool It Carol* a fallow period followed, during which he called upon his military knowledge for several army recruitment documentaries. Then in 1976 he had a cameo role in *Come Play with Me* and was asked by director Harrison Marks to perform in a hardcore sequence with young popsie Lisa Taylor, an actress half his age. 'I didn't have to persuade the old bugger at all,' commented Marks. 'He hadn't been laid for years!' Aylward subsequently starred, albeit anonymously, in a series of 8mm shorts with titles like *Super Sex Shop* and *Wet Dreams* and nude layouts (some with Mary Millington) in David Sullivan's top-shelf publications. Thereafter he seemingly disappeared off the face of the earth.

GENRE CREDITS: *I Like Birds* (1967), *School For Sex* (1968), *Cool It Carol* (1970), *Come*

Play with Me (1977), *The Playbirds* (1978)

Antony BALCH (1937-1980)

A legendary Wardour Street distributor, Antony Balch originally trained as a film editor and production assistant. In 1963 he saw the infamous American film *Freaks* (1931) and reportedly became a film distributor for the sole reason of finally bringing the movie to a British audience. Throughout his flamboyant career, Balch indiscriminately bought up sexploitation pictures, American oddities and European arthouse films by the shed-load for exhibition at his two London cinemas, the Jacey in Piccadilly Circus and the Times Baker Street. Besides his distribution business, Balch was a close friend of American 'beat generation' novelist William Burroughs and together they collaborated on two avant-garde shorts, *Towers Open Fire* (1963) and *The Cut Ups* (1966), the former featuring Balch masturbating in his poorly lit bedroom, a scene the censor seemingly slept through. It was Balch's dream to film the 'unfilmable' Burroughs novel *The Naked Lunch* with Mick Jagger in the lead role. What materialised instead, in 1969, was the strikingly weird portmanteau picture, *Secrets of Sex*, aptly retitled *Bizarre* in the US. He made only one other feature, a more traditionally structured horror-comedy called *Horror Hospital* in 1972, starring a pre-Confessions Robin Askwith. Balch died of stomach cancer in April 1980, aged only 43.

GENRE CREDIT: *Secrets of Sex* (1969)

Anna BERGMAN (1949-)

Born in Sweden, Anna first bared all in 1967 for the film *The Crooked World of Art*, but later realised she'd been hired for novelty value. 'Ingmar Bergman's daughter without her clothes on gave the film a lot of publicity,' she observed in 1976. She moved to London in the late 1960s and carved out a successful career as a model. She subsequently starred in a succession of well-received sex comedies, starting in 1975 with the Anglo-German *Penelope Pulls it Off*. Anna famously didn't get on with director Harrison Marks on the set of *Come Play with Me*. She complained to Equity, the actors' union, about the film's hardcore content and refused point blank to strip off, telling the *News of the World* that 'I'm fully dressed all the way through and I don't want to be associated with anything nasty!' She disrobed for several films thereafter, however, and in Denmark even appeared in two out-and-out hardcore movies, directed by Werner Hedman, in which her softcore nude scenes were intercut with anonymous hardcore close-ups. On safer ground, Anna starred in the first series of TV sitcom *Mind Your Language*, but departed in 1978 leaving Françoise Pascal to do the sexy stuff. In 1985, 14 million viewers saw her as a red-light girl in the coming-of-age TV movie *Dutch Girls*.

GENRE CREDITS: *Go On, Slip Off Your Dress!* (Germany 1973), *Penelope Pulls It Off!* (1975), *Adventures of a Taxi Driver* (1975), *Intimate Games* (1976), *Come Play with Me* (1977), *Agent 69 in the Sign of Scorpio* aka *Emmanuelle in Denmark* (Denmark 1977), *What's Up Superdoc?* (1978), *Agent 69 in the Sign of Sagittarius* (Denmark 1978), *Blue Paradise* (Italy 1980), *Nutcracker* (1982), *Doing Rude Things* (TV 1995)

Minah BIRD (1950-1995)

Afro-haired, Nigerian-born, Finland-educated, Minah Ogbenyealu Bird (sometimes spelt Byrd) was one of only a handful of black starlets (others were Venicia Day and Pauline Peart) who made an impact on British sex films during the 1970s. Her slim and slinky appearance made her a popular face on TV comedy shows throughout the decade and her figure was best showcased in boob-tubes, hotpants and platform boots. She proved to be the centre of attention in 1978's *The Stud* as a hip-gyrating disco queen and in 1979 published her steamy autobiography *Bye Bye Blackbird*, which caused a sensation when serialised in a Sunday newspaper. She faded into obscurity during the 1980s and fell on hard times. She died after a massive heart attack in her London council flat in July 1995 and, tragically, her body was not found for some weeks.

GENRE CREDITS: *The Four Dimensions of Greta* (1972), *Layout for 5 Models* (1972), *The Love Box* (1972), *Percy's Progress* (1974), *The Stud* (1978)

Timothy BLACKSTONE (1946-)

A tall, blond, blue-eyed (but not especially well-hung) hardcore porn actor, Blackstone was the nearest thing Britain had to a male Mary Millington, with whom he often worked. He was considerably more glamorous than many of his beer-gutted contemporaries and became a mainstay of porn magazine layouts throughout the 1970s. David Sullivan used Blackstone extensively in photographs advertising *Come Play with Me*, despite the fact he never appeared in the movie. Prior to his big screen career he was cast in several hardcore loops by John Lindsay, later enjoying his biggest film role as Julie Lee's slimy bisexual lover in *Emmanuelle in Soho* (1981). In May 2000 it was revealed that Blackstone, now a public relations man, is the brother of minister for culture Baroness Blackstone. Suing the *Sunday Mirror* for an article claiming that he had been arrested following an argument with his wife at their West London home, he was forced to give details about his various roles. 'I did some things I am not proud of today,' he told the prosecutor. 'You are raking over matters that happened in the seventies.' Blackstone neglected to mention that he had returned to Sullivan's fold in 1991, appearing in a sexy shoot for *Playbirds* magazine. 'I rather foolishly had a lapse,' he said.

GENRE CREDITS: *The Hot Girls* (1974), *Sex Express* (1975), *I'm Not Feeling Myself*

Tonight! (1975), *Confessions of a Driving Instructor* (1976), *Under the Bed!* (1977), *Let's Get Laid!* (1977), *Emmanuelle in Soho* (1981).

Gloria BRITTAIN

Gloria, a lisping, baby-voiced brunette, was a nude regular in the pages of David Sullivan's magazines, sometimes credited as an American model called 'busty Bibi Forbes'. Represented by agent Alan Selwyn, her first film role was uncredited and involved being burned alive on a flaming crucifix in *The Playbirds*. Middlesex-born Gloria was even called upon to play a topless schoolgirl in the ill-conceived *The Wildcats of St Trinian's*. With her minimal acting ability it's surprising (or then again, perhaps not) that she took the lead role in Kenneth Rowles' snooze-inducing *The Perils of Mandy*, cast again as an overgrown schoolgirl but this time with a hairdo that has to be seen to be believed.

GENRE CREDITS: *The Playbirds* (1978), *The Great British Striptease* (1980), *Mary Millington's World Striptease Extravaganza* (1981), *The Perils of Mandy* (video 1981)

Ava CADELL (1956-)

Ava was born Ildjko Csath in Budapest. In London, aged 18, she embarked on a career as a model, sometimes using the name Eva Chatt. Her cute, schoolgirl looks and big chest soon got her onto Page Three of the *Sun* and *Daily Mirror*, as well as dozens of glamour magazines, calendars and book covers. She also starred in a number of 16mm hardcore films directed by John Lindsay, most infamously, *Jolly Hockey Sticks*. Having won a contract to advertise Miners' Cosmetics, her explicit past was repeatedly exposed in David Sullivan's scandal sheet *Private National News* in 1976, the magazine hypocritically accusing the *Sun* of passing off a hardcore porn actress as a 'whiter-than-white former nurse turned model'. Ava weathered this storm in a D-cup and went on to appear in Peter Cook and Dudley Moore's *The Hound of the Baskervilles* (1977). After a walk-on in *History of the World Part 1*, she relocated to the USA in 1980 and became a hostess on the Playboy Channel. She also had small roles in *Smokey and the Bandit Part 3* (1983), *The Jerk, Too* (1984), *Commando* (1985) and a handful of B-movies. Now a certified clinical sexologist, Ava works from offices on Sunset Boulevard, makes regular appearances on radio and TV and has her own website. She has also written several books, including *Confessions of a Sexologist* and *Stock Market Orgasm*, and released an album, *The Soundz of Sex*, in 1995.

GENRE CREDITS: *The Hot Girls* (1974), *Confessions of a Window Cleaner* (1974), *Confessions of a Sex Maniac* (1974), *The Ups and Downs of a Handyman* (1975), *Outer Touch* (1979)

James Kenelm CLARKE (1941-)

James Kenelm Clarke was a BBC documentary filmmaker who worked on such TV shows as *Braden's Week* and *That's Life!* His cinematic début, made for his Norfolk International Company, was *Got It Made* (1974). Although often cited as a sex comedy, it's actually a glum drama about a well-heeled young lady (Lalla Ward) coming to terms with her lost childhood. Inexplicably retitled by over-zealous distributors as *Sweet Virgin*, there's not a single virgin in it. Legend has it that Clarke was only introduced to the lucrative delights of making sex films after directing a documentary on the 'X'-rated movie industry for the BBC's *Man Alive* series, broadcast in April 1975. Inspired by the programme, he made *Exposé*, featuring glamourpuss Fiona Richmond, quickly followed by two further Richmond collaborations. Clarke was perhaps the only British director who triumphed in producing professional-looking sex pictures with a fair amount of finesse and style. By the eighties his production company was pretty much washed-up and in 1982 he wrote and directed the underrated *Funny Money*, produced by Confessions impresario Greg Smith. His last movie, comedy thriller *Yellow Pages* (1985), was filmed in Los Angeles and Copenhagen. It sat on the shelf for three years before finally getting a Stateside release as *Going Undercover*. Also an accomplished composer, Clarke has contributed the musical score to several of his own movies as well as others, like *Vampyres* (1974) and *The Wildcats of St Trinian's* (1980).

GENRE CREDITS: *Exposé* (1975) (director/writer), *Hardcore* (1977) (director/co-writer/music), *Let's Get Laid!* (1977) (director/music), *Paul Raymond's Erotica* (1980) (producer)

Norman COHEN (1936-1983)

A Jewish Dubliner, Norman Cohen started his career as a film editor in the late fifties before moving to London in 1964 and hooking up with Greg Smith's theatrical agency. The two men became inseparable and immediately started collaborating on movie projects. After co-directing a low-budget mondo movie, *London in the Raw*, Cohen directed three documentary featurettes including *Brendan Behan's Dublin* (1966) and *The London Nobody Knows* (1967), all of which were critically acclaimed. Cohen's real forte, however, was comedy and his big break came when he helmed the movie version of *Till Death Us Do Part* in 1968. *Dad's Army* (1971) and *Adolf Hitler – My Part in His Downfall* (1972), also struck gold at the box-office. In 1974 he acted as associate producer on *Confessions of a Window Cleaner* and subsequently directed the next three movies in the series. Having moved to the US, he attempted to set up deals on other movie projects but without much success. After a triple heart-bypass operation in 1983, he died in California aged 47. 'We had wonderful times together,' reminisces Greg Smith. 'We used to see each other every day and I can honestly say it was a joy working with him always. I still miss him today.'

GENRE CREDITS: *London in the Raw* (1964) (co-director), *Confessions of a Window Cleaner* (1974) (associate producer), *Confessions of a Pop Performer* (1975) (director), *Confessions of a Driving Instructor* (1976) (director), *Stand Up Virgin Soldiers* (1977) (director), *Confessions from a Holiday Camp* (1977) (director)

Mary and Madeleine COLLINSON (1952-)

Mary and Madeleine were identical twin sisters from Malta (born to an English father) who created quite a buzz on their arrival in Britain in April 1969. Various modelling assignments, nude and clothed, culminated when they became *Playboy*'s very first twin Playmates in the October 1970 issue. Filmmakers sat up and took notice at once. Their threesome tussle with Chris Matthews in *Come Back Peter* was filmed nearly two years after the movie's initial release, and inserted into the narrative to increase its nudity quota on re-release in 1971. The sisters took the title roles in Hammer's *Twins of Evil* the same year, the roles giving them maximum exposure in the press and sealing their celluloid immortality. Hollywood soon took notice, but their one and only American film was the ultra-camp *Love Machine* (1971), based on the bestselling novel by Jacqueline Susann, in which they had a naked shower scene with John Philip Law. After a few more modelling jobs the twins returned home to obscurity. Today Mary runs her own business in Milan, while sister Madeleine resides in Bournemouth.

GENRE CREDITS: *Come Back Peter* (aka *Some Like It Sexy*) (1969), *Permissive* (1970), *Groupie Girl* (1971), *She'll Follow You Anywhere* (1971)

Heather DEELEY (1956-)

Suffolk-born, doe-eyed, bisexual Heather Deeley certainly made her mark in 1975, appearing in no less than five British sex films and being hailed as 'Britain's new succulent sex star!' A sixth film, *Pink Orgasm*, produced by David Grant and co-starring Victor Spinetti and *Deep Throat* star Harry Reems, was unfinished, however, and never saw the light of day. Despite being very pretty and a good actress – she played the lead in *Sex Express* (and participated in hardcore scenes for the American release, *Diversions*) – Deeley's reliance on cocaine made her difficult to work with and she only appeared in two further movies, the last being a tiny role in *Hardcore* in 1976. 'Heather had so much going for her,' recalls her one-time manager Alan Selwyn. 'She was only 16 or something when she started, but already was a very natural actress and was constantly in demand. I had fan letters pouring in for her every day, but she met this awful bloke who was into drugs and it ruined her. I sorted her out another movie, but she never turned up on set. She just totally vanished and nobody saw her again.'

GENRE CREDITS: *Erotic Inferno* (1975), *Pink Orgasm* (unfinished, 1975), *Girls Come First* (1975), *I'm Not Feeling Myself Tonight!* (1975), *Secrets of a Superstud* (1975), *Sex Express* (1975), *Intimate Games* (1976), *Hardcore* (1977)

Felicity DEVONSHIRE

At 17, London-born Felicity (nicknamed 'Fluff') turned down a Hollywood contract because she couldn't face being tied down to one career for ten years. Instead she opted for a saucier life back home in Britain. Breaking into modelling after a famous agent spotted her photograph in a local newspaper, she immediately signed to Top Models, an agency she shared with Sue Longhurst. Felicity became a regular face in adverts, magazines and Page Three of the *Sun* before finding her place in sex comedies. Well-liked in the industry, she could be called upon to put in a decent leading performance, such as in *Blue Belle*, and even inched her way into more mainstream titles like *The Magnificent Seven Deadly Sins* (1971) and Ken Russell's *Lisztomania* (1975). Married to an American lawyer, she was four months' pregnant when she filmed her final movie, *What's Up Nurse?*, in which she was encased in concrete from the waist down and was thrown into the North Sea. Despite expressing a desire to take on more serious roles, particularly in the theatre, she faded from view and concentrated on raising her family. In June 2001 Felicity was voted 67th most popular Page Three girl ever in a celebratory issue of the *Sun*.

GENRE CREDITS: *Sex and the Other Woman* (1972), *The Four Dimensions of Greta* (1972), *The Sex Victims* (1973), *Secrets of a Door to Door Salesman* (1973), *The Over Amorous Artist* (1974), *Feelings* (1975), *Blue Belle* (1975), *Intimate Games* (1976), *What's Up Nurse?* (1977), *The Kiss* (1977)

Diana DORS (1932-1984)

Britain's answer to Marilyn Monroe was born plain Diana Fluck in Swindon in 1932 and made her movie début in *The Shop at Sly Corner* in 1946. Signed to the Rank Organisation, early film successes like *The Weak and the Wicked* (1953), *A Kid for Two Farthings* (1955) and *Yield to the Night* (1956) established her as one of the most popular young actresses of her generation. However, a brief foray in Hollywood badly backfired and she hurriedly returned to Britain. As she piled on the pounds in the mid-1960s, the only roles that came her way were blowzy character parts, usually ageing good-time girls, nosy cleaners, frustrated housewives and brothel Madames. Dors' last husband was B-grade actor Alan Lake. The couple endured a turbulent marriage for nearly 16 years, appearing separately and together in some of the worst films ever made. During the seventies Dors continually lamented the state of British filmmaking, complaining bitterly that moviegoers were obsessed with pornography. But she appeared in more sex films – in Scandinavia as well as Britain – than any other British character actor. She converted to Catholicism in 1974, at which point her participation in 'X'-rated movies only accelerated. She even asked director Michael Winner to find her a really raunchy script which would give her the opportunity to strip off and rejuvenate her career (as would later happen to Joan Collins), but no-one was interested. In the last years of her life Dors was extremely close to pornographic model Mary Millington, while simultaneously lending her voice to a campaign to ban 'girlie' magazines from newsagents. She died of cancer on 4 May 1984, shortly after completing her scenes in Joseph Losey's *Steaming*.

GENRE CREDITS: *Baby Love* (1968), *Swedish Wildcats* (Sweden 1972), *The Amorous Milkman* (1974), *What the Swedish Butler Saw* (Sweden 1974), *Adventures of a Taxi Driver* (1975), *Keep it Up Downstairs* (1976), *Adventures of a Private Eye* (1977), *Confessions from the David Galaxy Affair* (1979) (+ performer of theme song)

Linzi DREW (1958-)

Bristol-born Linzi landed her first movie role as a frighteningly pink-haired party guest in *Emmanuelle in Soho* (1981), alongside her glamour model friend (and ex-flatmate) Marie Harper. Horror fans loved her as Brenda Bristols in the clever British sex film spoof *See You Next Wednesday* incorporated into the climax of *An American Werewolf in London* (1981). She subsequently worked for Ken Russell in *Salome's Last Dance*, *The Lair of the White Worm* and *Aria*. Following in Fiona Richmond's footsteps, Linzi contributed a long-running feature, 'Life with Linzi', to Paul Raymond's *Club International* magazine and in 1988 became the first female editor of British *Penthouse*. In 1992 she was imprisoned for four months for participating in the production of 'obscene' videos with her long-time partner, hardcore performer Lindsay Honey (aka Ben Dover). On her release Linzi published her funny autobiography *Try Everything Once Except ... Incest and Morris Dancing*. Linzi also handles the distribution and marketing of the Ben Dover videos and remains one of the best-liked women in British porn.

GENRE CREDITS: *Emmanuelle in Soho* (1981), *Death Shock* (video 1982), *Dirty Woman* (German video 1990), *An American Buttman in London* (US video 1991), *I Love Linzi* (video 1990), *Marie and Linzi's Fantasies* (video 1991), *Members Only – Volume 1* (video 1992), *I Love Linzi Too* (video 1994)

John M EAST (1932-)

East was born into a theatrical family, his grandfather being John Marlborough East (1860-1924), the silent film actor and director. East Jr was brought up by his mother with family friend Max Miller, whom East idolised. Through Miller he was given his first taste of showbusiness as a performer in the music halls. For three years, from 1958, East played the role of Polyte Le Mou in the West End production of *Irma La Douce*. He also regularly acted in films. On television he featured alongside Red Skelton, Tommy Cooper, Harry Worth and Morecambe and Wise, and enjoyed small roles in sitcoms like *On the Buses*, *Yus My Dear* and *Love Thy Neighbour*. But the BBC features department and, from 1972, his own public relations company took up most of his time. In 1977, while working on a radio series on British entrepreneurs, East met pornographer David Sullivan and, through him, Mary Millington. East and Mary became extremely close, with East acting as her dialogue coach. Having landed a bit-part in *The Playbirds*, East's behind-the-camera involvement in Sullivan's films culminated in his writing, producing and starring in 1981's *Emmanuelle in Soho*. After Mary's suicide, East produced and performed in two much-criticised Mary Millington 'tribute' films. He continues to crop up occasionally on radio and in newspaper articles.

GENRE CREDITS: *The Lustful Lady* (1977) (actor), *The Playbirds* (1978) (actor), *Confessions from the David Galaxy Affair* (1979) (actor), *Queen of the Blues* (1979) (actor), *Mary Millington's True Blue Confessions* (1980) (co-director/writer/narrator), *Emmanuelle in Soho* (1981) (actor/producer/writer), *Mary Millington's World Striptease Extravaganza* (1981) (producer/presenter), *Hellcats – Mud Wrestling* (1983) (producer/interviewer), *Foxy Female Boxers* (video 1983) (producer/interviewer), *Queen Kong – The Amazonian Woman* (video 1984) (producer/interviewer), *Sex and Fame – The Mary Millington Story* (TV 1996) (interviewee)

Rosemary ENGLAND

Rosemary was a late addition to the David Sullivan stable and the only one of his models to achieve anything approaching the status of Mary Millington. A plummy-voiced ex-magician's assistant from Bournemouth, Rosemary started her modelling career in her late teens using her real name Jada Smith. Her big smile and even bigger breasts endeared her to the aged judges of beauty contests and she rapidly became the most successful beauty queen in the south of England. Her seaside celebrity eventually brought her to the attention of Sullivan, who quickly made her a fixture in his publications. Renamed Rosemary England (because, Sullivan reasoned, she was the archetypal English rose), she was an instant hit with readers. She made her acting début (as a beauty queen, naturally), in *Confessions from the David Galaxy Affair*. Mary Millington's suicide in 1979 hit Rosemary hard and she vanished from the pages of *Whitehouse* the following year. She made only one further film, *Sex with the Stars*, using yet another name, Poula Grifith-Jada. She was apparently earmarked to play Sid Vicious' mother (!) in *The Great Rock 'n' Roll Swindle*, but this never materialised.

GENRE CREDITS: *Confessions from the David Galaxy Affair* (1979), *Queen of the Blues* (1979), *Sex with the Stars* (1980).

Adrienne and Malcolm FANCEY

Glamorous ex-actress Adrienne and her cigar-chomping brother Malcolm are the children of movie mogul Edwin J Fancey (1902-1980), who produced and distributed hundreds of exploitation films during the 1960s and 70s. After their father's retirement, Malcolm and Adrienne took over his New Realm company and continued to produce sex films, the final one being *The World is Full of Married Men* in 1979. They also made a million (literally) from their acquisition of Just Jaeckin's *Emmanuelle*. Malcolm retired from the film business, leaving Adrienne in charge, a year after Edwin's death. Incidentally, the name Negus-Fancey, which appears on the credits of several seventies' sex films, is the pseudonym of Edwin J Fancey's common-law wife, Olive Negus (*not* Adrienne and Malcolm's mother), who ran Border Films and Watchgrove Productions.

GENRE CREDITS FOR ADRIENNE FANCEY: *Some Like It Cool* (1961) (producer), *It's a Bare, Bare World* (1963) (producer)
GENRE CREDITS FOR MALCOLM FANCEY: *Secrets of a Door to Door Salesman* (1973) (associate producer), *The Over Amorous Artist* (1974) (associate producer), *I'm Not Feeling Myself Tonight!* (1975) (producer), *Girls Come First* (1975) (co-producer), *Under the Bed!* (1977) (co-executive producer), *The World is Full of Married Men* (1979) (co-producer)

Liz FRASER (1933-)

Liz (real name: Elizabeth Winch) is a busty blonde comedy actress who was immensely popular on film and television from the 1950s onwards. Her best movies include *I'm All Right Jack* (1959), *Two Way Stretch* (1960), *The Pure Hell of St Trinian's* (1961) and *Carry On Cruising* (1962). She was a very close friend of Sid James and starred as his girlfriend in the BBC's *Citizen James* show between 1960 and 1962. After a 12-year break from the Carry Ons, a supporting role in *Carry On Behind* (1975) marked her return to broad comedy and signalled the shape of things to come. The same year she signed to star in the revealing *Adventures of a Taxi Driver* with Barry Evans, the first of her six British sex comedies. Unlike many of her contemporaries, she was quite prepared to strip down to her undies and act in sexual situations; she still looked fabulous well past 40. She also starred alongside Mary Millington in 1979's *The Great Rock 'n' Roll Swindle*, but stayed covered-up. She continues to act on television, most recently as a guest star in *Last of the Summer Wine*.

GENRE CREDITS: *Adventures of a Taxi Driver* (1975), *Confessions of a Driving Instructor* (1976), *Under the Doctor* (1976), *Confessions from a Holiday Camp* (1977), *Adventures of a Private Eye* (1977), *Rosie Dixon – Night Nurse* (1978)

Derek FORD (1932-1995)

After a spell in the armed forces, Derek Ford became an accountant and, at 24, managed to wangle himself a job as clapper boy on a soap advertisement for Morton M Lewis' film company. He eventually became a partner in the business, but quit in 1960 after Lewis repeatedly refused to let him direct. He finally got his chance when he was approached by a filmmaker in a Soho pub to insert some new scenes into a duff Swedish sex movie, later released in the UK as *Paris Playgirls*. He also wrote radio plays for *Children's Hour* and, with his novelist brother Donald, scripted 12 feature films and over 50 TV shows, including popular series like *Adam Adamant*, *Z-Cars* and *The Saint*. A busy director and writer of sex films throughout the 1960s and 70s, his biggest success was undoubtedly *The Wife Swappers*, produced by Stanley Long in 1969. Not shy of stronger material, Ford regularly directed hardcore versions of all his early 1970s movies. Remembered as 'generally miserable' by many of his ex-colleagues, he only really seemed to come alive when directing sex scenes. 'He was a male nymphomaniac, if you can call him that,' recalled Ray Selfe. After the sex film era had ebbed away, Ford bummed around the bottom half of the film business trying to get several unfilmed projects off the ground. In 1984 he wrote the excruciating screenplay for *Don't Open Till Christmas* and was unceremoniously sacked as the movie's director after just two days. In a bid to sanitise his past, during the 1980s his CV desexualised several of his movies; *The Sexplorer* was listed as *Explorer* and *Sex Express* became plain old *Express*. His final film, made in 1990 and sitting on the shelf ever since, was *Urge To Kill* (aka *Attack of the Killer Computer*), in which a vengeful computer kills several young ladies, including one whose breasts explode under a sunbed. He died following a heart attack in W H Smith in Bromley High Street in 1995, leaving a legacy of British filth. 'He was a nice chap,' recalls one of his leading actors, Mark Jones, 'but he always acted like he was the studio carpenter, rather than a feature film director.'

GENRE CREDITS: *Paris Playgirls* (Sweden 1960) (additional direction/writing), *Saturday Night Out* (1963) (co-writer), *The Yellow Teddybears* (1963) (co-writer), *A Promise of Bed* (1969) (director/co-writer), *The Wife Swappers* (1969) (director/co-writer), *Groupie Girl* (1970) (director/co-writer), *Suburban Wives* (1971) (director/co-writer), *Commuter Husbands* (1972) (director/co-writer), *Keep It Up Jack!* (1973) (director/co-writer), *Sex Express* (1975) (director/writer), *The*

Sexplorer (1975) (director/writer), *What's Up Nurse?* (1977) (director/writer), *What's Up Superdoc?* (1978) (director/writer), *Erotic Fantasies* (Italy 1978) (co-director)

Tudor GATES (1930-)

A well-respected writer/director/producer who began his career in the theatre in 1954, Gates has had numerous plays performed on BBC Radio and on television and has written for popular series like *The Saint* and *The Avengers*. In 1966 he created the BBC TV 'anti-Mafia' series *Vendetta*. A shift into movies was prompted by an offer to co-write the screenplay for Roger Vadim's cult sci-fi romp *Barbarella* in 1967, filmed in Italy. The same year – also for Dino de Laurentiis – he co-wrote another comic-strip extravaganza, Mario Bava's *Diabolik*. Returning to Britain, he wrote three scripts for Hammer, injecting more than a little sex into their so-called Karnstein trilogy: *The Vampire Lovers*, *Lust for a Vampire* (both 1970) and *Twins of Evil* (1971). 'They were all good pictures of their genre,' he says. 'I saw them as straightforward, simple medieval morality tales.' Gates and his business partner Wilbur Stark then branched out into sex film production, for which they used the pseudonyms Teddy and Billy White. Their alter egos were an open secret within the industry and, by the time *Intimate Games* was released in 1976, Gates had reverted to his real name. After his successful stint in films, Gates returned to his first love – theatre. His dozen or so stage plays have included *Lyric for a Tango*, *The Kidnap Game* and *Who Killed Agatha Christie?* Still writing and working in the theatre today, he is also on the board of BECTU (Broadcasting Entertainment Cinematograph and Theatre Union), an independent union for some 25,000 members working in the British entertainment industry.

GENRE CREDITS: *The Love Box* (1972) (co-director/co-producer/co-writer), *The Sex Thief* (1973) (co-producer/co-writer), *Intimate Games* (1976) (director/writer), *Sex with the Stars* (1980) (writer)

Bob GODFREY (1921-)

Few directors associated with British sex films would ever get within a thousand miles of an Oscar, let alone win one. But Bob Godfrey has: four times Oscar-nominated and a winner in 1975 for his cartoon *GREAT – Isambard Kingdom Brunel*. Born in Australia but transplanted to Essex as an infant, Godfrey joined Peter Sacs at the famous Larkin Animation Studios in 1950 and four years later he and three of his colleagues set up their own company, Biographic Films, to produce television commercials. He branched out in 1965 with his very own business, Bob Godfrey Films (still going strong today), and between 1970 and 1981 directed six 'sextoons' and two animated inserts for David Grant productions, the second of which, *Pink Orgasm*, has never seen the light of day. Godfrey also directed the animated title sequence of *It's a 2' 6" Above the Ground World* in 1972, easily the most entertaining part of the whole movie. He's even been persuaded to make fleeting appearances in front of the camera: twice for Dick Lester and the Beatles and twice for Joseph McGrath. He's best known, however, for his legendary BBC children's series *Roobarb and Custard* (1974) and the BAFTA-winning *Henry's Cat* (1982), to which he also lent his distinctive vocal talents. His most recent cartoon short was *Millennium* (2000), documenting 1000 years of British history in 25 minutes. In April 2001, TV presenter Richard Madeley suggested that the man who animated the psychedelic *Roobarb and Custard* must have been 'on something'. Godfrey was incensed and demanded an apology from Granada Television. 'Drawing a green dog and a pink cat doesn't mean I was on drugs!' he stormed.

GENRE CREDITS: *Love and Marriage* (1970) (animation inserts), *Henry 9 Till 5* (1970) (director), *Kama Sutra Rides Again* (1971) (director), *I'm Not Feeling Myself Tonight!* (1975) (actor), *Pink Orgasm* (unfinished, 1975) (animation inserts), *Dear Margery Boobs* (1977) (director), *Dream Doll* (1979) (co-director), *Instant Sex* (1980) (no official UK release), *Bio Woman* (1981) (no official UK release)

Angela GRANT (1950-)

Also known as Angie Grant, this exotic-looking actress made her name as a Carry On glamour girl with small parts in *Follow that Camel*, *... Up the Khyber* and *Camping* before securing a more substantial role, as beauty queen Miss Bangor, in *Carry On Girls* (1973). Working on the latter, she came out in a rash after being sprinkled with soil and itching powder in the beauty pageant finale. Before she started acting, tawny Angela was a teenage fashion model for London's famous Lucie Clayton agency and by the late 1960s was posing topless for movies and magazines. Becoming the 'It' girl of her time, she oozed sex appeal and removed all for Derek Ford's *What's Up?* comedies in the late 1970s. Angela, who lives in Knightsbridge, now has a career as a public speaker, charity worker and tireless fund-raiser for the Tory party.

GENRE CREDITS: *A Promise of Bed* (1969), *Zeta One* (1969), *What's Up Nurse?* (1977), *What's Up Superdoc?* (1978)

David GRANT (1937-1991)

David Hamilton Grant was an incredibly prolific producer and distributor of seventies sex movies for his company, Oppidan Film Productions. He entered the business as a photographer but really made his name as the author of the controversial illustrated sex manual *Love Variations*, later turned into a dubiously motivated sex education film in 1969. From producing he progressed into screenwriting and directing, but with little or no flair. He took charge of filming all the hardcore sequences for his movies, but colleagues recall he had deep psychological problems, including a compulsion to watch other people having sex. He regularly took sex film actor Steve Amber to his home in Bray in order to film him shagging women he'd just picked up. Grant relished any opportunity to go on radio or TV to promote himself but remained a mystery; David Hamilton Grant wasn't even his real name. 'He was really called Andrew,' said his one-time business partner Ray Selfe, 'but he pinched the name David Hamilton from a French photographer of nudes. He'd never tell anyone his real identity. Most people just called him the Poison Dwarf.' As well as his 'X'-rated films, Grant produced the Peter Sellers/Spike Milligan disaster *The Great McGonagall* (1974) and the shorts *Escape to Entebbe* (1976), *Marcia* (1977), a satire on Harold Wilson, and *End of Term* (1977), a concert film starring children from the Barbara Speake Stage School with special guest Arthur Askey. After directing his last movie, *You're Driving Me Crazy!* in 1978, things went rapidly downhill. Despite owing thousands of pounds (he was a compulsive gambler), Grant diversified into video distribution with his World of Video 2000 company and in 1984 was gaoled for 18 months for distributing the 'video nasty', *Nightmares in a Damaged Brain*. On his release Grant spent much of his time in Cyprus and Turkey, allegedly making child porn films or dealing in hard drugs, depending on which newspaper reports you read at the time. Although missing for well over a decade, it is understood that he was murdered in 1991, very possibly the victim of a contract killing. 'I never really liked the man, but I respected his business abilities,' says Selfe. 'His life was so different from mine and he loved playing that King of Porn role, but the real trouble with him was that he was so inherently sleazy.'

GENRE CREDITS: *Love Variations* (1969) (director/producer/writer), *Love and Marriage* (1970) (director/producer/writer), *Au Pair Girls* (1972) (original story), *Sinderella* (1972) (executive producer/writer), *Snow White and the Seven Perverts* (1973) (executive producer/writer), *Secrets of a Door to Door Salesman* (1973) (producer), *The Over Amorous Artist* (1974) (producer), *Pink Orgasm* (unfinished 1975) (director/producer/co-writer), *Girls Come First* (1975) (co-producer/actor), *The Office Party* (1976) (director/producer/co-writer/actor), *Under the Bed!* (1977) (director/co-executive producer/co-writer), *The Kiss* (1977) (co-producer/co-writer), *Dear Margery Boobs* (1977) (producer), *You're Driving Me Crazy!* (1978) (director/co-writer/actor)

Pamela GREEN (1923-)

Britain's most naked glamour goddess of the fifties and sixties was born in Kingston upon Thames in 1923. She spent her formative years in Holland and in 1947 enrolled at St Martin's School of Art in London to study life and fashion drawing. One year later she started nude modelling to help her pay her tuition fees. Pam also toured with the Russian Ballet School and within 12 months her modelling and dancing were earning her more per hour than her artwork ever could. She made her West End stage début as a dancer in 1953 and it was while appearing in Bernard Delfont's *Folies Bergère* in 1957 that Pam first met theatrical snapper George Harrison Marks. They became lovers and went into business together, bringing out the incredibly popular glamour magazine *Kamera*. Although she never took full credit, it was undoubtedly Green who was the driving force behind the magazine. Still photographs led to 8mm films such as *Witches' Brew*, *Xcitement* and *Art for Art's Sake* (all 1958). Pam often donned a red wig to become her alter ego Rita Landre. In 1959 she had a small but crucial role in Michael Powell's notorious *Peeping Tom*. At the movie's London première in April 1960, a 40ft cut-out of Pam was displayed above the theatre with 'Introducing Pamela Green' illuminated in lightbulbs. In 1961 she was the leading lovely in Harrison Marks' début big screen movie, the quaint nudist travelogue *Naked – As Nature Intended*. She followed this with a small role as a saucy maid in *The Chimney Sweeps* (1963), Harrison Marks' only non-sex film. After eight years the Green-Marks partnership dissolved in 1965, the same year *The Naked World of Harrison Marks* was released. After the break-up Pam began a long relationship with Douglas Webb, the stills photographer on *Naked – As Nature Intended*. Throughout the seventies Pam carried on modelling and acting, landing a small role as a Parisian tart in *Legend of the Werewolf* (1974). In 1986 she relocated with Webb to Yarmouth on the Isle of Wight and they began running a photographic studio specialising in portraiture. Pam's skills as a retoucher and finisher were never more in demand. After Webb died, Pam began selling a mail-order video called *Never Knowingly Overdressed* (1997), a compilation of 500 still glamour photographs and five 8mm striptease films she had made with Harrison Marks. Recently in poor health, she still lives on the Isle of Wight.

GENRE CREDITS: *Naked – As Nature Intended* (1961), *The Naked World of Harrison Marks* (1965), *Doing Rude Things* (TV 1995)

Neil HALLETT (1925-)

A suave, handsome devil, usually cast as a slightly shady figure of authority. Avuncular in appearance, he looked like the sort of man who would be outwardly disapproving but would secretly have a stash of hardcore porn mags under his bed. Hallett initially came to prominence in the groundbreaking crime series *Ghost Squad* (1961-64), alongside actor and friend Ray Austin. When Austin turned his hand to directing he cast Hallett in two of his saucy sex films, *Virgin Witch* and *Fun and Games*. Hallett was a very close friend of Hazel Adair, who gave him roles in three movies, the last of which was *Game for Vultures* in 1979. He made frequent appearances in all the big TV action series, including *The Sweeney*, *The Professionals* and five times in *The Avengers*. Married to actress Tracy Reed (star of Donovan Winter's *The Deadly Females*), he retired to Spain in 1991.

GENRE CREDITS: *Groupie Girl* (1970), *Virgin Witch* (1971), *Fun and Games* (1971), *Can You Keep it Up for a Week?* (1974), *Keep It Up Downstairs* (1976) (+performer of theme song)

John HAMILL (1947-)

An extremely handsome, well-put-together stud muffin, in his youth Hamill was a champion bodybuilder, coming second in the Junior Mr Britain contest. After training as an actor at the Webber Douglas Academy, he enjoyed a long run in the stage farce *There's a Girl in My Soup* and landed the role of Dave Cartwright in TV's *Crossroads*. His film career initially bloomed with camp horror movies, including *Trog* (1969), *The Beast in the Cellar* (1970) and *Tower of Evil* (1971), although sex comedies would eventually become his bread and butter. In 1975 he produced and directed himself in a raunchy comedy entitled *Doing the Best I Can*. Unfortunately he ran out of money halfway through and the project was unfinished. Hamill's last British film was *Hardcore* in 1977, in which he has his wicked way with Fiona Richmond in the back of a fruit and veg lorry. A year later he had a supporting role in the Swedish thriller *Man in the Shadows* (aka *Black Sun*) and subsequently appeared in TV shows like *Doctor Who* and *The Professionals*. But the acting profession could not sustain him financially and he opened a furniture shop.

GENRE CREDITS: *The Over Amorous Artist* (1974), *Girls Come First* (1975), *Under the Bed!* (1977), *Hardcore* (1977)

Irene HANDL (1901-1987)

Born to a wealthy Austrian banker and aristocratic Frenchwoman, Irene didn't

Irene Handl shows Tony Booth her industrial-strength bloomers in Confessions of a Driving Instructor *(1976).*

take to the stage until she was 36 but was an immediate hit as the level-headed maid in the West End smash *George and Margaret*. She subsequently appeared in over 100 movies, including *The Belles of St Trinian's* (1954) and *I'm All Right Jack* (1959). On TV she was popular in sitcoms like *For the Love of Ada* (1970-1) and *Metal Mickey* (1980-3), usually playing cuddly grandmothers. She also wrote two outstanding novels in her mid-sixties, *The Sioux* and *The Gold Tipped Phitzer*, complete with bad language and sexual situations. She had no qualms about appearing in 'X' films either, but had a tendency to ad-lib if she thought the script wasn't up to much. On the set of *Come Play with Me*, a photographer asked if she'd mind having her photo taken with a topless Mary Millington and Penny Chisholm. 'Not at all,' she cheerfully replied. 'If I was a bit younger I'd get my tits out with them!' Irene also played opposite Mary in 1979's punk rock movie, *The Great Rock 'n' Roll Swindle*, and her last film role, though brief, was in *Absolute Beginners* (1986).

GENRE CREDITS: *Confessions of a Driving Instructor* (1976), *Come Play with Me* (1977), *Stand Up Virgin Soldiers* (1977), *Adventures of a Private Eye* (1977)

Linda HAYDEN (1953-)

One-time child actress (and graduate of the Aida Foster stage school) who made her cinema début, aged 15, as a teenage nymphette in 1968's *Baby Love*, and later gained notoriety as the sluttish Angel Blake, ringleader of a group of Devil-worshipping children in 17th century England, in *Blood on Satan's Claw* (1970). Frequently cast as a cruel, vindictive young bitch who exploited her sexuality for her own gain, Hayden reached the pinnacle of nastiness as the murderous secretary in 1975's *Exposé*. For a while she was extremely popular on TV, adding glamour to Charlie Drake and Dick Emery's comedy shows, and on the big screen was happy to shed her clothes as soon as the director called 'Action!' For many years the real-life partner of Robin Askwith, she faded from the big screen during the eighties. Her saucy career got a boost in the mid-1990s when she appeared in Jim Davidson's adults-only pantomime, *Sinderella*, and, although she now acts mainly in the theatre, Linda continues to have a huge cult following, particularly in the States.

GENRE CREDITS: *Baby Love* (1968), *Confessions of a Window Cleaner* (1974), *Exposé* (1975), *Let's Get Laid!* (1977), *Confessions from a Holiday Camp* (1977)

Helli Louise JACOBSON (1950-)

A Danish popsie, short on stature but big on boobs. Oddly shaped, with square shoulders, huge dark eyes and a mop of brown hair, Helli Louise (she later dispensed with her surname) started her glamour career in hardcore loops and feature films in Scandinavia – she played the lead role as a promiscuous, incestuous teen in *Daddy Darling* (1968) – before moving to London and modelling extensively for John Lindsay. Also appearing in television shows like *The Goodies* and *The Sweeney*, her most enduring role (due, in part, to endless TV repeats) is as a nude girl showering in *Carry On Behind* (1975). Surprisingly, in *The World is Full of Married Men*, her final British movie, she actually keeps all her clothes on. Helli has since worked for music promoter Harvey Goldsmith.

GENRE CREDITS: *Daddy Darling* (Denmark 1968), *Dagmar's Hot Pants* (Denmark 1972), *The Yes Girls* (1972), *Soft Beds, Hard Battles* (1973), *The Hot Girls* (1974), *Confessions of a Pop Performer* (1975), *The Ups and Downs of a Handyman* (1975), *Hardcore* (1977), *The World is Full of Married Men* (1979)

Mark JONES (1939-)

Shropshire-born Mark Jones was one of the few regular male leads in British sex films during the 1970s and wasn't bashful about being completely nude. At the Central School of Speech and Drama in the early 1960s, he was talent-spotted by visionary theatre director Peter Brook, who took the young actor under his wing. A star of the RSC and the Royal Court, and a heart-throb from playing the lead in the early seventies TV drama *Family at War*, Jones was an unlikely recruit to the world of British sex comedy. Bald on top, he was often required to wear a wig for his various slapstick roles and was most fun in drag in *Keep It Up Jack!* His extensive non-sex film work includes *Tell Me Lies* (1967), *Marat/Sade* (1968) (both for Peter Brook), *Connecting Rooms* (1972) with Bette Davis, *The Medusa Touch* (1978), *The Empire Strikes Back* (1980) and finally Derek Ford's horror epic, *Don't Open Till Christmas* (1984). During the 1980s he appeared in TV series *Buccaneer* and *Blott on the Landscape*, but he was last seen losing his wig in a bowl of soup in a Hamlet cigar commercial. Jones now resides in Cornwall, where he writes and is happy to remember his colourful sex film past. 'I wouldn't have minded a whole career of those films,' he chuckles. 'I loved the pretty girls and I'd do it all again!'

GENRE CREDITS: *Layout for 5 Models* (1972), *Keep It Up Jack!* (1973), *The Sexplorer* (1975), *Secrets of a Superstud* (1976), *Can I Come Too?* (1979)

Anthony KENYON

Anthony Kenyon and Monika Ringwald in *The Sexplorer* (1975).

Another male lead, slightly more mature than his contemporaries and usually sporting a hang-dog expression. Dubbed the 'British Harry *Deep Throat* Reems' during the mid-1970s, Kenyon wasn't backward in coming forward when required to participate in the hardcore scenes for the export versions of *Keep It Up Jack!*, *Sex Express* and *Secrets of a Superstud*. However, he is at his best (fully dressed) as the randy gamekeeper, Mellons, in 1976's *Keep It Up Downstairs*.

GENRE CREDITS: *Keep It Up Jack!* (1973), *Sex Express* (1975), *The Sexplorer* (1975), *Secrets of a Superstud* (1975), *Erotic Inferno* (1975), *Keep It Up Downstairs* (1976), *The Playbirds* (1978)

Queen KONG (1950-)

Born Deanna Booher in Running Spring California, Queenie was over 6' by the age of 13 and by 16 weighed an incredible 200lbs. Queenie decided to exploit her huge size and became the first female collegiate wrestler in America, first performing professionally aged 21. In 1980 she started a 300-strong troupe of like-minded female grapplers who fought in mud and oil for nightclub audiences throughout California. Queenie was famed for taking on all comers in the ring: big women, two men at a time, even defanged bears. David Sullivan caught her act on a trip to the US and paid Queenie to bring her bizarre attraction to the UK, which caused quite a storm. Queenie shocked viewers with an eye-opening interview on BBCTV's *Nationwide*, appeared on radio's *Woman's Hour* and on *Breakfast Time* sang (remarkably well, it must be noted) her theme song 'I Eat Red Meat'. As if to back up her claim, she later ate raw rump steak at Bayswater's Concordia Restaurant in a publicity stunt organised by John M East. She made two artless (but profitable) films for Sullivan. After semi-retiring from wrestling in the 1990s, flame-haired Queenie has acted (and been a stuntwoman) in numerous situation comedies, TV shows and movies, including *Spaceballs* (1987) and *Theodore Rex* (1995). Today Queenie is a grandmother who produces 'female domination' videos and organises 'fetish training' classes for her legion of fans.

GENRE CREDITS: *Hellcats – Mud Wrestling* (1983), *Electric Blue 10* (video 1983), *Foxy Female Boxers* (video 1983), *Queen Kong – The Amazonian Woman* (video 1984)

Alan LAKE (1940-1984)

Despite showing early promise, Alan Lake never made a lasting impression as a male lead and his choice of films was uniformly dreadful. His notorious heavy drinking and profound psychological

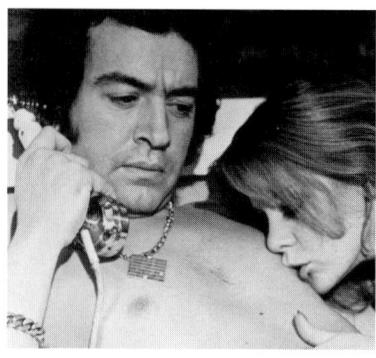

Medallion man Alan Lake with Mary Millington in *The Playbirds* (1978).

problems often made him unstable, violent, and unpredictable. On the set of *The Playbirds* he shocked his co-stars by punching an extra, but this sort of behaviour was not uncommon. In the early part of the decade he served 12 months for being an accessory to a violent assault. Rarely out of the tabloids for his hell-raising, Lake was most famous for being the third husband of faded 1950s film star Diana Dors. The couple worked together on several sex films and Dors even got him a tiny part in her Scandinavian movie *Swedish Wildcats*. Lake repaid her by trying to strangle her on location. By the late 1970s he seemed to have found his niche in British movies, playing 'medallion man' studs, jack-the-lads and ex-cons, but despite making a couple of neat guest appearances in TV shows like *Bergerac* and *Hart to Hart*, he was unable to shake off his seedy image. This was compounded by his final film role, as a serial killer with a psychopathic hatred of Santa Claus, in Derek Ford's *Don't Open Till Christmas* (1984). In October 1984, five months after the death of his wife from cancer, Lake shot himself through the head in his teenage son's bedroom.

GENRE CREDITS: *Layout for Five Models* (1972), *The Amorous Milkman* (1974), *Percy's Progress* (1974), *Swedish Wildcats* (Sweden 1974), *The Office Party* (1976), *The Playbirds* (1978), *Confessions from the David Galaxy Affair* (1979)

Me Me LAY (1952-)

Elegant, slim, long-haired Burmese actress with one of the best *double entendre* names ever. She first regularly appeared on British TV as 'paper master' Robert Harbin's sidekick on ATV's *Origami* (1968-72), before graduating to hostess on *Sale of the Century* with Nicholas Parsons. On the big screen, Lay featured briefly in *Crucible of Terror* (1971) and as a hooker in Burt Kwouk's 'Chinese nookie factory' in *Revenge of the Pink Panther* (1978). On the Continent, Lay was a mainstay of gore-filled Italian horror films, usually playing innocent-looking cannibal girls who make a meal of unsuspecting jungle explorers in films like *Deep River Savages* (1972), *Jungle Holocaust* (1977) and *Eaten Alive* (1980). Latterly billed as Me Me Lai, her final movie credit is Lars von Trier's *Element of Crime* from 1984.

GENRE CREDITS: *She'll Follow You Anywhere* (1971), *Au Pair Girls* (1972)

Julie LEE (1955-1983)

Born Julie Moxon in Sheffield to a Chinese mother and English father, Julie escaped to London when she was 24 and embarked on a desperate search for modelling and film work, scraping together enough cash for a boob job and various other operations. Posing topless at the Cannes Film Festival in 1979, she informed reporters that she had been offered leading roles in two sex comedies for sometime boyfriend Kenneth Rowles, *Weekend Bangers* and *The Ups and Downs of a Soccer Star*. Neither film materialised. Her luck changed in 1980 when she was introduced to David Sullivan, who quickly signed her up to appear in *Emmanuelle in Soho*. During rehearsals, however, it became apparent to everyone that she had absolutely no acting ability. Julie worked extensively as a high-class prostitute and cocaine dealer and in 1982, in a bizarre publicity stunt organised by John M East, agreed to marry a wealthy Egyptian businessman whom she had never met in return for one million pounds, a luxury house in Chiswick and a £20,000 Mercedes. In the early hours of 4 May 1983, she was driving back from a Maidenhead nightclub (where she had been placed second in a tacky beauty contest) and lost control of her Mercedes at the Datchet junction of the M4, sustaining major head injuries and appalling burns. She died at Wrexham Park Hospital six days later, aged 28.

GENRE CREDITS: *Emmanuelle in Soho* (1981), *Mary Millington's World Striptease Extravaganza* (1981)

John LINDSAY (1939-)

The founding father of hardcore pornography in Britain, Scots-born Lindsay left school at 18 and then studied at Glasgow School of Art, where he was particularly taken with the life classes. Lindsay then worked as a press photographer, first for the Scottish *Daily Herald* and then in London for the *Daily Express*. Shooting the female models for *Vogue* gave him his first taste of glamour photography and he rapidly moved onto *Penthouse*, among others. Blue movies were just a step away and Lindsay made his first 16mm sex film in 1966. He subsequently admitted to having made well over 4000 blue movies throughout the world, including such titles as *Schoolgirl Seduction*, *Convent of Sin*, *Girl Guide Rape* and *The Kinky Vicar*. Among his discoveries were Mary Millington, Ava Cadell, Pat Astley and Timothy Blackstone. In October 1974 he was found not guilty of 'conspiring to publish obscene films for monetary gain' at Birmingham Crown Court. The films in question had stirred up controversy not only because they depicted young women dressed as schoolgirls, but also because Lindsay made his films at Aston Manor Comprehensive School during the summer holidays with help from the randy caretaker and ex-head boy! After the ruling Lindsay opened London's first hardcore cinema clubs. His Taboo Club in Great Newport Street and London Blue Movie Centre in Berwick Street brazenly advertised homegrown hardcore films, either to watch on the premises or purchase for use on a home projector. In 1977 he was tried again, this time at the Old Bailey. Once more he was acquitted. Never shy about the nature of his business, Lindsay was twice filmed at work for the documentaries *Naughty!* (1971) and his own *The Pornbrokers* (1973). By the early eighties Lindsay was selling his films on videotape and in 1983 his premises were raided for the last time. At his subsequent trial he was found guilty of selling and exhibiting obscene material and gaoled for 12 months. On his release, tired of constant police harassment, he sold his businesses and moved to Kent with his second wife Penny and their twin daughters. Now a very private man, he was coaxed out of obscurity, amid much secrecy, to be interviewed for Channel 4's Mary Millington tribute in 1996.

GENRE CREDITS: *The Wife Swappers* (1969) (stills cameraman), *The Love Pill* (1971) (co-producer/writer), *Naughty!* (1971) (interviewee), *The Pornbrokers* (1973) (co-director/co-producer/photography/interviewee), *The Hot Girls* (1974) (co-director/co-producer/co-writer), *I'm Not Feeling Myself Tonight!* (1975) (co-producer), *Mary Millington's True Blue Confessions* (1980) (interviewee), *Sex and Fame – The Mary Millington Story* (TV 1996) (interviewee)

Stanley LONG (1933-)

Stanley A Long, the godfather of British cinema sex, was born in south London, the eldest son of the chauffeur to the Hovis chairman. He started his career as a freelance stills photographer and one day was hired to take photographs of the scantily clad dancers at London's Windmill Theatre. Thus began his long love affair with naked ladies. In 1958 Stanley set up in business with friend Arnold Louis Miller and together the two men produced glamour photographs and 8mm striptease films for their company, Stag. As well as making documentaries for the Ministry of Defence, Stanley produced his first cinema movie, *Nudist Memories*, at the age of 25, with a budget of £1000. Long and Miller cranked out more nudie successes like *Nudes of the World* and *Take Your Clothes Off and Live!* and their first all-out sex film, *Secrets of a Windmill Girl*, in 1966. After their partnership split, Long worked as a cameraman for ATV plus photographing and producing several movies for sexploitation director Derek Ford. His own directorial début was the hippy musical *Bread* in 1971. His production company Salon (a conflation of Stanley Alfred Long) then made a stream of popular comedies during the mid-1970s. Most successful of all was *Adventures of a Taxi Driver* in 1975, which grossed millions around the world. The same year Stanley set up his own distribution company, Alpha, after endless frustrations with other distributors ripping him off. He retired from full-time movie production in 1978 after the release of his final feature, *Adventures of a Plumber's Mate*, and thereafter concentrated on distributing other people's movies. He won an award for his trailer for David Cronenberg's *The Brood* and, when he sold Alpha in the early eighties, it was the biggest independent distribution company in Britain. 1983 saw the video release of *Screamtime*, a compilation film made up of three horror shorts he had directed two years previously with Michael Armstrong under the collective name Al Beresford. The Salon company is still in existence and is now one of the largest post-production facilities in Europe. 'I'm not ashamed of anything I've done and I'm very proud of my record in 40 years of the movie industry,' he says. 'I've had a very good life.'

GENRE CREDITS: *Nudist Memories* (1959) (photography), *West End Jungle* (1961) (unreleased) (co-producer/co-writer/photography), *Nudes of the World* (1961) (photography), *Take Your Clothes Off and Live!* (1962) (photography), *London in the Raw* (1964) (photography), *Primitive London* (1965) (co-producer/photography), *Secrets of a Windmill Girl* (1966) (co-producer/photography), *A Promise of Bed* (1969) (producer/photography), *The Wife Swappers* (1969) (producer/co-writer), *Groupie Girl* (1970) (producer/photography), *Naughty!* (1971) (director/producer/co-writer/photography), *Sex and the Other Woman* (1972) (director/producer), *On the Game* (1973) (director/co-producer), *Eskimo Nell* (1974) (co-director/producer), *It Could Happen to You* aka *Intimate Teenage Secrets* (1975) (director/producer), *Adventures of a Taxi Driver* (1975) (director/co-producer), *Adventures of a Private Eye* (1977) (director/co-producer), *Adventures of a Plumber's Mate* (1978) (director), *Peter Noble Introduces the Best of the Adventures* (video compilation 1981) (director/producer)

Sue LONGHURST (1943-)

'I've always considered myself to be a bit of a fraud really,' says Sue Longhurst. 'I just kind of wandered into acting.' Having trained at the London Academy, Sue was initially a music teacher but, egged on by her model sister, she was soon posing for magazines, record sleeves, book covers and TV commercials, as well as spending 18 months advertising John Player's cigarettes. At 27 Sue made her movie début as a schoolgirl in Hammer's *Lust For a Vampire* (1970). Then for two years she worked primarily in television: with Benny Hill and Dick Emery, on *The Good Old Days* and as replacement for Anne Aston on *The Golden Shot*. In 1972, she was offered an eye-catching supporting role in David Grant's *Secrets of a Door to door Salesman*. 'She was quite a bit older than some of the other girls we'd seen and David wasn't keen on her,' remembers Alan Selwyn. 'But I thought she was bloody good and persuaded him to give her a part and of course she was super.' This first sex film led to bigger roles in some of the most popular British sex comedies of the seventies. Always looking eager to please, Sue had the rare honour of taking Robin Askwith's virginity, while covered in soap suds, in *Confessions of a Window Cleaner* in 1974. Later that year she was invited to play the female lead opposite Scandinavian sex film habitué Ole Søltoft in the Swedish romp *A Man with a Maid*, released in the UK as *What the Swedish Butler Saw*. Returning to England, Sue continued to keep busy on screen, clocking up ten films in six years. Her last movie was Ray Selfe's *Can I Come Too?* in 1979. A very funny, charming lady, Sue retired from acting in 1981 and now lives on the south coast of England.

GENRE CREDITS: *Secrets of a Door to Door Salesman* (1973), *Keep it Up Jack!* (1973), *Can You Keep It Up for a Week?* (1974), *Confessions of a Window Cleaner* (1974), *The Over Amorous Artist* (1974), *What the Swedish Butler Saw* (Sweden 1974), *Girls Come First* (1975), *Keep It Up Downstairs* (1976), *Come Play with Me* (1977), *Can I Come Too?* (1979), *Doing Rude Things* (TV 1995)

Suzy MANDEL (1955-)

Suzy Mandel gets extra tuition from Robin Askwith in *Confessions of a Driving Instructor* (1976).

While Mary Millington was afforded top billing in *Come Play with Me*, it was actually fellow glamour girl Suzy Mandel who most impressed critics and audiences alike. Her well-educated manner and almost snooty confidence, coupled with a cherubic face and trim figure, endeared her to legions of sex film fans. A former lingerie model and stripper, Suzy made her mark on TV in *The Benny Hill Show* from 1974. She became a favourite of sex film directors, who were confident that she could deliver large chunks of dialogue. In just two years Suzy made six movies, including a couple for David Sullivan, who liked her so much that he named a racehorse after her. In 1979 she married movie financier Stanley Margolis and the couple emigrated to the USA. Across the Atlantic, Suzy's first American movie was the crazy sex comedy *Blonde Ambition* (1980), in which she was required to perform in hardcore scenes. Suzy angrily claimed that her sex scenes had been faked with a body double. Even so, she adored her new life in Hollywood and the major league celebrities surrounding her. Sadly, Suzy's acting career was not to last. Although her last two pictures were strictly 'clothes-on' affairs – the cult favourite *The Private Eyes* (1980) and a tiny role in silly safari B-movie *Mistress of the Apes* (1981) – she never worked again. Still living in America, she now resides in New York.

GENRE CREDITS: *Intimate Games* (1976), *Confessions of a Driving Instructor* (1976), *Come Play with Me* (1977), *The Playbirds* (1978), *Adventures of a Plumber's Mate* (1978), *You're Driving Me Crazy!* (1978), *Blonde Ambition* (USA 1980)

George Harrison MARKS (1926-1997)

By his own account, Harrison Marks teamed up in his teens with chum Stuart Samuels to form a music hall act, their jokes mainly pinched from other people. Variety, Marks claimed, was 'in his blood'. None of this was true, however; his first showbusiness experience involved lugging Pathé News cans around Ealing Studios. Having established himself as a theatrical photographer, he was working at the Prince of Wales Theatre when he met and fell in love with semi-nude dancer Pamela

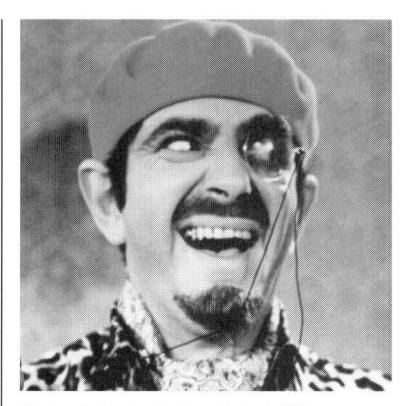

Master of disguise Harrison Marks in 1965.

Green. Together, their glamour pictorial *Kamera*, established in 1957, set the benchmark for British nude photography. Before long they were publishing four separate titles per week including *Solo*, *Femme* and *In Touch*. Marks shot his first glamour film in 1958, making Green a household name in black-and-white 8mm shorts like *The Window Dresser*. Three years later they made their début feature film, *Naked – As Nature Intended*. Marks discovered, and romanced, numerous other voluptuous models including Paula Page, Marie Devereux, June Palmer and Vicki Kennedy (aka Margaret Nolan). His partnership with Green broke up in 1965 and six years later his publishing and film empire collapsed when he was convicted at the Old Bailey of sending obscene material through the post. Broke and drinking heavily, he somehow continued to make 8mm films like *Apartment 69* and *Halfway Inn* and in 1976 was offered the chance to direct *Come Play with Me* by David Sullivan. Sadly, Marks had sold his share in the blockbusting movie to Sullivan and was soon skint again. While hardcore had never really been to Marks' taste, he was persuaded to direct several explicit films in Germany and Denmark in the late 1970s, released on the *Color Climax* label. His real name didn't appear on the credits and he was subsequently unable to recall the films' titles. Having been taken on as a photographer for popular British spanking magazine *Janus*, in 1984 Marks set about publishing his own magazine, *Kane*, from the studio in his Stamford Hill home. As a spin-off, he directed nearly 80 videos in ten years, titles like *Stinging Tails* (1992) and *The Spanking Game* (1993) selling by the bucketload, particularly in the US and Germany. By the mid-1990s he had been diagnosed with terminal bone cancer and he died in June 1997. His business is now run by his daughter, Josie, who is in charge of administering the spankings within the pages of *Kane*.

GENRE CREDITS: *Naked – As Nature Intended* (1961) (director/producer/co-writer/cameo appearance), *The Naked World of Harrison Marks* (1965) (director/producer/co-writer/actor), *Pattern of Evil* (USA 1967) (director/producer), *Otto and the Nude Wave* (Germany 1968) (actor), *Nine Ages of Nakedness* (1969) (director/producer/writer/actor), *Come Play with Me* (1977) (director/producer/writer/actor)

David McGILLIVRAY (1947-)

An actor, director, screenwriter and much-performed playwright, McGillivray began his career as a film journalist in 1966. For 12 years he reviewed films for the *Monthly Film Bulletin* (he was also assistant editor for a time) and in 1970 he began writing screenplays. McGillivray turned in inventive scripts for a clutch of Pete Walker shockers: *House of Whipcord* (1973), *Frightmare* (1974), *House of Mortal Sin* (1975) and *Schizo* (1976), and two for Norman J Warren: *Satan's Slave* (1976) and *Terror* (1978). But the handful of sex films McGillivray was involved with were less rewarding, mainly because his scripts were heavily tampered with. In the mid-seventies McGillivray wrote a sex comedy for producer Laurie Barnett, wonderfully entitled *Unzipper De Do Dah*, but despite a test sequence being shot the production collapsed. 'I've not opened the script since 1976 and I don't intend to,' he says. In 1982 he reawakened the slumbering genre of British sexploitation films for a series of articles in the now-defunct *Cinema* magazine. Ten years later these articles were brought together into a book entitled *Doing Rude Things*. 'That is my only achievement in life to date,' he says dryly. The book spawned a tongue-in-cheek BBC documentary, broadcast in May 1995, in which McGillivray appeared uncredited as a kinky High Court judge watching adult films at London's Prince Charles Cinema. Nearly 30 years on, McGillivray is unable to watch the films he wrote and appeared in. 'I always liked writing comedy bits for myself,' he recalls, 'but I can't bear to watch those films now because of my enormous sideburns. I modelled myself on the lead singer of Mungo Jerry. The shame is immense!'

GENRE CREDITS: *White Cargo* (1973) (actor/writer), *The Hot Girls* (1974) (actor/writer), *I'm Not Feeling Myself Tonight!* (actor/writer) (1975), *Doing Rude Things* (TV 1995) (interviewee), *Sex and Fame – The Mary Millington Story* (TV 1996) (interviewee)

Joseph McGRATH (1930-)

Glaswegian Joe McGrath was a reluctant contributor to British sex films. Legend has it that he was so bored with his 1975 movie *I'm Not Feeling Myself Tonight!* that he directed some of the scenes with his back to the performers. For his two other 'X'-rated movies McGrath declined even to use his real name. His non-sex movies weren't necessarily any better. In 1967 he co-directed the shambolic James Bond spoof *Casino Royale* and the seriously overstretched *Thirty Is a Dangerous Age, Cynthia*. Three years later McGrath brought together the most chaotic cast ever assembled for a British movie in *The Magic Christian*. The film bombed. Licking his wounds, McGrath turned to the 'X'-rated industry where he met producer David Grant and worked on several projects for Grant's Oppidan company, including *The Great McGonagall* (1975), *Escape to Entebbe* (1976) and *Marcia* (1978), all non-sex films, incidentally. On TV McGrath was infinitely more popular, especially with Peter Cook and Dudley Moore's *Not Only ... But Also* series (1965-70), for which he won the Guild of Television Producers Award for best comedy programme.

GENRE CREDITS: *Secrets of a Door to Door Salesman* (1973) (co-writer), *Girls Come First* (1975) (director/co-writer), *I'm Not Feeling Myself Tonight!* (1975) (director), *Pink Orgasm* (unfinished 1975) (co-writer)

Vicki (1950-) and Ann MICHELLE (1952-)

Vicki and Ann Michelle (real name Nathan) were raised in Chigwell by their parents and a German au pair who went on to become international film star Elke Sommer. Graduates of the Aida Foster stage school, the sisters made their joint movie début in 1970 in the devilishly sexy *Virgin Witch*. Previously Vicki had appeared in *The Haunted House of Horror* (1968) and had played the go-go girl opposite Dudley Moore in the West End hit, *Play It Again Sam*. Ann's earlier movies included small parts in the sex 'mockumentary' *Sex in Our Time* (1968) and *The Prime of Miss Jean Brodie* (1969). After the success of *Virgin Witch*, Ann found her niche in sex and horror, notably as a zombie biker chick in *Psychomania* (1971) and in Pete Walker's gruelling *House of Whipcord* (1973). Vicki, meanwhile, leaned more towards comedy. Throughout the 1970s she carved out a career working alongside Dick Emery, Les Dawson, Ken Dodd, the Goodies and the Two Ronnies. On TV both sisters starred alongside Mollie Sugden in the bizarre sci-fi sitcom *Come Back Mrs Noah* (1978). And, while Ann quietly retreated from acting in the 1980s, Vicki is still a popular face on TV and in stage farces. She is now forever identified with her role as saucy French waitress, Yvette, in the BBC sitcom *'Allo 'Allo* (1984-1992).

GENRE CREDITS: *Love in Our Time* (1968)

(Ann), *Virgin Witch* (1971) (Vicki and Ann), *Mistress Pamela* (1973) (Ann), *Cruel Passion* (1977) (Ann), *Young Lady Chatterley* (USA 1977) (Ann)

Mary MILLINGTON (1945-1979)

Mary Millington models a shell bikini in March 1973.

Born Mary Quilter in Middlesex to unmarried parents and raised just outside Dorking in Surrey, Mary married local butcher's boy Robert Maxted in 1964. A chance meeting with pornographer John Lindsay in a Kensington coffee shop in 1970 led to Mary playing the title role in *Miss Bohrloch*, the first of a dozen or so hardcore films she made both in Britain and on the Continent over a three-year period. Interestingly, Mary had her husband's blessing in pursuing her new career and they remained married until her death. Modelling for top-shelf magazines and working as a high-class prostitute throughout the early 1970s, Mary is said to have only plunged into porn in order to pay for medical treatment for her mother, who was dying of cancer. However, there can be little doubt that the uninhibited Mary really did love being the centre of attention. Mary's first big screen role came with a tiny cameo in *Secrets of a Door to Door Salesman* in 1973, but her part was left on the cutting-room floor. Other films rapidly followed but it was her love affair with porn publisher David Sullivan that finally broke her into the big time. Sullivan persuaded Mary to change her name to Millington and splashed her face, body and personality across all his magazine titles, including *Playbirds*, *Whitehouse* and *Park Lane*. Mary's overnight success was nothing short of phenomenal. Sackloads of mail arrived for her each week and Sullivan quickly installed her as the star attraction behind the counter of one of his sex shops in Norbury, south London. However, it was Mary's brief role as a saucy nurse in *Come Play with Me* that shot her into the sex stratosphere. Within the space of just two years Mary became the most bankable name at the British box-office with a string of record-breaking 'X'-rated movies. But with fame came unhappiness. Mary's sex shop was repeatedly raided by the Obscene Publications Squad and she complained bitterly of police threats and harassment. After the death of her beloved mother, Mary sank into depression, kleptomania and cocaine abuse. After being arrested for shoplifting on 18 August 1979, the police told her it was highly likely that she would be sent to Holloway. With a court appearance for an earlier shoplifting offence set for the following Tuesday, Mary made one last desperate phone call to her friend John M East, who dismissed her worries and bluntly told her she needed 'psychiatric treatment'. Mary rang off abruptly and on the morning of 19 August was found dead in bed by her husband. The cause of death was a deadly cocktail of paracetamol and alcohol. In a rambling suicide note to David Sullivan she wrote: 'The police have framed me yet again. They frighten me so much. I can't face the thought of prison.' She was 33. There has been a resurgence in interest in the Mary Millington phenomenon in recent years, including a fine Channel 4 documentary first broadcast in 1996.

GENRE CREDITS: *Secrets of a Door to Door Salesman* (1973), *Eskimo Nell* (1974), *Erotic Inferno* (1975), *I'm Not Feeling Myself Tonight!* (1975), *I Nöd Och Lust* aka *Private Pleasures* (Sweden 1975), *Intimate Games* (1976), *Keep It Up Downstairs* (1976), *Come Play with Me* (1977), *The Playbirds* (1978), *What's Up Superdoc?* (1978), *Confessions from the David Galaxy Affair* (1979), *Queen of the Blues* (1979), *Mary Millington's True Blue Confessions* (1980), *Mary Millington's World Striptease Extravaganza* (1981), *Doing Rude Things* (TV 1995), *Sex and Fame – The Mary Millington Story* (TV 1996)

Olivia MUNDAY (1951-)

Olivia was a well-endowed model and comedy actress very much in the Rosemary England mould. Based in Los Angeles for the early part of her career, she moved back to Britain in 1973 where her big bristols and shapely bum made her extremely popular with filmgoers. Olivia made her naked début in *Confessions of a Window Cleaner* and went the whole hog in a threesome with Mary Millington and Maria Coyne in her best movie, *Keep It Up Downstairs* in 1976. Retired from the acting profession, Olivia now works for a PR company in London.

GENRE CREDITS: *Confessions of a Window Cleaner* (1974), *Can You Keep It Up for a Week?* (1974), *Keep it Up Downstairs* (1976)

Chic MURRAY (1919-1985)

Chic Murray was a fast-talking working class Scot who became one of the most popular comedians of his generation. Touring the music halls with his saucy brand of humour and songs, he was once fêted as 'Britain's funniest man'. At the height of his fame he travelled Great Britain in a double-act with his 4'11" accordion-playing wife, Maudie. During his last decade or so, Murray's talents were regularly utilised for British sex comedies, which he relished. His best performance is as the bumbling village policeman in *The Ups and Downs of a Handyman*. Four years before his death

Murray's big movie break finally came with a polished performance as the headmaster in *Gregory's Girl* (1981).

GENRE CREDITS: *Secrets of a Door to Door Salesman* (1973), *Ups and Downs of a Handyman* (1975), *I'm Not Feeling Myself Tonight!* (1975), *What's Up Nurse?* (1977), *What's up Superdoc?* (1978), *Can I Come Too?* (1979)

Christopher NEIL (1948-)

A skinny, baby-faced leading man who, although born in Dublin, was raised in Manchester, Neil was pop-mad as a youngster and appeared in the West End production of *Hair* alongside singer Paul Nicholas. The two bonded immediately and in 1974 they starred as members of a pop group touring Spain in the Tudor Gates comedy *Three For All*. A year earlier Neil had made his sex film début in a supporting role in *The Sex Thief*, rapidly followed by *Eskimo Nell*. Between film work, Neil presented *You and Me*, the BBC2 under-fives programme, and produced three Top 20 singles for Nicholas. While starring as a roadie in ITV's *Rock Follies* in 1976, Neil was approached by producer Stanley Long to take over the leading role from Barry Evans in the second *Adventures* film. 'I thought long and hard about whether it could harm my career if people saw my bum on screen!' he later admitted. He was eventually persuaded to sign on the bottom line and was the top-billed star for the last two movies in the saucy trilogy. What's more, Neil wrote and performed the theme tunes to both his *Adventures* movies, the first written in collaboration with Nicholas. Since retiring from acting, Neil has produced top tunes for Dollar, Sheena Easton and Celine Dion.

GENRE CREDITS: *The Sex Thief* (1973) (actor), *Eskimo Nell* (1974) (actor), *Adventures of a Private Eye* (1977) (actor/composer), *Adventures of a Plumber's Mate* (1978) (actor/composer)

Françoise PASCAL (1949-)

Above: Françoise Pascal lets rip in *Keep It Up Downstairs* (1976).

Golden-skinned, high-cheekboned, Mauritian-born Françoise established herself in the UK during the 1960s and 70s as the archetypal sexy French bird, displaying plenty of *entente cordiale*. On television she had roles in *Coronation Street*, *The Brothers*, Kenneth Rowles' short-lived all-female action series *Go Girl* and, most famously, as saucy Gallic student, Danielle Favre, in LWT's dodgy sitcom *Mind Your Language* (1977-1979). She worked alongside Peter Sellers twice, in *There's a Girl In My Soup* (1970) and *Soft Beds, Hard Battles* (1973), which led to a short-lived affair with the star. In France she appeared in several offbeat horror movies, including Jean Rollin's *Les raisins de la mort* aka *The Grapes of Death* (1978). In the early 1980s she moved to Hollywood, but only bit parts came her way and she claimed to have supplemented her income by pushing cocaine. She eventually returned to the UK but weight problems and health worries, including colon cancer in 1993, knocked back her career. She currently resides in Hampshire with her son, Nicholas, from her relationship with actor Richard Johnson.

GENRE CREDITS: *School for Sex* (1968), *Loving Feeling* (1968), *Soft Beds, Hard Battles* (1973), *If You Don't Want It* (France 1974), *Keep It Up Downstairs* (1976), *Doing Rude Things* (TV 1995)

Paul RAYMOND (1925-)

In 2001 Paul Raymond, the self-proclaimed King of Soho, is one of the richest men in Britain, with a yearly salary of three and a half million pounds and a £650 million fortune built on nakedness. It's a far cry from his strict Roman Catholic childhood in Liverpool. Born Geoffrey Quinn, the son of a lorry driver, Raymond initially sought his fortune touring provincial theatres with a fraudulent mind-reading act. In 1951 he married Jean, a 20-year-old showgirl choreographer, and together they created Britain's first travelling variety show with bare girls. They eventually settled in London and in 1955 Raymond opened his now-legendary Soho striptease club, Raymond's Revuebar. His flashy, elaborate nude shows were an instant success and Raymond and his family could soon afford to live in an elegant house in Wimbledon and drive around in a black Rolls-Royce, plate number PR11. He branched out into top-shelf publishing with magazines like *King* and *Club International*, but it was his acquisition of tired men's monthly *Men Only* in 1971 that was to be his greatest coup. With model Fiona Richmond at the helm of the new-look title, *Men Only* became Britain's number one *glamour* magazine of the early 1970s. Raymond, by then separated from his wife, wooed Richmond and, despite a 20-year age gap, the two became London's most famous lovers. Uncredited, Raymond financed Richmond's three movies for James Kenelm Clarke but only ever put his name (literally) to one big screen project, 1980's *Paul Raymond's Erotica*, co-starring himself. The film was not a success and Raymond never dabbled with the cinema again, although his Revuebar was a preferred location for several other sex films. Since the mid-1980s Raymond has bought up vast tracts of land in the West End, becoming one of the biggest landlords in London. Since the death of his daughter, Debbie, from a drink and drugs overdose in 1992, Raymond has been somewhat reclusive. Now living in a penthouse behind the Ritz, he is rarely seen in public. In 2001 he stood down as chairman of the Paul Raymond Organisation and handed over his empire to his high-flying nephew, Mark Quinn.

GENRE CREDITS: *Exposé* (1975) (executive producer), *Hardcore* (1977) (executive producer), *Let's Get Laid!* (1977) (executive producer), *Paul Raymond's Erotica* (1980) (actor/executive producer), *Electric Blue Presents a Night at the Revuebar* (video 1982) (consultant)

Fiona RICHMOND (1945-)

Grocery tips from Fiona Richmond outside London's Classic Moulin cinema in April 1977.

The formidably brainy daughter of an Anglican vicar, Richmond was born Julia Rosamund Harrison in the rectory at Hilborough, Norfolk in 1945. The family later moved to a parish in Cornwall, where her mother taught in a Falmouth convent. Coming to London aged 20, Fiona became an airline stewardess and then a Playboy bunny, staying in the hutch for two years. In 1970 Fiona met the married porn mogul Paul Raymond when she auditioned for his saucy stage show *Pyjama Tops* at the Whitehall Theatre. She got the job and they soon became lovers, staying together for nearly six years. Fiona was regularly seen tearing around the streets of Soho in her yellow E-type Jaguar (number plate: FU2), a gift from her wealthy boyfriend. In 1971, with a new name dreamt up between them, Fiona was installed as a sexy columnist in Raymond's revamped *Men Only* magazine. In each issue Fiona was called upon to 'road test' men throughout the world but, unknown to her fans, the sexy exploits were completely fabricated. 'It was in the day of pretty nudes,' she said in 2000. 'There was nothing tacky or nasty about what I did. One critic said that if you could buy ladies in Sainsbury's, then you'd buy Fiona Richmond!' Her column spawned a series of popular paperbacks which gave Timothy Lea's Confessions books a real run for their money. Alongside her burgeoning writing career, Fiona was the headline attraction in a succession of Raymond-sponsored West End stage shows between 1970 and 1981, most famously *Let's Get Laid!* (1974), *Come Into My Bed* (1976) and *Women Behind Bars* (1977), co-starring such diverse actors as John Inman, Victor Spinetti and American drag queen Divine. Fiona's movie career began in 1974 when she played a French stripper in *Barry McKenzie Holds His Own*, but meatier film parts followed thanks to director James Kenelm Clarke, who starred her in a trio of well-publicised sex movies, beginning with *Exposé* in 1975. 'For a time in the seventies I felt that I'd explode because my life was so frenetic,' she admitted in 1984. 'I'd go from opening in a sex show to writing a book, giving interviews, planning a film, with no break at all.' After the bottom fell out of the sex film market Fiona returned to the stage, touring the UK in near-the-knuckle fare like *Space in My Pyjamas*, *Galactic Girl* and *Yes, We Have No Pyjamas*. In 1983 she married TV journalist James Montgomery and, at the age of 40, gave birth to a daughter, Tara. Film cameos continued in Mel Brooks' *History of the World (Part 1)* and the insane *Eat the Rich*, and Fiona even gained a measure of respectability as guest panelist on *Celebrity Squares* and *Blankety Blank*. Her last TV appearance was, curiously, as an uncredited extra in Jilly Cooper's *The Man Who Made Husbands Jealous* in 1995. Today she enjoys life as the respectable owner of a Hampshire bed and breakfast and a luxury hotel on the Caribbean island of Grenada.

GENRE CREDITS: *Exposé* (1975), *Hardcore* (1977), *Let's Get Laid!* (1977), *Electric Blue 001* (video 1979)

Monika RINGWALD

A petite European model and cover star of naturist magazine *Health & Efficiency*, Monika barely uttered a single word throughout her film career, due mainly to her heavy German accent. Her only sizeable role was as a sexually inquisitive alien in Derek Ford's *The Sexplorer* in 1975. 'She was a lovely girl but didn't have much of a sense of humour,' recalls her *Sexplorer* co-star and one-time agent, Alan Selwyn. 'Off screen she'd say to me in a monotone voice, "You are making me a big star, yes?"' Apart from her sex film work, Monika also appeared naked in Norman J Warren's horror classic *Satan's Slave* (1976), but the director had little idea how well-known she was. 'There was this dream sequence in *Satan's Slave* where she is being whipped,' Warren remembers, 'but she just wasn't registering any pain. All she did was moan, almost orgasmically. I had to say to her, "Monika, you've got to pretend this is hurting you. You're not meant to enjoy it!"' She finally retired from modelling in 1978 after her second marriage to a car dealer, and appears not to have kept in touch with any of her former colleagues.

GENRE CREDITS: *Secrets of a Door to Door Salesman* (1973), *Confessions of a Window Cleaner* (1974), *Percy's Progress* (1974), *The Amorous Milkman* (1974), *Confessions of a Sex Maniac* (1974), *The Sexplorer* (1975), *I'm Not Feeling Myself Tonight!* (1975), *Erotic Inferno* (1975), *Intimate Games* (1976), *What's Up Nurse?* (1977)

Kenneth F ROWLES (1945-)

At 16 Ken was hired as a runner for producer Laurie Green at Merton Park Studios. He later became editor on over 20 movies, including Jean Luc Godard's classic *Sympathy for the Devil* (1968) starring the Rolling Stones. Branching out in 1967, he set up his own production company, KFR Productions, and his first feature-length movie was Peter Sykes' spidery thriller *Venom* (1970), written by Donald and Derek Ford. The same year, Ken produced a way-ahead-of-its-time funky television series *Go Girl* starring Luan Peters, Françoise Pascal and Leena Skoog, filmed on location in Marbella and Benidorm. Sadly, due to internal wranglings with HTV, the 13-part series was never broadcast and only the innovative pilot episode survives. By the mid-seventies Ken was the brains behind a couple of hugely popular sex movies. His 1976 meisterwerk, *Take an Easy Ride*, ran for a whopping 48 weeks at the Pigalle in Piccadilly Circus. Ken was later responsible for documentaries about the Royal Family (*Tribute to Her Majesty*, 1986) and James Herriott (*Creature Comforts*, 1991). Currently the vice-chairman of the producers' and directors' section of BECTU, Ken is still heavily involved in the entertainment industry, embarking, among other things, on a new TV series on the history of the theatre entitled *Bright Lights* for international distribution.

GENRE CREDITS: *Up and Downs of a Handyman* (1975) (producer), *Take an Easy Ride* (1976) (director/producer/editor), *The Perils of Mandy* (video 1981) (director/producer).

Vicki SCOTT

A petite, curly-haired model from Glasgow, Vicki worked extensively as a lingerie model and in 1979 featured in the infamous British video *Sex Freaks*, as a Marilyn Monroe lookalike paired with the hugely endowed (reputedly 18") wannabe black porn star Long Dong Silver. She met David Sullivan the same year and became popular with readers of *Whitehouse* magazine. After the death of Mary Millington and the departure of Rosemary England, Sullivan was keen to promote Vicki and plastered her name all over the posters for the *Star Sex* reissue and *Emmanuelle in Soho*, despite the fact that her participation in both was pretty negligible. She stayed working for Sullivan for several years and in 1982 even roped in her sister to appear with her in *Hellcats – Mud Wrestling*. The following year the 'sizzling savage from Glasgow' donned a kilt and sporran and was brave enough to take an almighty pummelling in the boxing ring in *Foxy Female Boxers*. It was to be her last film. After marrying, Vicki retired to Scotland.

GENRE CREDITS: *Let's Get Laid!* (1977), *Adventures of a Plumber's Mate* (1978) *What's Up Superdoc?* (1978), *The Stud* (1978), *The Bitch* (1979), *Confessions from the David Galaxy Affair* (1979), *Can I Come Too?* (1979) *Sex Freaks* (video 1979), *The Great British Striptease* (1980), *Paul Raymond's Erotica* (1980), *Emmanuelle In Soho* (1981), *Hellcats – Mud Wrestling* (1983), *Fanny Hill* (1983), *Foxy Female Boxers* (video 1983)

Ray SELFE (1932-2001)

Ray Selfe was a jack-of-all-trades and self-confessed cinephile who, since the late 1940s, had viewed the British film industry from virtually every angle. Ray worked as an editor, producer, director, actor, cameraman, projectionist and even cinema manager, taking in well over 1000 features, shorts, documentaries, cinema trailers and videos. He will go down in history for producing and directing Britain's first ever 'X'-rated cinema advertisement for the 1968 launch of saucy film magazine, *Cinema X*. During the seventies Ray was the business partner of producer David Grant, and together the two men operated eight sex cinemas in London's West End from 1972 to 1978, including the Pigalle in Piccadilly Circus. The cinema rarely advertised itself in the press – incredibly lurid displays around its entrance were used to entice the customers in – but at its peak it was taking £4000 per week. Ray also worked with Grant on a string of 'X'-rated movies including *Under the Bed!* His son Howard is the producer of a Channel 4 sex films retrospective made in 2001. Sadly, Ray died in September 2001, just weeks before the publication of this book.

GENRE CREDITS: *Sweet and Sexy* (1970) (producer/photography), *The Four Dimensions of Greta* (1972) (associate producer/3D advisor), *White Cargo* (1973) (director/co-writer), *The Hot Girls* (1974) (actor/co-photography), *Under the Bed!* (1977) (producer), *The Kiss* (1977) (editor), *You're Driving Me Crazy!* (1978) (actor), *Can I Come Too?* (1979) (director/actor), *Emmanuelle in Soho* (1981) (director/editor of hardcore inserts), *Doing Rude Things* (TV 1995) (interviewee)

Alan SELWYN (1926-)

During World War II, Selwyn served in Combined Services Entertainment alongside Stanley Baxter and Kenneth Williams, later establishing himself as a music hall comedian and supporting player in films and TV. In 1972 he helped his friend David Grant to cast *Secrets of a Door to Door Salesman*. From then on he was responsible for casting established comedy actors and naked newcomers in dozens of sex movies. When necessary, he also scripted, produced, directed (often anonymously) and acted too, although he never considered himself a legitimate thespian. 'If they were stuck for an actor and needed to save time they'd ask me to fill in,' he says. In 1979 he relocated to Hollywood for five years, ghost-writing various TV shows. Back in the UK, he collaborated with Derek Ford on several projects, notably the book *Casting Couch*, published by Grafton in 1990 under the pseudonym Selwyn Ford. Of his sex film days Selwyn is dismissive. 'They are blank empty spaces in my life,' he admits. 'I had a bit of fun on a couple of them, but I don't consider them to be important at all.'

GENRE CREDITS: *Secrets of a Door to Door Salesman* (1973) (actor), *Keep It Up Jack!* (1973) (co-writer), *The Sexplorer* (1975) (actor/co-composer of theme song), *Secrets of a Superstud* (1975) (actor/co-director/co-writer), *Sex Express* (1975) (production supervisor), *The Office Party* (1976) (casting director), *Under the Bed!* (1977) (production supervisor), *You're Driving Me Crazy!* (1978) (actor/production supervisor), *Erotic Fantasies* (Italy 1978) (production controller), *Can I Come Too?* (1979) (actor/writer/producer), *The World Is Full of Married Men* (1979) (assistant to producer)

Lindsay SHONTEFF (1939-)

A Toronto-born director/producer/writer who has been based in Britain since the early 1960s. His first two British-made films were the creepy cult favourites *Devil Doll* (1963) and *Curse of Simba* (1964), both shot on fortnight-long schedules. By the end of the decade Shonteff was making pictures for his own production company, often with his wife Elizabeth Gray acting as producer. In 1969 Shonteff directed the grisly *Night after Night after Night*, an obvious precursor to his handful of sex films. Shonteff only dabbled in sexploitation movies, preferring to direct fruity tongue-in-cheek spy spoofs like *Licensed to Kill* (1965), *Number One of the Secret Service* (1977), *Licensed to Love and Kill* (aka *The Man from S.E.X.*) (1979) and *Number One Gun* (1990). It must be noted that Shonteff was responsible for one of the most spectacularly jaw-dropping sequences in British movie history. In *Licensed to Love and Kill* the hero (Gareth Hunt) is pursued by the 'Booby Girl' stripper (Sharon Burton). Twirling razor blades attached to her nipple tassels at high speed, she becomes a walking circular saw before inadvertently impaling herself on a wall! Disillusioned with the British film industry after the failure of his last film, *The Gunfighter*, in 1992, Shonteff returned to Canada, where he now teaches at a film school.

GENRE CREDITS: *Permissive* (1970), *The Yes Girls* (1971), *Big Zapper* (1973)

Ina SKRIVER

A striking Danish actress born, according to her CV, in 1950. Originally a stage and nightclub singer, Ina came to England in 1973 to pursue an acting career, initially appearing in television commercials and guesting on TV shows like *Space: 1999*, *The New Avengers* and *The Professionals*. Films included *Percy's Progress* (her début, 1974), *Rollerball* (1975) and *Voyage of the Damned* (1976). Happy to get naked, Ina revealed all in *Take an Easy Ride*, in which she played the leading role yet remained uncredited. Weirder still was her title role in José Larraz' *The Golden Lady*, an all-female spoof on the James Bond movies intended as the first of a series. Ina was asked to change her name to Christina World, which she did, apparently just so the movie's credits could read 'starring Miss World'. Rewriting her biography, she refused to acknowledge that Ina and Christina were one and the same person. But there were no more *Golden Lady* movies and she settled in Norfolk with her daughter. Her last film was *Victor/Victoria* in 1982.

GENRE CREDITS: *Percy's Progress* (1974), *Take an Easy Ride* (1976), *Emily* (1977)

Greg SMITH (1940-)

This eternally youthful, razor-sharp film producer started his career as a theatrical agent for MCA in the early 1960s. After that company folded, Smith set up his

Confessions producer Greg Smith.

own talent agency representing a varied list of new directors, producers and writers. In 1964 he met up-and-coming director Norman Cohen. The two friends became business partners and in 1970 formed Prophet Enterprises, producing their first feature film, *Dad's Army*. 'I was only an agent by default,' admits Greg. 'I always wanted to get into the movie business and after we made *Adolf Hitler – My Part in His Downfall* in 1972 the scales had tipped so much that I decided to concentrate on movies full-time.' Briefly married to actress Lynda Bellingham, who starred in two of his saucier movies, Smith established himself as one of the main players in the British film industry with the lucrative Confessions series (1974-7). Smith's other films include the Glam Rock extravaganza *You're Never Too Young to Rock* (1974), the remake of *The 39 Steps* (1978), *Funny Money* (1982) and Cannon and Ball's big screen flop *The Boys in Blue* (1982). He also produced (with Laurie Mansfield and Paul Elliot) the award-winning Buddy Holly tribute musical, *Buddy*, on the West End stage, which has been running continuously since 1989. Based at Shepperton Studios, Smith is now busier than ever with television series and movies, having produced new versions of *Twelfth Night* (1996), *Animal Farm* (1999) (rumoured to be the most expensive TV movie of all time, with a budget of $22 million) and *David Copperfield* (2000), as well as the Anjelica Huston film *Agnes Browne* (1999).

GENRE CREDITS: *Confessions of a Window Cleaner* (1974), *Confessions of a Pop Performer* (1975), *Confessions of a Driving Instructor* (1976), *Stand Up Virgin Soldiers* (1977), *Confessions from a Holiday Camp* (1977), *Rosie Dixon – Night Nurse* (1978) (executive producer)

Graham STARK (1922-)

A flat-faced comedy actor who played opposite Peter Sellers in six of the original *Pink Panther* movies. He contributed lovely, scene-stealing comic cameos as waiters, van drivers, taxi drivers and postmen to heaps of British pictures. In 1970 Stark directed the star-studded comedy short *Simon Simon* before moving onto his first feature, *The Magnificent Seven Deadly Sins* (1971), in which he also co-wrote the 'Lust' segment for Harry H Corbett and Felicity Devonshire. So popular was this stand-out sequence that it was reissued by Tigon as a 17-minute short in 1979. Stark considers his sex comedies rather disappointing ('I call them Z films,' he says), but nevertheless gave them his all. Aside from acting and scriptwriting, Stark has also had tremendous success as a portrait photographer and enjoyed some major exhibitions of his work

GENRE CREDITS: *Secrets of a Door to Door Salesman* (1973), *I'm Not Feeling Myself Tonight!* (1975), *Hardcore* (1977), *What's Up Nurse?* (1977) (also associate producer), *Let's Get Laid!* (1977)

Koo STARK (1956-)

Koo is the daughter of American moviemaker Wilbur Stark, who made a couple of early 1970s' sex films in the UK under the name Billy White. Koo followed in her father's mucky footsteps in 1975, aged just 19, when she appeared naked in *Les adolescentes*, filmed in Spain, before getting star billing in two fairly uneventful 'X'-rated British movies, *Emily* and *Cruel Passion* in 1977. The movie press were quick to dub her the English Sylvia Kristel, but her career as a naked starlet quickly stalled at the starting blocks. The same year a supporting role in a far more enduring movie, *Star Wars*, was wasted when all her scenes were deleted before the film's release. Five years later a romance with Prince Andrew was doomed from the outset when her soft-core past caught up with her. The tabloids had a field-day splashing raunchy lesbian stills of 'Koo Starkers' from *Emily* across their pages. Even *Electric Blue* helpfully put together a video of rehashed clips from her sex films. Throughout the Royal furore Koo kept her dignity and has since carved out a highly successful career for herself as a freelance photographer, working for publications like *Harpers & Queen*.

GENRE CREDITS: *Emily* (1977), *Cruel Passion* (1977), *Electric Blue 8* (video 1982)

David SULLIVAN (1949-)

David Sullivan spends some quality time with one of his models in this 1975 picture.

Born to working class parents on a council estate in Penarth, Cardiff in 1949, David Sullivan couldn't have come from much humbler beginnings. Because his father was in the RAF, the family had to relocate several times but eventually settled in Hornchurch, source of Sullivan's distinctive 'Essex man' accent. Sullivan was a born entrepreneur and, after graduating in Economics from London University's Queen Mary College, set himself up in business selling photographs of nude girls through the post. Before long he was making nearly a grand a week and working from his own premises in Forest Gate, over a sex shop catering for personal callers. By 1972 his firm had 50,000 customers and, amazingly, had cornered 90 per cent of the mail order business in Britain. A year later he launched his first girlie magazine, *Private*, the title pinched from its Scandinavian namesake. A rash of other magazines followed, notably *Whitehouse*, *Playbirds* and *Lovebirds*, all of which survive to this day. Sullivan was a millionaire by the age of 24 with a publishing empire second only to Paul Raymond's. After a chance conversation with George Harrison Marks in 1976, Sullivan was persuaded to part with some money for his first feature film, *Come Play with Me*. It went on to become one of the most profitable movies in British film history. Other films followed, but none matched the success of the first. As well as his movie business, Sullivan set about creating Britain's biggest chain of sex shops and by 1982 had 130 outlets throughout the UK. In recent years he has distanced himself from his sex empire and is now most recognised as the publisher of the *Sport* newspaper, launched in 1986. In 2001, Sullivan was listed by the *Sunday Times* as Britain's 51st richest man, with assets valued at over £500 million. That's still quite a way off Paul Raymond's fortune, but Sullivan is a great deal more visible, his high profile boosted by regular TV and radio appearances, his 58 per cent stake in Birmingham City FC and a £10 million neo-Georgian mansion in the Essex village of Theydon Bois. After the closure of the Millennium Dome he offered to buy it and turn the venue into the world's biggest casino, broadcasting live strip shows around the world. Strangely, his offer was rejected by Downing Street.

GENRE CREDITS: *Come Play with Me* (1977)

(executive producer), *The Playbirds* (1978) (executive producer), *Confessions from the David Galaxy Affair* (1979) (executive producer), *Queen of the Blues* (1979) (executive producer), *Boys and Girls Together* (1979) (executive producer), *Come Play with Me 2* (Switzerland 1980) (executive producer, English version), *Mary Millington's True Blue Confessions* (1980) (executive producer/interviewee), *Emmanuelle in Soho* (1981) (executive producer), *Mary Millington's World Striptease Extravaganza* (1981) (executive producer/co-writer), *Hellcats – Mud Wrestling* (1983) (co-director/executive producer), *Foxy Female Boxers* (video 1983) (director/executive producer), *Queen Kong – The Amazonian Woman* (video 1984) (co-director/executive producer), *Sex and Fame – The Mary Millington Story* (TV 1996) (interviewee)

Suzie SYLVIE (1956-)

A lusty blonde seventies' saucepot whose innocent eyes and fabulous smile enlivened many a film in the dying days of British sex movies. Blessed with a lovely sense of comedy, Suzie played against type in the nasty 'alien birth' sequence of the low-budget British horror movie *Xtro* in 1980, but returned to more familiar territory as an 18th century whore (albeit with a dubbed voice) in *Fanny Hill* (1983). Sometimes billed as Susie Silvie or Susan Silvey, she is now a fund-raiser for Food Relief International.

GENRE CREDITS: *Come Play with Me* (1977), *The Playbirds* (1978), *The Stud* (1978), *Can I Come Too?* (1979) *The World is Full of Married Men* (1979), *Sex with the Stars* (1980), *Fanny Hill* (1983)

Lisa TAYLOR

A Lolita-like hardcore porn performer who graduated from under-the-counter magazines and 8mm films, some directed by John Lindsay and George Harrison Marks, to features. Her uncredited hardcore scene with veteran actor Derek Aylward in

Lisa Taylor sends pulses racing in What's Up Superdoc? *(1978).*

Come Play with Me was cut to the bare minimum for cinema release and although her role in *Let's Get Laid!* was her largest to date, most of her saucy threesome ended up on the cutting-room floor. Not a bad actress, she even managed to master a passable Italian accent for David Grant's *Under the Bed!* Long since retired, Lisa is now married with children and living in the south of England.

GENRE CREDITS: *Come Play with Me* (1977), *Under the Bed!* (1977), *Let's Get Laid!* (1977), *What's Up Nurse?* (1977), *You're Driving Me Crazy!* (1978), *What's Up Superdoc?* (1978), *The Great British Striptease* (1980)

Edward Craven WALKER (1918-2000)

Edward Craven Walker may have been famous for his love of naturism, but he made his fortune as the designer of the Lava Lamp, one of the most evocative symbols of the 1960s. It took him many years to develop his invention (which he christened the Astro Lamp) and by the early 1970s no self-respecting hippy was without one. Walker served as a squadron leader during World War II and, after being demobbed, paid his first visit to the Isle of Levant off the southern coast of France. It was here that his love of naturism began. Back in Britain he became a frequent visitor to the nudist beach at Studland Bay in Dorset and decided to promote naturism through film. Using the pseudonym Michael Keatering, he produced and directed three titles (all shot overseas), the true intentions of which were mostly lost on the pop-eyed punters that went to see them. *Travelling Light* ran for six months in London's West End alone and all his films were widely distributed throughout the world. After the bottom dropped out of the nudie market, Walker bought a nudist complex in Dorset, the Bournemouth and District Outdoor Club, where he spent much of his free time. There was a resurgence of interest in Walker's Lava Lamps during the 1990s and at the time of his death, aged 82 his company Mathmos was manufacturing over 10,000 lamps per month.

GENRE CREDITS: *Travelling Light* (1959) (director/producer/photography), *Sunswept* (1961) (director/producer/photography), *Eves on Skis* (1963) (narrator/director/producer)

Pete WALKER (1939-)

'I hate tits,' claims exploitation mogul Pete Walker, 'except when they're in the bed next to you.'

Son of famed music hall star Sydney Walker and Gaiety girl Jesse Aymer, Pete Walker became Britain's youngest comedian at the age of 15, touring theatres and tatty strip joints around the country. Obsessed with movies – he was expelled from Brighton Grammar School for perpetually bunking off to visit the local fleapit – he had several small parts in films during the early 1960s. Around the same time, he began directing and distributing 8mm glamour films through his own company, Heritage Films. It's estimated that between 1962 and 1963 he made nearly 500 titles, each shot in half an hour. Walker's first feature film was the saucy *I Like Birds* in 1967, followed by the blockbusting *School for Sex* the next year. 'I didn't want to be known as a tit man,' he told David McGillivray a few years later. 'I didn't want to be Harrison Marks, never have done. I hate tits, horrible things. Except when they're in the bed next to you.' Unsurprisingly, psychological horror took over as Walker's preferred genre and his dastardly collection of explicit Grand Guignol thrillers soon earned him cult status. Sadistic films like *The Flesh and Blood Show* (1972), *House of Whipcord* (1973), *Frightmare* (1974), *House of Mortal Sin* (1975), *Schizo* (1976) and *The Comeback* (1977) are well remembered for some of the kinkiest violence ever seen in British movie history. Walker's final movie, *House of the Long Shadows* (1982), provided a showcase for some of the biggest names in horror – Vincent Price, Christopher Lee, Peter Cushing and John Carradine. However, the film was not a success and Walker soon retired from movie-making for good. Since the mid-1980s Walker has shrewdly invested in the property market and restored a number of traditional cinemas, including the Bognor Picturedrome and the Orpheus in Bristol.

GENRE CREDITS: *I Like Birds* (1967) (producer/director/writer), *School for Sex* (1968) (producer/director/writer), *Cool it Carol* (1970) (producer/director), *The Four Dimensions of Greta* (1972) (producer/director/actor) *Tiffany Jones* (1973) (producer/director), *Adventures of a Taxi Driver* (1975) (cameo appearance)

Norman J WARREN (1942-)

A real film aficionado who has been fascinated with movie-making from child-

Norman J Warren (far left) directing Simon Brent and Paula Patterson in Loving Feeling *(1968).*

hood, Norman John Warren was given his first cine camera on his 13th birthday and started making his own amateur films. His big break came in 1959 when he started work as an assistant for famed producers Anatole and Dimitri de Grunwald. From being a runner on the set of Sophia Loren's *The Millionairess*, he progressed to third assistant director on *The Dock Brief* (1962). 'I learnt an enormous amount in those days, especially from my time in the cuttings rooms,' he recalls. In 1965 he directed a short entitled *Fragment*, made as a show-reel to get people interested in his work. An offbeat tale about a young girl unable to cope with her feelings of first love, this 11-minute fantasy caught the eye of Indian producer Bachoo Sen, who gave Warren the opportunity to direct his first feature film, *Her Private Hell*, in 1967. The film was a huge success and *Loving Feeling*, a more ambitious sex film, also produced by Sen, came the following year. However, during the seventies, Norman's real passion was to become horror. His flesh and blood epics, *Satan's Slave* (1976), *Prey* (1978), *Terror* (1979) and *Inseminoid* (1980) have an enormous following and are considered cult classics both in the UK and US, thanks in the main to their reissue on video and DVD. Residing in London, he continues to work on movie projects and rightly deserves his reputation as the 'nice guy' of British exploitation cinema.

GENRE CREDITS: *Her Private Hell* (1967), *Loving Feeling* (1968), *Outer Touch* (1979)

Queenie WATTS (1926-1980)

A smoky-voiced cockney character actress, famed also for her jazz and blues singing (showcased, uncredited, in Lewis Gilbert's *Alfie*), Queenie was actually half-Romany, half-Scottish. She started performing at 14, made her movie début in *Sparrows Can't Sing* in 1963 and became very popular on TV in series like *Stars and Garters* and *Time Gentlemen Please!*. She played opposite fellow cockney comedian Arthur Mullard as Lily and Wally Briggs in seventies sitcoms *Romany Jones* and *Yus My Dear*; they also provided much of the comedy in the film *Holiday on the Buses* (1973). In 1975 Queenie was honoured with a tribute on *This Is Your Life*. She popped up in several British sexcoms, including two for David Sullivan, and towards the end of her life ran the Rose and Crown public house in Limehouse with her husband Slim. Her final TV role was the lead in Barrie Keefe's 1979 BBC play *Waterloo Sunset*, about an elderly woman running away from an old people's home. In fact, Queenie was dogged by ill-health and wasn't as old as she looked. She eventually succumbed to cancer, aged 54, in January 1980. Queenie died at home, in her beloved pub.

GENRE CREDITS: *The Best House in London* (1968), *Keep it Up Jack!* (1973), *Intimate Games* (1976), *Come Play with Me* (1977), *Confessions from the David Galaxy Affair* (1979)

Rita WEBB (1904-1981)

The archetypal abrasive, parrot-voiced cockney charwoman in innumerable films and TV shows, Rita was 4'10", with a 48" bust, 46" waist, 52" hips and a mop of flaming red hair. She regularly stole the show from the likes of Frankie Howerd, Tony Hancock, Dick

Emery and Benny Hill, cheerfully admitting that 'When they want an old cow, they always send for me, but I'm not out of work like the hundreds of actresses who depend on good looks and curves.' She was absolutely right. Born in Kilburn, Rita ran away from home at 14 to become a chorus girl, but as her weight increased her dancing career foundered. She was continually confused with fellow actress Queenie Watts but, unlike Queenie, refused to be a subject on *This is Your Life*. She made a delightfully perverse Maid Marion in *Up the Chastity Belt* (1971) and bawled her way through several sex comedies. The lasting memory she left with many of her colleagues was her fondness for swearing. 'She was hilarious,' recalls casting agent Alan Selwyn, 'but her language was absolutely foul.' Rita died in London, aged 77, six months before her final film, *Venom* (1982), was released.

GENRE CREDITS: *Zeta One* (1969), *The Nine Ages of Nakedness* (1969), *Percy* (1971), *Confessions of a Pop Performer* (1975), *I'm Not Feeling Myself Tonight!* (1975), *Come Play with Me* (1977), *Can I Come Too?* (1979)

Jenny WESTBROOK

Slim, serious-looking brunette who worked regularly with Benny Hill on his TV show during the 1970s. In just two years Jenny managed to pack in a bunch of sex film performances too, most notably as Nicole, the female lead, in her best movie, *Erotic Inferno*. The brutal scenes with her womanising lover, Adam (played by Michael Watkins), are incredibly effective and showcased her previously untapped potential. Jenny could have easily progressed with her acting career, yet instead opted to get married to a music impresario and retire to Hertfordshire to breed horses in 1976.

GENRE CREDITS: *Secrets of a Door to Door Salesman* (1973), *The Sex Thief* (1973), *Keep It Up Jack!* (1973), *The Amorous Milkman* (1974), *Confessions of a Window Cleaner* (1974), *Secrets of a Superstud* (1975), *Erotic Inferno* (1975)

Donovan WINTER (1933-)

A once-handsome B-movie actor turned one-man-movie-industry who, as well as performing, was a director, producer, editor, composer and writer for his own company, Donwin. His directorial début came with *The Trunk* in 1960, a taut frame-up thriller, and the following year Winter made his first sex film, a successful nudie cutie called *World Without Shame*. In 1965 he directed the most bizarre movie of his career, *A Penny For Your Thoughts* (aka *Birds, Dolls and Scratch*), documenting the ripe conversations of a group of women overheard in a public toilet, featuring Sheila (Confessions) White and Annette Whiteley from *The Yellow Teddybears*. Throughout the seventies he gained a reputation as the tough man of Wardour Street. Winter's last feature was *Give Us Tomorrow*, a ropey hostage thriller starring Sylvia Syms, only released (as part of a double-bill with Pete Walker's *Home Before Midnight* in 1979) after he sued distributors EMI. Winter's love/hate relationship with the British film industry is well documented and he hasn't made a film since.

GENRE CREDITS: *World Without Shame* (1961), *Come Back Peter* (aka *Some Like it Sexy*) (1969), *Escort Girls* (1974)

Christopher WOOD (1935-)

Wood's saucy Confessions books were the paperback publishing phenomenon of the seventies, selling well in excess of three million copies. Writing under the name Timothy Lea, Wood penned 19 instalments between 1971 and 1979, averaging two a year. After writing eight titles for

The paperback tie-in of Christopher Wood's *Confessions of a Window Cleaner*.

Sphere, he jumped ship in 1974 and took Timothy Lea to Futura for a further 11. Sphere, still smarting from Wood's betrayal, began their own, almost identical Confessions series written by 'Jonathan May' (aka Laurence James), thus creating a publishing feud that would last for over five years. Wood also used the *nom de plumes* of trainee nurse Rosie Dixon, stewardess Penny Sutton and teenage tearaway Oliver Grape for other companion series. His books continued to be regularly reprinted until the mid-1980s. In 1974 Wood was asked to adapt *Confessions of a Window Cleaner* for the big screen and the rest, as they say, is history. He also provided two of the most *double entendre*-saturated 007 screenplays: *The Spy Who Loved Me* (1977) and *Moonraker* (1979). Now living in France, Wood continues to write screenplays and novels.

GENRE CREDITS: *Confessions of a Window Cleaner* (1974), *Confessions of a Pop Performer* (1975), *Confessions of a Driving Instructor* (1976), *Confessions from a Holiday Camp* (1977), *Rosie Dixon – Night Nurse* (1978)

BIBLIOGRAPHY

Left: Fiona Richmond at the launch of *The Crisp Report* in October 1981.

Robin Askwith, *The Confessions of Robin Askwith* (Ebury Press 1999)

Denis Gifford, *The British Film Catalogue 1895 – 1985* (David & Charles 1986)

David Hebditch and Nick Anning, *Porn Gold* (Faber & Faber 1988)

The Longford Committee, *Pornography: The Longford Report* (Coronet 1972)

Linda Lovelace, *Inside Linda Lovelace* (Heinrich Hanau 1974)

David McGillivray, *Doing Rude Things: The History of the British Sex Film 1957-1981* (Sun Tavern Fields 1992)

Fiona Richmond, *Tell Tale Tits* (Javelin 1987)

Jonathan Rigby, *English Gothic: A Century of Horror Cinema* (Reynolds & Hearn 2000)

Robert Ross, *The Carry On Companion* (Batsford 1996)

Simon Sheridan, *Come Play with Me: The Life and Films of Mary Millington* (FAB Press 1999)

G L Simons, *A History of Sex* (New English Library 1970)

John Trevelyan, *What the Censor Saw* (Michael Joseph 1973)

Mary Whitehouse, *Quite Contrary: An Autobiography* (Sidgwick & Jackson 1993)

INDEX

Page numbers in bold indicate pictures.

A

Adair, Hazel 22, 81, 136, 211, 220
Adventures of a Plumber's Mate 19, 155, 164, 164-165, 223
Adventures of a Private Eye 18, 141, 154, 154-155
Adventures of a Taxi Driver 19, 21, 23, 29, 29, 131, 131-132, 139, 141, 208, 217, 223
Ain't Misbehavin' 186
Alfie 11, 52, 62, 107
Alfie Darling 163
Amorous Milkman, The 6, 20, 113, 113-114, 208
Are You Being Served? 8, 67, 212
Arkoff, Samuel 80, 112
Armstrong, Michael 20, 91, 11, 112, 154, 155, 211, 223
Ash, Leslie 161, 192
Askwith, Robin 2, 6, 7, 17, 18, 20, 21, 24, 27, 28, 28, 29, 30, 31, 66, 66, 82, 106, 107, 106-107, 108, 109, 118, 119, 119, 124, 131, 132, 139, 139, 140, 147, 148, 148, 157, 157, 160, 160, 162, 164, 169, 177, 180, 196, 207, 209, 209, 211-212, 213, 220, 224, 224
Astley, Pat 8, 18, 27, 151, 152, 163, 166, 167, 174, 212, 212, 222
Au Pair Girls 17, 21, 22, 84-85, 87, 106, 123
Austine, Nicola 18, 49, 97, 151, 152, 168, 169, 174, 177, 183, 193, 212
Aylward, Derek 46, 49, 212-213, 232

B

Baby Love 50, 50-51, 60, 129, 220
Balch, Antony 57, 58, 213
Belle, Annie 133, 134, 134
Bellingham, Lynda 19, 106, 139, 139, 140, 148, 230
Benny Hill Show, The 18, 224
Benson, Lindy 103, 164, 164, 174
Bergman, Anna 18, 126, 126, 132, 135, 151, 168, 169, 193, 213
Best House in London, The 49-50
Big Zapper 96-97, 97, 126
Bird, Minah 82, 88, 105, 213
Bitch, The 139, 173, 174, 178-180, 180, 192, 194
Blackstone, Timothy 121, 122, 145, 213-214, 222
Blue Belle 22, 133-134, 134, 215
Bond, Julia 138, 153, 157
Booth, Anthony 107, 118, 119, 119, 139, 157, 209, 220
Boys and Girls Together 180-181
Braun, Lasse 92
Briggs, Johnny 138
British Board of Film Censors/Classification (BBFC) 9-10, 12-13, 17, 22, 44, 55, 76, 89, 91, 93, 95, 100, 122, 152, 188, 195, 198, 200, 201, 202, 203, 204, 206-207, 209
Brittain, Gloria 182, 191, 201, 214
Bulloch, Jeremy 109, 109, 110

235

C

Cadell, Ava 103, 177, 178, 200, 214, 222
Caligula 196
Campbell, Martin 15-16, 91, 111, 135
Can I Come Too? 6, 22, 172-173, 224
Can You Keep It Up For a Week? 18, 22, 109, 109-110, 136, 211
Carry On Behind 16, 141, 217, 221
Carry On Camping 8, 9, 32, 156, 218
Carry On Emmannuelle 169-172, 170, 171, 174
Carry On England 169
Carry On Girls 20, 169, 211, 218
Carry On Nurse 153, 194
Chittell, Christopher 115, 115, 116
Clarke, James Kenelm 130, 149, 160, 214, 227, 228
Clinic Xclusive 19, 22, 81, 100, 211
Cohen, Norman 107, 108, 118, 119, 140, 147, 148, 214-215, 230
Collins, Jackie 162, 173-174, 178, 179
Collins, Joan 19, 29, 131, 139, 162, 163, 163, 174, 178-179, 180, 192, 192, 193, 216
Collinson, Mary & Madeleine 53, 53, 78, 215
Come Back Peter 20, 38, 52-53, 53, 102, 215
Come Play with Me 7, 8, 8, 19, 21, 22, 23, 27, 27, 29, 44, 49, 54, 134, 150-153, 152, 165, 170, 188, 196, 197, 199, 205, 208, 209, 212, 213, 220, 224, 226, 231, 232
Come Play with Me 2 197
Come Play with Me 3 197
Commuter Husbands 26, 29, 87-88, 88, 99, 133, 212
Confessions from a Holiday Camp 147, 156-158, 157, 158, 209
Confessions from the David Galaxy Affair 19, 21, 23, 175, 175-176, 177, 182, 197, 216
Confessions of a Driving Instructor 19, 118, 139, 139-141, 140, 147, 157, 169, 212, 220, 224
Confessions of a Pop Performer 21, 118, 119, 118-120, 139, 157
Confessions of a Sex Maniac 114-115, 203
Confessions of a Window Cleaner 2, 6, 7, 8, 17-18, 21, 22, 27-28, 28, 30, 84, 106, 107, 108, 106-109, 115, 118, 123, 134, 157, 196, 209, 214, 224, 226, 234, 234
Connock, Jim 11, 177
Cool It Carol 65-67, 66, 212
Corbett, Harry H 21, 105, 155, 168
Crossroads 20, 22, 79, 81, 87, 123, 211
Cruel Passion 159-160, 231

D

Deadly Females, The 220
Dear Margery Boobs 155-156
Death Shock 201, 207
Deeley, Heather 18, 26, 116, 117, 121, 122, 122, 135, 215
Deep Throat 23, 24, 25, 27, 73, 155, 196, 200, 209, 215, 221
Derek and Clive Get the Horn 212
Devonshire, Felicity 18, 22, 83, 86, 90, 94, 131, 134, 135, 153, 156, 215, 231
Doing Rude Things 208, 225
Don't Open 'Til Christmas 55, 85, 212, 217, 221, 222
Dors, Diana 6, 21, 50, 113, 114, 131, 132, 175, 215-216, 222
Dover, Ben 207, 216
Drake, Gabrielle 19, 75, 84, 87, 88
Dream Doll 181
Drew, Linzi 187, 188, 201, 207, 216

E

Eady Fund 12, 142, 196
East, John M 35, 176, 177, 184-185, 187-188, 191, 195, 216, 221, 222, 226
Elcoate Gilbert, Elizabeth 10, 33, 38
Electric Blue - The Movie 186-187, 202
Electric Blue videos 68, 117, 186, 202, 231
Emily 22, 134, 143, 146, 146-147, 159, 231
Emmanuelle 24, 133, 146, 170, 183, 189, 208, 217
Emmanuelle in Soho 27, 187-189, 190, 191, 194, 213, 216, 222, 229
England, Rosemary 175, 183, 216-217, 226, 229
Erotic Fantasies 78-79
Erotic Inferno 115, 115-116, 167, 208, 234
Escort Girls 38, 102
Eskimo Nell 15, 111-112, 112, 172, 211, 227
Evans, Barry 20, 29, 131, 131-132, 141-142, 154, 217, 227
Every Home Should Have One 14-15
Eves on Skis 40
Exposé 18, 129, 129-130, 214, 220

F

Fancey, Adrienne 174, 217
Fancey, Edwin J 35, 95, 217
Fancey, Malcom 174, 217
Fanny Hill 193-194, 232
Feelings 130-131, 194
Ferman, James 22, 188, 195, 206
Ford, Derek 26, 27, 29, 55, 58, 61, 75, 84, 87, 98, 99, 120, 122, 153, 168-169, 182, 217-218, 223, 228, 229
Ford, Donald 217, 229
Four Dimensions of Greta, The 29, 82-83, 89, 90, 95, 211
Foxy Female Boxers 195, 195, 229
Fraser, Liz 19, 132, 139-140, 142, 155, 157, 161, 169, 217
Fraser, Ronald 22, 105, 149, 151
Freeman, Mike 23, 200
Fun and Games 79, 79-80, 220

G

Games That Lovers Play 20, 48, 67-68, 68, 78, 186
Garden of Eden, The 9-10

INDEX

Gascoine, Jill 19, 118, 119
Gates, Tudor 16, 20, 25, 85, 86, 91, 112, 135, 181, 183, 192, 211, 218, 227
Gay, Russell 11, 39
Gay Man's Guide to Safer Sex 204
Girls Come First 27, 117-118, 208
Godfrey, Bob 63, 69, 70, 71, 81, 82, 89, 95, 155, 156, 181, 218
Godfrey, Tommy 21-22, 22
Got it Made 214
Grant, Angela 218
Grant, David 14, 26, 27, 63, 69, 82, 84, 89, 93, 95, 96, 103, 115, 117, 137, 138, 142, 143, 145, 156, 167, 204, 215, 218-219, 223, 225, 229, 232
Great British Striptease, The 182, 191
Green, Hughie 118, 168, 169
Green, Pamela 10-11, 36, 37, 45, 210, 219, 224
Groupie Girl 58-60, 59, 65, 132
Growing Up 63
Guest, Val 22, 84-85, 87, 106, 108, 108, 118, 123, 211

H

Hallett, Neil 76, 79, 109, 136, 137, 219-220
Hamill, John 20, 103, 117, 145, 149, 220
Handl, Irene 21, 140, 148, 151, 155, 220, 220
Hardcore 14, 19, 149-150, 150, 208, 215, 220
Hare, Doris 118, 119, 140, 157

Hayden, Linda 2, 28, 28, 50, 51, 108, 129, 129, 130, 140, 157, 220
Hellcats - Mud Wrestling 6, 194-195, 229
Henry Nine 'Til Five 70-71, 82, 89
Her Private Hell 15, 15, 46-47, 47, 51, 56, 57, 116, 177, 233
Herbert, Henry 22, 147
Hot Girls, The 102-103
Hugs and Kisses 13

I

I Like Birds 46, 233
I'm Not Feeling Myself Tonight! 6, 14, 16, 29, 127, 127-128, 168, 225
Insatiable 186
Initiants, The 202, 202
Intimacy 209
Intimate Games 134-136, 218
It Could Happen to You 128-129
It's a Bare, Bare World 40-41, 41
It's a 2'6" Above the Ground World 104, 212, 218

J

Jacobson, Helli Louise 21, 103, 119, 123, 123, 220-221
Jones, Mark 20, 26, 26, 88, 98, 98, 120, 121, 172, 217, 221
Joseph Andrews 21, 193

K

Kama Sutra Rides Again 81-82, 156
Keatering, Michael *see* Walker, Edward Craven

Keep It Up Downstairs 6, 28, 136, 136-137, 137, 174, 208, 211, 221, 226
Keep It Up Jack! 7, 26, 26, 29, 98, 98-99, 122, 221
Kenyon, Anthony 20, 116, 121, 132, 133, 136, 221, 221
Kiss, The 156
Kong, Queen 194, 195, 221
Kristel, Sylvia 17, 133, 134, 146, 170, 189, 189, 231

L

Lady Chatterley's Lover 189, 189-190
Lahaie, Brigitte 185, 186
Lake, Alan 19, 88, 114, 138, 138, 166, 175, 175, 215, 221-222, 222
Last Tango in Paris 24, 155
Lawson, Leigh 20, 104, 105
Lay, Me Me 84, 222
Layout for Five Models 88-89
Le Mesurier, John 21, 107, 148, 153, 161
Lee, Julie 124, 187, 188-189, 191, 213, 222
Leigh, Malcolm 48, 67, 68, 78, 79
Leon, Valerie 64, 109, 123
Let's Get Laid! 17, 121, 160, 160-161, 232
Lewis, Morton 133, 217
Licensed to Love and Kill 212, 230
Lifetaker, The 21
Lindsay, John 19, 24, 26, 73-74, 77, 91-93, 103, 166, 182, 198, 200, 212, 213, 214, 221, 222-223, 226, 232
Lloyd, Sue 123, 125, 163, 179
London in the Raw 13, 13,

42, 42-43
Long, Stanley 6, 8-9, 11, 13, 14, 15, 16, 18, 19, 20-21, 23, 28, 29, 33, 35, 38, 39, 42, 43, 45, 55, 56, 58, 59, 61, 73, 74, 86, 97, 111, 112, 124, 128, 129, 131, 132, 141, 142, 152, 154, 155, 164, 165, 182, 205, 209, 211, 217, 223, 227
Longhurst, Sue 7, 7, 23, 26, 26-27, 93, 94, 98, 98, 99, 103, 107, 107, 108, 109, 114, 117, 136, 137, 137, 172, 215, 223-224
Love and Marriage 69, 69
Love Box, The 85, 85-86, 91, 181, 183
Love in Our Time 47-48, 48, 225
Love is a Splendid Illusion 56-57
Love Pill, The 14, 20, 76-77, 77, 168, 204
Love Variations 14, 62-63, 69, 82, 84, 128, 204, 218
Lovers' Guide, The 203-204, 204
Loving Feeling 25, 51, 51-52, 56, 177, 233
Lumley, Joanna 19, 20, 67, 68, 186
Lustful Lady, A 158-159

M

Macaskie, Charles 10, 14, 32, 37
Mandel, Suzy 8, 18, 22, 27, 135, 139, 151, 152, 164, 166, 167, 224, 224
Manning, Bernard 182, 191
Marks, George Harrison 11, 27, 27, 36, 36, 37, 41, 44-

237

45, 53-55, 150-151, 152, 152, 165, 169, 201, 212, 213, 219, 224, 224-225, 231, 232, 233
Mary Millington's True Blue Confessions 180, 184, 184-185, 199, 199
Mary Millington's World Striptease Extravaganza 190, 191-192
Maynard, Bill 82, 107, 108, 118, 119, 140, 157
McGillivray, David 12, 14, 16, 17, 24, 25, 29, 94, 95, 102-103, 127-128, 196, 199, 207-208, 209, 225, 233
McGrath, Joseph 93, 117, 127, 218, 225
Men Only (magazine) 18, 123, 130, 157
Meredith, Penny 123, 157
Michelle, Ann 48, 75, 76, 99, 100, 159, 189, 225-226
Michelle, Vicki 19, 75, 76, 76, 225-226
Miller, Arnold Louis 11, 33, 39, 42, 43, 45, 63, 100, 223
Miller, Mandy *see* Quick, Angie
Miller, Nat 9, 10
Millington, Mary 6, 7, 8, 18-19, 19, 21, 23, 27, 29, 31, 39, 94, 116, 124, 127, 135, 136-137, 144, 151, 152, 152, 165, 166, 166, 167, 168, 169, 175, 175, 176, 176, 177, 180, 184, 184-185, 187, 191, 200, 203, 208, 212, 213, 216, 217, 220, 222, 222, 224, 226, 226, 229
Mitchell, Christopher 168, 168

Miss Bohrloch 226
Mistress Pamela 99-100, 100
Monique 60, 60-61,
Munday, Olivia 18, 109, 137, 226
Murray, Chic 93-94, 123, 124, 127, 226-227

N

Naked – As Nature Intended 6, 10, 11, 28, 36-37, 40, 44, 54, 219, 224
Naked World of Harrison Marks, The 13, 44, 44-45, 219
Naughty! 73, 73-74, 97, 223
Negus, Olive 95, 217
Neil, Christopher 18, 20, 25, 154-155, 164, 164, 227
Night, after Night, after Night 65, 166, 230
Nine Ages of Nakedness, The 25, 53-55, 54, 55
Nolan, Margaret 41, 41, 50, 169, 224
Not Tonight Darling! 74
Nudes of the World 10, 11, 37-38, 223
Nudist Memories 33-34, 35, 223
Nudist Paradise 10, 31, 32, 31-33
Nudist Story, The 8, 34, 34-35
Nutcracker 192, 192-193
Number One of the Secret Service 230

O

Obscene Publications Act 1959 13, 200, 202-203, 206
Office Party, The 27, 137-139, 138, 145

O'Hara, Gerry 130, 173, 194
On the Game 21, 23, 97-98
Outer Touch 64, 177-178, 178
Over Amorous Artist, The 103-104

P

Paige, Elaine 19, 165
Pascal, Françoise 49, 52, 136-137, 199, 213, 227, 227, 229
Parry, Ken 99, 100, 151, 154
Paul Raymond's Erotica 160, 185-186, 227
Penelope Pulls It Off! 23, 126, 126, 213
Percy 17, 22, 28, 71, 72, 71-73, 104, 168
Percy's Progress 22, 104, 105, 104-105, 143, 168, 230
Perils of Mandy, The 201, 214
Permissive 65, 65, 88
Personal Services 205, 205
Pink Orgasm 117, 215, 218
Playbirds (magazine) 166, 188, 205, 213, 226, 231
Playbirds, The 165-167, 166, 175, 180, 184, 199, 212, 214, 216, 222
Pornbrokers, The 91-93, 92, 223
Primitive London 13, 43, 43-44
Promise of Bed, A 29, 55-56, 56

Q

Queen of the Blues 176, 176-177, 191, 201, 203
Quick, Angie 186, 187, 191, 193

R

Raymond, Paul 18, 74, 149, 160, 169, 185, 202, 216, 227-228, 231
Reluctant Nudist, The 41-42
Richmond, Fiona 6, 17, 17, 18-19, 31, 129, 129, 130, 149, 150, 160, 160, 185, 202, 214, 216, 227, 228, 228, 235
Ringwald, Monika 120, 120-121, 221, 228
Rise and Fall of Ivor Dickie, The 204
Rita, Sue and Bob Too 205, 206
Robinson, Cardew 8, 54, 77
Roe, Willy 151, 165, 175, 176, 180, 187
Rogers, Peter 66, 72, 104, 169, 170, 187
Rosie Dixon - Night Nurse 22, 161-162, 208
Rowles, Kenneth 123, 124, 142-143, 144, 201, 214, 222, 227, 229

S

School for Sex 17, 25, 46, 49, 66
Scott, Vicki 168, 169, 179, 182, 193, 194, 195, 229
Secrets of Sex 28, 57, 57-58, 213
Secrets of a Door to Door Salesman 7, 17, 22, 93-94, 94, 114, 124, 223, 226, 229
Secrets of a Superstud 132-133, 133, 221
Secrets of a Windmill Girl 45, 45-46, 47, 223
Selfe, Ray 12, 15, 17, 25-26, 27, 28, 69, 70, 83, 94, 95,

INDEX

96, 117, 138, 145, 156, 167, 172, 188, 217, 219, 224, 229
Sellers, Peter 100-101, 227
Selwyn, Alan 26, 121, 133, 137, 173, 215, 223, 228, 229-230, 234
Sen, Bachoo 47, 56, 116, 233
Sex and the Other Woman 86, 86-87
Sex Farm 100
Sex Express 26, 121-122, 122, 215, 217, 221
Sex Freaks 229
Sex Play 22, 110, 110-111
Sex Thief, The 15, 16, 20, 25, 90, 91, 111, 135, 211, 227
Sex Victims 90, 141
Sex with the Stars 182-184, 183, 192, 217
Sexplorer, The 64, 120, 120-121, 133, 204, 217, 228
Sextet 141
Sexy Secrets of the Kissogram Girls 197, 202
Sexy Secrets of the Sex Therapists 202
She'll Follow You Anywhere 77-78, 78
Shonteff, Lindsay 65, 80, 81, 96, 166, 212, 230
Sinderella 89, 96
Singleton, Valerie 37-38
Skriver, Ina 143, 147, 230
Smith, Greg 8, 17, 19, 21, 27-28, 28, 106, 107, 108, 108-109, 117, 131, 139, 140, 147, 148, 156-157, 158, 161, 201, 209, 211, 214, 230, 230-231
Snow White and the Seven Perverts 95-96
Soft Beds, Hard Battles 100-101, 227
Søltoft, Ole 24, 84, 224
Some Like it Cool 35, 35
Spanish Fly 28, 124, 125, 168
Stand Up Virgin Soldiers 147-149, 148
Stark, Graham 21, 153, 160, 231
Stark, Koo 19, 23, 143, 146, 146, 147, 159, 231
Steel, Anthony 149, 160
Story of O, The 24, 209
Stud, The (1974) 112-113
Stud, The (1978) 8, 29, 162-164, 163, 170, 173, 174, 178, 192, 213
Suburban Wives 74-75, 75, 84, 87, 99
Sullivan, David 14, 19, 27, 92, 150-151, 152, 165, 166, 175, 176, 177, 180, 182, 184, 185, 186, 187, 188, 189, 190, 191, 194, 195, 197, 199, 200, 203, 205, 206, 207, 209, 212, 213, 214, 216, 221, 222, 224, 226, 229, 231, 231-232, 233
Sunswept 38, 40
Sweet and Sexy 15, 69-70, 70, 74
Sylvie, Suzie 163, 172, 174, 183, 183, 193, 232

T

Take An Easy Ride 142-145, 143, 201, 229, 230
Take You Clothes Off and Live! 39-40, 223
Taylor, Lisa 145, 160, 167, 169, 182, 212, 232, 232
Tenser, Tony 48, 60, 112
That Kind of Girl 11, 12
There's a Girl in My Soup 87,

100, 227
Tiffany Jones 89-90
Tobias, Oliver 20, 162, 163, 163, 164, 179
Todd, Bob 21, 119, 123, 124, 151, 181
Travelling Light 10, 33, 38, 40, 232
Trevelyan, John 10, 11, 13, 14, 15, 36, 37, 55, 58, 60, 70, 71, 84

U

Under the Bed! 145-146, 229, 232
Under the Doctor 141-142
Ups and Downs of a Handyman, The 21, 123, 123-124, 209, 226

V

Vampira 21, 212
Virgin Witch 22, 75-76, 76, 79, 220, 225

W

Walker, Edward Craven 10, 11, 33, 38, 40, 232
Walker, Pete 46, 49, 66, 83, 89, 95, 106, 123, 211, 212, 225, 232, 232-233, 234
Warren, Norman J 15, 16, 25, 47, 51, 52, 116, 177, 178, 228, 233, 233
Watts, Queenie 21, 50, 135, 233
Webb, Rita 21, 54, 119, 127, 173, 233-234
West End Jungle 12, 42
Westbrook, Jenny 18, 98, 114, 116, 234
What's Good For the Goose 25
What the Swedish Butler Saw

7, 224
What's Up Nurse? 22, 153-154, 168, 208, 215
What's Up Superdoc? 24, 168, 168-169
White Cargo 94-95
Whitehouse, Mary 14, 15, 22, 24, 63, 72, 112, 198, 200, 201, 206
Whitehouse (magazine) 188, 195, 205, 212, 216, 226, 229, 231
Wife Swappers, The 6, 8, 14, 23, 26, 28, 61-62, 62, 74, 75, 85, 128, 142, 144, 217
Williams, Omar 207
Wilt 205, 207
Window Cleaner, The 48-49
Winter, Donovan 11, 38, 39, 52, 53, 102, 234
Winters, Bernie 133, 175, 191
Wood, Christopher 17-18, 106, 107, 108, 110, 117, 140, 161, 234
Wood, Teresa 138, 145, 164
World Is Full of Married Men, The 173, 173-174, 217, 221
World Without Shame 38-39, 39

Y

Yellow Teddybears, The 12, 234
Yes Girls, The 80, 80-81
You're Driving Me Crazy! 167-168, 219

Z

Zapper's Blade of Vengeance 97
Zeta One 17, 21, 63-65, 64